The Kalamazoo Automobilist

To Daniel

For the old days
at Checker - hope
you enjoy.

David Glyer

~

The Kalamazoo Automobilist

1891–1991

BARLEY, BLOOD, CANNON, CHECKER, CORNELIAN, DORT,
GREYHOUND, HANDLEY, HANDLEY-KNIGHT, KALAMAZOO, LANE,
MICHIGAN, PENNANT, REED, ROAMER, STATES, AND WOLVERINE

David O. Lyon

NEW ISSUES PRESS

WESTERN MICHIGAN UNIVERSITY

2002

ISBN   0-932826-83-0

Editor: Thomas H. Seiler
Designer: Elizabeth King
New Issues Press Director: Herbert Scott

〜

A special tribute to those who provided generous financial support
to Western Michigan University to facilitate the publication of
The Kalamazoo Automobilist:

  The Kalamazoo Antique Restorers Club
  The Kalamazoo County Historical Society
  Dick Walters — Walters-Dimmick Petroleum Inc.
  Mr. and Mrs. Philip Renuart
  Mr. and Mrs. Robert Packer
  Mr. and Mrs. Ronald Elenbaas
  The Philip Hissong Family
  Gene N. Sahr — Sahr Building Supply, Inc.
  Orrin B. Hayes, Inc. — Oldsmobile–Jeep–Mazda–Mercedes-Benz
  Richard and Janet Saddler — Uneek Restorations
  John Bright and Bonnie Dumlao

Printed in the United States of America

With deepest appreciation to my wife Jane Ann
who tolerated, with good nature, twelve years of an obsession,
and provided personal support in all aspects of the endeavor.

Contents

Preface

"A man who couldn't sell this car
couldn't sell gold dollars for eighty cents."

—Michigan advertisement

The *Kalamazoo Automobilist: 1891–1991* was written for the people of Kalamazoo: the interested citizen, the regional historian, and the automobile enthusiast. Once said, that purpose drove both the organization and the content of the book.

I was politely admonished for the title. "It sounds like a magazine," commented John Conde, referring to an early automobile publication, *The Automobilist.* "Can't you find something a bit more inventive?" But the title truly identifies the purpose of this book: to write an historical account of automobile manufacture in Kalamazoo, and to relate that tale to automobiling in and around this midwestern town.

Two events in the story stand like bookends at either end of the one hundred year span. We open raucously with the rumble of Jay Rhode's steam carriage across the tracks and down Rose Street in the spring of 1891, showing the potential of a self-propelled vehicle. We close dramatically with the rumble of semi-trucks across the tracks and down Pitcher Street in December 1991, removing the last automobile dies and presses from Checker Manufacturing. In between is the story of life—from the suicidal depression brought on by financial despair to the unbridled exhilaration brought on by success. The tale is written with attention to accuracy, but with great respect for each person's life exposed in these pages, and for surviving family members who are occasionally surprised by the deeds of their ancestors.

The *Kalamazoo Automobilist* is about the manufacture of automobiles, and true to that purpose, it includes much of the mechanical specifications of these vehicles. Certainly, a measure of success of a self-propelled vehicle is reflected in the quality of its engineering. In turn, that purpose is balanced with the human story, using the text to concentrate on the people and events behind these vehicles.

In the spirit of the "automobilist," several pages are dedicated to descriptions of general aspects of the automobile industry that might be well-known to the automotive historian, but not the

Kalamazoo resident. The text includes a brief history of Louis Chevrolet, descriptions of the Indianapolis 500 race and the characteristics of the early steam-powered Locomobile, placing relevant aspects of these stories within the context of Kalamazoo history. A brief history of the "cyclecar" and the "light car" also serves to enhance the reader's appreciation of the brief saga of Howard Blood's wonderful Cornelian and his dreams of success.

The decision to write about the "Kalamazoo automobilist" demanded a full account of the Michigan Buggy trials. It is a tale almost without reference to the mechanics of automobiles, but one that exposes Kalamazoo's struggle in the automobile industry at a time when Henry Ford's success allowed him to raise the daily wage to five dollars. In the same spirit of the automobilist, two stories, the first concerning the Cornelian and the second the Kalamazoo truck, were written by people who lived the episode described in those pages. Finally, the book includes a history of the Kalamazoo Rail and Velocipede Company, an enterprise that has a tangential relationship to the automobile at best, but a long history in the Kalamazoo community.

Given its intent as a history for Kalamazoo residents, the book seeks to associate automobiling with the landmarks of the Kalamazoo community. This notion became particularly important in the color signature, as color photographs of relevant automobiles are juxtaposed with period postcards of Kalamazoo, perhaps the only source of early color photography. Photographs of automobiles not built in Kalamazoo are also included in the signature, as these illustrate relevant aspects of local history.

Early in the development of the manuscript, a decision was made not to interrupt the story with footnotes and other forms of affirmation of substance and fact, but to provide a list of pertinent references at the end of each chapter. Newspaper articles, automotive periodicals, company sales brochures, and reference books are presented in order corresponding to their reference in the text. These materials are readily available in libraries and museums, and the reference titles are sufficiently clear to identify the source of the information in the text without reference footnotes.

The extraordinary *Standard Catalog of American Cars 1805–1942* by Beverly Rae Kimes and Henry Austin Clark, Jr. is an appropriate reference for almost every chapter. The history presented here, however, is occasionally at odds with the story documented in the *Standard Catalog*. Kimes and Clark did not enjoy ready access to the newspapers, libraries and museum collections in Kalamazoo; the noted discrepancies are well documented and believed to be correct as written. Many of the discrepancies are derived from the intermingling of facts in the history of the Blood, Michigan and Cannon automobiles. Since historical accounts are not always read in sequence—readers often select an isolated chapter of interest—the story of the interplay among the companies was explained briefly in each chapter pertaining to that particular company. The decision tolerates a certain amount of redundancy in exchange for a guarantee that the explanation of the interaction in the histories not be lost regardless of the sequence in which the material is read. The story also is told in the figure legends and the captions of the color photo signature, often repeating the information in the text, but providing access to the tale even with the most casual of reviews.

Interestingly, most automotive histories are published in a "popular" rather than "scholarly" genre, so that specific references are often difficult to find. Ross Collier, a journalist at *The Kalamazoo Gazette* during the 1930s created a series of index cards for the 1937 centennial publication of the *Gazette*. This card file is now in the holdings of the Western Michigan University archives, and the cards cite newspaper reports of important events in the history of the city. Collier did not always identify the paper, and never did he provide the page, but his brief summaries of events and the date of the publication were an important step in the initial search for information. The Ross Collier collection referenced several major newspapers published in Kalamazoo during the one hundred year period of this book. Each newspaper in turn became both reporter and participant in this story.

The *Kalamazoo Gazette*, the first newspaper in the city, was founded in 1837 when Henry Gilbert moved his weekly newspaper to Kalamazoo. The *Weekly Michigan Statesman and St. Joseph Chronicle* was founded by Gilbert in 1833, and when the United States Land Office moved from White Pigeon, Michigan to Kalamazoo, Gilbert followed with his weekly publication, changing the name in the course of the move. During the ensuing years, the newspaper had an number of editors as well as changes in format, direction and font. Major improvements were made in 1898 when Ford B. Rowe purchased the paper and installed modern printing equipment and other improvements under his hand helped to maintain a steadfast readership. In 1925 the paper moved into the beautiful Indiana limestone structure designed by Albert Kahn and built on the corner of Burdick and Lovell Streets where the paper remains to this day.

During its early days, the paper was known as the *Kalamazoo Gazette* until January 1897, when "The" was added to the formal name, making the title *The Kalamazoo Gazette*. Except for the period from March 21, 1900 to December 31, 1903 when it was known as *The Kalamazoo Gazette-News*, and another brief period in 1916, the name remained as *The Kalamazoo Gazette* until May 1, 1951 when the word "the" was dropped. The *Gazette* is a primary reference, and the citations in the various chapters reflect these changes in the use of "The" in the title.

A second paper came to Kalamazoo in 1844 when Henry B. Miller founded the *Kalamazoo Daily Telegraph*, which was published on a daily basis for the urban clientele and on a semi-weekly basis for area farmers. The words "Daily" or "Evening" were often added to the title just after the turn of the twentieth century. Edward N. Dingley, former editor of the *Levenworth Kansas Times*, arrived in Kalamazoo in 1888 to assume the position of managing editor of the *Telegraph*. Dingley was a graduate of Yale College and the Columbia College Law School. He was an aggressive writer, a bit self-righteous to be sure, but he was knowledgeable and his opinions were probably more often correct than not. His writings provide a rich account of the times.

The *Telegraph* grew in stature and by 1908 it was well-respected, prosperous and aptly equipped with modern printing equipment. The paper resided at 116–118 West South Street, a building that still stands in the city. In the same year and reportedly as the result of an ambiguous will, M. Henry Lane and Victor Palmer, executives at the Michigan Buggy Company, took control of the *Telegraph*. Dingley found the new owners objectionable, and later claimed their purchase was at the bottom of Michigan Buggy's problems. He resigned his position at the *Telegraph* and founded another newspaper, the *Kalamazoo Evening Press*. Coincidentally, that paper was located at 114–118 West South Street, in the same building as the *Telegraph*, but with a difference of a single number in the address. In spite of the neighboring facilities, the competition between the two papers was not amicable. According to Mr. Dingley, the move created a battle not unlike Gettysburg, "resulting in shattered hopes, broken spirits and shaken nerves." The battle lasted from February 1909 to May 1911 when a truce was negotiated. The two papers, the *Kalamazoo Telegraph* and the *Kalamazoo*

Evening Press, were joined to form the *Kalamazoo Telegraph-Press*. Edward Dingley assumed the position of managing editor of the combined papers, but the truce did not last a year.

Edward Dingley's relationship with Palmer and Lane had not improved, and on October 2, 1911, Dingley resigned as managing editor of the *Kalamazoo Telegraph-Press*. For a second time, he founded a new paper, the *Progressive Herald* which was located in suite 211 of the Peck Building. His challenging editorials about political and social issues in Kalamazoo appeared on the *Herald's* pages through 1916. In 1917 Thomas P. Gleason became editor and the *Progressive Herald* moved to 123 Portage Street. Subsequently, Dingley moved to Washington, D.C.

Few if any of the *Kalamazoo Evening Press* issues survive, but almost every issue of the *Telegraph* and the *Telegraph-Press* remain, providing ample record of local history until the paper was sold in 1916. Not much of the *Progressive Herald* survives, but the small amount of extant text is historically rich and the editorials insightful.

The competition between local newspapers came to an end in 1916, when *The Kalamazoo Gazette* purchased the *Kalamazoo Telegraph-Press*. According to Mr. Dingley, the *Telegraph-Press* could not recover after it fell into "alien hands" from Battle Creek, Michigan in 1912, resulting in "the rape of the old *Telegraph*." For a brief period the consolidated paper was titled *The Kalamazoo Gazette-Telegraph*, an identification used in the city directory through 1919, well after the paper returned to its former name *The Kalamazoo Gazette*.

The last significant publication in Kalamazoo was the *Advocate*, founded in 1906 as the *Trades Union Advocate* and, as the name implies, it served the purposes of developing unions among the skilled trades. M. Henry Lane sold his interest in the *Kalamazoo Telegraph-Press* in the spring of 1912, and in June 1913 he purchased the *Advocate*, changing the name to the *Kalamazoo Advocate*, with offices at 230 North Burdick Street. Harlan E. Babcock, appointed editor at the *Telegraph-Press* after Dingley's resignation, left the *Telegraph-Press* after it was sold, and was appointed editor of the *Advocate* after Lane bought it. Eventually, the paper was moved to Kalamazoo's industrial district at the corner of Reed Avenue and Fulford Street, close to Michigan Buggy. The *Advocate* is cited occasionally by name in the present text, but it is not in the reference sections. Lane's sale and rapid purchase of newspapers in 1912–1913 as well as H. E. Babcock's editorial involvement in both the *Telegraph-Press* and the *Advocate* occasionally create some confusion in reference to these newspapers.

With local newspapers as a primary reference source, *The Kalamazoo Automobilist* seeks to serve as a compendium of resources about the automobile and its manufacture in Kalamazoo. Surely, all of the references are not documented, but after twelve years of research, a great percentage of the extant reference material about Kalamazoo automobiles from 1891–1991 is cited within its pages.

Acknowledgments

Very little in this world can be accomplished alone, and compiling the information and preparing this manuscript was no exception. First, I thank my wife Jane for her support, encouragement and her tolerance of an activity that has been an obsession for over a dozen years. We enjoy the antique car hobby together and the development of this manuscript has been an extension of that part of our lives.

I would like to thank Yvonne Rumery for reading and formatting the first draft and setting the initial format of the text. The major work of formatting the final text and integrating the photographs was accomplished by Elizabeth King who served not only as designer and editor, but as counselor through complex and often arduous stages of preparing the text.

All of the material for some parts of the book, noticeably the Michigan Buggy trial, was drawn from the resources at Western Michigan University. Of the staff of the University Archives and Regional History Collections, I am most grateful to Wayne Mann, former Director; Barb Taflinger, former Curator; Sharon Carlson, Director; Sue Husband, Regional History Curator; and Shirley Campbell, Assistant Curator.

Much of the content of this work was drawn from the resources made available from museums, libraries and personal collections across the United States and in Great Britain. These professionals are an impressive group, who readily share information, answer questions and fill requests promptly and graciously.

My sincere appreciation is extended to Kim Miller, Librarian, Antique Automobile Club of America; John Emory, Archivist, Auburn-Cord-Duesenberg Museum; Carol Martinkus at Borg Warner Company; Rod Walton at the Checker Motor Corporation Archives; Linda Busse, Director of Public Affairs, and Margaret Gifford, Director of Membership Services, Automotive Hall of Fame; Mike Spezia, President, Thomas Kayser, and Linda Reames, Administrative Assistant, Gilmore Car Museum; Dale Wells at the Gilmore Classic Car Club Museum Library; David Moroknek and Donald Donaldson at the Indianapolis Motor Speedway Hall of Fame Museum Library; Katherine Larson, Local History Specialist, Kalamazoo Public Library Local History Collection; Paula Metzner, Collections Manager, Kalamazoo Valley Museum; Dr. Charles Lindquist, Curator, and Jan Richardi, President, Lenawee County Historical Society; William J. Lewis, The Lewis Automotive History Collection; Karl Ludvigsen, Ludvigsen Library Limited; Ron Grantz, former Curator and Mark A. Patrick, Curator, National Automotive History Collection, Detroit Public Library; Jackie Frady, Executive Director, Janet Ross, Librarian and Sandy Saunders, Support Services Manager, National Automobile Museum; The William F. Harrah Foundation; Stuart Mc Dougall, Librarian, Automobile Reference Collection, The Free Library of Philadelphia; Mark Oudersluys, Pharmacia Inc. Archivist; Maggie Snyder, Curator, Vicksburg Historical Society, Vicksburg Museum; and George D. Kanaan, The Walter O. MacIlvain Collection, *The Bulb Horn* magazine. Finally, in this list is Henry Blommel, Auburn-Cord-Dusenberg enthusiast and historian, and Ralph Dunwoodie who has an extensive and well-indexed library and who searched the periodicals and provided copies of trade magazines at reasonable cost.

I enjoyed the assistance of a number of people in the antique automobile hobby, who provided photographs, information and encouragement. I am indebted to Ann Bothwell, Ralph Borton, Buck Boudeman, Jim Cesari, Bill Cuthbert, Norm Jones, Dan Kamerman, Norm Knight, Basil Lewis, John McMullen, Dick and Jo Reames, Al Rohrstaff, Virgil Ronkin, Dick Saddler, Stefan Sarenius, Bruce Uhrich, Kent Van Emst and Dale Wells.

I owe much to Susan Hickmott, a granddaughter of Frank Lay, who educated me about the history of the Lay and the Lane families; Fred and Martha Blood Zeder who provided material and information about Howard Blood and the Blood family; and Buck Boudeman for information about his family. I am indebted to Bob Hayes II, president of the Orrin B. Hayes Oldsmobile dealership in Kalamazoo for sharing photographs from the Hayes family collection. I am also indebted to Robert Gregorson of the Kalamazoo County Parks Department for a tour of the Markin home and grounds and Al Barberry, former Checker employee, for his insight into Morris Markin's life. John Conde, noted author and automotive historian, provided invaluable assistance and direction, and, in many respects, served as guide and mentor.

Finally, I am grateful to Diether Haenicke, past president of Western Michigan University, for granting me a development leave during the fall semester of 1998 that allowed me to complete the final draft of the manuscript.

The thought of a book began in 1986 when I stopped at the University archives, then in Waldo Library at the center of the Western Michigan University campus. It was raining, and I was getting drenched walking back to my office with an hour before my next meeting. I literally wandered into the archives to get out of the rain. Given my interest in antique automobiles, I began a casual search through the reference sources and found an article on the Kalamazoo car in the *Kalamazoo Telegraph*. I was hooked on the project. I was the editor of the *Arc & Spark*, a newsletter of the Kalamazoo Antique Auto Restorers Club, and I began writing brief articles about automobile manufacture in Kalamazoo for that publication. Many readers responded with interest and it was clear that the material had a ready audience. I began scheduling additional visits to the archives between meetings, digging deeper into the early newspapers and writing brief accounts of what I found.

The search continued and the list of references and pile of photographs grew over the years as did my interest, circle of friends and associates in the automobile hobby and the Society of Automotive Historians. I talked about the subject matter wherever I went, and found considerable support from people in the hobby and for that I am most grateful, even though I have not identified everyone I met along the way. My thanks to those in the hobby for their positive support, their insatiable interest in history and their robust enjoyment of antique automobiles, for making this endeavor more than just a hobby and a diversion from life for me.

~

Photograph Credits

The following abbreviations have been used to identify the source of the photographs in the text and to acknowledge that these photographs are reproduced here with permission, appreciation and courtesy of the institution or individual so identified.

ACA: Courtesy, Antique Automobile Club of America Library, Hershey, PA.

ACD: Courtesy, Auburn-Cord-Duesenberg Museum, Auburn, IN.

BCC: Courtesy, Bill Cuthbert, Santa Maria, CA.

BFC: Courtesy, Bothwell Family, Woodland Hills, CA.

BWC: Courtesy, Borg-Warner Company, Chicago, IL.

CAG: Courtesy, Chris & Ann Garlitz, Lansing, MI.

CMC: Courtesy, Checker Motors Corporation archives, Kalamazoo, MI.

DOL: David O. Lyon, Lawton, MI.

FAM: Courtesy, Automotive Hall of Fame, Dearborn, MI.

GCA: Courtesy, Gilmore Car Museum, Hickory Corners, MI.

IMS: Indianapolis Motor Speedway Hall of Fame Museum, Indianapolis, IN. Photos used with permission of IMS properties.

JCC: Courtesy, John A. Conde, Bloomfield Hills, MI

JLC Courtesy, Jim & Loretta Cesari, Palo Alto, CA.

JMC Courtesy, John McMullen, Lapeer, MI.

KLL: Courtesy, Kalamazoo Public Library, Local History Collection, Kalamazoo, MI.

KLM: Courtesy, Kalamazoo Valley Museum, Kalamazoo, MI.

LCM: Courtesy, Lenawee County Historical Museum, Adrian, MI.

LLL: Courtesy, Karl Ludvigsen Library Limited, London, UK.

NAC: Courtesy, National Automotive History Collection, Detroit Public Library, Detroit, MI.

NAM: Courtesy, National Automotive Museum (The Harrah Collection), Reno, NV.

OBH Courtesy, Orrin B. Hayes, Kalamazoo MI.

PFL: Courtesy, Automobile Reference Collection, Free Library of Philadelphia, Philadelphia, PA.

RRC: Courtesy, Richard Reames Family, Kalamazoo, MI.

UJA: Courtesy, Pharmacia (formerly Upjohn Company) Archives, Portage, MI.

WMU: Courtesy, Western Michigan University Archives and Regional History Collections, Kalamazoo, MI.

Introduction

1791–1891

The melting winter snows and the early spring rains collect in the water shed to the east of Homer, Michigan and then drain into the streams that eventually flow together forming the Kalamazoo River. The river runs westward, then south to Kalamazoo, north again to Allegan, and, finally, empties into Lake Michigan near the once proud port of Singapore just south of Saugatuck. Before the arrival of the railroad and the motorcar, this watery avenue was the only major transportation artery in the south central and western part of Michigan. From the days of the first settlement until the turn of the twentieth century, canoes, barges, flatboats, and later steam boats sailed the lower fifty miles of river carrying passengers and transporting goods.

In the early years, before the dams were built and the river tamed for industrial use, the river shallows just east of Kalamazoo created turbulent rapids that forced early travelers to beach their vessels and portage their cargo. The land nearby was hospitable and provided both an area for respite and a place for barter among the river traders. These two simple characteristics of the region—rapids to interrupt the river journey and land hospitable for rest—created the essential ingredients for the growth of the village that was to become Kalamazoo.

According to legend an old Frenchman known only by his last name, Numaiville, built the first trading-hut in 1823 on the land that was to become Kalamazoo just north of the river. He could neither read nor write, but kept his accounts with a form of hieroglyphics and drawings. The land near the river was heavily wooded, dominated by stands of oak and accented with a few majestic pines. These stands were interlaced with grand prairies and bottom land of rich black soil that James Fenimore Cooper's *The Oak Openings* made famous. Prairie Ronde was the largest at 20,000 acres, the Gull Prairies next at nearly 3,000 acres, followed by Gourdneck to the south at 2,500 acres. The natural beauty of the land was enhanced by conspicuous symmetrical mounds on the Gull Prairies and the area that would become Bronson Park in Kalamazoo. These mounds were the only extant evidence of an ancient people, known only as the mound builders, whose civilization stretched well down the Mississippi valley into Missouri.

The area was abundant with game. Fur bearing animals, fish, and flocks of wild fowl provided an attraction for the sportsman, meat for the larder, and pelts for barter among the indigenous tribes and the newly arrived pioneers. In spite of the reputation of the pioneers for self reliance, historians claim that "everybody borrowed and everybody lent and by it, business was kept prosperous." A nondescript currency called dicker, consisting of various and sundry paper notes of numerous denominations, sizes, and affiliations, was also a major part of the economy before a true currency arrived in the region. Deer was the primary source of meat, and it was these animals in their periodic migrations seeking the paths of least resistance across the land leading away from the river that defined the trails in the region. The Potawatomie Indians who populated the area followed the same trails and it was not surprising that these paths in turn were marked by the surveys of the 1830s. The Washtenaw trail, the primary roadway across the lower part of the state from Detroit to Chicago, was created in a similar manner, and locally these same paths would become the primary roads into the growing village. One trail led west along West Street (the present-day Westnedge Avenue) through Kleinstuck Preserve and out Oakland Drive. The northern track followed Douglas Avenue and a third veered off to the east toward Gull Road and the Gull Prairies.

Most of the early inventors, manufactures, and investors came across the Washtenaw trail from the east in two distinct migrations. The first group represented a particularly strong stock of immigrants who were displaced from New York State in an area that comprised the Holland Purchase, the Morris Grant and the Pulteney Estate, all of which were held as a monopoly by the Holland Land Company. These were industrious people, but there was no market for the farming and manufacturing abundance they produced. Their indebtedness for the land and the compound interest on their mortgages quickly increased until most lost their property to foreclosure.

Nineteenth-century historians described these pioneers as neither "purse proud families" nor "rainbow chasers," but people with strong arms, iron wills and relentless energy. For many, the trip began in central New York State, a week's journey west on the Erie Canal to Buffalo, and then across Lake Erie aboard the steamer United States to Detroit, the city that served as the rendezvous for immigrants moving west. There they were outfitted for the overland trip by oxcart on the Washtenaw trail and those destined for Kalamazoo bumped along that trail for fourteen days.

The second migration, just after the Civil War, was fueled by the post-war inflation that raised both the price and profit of many concerns within the city and attracted other entrepreneurs and industrialists, and brought to the city a swelling number of settlers. This wave of settlers was characterized by early writers as a people with "humanity as their distinguishing trait," but they also had both the grit and the skill to develop the many industrial concerns that grew in Kalamazoo including those related to the automotive manufacturing enterprise. The availability of the Kalamazoo river for transportation, and its ability to be diverted to create power as an ingredient in the manufacturing process, provided the basic needs for a growing industrial enterprise. The arrival of the railroad in 1846, the founding of the Kalamazoo Gas Light Company in 1855, the construction of drainage sewers in 1881, and the development of the magnificent water system with deep wells and a sophisticated steam pumping station provided not only the basic needs for manufacturing, but also the amenities of life that none of the neighboring cities could duplicate.

The Potawatomie Indians held title to the lands of Kalamazoo County until the Chicago treaty of 1821. That agreement committed $5,000 per year to the tribe for the next twenty years and another $1,000 per year for a blacksmith and a teacher. Also in that agreement the tribe ceded to the United States all of the lands south of the Grand River except for five reservations and one in Kalamazoo County that included the present site of the city of Kalamazoo. That area was called the Match-e-be-nash-e-wish reserve and the treaty is the basis for all land titles in Kalamazoo county.

In September of 1827 the lands identified in the Chicago treaty of 1821 were exchanged again for the Nottawasepee reservation in St. Joseph county and the lands in and about Kalamazoo that were ceded to the government. The final treaty of 1833 removed the last vestige of land ownership from the Indians. The chief at the time, identified as Saginaw or Noonday, was known for his countenance and his gentle manners. He was often seen assisting his squaw in mounting her pony and under his leadership the departure of the Potawatomie was peaceful, although conducted under military surveillance.

The village was founded first in 1829 by Titus Bronson under his own family name, but when the village of 1000 residents was incorporated in 1836, it was registered as Kalamazoo, "where the river boils in the pot." The name "Kalamazoo" is of Indian origin and derived from Kee-Kalamazoo meaning "it boils like a pot," or "boiling pot," a reference to the rapids and small eddies on the surface of the river that created a boiling appearance as it flowed through the valley in which the village nestled. In addition to its meaning, the new name was also preferred because another village named Bronson already existed in Branch county. The change so depressed Titus Bronson, however, that he sold off his lands and other interests and moved to Davenport, Iowa.

The "boiling pot" is the area where our story begins and the tale that unfolds is an account of both success and failure. The history of each of the participants reveals a life of great pride and accomplishment, occasionally interrupted by times of despair and great tragedy. The story is also the account of a struggle against the economic odds and, on occasion, the vicious deeds of the corrupt. Finally, it is a tale of the genius of the inventor and the eternal optimism of the investor, but it is forever a human story of men and women who sought wealth and fame in the manufacture and exploitation of the gasoline-powered vehicle known at the turn of the twentieth century as the "horseless carriage."

The Kalamazoo Automobilist is a story of what was and what might have been in this midwestern town had circumstances been just a little different. It is also a tale containing threads similar to those played out in many cities and towns across the country during the glorious century of the motor car from 1891 to 1991.

REFERENCES

Ethel Balls and Marie Lassfolk. *Living in Kalamazoo*, Kalamazoo, MI: Ihling Bros. Everard Company, 1958.

James P. Craig. *Picturesque Kalamazoo*, Evansville, IN: Whipporwill Publications, 1984. (reproduction)

Willis F. Dunbar. *Kalamazoo and How It Grew*, Kalamazoo, MI: Western Michigan University, 1959.

David Fisher and Frank Little, (eds). *Compendium of History and Biography of Kalamazoo County*, Chicago, IL: A. W. Bowen & Co., 1905.

Nick Kekic. *A Fine Place For a City: Titus Bronson and The Founding of Kalamazoo*, Kalamazoo, MI: Oak Opening Press, 1984.

Roger Kullenberg and David Hager. *Looking Back; A Pictorial History of Kalamazoo*, Marceline, MO: Heritage House Publishing, 1994.

Brenden Henehan. *Walking Through Time: A Pictorial Guide to Historic Kalamazoo*, Kalamazoo, MI: Kalamazoo Sequoia Press, 1981.

Larry B. Massie and Peter J. Schmitt. *Kalamazoo: The Place Behind the Products*, 2nd ed. Sun Valley, CA: American Historical Press, 1998.

Fred McTaggart. *Kalamazoo County: Where Quality is a Way of Life: A Contemporary Portrait*. Windsor, ONT: Windsor Press, 1989.

Part I

THE PROMISE OF
THE HORSELESS CARRIAGE

1891–1910

≈

Chapter 1

J. B. Rhodes, Dean of Kalamazoo Automobilists

1891–1934

*"…most lucrative invention,
an oil dispensing bottle from a Mason jar…"*

—*The Kalamazoo Gazette*

Kalamazoo offered great promise at the close of the Civil War, and David Rhodes and Abigail Slack, married in 1846, were part of a group of industrious and inventive pioneers who moved west to Michigan in the boom years of the late 1860s. David settled in Kalamazoo while his three brothers, Peter, O. E., and William, built homes in Hamilton, Oshtemo, and Cedar Springs respectively. His sister, Mrs. John Baxter, settled in Bloomingdale. Abigail was a strong woman, working long hours on the farm and giving birth to six healthy children: Irvin, Jay, Bert, Elizabeth, Ella, and Celia. Jay, born on March 2, 1865, and his younger brother Bert, born just four years later on July 25, would make a substantial impact upon the economy associated with the horseless carriage in the growing city of Kalamazoo.

Jay B. Rhodes began his career as an inventor in 1878 when, at the age of thirteen, he left the farm to serve his apprenticeship as a machinist and a tool maker. His first invention was a simple garden seed thresher powered by a belt wrapped around the family grindstone and cranked by his younger brother, Bert. During his lifetime, Jay Rhodes filed 232 patents for a variety of inventions, although only ten of those proved to be financially worthwhile.

Jay Rhodes' most impressive invention was an operable steam wagon, that, according to newspaper accounts, was completed in 1891, thus making his invention the earliest self-propelled vehicle to travel the streets of Kalamazoo, although predated eighty-six years by inventors elsewhere. He intended to perfect this steam wagon to provide commercial transportation to Gull Lake and to Hunt's Tavern, a popular road house in the Kalamazoo area during the "Gay Nineties." Rhodes enjoyed recounting tales of the wild rides down Rose Street on Sunday afternoons, with the big vehicle rumbling and snorting along as the crowds cheered his daring exploits. The vehicle was a sight to behold with its huge iron wheels and hissing steam valves, but it was not without its troubles. It seemed to run out of breath about every three blocks and Rhodes later surmised that the boiler was not large enough to maintain sufficient pressure for continued service. With each pause in power, he would wait for it to "steam up again" before setting off on another short spurt at breakneck speed. "I've gone over the railroad tracks down on Rose Street faster than any train that ever came across it," exclaimed Rhodes in a 1928 interview with *The Kalamazoo Gazette*.

Fig. 1-1. Jay B. Rhodes from The Kalamazoo Gazette, *circa 1928. (DOL)*

Unfortunately, Rhodes fell ill during this period and was unable to maintain the steam wagon or to establish his planned bus line to Gull Lake. Although he claimed to have $3,500 invested in this steam wagon, he eventually sold the vehicle to Jack Le Dick of Oshtemo for the grand sum of $150. Le Dick was unable to convert the big machine into a pleasure vehicle and the engine was consigned to labor as part of a spraying outfit in the fruit orchards near South Haven, where it was still in use well into the Great Depression. Rhodes built a second engine capable of developing 125 pounds of pressure intended for installation in another road wagon, but was forced to sell this one to U. K. Balch who converted it for use in a launch on Long Lake.

Rhodes worked as a mechanical engineer at the Austin Manufacturing Company in Chicago where he developed dozens of contrivances for the horseless carriage, but never built another vehicle. He was still on the company payroll when he returned to Kalamazoo in 1903 to settle permanently on Douglas Avenue. About this time he invented a mechanical swimming frog and a wooden minnow that he manufactured and sold through the Kalamazoo Fishing Tackle Company from 1903 through 1905. He subsequently sold the concern to William Shakespeare, and Rhodes' rendition of the birth of the Shakespeare Company compares favorably with Shakespeare's own description. According to Shakespeare, during the summer of 1895, he came upon an erstwhile inventor attempting to cast with a crudely made fishing reel. He paused, laid down his school books, and asserted with much confidence that one day he would build a reel that would work. In spite of the laughter and ridicule from the two men, he kept that vow, built the reel on a jeweler's lathe, and the Shakespeare Company was incorporated in 1905 to manufacture fishing reels, rods, and assorted tackle. Over the next ten years the company diversified its production to supply carburetors to local motorcar manufacturers.

Rhodes' most important invention was a compressed air-powered lift for dumping railroad cars. This particular device was a major convenience in the construction of the Panama Canal and helped the allied effort during World War I. Rhodes was an adventurer, was known to have visited the Panama Canal site on several occasions, and often stayed for months at a time returning with artifacts that he had found there. He enjoyed recounting the tales of the typhoon of September 17, 1908 just off San Salvador and how he survived that tropical storm by clinging to the mast for eighteen hours as waves swept across the deck. Three sailors died that day, but that did not deter

Jay from returning to the canal construction site on future occasions.

Rhodes' most ingenious invention was a road guide that operated through a gear arrangement connected to the front wheel of the car similar to a speedometer. As the front wheel turned, a set of brass discs turned more slowly than the wheel, but to scale of the distance traveled by the automobile. Openings in the discs allowed light to pass through an opening at a preset point in the cycle and that contact was used to set off a gong. Simultaneously, the signal "RT" or "LT" was illuminated on the dash of the car, instructing the driver to turn either right or left.

The guide, of course, had to be set previously by someone familiar with the route. Rhodes claimed that the instrument was infallible and was never off by more than two or three feet during the several years that he used it. Unfortunately, the development of highway makers, road signs, and maps rendered his invention valueless. "I was just too late with it," commented Rhodes during the 1928 interview with the *Gazette*. He had invested $25,000 and an incalculable number of hours in developing the device.

Rhodes' most lucrative invention was an oil dispensing bottle made from a simple "Mason" fruit jar. Designed for pouring lubricants into an automobile crank case, it fit a tubular spout into a dome shaped chamber that attached to the bottle with the ring normally used to hold the jar lid. The patented design included a small brass air vent soldered into the chamber that allowed the passage of air into the bottle thus enabling the free discharge of the lubricant through the spout. The vent's convenient location allowed the vent to be "fingered," as Rhodes expressed it in the patent application; that is, the user could cover the opening with an index finger, thereby con-

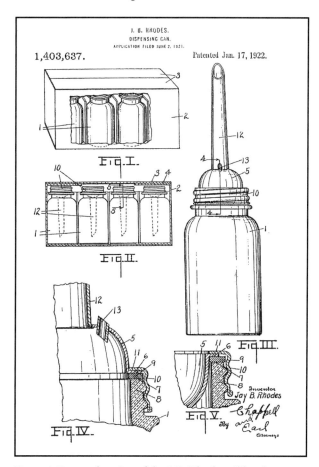

Fig. 1-2. Patent drawing of the J. B. Rhodes oil bottle, patent # 1,403,637, granted January 17, 1922. The air release valve mounted in the neck ring, is identified as point #13, Figures III and IV. Figures I and II in the same drawing show the manner in which the bottles might be packaged for shipping. (DOL)

trolling the passage of air into the container and in turn controlling the discharge rate of the oil. This arrangement also allowed the bottle to be refilled easily through the spout as the lubricant would not leak through the vent. Two similar patents were submitted; one on December 27, 1920 and the other on June 23, 1921. Both were granted on January 17, 1922. The first showed the detail of the brass vent, while the second included the packaging feature made possible by removing the spout, inverting it into the bottle and securing it with the neck ring. The finished product could then be shipped to buyers utilizing the same cartons in which the bottles were received from the glass factory. Rhodes' penchant for reusing materials was but one of his traits that was reminiscent of Henry Ford. Two subsequent designs were manufactured under this patent, both using a cone-shaped rather than a tubular spout as used in the original patent. In one design the brass vent tube was located in the chamber at the base of the spout; in the other, it was located about one third up the side of the spout.

Rhodes manufactured thousands of these bottles in his plant at 145 E. Kalamazoo Avenue where he employed a crew of workers to roll and solder the spout and the small brass opening in its base. The bottles were shipped to Kalamazoo by the carload and the finished product was then delivered throughout the United States and foreign countries. The early "Mason" jar bottles measured 8½" tall, with an abrupt shoulder at 6½" from the base. This bottle included the inscription, *THE "KALAMAZOO," JAY B. RHODES COMPANY.* The second bottle had a contoured shape similar to an early milk bottle. It also measured 8½" tall, but had a gradual taper beginning at 4½" from the base and expanding again at the mouth. This bottle read *JAY B. RHODES CO., Kalamazoo Mich.* Reportedly, the profits from this invention were enormous and the 1928 *Gazette* account unabashedly reported that the money "poured in," allowing Rhodes to retire by 1928 to amuse himself with mechanical inventions and enjoy his splendid summer home at Gun Lake.

The design and manufacture of oil dispensing bottles created much interest among the members of the Rhodes family. David D. Lewis, son of John Lewis and Jay's sister, Ella, applied for a patent in February 1924 for another oil bottle design. In this design, the long narrow air vent was soldered inside the tubular spout and had a more finished appearance than the Jay Rhodes designs, since there was no external vent. This arrangement, however, did not allow for the finger control of the oil flow that Jay Rhodes had thought so important. The Lewis patent was granted on September 23, 1924 and the bottle and spout were manufactured, and sold along with other automotive supplies from 1924 through 1926 at the David D. Lewis Co., 323 North Church Street in Kalamazoo. The spout is identified by the inscription, *D. D. Lewis Co. Kalamazoo Mich. Pat'd Sept 23, 1924,* around the top ring.

Jay's brother Bert filed articles of incorporation for the Acme Universal Joint Company on March 12, 1909, a company that continued to operate at 1908 Reed Street until 1923. Subsequently, he manufactured automatic oilers and other automotive supplies at 301 West Cedar Street until 1929. Bert also was an erstwhile inventor and held patents for universal joints as well as oil dispensing bottles. He filed patents for two dispensing bottles, both in 1925, although neither was granted until the spring of 1928. The first was a glass bottle and spout with a side opening in the neck, that was closed with a cork fitted with a vent tube. Interestingly, the patent drawing for this bottle includes the horizontal quart line with a vertical arrow and the instruction: *fill to line above arrow point, one full liquid quart.* This feature later became a standard in the industry. Bert's second design was similar to Jay's, except that the vent hole had a "tongue-like" baffle covering the vent on the inside of the spout. Bert's dispensing bottles are much less ornate than Jay's designs, as he used only a simple identification, *B. O. Rhodes Mfg. Co. Kalamazoo Mich.,* around the base of the bottle. A dispensing bottle with the patented Bert Rhodes spout was sold subsequently by Childs Equipment Company of Battle Creek, Michigan. The patent records between 1917 and 1940 reveal only four basic designs for oil dispensing bottles using a quart bottle and a screw-on spout, and all but one of these was filed by a member of the Rhodes family.

In some respects, the history of Jay B. Rhodes, his manner and appearance, resembles that of Henry Ford, including the reports of his ability to repair broken watches at an early age, his penchant for collecting curious objects, and his interest in making farm work easier. Like Henry Ford, Rhodes enjoyed the outdoors, and Jay and his brother Bert often went hunting for squirrel, an activity that almost cost him his life. A newspaper story in the fall of 1925 indicated that he and Bert were hunting near Shelbyville and each man had followed a different course in search of game. When Jay crept through the brush, his brother thought it was a squirrel and fired at the sound, striking Jay on the side of the head near the eye. Fortunately, the shotgun pellets were not fatal and almost all were removed by Dr. Rush McNair, one of Kalamazoo's best known surgeons and a prominent investor in the Blood Brothers bicycle shop.

Jay Rhodes died at the age of sixty-six on October 12, 1931, about the same time his first steam engine died in the orchards of South Haven. His legacy includes the Jay B. Rhodes Dispensing Bottle Company, that remained for another few years after his death, as well as numerous inventions as small as the safety razor and as large as the construction equipment that was used in well drilling and road construction and made the completion of the Panama Canal possible. Rhodes was the premier inventor in Kalamazoo and the first to build and drive a self-propelled vehicle on the streets of the city in 1891. His relationship with other citizens of the city is unknown, but he must have been well known within the Kalamazoo circle of mechanics and inventors, including Clarence and Maurice Blood, the first to design and manufacture a gasoline-powered horseless carriage in the city.

REFERENCES

Ross Collier. *Ross Collier Collection*. Regional History Collections, Western Michigan University, A–1911.

Jay B. Rhodes, Kalamazoo Inventor. *The Kalamazoo Gazette*, January 29, 1928.

Larry B. Massie and Peter J. Schmitt. *Kalamazoo: The Place Behind the Products*. 2nd ed. Sun Valley, CA: American Historical Press, 1998.

Jay B. Rhodes. "Dispensing Can, Patent #1,403,636 Issued." *United States Patent Office*, January 17, 1922.

Jay B. Rhodes. "Dispensing Can, Patent #1,403,637 Issued." *United States Patent Office*, January 17, 1922.

Jay B. Rhodes. "Shipping Case and Tray, Patent #1,431,255 Issued." *United States Patent Office*, October 10, 1922.

David D. Lewis. "Dispensing Can, Patent #1,509,360 Issued." *United States Patent Office*, September 23, 1924.

Bert O. Rhodes. "Dispensing Receptacle, Patent #1,667,821 Issued." *United States Patent Office*, May 1, 1928.

Bert O. Rhodes. "Dispensing Can, Patent #1,667,822 Issued." *United States Patent Office*, May 1, 1928.

Bert O. Rhodes. "Dispensing Can Patent #1,817,322 Issued." *United States Patent Office*, August 4, 1931.

Jay B. Rhodes Badly Hurt. *The Kalamazoo Gazette*, October 18, 1925.

Chapter 2

The Horseless Carriage
Arrives in Kalamazoo

1900–1905

"It has come! The first Locomobile
to be owned in this city."

—*The Kalamazoo Gazette*

A light snow was falling on the afternoon of January 24, 1900 when the shiny new Locomobile arrived by rail from Watertown, Massachusetts. The content of the shipping crate was half-veiled by the protective wrappings and the employees at the express office poked and tugged at the container to get a view of the first horseless carriage in Kalamazoo. As they did so, they spoke in hushed tones of wonderment, quizzing one another about the probable cost of the marvelous machine.

The *Gazette's* response the next day, January 25, 1900, was simple: *"It has come! The first Locomobile to be owned in this city."* The reporter then went on to assert that Kalamazoo was now the equal of Chicago, host of the first American race for gasoline-powered automobiles in 1895.

The crate arrived addressed to George W. Taylor, a local clothier, and, after initial inspection by the employees at the express office, was promptly carted off to Taylor's residence on South Park Street. There, the protective wrappings were torn away to reveal the automobile, finished in black with red trim, wheels, and gearing. It was a day of wonder for all who saw it, and according to the *Gazette* story on January 25, 1900, one onlooker praised the vehicle as a "machine with an ornate design and a natty shape."

The inaugural drive was set for April 1, 1900, but George Taylor was not the first to drive his own car. Later accounts put the steering gear in the hands of W. E. Upjohn, locally known for his severe case of "horselesscarriageitis," a term often used facetiously by the local press to identify individuals with an uncommon interest in, or penchant for, the new self-propelled horseless carriage. Reportedly, the car was driven down Main Street where its arrival was documented by a local photographer. Frank Burtt also had his first ride that spring, with Ed Taylor, George's son, at the

Fig. 2-1. The horseless carriage arrives in Kalamazoo. The view is down Main Street, looking east, with a carriage emerging from Portage Road to the right. The Locomobile, the first manufactured automobile to appear on the streets of Kalamazoo, can be seen on the street, just to the left and below the FOLZ sign in the photograph. There is a man standing next to the car. W. E. Upjohn is presumed to be at the helm. (WMU)

helm. The occasion was a memorable one for Frank Burtt and he recalled his part in the historic event to a reporter in an interview with *The Kalamazoo Gazette* on February 21, 1937:

> I was called by Ed Taylor and asked to come to their home to see why they could not get water
> up into the boiler. On my arrival I could see the boiler was already filled, so Ed fired up and
> took me for a ride south on Park Street to the Oaks, just south of Vine Street, and then back
> home again. It didn't take long.

After the inaugural run, W. E. Upjohn badgered and cajoled George Taylor throughout the month until he finally persuaded Taylor to sell the Locomobile, although reportedly Taylor immediately ordered another of the same make and color. Most residents of Kalamazoo in 1900 considered the horseless carriage a plaything for the rich, and driving was treated as a sport. Upjohn did more than just drive about Kalamazoo, for he used the vehicle in his sales for the Upjohn Pill and Granule Company. He once drove the car to Buffalo, New York, a distance of some seven hundred miles without an accident and with only a few stops for repairs. He kept the Locomobile for another two years before trading it for a bigger and more powerful White steam car.

Some reviews of the early Locomobile contend that the $600 price tag only made it appear to be a bargain, for neither the design nor the construction was considered sturdy. It was built from a horse-drawn carriage body, including the holes in the leather dash for reins, and was mounted on a welded bicycle frame with tiller steering. A twin-cylinder steam engine provided direct power to the rear wheels by chains, but the small boiler mounted beneath the seat limited the driving range to around twenty miles. Finally, the lubrication system was considered primitive even for that era. Despite the mechanical limitations and short cruising range, over four thousand of these runabouts were sold by May of 1902, making the Locomobile one of the most popular automobiles in America at the start of the twentieth century.

The Locomobile company of America was incorporated in 1899 by John B. Walker, publisher of *Cosmopolitan* magazine, and Amzi L. Barber who had made a fortune in asphalt. Walker was a crafty businessman, for he purchased the company from the Stanley brothers, subsequent builders of the Stanley Steamer, at a cost of $250,000 and then sold half interest in the enterprise to Barber for the same amount of money. The new business relationship between Walker and Barber could not last long in these circumstances, and within months a quarrel resulted in the demise of the partnership. Barber retained the Locomobile name, and Walker erected a factory in Tarrytown, New York to build the same car under

Fig. 2-2. William Blaine, reportedly associated with the Church Manufacturing Company, is shown chauffeuring W. C. Moran on his rural mail route near Adrian, Michigan, circa 1903. Blaine was intent on showing the car's durability in the snow, and as a precaution had attached chains to the rear wheels. This Murray automobile is the same model owned and driven by Rev. Blekkink. About 225 of these automobiles were built. (LCM)

the name Mobile. Interestingly, a Mobile was the third car sold in Kalamazoo on April 10, 1901, when it was delivered to Oscar K. Buckhout, owner of a local chemical company that supplied embalming fluid to Kalamazoo morticians.

Steam cars such as the Mobile, Locomobile, and White played an important role in early motoring in Kalamazoo. Almost all gasoline-powered cars prior to the introduction of the electric starter by Cadillac in 1912 had to be started with the very troublesome and often dangerous engine crank that was responsible for crippling and in at least one case killing a careless novice. Although starting a steam-powered vehicle could be a lengthy and complex process, it required no cranking, and once started, the car was quiet and free of vibration. Steam power also provided continuous acceleration without the pesky gearbox so troublesome to the first time "automobilist." Failure to coordi-

Fig. 2-3. 1902 Mobile similar to that purchased by Oscar K. Buckhout, who owned the third car in Kalamazoo. (DOL)

nate steering and gear selection in the early horseless carriage was the cause of many accidents, and the poor driving skills of the novice were well-documented in the Kalamazoo press.

On July 9, 1903 the congregation of the Second Reformed Church invested in a new Murray automobile for their pastor, Rev. E. J. Blekkink. Reverend Blekkink was very popular among his parishioners, and they contributed to the purchase of the car and constructed a small building behind the church to house the vehicle. The five-horsepower Murray, built appropriately by the Church Manufacturing Company in nearby Adrian, Michigan, was finished in black enamel with black leather seating and sold for $600. The Murray featured a buggy style carriage mounted on a 67.5" wheelbase with side-tiller steering and wire wheels. While reports indicate that the Murray was a well-made automobile, financial difficulties forced the company to close in late 1903 after production of only 225 cars. At the time of delivery the good Reverend commented as follows to the *Kalamazoo Telegraph*, "A horse and carriage are a little bit behind the times, and an automobile is more convenient, less expensive and easier to care for."

The purchase was the first in the midwest for the purpose of assisting a minister with his church-related duties. The Reverend took delivery on July 12, 1903 and, at 6:00 p.m. the very next day, had his first accident. The article in the *Kalamazoo Telegraph* on July 16 was entitled "His Auto Bucked," and described what is likely the first automobile accident in Kalamazoo:

> About 6 o'clock last evening Mr. Blekkink gave a pretty exhibition of the possibilities of an
> auto when properly governed in turning corners. West on Academy Street the machine hummed

merrily along. Near West Street, a street car waited on the corner, as did a five-foot pile of stone curbing and a fire hydrant. With a majestic pull at the steering gear in the wrong direction, Mr. Blekkink ignored West Street and the street car, and landed squarely in the front yard of E. R. Burrell. The auto, unable to travel as fast as Mr. Blekkink over the curb stones and the city hydrant, remained wedged in the inconvenient chaos and required the united efforts of several bystanders and Mr. Blekkink to extricate it. An unexpected shake up was the extent of Mr. Blekkink's injuries. The auto was soon in commission again, although one wheel was badly out of shape and the handsomely enameled box marred.

During the first several years of the twentieth century, reports of automobile purchases by Kalamazoo residents often appeared in the local press and the following are cited in the *Ross Collier Collection*: April 19, 1901—"auto number three has arrived as O. K. Buckhout takes delivery of a Mobile steam car"; May 27, 1902—"Arthur L. Pratt receives a new Packard from Warren, Ohio and

it's a hummer"; August 1, 1902—"Dr. Edward Ames, takes delivery of a gasoline Locomobile, and is first doctor to use an auto on city streets"; May 16, 1903—"F. N. Rowley ordered a new 24 horsepower auto"; June 17, 1903—"Archibald Campbell has a new Orient Buckboard." Campbell was especially proud of his Orient Buckboard, and on August 1, 1903, challenged other owners of light machines to a five-mile race at Recreation Park. The Orient Buckboard had been very successful at New York City's Empire City Track, and Campbell was very confident in his vehicle's capability.

Fig. 2-4. The Orient Buckboard was a popular car in early Kalamazoo and was sold by Harry Harlow, the first true automobile dealer in the city. Note the statement: "Patented March 10, 1903" indicating that this vehicle was sold under the protection of the Selden patent. (DOL)

The opening of the St. Louis Exposition in the summer of 1904 created an opportunity for some of the more adventurous of Kalamazoo's residents. M. B. Flenner and L. D. Cooley planned to make the trip in Mr. Cooley's 1904 curved-dash Oldsmobile, and they expected that the round trip and the exposition would occupy about two weeks. The Oldsmobile was small but reliable, and, according to the local press, they anticipated to make the run with no more than the customary amount of trouble. Reportedly, a Cadillac, a Winton and a French-built Panhard were leaving Cleveland at about the same time. The August 4, 1904 issue of the *Telegraph* reported:

> The gentlemen from Kalamazoo form a part of the vast number of autos that are puffing along the country roads to St. Louis from almost every part of the country. A large party is going in touring cars from Chicago to meet the big crowd which is now on its way from New York City, and other points in the east.

The Kalamazoo populace was discovering the joys as well as the sorrows of automobile ownership. Many new cars were being sold, and both men and women were learning to drive. On July 4, 1904 the city sponsored its first parade of fifteen locally-owned cars as well as other vehicles invited from as far away as Chicago. By August 1904, there were about thirty automobiles running around Kalamazoo and additional deliveries were anticipated before the close of the driving season. By the following summer, automobile ownership had climbed to fifty-two, including the

Fig. 2-5. M. B. Flenner and L. D. Cooley on the morning of August 4, 1904 just before leaving Kalamazoo to drive to the St. Louis Exposition in Mr. Cooley's curved-dash Oldsmobile. This photograph is occasionally identified incorrectly as the Blood brothers in an early Blood car. (KLL)

Oldsmobile shuttle bus to the Nazareth Academy just east of the city. An automobile census for 1905 published in the *Gazette* in January of 1937, identified the various makes owned and operated by Kalamazoo residents at that time.

The Michigan, the Cannon, and the Blood were built in Kalamazoo with all the rest built in

MAKE	#	MAKE	#	MAKE	#
1. Michigan	8	6. Franklin	3	11. Thomas Flyer	1
2. Cannon	6	7. Blood	2	12. Pope-Toledo	1
3. Oldsmobile	6	8. Ford	2	13. Pope-Tribune	1
4. Cadillac	5	9. Kensington	2	14. Knox	1
5. White	5	10. Buick	1	15. Hayes-Apperson	1
				16. Home	1

Michigan or Ohio except for the Kensington, built in Buffalo, New York, and the Franklin built in Syracuse, New York. The Home owned by Charles Payne is a puzzle. There was a Home Manufacturing Company in Chicago, but it was not established until 1916, and manufacture of any vehicle is doubted. Perhaps the reference was used to identify a "home-built vehicle." The fact that Mr. Payne was a machinist at the Michigan Automobile Company adds some credence to that notion.

Many of the cars belonged to local notables and automobile manufacturers. Frank Fuller, a founder of the Michigan Automobile Company, and Ralph E. Balch, O. A. LaCrone, and A. H. Rockwell—all local physicians—each owned the very popular Michigan. Frank Burtt, president of

Burtt Manufacturing that built the Cannon; Warren Cannon, designer of the Cannon; and James C. Hatfield, secretary of the Kalamazoo Corset Company, owned Cannon automobiles. Maurice Blood, president of Blood Brothers Automobile and Machine, and local chemist O. K. Buckhout each owned one of the two Blood cars. Charles Clarage, founder of Thomas Clarage Foundry;

Benjamin VanBochove, chairman of VanBochove Building and Real Estate Company; William O. Harlow, owner of a local sporting goods store (that later became a Cadillac dealership); F. J. Welsh, a physician; and Derk Yomkerman, a veterinarian, owned Cadillacs. Tilden Robb, of Locher and Robb Sporting Goods, a company that became one of the first dealerships in Kalamazoo, owned an Oldsmobile. W. E. Upjohn, president of the Upjohn Pill and Granule Company, owned the steam-powered White purchased from the factory in Cleveland, Ohio after he sold the Locomobile he bought from George Taylor back in 1900.

Ownership represented one auto per one thousand residents in Kalamazoo, and according to the 1904 *Telegraph* article on "Automobilists," that was an excellent record for a city the size of Kalamazoo, given the development of automobiling by that time in Michigan. The initial claim that Kalamazoo was the equal of Chicago, made by the *Gazette* when the first Locomobile arrived in

Fig. 2-6. W. E. Upjohn at the controls of the Locomobile that he purchased from George Taylor, circa spring 1900. This photograph was taken on the road to Vicksburg by Archibald Campbell. This car was built from a horse-drawn carriage, and note the openings for reins in the leather dash, especially clear on the upper right of the dash. (WMU)

1900, was perhaps a bit presumptuous, but by 1905 the number of Kalamazoo automobilists exceeded those in most nearby towns.

Several Kalamazoo women also learned to drive in this period and, while many of these enthusiasts were wives of well-known male automobilists, most seemed to own their own vehicles. Mrs. Derk P. Yomkerman was the first woman driver in the city starting in the 1903 season. She often drove her beautiful one-cylinder Cadillac touring to Grand Rapids, Jackson, and South Haven, which at the time were all treks of considerable challenge. Mrs. Winifred Upjohn Smith began driving in 1904 and was often seen in her White steamer as was Mrs. C. H. Swindel. The Swindel family owned three different automobiles over a three year period. Woman automobilists, or the

Fig. 2-7. The man behind the wheel of the White Steam car, circa 1905, is believed to be W. H. Upjohn, vice-president of the Upjohn company and son of W. E. Upjohn. (UJN)

"fair chauffeurs" as they were occasionally identified in the local papers, often preferred steam cars at the time because of their enormous power, convenient regulation, and ease of starting. In spite of the convenience of steam, however, Mrs. Boudeman purchased an eighteen-horsepower Rambler in 1905 and Mrs. J. W. Ryder began driving her Maxwell in 1906. The local paper noted that not one of the "women chauffeurs" had been charged with an accident.

Automobile manufacturers recognized quite early the potential for sales to women. The first automotive advertisement for Haynes-Apperson appeared in *Life* magazine in July 1903 and placed two plainly-dressed women in the back seat, a staid appearance in stark contrast to the flamboyant bicycle advertisements of just a few years before. An advertisement for Oldsmobile, that appeared in *Life* magazine for August 1905, however, shows a woman at the tiller with scarf flying in the wind and a male companion at her side. Subsequent advertising by most of the major companies included scenes of women driving alone on rural roads, picnicking in a bucolic countryside, or sitting at the wheel talking with friends by the country club, all of which created the impression of freedom and independence that only the automobile could provide.

The sorrows of automobile ownership also became apparent to many citizens, and some sold their newly-purchased vehicles after a brief ownership. As early as January 1905, the secondhand auto was recognized as an article of commerce, and businesses began appearing in Kalamazoo for the sole purpose of selling used cars. Apparently a number of citizens had purchased an automobile only to find that they were unable to maintain it. A *Gazette* article on January 5, 1905 quoted one dealer as follows:

> Automobiling, like every other new sport, has been overdone, and people are tiring of it in
> droves…. There are, however, a lot of people who ought never have taken up the sport, who

are continually getting into it, and they furnish the quitters. They think that the automobile is as easy to drive as a tired old horse and that it costs nothing more than the price of a few gallons of gas to run it. They want to run it all the time and drive it at top speed, and then they are surprised when it breaks down and needs repairs… the automobile is above all an article of utility, and its use must continue to increase indefinitely.

The introduction of the horseless carriage into Kalamazoo was in the hands of George Taylor and W. E. Upjohn, but the Blood brothers certainly fueled interest in the automobile with the early manufacture of the Blood car that would stimulate both the production and purchase of the gasoline-powered motor vehicle.

∽

REFERENCES

George W. Taylor's Horseless Carriage. *The Kalamazoo Gazette*, January 25, 1900.

Frank Burtt Got First Patent as a Boy. *The Kalamazoo Gazette*, February 21, 1937.

George W. Taylor Owned First Automobile. *The Kalamazoo Gazette*, February 13, 1912.

Locomobile Steamers, Started with the Stanleys. *Old Cars Weekly News and Market Place*, August 10, 1989, pp. 14–15.

Automobile Number Three. *Kalamazoo Evening Telegraph*, April 19, 1901.

Auto for a Minister. *Kalamazoo Evening Telegraph*, July 9, 1903.

His Auto Bucked. *Kalamazoo Evening Telegraph*, July 16, 1903.

Ross Collier. *Ross Collier Collection*, Regional History Collections, Western Michigan University, A-1911.

Auto Race. *Kalamazoo Evening Telegraph*, August 1, 1903.

Start For St. Louis in Morning. *Kalamazoo Evening Telegraph*, August 4, 1904.

Roger Kullenberg and David Hager, eds. *Looking Back; A Pictorial History of Kalamazoo*. Marceline, MO: Heritage House Publishing, 1994.

____. *Through the Years*, Marceline, MO: Heritage House Publishing, 1999.

To Open With Big Automobile Parade. *The Kalamazoo Gazette*, July 2, 1904.

First Auto Arrived in 1900; Fifty-Two Cars in 1905. *The Kalamazoo Gazette*, January 24, 1937.

Beverly R. Kimes and Henry Austin Clark, Jr. *Standard Catalog of American Cars, 1805–1942*, 3rd ed. Iola, WI: Krause Publications, 1996.

Automobilists in Kalamazoo. *Kalamazoo Evening Telegraph*, August 13, 1904.

Kalamazoo Women Take to Out-of-Door Sports. *The Kalamazoo Gazette*, August 12, 1906.

Yasutoshi Ikuta. *The American Automobile; Advertising From the Antique and Classic Eras*. San Francisco: Chronicle Books, 1988.

Old Automobiles. *The Kalamazoo Gazette*, January 5, 1905.

Larry B. Massie and Peter J. Schmitt. *Kalamazoo The Place Behind the Products*, 2nd ed. Sun Valley, CA: American Historical Press, 1998.

Fig. 3-1. This blacksmith shop, photographed circa 1891, was almost directly across the street from the Kalamazoo Cycle Shop located at 210 North Rose Street. One might imagine that the man with the doctor's bag on the left is Dr. Rush McNair. His office was at 1439 East South Street, several blocks to the south and to the east of Rose Street. Before the introduction of automobiles, Dr. McNair rode a bicycle when making house calls and perhaps had just left his bike for repair at the Blood brothers shop when this photograph was taken. (WMU)

Chapter 3

The Blood Brothers Build
the First Horseless Carriage

1891–1906

*"…if its home roads are heavy,
the car will be strongly driven."*

—Hugh Dolner

North Rose Street in Kalamazoo was a simple dirt road with a few scattered shops and wooden sidewalks when the Blood brothers opened their bicycle shop in the unpretentious building at 210 North Rose Street in the spring of 1891. The Kalamazoo Cycle Company was incorporated that year with a capital stock of $10,000 provided by Dr. Rush McNair who was named president of the concern. Maurice Blood was named secretary, and Maurice's younger brother, Clarence, was named manager. Clarence was a mechanic of some repute, and though always associated with the company, he never rose above the role of chief mechanic or manager. Eventually, Maurice's son, Howard, and not Clarence, would be the vice-president of the Blood Brothers enterprise. Little is known about the Blood family in those early years, but surviving photographs show them gathered on the porch at Maurice's Woodward Avenue home in the summer, or with a favorite pet in their well-kept gardens, creating the image of a gentle, family-oriented people with a strong work ethic.

Clarence C. Blood was born in Fillmore, Minnesota, on December 11, 1859 and moved to Kalamazoo with his parents, Mr. and Mrs. Orville T. Blood, and elder brother, Maurice, in 1862. A second brother, Charles, and two sisters were also born within the decade of the 1860s. Charles eventually moved to Boston, Massachusetts, and was known to have sold Michigan automobiles there, but little else is known of his activities. Orville Blood owned and operated an implement business on North Burdick Street, and there is some indication that he left the midwest for California prior to 1890. Clarence completed his schooling in Kalamazoo and at the age of eighteen set off for Petoskey, Michigan, to learn the wood-working trade. He was a skilled craftsman who had gained recognition for making improvements in tooling for the industry and who enjoyed a wide reputation when he returned to Kalamazoo to take a position with the Fuller brothers' firm, manufacturers of broom handles, rolling pins, and potato mashers. He also may have left Kalamazoo for the west coast and possibly New York during these years, returning to Kalamazoo in 1891. Clarence married Nannie Wilson of Petoskey in 1888, but she died thirteen years later in 1901. He

Fig. 3-2. The scene is at the corner of Rose and West Main Streets, circa 1890, just south of the Kalamazoo Bicycle Shop. Note the dirt streets. (WMU)

was married again in 1910 to Etta M. Gardner, and they lived together with two sons, Edward and Lawrence, at 132 Catherine Street in Kalamazoo, a residence he maintained well after his retirement. Etta died in 1928 and Clarence passed away in 1949 at the age of eighty-nine, a well-recognized pioneer in the automobile business.

Maurice Blood was born on August 16, 1851 in Hollis, New Hampshire, and moved with his parents to Minnesota and then Kalamazoo where he, too, completed his schooling. He also made the trek to Petoskey, Michigan, to learn woodworking, and it was there that his son Howard was born on February 26, 1886. Subsequently, Maurice returned to Kalamazoo, and he and his wife, Mary, resided at 813 South West Street (Westnedge Avenue) where his second son, Wallace, was born. They later moved to 435 Woodward Avenue, a residence where he lived until his death on

May 8, 1917 at the age of sixty-five. Maurice was also employed by the Fullers, although his position in the company was in sales rather than manufacturing, and from 1889 to 1891 he traveled to nearby towns selling a variety of wooden utensils manufactured by the Fuller company. Perhaps it was the competition for the manufacture of wooden goods before the turn of the twentieth century, perhaps it was the tedium of traveling with a new son at home, but more likely it was Maurice's recognition of the potential of the fledgling bicycle industry that led him to found the Kalamazoo Cycle Company. First, he persuaded Dr. Rush McNair, a local physician, to provide the financial backing and serve as president of the company. Then he persuaded Clarence to return to Kalamazoo to provide the mechanical expertise required for the manufacture and repair of the bicycles. The Kalamazoo Cycle Company was housed at 208–210 North Rose Street. In that facility, the Blood brothers manufactured the Fortune cycle, sold the Crown and the Waverley bicycles and repaired all manner of bicycles.

Maurice was an astute young man. It was at his urging that the family entered first the bicycle business, and then automobile manufacturing, and the rapid developments in the history of the modern bicycle serve to show Maurice's responsiveness to the potential of the industry. Bicycle history begins in 1816 with the construction of the "Hobby Horse," a cumbersome wooden contraption that was propelled along by the rider's feet pushing against the ground. Little advancement occurred in the next fifty years, until the velocipede was developed in 1869. The velocipede had pedals attached to the front axle that could be used to power the front wheel. The next development was "The Ordinary" with its sixty-inch front wheel and small rear wheel that emerged from England in 1872 mounted on hard rubber tires. The large front wheel provided a wonderful mechanical advantage that was lacking in the velocipede, but these machines were very unstable. Injuries from "taking a header" were not uncommon when the rider was thrown from the towering cycle. The risks, however, were not all rider-related, for "country bumpkins" took great delight in thrusting sticks into the spokes of the high-wheel cyclist. Frank Burtt was an avid cyclist and was instrumental in forming a chapter of the American Wheelmen in Kalamazoo, both for social reasons and for protection from these wanton attacks.

The invention of the chain-driven "safety bicycle" in 1885, the development of the pneumatic tire by John Dunlap in Belfast, Ireland, in 1889, and the subsequent decrease in the cost of production led to a bicycle craze in the United States during the decade just before the turn of the twentieth century. By 1896 there were over four hundred bicycle manufacturers in the United States, including the Kalamazoo Cycle Company. The February 1896 issue of *Outing* magazine described the status of the industry in the following terms:

> The cycle trade is now one of the chief industries of the world. Its ramifications are beyond ordinary comprehension. Its prosperity contributes in no small degree to that of steel, wire, rubber and leather markets…. Nearly every season since 1890 has witnessed a doubling of the number of our factories… yet the supply… was unequal to the demand…. [T]he prospects are that the field offers reasonable prosperity to all makers of high-grade products.

Dr. Rush McNair had invested in the Bloods' bicycle shop, but the good doctor's stake was not largess, for the choice of transportation in Kalamazoo in 1891 was the horse, the horse-drawn street car, or the bicycle, and around town he preferred the last. In the late 1800s, physicians were not members of the monied class, and low-cost transportation was essential. The Bloods also built a bike carrier to transport a doctor's medical bags and emergency case. A stock company was formed to sell the carrier, but McNair complained that he had invested a year's wages in the idea and had seen no return on his investment.

Bicycles bridged the gap between the horse and the automobile, although each was not without its own challenges. McNair described one of his escapades in a 1937 interview with *The Kalamazoo Gazette:*

> One night I rode my bike off a bridge, down ten feet and over a dry ditch in East Walnut Street. I struck the gravel, empty cans and bottles and looked up just in time to see the bicycle coming down to deal me a cracked rib.

Stories about travel by horse and bicycle were engaging, but the convenience of the automobile grew quickly, and by 1912, the motorcar was the first choice of the physician. According to a report in *The Kalamazoo Gazette* in February of 1912, one manufacturer reported that over 16,000 automobiles, representing about one-third of their production, were in the hands of physicians.

The bicycle offered entertainment value as well, and evening rides to Gull Lake and other resorts some twenty miles outside of Kalamazoo were commonplace. Curiously, business records show that the rise of bicycle sales interfered with theater attendance, book sales, and piano sales, all of which declined during the decade.

Advertising for the bicycle was enhanced by the lithographic process that developed coincidentally with the bicycle, and by 1890 the sale of bicycles was promoted by dazzling color posters. The advertisement that the Kalamazoo Cycle Company used in the 1896 City Directory was typical of the period and featured an ethereal young woman in stylish bloomers astride a Waverley bike. The

message was clear; a woman could retain her femininity riding a bicycle, the only conveyance that provided personal freedom within the financial constraints governing many females in that era.

The Blood brothers sold and repaired bicycles from 1891 to 1901 at their shop on North Rose Street, but at the beginning of the twentieth century their interests turned to the horseless carriage. In a statement to the local *Telegraph* on October 20, 1900, Maurice Blood

Fig. 3-3. The lithographic process developed coincidentally with the bicycle and new bicycles were often promoted with dazzling color posters. This poster was painted by an American artist and depicts both the freedom and the healthy family activity offered by the Crown bicycle, a model sold by the Bloods. (HCL)

predicted that the auto industry would become the nation's largest and that Kalamazoo might be one of the centers of that growth. Maurice had been smitten with an intense interest in the horseless carriage, and his public pronouncement of the wonderful potential in automobile manufacture also suggests that he and his brother were already hard at work building a functioning model of the gasoline-powered horseless carriage. Within the next eighteen months they sold the bicycle business and turned their attention to the development and sale of automobiles.

On April 14, 1901 the Blood brothers delivered a Mobile steam carriage to Oscar K. Buckhout, a local chemist. This Mobile was the third car to arrive in Kalamazoo, and, since George Taylor had purchased the first two Locomobiles in Kalamazoo directly from the factory, the purchase and delivery arrangements of the Mobile made by the Blood brothers makes them the first "automobile dealership" in the city.

The Blood brothers are perhaps the least well known of the early Kalamazoo automobile manufacturers, and yet they were among the most productive, and credited with a number of "firsts" in the industry. Maurice E. and Clarence C. Blood began tinkering with automobiles perhaps as early as 1899 or 1900, and they successfully built the first gasoline-powered horseless carriage manufactured in Kalamazoo. There is some disagreement about whether Warren Cannon should be credited with that accomplishment, as Frank Burtt claimed in a *Gazette* interview in 1937. Warren Cannon may have started building his car as early as 1900, but the *Kalamazoo Morning Gazette* on October 22, 1902 verified that the Bloods completed an operative gasoline-powered vehicle no later than June of 1902, and suggested that they had tested the car well before that date. Cannon did not complete his vehicle until the fall of the same year.

That first Kalamazoo-made car was designed and built in its entirety by the Blood brothers, except for the motor, which was a French-made de Dion-Boutan single cylinder 3.3 horsepower air-cooled engine. The history of Albert de Dion and the de Dion-Boutan manufacturing enterprise that he founded rivals the history of any of the manufacturing companies in this country. Count Albert de Dion, born on March 9, 1856, was tall and handsome, with a reputation for charming manners and a facility with the rapier and the dueling pistol. He was educated at the finest German schools, a gambler of some repute, and a popular playboy among the French social elite in spite of his association with smelly internal combustion engines. He played an immense role in the development of automotive transportation with 394 engineering patents, building the first V-8 engine in 1908 and the magnificent fork and blade configured engine used in the early Lincoln. Two of his major accomplishments had a direct effect upon automobile manufacture in Kalamazoo, Michigan.

The first of these accomplishments was a one-cylinder air-cooled engine built in 1889. The de Dion-Boutan Company claimed to have over 20,000 of these engines in service by the end of 1900. Thousands were installed in motorized three-wheel cycles and others were sold to automotive companies throughout the world. Company patent policy was generous as a license was extended to all who inquired and engines were provided to over 140 companies, including Darracq, Delage, and Opel in Europe, and Packard, Peerless and Pierce Arrow in America. Considering that the Waverley bicycle was sold in Paris as well as in the Kalamazoo Cycle shop, it is not surprising that the Blood brothers, living in a small midwestern town at the turn of the twentieth century, knew about de Dion and started creating their automobile with a French-built engine.

The second of the de Dion developments was an independent rear suspension, patented in 1893, that had three features: 1) a solid axle shaft connecting the two rear wheels, 2) a differential and gear box mounted directly to the chassis above the rear axle, and 3) two half shafts with a universal joint at either end connecting the differential to the rear wheels. This sophisticated design was used on many de Dion-Boutan cars and was an essential part of the Blood brothers' early Blood car and the later Cornelian race car, built by Maurice's son Howard, that appeared in the 1914 Kalamazoo one hundred mile race and the 1915 Indianapolis 500 race. This suspension geometry was remarkable for 1893, and the fact that it is found in many modern vehicles including the 1976 Formula I Ferrari race car attests to the genius of its design.

The first Blood-built gasoline-powered automobile, or quadricycle, was nothing more than a small cart built according to bicycle technology of the day. It had a wheel base of forty-eight inches, and a gauge width between the wheels of thirty inches. The wheels were twenty-eight inches in diameter and the tires 1¾" wide, approximately the size of a balloon bicycle wheel and tire. It was a primitive affair, powered by the de Dion engine driving the rear wheels by a bicycle chain, and yet the engine was powerful enough to make the car a good hill climber. The car weighed 360 pounds with seating for only two passengers, and was equipped with flexible running gear, making it as comfortable on rough roads as an ordinary automobile. The exhaust was well muffled, but technology of the day dictated a bypass of the muffler to release back pressure thereby gaining more power. A single lever was used to regulate speed, change gears, and set the brake. The vehicle provided a top speed of twenty miles an hour on "smooth pavement" and Maurice Blood clocked 1,500 to 3,000 miles in his quadricycle during the summer of 1902 before it was discarded. There is

no indication that more than one example of this little vehicle was built. Maurice Blood used this car much as one would use a bicycle to run errands about town, including the two-mile trip from the cycle shop to his residence on Woodward Avenue for his noon dinner break. These trips were always eventful and often attracted onlookers who crowded around the vehicle, impeding his progress.

The Blood brothers also built a three-wheel pedal powered "carry-cycle," that had a seat for the driver above the single rear wheel and a bench seat in front to carry passengers; hence the

Fig. 3-4. The "carry-cycle" prototype was the second horseless carriage built by the Bloods and was finished in the fall of 1902. The Blood car was identified in Motor Age, *August 28, 1913, as the first cyclecar built in the United States, although that particular terminology was not used in the industry until at least 1910. This car was predated by the Orient Buckboard, built in Waltham, Massachusetts, from 1899–1905, which was similar to the Blood, but lacked some of the elements of the cyclecar concept. The Blood brothers built and sold about one hundred of these vehicles, almost six months before Henry Ford began manufacture of his first Model A runabout. (WMU)*

name "carry-cycle." The arrangement required the driver to turn the front axle and the passengers in order to steer the vehicle. These three-wheel cycles were built at the bicycle shop and were very popular on the board walk at Atlantic City and other ocean-side resorts.

On October 22, 1902 the Blood brothers completed the second of their light autos by adapting the "carry-cycle" to engine power. A second wheel was added on the rear, and a 3.3 horsepower engine of the de Dion-Boutan type was mounted above the rear axle. The *Gazette* report in October 1902 identifies the engine as being built by the Bloods. The fact that engines of similar design and description to the de Dion continued to appear in their cars, however, suggests that they might have continued to use the de Dion engine, since machining their own engines as early as 1902 would have been a considerable challenge.

As with the first vehicle, power for the "carry-cycle" was transmitted to the rear wheels by bicycle chains providing two speeds forward and no reverse. Control of the vehicle was by a single lever. Low gear was engaged by pulling the shift lever back about one inch and high gear was engaged by pulling it back to its limit. The brake was engaged by pushing the lever forward, releasing the transmission, and setting the brake on the rear axle. Vehicle speed was varied by twisting the grip on the lever to advance and retard the spark, thereby controlling engine speed. A button mounted at the end of the control lever was used as an engine shut off. These general operating characteristics were also found on the Blood cars that followed. This second car weighed three

hundred pounds and was mounted on a forty-five inch wheelbase with twenty-eight inch wheels and 1¾" Hartford single tube tires. It had seating for three passengers rather than two, as in the first model.

The brothers manufactured and sold about one hundred of these three passenger "carry-cycle" cars for $400 each. Recall that the Duryea company is recognized as the first automobile manufacturer for building thirteen cars of the same design in 1896; so the Bloods, while not the first, were among the first wave of pioneer automobile manufacturers in this country. Henry Ford had not yet built one hundred cars, as manufacture of the Model A runabout did not begin until June 1903, almost six months after the Bloods finished their first production run.

The manufacturing success that they found with this second vehicle was the basis for the plans of incorporation concluded on December 30, 1902 with Frank D. and Charles D. Fuller at the Kalamazoo Cycle Company. One can only imagine the excitement and perhaps a hint of trepidation as the group huddled about the coal stove on that frosty evening to form the Michigan Automobile Company Limited for the manufacture and sale of the horseless carriage in Kalamazoo. The company was incorporated with $50,000 of preferred stock and $100,000 of common stock. Charles D. Fuller was named chair-

Fig. 3-5. The third gasoline-powered horseless carriage was completed by the Blood brothers in late 1902 or early 1903. This car was identified as the Blood in the 1903 February issue of the Cycle and Automobile Trade Journal and was the forerunner of the "Little Michigan." The Blood was further refined with fenders, driving lamp, and leather-tufted seating and sold under the name of Michigan by the Michigan Automobile Company. The man on the left is thought to be Maurice Blood and the man on the right, in the ill-fitting suit and with a repair in the left pant leg, is believed to be Clarence Blood. (WMU)

man, Frank D. Fuller was named secretary, and Maurice E. Blood was named treasurer. Together with W. E. Upjohn and Dallas Boudeman, these men comprised the board of directors. The company was the first automobile manufacturer in Kalamazoo, and the first for which W. E. Upjohn would serve as treasurer or member of the board, a role he played for many other automobile manufacturers in Kalamazoo. Clarence Blood's name was conspicuously absent from the list of company officers, and, although involved in the various Blood enterprises, he never served on the board of directors. At the time of incorporation, the Michigan Automobile Company planned to continue production of the Blood "carry-cycle."

On February 9, 1903 the Michigan Automobile Company Limited acquired the big Montgomery Ward factory on the northeast corner of Prouty and North Pitcher Streets and immediately installed modern machinery for the employ of one hundred skilled craftsman. During this period, circa February 1903, Maurice and Clarence Blood designed and built a third vehicle, appropriately described as a "runabout," that they called the Blood. This vehicle was intended to replace the "carry-cycle." The runabout was powered by a 3.3 horsepower air-cooled engine mounted at the rear axle. It transmitted power to the rear wheels by roller chains, and, as with their previous models, the transmission provided two speeds forward, but for the first time offered a reverse. The twenty-eight inch wheels were mounted with heavy duty two-inch Dunlap tires. The company promised twenty miles an hour over good roads and one hundred miles on a tank of gas. The car weighed four hundred pounds and sold for $450. This "runabout" was listed in the *Cycle and Automobile Trade Journal* as late as April 1903 as the Blood, but in the same issue, using the same image, the company advertisement identified the car as Michigan Automobile Company's 1903 Model. Clearly there was consideration to replace the Blood name, and the April 1903 issue of *Motor Age* published an announcement that the name of the car would henceforth

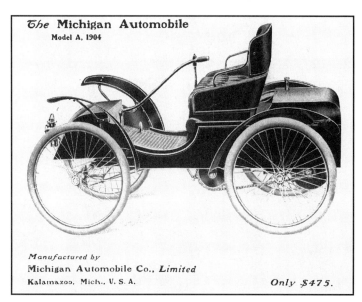

Fig. 3-6. The 1904 Michigan was built by the Michigan Automobile Company, operated in partnership by the Fullers and the Bloods, but was clearly the direct descendent of the Blood car. Letters from owners of these cars indicate that they were far more capable than the description of "a somewhat unreliable toy" proposed in another publication. (DOL)

be the Michigan. The car was subsequently refined, and in May 1903, the Michigan appeared in *Motor*, with the addition of fenders, driving chain cover, a driving lamp, and styled leather seating.

The Michigan was designated as the Model A, and production began in late spring of 1903. By the end of July, the company was producing one vehicle a day with expectations that production would rise to ten cars a week by September. The Michigan had a fifty-four inch wheel base, thirty-six inch gauge and was powered by a 3.3 horsepower air-cooled engine driving the rear wheels by chains through a two-speed transmission. There appeared to be little difference between this car and the Blood runabout except it was now described as having no reverse gear. According to the company, the machine was light enough so that it could be pushed rearward or the front end lifted to reverse its direction. A single side-mounted control lever was moved forward to select low gear and back to engage high gear. The engine speed was controlled by twisting the grip of the gear selector to retard or advance the spark, and speeds up to twenty miles an hour were possible. The precise control of the spark advance was considered a major feature of reliability, and the company literature included the comment that "Lovers are especially requested to take note of this feature."

Clearly, the automobile provided a sense of freedom that many had not known before; this idea provided a basis for the advertisement of these cars. The Michigan was finished in either red or black with crimson wheels, elaborate striping, floral designs, and a coat of arms on the dash. The company sold approximately 150 of these cars at a cost of $450 each. One of the first Michigan cars was purchased by Dr. A. H. Rockwell of Kalamazoo, who used it for house calls, and another by D. C. Olin, who used it for errands about the city until 1911. Other cars were shipped throughout the country from California to Massachusetts.

"The Car of Power" was the slogan of the company, and Frank Fuller, manager of the concern, sold the car in the press every time he got the opportunity. "The Michigan can climb any hill out of Kalamazoo," he claimed, "and do it with two persons, the capacity of the auto. It will easily make twenty miles an hour and I am satisfied it will roll up to twenty-five miles an hour on level road." During this era, buyers were also prone to write manufacturers with kudos about newly-acquired vehicles and the following curious testimonial from a letter dated July 30, 1903 was used in a company advertisement in *The Automobile* on August 8, 1903.

> I have run my machine up to yesterday about 460 miles and outside of the carburetor working bad at times it has never made a skip and will do all and more than it is represented to do.

—Name given on request—

C. W. Brown, a sales agent for the Michigan in Winnipeg, Ontario, also reported in the December 3, 1903 issue of *Motor Age*, on his test drive of the vehicle from Winnipeg to Balmoral, Ontario:

> The 80 miles were made in a little over 5 hours' running time. The roads were rough at first, but further along were excellent. On one stretch of road near Stonewall a distance of 9 miles was made in 25 minutes. There was no accident to delay the travelers on the entire trip, and although some trying pieces of road were encountered, the car went over them without trouble.

Another letter, from a prominent New York dealer and dated August 4, 1903, was published in an advertisement in *Motor Age*, on August 20, 1903:

> We like it very much, and I must say that it more than comes up to my expectations. It seems to have lots of power to spare. I ran it around Central Park and tried it on some of the hills and did not have an occasion to use the low gear.

There was little change in the Michigan Model A for 1904. Improvements were made in the rear springs, a larger cooling fan was added and heavier structural components were used, but the basic design and power train remained the same. The cost of the car was raised to $475.

Sometime after the end of the production run of the 1903 model and the beginning of the 1904 run, Maurice and Clarence Blood left the company. In March 1904, the brothers established the Blood Brothers Automobile and Machine Company at Ransom and North Pitcher Streets, near the South Haven Railroad crossing, to manufacture automobiles and automobile parts.

The demise of the Blood-Fuller partnership appeared to be as sudden as it was final. The Fuller brothers and the Michigan Automobile Company remained in the Montgomery Ward factory. The Fullers added $50,000 in capital stock to the Michigan Automobile Company Limited, and the former limited company was given up. The position of treasurer, previously held by Maurice Blood, was assumed by W. E. Upjohn. The explicit reason for the separation of the two families is unknown, but new models, larger than the Model A, were planned for 1904 and a divergence of opinion about the mechanics for the 1904 models may have been a key feature in the demise of the partnership. An announcement of the forthcoming Michigan powered by a twelve-horsepower engine appeared in *The Horseless Age* on March 30, 1904, just four days after the announcement of the Blood brothers' departure.

The personal chemistry for this partnership could not have been ideal. The Blood brothers had both been employed by the Fuller family and had left to found their own bicycle company where they built and repaired bicycles for almost ten years. There they designed and built three different automobiles, the second of which they manufactured and sold under the Blood name. They became partners with the Fullers only to find that they had but one voice on the Board of Directors and that the name of the automobile they designed and built would not be the Blood, as they had planned, but "The Michigan." This turn of events in the control of the manufacturing enterprise would not have worn well for the talented and independent Blood brothers. The separation was announced in the March 26, 1904 issue of *The Automobile*, and by June of 1904, the fourth generation Blood car and the second generation Fuller-built

Fig. 3-7. The magnificent 1905 Blood automobile was ahead of its time with the engine mounted under the hood and a four-speed sliding gear transmission mounted directly to the differential. While much is known about the mechanical aspects of these cars, little is known about the extent of the production run. (NAC)

Michigan were both on the road. These cars were not similar in appearance and were radically different in design and mechanical layout, again suggesting that the separation was founded on a disagreement about the design and construction of the planned Michigan to replace the Model A.

The newly-developed Blood automobile received a very positive review from the editors of the *Cycle and Automobile Trade Journal* in the January 1905 issue of that publication. Hugh Dolner made a special trip to Kalamazoo to test the new Blood car and began his introduction with a strong statement about manufacturing quality and the Kalamazoo environment:

> It will always be noticed that a car suits the locality in which it is produced, and if tested by its originators in rough country is sure to be a good hill-climber, and if its home roads are heavy, the car will certainly be strongly driven. The Blood brothers, two highly ingenious and expert mechanics and machine designers, are located at Kalamazoo, Mich., in a district of fine farms, owned by farmers of easy circumstances, and the large roomy, low-priced tonneau car designed by these two brothers is strongly driven at four forward speeds and has a unique tonneau body, very readily convertible into different forms, so that it can serve either as a passenger carriage or for transportation of material.

The Blood car, weighing 1,700 pounds, was mounted on a chassis with a ninety-inch wheelbase and rode on thirty-inch wheels with 3½" tires. The engine, consisting of a pair of 5" x 5" opposed cylinders, was mounted beneath the hood, rather than under the body as in the Fuller-built Michigan. The Bloods are credited with building the first car in the industry with an engine mounted in this manner. A long drive shaft with universal joints at either end connected the motor to the "change gear box," or transmission, mounted just in front of the "balance gear box" or differential all in one rigid integral supporting frame at the rear of the car. This arrangement followed the de Dion-Boutan geometry. The universal joints were described by Dolner as "decidedly novel, all hardened, self-lubricating, very strong and very durable," and he believed the quality predicted the successful future of the company.

The steering was mounted on the right, typical of the era, but the shift lever for the four-speed sliding gear transmission was mounted inside the car and to the left of the driver. The latter arrangement was atypical of the era as many cars continued to mount the transmission controls outside the car on the right, including such makes as the Buick as late as 1911. A single outside-mounted lever controlled the clutch and the rear brakes, thus putting speed control on the left of the steering wheel and braking and clutch on the right, which divided control of the car between the driver's two hands and allowed easy access in and out of the car by the right hand opening.

The test drive for *Cycle and Automobile Trade Journal* was handled by one of the sons, presumably Howard Blood, who gave an expert demonstration, changing gears flawlessly and, contrary to the usual practice, making speed changes by operating the spark advance rather than the throttle. The 1904 Blood vehicle sold at $1,500, and an almost identical model followed in 1905 on a ninety-two inch wheel base at $1,800. In spite of the apparent success, however, the Bloods chose to show automobile parts, rather than their car, at the New York and Chicago shows in the winter of 1905, perhaps foretelling the future direction of the company. On October 12, 1906 the Blood brothers ceased automobile production, and The Blood Brothers Machine Company was incorporated in Kalamazoo for the purpose of manufacturing universal joints.

Howard Blood's presence as "test driver" for the 1904 model at the age of eighteen also predicted his success and eventual rise to executive positions with Borg-Warner. But first, he had an innovative car to design and build that would prove worthy in head-to-head competition with the biggest and finest racing machines of the era.

REFERENCES

Auto Industry Here Made Its Start in 1902. *The Kalamazoo Gazette*, October 18, 1925.

Maurice Blood Taken by Death. *The Kalamazoo Gazette*, May 9, 1917.

Ross Collier. *Ross H. Collier Collection.* Regional History Collection, Western Michigan University, A-1911.

Eugene A. Sloane. *The Complete Book of Bicycling.* New York: Trident, 1970.

Cycling Trade Notes. *Outing*, February 1896, No. 5, pp. 87–92.

Dr. McNair Recalls Horses and Bicycles of Long Ago. *The Kalamazoo Gazette*, February 21, 1937.

Says Physicians Are Largest Auto Users. *The Kalamazoo Gazette*, February 20, 1912.

Jack Rennart. *100 Years of Bicycle Posters.* New York: Harper and Row, 1973.

Manager of Kalamazoo Cycle Predicts Auto Industry Will Be Greatest in Nation. *Kalamazoo Daily Telegraph*, October 20, 1900.

Kalamazoo Cycle Co. *The Motor Age*, June 12, 1902, p. 17.

Automobile No. 3. *Kalamazoo Daily Telegraph*, April 19, 1901.

The Kalamazoo Cycle Co. *The Horseless Age*, November 5, 1902, p. 519.

Smallest Car in the World. *The Kalamazoo Morning Gazette-News*, October 22, 1902.

Frank Burtt Got First Patent as a Boy. *The Kalamazoo Gazette*, February 21, 1937.

Griffith Borgeson. "The Automotive World of Albert De Dion." *Automobile Quarterly*, Vol. 15, No. 3, 1977, pp. 266–85.

_____. "A Marque is Born—The Early Products of De Dion-Boutan." *Automobile Quarterly*, Vol. 15, No. 3, 1977, pp. 290–303.

_____. "De Dion-Boutan." *Automobile Quarterly*, Vol. 22, No. 2, 1984, pp. 196–97.

A Kalamazoo Quadricycle. *The Automobile and Motor Review*, June 14, 1902, p. 15.

Kalamazoo Pioneer in Automobile Industry, Cars Made Here in 1901. *The Kalamazoo Gazette*, February 20, 1912.

Beverly R. Kimes and Henry Austin Clark Jr. *Standard Catalog of American Cars, 1805–1942 3rd ed.* Iola, WI: Krause Publications, 1996.

Claim America Cyclecar Pioneer. *Motor Age*, August 28, 1913, p. 19.

$400-Blood Automobile. *Cycle and Automobile Trade Journal*, February 1903, p. 170.

George S. May. *A Most Unique Machine, The Michigan Origins of the American Automobile Industry.* Grand Rapids, MI: William B. Erdmans, 1975.

The Blood Gasoline Car. *Cycle and Automotive Trade Journal*, April 1903, p. 86.

Getting Ready to Manufacture Those Autos. *Kalamazoo Daily Telegraph*, February 9, 1903.

Will Make Automobiles. *The Kalamazoo Evening Gazette-News*, December 28, 1902.

The Michigan Automobile Co. Ltd. *The Horseless Age*, January 14, 1903, p. 111.

The Michigan Automobile Co. Ltd. *The Automobile Review*, January 15, 1903, p. 32.

Harold Crews. "Evolution of the Michigan." *The Horseless Carriage Gazette*, January–February, 1962, pp. 16–20.

The Michigan Runabout. *Motor Age*, May 28, 1903, p. 19.

New Machine the Michigan. *The Horseless Age*, April 15, 1903, p. 490.

"Michigan" Gasoline Runabout. *The Horseless Age*, June 3, 1903, p. 652.

The Michigan Automobile. *The Automobile*, July 25, 1903, p. 64.

The Michigan Automobile Model A, Company Sales Brochure, 1904.

Michigan Runabout. *The Automobile Review*, May 1, 1903, p. 173.

To Make Ten Cars a Week. *The Motor World*, August 20, 1903, p. 773.

Michigan Air Cooled Car. *Cycle and Automobile Trade Journal*, April 1903, pp. 72, 74.

A Good Automobile for $450. *Cycle and Automobile Trade Journal*, April 1903, p. 111.

Michigan Gasoline Runabout Model A. *The Horseless Age*, February 10, 1904, p. 168.

New Auto "Michigan." *Kalamazoo Daily Telegraph*, July 25, 1903.

We Offer You For $450, The Michigan Automobile. *Cycle and Automobile Trade Journal*, August 1903, p. 111.

We Offer You for $450, The Michigan Automobile. *The Automobile Review*, October 15, 1903, p. 9.

The Michigan Automobile. *The Automobile*, August 8, 1903, p. 53.

Testing the Michigan. *Motor Age*, December 3, 1903, p. 11.

The Michigan Automobile. *Motor Age*, August 20, 1903, p. 34.

The 1904 Michigan Car. *Cycle and Automobile Trade Journal*, January 1904, p. 134.

Some Pointers About the Michigan Automobile. *The Automobile*, February 20, 1904, p. 78.

Michigan Runabout. *The Automobile*, February 27, 1904, p. 259.

Maurice E. Blood and Clarence C. Blood. *The Automobile*, March 26, 1904, p. 364.

Recent Incorporation. *The Motor World*, March 13, 1904, p. 1069.

The Michigan Automobile Co. *The Horseless Age*, March 30, 1904, p. 373.

New Touring Car. *Kalamazoo Evening Telegraph*, March 19, 1904.

Will Exhibit at Auto Show. *Kalamazoo Evening Telegraph*, January 3, 1905.

Hugh Dolner. "The Michigan Company's 1905 Cars." *Cycle and Automobile Trade Journal*, January 1905, pp. 117–20.

Fig. 4-1. Frank Burtt poses with his ordinary style bike with which he toured the eastern United States, circa 1890. (DOL)

Chapter 4

The Burtt
Manufacturing Company

1902–1912

*"Manufacturers of the
'KALAMAZOO' Automobile."*

—Burtt Advertisement

The Burtt family had a long, successful tradition in the iron foundry and furnace manufacturing business. William Burtt was an anchorsmith in Clintonville, New York, earning over $3,000 a year for his craft when, in 1854, Burtt moved to Michigan with his son, William Jr., then thirty-four years old. They brought with them $20,000 in gold for operating capital. "The money was not their best endowment for their work here, however," wrote a biographer in 1906. "That was found in their sterling manhood, their commanding enterprise and their accurate business sense." Before the death of the elder Burtt in 1861, the family built the Eagle Foundry, the first blast furnace and iron works in southwest Michigan. One of their first successes was the construction of a seventy-horsepower steam engine to power the Stockbridge Mill at the mouth of the Kalamazoo River.

William Burtt Jr. had married Martha Thorn from Vermont in 1847 and, over the next ten years, she gave birth to three sons and one daughter: Charles T., James M., Helen M., and Frank. Frank Burtt was born on August 31, 1855 in a house on the southeast corner of Cedar and Park Streets in Kalamazoo. He attended public schools in Kalamazoo and graduated from Kalamazoo College in 1876. Although he never studied mechanics, he was an energetic and mechanically skilled inventor who filed a large number of patents during his lifetime. At the age of thirteen he invented and obtained a patent for a planter, and he subsequently contracted with area farmers to plant clover seed, a familiar tale of enterprise in the chronicles of the nation's early inventors.

Frank was an avid cyclist and, in September of 1878, he purchased a used Columbia ordinary-style bike with a fifty-two inch front wheel, from William Wagner for $72.50. According to Burtt, the cycle had been purchased originally by two brothers who paid for it with money that did not

belong to them and who had to return the bike to Wagner. A number of other young men—
Charles Fisher; Bert Howard of Colman Drug Company; Robert Clarage, later president of Columbia Steel Tool Company; Chauncey Strong, later a clerk with the city and then with J. L. Sebring
Company; Ben Bush; Goddie Israel; and Addison Pengelly—also purchased ordinary style bikes,
and together they formed a bike club that was located over Bell's grocery store at the corner of

Main and Burdick Streets. They often rode to Gull Lake and
Battle Creek, although their most frequent trip was to Long
Lake where they enjoyed dinner at Nate Spicer's restaurant.
Burtt also raced bicycles, and in 1879 won Kalamazoo's first
bicycle championship.

In June of 1899, Frank Burtt left Kalamazoo on a bicycle
trip through Ohio, New Jersey, Rhode Island, Connecticut,
and Massachusetts to advertise, display, and promote the
sale of a twist drill produced by the Eames Machine Company. He carried the fourteen-pound device on the back of
his bike and, considering the condition of the roads before
the turn of the twentieth century and the energy required
to maintain speed on the ordinary bicycle, the trip had to
have been a considerable undertaking. After his return in
October of the same year he left the company, worked on

Fig. 4-2. Frank Burtt, circa 1910. (DOL)   the river barges for a spell, carrying bog ore for the local
blast furnaces, and subsequently established his own ma-
chine shop at 121 Exchange Place, the present site of the *Kalamazoo Gazette* building. There he
provided general machine shop work and was often called upon to repair the *Gazette's* presses.

Frank Burtt was smitten with automobiles after his ride in Ed Taylor's Locomobile in the spring
of 1900. He described that trip briefly in his 1937 interview with the *Gazette*: "We went south on
Park street to the 'Oaks' just south of Vine Street and then returned to the Taylor place." A year

later, in early 1901, Burtt bought
the patent to the Schau Cold-Set
Tire Setter, a device that was used
to stretch the solid rubber tires
over buggy wheels. In the same
year he incorporated the Burtt
Manufacturing Company and
moved to 128 Edwards Street at
the corner of Water Street to
manufacture and sell this device.

Walter Cannon, a resident of
nearby Vicksburg, was an expert

*Fig. 4-3. The advertisement that appeared in the 1904 Kalamazoo di-
rectory. Note the statement "Manufacturers of the Kalamazoo Automobile." There was a Kalamazoo, but it was built by the Michigan Buggy
Company, not by the Burtt Manufacturing Company. (DOL)*

machinist and a good friend of Burtt's. He previously had joined with M. B. Williams to form the
Automatic Machine Company. Since Williams was not actively involved in the business, Cannon
and Burtt combined the Burtt Manufacturing Company and the Automatic Machine Company

and incorporated the venture on October 8, 1902 as the Burtt Manufacturing Company with $10,000 in capital stock.

Cannon had been working on the development of a gasoline-powered vehicle since 1900 and he finally completed his first car, which he called the Cannon, in October of 1902. The reorganized Burtt Manufacturing Company continued the work of the Automatic Machine Company by manufacturing the I. X. L. stationary gasoline engine. Burtt brought the Schau Cold-Set Tire Setter, and

Cannon brought his newly-developed Cannon automobile to the new company, creating a formidable union at the time. Stockholders and officers were Frank Burtt, president; his brother James M. Burtt, vice-president; William B. Cannon, secretary-treasurer; and T. W. Resch of Detroit, sales manager. M. B. Williams, formerly associated

Fig. 4-4. The image is the 1904–05 Cannon Flyer that appeared in the Michigan Buggy Company catalog in 1904. This photograph is from the entry in the Burtt Company sales literature for 1905. (DOL)

with the Automatic Machine Company and a respected business man in the community, supervised the general office work.

The first Cannon car was well designed except for the engine that had been supplied by another manufacturer. In an effort to resolve the problem, Burtt and Cannon, together with Frank Lay and Henry Lane, owners of the Michigan Buggy Company, went to Chicago to inspect a car there, and after that inspection had a model shipped to Kalamazoo. Although the car was well constructed, it was simply not rugged enough for the infamous Michigan roads and they sent it back to the Chicago firm. Eventually, Warren Cannon turned to the Blood brothers for an engine when manufacture of the Cannon "Flyer" began in 1903.

The Flyer bodies were built by Charles Ford at his Fulford Street factory. The paint, in either Automobile Red or Brewster Green, and the black or russet hand-rubbed leather seating was completed by the Michigan Buggy Company just around the corner at Reed and Factory Streets. The stylish fenders were made of patent leather stretched over a wire frame. Information in the local press reported that all mechanical parts were built by the Burtt Company, although there is some indication that the runabout was powered by a one-cylinder "Michigan-style" air-cooled engine. A photograph of this engine appears in the February 27 issue of *The Automobile* in 1904, and is believed to be the work of the Blood brothers. It was used in the second of the Blood vehicles and was the same engine installed in the 1903 and 1904 Michigan car, built by the Michigan Automobile Company under the direction of the Fuller and Blood families. Some confusion stems from the Cannon being advertised in the Michigan Buggy catalog for 1904, featuring their extensive line of horse-drawn vehicles and sleighs. This display helped the Burtt Manufacturing Company sell about forty of these cars the first year.

In February of 1904, *Motor Age* and *The Automobile* reported that the Cannon car was produced cooperatively by the Burtt Manufacturing Company and the Michigan Buggy Company.

"CANNON" No. 3.   Four Passenger Light Touring Car

Fig. 4-5. The magnificent 15 horsepower Cannon with side-entrance tonneau, is similar in appearance and mechanical detail to the 1903 Model A Ford. The Ford sold for $850, and the Cannon for $1,350, a considerable difference at the time. This image is from the Burtt Company sales literature. (DOL)

Just a year prior to this announcement, Henry Lane had released information pertaining to the construction of a car by Michigan Buggy that was to be named "The Kalamazoo." Lane described the vehicle's characteristics, and reportedly at least two experimental models were built. The runabout was powered by a five-horsepower engine, and a larger vehicle intended for country roads was powered by a seven-horsepower engine, the same configuration used for the Cannon. In a 1937 interview with the *Gazette*, Burtt made no mention of "The Kalamazoo." Considering Lane's expressed caution in his newspaper report, he may have abandoned the idea of building the Kalamazoo in favor of a cooperative effort between Michigan Buggy and Burtt Manufacturing. Burtt also used the expression "manufacturers of the 'Kalamazoo' automobile" in advertising, referring to his own company, but the expression seems to be a reference to the Cannon as the "prestigious car" of Kalamazoo rather than a car by the name of the "Kalamazoo."

The 1904 Cannon Flyer was a stylish runabout with a seventy-inch wheel base, mounted on twenty-eight inch wooden artillery type wheels fitted with 2½" diamond tires. The one-cylinder seven-horsepower engine was set horizontally beneath the seat. An attractive radiator with a gentle French curve was front-mounted and the company claimed its two-gallon capacity was large enough that no steam would ever be noticed. The oiling mechanism was mounted above the engine and was sufficient for five hundred miles of driving. Cars of this era had no oil pump or recirculating feature for lubricants. Typically, the oil was slowly dripped on engine bearings and either captured in the pan at the bottom of the engine, drained and poured back into the oil reservoir, or simply allowed to drip onto the roadway and replenished periodically.

Power to the rear wheels of the Cannon was by a chain drive through a two-speed planetary transmission with reverse. The planetary transmission was typical for the period and was later used on Henry Ford's Model T. The name refers to the arrangement of a small gear circling a larger gear as a planet might circle the sun. Such a transmission was operated by bands that were drawn tight around a spinning hub engaging the gear either by depressing a pedal or moving a lever. Cannon also used a sliding gear transmission. In this case a shift lever is used to move the position of the gears relative to the drive shaft and thereby engage the gear for speed or power. Top speed for the Cannon was rated at thirty-five miles an hour. Steering was by a hinged tiller attached in the middle of the car allowing operation from either side of the seat. The throttle lever, which regulated the amount of gas to the engine, and the spark lever, which retarded the spark for slow running or advanced the spark for fast running, were mounted on the steering post. The price of this car was $650, with leather seating, two side lamps, horn, pump, and tools.

The five passenger model was powered by a fifteen-horsepower, two-cylinder engine; according to Cannon if one cylinder gave out, the other would be sufficient to drive the car home. Power to the rear wheels was provided by roller chains through a modified planetary and selective gear transmission, providing four forward speeds and reverse. In addition to the side-mounted brake and a shift lever for high and low gears, a second gear lever was mounted amidship inside the car. This second lever gave a choice of either a ten miles an hour gear speed for the flat roads, or a three miles an hour gear speed for hill climbing. The wheel base was 84½" and the car rode on thirty-inch wheels with three-inch diamond pattern tires. Steering was by a right-mounted steering wheel with the spark and throttle mounted on the steering post.

The five passenger cars sold for $1,350 and were offered in three styles, which, according to Burtt, included the first side-entrance tonneau in the country. The "tonneau" is the open seating area of the vehicle, and on many early automobiles passenger access was through a rear-mounted door. After a rain, when the dirt streets had turned to mud, cars with a rear-entrance tonneau backed up perpendicular to the wooden sidewalk to allow passengers to enter the rear door without walking in the mud; this inconvenience was avoided with the side-entrance design. Burtt anticipated a production run of fifty of the fifteen-horsepower cars and five hundred of the seven-horsepower cars. Interestingly, the large fifteen-horsepower model was very similar to Henry Ford's 1903 Model A; however, the Model A sold for only $850 with a production run of 685 cars during the nine months between June 1903 and March 1904.

Locally, Charles B. Hays purchased two of the single seat "Flyer" models to be used as a part of the campaign to develop the Hays Park area on the south side of the city. Hays had purchased this land in 1899, and built over one hundred affordable homes with proper heating, lighting, and sanitary plumbing. The development attracted a number of paper mills as well as the Burtt Manufacturing Company, the Charles Ford Body Factory, the Michigan Buggy Company, and the Kalamazoo Railway Supply Company to the area and was considered very beneficial to the city. The Cannon was sold locally to many citizens and also shipped to Detroit, Chicago, Kansas City, and Buffalo.

Frank Burtt built at least two custom cars, one for himself and the other for James C. Hatfield, then secretary of the Kalamazoo Corset Company. Burtt built the first car using the same engine, running gear, and chain drive found in the production Cannon vehicles, but the engine was mounted in front of the dash rather than beneath the seat. This particular car was later made into a truck and driven to south Texas. The second car that was built for Hatfield had a four-cylinder engine, chain drive and a four-speed sliding gear transmission. It was a massive vehicle with a large fly wheel allowing the engine to turn at slow speeds without missing, and Hatfield usually won the local "slow races" that were popular at the time the car was built. The car also sported a large full windshield, not typical for the period, and a handsome Victoria top. The top is named after Queen Victoria, and is reminiscent of a royal carriage, appearing like a "clamshell" over the rear tonneau of the car leaving the driver's area open. Hatfield's Cannon car compared well in size and accoutrements with other luxury cars of the era.

Fig. 4-6. This building is the Burtt Manufacturing Company factory believed to have been located at the southwest corner of Fulford and Clinton Streets. (DOL)

The company did very well in 1904 and Burtt bragged that the Cannon car was so popular that the company had fallen behind in filling orders. The prosperity was sufficient to convince Burtt in late 1905 to build a new and much larger factory at Clinton and Fulford Streets just around the corner from Michigan Buggy. Despite the fact that the ever-optimistic Burtt boasted that the 1905 models were lighter and more powerful than previous vehicles, production ceased sometime in early 1906.

In his 1937 interview with the *Gazette*, Burtt suggested that the financial climate in 1906 simply was not conducive to the growth of automobile manufacturing in Kalamazoo. Other writers have suggested that the success of the local paper mills drew off available venture capital, leaving little for development of the automobile industry. Interestingly, the three automobile manufacturers in Kalamazoo at this time—Burtt, Blood Brothers, and Michigan—all diverted their manufacturing to automobile-related products, rather than automobiles, around 1906–07.

Burtt did continue to manufacture stationary engines for the next several years, but could not resist the challenge of automobile manufacturing. In December of 1909, Burtt disclosed his plans to build a chassis for a light-duty truck and several automobile models. A four-cylinder forty-horsepower air-cooled engine and chain drive were planned for these vehicles and the truck was designed to carry 1,500 pounds, making it suitable for milk, groceries, and other small delivery requirements. In typical Burtt style, his pronouncement about the vehicle, published in the December 19, 1909 issue of *The Kalamazoo Gazette*, was filled with enthusiasm:

> No cars of this description are now being made and the manufacture of the Burtt car will
> occupy a place unique in the annals of the development of the gasoline propelled delivery
> vehicle in this country. The tonneaus are the work of some of the best designers in Detroit.
> Any style body will be made to be mounted on the standard Burtt chassis.

While Burtt claimed to have built some examples of this car, no evidence of the manufacture of this vehicle exists.

In less than two years, on September 29, 1911, he announced plans to organize another company with capital stock of $100,000 and plans to erect a large factory for manufacture of a street cleaner he had invented. This suction-type device deposited refuse into a large bag for disposal, was operated by a gasoline engine, and mounted on an automobile frame. Although not reported as such, he may have intended to incorporate the design for the cleaner into the previously planned

light truck chassis. He claimed that the street cleaner was capable of cleaning forty miles of streets in a twenty-four hour period.

Sadly, on February 22, 1912, the Burtt Manufacturing Company was closed by a judgment of involuntary bankruptcy brought about by a creditor's petition in

Fig. 4-7. Frank Burtt's early residence, located at 939 Washington.(DOL)

federal court in Grand Rapids, Michigan. The ever-optimistic Burtt was undaunted, predicting another reorganization with increased capital to manufacture gasoline engines that he had designed in 1909. According to the *Gazette* of December 19, 1909, these engines were well respected in the industry and sold well in Europe, Canada, and the United States. Interestingly, in 1909 the Michigan Buggy Company began manufacturing cars within a few blocks of the Burtt Manufacturing Company. In spite of their former association with Burtt, they preferred to order their four-cylinder engines from the Hazard Motor Manufacturing company of Rochester, New York.

Frank Burtt's activities from 1912 to 1917 are not well known, although he continued to be listed as the president of the Burtt Manufacturing Company. The company's moves from the big plant at Fulford and Clinton Streets to a downtown office and then to office number 313 in the Park building suggest a steady decline in business and productivity. The activity does suggest, however, that Burtt continued to manufacture what appeared to be a reliable forty-horsepower engine, but local manufacturers seemed unconvinced of its worth. Ironically, Frank Burtt's wife, Harriet, was killed by an automobile on June 3, 1923, as she walked home from a friend's house. She was sixty-four years old.

Burtt joined the faculty of Kalamazoo Central High School in 1917 where he taught in the manual arts training department. He continued to work there through 1926, retiring at the age of seventy-one. Ten years later he was still active, and his teaching stint must have left its mark. In the 1937 interview with the *Gazette*, he described his invention of a machine for cleaning blackboard erasers in, as he described it, "a sanitary and business-like manner." He intended to manufacture this device, but the extent of his success in this venture is unknown.

Frank A. "Dad" Burtt died on March 10, 1952 at the age of ninety-six. He was a dreamer, an inventive genius and a pioneer in the automobile industry in Kalamazoo. His failures diminish neither his talent nor his dedication, but serve instead to embellish the success of those who continued to thrive in this young and competitive marketplace. The Cannon automobile survived for only five years, 1902 through 1906—a vehicle of some promise that might have survived if the financial times had been supportive.

~

REFERENCES

David Fisher and Frank Little, eds. *Compendium of History and Biography of Kalamazoo County, Mich*. Chicago: A. W. Bowen, 1906.

"Firsts" in Kalamazoo. *The Kalamazoo Gazette*, October 18, 1925.

Frank Burtt Got First Patent as a Boy. *The Kalamazoo Gazette*, February 21, 1937.

Burtt Manufacturing. *Kalamazoo City Directory*, Kalamazoo: Ihling Bros. & Everard, 1904, p. 7.

Automatic Machine Co. *The Kalamazoo Gazette-News*, January 5, 1902.

The Burtt Manufacturing Company. *The Horseless Age*, October 15, 1902, p. 440.

The Schau Cold Set Tire Setter. *The Vicksburg Commercial*, August 15, 1902.

Will Build Automobiles. *The Kalamazoo Gazette-News*, October 8, 1902.

Gazette of 1904 Tells of First Motor Industry. *The Kalamazoo Gazette*, October 18, 1925.

The Cannon Automobiles. Burtt Manufacturing and Michigan Buggy Company Sales Brochure, 1904.

The Michigan Runabout. *The Automobile*, February 27, 1904, p. 259.

Michigan Buggy Co. High Grade Carriages for the Trade. Michigan Buggy Co. catalog, 1904.

Burtt Mfg. Co. and Michigan Buggy Co. *Motor Age*, February 11, 1904, pp. 13–14.

Cannon Automobiles. *The Automobile*, February 13, 1904, pp. 190–92.

Michigan Buggy Company Announces The Kalamazoo. *The Horseless Age*, August 5, 1903. p. 158.

Cannon Runabout. *The Automobile*, February 20, 1904, p. 53.

George S. May, *A Most Unique Machine*. Grand Rapids, MI: William B. Eerdmans, 1975.

Cannon Runabout and Tonneau. *Cycle and Automobile Trade Journal*, March 1904, p. 89.

Cannon Gasoline Cars. *Cycle and Automobile Trade Journal*, April 1904, p. 88.

The Burtt Manufacturing Co. *Cycle and Automobile Trade Journal*, February 1905, p. 205.

To Erect New Factory Plant. *The Kalamazoo Gazette*, August 4, 1905.

Automobile Specifications. *Motor*, January 1906, pp. 22, 82.

Burtt Manufacturing. *Kalamazoo City Directory*, Detroit: R. L. Polk Co., 1908, p. 2.

Kalamazoo to Have New Auto Industry. *The Kalamazoo Gazette*, December 19, 1909.

Suction Cleaner for Streets to be Made by Kalamazoo Company. *The Kalamazoo Gazette*, September 29, 1911.

Burtt Manufacturing Co. Declared Insolvent. *The Kalamazoo Gazette*, February 23, 1912.

Local Woman, Struck Down by Auto, Dies. *The Kalamazoo Gazette*, June 3, 1923.

Frank Burtt Dies; Early Auto Maker. *Kalamazoo Gazette*, March 10, 1952.

Chapter 5

Rough and Tumble Vicksburg

1899–1904

"… plain and unvarnished, like Truth itself, yet it has a neat and business-like appearance which gives it standing among vehicles of the same nature."

—*Kalamazoo Telegraph*

The fall of 1902 was an exciting time for automobilists in Kalamazoo, Michigan. Several horseless carriages had been delivered to prominent residents of the community and their presence on the streets of the city was almost a daily occurrence during the driving season. The Blood brothers were feverishly working on their second automobile and Walter C. Cannon was testing and refining his machine. M. Henry Lane and Frank Lay of the Michigan Buggy Company were also considering construction of a gasoline buggy, but had not yet announced their plans.

In nearby Vicksburg, Michigan, Theodore A. Ells had built a machine of his own design. He was, according to the *Kalamazoo Telegraph* of August 9, 1902, "…a plain, matter-of-fact man… an unrecognized genius." The Ells vehicle was a familiar sight on the country roads in and around Vicksburg in the fall of 1902, and Ells often drove his motorcar to Kalamazoo for pleasure as well as business.

Vicksburg, Michigan, located just southeast of Kalamazoo, was a thriving village of about one thousand residents in the late 1800s. The town served as the stopping place for teamsters and mule skinners who hauled agricultural goods and distillery products to the logging camps north of Allegan, Michigan. On the return trip they brought pine lumber, shingles, and other building supplies for the dealers on the southern prairies. These were rough and tumble men whose exploits and occasional brawls around the town's infamous distillery were part of the local legend. At least one of the incidents involved gun fire and one or more of the bullets hit Ells' popcorn machine. While some suggested that these tales gave the town a "black eye," the fierce competition and rivalry also ignited industrial growth in the area.

Fig. 5-1. Main Street, Vicksburg, Michigan, circa 1905. One might imagine that the small vehicle on the left is the Clark steam carriage. (DOL)

Theodore A. Ells moved to Vicksburg just before the turn of the twentieth century and purchased the J. J. Carney building on the north side of Prairie Street. There he opened a confectionery where he sold candy, ice cream, and tobacco products. Business was good and Ells appeared to be a popular and successful businessman. Many references identify him, almost affectionately, as "Popcorn Dick." He was also a progressive businessman for in 1899 he purchased and installed in his place of business a Wolverine engine—possibly from Grand Rapids, Michigan—for the purpose of freezing ice cream. Reportedly this engine was not satisfactory and was soon replaced with a three-horsepower Oldsmobile engine that apparently provided the required service.

The car that he built received a glowing review in the August 9, 1902 *Kalamazoo Telegraph*:

> The sample which Mr. Ells has built for his own use is plain and unvarnished, like Truth itself, yet it has a neat and business-like appearance which gives it standing among vehicles of the same nature…. Ever since the automobile craze started Mr. Ells has been a student of that branch of mechanical ingenuity…."

Theodore Ells began the construction of his automobile in the winter of 1902. A gasoline engine, frame, and wheels were obtained from various manufacturers, and then assembled according to his design. The wooden artillery-style wheels were a special order from a St. Louis company and were fitted with heavy pneumatic tires. Ells touted the wheel construction and the tires as being superior for country travel compared to the light wire-spoke wheels used on many vehicles in that period. The *Telegraph* review described his work as follows:

> The devices for stopping, starting, quick handling of power and perfect control of the auto, are all of Mr. Ells' own designing. He is now at work upon the plans for a gasoline motor of superior motive power and light weight and expects soon to undertake the manufacture of automobiles for commercial use.

The fate of the Ells automobile is unknown, and there is no evidence that he built more than the one example. He sought funding for his venture, and he was quoted in the same 1902 *Telegraph* article as saying that "the merit contained in his auto [was] such, that success would follow if launched by a company properly capitalized." Ells considered the car to be far superior to those machines built for speed alone, and he thought it particularly well designed for use on the primitive roads outside Michigan cities. He estimated that $25,000 would be sufficient to start manufacture, an amount that is just over twice that needed by the Blood brothers to start the Kalamazoo Bicycle Company in 1891. The discrepancy suggests that Ells did not understand the amount of financial backing required for the manufacture of a gasoline-propelled horseless carriage.

One might wonder how the owner of a candy store was able to build a gasoline-powered horseless carriage in 1902. Early issues of some of the motoring magazines, for example the August 6 issue of *The Horseless Age* in 1902, carried a description of the Brecht chassis and running gear that were built in St. Louis, Missouri. The Rutenber engine, built in Logansport, Indiana, was also available at this time and was considered one of the most reliable American-made engines just after the turn of the twentieth century. The famous one-cylinder air-cooled de Dion-Boutan engine, manufactured in France, was also available through dealers in Boston, Massachusetts. The latter engine had been purchased by the Blood brothers in Kalamazoo. By 1903, available magazines such as *The Automobile* were filled with advertisements for engines, carburetors, radiators, running gear, castings, body components, instruction books, and other essentials for the construction of a horseless carriage. Ells is known to have purchased and maintained both a Wolverine and an Oldsmobile engine prior to the construction of his vehicle, so he was not a stranger to the concepts and operating characteristics of the internal combustion engine. There is every reason to believe that he would have been aware of the various sources of commercially available engines, running gear, and chassis components necessary for the construction of a gasoline-powered automobile.

Fig. 5-2. Theodore A. Ells, circa 1902. (DOL)

The construction of gasoline-powered vehicles by the town blacksmith or village craftsman was not commonplace just after the turn of the twentieth century, but neither was it a complete rarity. The availability of suppliers and Ells' reference to the St. Louis company suggest that the Brecht Company may have been the source of his reported genius and the car that the *Telegraph* reporter tagged with an appearance "like Truth itself." Whatever the source of his automotive components, however, one can only imagine the sheer excitement in building an operable automobile in 1902, the joy of travel in a vehicle built by one's own hand, and the immense frustration at the failure to find the necessary funding to begin manufacture of a machine that appeared to have such business potential.

Theodore Ells was not the only automobile builder in Vicksburg. Brothers Vern C. and Omer E. Clark arrived in Vicksburg in 1898, about the same time Theodore Ells arrived, and established the Clark Brothers Company for the purpose of building a feed water-regulating device. This regulator was a simple float arrangement with an attached valve that regulated water flow similar to the control found in a modern toilet. In an effort to demonstrate this invention, credited to Omer, and to attract attention to the Clark Brothers Company, Omer also designed and built two steam cars. These two cars were not the earliest self-propelled vehicles built in the Kalamazoo area, but they were the first to be successfully driven and sold. Both vehicles were fitted with the Clark regulator alarm column that maintained the water supply at a predetermined level, making it impossible for the vehicle to boil dry.

The two Clark steam-powered vehicles are believed to be of the runabout style that were quite standard in design for the period. One of the two examples was shipped to Chicago for display in June of 1901, a decade after the Rhodes steam wagon ran Rose Street, but a full year before the Blood brothers had an operable gasoline-propelled vehicle on the road. The Clark automobile was subsequently sold there for $750. The report in *The Vicksburg Commercial* concluded that the price was a tribute to the vehicle, since the car had been run five hundred miles and the same amount of money was sufficient to purchase any one of a number of standard makes available at the show. As a result of the display and the sale, *The Commercial* reported that the Clark Brothers Company

Fig. 5-3. The Brecht Automobile Company of St. Louis, Missouri advertised this runabout body and running gear in the August 6, 1902 issue of The Horseless Age. *The angle iron frame is hung on semi-elliptic springs over wooden artillery-type wheels mounted with 3" x 30" pneumatic tires. Perhaps this is the car that caused the* Gazette *reporter to describe the Ells's auto as "simple, plain and unvarnished, like Truth itself." (DOL)*

obtained a large contract for automobile steam regulators from one of the largest automobile manufacturers in the west.

References in *Water Over the Dam* cite a report in *The Commercial* that Omer and Vern Clark drove the second machine to Ohio around July 17, 1901. It was a trip of 250 miles, and they had planned to drive about 125 miles each day. Considering the quality of the Michigan roads, which were notoriously poor at the time, their planned trip was a considerable undertaking and the anticipated mileage had to be extremely optimistic. Their successful return was documented in *The Commercial* on August 25, 1901 and the two men reported only that "they had a nice time."

There is no record of the eventual disposal of the second car, nor any indication that the Clark brothers built more than the two examples. Apparently, the brothers were well satisfied with the original intent of the company to manufacture water control devices and had built and driven both automobiles just to promote the company and for their own recreation and enjoyment.

Carson Durkee was another of the erstwhile inventors in Vicksburg, and had arrived in town well before the turn of the twentieth century. He was an agent for the Dentler Bagger Company and proprietor of the Durkee House, one of four hotels in the village. There he offered both elegant lodging and extravagant entertainment. He hired a dance band for the grand opening of his hotel in 1882, charging fifty cents for dancing and seventy-five cents for an oyster dinner for two. This first gala affair was so successful that the Durkee house continued to be the local center of entertainment throughout most of the "Gay Nineties" and was often the site of carnivals and traveling shows that visited Vicksburg around the turn of the century.

Carson Durkee was also a mechanic. According to a report in *The Kalamazoo Gazette* on August 4, 1933, he had finished construction of a gasoline-powered vehicle in 1903, the same time that the

Fig. 5-4. The 1903 Durkee horseless carriage as it appeared in 1933. The only known record of this vehicle is The Kalamazoo Gazette *article in 1933. Its whereabouts after restoration in 1933 is unknown. (DOL)*

Michigan was being advertised and sold through national publications. Durkee had begun his work about the same time as the Blood brothers, and in 1899 he started hand-turning many of the parts for the car from special castings. The vehicle he eventually built had a small open body with a buggy-type seat, buggy springs, and buggy wheels fitted with iron tires. The 1500 pound vehicle was propelled by a small air-cooled engine, of an unknown source, and was equipped with a side oiler that required about half a pint of oil every three hundred miles. Replenishing the engine oil was typical for motorcars of the period; even Henry Ford had yet to develop a system for recirculating the lubricants in the engines he built. The air-cooled engine was mounted beneath the seat, and power to the rear wheels was provided by a two-speed planetary transmission. Steering was by a right-hand mounted wheel, and the small gasoline tank and tool box were enclosed in the front compartment. These characteristics were also typical of early vehicles.

While the Durkee car was built to start with a hand crank, the newly-built engine was tight and he was unsuccessful starting the car in this manner in his first outing. The car was pulled up a hill by a horse so that the engine could be spun fast enough to start as it coasted down the incline. One might assume that amid the cheers, cries of "get a horse" could be heard during that inaugural run. After the initial break-in run that day, Durkee apparently made numerous trips around Vicksburg and these excursions always attracted a crowd. Reportedly, the vehicle was capable of running at about seven miles an hour and carried sufficient gasoline for a range of seventy-five miles. The driving range of the vehicle was important since gasoline was not readily available in Vicksburg in 1903. *The Gazette* reported in 1933 that Durkee spent about $3,000 developing this machine and that he built a second vehicle that he sold to a monied family in Port Huron, Michigan.

Fig. 5-5. The scene portrays West Michigan Avenue looking east toward Portage Street at the time when Theodore Ells drove to Kalamazoo seeking financial investors. One can easily imagine this scene when Ells parked his car below the KOOLS sign on the left-hand side of the street on his way to visit one of the local banks. (WMU)

The August 4, 1933 issue of *The Kalamazoo Gazette* also reported that the engine installed in the Durkee motorcar was built by the Michigan Buggy Company in 1899 according to Durkee's specifications. Such a claim is doubtful. There is no other independent evidence that the Michigan Buggy Company ever built an engine or drive train for an automobile during any period of the company's existence. The Michigan Buggy Company flirted with the construction of an automobile in 1903, when the Durkee was being completed—a car that was to be called the Kalamazoo—but their own 1904 catalog featured the Cannon automobile constructed as a joint venture with the Burtt Manufacturing Company. At the same time, the Blood brothers, in conjunction with the Fuller family, built the Michigan automobile and it also was powered by a one-cylinder air-cooled engine. Other sources make reference to the Cannon automobile using a "Michigan-style" one-cylinder air-cooled engine, but those most likely refer to the engine used in the Michigan motorcar built by the Bloods and the Fullers. A photograph of the Michigan air-cooled motor, rated at 3.3 horsepower, appears in the February 27, 1904, issue of *The Automobile*. This motor is assumed to be the work of the Blood brothers and would have been built in the fall of 1902, and thus available for installation in the Durkee in 1903. Finally, The Michigan Motor Company was established in Grand Rapids in 1904, but little is known of the engine availability or its length of production.

The Michigan Buggy Company was involved in the manufacture of the Cannon, but not the construction of either the "Little Michigan" or the Durkee. Many newspaper reports and subsequent historical references confused the early "Little Michigan" that was built in 1903 and 1904 with the "Mighty Michigan" built by the Michigan Motor Car Company that was owned by the Michigan Buggy Company during the period 1909–13. These sources often indicate that both of the Michigan cars were built by Michigan Buggy. *The Kalamazoo Gazette* report in 1933 seems to reflect that same confusion.

The Durkee vehicle was eventually stored in a railroad tie shed near Vicksburg, Michigan, where it was discovered in 1933 following Durkee's death. Duane Hopkins, a local mechanic, restored the car to running condition and it was placed on display. The present location of the vehicle is unknown and its existence is not recorded in *The Standard Catalog of American Cars* or other recognized automobile encyclopedic references. This car is yet another example of the hundreds of cars built by local craftsman who were unable to meet the enormous financial and technical challenge of organizing the commercial manufacture of a horseless carriage.

REFERENCES

T. A. Ells of Vicksburg. *The Horseless Age*, August 6, 1902, p. 204.

In Early Days; Vicksburg Was Known as Brady. *The Kalamazoo Gazette*, February 11, 1914.

Invented an Auto. *Kalamazoo Evening Telegraph*, August 9, 1902.

Grace Molineaux, ed. *Water Over the Dam*. Vicksburg, MI: Vicksburg Commercial, 1972.

C. H. Wendel. *American Gasoline Engines Since 1872*. Osceola WI: Crestline Motorbooks, 1994.

The Brecht Automobile Parts. *The Horseless Age*, August 6, 1902, p. 149.

Clark Brothers. *The Vicksburg Commercial*, June 21, 1901.

The Clark Steam Automobile. *The Vicksburg Commercial*, June 28, 1901.

Omer and Verne Clark Arrive Home. *The Vicksburg Commercial*, August 21, 1901.

1903 Automobile, Unearthed Again in Use. *The Kalamazoo Gazette*, August 4, 1933.

The Michigan Runabout. *The Automobile*, January 27, 1904, p. 259.

Michigan Vehicles, Michigan Buggy Company Sales Brochure, 1904.

Beverly R. Kimes and Henry Austin Clark, Jr. *Standard Catalog of American Cars, 1805–1942 3rd ed*. Iola, WI: Krause Publications, 1996.

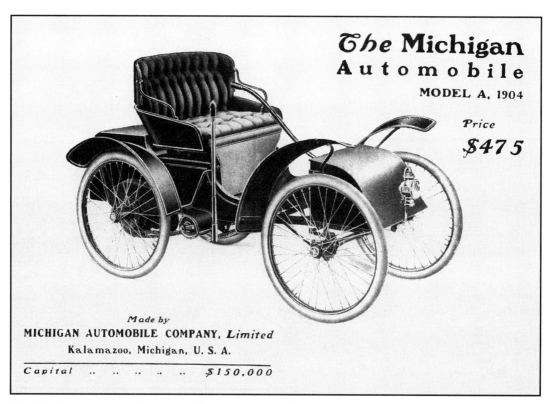

The Michigan
Automobile
MODEL A, 1904

Price
$475

Made by
MICHIGAN AUTOMOBILE COMPANY, *Limited*
Kalamazoo, Michigan, U. S. A.

Capital $150,000

6-1. The Blood car evolved into the Michigan light runabout, nicknamed the "Little Michigan" and designated as a Model A. The Michigan was powered by a 3.3 horsepower air-cooled engine. Images of this vehicle began to appear in articles in Cycle and Automobile Trade Journal *as early as April 1903. The company produced about one hundred of these automobiles in 1903 and perhaps another fifty in 1904. This image is from the 1904 Michigan Company sales catalog. The Blood brothers left the company in early 1904 to manufacture a new Blood car, and the Fullers designed another Michigan that was on the road by June 1904. (DOL)*

Chapter 6

Fuller Brothers
Manufacturing

1903–1958

"The Michigan—
The Car of Power"

—Company Slogan

George P. Fuller, king of the washboard, was born November 21, 1934 in Yates County, New York, married in 1857, and eventually moved westward to Wisconsin. He invented the ubiquitous washboard that the family company manufactured and sold in abundance under thirty-five brand names, including by 1892, $1.8 million sales of the celebrated "Northern Queen." Fuller began manufacturing washboards, driers, and other woodenware in 1885 in Minneapolis, Minnesota; the family then moved to Kalamazoo in 1888 to take advantage of the good business climate.

Frank D. Fuller, son of George, was the family envoy. He started his career as a teacher in Wisconsin, then spent five years in the legal profession and was in the process of rejoining the family business when he visited Kalamazoo on December 14, 1887. He purchased two acres where the Grand Rapids and Illinois tracks intersected with the Lakeshore rails north of the city, and there the family constructed a large brick building. They purchased a million linear feet of basswood and hired fifty workers to begin the manufacture of the indispensable washboard. The company continued to grow and reported a work force of eighty and annual sales of $130,000 by July of 1891, sending washboards throughout this country, and to Britain, Australia, and South America.

In December of 1891, fire struck the Fuller Company factory damaging the goods on the second floor and much of the structure. Hose Cart #3 had been summoned, but in the process of reeling off the hose, a stream of water sprayed the horses and they took off with the cart, running along the tracks, across Paterson Street, and then south to Bush Street where the cart was dumped. The horses were not hurt, but the melee interfered with the firefighting. Damage to the building was estimated at $10,000, and the factory was closed for a month.

49

The following incident conveys the general climate on the factory floor when it reopened its doors. On St. Patrick's Day, March 17, 1892, several men appeared at the factory wearing green ties, and announced that they were exercising their American privilege of the "wearing of the green." Soon after their arrival a representative of management approached each man with a mandate: "take off that green or quit work at once." All removed their ties except Percy Cannon, Frank Broughton, and John Milbach, and each in turn was subsequently fired for their insubordination. The *Gazette* reporter was unable to reach a member of the Fuller family to obtain comment at the time.

Fig. 6-2. The original Blood/Michigan was designed and built by the Blood brothers just prior to or just after the incorporation of the Michigan Automobile Company in December 1902. This car has no fenders or driving lamps and the seating is minimal at best. A manufacturer's picture and description of this car as a Blood appears in Cycle and Automobile Trade Journal, *in April 1903, and as the Michigan in an advertisement in the same issue, and again under automobile news in the* Automobile Review, *May 1, 1903. (KLL)*

A year later, the Fullers sold the washboard factory to the American Washboard Company. The family remained active in manufacturing during this period, although their efforts were scattered and purportedly even extended into coal mines in the state of Kansas. Reportedly, on December 30, 1893 they established the town of Fuller, Kansas, and anticipated the construction of some thirty houses and a hotel before the close of 1894. A year later George announced a $200,000 contract to supply coal to the street railways and stockyards in Kansas City. In spite of such apparent business success, the name "Fuller" is not listed as a town in Kansas. The Fuller Manufacturing Company, owned by Charles D. Fuller, and manufacturers of the Yankee drill grinder, was sold in 1900 to a Grand Rapids company. Charles turned his many talents to inventing, and in 1901 he devised a machine for hulling beans that he sold to the American Hulled Bean Company of Battle Creek, Michigan. Other activities followed, including the presidency of Sperry Hardware, an interest in the Munising Paper Company, and investments in the Korn Krisp Company of Battle Creek.

George P. Fuller died on April 11, 1901 after a two-year illness that had slowed his activities, but not made him bedridden. He was mourned by a community that respected him for his intelligence, kindly manner, and literary abilities. The obituary in the April 11, 1901 issue of the *Gazette* stated that he was survived by his widow, but curiously did not give her name. The three sons, Charles, Fred, and Frank, were mentioned individually. Fuller also left behind a volume of religious and poetic writings that was well respected for its literary contribution.

The developing automobile industry also attracted the energetic Fullers, and when the Blood brothers began producing a small gasoline-powered vehicle, the Fuller family regrouped in Kalamazoo and approached the Bloods with an investment proposal. Subsequently, The Kalamazoo Automobile Company Limited was founded in the Blood brothers' bicycle shop on December 30, 1902. Charles Fuller was named president, Frank D. Fuller, secretary, and Maurice Blood, treasurer. W. E. Upjohn and Dallas Boudemen were appointed to the board.

Initially, the car that was to be manufactured by the company was to be called the Blood, but a decision was made early in 1903 to rename the car the Michigan. In spite of its slogan, "The Car of Power," it is often called the "Little Michigan" to differentiate it from the Mighty Michigan produced by the Michigan Buggy Company from 1909 to 1913. In spite of its diminutive size, many owners reported that it was both strong and agile with documented testing over rough roads. The following testimonial was sent from Chattanooga, Tennessee, December 28, 1903:

> In reply to yours of recent date will say that the "Michigan" you sold me is a good machine and a sure hill climber. I have not found the hill yet that has taken all the power to ascend. I have had it ten weeks today and has not cost me one cent for repairs, never refused to start, go where I want it to and come home again. Saturday night I returned home from a 10 days hunt, from Cumberland Mountains, two of us, a tent, cooking utensils, a 300 lb. deer, some squirrels and mountain pheasants on and in the little Michigan. We covered 38 miles in 2 hours and 17 minutes.

The Michigan runabout was a light car intended to occupy a place between the voiturette, an early two-seat touring car without a top, and the "unsociable motor bicycle" and to sell at a low price. From all reports the Michigan seemed to fill that niche quite well. These cars were powered by a single-cylinder air-cooled engine using a belt-driven aluminum fan for cooling. Power was conveyed by chains to the rear wheels via a two-speed transmission with no reverse. Weight was 575 pounds; the steering was by tiller; and seating was described as ample for two. The car sold for $450 in 1903 and $475 in 1904, although there was little difference between the two models.

The eventual founding of the Michigan Automobile Company of Grand Rapids, incorporated to sell automobiles, created additional confusion that often haunts the history of these firms, as do other references to firms using similar titles with the Michigan name. The change in the name of the car was the first hint of potential dissatisfaction between the Blood brothers and the Fullers, and there was some confusion in 1903 about the style of the automobile to be offered. The "Blood" car was listed by name as the vehicle made by the Michigan Automobile Company and was shown in the trade journals in April 1903, but it was subsequently displayed in other journals under the name of "Michigan." In April of 1903, the *Cycle and Automobile Trade Journal* carried an advertisement for the Michigan that showed the Blood car with neither fenders nor driving lamp. At the same time it published a picture and a description of the Michigan that showed the new Model A with fenders and a lamp. Similar contradictions appeared in other journals into May of that year.

Perhaps the slowness of the mails and the preparation of the publications created the spurious record, but within a year the two families separated to establish their own companies, although it is not known whether the separation was amicable or rancorous. On March 19, 1904 an article appeared in the *Kalamazoo Telegraph-Press* that a new Michigan was being developed with a twelve-horsepower motor. According to that press release, the car was designed by F. D. Fuller and W. E.

Fig. 6-3. The 1904 Model D Michigan, designed by F. D. Fuller and W. E. Russell, was the first automobile built exclusively by the Fuller family and the second car built by the Michigan Automobile Company. More substantial than the "Little Michigan" Model A, it was equipped with proper steering gear, a two-speed planetary transmission and a two-cylinder twelve-horsepower engine. This four-passenger model, with rear-entrance tonneau, painted with fifteen coats of light automobile red, trimmed in wine color, and finished with deep green leather seating, sold for $1,000. About thirty of these cars were built, including tonneau and runabout models. (DOL)

Russell who had spent considerable time at the Chicago Car Show in January making an exhaustive study of over two hundred cars. There was no mention of the Blood brothers.

Subsequent to this article, the old Michigan Limited Company was set aside and a new Michigan Automobile Company Limited was incorporated with an additional $50,000 in investment capital. W. E. Upjohn assumed the treasurer's position that Maurice Blood had vacated.

One can only imagine the force of these strong-willed men who held equally strong beliefs in their abilities to satisfy the mechanical requirements for manufacturing a quality horseless carriage. It was an era when some people continued to laugh at these motorized buggies as passing fads. But these gentlemen were simply too successful to bend easily to the opinions of others, and the variance in the design of the automobiles that each family eventually produced after the separation offer some insight into the potential rift between the Bloods and the Fullers.

The Model A Michigan, nicknamed the "Little Michigan," is also described within the Blood story, for it was truly their car. The Model A Michigan was derived from the original Blood car and was not a design of the Fuller brothers. The Model D Michigan car was the first to be built by the Fuller-controlled Michigan Automobile Company. It was larger and more substantial in appearance than the first, weighing 1,400 pounds, with seating for five on a 78" wheel base. The engine

Fig. 6-4. The 1904 Model D runabout without tonneau. The rear seat, or tonneau, was removed and the runabout was created with rear decking supplied by the manufacturer. The runabout sold for $900. (DOL)

consisted of two 4.5" x 5" opposed cylinders lying horizontally in the chassis with a planetary transmission offering two forward speeds and reverse. The car was listed for $1,000 when production began on June 1, 1904 and was limited to about thirty examples. The first carload of these autos was sent to the Newark Automobile Company on July 9, 1904. The low production run suggests that this was the transition model between the Blood and the Fuller-designed automobiles, possibly incorporating some of the mechanics from each.

Perhaps Maurice and Clarence did not like the design and left the company in protest, or Frank and Charles Fuller may not have liked the Blood design ideas; in any case, the Fullers ceased production of the Model A, quickly turning to a design of their own. Whatever the circumstance, Model D seemed to be well-received by those who purchased it, and it was later described by Hugh Dolner, a prolific and opinionated writer for the *Cycle and Automobile Trade Journal*, in January 1905, as "…one of the most durable cars for $1,000 on the market. [It] is a beauty in appearance [and] an easy running and easily controlled machine [that] possesses high speed."

The Model D was said to be 50% more powerful than other cars on the market in its price range. The car won a two-mile race in three minutes and twenty seconds at Kalamazoo's newly-constructed Recreation Park. According to the report in the *Kalamazoo Evening Telegraph* on July 5, 1904 and again in the September 1904 issue of *Cycle and Automobile Journal*, the Michigan soundly defeated a ten-horsepower Pope-Hartford.

In their sales brochure for the Model D, the company included an interesting description of the automobile and automobiling in 1904:

> Automobiling is the King of sports and the queen of amusements. It is a rational form of open
> air enjoyment, appealing to the best side of our natures. It is the strong man's delight—this
> mounting the cab and riding away with the strength of Hercules and the speed of Pegasus. It is

Fig. 6-5. The 1904 Michigan Model D chassis. The twelve horsepower engine is mounted on the left, with the round tank on top of the engine for the drip oil system, and the large tank behind the steering wheel for gasoline. The Model D is driven by a single chain running from the engine to the differential. The large canister at the rear of the car is the muffler; made of sheet metal and asbestos, and weighing twenty pounds, it was described as being very effective. The 1904 model was equipped with rear brakes. Note the step for the rear-entrance tonneau. (DOL)

the woman's rare treat, rolling away through the country or down the shady avenue. And the children—well, if anyone enjoys an auto' trip, it is the little men and women.

It is become too, a distinctively *fin-de-siecle* thing. Riding and driving with horses has been and no doubt always will be a favorite means of pleasure. No rational man, howsoever an enthusiastic automobile lover, will deny that. But a good auto' goes far beyond the capabilities of a good horse, possesses so much greater speed, endurance and strength, that one only has to become familiar with this twentieth century mode to become, also, an ardent admirer of it. True, there are arguments pro and con, and to a lover of horseflesh, no arrangement of cylinders, pistons, cranks and levers can satisfy the feeling that exults in the ability to curb and command the nobelist of animals, and make them subservient to the human will. But who that has not done it can feel the thrill of power and command which comes to the man who throws in the clutch and speeds away over the hill and down the steep and off on the long stretch, leaving behind the puny horse and everything else on the road! Indeed one must be careful, or this conscious superiority breeds a spirit of arrogance—so often the concomitant of power.

After the favorable reception by the press and the public of the 1904 Model D, in November of that year the company introduced a third generation of cars: the 1905 Michigan Model D and Model E. Once again these cars were larger than the previous models, and the design included a front hood, although the engine was still tucked beneath the seat.

The 1905 Model E chassis had an 86" wheelbase and rode on 30" x 3½" tires, with the graceful "King of Belgium" side-entrance tonneau, beautifully trimmed and upholstered in leather with seating for five. This model used an engine similar to the previous series, although the bore had been increased to 4⅝" with the same 5" stroke. It had the same planetary transmission and chain drive as the 1904 model. Gear changes were made by an outside right-mounted lever; rearward for low, and forward for high. There were three pedals on the floor: an emergency brake with a ratchet retainer on the left, a standard brake in the middle, and reverse gear engagement on the right. This model weighed 1,700 pounds and sold for $1,250.

The 1905 Model D was slightly larger than the previous year's Model D and slightly smaller than the 1905 Model E. Sitting on an 80" wheel base and weighing 1,675 pounds, it sold for $1,100. As in 1904, this Model D offered a detachable rear-entrance tonneau and could be converted to a sporty-looking roadster with the addition of a rakish rear cover.

Standard finish for the 1905 Michigan was a medium Brewster green on the body with light red for wheels and running gear. Body and running gear either entirely in red or

Fig. 6-6. Members of the Fuller family are shown on a Sunday afternoon drive in Kalamazoo in a 1904 Model D. Note the carriage front on this vehicle which differentiates it from the Model D introduced in November 1904. (DOL)

Brewster green were also options, and other colors could be ordered if desired. The Model D was offered with a five-passenger touring, runabout or the special doctor's runabout body. The latter included a special square rear deck for the storage of a physician's bag and related equipment. Prices for both the D and the E models included two side brass oil lamps, brass horn, tools, pump, and tire repair kit. At the time the new models were introduced in November of 1904, William E. Russell, designer and superintendent for the Michigan, expected production of about 250 cars for both models during 1905.

Advertising photographs for both 1906 and 1907 show an automobile that differed little in appearance from the 1905 model. Sometime during 1907, a decision was made to cease automobile manufacture, and in January 1908, the announcement appeared in the press that the company would concentrate on the manufacture of transmissions, simultaneously with the announcement that they had a $50,000 order for transmissions from one of the leading automobile manufacturers. During 1908 they offered two planetary transmissions, one rated at six to twelve horsepower, and the other rated at twelve to twenty horsepower. In a 1912 interview with the *Gazette*, Charles Fuller commented that the production of the Michigan automobile was a losing proposition and placed the decline of automobile manufacture in the following perspective:

The business at the time was undeveloped—almost in the raw state so to speak—and the cost of production was something awful. There were no factories devoted to the manufacture of parts as there are now. Every auto manufacturer had to manufacture his own parts and all his machinery which ate up every cent of what is now profit. After stopping the manufacture of autos we began manufacturing auto transmissions, in which industry the Michigan Automobile company is now successfully engaged.

Fig. 6-7. The Michigan light touring car, Model D for 1905, was first introduced in November 1904. It was available in a rear-entrance tonneau, painted in Brewster Green with red trim and fine leather seating. The Model D has a modern look with a full hood, although the engine, now rated at fourteen horsepower, was installed beneath the front seat, as was done with the 1904 model. This model sold for $1,100. (NAC)

On December 31, 1912, the company changed its name from Michigan Automobile Company Limited to Fuller and Sons Manufacturing Company because of the confusing similarity between the former name and Michigan Buggy's new subsidiary, the Michigan Motor Car Company, incorporated the same year. A personal letter from a member of the Fuller family indicates that the Michigan name was given to Lay and Lane, owners of Michigan Buggy, in 1909 when they began manufacture of the Michigan. Under the new Fuller identification, transmission construction was gradually changed from applications for motorcars to heavy duty transmissions, first for taxi cabs (including Checker and Yellow) and then trucks. The last passenger car transmissions were built by Fuller in 1923.

In 1919, the company began to dismantle the old Montgomery Ward building—built in 1888—and invested $200,000 in the construction of a new factory. They also purchased a 150' x 200' building from the South Michigan Brick Company for a foundry with an anticipated daily capacity of thirty castings. Even then, the company planned to build another foundry with the most modern equipment. This construction was followed by a series of advertisements that appeared in *The Kalamazoo Gazette* for the sale of mortgage bonds paying a 7% return. Frank D. Fuller was company president at this time, and the confidence of the company is reflected in the humor of the advertisements that appeared in *The Kalamazoo Gazette* on December 24, 1924. They described Walter P. Fuller as secretary: "He is on the job at work every day"; W. E. Upjohn as treasurer: "He is president of the Upjohn Company"; Frank D. Fuller, as president: "He is some good, too." The levity of the advertisement is in stark contrast to the firing of three men for wearing green ties to work on St. Patrick's Day in 1892. The company's reputation for product quality continued to increase, and by 1925 they supplied the transmissions for eighty-five manufacturers of taxi cabs, buses, and trucks.

On April 20, 1929, Fuller and Sons Manufacturing Company was acquired by the Unit Corporation, a group of Chicago investors who sought to combine the Fuller Company with three other automobile parts suppliers. This purchase was an industrial and not a stock transaction. Unity owned the plant, the equipment, and the material goods, but control of the entire stock holdings was obtained subsequently by another purchase for $1.25 million. The Great Depression followed the market crash in the fall of 1929, and vehicle production plummeted, sapping the strength of

the company. On May 16, 1932, a majority of the board of directors of the Fuller and Sons Manufacturing Company applied to the courts for dissolution of the company. Judge George V. Weimer granted the petition and placed the company in receivership under the control of J. Seton Gray, a consulting engineer from Wisconsin. The economic charts had shown a downward spiral: the work force had fallen to eighteen employees, and cash assets had dropped to $303.76. The future looked dismal. The next two years would be critical for the company. Gray held the company together by purchasing steel and other necessary materials based on his reputation and personal credit. He offered thirty days to those from whom he sought credit, and demanded payment within fifteen days from those to whom he extended credit. The fifteen-day differential between credit and debits created the financial float that he needed and business improved slowly. By 1933, although still in receivership, the workforce had grown to one hundred employees. When automobile production finally showed an upturn in 1934, the heavy-duty transmission that they had been quietly developing found ready markets with General Motors, International Harvester, White, and Mack trucks. The company was reorganized in 1934 as the Fuller Manufacturing Company and by then its payroll had reached three hundred. Seton Gray finally brought the firm out of receivership in 1936. The public stock offerings that

Fig. 6-8. *The Michigan light touring Model E for 1905, mounted on an 86" wheelbase, was available as a four-door touring with a side-entrance tonneau, a runabout, and a special doctor's runabout. The doctor's car had a large box at the rear for carrying medical supplies and instruments. The standard finish was Brewster Green with red trim and running gear, but an all-red or all-green finish was an available option. This model sold for $1,250. (NAC)*

year brought in $386,000 that was sufficient to pay off all of the old creditors. Gray had accomplished what many other manufacturers had failed to do during this critical period and he remained with the company.

The company used the finest high-speed gear cutting machines in temperature-controlled rooms to produce castings machined within tolerances of .0001". The result was a transmission for heavy-duty vehicles that was more quiet and more easily operated than any other product on the market. During the decade of the 1930s, the company had returned from the brink of bankruptcy, and paid back every one of its creditors. By 1937 the company's market extended from Kalamazoo to Baghdad, and by 1941 annual sales exceeded $5 million, an increase of 96% above the previous year. As the United States entered World War II, Fuller and Sons Manufacturing Company was one of the premier manufacturers of transmissions for military vehicles.

In 1950, Fuller began producing the Roadranger Transmissions, a trade name applied to the combination of a four-or five-speed transmission with an auxiliary two-or three-speed transmission, giving flexibility of range from eight to ten gear ratios using fewer gears than were used in their competitors' products. Production soon out-distanced capacity and, in 1951, another fifty acres of land were purchased off Mosel Avenue north of Kalamazoo and a new factory was constructed to build the newly-developed single shaft Road Ranger transmissions. In 1953, Fuller purchased Shuler Axle Company of Louisville, Kentucky. Then on July 31, 1958, Fuller Manufacturing Company and its subsidiaries, Unit Drop Forge and Shuler Axles were acquired by Eaton Manufacturing, presently designated as the Eaton Corporation.

Fig. 6-9. The Fuller manufacturing buildings were completed circa 1922 on North Pitcher Street in Kalamazoo. The first automobile in the line of cars appearing on the street is a 1937 Oldsmobile, dating this photograph circa 1937–40. (WMU)

The company followed with the introduction of the revolutionary Twin Counter-shaft Roadranger Transmission in 1963. In this design, there are two counter shafts with a "floating" mainshaft making possible a transmission of short length, light weight and high capacity. These transmissions, capable of handling up to 1,250 pounds of torque and 420 horsepower, were well received by truck manufacturers and, by the start of the 1977 calendar year, over one million of these transmissions had been manufactured. The company continued to provide over 60% of the heavy-duty truck transmissions on the road during the 1980s.

REFERENCES

The Loss is Great. *The Kalamazoo Gazette Morning News*, October 4, 1891.
Smoking Washboards. *The Kalamazoo Gazette*, December 4, 1891.
Their Mandate. *The Kalamazoo Gazette*, March 29, 1892.

Beverly R. Kimes and Henry Austin Clark, Jr. *Standard Catalog of American Cars, 1805–1942 3rd ed.* Iola, WI: Krause Publications, 1996.

Ross Collier. *The Ross Collier Collection.* Regional History Collections, Western Michigan University, A-1911.

More Than an Ordinary Man. *The Kalamazoo Morning Gazette-News*, April 11, 1901.

Smallest Car in the World. *The Kalamazoo Morning Gazette-News*, October 22, 1902.

The Kalamazoo Cycle Company. *The Horseless Age*, November 5, 1902, p. 519.

Will Make Automobiles. *The Kalamazoo Evening Gazette-News*, December 28, 1902.

Kalamazoo Enters the Field. *Motor Age*, January 8, 1903, pp. 26–27.

The Michigan Automobile Company Ltd. *The Horseless Age*, January 14, 1903, p. 110.

The Michigan Automobile Company Limited. *The Automobile Review*, January 15, 1903, p. 32.

Getting Ready to Manufacture Those Autos. *Kalamazoo Daily Telegraph*, February 9, 1903.

$400—Blood Automobile. *Cycle and Automobile Trade Journal*, February 1903, p. 170.

The Michigan Automobile Co. *Motor Age*, April 9, 1903, p. 21.

The Blood Gasoline Car. *Cycle and Automobile Trade Journal*, April 1903, p. 86.

A Good Automobile for $450. *Cycle and Automobile Trade Journal*, April 1903, p. 411.

The Michigan Air Cooled Car. *Cycle and Automobile Trade Journal*, April 1903, pp. 72, 74.

Named Its Machine "The Michigan." *The Horseless Age*, April 15, 1903, p. 490.

Michigan Runabout. *The Automobile Review*, May 1, 1903, p. 173.

The Michigan Light Runabout. *Cycle and Automobile Trade Journal*, May 1904, p. 151.

Michigan Light Touring Car. *The Horseless Age*, May 11, 1904, p. 514.

Newly Developed Automobiles and Parts. *Motor Age*, May 28, 1903, p. 19.

"The Michigan" Gasoline Runabout. *The Horseless Age*, June 3, 1903, p. 652.

The Michigan Automobile. *The Automobile*, July 25, 1903, p. 64.

New Auto "Michigan." *Kalamazoo Daily Telegraph*, July 25, 1903.

The Michigan Automobile. *Cycle and Automobile Trade Journal*, August 1903, p. 111.

The Michigan Automobile. *The Automobile*, August 8, 1903, p. 53.

Michigan Automobile. *Motor Age*, August 20, 1903, p. 34.

To Make Ten Cars a Week. *The Motor World*, August 20, 1903, p. 773.

We Offer You for $450; The Michigan Automobile. *The Automotive Review*, October 14, 1903, p. 9.

Testing the Michigan. *Motor Age*, December 3, 1903, p. 11.

The 1904 Michigan Car. *Cycle and Automobile Trade Journal*, January 1904, p. 134.

Michigan Automobile. *Automobile Review*, January 9, 1904, p. 11.

Michigan Model A. Company Sales Brochure, January 1904.

Michigan Gasoline Runabout, Model A. *The Horseless Age*, February 10, 1904.

The Michigan Automobile Co. of Grand Rapids. *The Automobile*, February 20, 1904, p. 243.

The Michigan Automobile Company of Grand Rapids. *Motor Age*, February 18, 1904, p. 21.

Some Pointers About the Michigan Automobile. *The Automobile*, February 20, 1904, p. 78.

The Michigan Runabout. *The Automobile*, February 27, 1904, p. 259.

Recent Incorporation. *The Motor World*, March 17, 1904, p. 1069.

New Touring Car. *Kalamazoo Evening Telegraph*, March 19, 1904.

M. E. and C. C. Blood Formerly of Michigan Automobile Co. *The Automobile*, March 26, 1904, p. 364.

Michigan Light Touring Car. *The Horseless Age*, March 30, 1904, p. 373.

The Michigan Light Runabout. *Cycle and Automobile Trade Journal*, May 5, 1904, p. 151.

The Michigan Light Touring Car. *The Horseless Age*, May 11, 1904, p. 514.

Races and Ball Game. *Kalamazoo Evening Telegraph*, July 5, 1904.

Two Cylinder Michigan. *Motor Age*, July 28, 1904, pp. 18, 23.

The Michigan; The Car of Power. *Cycle and Automobile Trade Journal*, July 1904, p. 126.

First Shipment. *The Automobile*, July 16, 1904, p. 78.

Is Behind in Orders. *Kalamazoo Evening Telegraph*, August 27, 1904.

Michigan Light Touring. *Cycle and Automobile Trade Journal*, September 1904, p. 117.

At the Automobile Races. *Cycle and Automobile Trade Journal*, September 1904, p. 39.

Hugh Dolnar. "Blood Brothers Side Entrance Tonneau Touring Car." *Cycle and Automobile Trade Journal*, November 1904, pp. 130–37.

Michigan Light Touring Car Model D. Company Sales Brochure, June 1904.

$50,000 to be Added to Michigan Automobile Capital. *Kalamazoo Evening Telegraph*, September 26, 1904.

Michigan Light Touring Car Models D and E. Company Sales Brochure, September 1904.

Michigan Light Touring Car. *The Automobile*, November 5, 1904, p. 526.

New Michigan. *Cycle and Automobile Trade Journal*, December 1904, p. 132.

The Michigan Light Touring Car—Car of Power. *Cycle and Automobile Trade Journal*, January, 1905, pp. 12–13.

Will Exhibit at Auto Show. *Kalamazoo Evening Telegraph*, January 3, 1905.

New Michigan Cars. *The Automobile*, January 7, 1905, p. 17.

Michigan Light Touring Car. *The Horseless Age*, January 11, 1905, pp. 56–57.

The Michigan Light Touring Cars. *The Automobile*, January 14, 1905, p. 183.

The Michigan Model E. *The Horseless Age*, January 11, 1905, pp. 50–51.

$1,100 Michigan. *The Automobile*, January 11, 1905, p. 52.

New York Auto Show. *The Horseless Age*, January 18, 1905, p. 71.

Michigan Automobile Company. *The Automobile*, January 21, 1905, p. 129.

Michigan Descriptions. *Cycle and Automobile Trade Journal*, March 1905, pp. 83, 88.

"Michigan" Doctor's Runabout, Price $1,000. *Cycle and Automobile Trade Journal*, May 1905, p. 118.

F. D. Fuller. *The Automobile Review*, February 11, 1905, p. 276.

Michigan. *The Automobile Review*, February 11, 1905, pp. 162–63.

The Michigan Doctors' Car. *The Horseless Age*, April 5, 1905, p. 415.

A Michigan Doctor's Runabout. *Auto Topics*, April 8, 1905, p. 2026.

Doctors' Runabout. *The Automobile*, April 8, 1905, p. 469.

The Michigan Light Touring Car. *Cycle and Automobile Trade Journal*, June 1905, p. 202.

The Michigan Light Touring Car. *Motor Way*, October 12, 1905, p. 21.

Michigan Gasoline Car. *Cycle and Automobile Trade Journal*, March 1906, p. 116.

Michigan Gasoline Car. *Cycle and Automobile Trade Journal*, March 1907, p. 193.

Increased Capital Stock. *Cycle and Automobile Trade Journal*, May 1907, p. 47.

Michigan Auto Co. to Build Only Special Automobile Parts. *Cycle and Automobile Trade Journal*, January 1, 1908, p. 198.

Michigan 1909 Planetary Transmissions. *Cycle and Automobile Trade Journal*, September 1908, p. 114.

Kalamazoo Pioneer in Automobile Industry "Cars" Made Here in 1901. *The Kalamazoo Gazette*, February 20, 1912.

Names Cause Confusion. *The Accessory and Garage Journal*, March 1913.

Howard Crews. "Evolution of the Michigan." *The Horseless Carriage Gazette*, January–February, 1962, pp. 16–20.

Claim America Cyclecar Pioneer. *Motor Age*, August 28, 1913.

Big Addition Will Be Erected at Once to Fuller Factory. *Kalamazoo Telegraph-Press*, August 19, 1915.

Will Provide Jobs for Over 1,000 People. *The Kalamazoo Gazette*, December 27, 1919.

Fuller & Sons Buy 10 Acres. *The Kalamazoo Gazette*, February 9, 1920.

New Plant for Fuller Company. *The Kalamazoo Gazette*, January 30, 1920.

The Remaining First Mortgage 7% Bonds. *The Kalamazoo Gazette*, December 17, 1922.

A Few Words From Fuller & Sons Manufacturing. *The Kalamazoo Gazette*, December 24, 1924.

Auto Industry Here Made Its Start in 1902. *The Kalamazoo Gazette*, October 18, 1925.

Transmissions Made Here For 85 Motor Cars. *The Kalamazoo Gazette*, October 18, 1925.

Fuller Plant Sold to Unit Corporation. *The Kalamazoo Gazette*, April 20, 1929.

Receiver Asked For Fuller Firm. *The Kalamazoo Gazette*, May 16, 1932.

Two Firms Will Pay Back Taxes. *The Kalamazoo Gazette*, July 29, 1933.

Let Contract for $125,000 Work At Mill. *The Kalamazoo Gazette*, June 29, 1933.

George S. May. *A Most Unique Machine, The Michigan Origins of the American Automobile Industry*. Grand Rapids, MI: William B. Erdmans, 1975.

Continues Fuller Firm in Receivership. *The Kalamazoo Gazette*, May 13, 1933.

Feeling of Confidence Growing as 1933 Passes. *The Kalamazoo Gazette*, January 1, 1934.

Trucks Provided Quiet Gears by Fuller Company. *The Kalamazoo Gazette*, June 24, 1933.

Fuller Company 35 Years Old, At New Peak Today. *The Kalamazoo Gazette*, January 24, 1937.

Fuller Company Net Sales Reach Five-Year Peak. *The Kalamazoo Gazette*, March 27, 1942.

Fuller Plans Expansion. *The Kalamazoo Gazette*, May 1, 1942.

James C. Peterson. "Fuller of Kalamazoo." *Automotive History Review*, No. 12, Summer 1980, pp. 15–18.

Office of the *Michigan*

Buggy Company,

January 31st 189*3*

ANNUAL REPORT.

TO THE HONORABLE SECRETARY OF STATE OF THE STATE OF MICHIGAN:

In accordance with Section 12 of Act No. 232, Public Acts of 1885, the undersigned, being a majority of the Directors of the *Michigan Buggy Co.* Company, respectfully submit the following report of its condition on the *24th* day of *January* 189*3*

1. The amount of Capital Stock is - - - - - - - - - -	$100,000
2. The amount of Capital actually paid in is - - - - - - - -	100,000
3. The amount invested in Real Estate is - - - - - - - -	77,665.84
4. The amount of Personal Estate is - - - - - - - -	133,162.63
5. The amount of the Debts of the Corporation is - - - - - -	84,560.75
6. The amount of the Credits of the Corporation is - - - - -	149,709.50

And the annexed list is a true statement of the names of the stockholders, and the number of shares held by each at the date of this report:

M Henry Lane

Frank B Lay } Majority of Directors.

I, *Frank B Lay*, do solemnly swear that I am the Secretary of the above named corporation, and that the matters set forth in the foregoing report are true and correct, to the best of my knowledge and belief. And further, that the above signatures are those of a majority of the Directors of said corporation.

Frank B. Lay

Subscribed and sworn to before me, this *31st* day of *January* 189*3*

W F Cowlbeck

Notary Public in and for *Kalamazoo* County, State of Michigan.

(When the affidavit is made before an officer of another State than Michigan, it must be authenticated.)

STOCKHOLDERS' NAMES.	SHARES OF STOCK HELD.	STOCKHOLDERS' NAMES.	SHARES OF STOCK HELD.
M. H. Lane	1250		
F. B. Lay	1250		
Geo. T. Lay	750		
Ida E. Lane	750		

Fig. 7-1. The 1893 annual report for the Michigan Buggy Company. M. Henry Lane was president and Frank B. Lane was secretary-treasurer, both serving as company directors and each holding 1250 shares of stock. George T. Lane (Frank's father and vice-president) and Ida Lane (Henry Lane's wife and the daughter of George T. Lane) each held 750 shares, dividing the total interest in the company equally between the two families. (DOL)

Chapter 7

The
Michigan Buggy Company

1883–1909

"Built of carefully selected materials
by skilled mechanics"

—Company Catalog, 1885

Celery, windmills, and horse-drawn vehicles were the major products of the fledgling Kalamazoo economy in the late 1800s, as the growing might of the paper industry would not be felt in the area until the turn of the twentieth century. When M. Henry Lane arrived in the Kalamazoo area, the horse was king and the manufacture of horse-drawn vehicles and cutters created a national reputation for the city. By 1890 Kalamazoo boasted a half-dozen vehicle companies. The Lull and Skinner Company, founded in 1878, employed about two hundred men and built vehicles, sleighs, and cutters in a variety of finishes and styles. The Cash Supply and Manufacturing Company, at 201–206 North Rose Street, was established in 1880 by Frank J. Henry, and manufactured vehicles and harnesses appropriate to the needs of farmers and stockmen. By 1900 this company rivaled Montgomery Ward in its mail order business. The American Carriage Company, founded in 1887, employed 125 craftsmen and had an annual production of five thousand vehicles and three thousand sleighs. The Kalamazoo Carriage and Harness Manufacturing Company, located on East Ransom, was perhaps the only company in the nation that offered a free thirty-day trial period on every vehicle delivered through its direct sales department. The Kalamazoo Wagon Company, founded by M. Henry Lane in 1881, employed about one hundred workers and was located just across the street from the site of the Michigan Buggy Company that began operation in 1883.

M. Henry Lane—"M" standing for Moses, a name he detested and often refused to disclose to the curious—was born in 1849 in Cayuga, New York. He was a traveling man, as the salesmen of the day were called, and after the Civil War served as the Michigan region manager for the New York Wagon Company in Cortland, spending much of his time in and around Kalamazoo. He was

Fig. 7-2. The residence of George T. and his second wife Elizabeth Lay in Allegan, Michigan, circa 1880. (DOL)

described as energetic, outgoing, and rather boisterous by some, even bordering on the obnoxious by others. He had an excellent business sense and was an aggressive, persuasive salesman with considerable experience in the sale of horse-drawn vehicles. On one of his trips to Allegan, Michigan, he met and fell in love with Ida Lay, the youngest of the four children of George T. Lay and Mary E. Barber. M. Henry Lane and Ida Lay were married on December 11, 1878.

Henry Lane, Frederick W. Myers, and Ira V. Hicks formed the Kalamazoo Wagon Company in 1881. Later Lane left the wagon company to join his father-in-law, George T. Lay, who served as vice-president, and his brother-in-law, Frank B. Lay, who served as secretary-treasurer when they founded the Michigan Buggy Company in 1883. This close family arrangement was conducive to success and Michigan Buggy Company prospered immediately.

George T. Lay, the elder statesman of the company, was born October 28, 1822, near Lockport, New York, and was one of eight children who comprised this energetic family. His brother Horatio studied to become a physician and opened the Health Reform Institute in Battle Creek, Michigan, later known as the old "water cure sanitarium," from which grew the Michigan Sanitarium. Abner Lay, their father, moved the family to Erie, Pennsylvania in 1832, and George, the epitome of pioneer stock even at the age of ten, drove six head of cattle and twenty sheep over 150 miles through the blustery snow of a Pennsylvania winter from Lockport to Erie. By the age of twenty-one he had grown to a towering 6'5" handsome, broad-shouldered giant with flashing red hair, a memorable sight among smaller men. When he left home that year, he traveled to Jackson, Michigan, the terminus of the Michigan Central Railroad, and eventually arrived in Allegan, Michigan in 1844. George spent the next several years working on a logging boat, the "Pioneer," which plied the Kalamazoo River south of Allegan, hauling lumber from the nearby mills and returning with supplies for the logging camps. His industry, perseverance, and general frugal nature allowed him to purchase and clear almost 166 acres of prime farm land, and on October 5, 1851, he married Mary E. Barber of Allegan. From this union came four children, Ella (Mrs. Ezra Brackett), Ida (Mrs. Henry Lane), Alta (Mrs. J. C. Clemens), and Frank Barber Lay. After Mary's death on November 27, 1862, George T. Lay remarried some two years later on April 5, 1864. Noted for his industry and integrity, as well as his productive orchards and finely bred horses, George T. Lay was a man of considerable social acclaim and financial wealth. He owned several homes, gave each of his children a farm at the time of their marriage, and was the major stockholder in the Michigan Buggy Company when it was founded. Lay died on March 16, 1901 at his home in Allegan, survived by his wife, son Frank, brother Horatio, and three daughters Ella, Alta, and Ida.

The legacy of George T. Lay was one of hard work, honesty, and integrity; these exact words described his son Frank, who was known as a man "whose handshake was his bond." Frank Barber Lay, born on November 29, 1856 in Allegan County, grew in moral, if not physical, stature; unlike his father, he was quite short. He attended public schools in the area and in 1878 graduated from the University of Michigan with a concentration in law. He entered the manufacturing business with his father and married Mary Belle Barclay in 1879. They resided in a home outside of Hopkins where his son George T. Lay, named after his grandfather, and daughter Vera Lay were born in 1881 and 1883 respectively. Reportedly, Mary Lay did not like this home and the family moved to Kalamazoo soon after when Frank became associated with the Michigan Buggy Company. They purchased a house at 309 Elm Street, and subsequently a very solid, but con-

Fig. 7-3. Residence of Frank Lay, Sr. on South Street, Kalamazoo, Michigan, circa 1910. (DOL)

servative home at 523 West South Street. Three more children were born in Kalamazoo: Evelyn in 1895; Frank Barclay (often called Frank, Jr. because he had the same middle initial as his father); and Robert, born in 1898. George T. and Frank Barclay later became associated with Michigan Buggy. Evelyn attended Smith College, received a master's degree from Columbia College, and was later employed by Western Michigan University. Robert's activities are not well documented. (Frank's son George is identified without the middle inital "T" from this point on.)

The three men—M. Henry Lane, George T. Lay, and Frank B. Lay—and their families were quite close before George T.'s death in 1901. Henry Lane had married Ida Lay (daughter of George T. and sister of Frank), and Ida, who was described as "a real character," and Frank Lay's wife Mary Barclay were also very close friends. When a son was born to Henry and Ida, they named him Frank in honor of her brother. This was the only son born to the Lanes, and when the boy later tragically died, it seemed to change all their lives, as well as the relationship between the Lane and the Lay families, forever.

The two families owned all of the stock in the Michigan Buggy Company, valued at $75,000 in

Fig. 7-4. The "Lane Castle," residence of M. Henry Lane, on the southwest corner of Main and West Streets (Westnedge Avenue). This house was built before 1900 at a cost of $75,000 and the withdrawal of company funds for its construction was a part of the wedge that finally separated the Lay and Lane families, in spite of their relationship through marriage. It was demolished after World War II. (WMU)

1883, when the business began in a small factory they built just north of the city. But their investments were not limited to Michigan Buggy; together and individually, Henry Lane and Frank Lay owned an enormous amount of land throughout the city. They also founded and were the major stockholders in the Comstock Manufacturing Company, and owned and operated the Riverside Pony farm, "the famous Tony Pony line," as well as being the major forces behind the electric trolley cars that came to Kalamazoo in 1893. In 1895, they organized a company to construct the Chicago and Kalamazoo Terminal Railroad, a planned beltline around the city, although there was much dispute about the contribution of this endeavor to the community. Kalamazoo was a popular horse-racing town, and the Lays raised well-regarded racing horses. Three of their animals— "Cashwood," "Stormwood," and "The Puritan"—were among the many champions who regularly turned winning times at the local track. Henry Lane was also a horse fancier, and when National Park, a racetrack south of Washington Square near Hays Park, was subdivided for homes in 1902, Frank Lay and Henry Lane were members of the investment group that bought the farm on East Lake Street, site of the present-day Kalamazoo County Fair Grounds. There they built a race track they named Recreation Park. Michigan Buggy was building a new plant in the Hays Park area, and the platting of the area for homes, including Lay and Lane Boulevards as well as Palmer Avenue, was advantageous for them in terms of home sites for their employees. The development of the race track off Lake Street represented another investment opportunity.

Victor L. Palmer was the other executive officer of the company and also prominently aligned with the business community in Kalamazoo. Born on April 8, 1871, in St. Joseph County, Palmer

Fig. 7-5. The residence of Victor Palmer at 320 South West Street (later Westnedge Avenue). Palmer, who served as secretary-treasurer of Michigan Buggy, was at the center of the eventual bankruptcy of the firm. He lived here until his death in 1924. (DOL)

was educated in Kalamazoo. At the age of seventeen, he joined Burnell and Son in Kalamazoo, married Mary E. Barnard in 1893, and subsequently accepted the position as head of sales with Michigan Buggy in 1894 at the age of twenty-three. His organizational skills and financial planning abilities must have been considerable, because he, and not Frank Lay or Henry Lane, was credited with reorganizing the company following the fire in 1902 and for organizing the company to manufacture gasoline-powered automobiles in 1909.

Palmer rose to the position of secretary-treasurer and manager of sales, and by 1913, at the age of forty-two, he was considered the major influence in determining the financial direction of the company. He was a well known and respected member of the community, with memberships at the Park Club, and the Kalamazoo Country Club. He also served as a director at several banks, the *Kalamazoo Telegraph-Press,* and several other businesses in the city.

The history of the Michigan Buggy Company is one of accomplishment and product quality. They employed about three hundred workers and built close to 1,400 vehicles during that first season of production in 1883. The original plant included only 60,000 square feet of space, but production grew steadily and an additional building of 48,000 sq. ft. was added in 1886. Annual production during the last part of the decade reached 19,000 vehicles, including 10,000 road carts, 4,000 buggies, and 5,000 cutters. Their product was described in the 1885 catalog in the following terms: "Our vehicles are built of the most carefully selected material, by skillful mechanics, under the personal supervision of men with acute perception and vast experience."

The Timkin Spring Top Buggy, number sixty-five, a neat and stylish turn-out, offered a piano-case square body, velvet carpet, leather seating, and a hand-rubbed leather top. The shafts were fully leathered and silver-tipped, and the body finished in black with carmine trim. There were few rivals in the industry for quality of material, precision of fit, and luster of finish.

Henry Lane and Frank Lay were strongly principled businessmen and not hesitant to make their demands in a forthright manner. The following incident with a railway company reveals a streak of their occasional obstreperous nature and perhaps some insight into the growing friction in their relationship. According to the "rule of the rails," once a customer had begun to unload a rail car, the unloading had to be completed within forty-eight hours or the party had to pay two dollars per day to the car rental company. The incident began when the Michigan Buggy Company began to unload a coal car at

Fig. 7-6. In 1891 Michigan Buggy built the largest exclusive carriage factory in the country in the form of a hollow square. There was much speculation concerning its site with various people purchasing lands that they hoped would turn a profit by being near the factory. This building was southeast of the intersection of the Michigan Central and Lake Shore tracks and at the intersection of Porter and Willard. This factory survived the fire of 1896, but was destroyed in the great fire of 1902. (WMU)

noon on a Friday in 1892, but the men were unable to complete the task by Monday noon of the next business day. When the rental company called for the two dollar rental payment, it was refused by Michigan Buggy. When the rental company agent and a trainman showed up at four o'clock that afternoon to claim the car, they found that Messrs. Lane and Lay had chained it to the rails, and that they had placed heavy timbers across the tracks and plugged the coupling pin socket with mud. There were reports of a physical altercation between Lay, Lane, and the two men from the rental company, and one report indicated that Henry Lane took a blow to the face. Lane later denied the story, but in any case it provided a sufficient diversion to delay the agents in order to get the car unloaded. The event serves to illustrate the rough and tumble nature of the business and the businessmen who competed within it. Henry Lane later complained of the incident to the *Gazette* and the paper reported the altercation on March 5, 1892: "This firm claims we furnish over 800 cars of freight per year, and we think it pretty small business when we cannot be allowed a little lee time at busy times when unloading cars."

The size of the Michigan Buggy plant continued to grow with the company's success. Another major addition to the plant was constructed in 1889, and then it almost doubled again in size in 1891 with additions to the factory building at the intersection of the Michigan Central and Lake Shore railroad lines. It was touted as a building that eclipsed all plants in the city and was the largest in the country used exclusively for the manufacture of carriages. There was considerable land speculation during this period. Local real estate brokers Cowgill and Miller offered a new housing plat just east of Mill Street that the *Gazette* advertisement of December 30, 1891, cited as having an exclusive "Riverside and Factory View," and the attraction described as "[T]he largest factory of the kind in the world. Other factories to be built, also Belt Line railroad. Money invested in this property will double in the next twelve months."

As late as 1910 Lay and Lane owned a considerable amount of land along the Michigan Central tracks and the river east of Mill Street, but they never built in the area described in the advertisement. The new factory they built before the turn of the twentieth century was at the Porter and Willard Street intersection when the latter street extended east to intersect with Porter.

After the major construction of 1891, some of the firm's manufacturing was still carried on in the original

Fig. 7-7. In 1899 Michigan Buggy added a second building to the company plant and it was described as comprising the east wing and being fully as large as the original factory. Together these two structures were described as covering half-a-square south of the Michigan Central tracks and east of the Lake Shore tracks. Fire broke out in this building in 1902, and by the time the firemen arrived, the second and third floors of the new structure were in flames. (WMU)

wooden building that stood on Porter Street north of the Michigan Central tracks. Tragedy struck, however, when that building burned on Thursday evening, August 13, 1896, with an estimated loss of $50,000 to $60,000. The company carried a minimal insurance policy of only $10,000. Frank Lay thought the cause to be spontaneous combustion, perhaps heat generated from damp straw near the pony barns or damp sawdust near the mill. The band of firefighters was small for such a large fire, but according to the report in the *Kalamazoo Daily Telegraph*, "every 'pipeman' stood his ground against the blaze." While the building was destroyed, the bucket brigade was able to save both the railroad switch tower and the buildings of the nearby Kalamazoo Wagon Company. Most observers agreed that there was no chance to save this wooden structure. The plant, built south of the tracks in 1891*(fig. 7-6)*, survived.

A second wing was added to the remaining structure in 1899. Fully as large as the main building, constructed of brick, and fully steam-heated, it was considered one of the most modern plants of the era. The complex consisted of two buildings joined at the junction of the Michigan Central and Lake Shore Roads, and the "immense and wondrous factory," as it was called when built in 1891, was now referred to as the "old factory" when the new brick building was completed in 1899.

This new complex was also destroyed by fire on the very cold evening of January 17, 1902. The fire was one of the worst in the history of the city, at least since the great Dewing fire of 1895. In spite of the frantic work of Chief Healy and his "grim faced men," the two local papers, reporting on January 17, 1902, billed the disaster as a failure of men and equipment. "For the third conspicuous time," they reported, "the equipment and size of the Kalamazoo fire department proved utterly inadequate to the task of coping with a big fire." While the firemen did not save the plant, they did save the small houses around the plant, and no one was hurt except for minor injuries.

The cause of this blaze was never determined. Employees reported that never before had the plant been so loaded with supplies and finished products. About $200 worth of buggy tops and wheels, along with thirty Shetland ponies pulled from an attached barn, were saved that night. An estimated crowd of 5,000 watched, as the fire scorched their faces and the bitter wind chilled their backs. The fire spread rapidly, and the firemen were successful for a brief period in keeping the flames from the paint shop and its flammable contents, but the heat of the fire was so intense that it eventually melted the steel fire doors and the flames

MICHIGAN BUGGY COMPANY

Fig. 7-8. Following the great fire of 1902, Lay and Lane constructed a magnificent plant at Reed Avenue and Factory Street just east of Lane and Lay Boulevard in the Hays Park area. This photograph appeared often in company advertisements and is believed to be an artist's rendition of the structure as it has far greater prominence than the actual building. (DOL)

reached the varnish and other accelerants. A series of explosions followed and the northwest corner of the building crashed to the ground, narrowly missing the two hose-crews on the north side. The awful night was described poetically by the *Telegraph* reporter on January 17, 1902:

> From every side the red faced demon could be seen, grinning, smiling in anticipation of the feast before him. The long hungry forked tongues leaped from window to window and from floor to floor. Onward and upward leapt the flames destroying everything before them, at times leaping high into the air and again bursting forth as though in joyful exaltation. Steadily the roar of the flames increased, broken only by the crash of an occasional wall.

In the aftermath, Henry Lane placed the incidental loss of the structure and its contents at $200,000 and the business and production loss at $800,000. The social disruption, in terms of the $20,000 monthly payroll and the subsequent failure to meet house rent, grocery and butcher bills by the unemployed workers, was estimated to impact over a thousand men, women, and children who depended upon the company for their livelihood. The company paid its employees on the fifteenth of each month, so the workers were due almost a month's pay at the time of the fire. All records of the amount due the workers and creditors alike were destroyed in that fire, a circumstance that was bound to create a severe hardship for those families without money for food and fuel in the midst of the winter snows. The leaves would turn and snows would threaten again before these same workers would begin work on another Michigan Buggy vehicle.

Lay and Lane moved quickly after the fire, setting up offices in a local hotel called the American House and making plans for reconstruction. Fortunately, the building was insured through the Garrett Agency at $57,400 and the Rankin Agency at $30,000 with the risk spread across more than thirty companies from Philadelphia to London. "A life-long work gone skyward," commented Henry Lane as he gazed upon the ruins and rubbed his injured hand. It had been badly pinched in a door during the fire and would not function well for some time.

The site of the burned factory was subsequently sold to the city for $15,000 as a rail terminal and loading area, a proposal approved in a Monday night session of the city council on April 28, 1902. The proposed sale was led by Dallas Boudeman who presented the recommendation, not as a stockholder, but as a concerned citizen. Using what he called a "good straightforward common sense speech," he argued that the city should purchase the site to hold the industry in Kalamazoo and bolster the economic strength of the community. Many of the workers had already left the city to find work elsewhere and would return once the new plant was built and manufacturing could begin again. The members of the council apparently agreed, for the proposal was passed with nine in favor and only one dissenting voice. Alderman Levy argued strenuously that, while he was sympathetic with the company's situation, he did not believe that public money should be used to help any private institution in the city.

The accumulated funds from the insurance policies and the land sale to the city were used to purchase land from Charles Hays in the Hays Park area being developed south of the city at Reed Avenue and Factory Street in order to construct a marvelous new facility just within the limits of the city. The memory of the two plant fires had not been forgotten, and Henry Lane and Frank Lay opted for using cement as the primary construction material, although cement as a building material was not quite out of the experimental stage in 1902. Board walls were first constructed and then the cement was poured down between these forms and allowed to cure. The two main three-story buildings were 200' x 80', and 200' x 50', while the cross buildings were 100' x 60'. The floors between the stories were made of three thicknesses of hardwood. The finest sprinkling system available was installed, together with other special fire protection, including an immense fireproof vault sixteen feet square and two stories high that was set on the northwest side of the plant, so that if the plant caught fire, the papers of the firm would be safe. Finally, a separate power building was constructed adjacent to the main building and the cotton stuffing for the upholstery and similar flammable supplies were kept in another separate building so that if it caught fire no harm would come to the main structure.

Manufacturing plans were detailed and specific. Green wood was unloaded from rail cars at one end of the building, moved by hand-truck into the drying kilns, and then on to the wood shaping department. The final pieces were carried to the second floor on an elevator, fitted together according to the style of vehicle, and then moved to the finishing department adjacent to shipping. While the process could not be considered a moving production line, the movement of the raw materials was regulated through a sequence of steps that required minimal energy and maximum efficiency and almost eliminated the need for roustabouts whose sole purpose was to move unfinished goods from one manufacturing point to the next. The main offices were located on the northwest corner of the plant and were handsomely furnished. The great plant was considered one of the most modern, spacious, and sanitary manufacturing plants in the state when it was completed in October of 1902. The manufacture of sleighs and cutters for the winter season began immediately.

Soon after the completion of the new plant, Michigan Buggy Company announced its intentions to build a new lightweight horseless carriage for the businessman's use. The news in the *Kalamazoo Telegraph* of February 1903 described a small machine of approximately six hundred pounds capable of speeds around fifteen miles an hour. Later reports in July of the same year indicated that sample autos were already being tested and two models, one with a five-horsepower engine for city use and the other with a seven-horsepower engine for country touring, would be marketed soon. Plans called for a vehicle that was to be known as "The Kalamazoo" and that would be similar in appearance and style to the 1903 Cadillac, but no evidence of eventual manufacture exists.

In his 1937 interview with *The Gazette*, Frank Burtt recalled a trip he had taken with Henry Lane and Frank Lay in 1902 to review an automobile in Chicago, and that they had a sample of this machine delivered to Kalamazoo. In further evaluation of the construction they decided that it was not worthy, and returned it to the Chicago builder. Clearly, Henry Lane and Frank Lay were interested in automobile manufacture and no doubt their interests were stimulated by the appearance of the attractively finished Michigan manufactured by the Fuller brothers and Maurice and Clarence Blood, as well as the Cannon built by the Burtt Manufacturing Company, a machine for which Michigan Buggy provided the final coach work and painting.

Henry Lane reported the prospects for the new car to the *Kalamazoo Telegraph* on July 15, 1903:

> We will soon have a good supply of autos on the market, but we are going about it very carefully. A great many thousands of dollars have been lost in the automobile business and we don't intend to take any chances. We are thoroughly testing our machines and intend to perfect them in every way possible before putting them on the market.

Lane was a capable businessman, and his report to the local press was not idle conversation. Eventually Michigan Buggy did produce a car, and later Lane alone organized a truck manufacturing firm, but he was not prepared to launch either of these endeavors in 1903. Perhaps his conservative approach, the suspect business climate, or the published threats by the Selden patent group prevented him from making the investment, but the "Kalamazoo" never reached production.

The Michigan Buggy catalog display of its 1904 line provides some insight into the decision of the company. The forty-three page catalog had a cover of lavender blending to purple, large gold letters, and a gold border. The word "Michigan" and "1904" appear on the front cover, and the word "Kalamazoo" appears on the back. The intricate styling of "Kalamazoo" is believed to have been designed for use on the gasoline-powered horseless carriage that Lane described in the paper. Considering the number of drawings and vehicle descriptions for that catalog, planning and typesetting must have begun late in the fall of 1903, shortly after the announcement of the plans to build the Kalamazoo. Since the catalog contained only horse-drawn vehicles built by the Michigan Buggy Company, there was no need for the word "Kalamazoo," identifying the place of manufacture and appearing on the back cover, to have been so decorative.

On page forty-three of the catalog is a Cannon Runabout, also not unlike the 1903 Cadillac in

Fig. 7-9. Across the top of the photograph, looking southward, is the Michigan Buggy plant, circa 1964. Note that the artist's rendition of the building in Fig. 7-8 has twenty windows along the west wall, while the photograph shows only fourteen windows along the same side of the building. (DOL)

appearance, as Lane had described the Kalamazoo. The accompanying description makes clear that the design and manufacture of the Cannon was by the Burtt Manufacturing Company of Kalamazoo. The July 1903 report by Michigan Buggy indicated their intentions to make certain that the horseless carriage which they produced would be thoroughly tested before marketing, and perhaps it was those tests that led the company into a cooperative relationship with the Burtt Manufacturing Company rather than manufacturing the Kalamazoo.

Sometime during the first decade of the twentieth century, the relationship between Henry Lane and Frank Lay began to deteriorate. There is no evidence that Palmer instigated any of the difficulty, but in retrospect, the loss of the guiding hand of George T. Lay, the elder statesman of the firm, in March of 1901 may have allowed the rise of animosity in their relationship. The issues, whatever they were, came to a head in 1911, when Henry Lane was removed as president of Michigan Buggy, thereby restricting his influence on company policy. Interestingly, in 1909 and 1910, Henry Lane was listed in the city directory as president of the *Kalamazoo Telegraph Press* rather than as associated with Michigan Buggy. He was succeeded by Frank Lay with his sons, Frank Jr. and George—now grown and experienced—in the roles of company vice-presidents. The exact reason for the difficulty is unknown, although the 1902 fire, the construction of the new plant, a potential debate over building the "Kalamazoo" car, a conflict about withdrawals of money from the business, and the decision to build the Mighty Michigan beginning in 1909 were all sufficient to strain even the best of family relationships. Family descendants are not sure of the cause, although Edward Dingley blamed it on Lane's purchase of the *Kalamazoo Telegraph Press.* Whatever the cause, the animosity between the two families was not resolved until sometime after 1920.

The demand for Michigan Buggy products continued to climb after the new plant was built, but the pace of manufacture was unable to match the demand, and in the fall of 1906 another three-story building measuring 225' x 80' was added to the already large complex. This building was made of concrete block set on a concrete foundation and was fully equipped with automatic sprinklers. The total workforce was increased at the same time from 350 to 500 employees with the addition of well-established artisans and mechanics. The company anticipated that the added space would allow them to increase annual production from 20,000 to 35,000 vehicles, and a portion of the new space was also devoted to the manufacture of wheels, making the entire Michigan Buggy vehicle a Kalamazoo-made product. In addition, 15,000 to 20,000 wheel sets, consisting of a matching set of four wheels, were ordered annually by other suppliers.

The sale of horse-drawn vehicles soared, and in 1910 alone the company sold over $1 million worth of merchandise to a single dealer, Edward Gerber of the Pennsylvania Sales Corporation, who would eventually have a major impact upon the future of Michigan Buggy. Consideration of building the Kalamazoo automobile had not been forgotten, and the prosperity at the end of the first decade of the twentieth century convinced the company directors to begin the manufacture of a gasoline-powered automobile. Discussions began sometime in 1908 or 1909 when two drafts-man were hired. The manufacture of the Michigan began in late 1909, although only a few of these cars were sold, and it was not until the beginning of 1910 that actual production began. Exciting as the decision may have been at the time, it would prove to be the demise of one of Kalamazoo's most respected and well known companies.

REFERENCES

The World of Wheels. *Kalamazoo Telegraph*, [no date], 1887.

Kalamazoo Carriages Have National Reputation. *Kalamazoo Evening Telegraph*, June 19, 1902.

Larry B. Massie and Peter J. Schmitt. *Kalamazoo: The Place Behind the Products*, 2nd ed. Sun Valley, CA: American Historical Press, 1998.

Personal Letters. From Susan Hickmott, daughter of Evelyn Lay Hickmott, the daughter of Mary Barclay and Frank Lay Sr.

David Fisher and Frank Little, eds. *Compendium of History and Biography of Kalamazoo County Mich.* Chicago: A. W. Bowen, 1906.

Henry Thomas. *A Twentieth Century History of Allegan County, Michigan.* Chicago: Lewis Publishing, 1907, p. 89.

Crisfield Johnson. *History of Allegan and Barry Counties, Michigan.* Philadelphia: D.W. Ensign Co., 1880, p. 288.

Death Claimed Him. *Allegan Chronicle*, March 16, 1901.

Frank B. Lay, Old Resident of the City, Dies. *The Kalamazoo Gazette*, October 6, 1933.

Death Takes Heavy Toll in 1933. *The Kalamazoo Gazette*, January 1, 1934.

Ross Collier. *Ross Collier Collection.* Regional History Collections, Western Michigan University, A-1911.

It Is Coming. *Kalamazoo Telegraph Gazette*, March 6, 1891.

Death Claims Victor Palmer at Home Here. *The Kalamazoo Gazette*, June 14, 1924.

Michigan Buggy Company, Kalamazoo. Company sales catalog, circa 1885.

Chained the Car Down. *Kalamazoo Gazette*, March 5, 1892.

Kalamazoo Real Estate Advertisement. *Kalamazoo Gazette*, December 30, 1891.

Immense New Brick and Stone Factory. *Kalamazoo Gazette*, December 30, 1891.

Nothing But Ashes. *Kalamazoo Daily Telegraph*, August 14, 1896.

Destroyed by Flames. *The Kalamazoo Gazette*, January 17, 1902.

Big Fire Costs $200,000. *Kalamazoo Evening Telegraph*, January 17, 1902.

Will Purchase the Property. *The Kalamazoo Morning Gazette-News*, April 29, 1902.

120,000 Feet of Floor Space. *Kalamazoo Evening Telegraph*, May 18, 1902.

Great Plant. *Kalamazoo Evening Telegraph*, October 18, 1902.

Michigan Buggy. *The Horseless Age*, August 12, 1903, p. 183.

Horseless Carriages. *Kalamazoo Evening Telegraph*, February 16, 1903.

Frank Burtt Got First Patent as a Boy. *The Kalamazoo Gazette*, February 21, 1937.

Kalamazoo; Name of New Automobile. *Kalamazoo Evening Telegraph*, July 15, 1903.

Michigan Buggy Co. High Grade Carriages for the Trade.

Michigan Buggy Co. catalog, 1904.

Buggy Works to Be Doubled. *The Kalamazoo Gazette*, September 5, 1906.

Michigan Motor Car Company. *The Progressive Herald*, May 10, 1913.

Investigation of Affairs of Michigan Buggy Company Awaited With Intense Interest. *The Progressive Herald*, August 9, 1913.

**Motor Car Will Be King
For Week In Kalamazoo**

Fig. 8-1. The Kalamazoo Automobile Show of 1910 was the first of a series of annual automobile events in Kalamazoo designed to attract the socialites and, of course, potential automobile buyers. The Armory was decorated with lights and colored paper, and local orchestras were hired to set the musical tone. The mood of the show is reflected in this advertisement from The Kalamazoo Gazette *for the 1914 show, with visitors attired in tuxedos and formal gowns. Similar large-scale newspaper advertisements first appeared in 1910 and continued to be used to inform the public of the great event. (DOL)*

Chapter 8

Automobiling

1900–1910

"Flashy, gaudy, brassy-lookers don't prove the best. Look to the heart and life of it.…
A balky horse will go—but a balky, fussy, bothersome, expensive automobile is worse
and you want the other kind."

—W. O. Harlow

Enthusiasm for and interest in the automobile grew steadily in Kalamazoo after the turn of the century. By 1905, just ten years after the great *Chicago Tribune* race had been won by the Duryea, automobile manufacture in the state of Michigan was already far ahead of other states, and even then the city of Detroit was recognized as the "banner city" of the young industry. Locally, the horse-drawn vehicle industry had carried the community for years and Maurice Blood and others assumed that success in the automobile business would follow. Only the automobile industry, with its complex and integrate mechanical demands, provided the potential for much needed employment growth. The contributions of the sewing machine, typewriter, and bicycle industries were well noted, and a *Kalamazoo Telegraph* article on July 23, 1904 quoted a Kalamazoo businessman as saying, "We have large factories employing female help and we appreciate them, but we need now more than ever to get those (automobile manufacturers) giving employment to a high class of skilled mechanics in order to maintain a just equilibrium."

There were three automobile manufacturers in Kalamazoo in the period from 1902 through 1907, as the plants building the Blood, the Michigan and the Cannon were humming with productivity. Henry Lane and Frank Lay of the Michigan Buggy Company had announced their intent to build the "Kalamazoo" car in the summer of 1903, and Theodore Ells of Vicksburg, who had built a car in 1902, was still seeking financing to launch his manufacturing dreams. Reportedly, W. E. Oswald of Kalamazoo built a four-wheel drive vehicle powered by a Buffalo engine, and there is some suspicion that Charles Payne, a machinist at the Michigan Automobile Company, also built an operative vehicle. The *Vicksburg Commercial* documented that Carson Durkee from nearby Vicksburg had built a gasoline-powered machine, and that the Clark brothers, also of that city, built and drove two steam-powered automobiles. The purchase and operation of a variety of auto-

Fig. 8-2. The scene is Main Street, Kalamazoo, looking east toward Portage Street, circa 1900. The residents of Kalamazoo depended on the street car, horse and buggy, and the bicycle for transportation before the arrival of the motorcar. (DOL)

mobiles by residents of the city and the attempts to build automobiles created considerable activity in and around Kalamazoo. According to the men who tried to build the industry, however, the conditions did not exist in the city. Neither the investment capital nor the sources of mechanical parts were sufficient to support the required growth in manufacturing necessary for the automobile industry to succeed.

Use of the automobile for both business and pleasure was limited by the quality of the roads in and around Kalamazoo, and street improvement was a major concern in the spring and summer of 1903 when the city government sought to replace the creosol-treated woodblock paving used on many streets with a superior material. Bids were obtained from several companies and three types of paving materials were in the offing for street improvement. Red paving bricks were laid on Water Street between Rose and Burdick in May of 1903; concrete was being laid near Edwards Street during the same period; and asphalt pavement, a process new to southwest Michigan, was being used on South Burdick Street between Lovell and Cedar Streets. In the last process, the roadway was first graded, a coarse layer of stone was then put down, followed by two layers of finely crushed stone that were rolled until a level surface was obtained. A mixture of tar was then spread on the stones and covered by a layer of stone that was again rolled to a smooth finish. The Barber Asphalt Company was awarded the bid at $2.05 per square yard to pave West South Street and South Park Street in this manner. Curiously, some residents on South Street opposed the street improvement.

While the primary city streets in Kalamazoo were finished in a variety of hard surfaces, most of the country roads were dirt and the best were graded gravel. The best suburban road surface between the city and Long Lake was considered fair. Improved roads to Gull Lake made the resort area very popular, drawing families from Kalamazoo, and Battle Creek, Michigan, as well as Dayton, Toledo, and Cincinnati, Ohio. There were no golf courses, tennis courts, or baseball diamonds, so the young people had to be content with amusing themselves with swimming, boating, and general social activities. Two boats, the "Search Light" and the "Kalamazoo," a steel-hull steamer owned by Captain Cline, were refurbished for the 1904 season to provide leisurely romantic trips about the lake. The newspaper regularly reported the names of the visitors and their activities at the lake. For instance, a merry company of school girls from Battle Creek was reported as occupying the Morgan Cottage, and Captain Cline noted that most of the girls wore glasses or "effectors" as he called them. The good captain suggested that as young men were scarce, the young ladies needed glasses because they strained their eyes searching every little speck on the water for an available companion.

The construction at the lake was also of primary interest and seasonal improvements were duly reported in the local newspapers: "Work is progressing nicely on the Humphrey cottage which was built at a cost of $8,000… James Dewing was also erecting a summer residence at a cost of $5,000 and Dr. Crane's cottage was being built at a cost of $1,500… Moses (Henry) Lane built a summer home on the island and had purchased a thirty foot steam launch."

Moses Henry Lane (he preferred Henry) was often driven to the lake by his "coachman." The "comings and goings" of other Kalamazoo personalities were also noteworthy. Reports such as: "Dr. J. T. Upjohn came Friday for a stay," or "Mrs. Arthur Prentice of Kalamazoo will entertain a party of twenty-four ladies on Thursday next at her cottage," were commonplace. While Gull Lake was certainly accessible by bike, horse, or horse-drawn carriage, access to the summer pleasures of boating, fishing, and just lounging on the beach was considerably enhanced by good roads, the growing availability of motorcars, and the public conveyance provided by the Michigan Traction Company.

Work on suburban roads and city pavement continued. By the fall of 1904 the roads in every direction about Kalamazoo were being graded with the anticipation that all roads would have a solid gravel bed and be suitable for all manner of self-propelled vehicles. By 1915, as reported in the February 25 *Telegraph*, Kalamazoo County was regarded as a model for the state, and the work in the county was cited as an example of the best in the science of road building. Road improvement was often recorded by reports in the local press of the comings and goings of various automobile parties during the driving season. On May 8, 1902, for example, the *Gazette* reported, "a party of eight, which had left South Bend at 7:30 a.m., drove through town at 4:00 p.m. during a hard rain on their way to Otsego." On March 17, 1904, the *Telegraph* reported that "E. C. Adams of Battle Creek and Frank H. Wilson of the Slover and Wilson Agency in Kalamazoo drove from Battle Creek in just over two hours, and covered the last few miles from Comstock in twenty minutes in spite of the eight inch snow fall."

Driving an automobile on country roads was often a perilous experience, not only because of weather conditions but also because of hazards created by the local citizenry. In August of 1906, sixty cars were returning to Grand Rapids from the Venetian celebration in Holland, and, given the very poor illumination provided by the automobile gas lights, they almost ran into a pile of railroad ties laid across the road just outside Zeeland, Michigan. The affair was reminiscent of the "country bumpkins" who took pleasure in running sticks into the spokes of the high-wheel ordinary bikes as members of the American Wheelmen plied the country roads in the 1890s. In this instance, a pile of ties was found behind the barn of a resident near the roadway. There was great animosity toward bicyclists just before the turn of the twentieth century, and a similar feeling about automobilists existed among rural residents of the state. Much of the animus was blamed on the automobilists and their lack of understanding of horses. The auto drivers seemed to have a

penchant for racing past a horse-drawn vehicle at high speed, frightening the animal and causing a run-away. By 1910, how-ever, those attitudes began to change, for the demand for im-proved roads by auto-mobilists was a great service to the farmer, and to those living in outlying villages who were interested in reaching city markets

Fig. 8-3. This postcard depicts Lovers Lane, one of the narrow dirt roads that existed just south of Kalamazoo, circa 1910. (DOL)

and the railroad connecting them to other points across the state.

The first active campaigning for improved roads was initiated by the Michigan Division of the League of American Wheelmen at the height of the bicycle craze in 1893. Their activity resulted in the passage of the county road law that year. Horatio Earle, an avid bicyclist and member of the American Wheelmen, was appointed chairman of the organization's good roads committee in 1898 and on July 4, 1900 Earle held the first Good Roads Congress at Port Huron, Michigan. The event was highlighted by a parade of horse-drawn road graders, dump wagons, and other con-struction equipment. In 1901, Earle was elected state senator and immediately drafted legislation for road improvement. After an initial failure in 1903, the legislation was finally enacted in 1905.

The act of June 1, 1905 marked the beginning of widespread road improvement in Michigan. It created the State Highway Department, and its first commissioner was none other than Horatio Sawyer Earle. The original budget for the department was only $5,000, but Earle was a vigorous advocate and his successful campaign for road improvement earned him the nickname "Good Roads Earle." Provisions of the act created a state-reward system that allowed counties and town-ships to recoup up to $1,000 per mile for road improvement. The act also established a fee of $2 for an auto license and $1 for a driver's, or chauffeur's, license as it was called at the time. It set the speed limit for automobiles at twenty-five miles an hour in the country, fifteen miles an hour in residential areas, and eight miles an hour in a city's business district.

With the purchase of a vehicle license, each motorist was given a small round metal tag to be fastened to the dashboard at the time of registration. The owner was required to display the same tag number on a "plate," measuring 6" x 14", attached to the rear of the car. The "plate" was not issued by the state, and most were fashioned of leather by local craftsmen. Four-inch house numbers were then pinned to the plate. As a result, there was considerable variability in their appearance. These first plates, or "leathers" as they are sometimes called, continued through 1909, until the rectangular porcelain plates were introduced by the state in 1910; those in turn continued through 1914. The tin plate now in use was introduced in 1915, and that basic design with some variation in size and trim has remained about the same ever since.

There were 2,188 vehicles registered in Michigan in 1905 and an estimated 68,000 miles of roadway, although only 245 miles provided a paved surface. The roads of Michigan were infamous, and as late as 1920 the challenges of poorly constructed highways in the state were the butt of jokes and published com-

Fig. 8-4. This post card of the wishing tree by Wall Lake near Kalamazoo is dated July 31, 1914. The road is typical of the era and the following passage from the Goodrich Tire Company tour book, circa 1913, describes many of the area roads as follows: "Roads for the next few miles sandy, poor and not well defined; numerous turns are best identified by following main traveled road, avoiding more sandy forks and poorer side roads." (DOL)

plaints. Perhaps the challenge of driving over these roads instigated the common practice of referring to automobiling or chauffeuring as a sport akin to other outdoor activities such as horseback riding, canoeing, or swimming. The brisk pace in the open air was often thought to be conducive to improved circulation and mental health, and doctors occasionally prescribed motoring as a remedy for a variety of ills. In contrast, reports of "motorpathea cerebralis" also reached the news—as for example, in the *Telegraph* on April 9, 1904—with some doctors claiming that the jolting and swinging of the early cars upset normal equilibrium thus causing unsteadiness of gait. Such claims of disorientation were regarded as nonsense by the manufacturers, who claimed that driving strengthened the nerves, hardened the muscles, and braced the lungs.

Interest in the automobile for commercial use appeared as early as 1903 when a five-ton LaFrance gasoline-powered chemical and hose truck was placed on display in Kalamazoo. These machines were said to be in use in many large cities (the same vehicle was on display in Battle Creek), but there is no indication that the vehicle was purchased by the city of Kalamazoo at this time. The use of the automobile as a commercial vehicle in Kalamazoo began on April 14, 1905, when William Harlow announced the start of a livery service, with cars rented by the hour or the day with a driver furnished, making Harlow the first owner of a taxi business in the city. On April 22 of the same year, Kalamazoo's first motor bus, built by the Oldsmobile Company, began offering service in and around the city and out to Nazareth Academy on Gull Road. A round trip ticket was thirty-five cents and a one-way ticket twenty-five cents; the trip was said to take only twelve minutes. By 1915,

82 THE KALAMAZOO AUTOMOBILIST

Fig. 8-5. The Goodrich Tire Company published a road directory in 1913 that provided a description of the roads to be followed between identified cities. The following passage described the roads along the Lake Michigan shoreline west of Kalamazoo: "The short route from Holland to Grand Haven along the lake has several miles of deep sand, making it impractical for the stranger to use it. For that reason only the longer route to Grand Haven, which goes inland a considerable distance, is given in these notes. Heavy cars, especially in dry weather, would find it difficult, or more frequently impossible, to make the short lake route." The driver in the scene depicted here apparently failed to heed the warning and a team of horses has been summoned to haul the automobile from the deep sand, circa 1913. (WMU)

there were three transportation services in the city. The Kalamazoo Taxicab Company was formed in March of 1914, and put eight small Model T Ford "jitneys" in service. By that fall the Kalamazoo Hack and Bus Company had fourteen different vehicles in operation, and a year later Mr. and Mrs. W. J. Forrest established the Jitney Bus line with Mrs. Forrest, owner of a local millinery business, serving as the first woman jitney driver in Kalamazoo.

Motoring in 1905 also meant auto maintenance, and, for new automobilists, newspaper articles often provided information about driving technique and preventive measures. The following list of tools and equipment was recommended: spark plug wrench, large and small screwdriver, cutting pliers, large and small file, hammer, medium-size tin punch, large and small cold chisel, spanners to fit the most important nuts on the car, large and small adjustable wrenches, hack saw, small hand vise, oil syringe, tire levers, jack, tire pump, and gasoline. In addition, the following supplies were recommended: funnels for water and gasoline; spare inner tubes (carried in a canvas bag); cement and patches; valve parts; pieces of rawhide to repair cuts; french chalk; and canvas.

There was no roadside service, and Frank Wilson, in spite of public admonishment and criticism for providing an unwanted service, was the only professional, independent auto mechanic in Kalamazoo when he opened a garage at 425 East Main Street in 1905. Many still believed the automobile to be a passing fancy that did not warrant an exclusive repair shop. Years later his son, John Wilson, recalled that the major tools on hand in the shop consisted of a bench vice and a bunch of wrenches. Gasoline sold for nine cents a gallon and was drawn in measured containers from one-hundred gallon tanks stored outside the building. The state passed a law at the time requiring each garage employee to have a license and to designate the make of cars that he expected to repair and drive. Frank listed the Cadillac, Buick, Oldsmobile, Rambler, and Elmore (built in Clyde Ohio, 1899-1912), as well as the Kalamazoo-built Cannon and Michigan.

John Wilson also recalled the first automobile "slow race" in 1905 between the "Red Devil" and the "White Ghost." The practice of naming automobiles in this manner, as though to endow them with a personality, was prevalent at the time. This event featured a specially built Cannon automobile—owned by James C. Hatfield, secretary of the Kalamazoo Corset Company—that may have been one of the largest passenger cars ever built. It weighed 4,500 pounds and was so tall that a man standing at the rear of it could not touch the top of the rear seat, let alone the top of the car. A large flywheel allowed the engine to turn over at a very slow speed without stalling and to move the car along at a speed so slow that it almost stood still. According to Wilson, when the others had crossed the finish line, the Cannon, with driver D. C. Olin (a former bicycle racer and one of the leading automobilists of the day), was not even in sight.

The first fatal accident in Kalamazoo is noteworthy because of its occurrence, the victim's identity, and the fact that there were only thirty vehicles in the city at the time. Late in the afternoon of May 6, 1904, George W. Parker was hit by an automobile driven by a Mr. Paterson. Parker died twenty-four hours later. George Parker, father of Harry B. Parker, was in Kalamazoo to be near his son while he recuperated from an operation. The son was then city editor of the *Telegraph-Press*, and moved slowly after receiving a telephone call that a man had been run down in front of the Burdick Hotel by one of Kalamazoo's few automobiles. He found his father, seriously injured, on the floor of the nearby drug store. The blow from the vehicle had collapsed several ribs.

George Parker was a local hero well-known in the community through his wife's family as well as through his son. He had a reputation as a world traveler and bon vivant who reputedly had made and lost a million-dollar fortune six times over while working at various occupations from Paris to San Francisco. Born in Medina, New York in 1839, he was attracted to Kalamazoo for business reasons. Curiously, Parker had rescued a young woman from a runaway horse in almost the same spot on that Kalamazoo street where he was hit. She was Miss Ellen Parker, daughter of United States Marshall John Parker, and shortly after the rescue, they were married in 1861.

The accident was a milestone in the city, and later that summer, on August 13, 1904, the *Kalamazoo Evening Telegraph* carried the following safe driving advice with special emphasis on the steering and braking functions of the car:

> A car which may be promptly stopped and accurately guided is never a source of danger of itself....The driver should be as quick at applying his brakes at the sign of danger as he is to close his eyes at the near discharge of a gun. He should be as able to find the two brakes in the dark as he is to find his way to his mouth. The next most important thing of course is to be able to steer, and this cannot be mastered unless the vehicle is in motion, and therefore should be practiced at low speeds until the driver can perform the act without mental process being performed between the direction desired and the wheel movement. As long as there is any conscientious thought, the driver is not qualified. The essence of safe motor-car operation lies in the automatic and instantaneous response by the driver to visual stimuli relevant to stopping and guiding of his car.

In spite of the sound advice, Kalamazoo's second automobile accident followed just five days later.

Learning to drive was a project of self-instruction for many in those years just after the turn of the twentieth century and controlling the various features of an automobile was not an easy task for a citizenry unfamiliar with machinery and unaccustomed to the required eye-hand coordination. Many accidents were simply the result of driver error and confusion about the maneuvers required to direct the vehicle in the proper direction.

Fig. 8-6. Another section of the 1913 Goodrich tour book provides an apt description of the circumstance, entitled "Mr. Lee's Auto": "Sandy, but otherwise fairly good roads greater part of the way to Muskegon; roads between Holland (or Grand Haven) and Grands Rapids good in dry weather, but difficult—or practically impassable—after long rains at any time of year, especially in wet seasons." (WMU)

The rise in automobile usage and the increasing incidence of automobile accidents on the streets of Kalamazoo resulted in several conflicts between those driving horses and those driving the "new machines." Anti-automobile legislation was introduced at the state level as early as June 1903. Restrictive ordinances were proposed in the Kalamazoo Council and reported in the *Telegraph* on July 7, 1903, including such provisions as "...six miles an hour on the level, four miles an hour around corners and across streets, a dead stop when horses are fractious and a penalty attached of $30 or 30 days in jail or both."

L. D. Cooley was an active and very vocal automobilist. He carried with him various court decisions that he was quick to share with any willing listener. One of his favorites was a decision passed down by Judge Monk of Kokomo, Indiana, in reference to the exclusion of steam-powered automobiles from the streets. Excerpts of that decision were published in the *Kalamazoo Telegraph* on July 16, 1903:

> Persons making use of horses as a means of travel or traffic by the highways have no rights therein superior to those that make use of the public ways... Horses may be and often are frightened by the newly-adopted locomotion, but it would be as reasonable to treat the horse as a public nuisance for its tendency to shy and be frightened by unaccustomed objects as to regard the vehicle propelled by new methods of locomotion as a public nuisance from its tendency to frighten horses.

The confrontation between those using horses and those driving automobiles continued for the next several years, and in January 1905, with James C. Hatfield as chairman, several automobilists established an automobile club that they hoped would have a hand in drafting city ordinances.

Hazards and liabilities for automobilists were also quite clear, and the development of fledgling automobile insurance companies and the benefits of insurance were major topics of discussion among area automobilists by the summer of 1903. The idea of insuring automobilists was just beginning. A standard policy cost $100 and offered $5,000 liability per person and $10,000 per accident. The July 13, 1903 *Telegraph* quoted an agent as saying, "For $100 a year the dashing chauffeur may knock a man sky high, put an arm or a leg out of business, or play hob with a man's anatomy generally and the insuring company will stand the damage, within certain bounds."

Fig. 8-7. A combination of poor gravel roads, excessive speed, and the limited skill of novice automobilists often resulted in a broken vehicle and this one is an awful mess. The simple design and the chain drive place the photo, circa 1910. (WMU)

Automobiles continued to arrive in Kalamazoo, but development of the "automobile dealership" and the necessary service network grew slowly. The first two cars in Kalamazoo, owned by George W. Taylor, a local clothier, and W. E. Upjohn, president of the Upjohn Pill and Granule Company, were ordered directly from the manufacturer, removing both the profit and the service responsibility of a dealer. The Blood brothers are credited with being the first to arrange for an automobile sale in 1901 to Oscar K. Buckhout, the owner of a local chemical company, technically making them the first automobile dealers in the city. However, they turned their attention almost immediately to the manufacture and not the sale of the horseless carriage.

There are two milestones in the development of automobile sales agencies. The first was the establishment of a true dealership organized by William O. Harlow, and the second was the construction of the first modern agency by Harry B. Parker some ten years later. Both Harlow and Parker remained leaders in the automobile business until the mid-thirties.

Harlow was born in Crescent City, Iowa, on November 6, 1878 and moved to Kalamazoo with his widowed mother in 1893. He attended Kings Business College and attained a modicum of fame in the city as a bicycle racer during the "Gay Nineties." In 1904 he began selling the Cadillac and Orient Buckboard (along with fishing tackle, bicycles, guns, ammunition, and other sporting goods, as well as phonographs) from the Kalamazoo Sporting Goods store that he and William Locher owned at 111 South Rose Street. The sale of automobiles was essentially a sideline at the time, and the service department for the repair of these vehicles was located in the alley behind the store. His first Cadillac was sold to D. C. Olin, the bicycle racer/automobilist and a local dry goods dealer. In 1904, Olin bought out Locher's interests and, along with Harlow, became associated with W. S. Daniels, proprietor of the Michigan Automobile Company of Grand Rapids, to form the Kalamazoo Automobile Agency. Still located at the sporting goods store, they offered many of the leading marques and their advertising slogans were listed in the *Telegraph* on March 26, 1904: the Pope Toledo—"the automobile deluxe"; The silent Cadillac—"America's best small car"; Columbia—"town carriages of refinement"; Pope-Tribune—"the swellest runabout"; Stevens-Duryea—"the doctor's favorite"; the Orient Buckboard—"the lowest priced runabout"; and the Winton—"a car of reputation."

Fig. 8-8. *The view is down South Rose Street, circa 1905. Harlow's sporting goods store is just distinguishable in the middle of the photograph. The sign on the second building reads "Harlows" and the small car in the street is believed to be an early Cadillac. (WMU)*

Harlow, an active salesman, offered advice to potential buyers in the March 26, 1904 *Gazette:*

Flashy, gaudy, brassy-lookers don't prove the best. Look to the heart and life of it.... A balky horse will go—but a balky, fussy, bothersome, expensive automobile is worse and you want the other kind. Investigate and talk with us. New catalogues ready. Let us advise you.

Harlow introduced the first Buick in Kalamazoo at the city's inaugural automobile show in 1910, and he holds the record for selling the greatest variety of makes, many of which had a brief production run. At one time or another, he was the dealer for the Apperson, Buick, Cadillac, Columbia, Dort, Durant, Ford, Harroun, King "8," Kissel, Liberty-Six, Lion-40, Moon, Oakland, Oldsmobile, Orient Buckboard, Pope-Tribune, Pope-Toledo, Stevens-Duryea, Star, Stutz, White, and Winton. He owned one of the largest dealerships in Kalamazoo with 15,000 square feet of space at 426 West Main Street, extending north with frontage on 427–429 Water Street. At the time of dealership's construction, Harlow pledged that he would provide "an active and up-to-date automobile agency, of the same standard as other cities supporting automobile stores and garages." In 1920, Harlow sold this agency to Thomas Orrell who planned to sell Franklin and Oakland cars, as well as Kalamazoo trucks, from this location.

In 1904, there was only one other dealership in addition to Harlow's agency in Kalamazoo: the Slover and Wilson Agency, located at 208 North Rose Street. Slover and Wilson offered eight models of the Rambler from $650 to $1,350, and they published the first automobile advertisement in Kalamazoo, complete with a picture of the Rambler, in the *Kalamazoo Evening Telegraph* on March 17, 1904, the day the Rambler arrived in the city. Slover and Wilson had been in the bicycle business and manufactured and sold bicycles from the same North Rose Street site that housed the Kalamazoo Cycle Company from 1891–1902 under the auspices of the Blood brothers. The Rambler dealership was successful, although Frank Wilson severed the partnership and left the dealership in 1905 to open his own garage and auto repair shop at 425 East Main Street.

The initial enthusiasm for the manufacture of automobiles began to wane in 1906, and the three original manufacturers—Frank Burtt, the Fuller brothers, and the Blood brothers—all turned to building automobile engines, transmissions, and universal joints respectively, rather than automobiles. The papers were filled with the news of declining business on Wall Street, and it was clear that the climate was not conducive to attracting large amounts of venture capital over and above the large investments made to the growing paper industry in the city. After the withdrawal of these men from the industry, there were few major changes in the automotive world in Kalamazoo until the subsequent introduction of the Mighty Michigan automobile in 1909 and the Great Automobile Show of April 7–9, 1910.

The first Kalamazoo auto show was organized by William A. Donaldson, advertising manager of *The Kalamazoo Gazette*. One can only imagine the financial return to the paper as the *Gazette* was filled with full-spread advertisements in early April of 1910. Local newspaper advertising had been very scant before that date, but in 1910, the Thomas Jeffery Company, maker of the Rambler automobile, praised the newspapers for increased automobile sales. The 1910 automobile show was promoted by J. H. Dore, owner of the Dore Auto and Machinery Company and agent for the Maxwell car. The show marked a major change in the sale of automobiles in Kalamazoo as auto sales increased dramatically during this period and there was much talk about how the "Kazooks had been smitten with the dread Automobilitist disease." The paper included a complete description of the stages of the disease from initial inquiry, to first purchase, to the final stage of "bought another car."

The three-day event was held at the Armory Hall on North Burdick Street just across from the Rickman Hotel. The dingy interior of the Armory was decorated with red and green banners and special lighting was installed to reflect off the nickel and brass of the wondrous machines. One of the features of the show was the Detroit Electric, sold by the Kalamazoo Motor Company, owned and operated by Thomas Orrell at 114–116 West Water Street. The electric cars always attracted women drivers, and the Detroit was especially admired for its beautiful enamel finish, silver trimmings, and handsome upholstery. Orrell also sold the K-R-I-T, the Mitchell, and the Brush from that agency. An interesting feature of the Brush display was the use of mirrors under the car, which allowed visitors to inspect the underside without crawling beneath the vehicle. Other attractions included a White gasoline-powered car with a torpedo body (probably the only one ever seen in Kalamazoo), a display for the Dayton airless tire, the Elliott Carbide-Feed Acetylene storage generator for lighting, as well as a display of lubricants by Steve Marsh of the Standard Oil Company. This grand affair attracted not only residents of Kalamazoo, but the incoming trains were filled with visitors from Three Rivers, Battle Creek, Coldwater, and Union City. The society night scheduled for Friday featured orchestral music by the Lyon ensemble, a particularly special highlight.

There were twenty-five cars in all on display. George Boyle's agency at 107 North Church offered an E.M.F. "30" and a Flanders "20" and reported sales of five E.M.F.s during the show, including one to Dr. Cornish of Lawton and another to Judge Knappen of Kalamazoo. J. H. Dore showed two Maxwell cars from the agency on Portage and Washington Streets and he sold three vehicles, although the names of the purchasers were withheld by request. William O. Harlow, who was still selling cars from the 111 South Rose Street address, advertised eighteen different models in stock,

Fig. 8-9. The Kalamazoo Motor Company was owned by William Orell and was located at 114-116 West Water Street where Orell sold the Brush, K-R-I-T, Mitchell, Oldsmobile, and the Detroit Electric. Orell displayed the Detroit Electric at the auto show in 1910 and it was well received, particularly by the women attending the show. The car in the photograph is a 1910 K-R-I-T, built in Detroit, Michigan. This dealership portrays the modest "storefront" agencies that existed at this time. Note the wooden container for gasoline storage on the right of the building. (WMU)

but displayed three Buicks, and sold a number of cars. He also refused to divulge the names of purchasers. Dallas Boudemen showed a Regal and sold one the first night to W. L. Wheatley of Plainwell. The Russell and Albrecht Agency at 425 East Main Street, which sold both the Overland and the Stanley Steamer, brought two Overland automobiles and reported three sales to residents of Kalamazoo. The Philip Glass agency, located at 310 East Water Street, displayed two Model T Fords, which were then available in colors other than black, and reported selling six cars to residents of Kalamazoo, Dowagiac, and Schoolcraft. F.N. Milliman at 115 Eleanor Street displayed the Reo, "The Handsomest Car Shown in Kalamazoo." By midday of the final day, fifty-three cars had been sold to customers from Three Rivers to South Haven, with a value of $50,000. The success of the show led to the founding of a dealers' organization with William Harlow as president. George Boyles, W. L. Weber, and Thomas Orrell were named members of a board that would organize an annual show and other events of special interest to the lovers of the sport. The Kalamazoo Automobile show would become an annual event.

Harry B. Parker was one of the most well known and celebrated of the early automobile dealers in the city, although he did not begin selling automobiles until after the inaugural Kalamazoo Automobile Show. Born in Detroit on August 11, 1882, and the only son of the four children born to the Parkers, he came to Kalamazoo at the age of fifteen and secured a position as "handy boy" in the offices of the *Kalamazoo Telegraph*, eventually rising to become city editor for the paper. In 1909 he became associated with *The Press*, managed by Edward N. Dingley (who, as we will discover, was probably the most principled editor in the city), and subsequently worked for the *Telegraph-Press*, when the two papers were combined. On Friday, May 7, almost exactly one year after the death of his father in an automobile accident, Harry Parker was hit by a street car coming down West Main Street between Woodward and Stuart Streets. Parker's horse had become unmanage-

able, rearing and then running in front of the street car. Parker was badly bruised when he hit the wooden blocks that served as pavement, but not seriously hurt. The incident would foretell a life of accomplishment and curious adventure— something always seemed to be happening to Harry Parker—and he was considered one of the great raconteurs. Many of his most interesting anecdotes concerned his infamous Stanley Steamer automobile.

Parker had purchased his first car while still employed at the *Telegraph-Press*. He saw an advertisement by Russell and Albrecht for some used bargains and finally settled on a Stanley Steamer. He tinkered with the car for about a week before he was able to get it to run reliably, and his first venture with the car was a brief family tour to Comstock, some ten miles east of Kalamazoo. His report appeared many years later in a *Gazette* interview on October 18, 1925, in which he confessed sheepishly, "When nearing Comstock, I looked down and my trouser legs were on fire. I soon extinguished the blaze, but my wife and children returned to Kalamazoo by interurban."

Fig. 8-10. The Kalamazoo Automobile Show of 1910 was highly publicized through a special section of The Kalamazoo Gazette, on April 6, 1910, and it was clear that the promoters were intent on attracting women. It was one of the major social and business events in Kalamazoo during the first decade of the 1900s and marked the beginning of the period of the automobile as a means of reliable transportation. (DOL)

Harry Parker and his young bride had eloped in 1903, and she must have been both a patient and understanding woman, for one incident followed another with Harry and his famous Stanley. The next encounter was a trip to South Haven with Dr. and Mrs. Walter den Bleyker. The two couples left Kalamazoo at 5:00 a. m., but did not arrive in South Haven until 10:00 that evening. On the way they encountered many horses, and the hissing of the engine caused five of the animals to run away, dragging their angry drivers with them. Harry blew five boiler safety plugs and lost the copper engine case in the mud. "We all came back on the train," he lamented, "and I had to buy a new engine, boiler and other equipment that cost as much as I had paid for the car."

After the steamer was repaired, Harry drove the family down to the Michigan Central Station to meet his father-in-law. "After entering the depot, I heard a scream which I recognized as my wife's," he said, and as he ran out the door he saw the Stanley running down Burdick Street with his wife and children in the rear seat. His wife was desperately trying without much success to steer the runaway automobile. Apparently, a pipe had broken that allowed the released steam into the piston without going through the control valve so that the car ran as long as there was steam pressure. Finally Harry was able to catch the car and he jumped aboard. He turned off the fire under the boiler, but the car continued to gain speed as they rounded the corner near the Rickman Hotel.

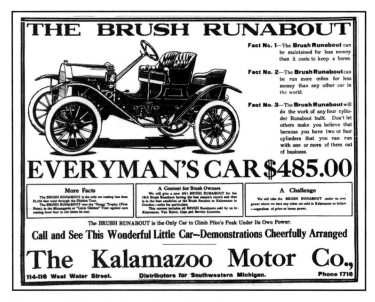

Fig. 8-11. *William A. Donaldson of* The Kalamazoo Gazette *promoted the Automobile Show and discovered an enormous increase in automobile advertising in the* Gazette. *Such displays, particularly full-page advertisements, were very scarce before the 1910 show. The Brush Runabout was sold by William Orell at the Kalamazoo Motor Company, 114-116 West Water Street. (DOL)*

The steam finally dissipated and the car came to a stop on Kalamazoo Avenue. Parker reported, rather dryly, "Mrs. Parker and the children walked home."

After his wife and children departed, Parker again fired up the boiler. The water level in the boiler was low, the steam pressure skyrocketed to four hundred pounds, and he was off on another wild ride. The car went through the side door of a garage and out the front, round and round he went several times until one of the mechanics, who thought Parker was playing games, hopped on board and threw the transmission into reverse. That maneuver accomplished little, for the car began to run in reverse at the same speed it had been going forward, smashing into the rear wall and into the grease pit. "That was the end of the Steamer," he said with a smile and one wonders if the demise of the "Demon Stanley" did not also save his marriage.

In 1910 Parker was debating about investing in another publishing opportunity in one of the western states, when A. E. Rose, owner of the Kalamazoo Auto Sales Company at 112 North Edwards Street, offered to sell the company if Parker would pay the rent and a commission of $100 for each car sold. The company had been bankrupt in 1909 and Parker, investing his total savings of $400, took over the business and began selling the Overland and the Hudson. He was able to complete $55,000 in gross sales the first year and pay off Rose.

He then went to the bank for another $5,000, and the bank officers gave him a fatherly talk about the transitory nature of the automobile business. Parker's persistence was rewarded with a loan and around 1912 he built one of the first show rooms on Main Street, much to the chagrin and opposition of the citizenry who scoffed at the depth of his involvement in the foolish automobile enterprise. Parker dropped the Hudson in 1916, but continued with the Overland and then the Willys Knight until 1921. At that time he moved to the Maxwell, the predecessor of the Chrysler, that he introduced to Kalamazoo when W. P. Chrysler began production in 1924.

Parker resided in Kalamazoo for most of his life at 1546 Spruce Drive, where he and his wife raised their seven children. He had an established reputation as an automobile dealer who sold fifteen different makes of cars in his lifetime, reaching sales figures of 16,000 new cars. In 1924 alone, his sales of the newly introduced Chrysler automobile reached $1.2 million. He was an accomplished flutist, a member of the Kalamazoo Symphony Orchestra, a founder of the Humane Society, a second commodore in the Gull Lake Yacht Club, and a competent horseman. He died suddenly of heart failure in 1936 in the office of his friend and physician, Walter den Bleyker.

As the first decade of the twentieth century came to an end, the automobile world in Kalamazoo seemed to settle down. The magnificent car show that year was very successful and served as the defining event that turned the automobile from a curiosity for parades, slow races, and recreation to a vehicle of commerce, transportation, and work. By 1910, business reports began to appear touting both the efficiency and the cost-saving aspects of the car and contending that the reliability of these vehicles made them suitable for use as emergency vehicles. The farmer, who once despised the automobilist and his horseless carriage, now recognized the relationship between the demands of the automobilists and good roads. The roads were passable, still not first class, but sufficient to open product transport to the farmer's own emerging markets. The initial enthusiasm in, and attempts at, the manufacture of automobiles by Frank Burtt, the Bloods and the Fullers dissipated and they turned to other manufacturing interests, although the very optimistic Burtt was still proposing new endeavors in vehicle manufacture. The Michigan Buggy Company had just begun to manufacture the Michigan in 1909, and the history of that company would define another legacy for the community. In its demise, Michigan Buggy would give rise to yet another chapter in the story of automobile manufacture in Kalamazoo. But for the moment, concluded the *Kalamazoo Telegraph*, on March 12, 1910:

> The automobile is no longer considered a luxury that it was in its experimental days—today,
> to many at least, it is a necessity. This year will break all records. Kalamazoo has arrived as the
> legitimate automobile headquarters for southwestern Michigan.

REFERENCES

Automobile Industry. *Kalamazoo Evening Telegraph*, July 23, 1904.

Beverly R. Kimes and Henry Austin Clark, Jr. *Standard Catalog of American Cars, 1805–1942 3rd ed.* Iola, WI: Krause Publications, 1996.

Clark Brothers. *The Vicksburg Commercial*, June 21, 1901.

The Clark Steam Automobile. *The Vicksburg Commercial*, June 28, 1901.

Asphalt Pavement. *The Kalamazoo Gazette-News*, April 28, 1903.

Progress of Paving. *Kalamazoo Evening Telegraph*, May 26, 1903.

Pavement Progress. *Kalamazoo Evening Telegraph*, June 11, 1903.

Season on at Gull. *Kalamazoo Evening Telegraph*, July 2, 1904.

Gull Lake the Beautiful. *The Kalamazoo Gazette*, July 3, 1904.

Ross Collier. *Ross Collier Collection*. Regional History Collections, Western Michigan University, A-1911.

Kalamazoo Good Roads Are Model for the State. *Kalamazoo Telegraph*, February 25, 1915.

Automobilists Put in Peril. *Kalamazoo Evening Telegraph*, August 3, 1906.

Have Come for Good, Many Autos Seen in Kalamazoo. *Kalamazoo Evening Telegraph*, April 2, 1904.

Relation of Automobile to Good Roads Improvement. *The Kalamazoo Gazette*, April 9, 1910.

American Farmer and the Automobile. *The Kalamazoo Gazette*, April 9, 1910.

Larry Massie. "Thank 'Good Roads' Earle for Today's Highways." *Kalamazoo Gazette*, January 29, 1989.

Harold Cook. *The Michigan License Plate Collectors Association Presents; The Michigan Book*. Milford, MI: Michigan License Plate Collectors Association, 1995.

New Automobile Disease. *Kalamazoo Evening Telegraph*, April 9, 1904.

Automobile Engine. *Kalamazoo Evening Telegraph*, July 16, 1903.

Route Book. *Michigan and Chicago to Cleveland and Reverse*. Goodrich Tire Company, circa 1913.

Taxicabs Placed in Service by the Kalamazoo Taxicab Company. *Kalamazoo Telegraph-Press*, March 7, 1914.

Unexcelled Taxi Service Afforded City by Kalamazoo Hack and Bus Company. *The Kalamazoo Gazette*, August 2, 1914.

Kalamazoo Woman Jitney Bus Driver; Her Hubby Conductor. *Kalamazoo Telegraph-Press*, April 9, 1915.

Automobilist in Kalamazoo. *Kalamazoo Evening Telegraph*, August 13, 1904.

First Garage Started Here 20 Years Ago. *The Kalamazoo Gazette*, October 18, 1925.

Automobile Repairing Is an Art in Itself. *Kalamazoo Evening Telegraph*, March 12, 1910.

Death of G. W. Parker. *The Kalamazoo Gazette*, May 9, 1904.

To License All Drivers. *Kalamazoo Evening Telegraph*, June 27, 1903.

Ordinance on Autos. *Kalamazoo Evening Telegraph*, July 7, 1903.

Automobile Decisions. *Kalamazoo Evening Telegraph*, July 16, 1903.

Automobile Insurance. *Kalamazoo Evening Telegraph*, July 13, 1903.

Automobile No. 3. *Kalamazoo Daily Telegraph*, April 19, 1901.

Automobile Announcement. *Kalamazoo Evening Telegraph*, March 16, 1904.

Leading Autos. *Kalamazoo Evening Telegraph*, March 16, 1904.

Are You Interested in Automobiles? *Kalamazoo Evening Telegraph*, March 26, 1904.

All Standard Cars Handled in Kalamazoo. *The Kalamazoo Gazette*, October 18, 1925.

The 1904 Rambler Arrived Today. *Kalamazoo Evening Telegraph*, March 17, 1904.

1904 Rambler Automobiles. *Kalamazoo Evening Telegraph*, March 26, 1904.

Get What You Pay For. *Kalamazoo Evening Telegraph*, March 12, 1910.

Rambler Sings Praise, Ads in Daily Newspapers. *Kalamazoo Evening Telegraph*, March 12, 1910.

Dread Disease, Automobilitis Stings Kazooks. *Kalamazoo Evening Telegraph*, April 8, 1910.

Remarkable Epidemic—Automobilious Fever. *The Kalamazoo Gazette*, April 9, 1910.

Kalamazoo Auto Show Open Hundreds Throng Armory to View Display of Machines. *The Kalamazoo Gazette*, April 8, 1910.

Buyer Can Find His Desire at the Auto Show. *The Kalamazoo Gazette*, April 9, 1910.

All in Readiness for Auto Show. *The Kalamazoo Gazette*, April 9, 1910.

Auto Exhibit Big Success. *The Kalamazoo Gazette*, April 9, 1910.

Auto Sales Best Ever. *Kalamazoo Evening Telegraph*, April 9, 1910.

Automobile Dealers Form Association. *The Kalamazoo Gazette*, April 9, 1910.

Harry Parker is Injured. *Kalamazoo Evening Telegraph*, May 8, 1905.

Harry Parker Led in Sale of Autos on Large Scale. *The Kalamazoo Gazette*, October 18, 1925.

Kalamazoo's Great Motor Display. *The Kalamazoo Gazette*, April 6, 1910.

Howard J. Cooper and D. O. Harlow Veteran Dealers. *The Kalamazoo Gazette*, January 24, 1937.

Harry B. Parker Dies Suddenly After Heart Attack. *The Kalamazoo Gazette*, March 22, 1936.

On Automobile Row. *Kalamazoo Evening Telegraph*, March 12, 1910.

Part II

THE PROMISE
IS SHATTERED

1910–1917

~

Fig. 9-1. This photograph seems to epitomize the character of the Blood family of talented yet mischievous and strong-willed mechanics. The image shows several men, including Clarence, third from the left, and his son Edward (believed to be the second from the left), in front of a dredging machine that has broken through a bridge somewhere near Buchanan, Michigan. It is a curious photo of a group of men who sought a photographer to venture into the countryside to have their picture taken in front of what had to be a substantial error in judgment. The story includes a conflict between the local constable and the foremen, the former threatening arrests and the latter threatening a charge of trespassing. The confrontation ended in a stand-off. (WMU)

Chapter 9

The Cornelian Light Car

1913–1934

The easiest ride of them all, a beautiful streamline and fast as a bullet.
—Cornelian advertisement

The Bloods were people of family, rather than notoriety, for their names were never found on the published guest lists for the grand social events in Kalamazoo. They were not members of the Park Club, the Kalamazoo Country Club, or the gentlemen's horse racing circuit at Recreation Park. They lived a quiet and comfortable life in their residence on Woodward Avenue, tending an attractive garden and gathering with the children and relatives on the front porch on Sundays and holiday celebrations. The Blood name had a national reputation for mechanical skill and quality of manufacture, and the intense but friendly competition between father and son in the summer of 1913 to build an innovative cyclecar was not surprising. What was surprising was that the "upstart son," Howard E. Blood, at the age of twenty-six, triumphed in the competition against his more experienced father, building a distinctive and innovative light-duty automobile of the cyclecar class.

The father was one of the original founders of the Michigan Automobile Company in 1902 and had considerable experience in the development of lightweight, reliable vehicles. Maurice had designed and built the first cyclecar in the United States, and in 1903 had invented a universal joint that the Blood Brothers Machine Company was still building in 1913.

Maurice and Clarence Blood are the brothers identified in the company name of Blood Brothers Machine Company. Howard Blood, Maurice's son, would not be included in a reference to the brothers, except as an employee of the company. The Blood brothers quit automobile manufacturing in 1906 to concentrate on the manufacture of the universal joint and other automobile parts. In the fall of 1913, the trade papers were full of articles about the impending "cyclecar movement" in this country, and at the age of sixty, Maurice began tinkering with automobiles once again. He returned to his original design using the same narrow 36" tread, single-cylinder air-cooled engine and friction drive that had been used on the first of the Blood cars built in 1902. Unlike his original

Fig. 9-2. The 1914 Mercury cyclecar, the first cyclecar to be sold in Detroit at a cost of $375, illustrates the American interpretation of a European concept. The car, of unibody construction, rode on a 100" wheelbase with a narrow 36" tread. The engine was a small twin-cylinder DeLuxe rated at 9.8 hp. Power was transferred to the rear wheels through a friction transmission via a copper-studded V-belt, visible on the outside of both cars in the foreground. The company offered three models: the two-seat model with tandem seating shown in the left foreground; a monocar designed for the salesman on the right; and a small delivery vehicle seen in the background. Interestingly, the Mercury was selected as the driver-training vehicle by the Michigan State Automobile School. The company lasted less than one year, from November 1913 to August 1914, but the vehicle epitomizes the concept and the craze that captured the imagination of this country in 1913 and 1914 and led Howard Blood to build the Cornelian. (DOL)

car, the 1913 model had tandem seating in which the passenger sat behind the driver. Interestingly, this arrangement was just the opposite of his second car, the 1902 "carry-cycle," in which the driver sat behind the passengers.

Maurice built just one example in 1913, but like many other cyclecar developers, he is credited with having toured through fourteen states with this experimental model in an effort to show both the pleasures and reliability of his cyclecar design.

The cyclecar concept was imported from Europe, where cars were taxed based upon engine displacement. The first American-built cyclecars reached the marketplace in early 1913. There were over 1.1 million horse-drawn vehicles sold in this country in 1913, and the potential to replace these vehicles with a reliable, inexpensive, gasoline-powered motorcar provided enormous incentive for a growing industry. What might be best described as the "cyclecar movement or craze" gathered momentum that swept the country in 1913 and reached a peak in interest and production in late 1913 and early 1914. A *Gazette* article in August 1913 proclaimed: "Poor Man's Auto is Here At Last." The cyclecar concept died almost as quickly as it arose, and, as the story unfolds, Howard Blood, inadvertent as the intent might have been, contributed to that demise.

The cyclecar was a nimble machine weighing from 350 to 1,000 pounds, built on a wheelbase of 80" to 102" and powered by a small displacement engine. Many had a tread width of 36" and their

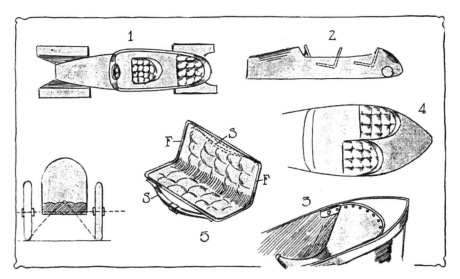

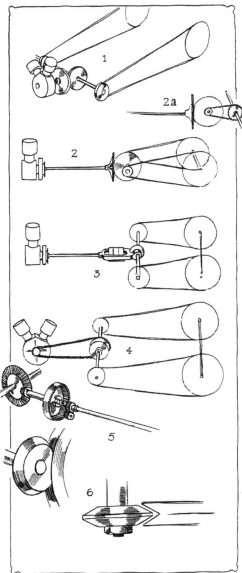

Fig. 9-3 (above). Cyclecars used a number of seating variations to squeeze two people in a small narrow chassis. This figure was taken from the January 15, 1914 issue of The Automobile. Points of interest include: (1) the tandem seating scheme used in the Imp cyclecar placing the front seat in the middle and the feet of the rear passenger on either side of that seat, allowing the wheel base to be short and the seats low; (2) the side elevation showing the tandem seating arrangement with the passenger's feet beneath the front seat in the vehicle as typically used with a 36" tread; (3) the hammock style seat used in many cars because of its economy of construction, consisted of a piece of leather stretched loosely between cross supports and proved quite comfortable; (4) the staggered seat design, offsetting the passenger seat to the rear by 10", used in the Dudley and Falcon cyclecar to get the effect of conventional side by side seating within the narrow 36" tread width; (5) the Cornelian seat, using a conventional side by side configuration, made of leather stretched across a rigid frame [F] and mounted on springs [S] both underneath and at the back of the frame, providing a very comfortable ride.

Fig. 9-4 (left). The cyclecar concept was one of simplicity and economical construction and power to the rear wheels was often by exterior drive belts so as not to impinge on the limited passenger space with a narrow 36" tread design. This figure was taken from the January 15, 1914 issue of The Automobile. The points of interest include: (1) showing a friction drive just behind the motor with a long exterior belt drive to the rear wheels that was used on 70% of the cyclecars announced in January 1914; (2) showing a friction drive with the transmission axle amidships and two exterior mounted drive belts to the rear wheels; (2a) showing the same arrangement with a single chain drive to the rear wheels; (3) showing a two-speed planetary transmission and gearset mounted amidships with an exterior drive belt to the rear wheels; (4) showing a chain drive from the motor to a gearset on a jack shaft, and an exterior mounted drive belt to the rear wheels; (5) showing a planetary transmission with a drive shaft through the middle of the car as used on the Cornelian; (6) the roller pinion drive used on the Duryea car which was inexpensive and avoided the use of belts.

size was touted as a convenience, for it could be driven through the front gate and stored on the front porch. "Why should one carry 3,000 pounds about in a car to carry two persons when five hundred pounds can do it even better?" asked the editors of *The Cyclecar*.

In January 1914, an article in *The Automobile* offered the following conclusion about cyclecars:

> [Cyclecars] have proven themselves competent to meet road conditions in a way that compares with motor vehicles which have been previously developed. They have made 50 miles per hour on good roads and have ploughed for hours through snow, gumbo mud, pouring rain, over steep hills, through deep sand and, in short, have been able to negotiate road conditions which were extreme.
>
> These tests have proven that it is possible to make a cyclecar of as great comfort as a real touring car, and equal roadability; that these cars are wonderfully reliable through the very simplicity of their mechanisms and that they can be run for one-half to one-fourth of the upkeep of the cheapest light cars.

The formal definition of a cyclecar offered by the American Cyclecar Manufacturers Association meeting in 1914 was simple: "a vehicle with four wheels, and an engine displacement of less than seventy-one cubic inches." Larger vehicles, similar in design and characteristics to a full-size automobile, although smaller in size and power, were identified as "light cars." *The Automobile*, January 15, 1914, made the following dichotomy between the "cyclecar" and "light car":

> The first type aims at new construction, simpler mechanisms and lower manufacturing and upkeep cost than has been attained by any former motor vehicle. This type is the real cyclecar. The other type aims at building a motorcar in all its general specifications, this car being lighter and smaller than previous cars have been and hence a lower upkeep proposition than former products. The light car therefore comes under the motorcar head and is dealt with in that class.

The accommodations in both the cyclecar and the light car were for two people with the seating usually, but not always, side by side in a light car and either staggered or in tandem fashion, one behind the other, to accommodate the narrow track and body width of the cyclecar. The cyclecar was usually powered by a small motorcycle engine and many were chain or belt driven. Often the belt was looped around a power take-off on the side of the engine and ran along the body of the car to a drive wheel attached to the rear axle. The exposed drive belt gave many of these cars a "home-made" appearance.

Unfortunately, manufacturers did not hold to a precise definition between the dichotomies of "cycle" and "light" and the specifications of any particular car might blur that distinction. The Blood-built Cornelian cyclecar was one that had characteristics of both, and with little effort in the spring of 1914, Howard moved the Cornelian from the cyclecar class to the light car class with the addition of a new four-cylinder engine, full front fenders, and other changes in the body.

The cyclecar enjoyed a strong romantic following and many of the cars bore whimsical names such as O-We-Go, LuLu, Covey Bear, Dudly Bug, Imp, Cricket, Little Princess, Carnation, Zip, and Peter Pan. Howard Blood was not without his appeal to romance and whimsy by using a child's rhyme to promote the cyclecar concept. He liked to define the cyclecar as the automobile's younger brother or the motorcycle's older brother. The following verse, taken from a old time child's game, appeared at the top of a company publication:

How many miles to Barley Bright?

Three score and ten.

Can I get there by candle light?

Yes, there and back again.

If you use the Cornelian Cyclecar.

Cyclecar clubs were formed in many cities to sponsor outings, tours, and races. Publications devoted to promoting these vehicles, such as *The Cyclecar* and *Cycle Car Age,* fueled the enthusiasm. Cyclecar companies seemed to sprout up everywhere in 1913 and 1914, and as many as thirty were started in Detroit alone during the six-month period from the fall of 1913 to the spring of 1914. Most survived less than a year, and the haste by many builders to market a vehicle often led to poor design, flimsy construction, and unreliable mechanical components. In some cases frames of soft pine and cheaply built engines brought these cars to a standstill and dimmed the enthusiasm of the owner after only several hundred miles of ownership. Grayson reports that as early as April 1914, *The Horseless Age* warned the industry of the impending negative reputation resulting from such hurried construction, and by the summer of 1914 widespread criticism of the cyclecar's shoddy construction and poor performance predicted its demise. There were many quality cars built by established companies, but the industry was painted with a broad brush and attempts to change the negative impressions of many potential buyers in the summer of 1914 fell on deaf ears. Production declined steadily after 1914, and many of the companies were short lived, producing fewer than one hundred cars. By the time the United States entered World War I in 1917, the concept, the cars, and the manufacturers had disappeared from the American marketplace. The cyclecar design continued in Europe, but it was not until after World War II that any critical mass of small cars would become available in this country. The American Austin, built in the 1930s in Butler, Pennsylvania, is perhaps the only exception to that generalization.

The activity in Kalamazoo became known nationally when the December 1913 issue of the *Automobile Trade Journal* listed an experimental cyclecar under the Blood Brothers Machine Company name, indicating only that it was powered by a two-cylinder engine with seating for two people. This car was designed by Maurice Blood. A separate cyclecar under the Cornelian Company name, powered by a two-cylinder four-horsepower engine with seating for two and selling at $400 was also identified in that issue. This car was the design of Howard Blood. The cyclecar that Howard built and named the Cornelian that autumn was both superior to and more developed than his father's design. At the invitation and insistence of the elder Blood, Howard Blood's Cornelian Company merged with the Blood Brothers Machine Company for the purpose of manufacturing the Cornelian. Subsequent publications referred to the Cornelian Department of the Blood Brothers Machine Company. The elder Blood commented as follows in an interview with *The Kalamazoo Gazette*, on November 28, 1913:

> The more I see of my son's machine, the more I am impressed with its remarkable simplicity
> and effectiveness…. Whereas most light cars throw the passengers about a good deal and are
> uncomfortable, the Cornelian suspends the seat on special springs, independently of the body,
> and the result is a little car which rides easier than many big cars.

Howard was born in Petoskey, Michigan on February 26, 1886, while Maurice was learning the woodworking trade in that city, and clearly he had grown to become his father's pride. Howard is

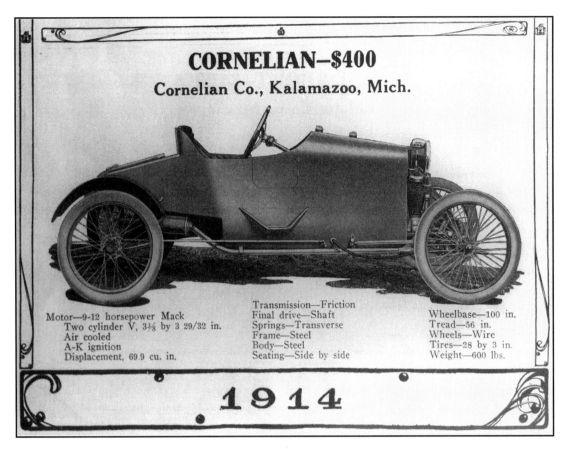

CORNELIAN—$400

Cornelian Co., Kalamazoo, Mich.

Motor—9-12 horsepower Mack
  Two cylinder V, 3⅜ by 3 29/32 in.
Air cooled
A-K ignition
Displacement, 69.9 cu. in.

Transmission—Friction
Final drive—Shaft
Springs—Transverse
Frame—Steel
Body—Steel
Seating—Side by side

Wheelbase—100 in.
Tread—56 in.
Wheels—Wire
Tires—28 by 3 in.
Weight—600 lbs.

1914

Fig. 9-5. The early Cornelian cyclecar from The American Cyclecar, *January 1914. Howard Blood built several models of this car with similar body styles: the first with motorcycle fenders on the front wheels, a second with flat fenders above the tires, and this one without fenders. This particular model was equipped with a Mack two-cylinder air-cooled engine mounted outside of the body, and a Ford Model T front axle. This car is similar to the cyclecar Howard Blood drove to Detroit to show to Henry Ford. Note that it is a product of the Cornelian Company of Kalamazoo and not the Blood Brothers Machine Company. This car is believed to be largely experimental as the detail varies among extant photographs. Perhaps five or six of these cars were built for testing and display at the Chicago and New York Automobile shows. (NAC)*

described by family descendents as shy, modest, and an accomplished student. He completed his education in Kalamazoo, no doubt mixing it with experience at the Blood Brothers Machine Company, where he built the first Cornelian. He graduated in mechanical engineering from the University of Michigan in 1909 and was great friends with a classmate, Fred Zeder, one of the foremost engineers of the Chrysler Corporation, vice-chairman of the board, and head of engineering at Chrysler until his death in 1952. The two men graduated at the head of their class, although according to Zeder family members, neither man would disclose the order of that honor.

Howard married Edith C. Goodrich on June 24, 1910. The "C" stood for Cornelian, and historians and members of the family alike agree that the Cornelian automobile was named after Howard's wife, although there is some disagreement about whether it was his offer or her demand. Considering the romanticism of the cyclecar, one prefers to believe that the Cornelian name was his sentimental offer. Some writers claim that the Cornelian name was derived from Cornell University, but no record has been found of Howard's attendance or graduation from that institution. Finally, others have suggested that Cornelian is an alternative spelling of carnelian, a reddish, semi-transparent stone, and that the name was used as a reference to that semi-precious variety of quartz. Interestingly, Howard Blood used the analogy at the bottom of the letterhead for the Blood Brothers Machine Company in 1914 when he referred to the Cornelian as: "A little gem you can't afford to be without and can afford to have," but there is no other evidence to substantiate this conjecture that the name is related to carnelian.

The cyclecar, that Howard Blood began building in May of 1913 and completed the following fall, received rave reviews in national automotive journals, and in September 1913, *The Kalamazoo Gazette*, proclaimed that Howard was "the inventor of a new cyclecar." The body of the Cornelian was formed from welded metal plates and steel ribs that served as both body and frame, and the all-steel body was finished in baked enamel. The car was powered initially by a two-cylinder, air-cooled, nine to twelve horsepower V-type Mack engine. Subsequently, Howard mounted the Spacke V-type air-cooled engine in the Cornelian; this popular motorcycle engine was also rated at nine to twelve horsepower and used in many cyclecars on the market in 1913. The engine was just behind the front axle outside of the body that was drawn and finished to a tight wedge. A single driving lamp was mounted at the nose of the wedge just above the engine and the front tires were covered by motorcycle-style fenders. The innovative sliding gear transmission provided two forward speeds and re-

Fig. 9-6. Howard Blood from The Kalamazoo Gazette, *circa 1913.*

verse, using only three gears when most transmissions used six or more to accomplish the same end. Power from the engine was by shaft drive, running through the middle of the car. The clutch and gear controls were incorporated into a single pedal at a substantial cost savings. The throttle was controlled by a foot pedal and the spark advance by a lever on the steering column. A cross-spring suspension system was used in place of the rear axle and the seat was suspended on two half elliptical springs, which gave the car an easy, comfortable ride.

Three additional models of this cyclecar were built during November of that year for display at the Chicago and New York auto shows in early 1914 and eventual production of this cyclecar reached twenty-five examples. At the Chicago show, the Cornelian was initially placed beside the Coey Bear, a widely advertised vehicle built in Chicago. So much attention was paid to the Cornelian, particularly by other engineers, that the Chicago-built vehicle was moved to a less conspicuous part of the coliseum. The Cornelian was also very well received at the New York show and a company there sought a single contract for one thousand cars in 1914, while a group of Boston investors wished to purchase the entire production run in 1914 if the cars could be sold exclusively in the northeast. Automobile agents from every state in the Union sent requests for sales agreements to Kalamazoo. Nationally, the Cornelian received plaudits from William Stout of *Motor Age*, in January of 1914. Stout worked for the Imp Cyclecar Company in Auburn, Indiana and was very familiar with the design problems of these cars. He gave an enthusiastic report of the car's performance after a test run of about ten miles in and around Kalamazoo:

Fig. 9-7a & b. These very rare photographs show Howard Blood behind the wheel of his first cyclecar, circa November 1913. In the photo at left, his father, Maurice, stands by the car and his cousin, Lawrence, is seated in the passenger seat. Eventually Maurice persuaded his son to merge the Cornelian Company with the Blood Brothers Machine Co. and produce the Cornelian under the family name. (DOL)

Blood Brothers of Kalamazoo Michigan, are bringing out a cyclecar, a side-by-side seater, absolutely new in construction throughout and wonderfully simple, developed by H. E. Blood. The cyclecar reached 35 miles per hour on very rough roads, plowed through mud halfway up to the axles and climbed a very steep hill with ease. The Cornelian cyclecar offered good road manners, and the unusual one piece spring-mounted seat provided good road comfort.

It was early in November 1913, when Howard made his successful, but fateful, journey to Detroit to show the Cornelian car to Henry Ford, who reportedly was much impressed with this diminutive vehicle. The trip itself proved the capabilities of the little car, as the journey was completed without a single mishap, except for a broken clutch pedal, which was quickly fixed and did not seriously delay the trip. Howard drove the Cornelian to Detroit over notoriously bad Michigan roads, passing many cars of greater size and power, and on the return trip he covered the last two miles from Battle Creek in deep mud that at times was up to the wheel hubs. When he pulled into Kalamazoo late Sunday afternoon the vehicle was covered with so much mud that identification of the car as the Cornelian was difficult. The Cornelian used a mere twelve gallons of gasoline and less than two quarts of oil in traversing three hundred miles. Interestingly, the name of the Cornelian engineer who accompanied him was S. W. Cushman, a famous name in early stationary engines and motorscooters in the 1950s.

The fateful part of the trip to visit Henry Ford occurred in Detroit when Howard parked the

Cornelian in front of the Ford factory. This particular model had a front axle from a Model T Ford, and no doubt included the Ford script stamping that may have made the Cornelian appear similar to a small Model T. Inadvertently, that small act by Howard Blood started a rumor that quickly reverberated through Detroit and the industry that Henry Ford was experimenting with a cyclecar.

Surely, that rumor contributed to the demise of the cyclecar, for the threat made by the cyclecar that competed in price with the Model T was apparent to Henry Ford. In retaliation, Ford built in 1914 a lightweight version of the famous Model T, about three-quarter size, including a scaled-down Ford running gear. When it was complete, Henry instructed his son, Edsel, to park the car in front of the Pontchartrain Hotel in downtown Detroit, where it drew large, curious crowds. The Ford Motor Company was the single most powerful force in the industry in 1914 and that simple display and its implied threat of competition from Henry Ford ended the cyclecar era in Detroit.

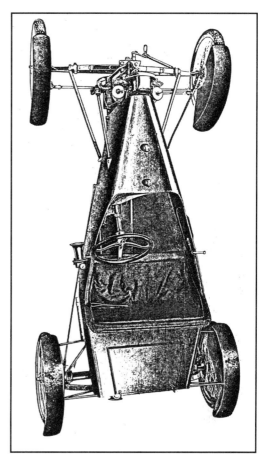

Fig. 9-8. The image shows a top view of the cyclecar that Howard Blood and Sam Cushman drove to Detroit in the fall of 1913 to show to Henry Ford. Note the wedge design and the way in which the Spacke V-type engine is mounted at the front of the wedge just behind the axle. This image shows motorcycle fenders on all four wheels, that differs from the other photograph, shown in Fig. 9-5. It also makes clear the small amount of space reserved for driver and passenger. (DOL)

During the same period, Ford decreased the price of a Model T from $550 in 1913, to $490 in 1915, to $440 in 1916, and then to $360 in 1917. The price of most cyclecars ranged from $300 to $400 and Ford's consistent price reductions eventually removed the price advantage that the cyclecars had enjoyed when first introduced.

On January 5, 1914, just two days after the very successful New York cyclecar show, Henry Ford proclaimed the $5 work day and 10,000 men appeared at the gates of the Ford factory. Once again, a single pronouncement from Henry Ford illustrated the influence of the Ford name, producing an immediate societal change. The marketplace for the cyclecar was lost. The combination of the cyclecar's wounded reputation, the loss of a significant part of the price advantage, and direct competition from Henry Ford slowed the cyclecar industry in 1914 and eventually brought it to a halt by the time America entered World War I in 1917.

On January 17, 1914, when the cyclecar concept was still at its peak of popularity and potential, the Bloods received the necessary papers from Lansing to increase their capital stock from $75,000 to $225,000 and the number of employees at the Ransom Street plant rose from 200 to 250. The announcement of the cyclecar industry and expansion of the Blood Brothers Machine Company produced quite a stir in Kalamazoo, but the competition with the giant Ford Motor Company was

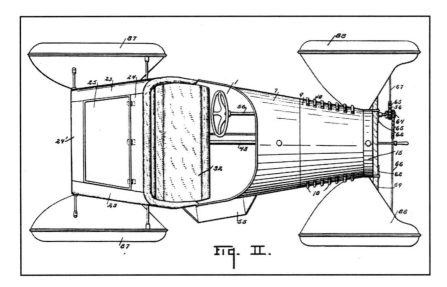

Fig. II.

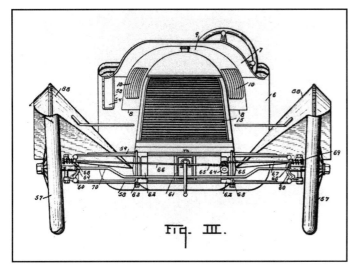

Fig. III.

Fig. 9-9 II, III & IV. These patent drawings show the changes made in the Cornelian as Howard Blood moved it from the cyclecar to the light car class. Figure II shows the full "ridge board" fenders and the interesting right-side step plate. Figure III shows the front view of the Cornelian and the spring arrangement that replaced the Model T Ford axle Howard had used on the cyclecar. Figure V shows the placement of the Sterling engine, now under a full hood, relative to the front wheels, flywheel, and universal joint on the drive shaft. The transmission was bolted to the differential and does not appear in the drawing. Note the location of the fuel tank just above the steering shaft. (DOL)

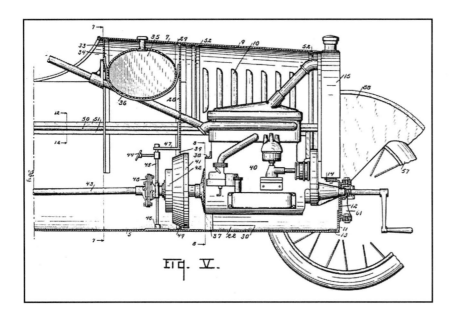

Fig. V.

Fig. 9-10. The second generation of Cornelian cars, the lightcar, had a Sterling engine with four cylinders and overhead valves fully enclosed under a hood. This photograph was taken in April 1914 in front of the Library in Kalamazoo for The Kalamazoo Gazette *article on the introduction of the Kalamazoo-built Cornelian. The photograph appeared again in the July 1914* Gazette *article describing the planned 10,000 mile endurance run. Note the step plate used on this model that was changed soon after this for the 1915 model. Note also the line of the cockpit dropping in a rakish manner from the dash to the seat back, a design feature that was also a part of the body style of the cyclecar. The total production run for this first model lightcar is unknown, but the best estimate is about one hundred since there were twenty-eight on the plant floor in the summer of 1914. (KLL)*

looming very large. Members of the Blood family had always been astute observers of the industry, and Howard responded quickly to the warnings about cyclecars. In April of 1914, Howard ceased construction of the cyclecar and turned his attention to finding another niche in the marketplace by developing an automobile in the more powerful light car class. This light car was also named the Cornelian.

The new Cornelian light car was introduced in Kalamazoo on April 12, 1914 with a selling price of $410, plus $25 for top and windshield. Gas driving lamps and side lights were standard and electric lights were available at extra cost. The car was capable of running eighty miles an hour while delivering thirty-five miles per gallon. The company advertisements touted the car as "the easiest rider of them all; a beautiful streamline and fast as a bullet." The "uni-body" construction was formed from steel plates ranging in thickness from twenty to twenty-four gauge. These plates were then reinforced with steel ribs and bulkheads, all electrically welded in place. The resilient body was finished in baked enamel and provided ample room for two passengers. The bench seat measured thirty-nine inches wide and sixteen deep and was supported by a spring at the leading edge of the cushion. The distance from the seat back to the dash was forty-four inches, providing a roomy cockpit for such a small car. Steering was on the left, and the gearshift on the right, with the gas, brake, and clutch arranged right to left according to practice. The spark advance in the lightcar was automatic, a feature not found on the popular Model A Ford some fifteen years later. A carburetor air adjustment, also a novel convenience item, was mounted on the dash. Finally, the fenders were described as "ridge board," coming to a point at the top and designed to splash the mud and water from the road outward and away from the car's body.

The Cornelian light car was powered by a four-cylinder, 103 cid overhead valve engine rated at thirteen horsepower, although that rating was later increased to eighteen. All castings were from the finest Chrome-Vanadium drop forging process and the engine weighed just 190 pounds.

Another unique aspect of the Cornelian design was the sliding gear transmission with two forward speeds and reverse, but utilizing only three gears. The transmission was mounted directly to the differential and then both components were bolted to the body of the car following the early de Dion design. The same design was used on the Ferrari race car in 1972. The power from the engine to the transmission was by shaft drive, and power from the differential to the rear wheels was transmitted by two short shafts with universal joints at either end. The extensive use of the universal joint, with claims of no power loss, was not surprising given its manufacture by Blood Brothers Machine Company.

The design meant there was no rear axle on the Cornelian: the car rode on two transverse springs, one below and one above the two short shafts, so that the entire rear end floated. The universal joints compensated for changes in the relative position of the wheels and the differential. Howard changed the design of the front end,

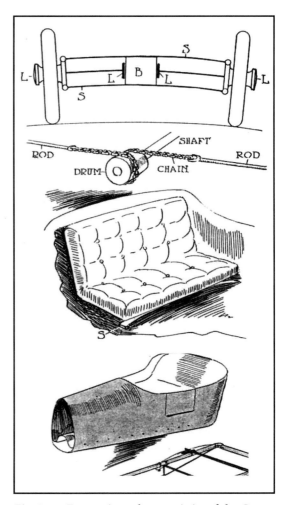

Fig. 9-11. Four unique characteristics of the Cornelian light car are the suspension, the steering, the seating and the body construction. The figures are from The Automobile, *April 30, 1914, p. 320 and May 14, 1914, p. 1013. Descriptions shown are from top to bottom. (1) The rear axle construction followed the de Dion Boutan configuration. The differential [B] is attached to the rear wheels with two short shafts with universal joints [L] at either end. The wheels are connected across the body by two springs [S], eliminating the need for an axle. (2) The steering shaft terminates on a drum that is wrapped with a short piece of chain, and the chain in turn is connected to rods that are attached to the wheels. The steering wheel turns the steering shaft and drum pulling the chain in one direction or another, turning the wheels either left or right, similar to the steering mechanism on a soap box derby car. (3) The seat was hung in a metal frame that was then mounted to the body with leaf springs [S] providing a comfortable ride. (4) A uni-body construction was used. (DOL)*

removing the previously used Ford Model T front axle on the cyclecar. He replaced the axle with a transverse spring similar to the arrangement on the rear suspension. This four-wheel independent suspension system offered a comfortable ride, exceptional handling qualities, and minimal unsprung weight.

In the summer of 1914, Howard mapped out a 10,000 mile reliability excursion for the Cornelian to be driven by Dr. C. G. Percival, president of the Cyclecar Club of New Jersey and one of a few noted "official tourists" in the country. The tour would start in Portland, Maine, run across the country by the southern route, then north to Portland, Oregon and then across the rough trails to Alaska, returning to Kalamazoo across Canada. The test car was selected from one of twenty-eight cars on the factory floor and was not modified. The trip was conducted under the auspices of the Kalamazoo Commercial Club and a "Made in Kalamazoo" streamer was planned to provide advertising along the way. The success of this venture is unknown, as there were no published reports of the test in either the national or local press.

Howard was competitive and bent on showing the capabilities of the Cornelian. The following fall, he stripped the fenders from a production model Cornelian and entered it in the first one hundred mile automobile race to be held in Kalamazoo, Michigan. The success of the car in the September race of 1914 attracted the attention of Ray Perrigo of nearby Allegan, and the opportunity for plant expansion in Allegan was offered to the Blood firm in October of 1914. At Ray Perrigo's insistence a town meeting was called by Judge Thompson at the local roller rink in late October of 1914. During that meeting, Howard Blood talked about the company's history and accomplishments, a history that included the excellent showing in the Kalamazoo race against much larger cars. He also included testimony that the Cornelian had driven up Bushong Hill west of Allegan in high gear with an estimated speed at the crest of fifteen miles an hour. Only the Model T Ford had duplicated that hill-climbing feat, and the comparison documented the credible performance of the Cornelian.

Howard did not request an incentive bonus, but only a sufficient amount to pay for moving the factory to Allegan, estimated at $25,000, plus a stock subscription of $75,000. A number of discussions ensued among the members of the business community and initially only the Cornelian production was planned for the Allegan site. Eventually, sufficient money was raised and, over the objections of the Kalamazoo Commercial Club, an agreement was struck with the Allegan Boosters on December 26, 1914 and a new mortgage for the Allegan Glass factory was granted to the Blood Brothers Machine Company. The entire operation of the company moved to Allegan in early 1915, a move inconvenient for many as available housing was scarce. Howard Blood moved in temporarily with the J. C. Steins, while Maurice Blood commuted from Kalamazoo on a daily basis; the employees had to find meals and lodging as best they could.

The company was very busy during this time, continuing to manufacture the Cornelian and the universal joint. By 1915 the company was running three shifts a day in an effort to meet the monthly production demand of 3,500 universal joints from truck and automobile manufacturers. The company employed about one hundred men under a revised salary plan, perhaps offered as a result of Henry Ford's improved wage. Under the new plan, the employees were paid at the same rate for the new eight-hour day as they had been under the old ten-hour schedule. The company expected eight hours of conscientious work and after that employees could do as they wished,

Fig. 9-12. This photograph appeared in the 1915 Indianapolis 500 Race program, but similar photographs appeared in Motor World *and* The Automobile *in April of 1915. This particular car is believed to be the last model of the Cornelian. The photograph shows a number of design changes from the 1914 Cornelian, including full length running boards, and a longer hood with additional cooling vents. The most prevalent change is that the door line comes straight back from the dash, giving the vehicle a more refined and less sporty appearance. The door is also much taller on this model than the previous models. This style Cornelian was built in Allegan, Michigan, and production is estimated at 100 to 150 cars. (DOL)*

including participation in company-sponsored baseball leagues and other activities. The scientific approach to shop management at the company was well respected and Howard was a celebrated speaker in Kalamazoo on the subject.

Advertisements for the Cornelian reflected the company's optimism, with predictions of a production run of twenty-five hundred cars in 1915, and cars were being sent to a few selected dealers in March, April and May of that year. At the same time, the previous fall's racing success at Recreation Park in Kalamazoo led Howard to seek support from Louis Chevrolet for entry of the Cornelian into the 500 mile race at Indianapolis, Indiana, in May of 1915.

In spite of success, plaudits from other engineers, and very positive, but limited, success on the track, the Blood company produced only 100 to 150 of the Cornelian light cars before leaving automobile manufacturing on September 29, 1915. This brought the total number of cars of all types built by Howard Blood to fewer than three hundred.

Reasons for the demise of the Cornelian are probably threefold. First, the profit from making universal joints was substantial, and the company had a ready market for every universal joint it could manufacture. Second, the demand for vehicles meeting the light car specifications was beginning to subside in 1915, partially because of Henry Ford's decrease in the price of the Model T and his published intent to compete in the field with a smaller version of the Model T. The early poor reputation of the cyclecar continued to plague the industry, a reputation that manufacturers could not shake even with changes to the light car designation. Third, later events suggest that Howard Blood's attention to the production of the Cornelian may have begun to wain after the Indianapolis race in the spring of 1915. His father, Maurice, may also have been ill, as he died just eighteen months later on May 14, 1917. The outbreak of war in Europe may also have been on Howard's mind, for he enlisted in the United States Air Force in August, 1917. He served with the rank of captain, was Field Commander at McCook Field (now Wright-Patterson) in Ohio from September to November 1918, and was discharged in March of 1919. He may never have returned to Allegan, since after the war he worked in Detroit where he organized the Norge Corporation, and by 1936 he was first vice-president of Borg Warner Corporation, president of the Norge Division, the Detroit Gear Division, and Detroit Vapor Stove Division of Borg Warner.

Howard's withdrawal from the company was accompanied by a complete withdrawal of other members of the family before the end of World War I, leaving the Blood Brothers Machine Company under the direction of others outside of family. Clarence Blood was still a board member of Blood Brothers Machine Company in 1916, but his relationship with the company was severed in 1918 soon after the death of his brother. He subsequently designed and built various tools for local manufacturers, but in 1929 he left the Kalamazoo area for the east coast. Wallace Blood, Maurice's second son, who had returned home after the company move to Allegan in order to assist with the unprecedented demand for the Cornelian, also left the company around 1917; he was later a member of the *Motor Age* staff. The company continued to prosper until the Great Depression of 1929, which it survived, although the company president jeopardized it with his reckless spending.

The Blood company continued to produce essentially the same universal joint from 1904 through 1932 supported by two changes in the industry that provided opportunity. First, as road speed increased, the automotive industry demanded improvements in universal joints. The Blood company was able to capitalize on the demand by adding a lubrication system, bronze washers, and needle bearings to their original design. Second, changes in agriculture provided a second marketplace for their product with the advent of "power farming" in the early 1920s. Before the introduction of the small gasoline-powered farm tractor, the big steam-driven tractor was used only as a source of mobile power for belt-driven machinery and to move planting and harvesting implements across the fields to sites as they were needed. These tractors served not as a source of mobile work, but as a source of stationary power that could be moved from one place to the other. The gasoline-powered farm tractor not only hauled the equipment about the farm, but powered the same equipment to plow, disc, and plant the fields. The power driveline connections between the tractor and the many moving parts of these implements required a variety of universal joints, thus expanding the market for the universal joints of the Blood Brothers Machine Company.

Thus the Blood company, now without family influence, capitalized on the new demands for universal joints and in the mid-thirties increased the size of the Allegan factory from 33,500 to 45,500 square feet, adding modern manufacturing equipment. As the marketplace grew, the company became a valuable commodity in itself. On December 10, 1936, the company was merged with the Standard Steel Spring Company of Pennsylvania and, eventually, the Blood Brothers Machine Company became part of Rockwell International.

REFERENCES

Howard Blood, Kalamazoo Man Is Inventor of New Cycle Car. *The Kalamazoo Gazette*, September 21, 1913.

Claim America Is Cyclecar Pioneer. *Motor Age*, August 28, 1913, p. 19.

Cycle Car, Poor Man's Automobile, At Hand. *The Kalamazoo Gazette*, August 24, 1913.

Answers to Inquires Concerning Cyclecar Construction. *Motor Age*, September 11, 1913, p. 27.

William B. Stout. "Cyclecar Development." *Motor Age*, September 11, 1913, pp. 24–27.

Principles in American Cyclecar Construction. *The Automobile*, January 15, 1914, pp. 165–69.

Cycle Cars Ideal Means For Touring. *The Kalamazoo Gazette*, December 28, 1913.

Cornelian 2-Pass. Runabout, $400. *Automobile Trade Journal*, December 1913, p. 220.

Springs and Suspensions For 1914. *The Horseless Age*, January 14, 1914, pp. 88–89.

William B. Stout. "Feeling The Pulse of The New Industry." *Motor Age*, January 15, 1914, pp. 7–15.

Other Michigan Cyclecar Makers Have Variety of Models. *The Automobile*, January 15, 1914, p. 172.

Gleanings From the Cyclecar Factories. *Motor Age*, June 4, 1914.

The Cornelian Cyclecar, Sales Brochure, circa February 12, 1914.

Advent of Cyclecar Great For Motoring. *The Kalamazoo Gazette*, December 13, 1914.

Cyclecar Popularity Considered Remarkable. *Kalamazoo Telegraph*, January 31, 1914.

Stan Grayson. "The Little Cars That Couldn't." *Automobile Quarterly*, Vol. 12, No. 4, 1974.

Blood Bros. Machine Co. *The Horseless Age*, December 31, 1913, p. 1123.

Blood Brothers' Machine Company to Manufacture New Cyclecar in Kazoo; Regarded as Big Success. *The Kalamazoo Gazette*, November 28, 1913.

Cornelian Cyclecar. *The American Cyclecar*, January 1914, p. 11.

Cornelian Has Novel Transmission. *Automobile Topics*, January 17, 1914.

Only Three Gears in Cornelian Gearset. *Motor World*, April 21, 1915, p. 20–21.

Year 1914 Promises to Be Year of The Cyclecar. *The Kalamazoo Gazette*, December 10, 1913.

Great Boom Strikes Blood Machine Firm. *The Kalamazoo Gazette*, January 14, 1914.

Steering Gear Designed Especially For Cyclecars. *The Automobile*, January 15, 1914, p. 183.

Kalamazoo Cyclecar Makes Great Showing on Trip to Detroit. *The Kalamazoo Gazette*, November 18, 1913.

New Ford Car? *The Horseless Age*, June 10, 1914, p. 891.

Latest Cornelian Car Harbinger of Big Industry For Kalamazoo. *The Kalamazoo Gazette*, April 12, 1914.

Cornelian Enters the Light-Car Field. *The Automobile*, April 30, 1914, p. 320.

Cornelian Light Car Described in Detail. *The Light Car*, October 13, 1914, p. 16.

Designing a Body For a Cyclecar. *The Automobile*, May 14, 1914, pp. 1012–13.

Cyclecar Development. *Motor Age*, June 4, 1914.

Little Kalamazoo Car to Make 10,000 Mile Cross-Country Trip. *The Kalamazoo Gazette,* July 21, 1914.

Kalamazoo Cyclecar and Spring Companies Busy. *The Horseless Age,* September 9, 1914, p. 385.

Cornelian to Be Removed to Allegan. *The Horseless Age,* October 28, 1914, p. 1.

Blood Brothers May Move. *The Automobile,* October 29, 1914, p. 826.

Allegan Gets Blood Bros. Plant. *The Automobile,* December 31, 1914, p. 1280.

Cornelian Completes Move to Allegan. *Automobile Topics,* March 13, 1915.

Blood and Ross to Talk on Efficiency. *The Kalamazoo Gazette,* February 3, 1914.

Speakers Give Joint Lecture on Efficiency. *The Kalamazoo Gazette,* February 5, 1914.

Cornelian 2-Pass. Roaster, $425. *Automobile Trade Journal,* June 1914, p. 160–61.

Cornelian 2-Pass. Roadster, $435. *Automobile Trade Journal,* December 1914, pp. 172, 185.

Body Acts as Frame in New Cornelian. *The Automobile,* April 22, 1915, p. 726–27.

The Cornelian—A Unique Light Car. *Horseless Age,* June 16, 1915, p. 814.

The Cornelian Is a Masterpiece of Light Car Construction. *Automobile Trade Journal,* June 1915, p. 115.

Chevrolet to Drive in Indianapolis. *The Horseless Age,* March 10, 1915, p. 328.

Blood Brothers Discontinue Cornelian. *The Automobile,* September 30, 1915, p. 626.

History of Wright Air Base, Wright Air Museum Brochure, Dayton, Ohio.

Herbert. S. Chase. *Who's Who in Michigan.* Munising, Michigan: Who's Who in Michigan, 1936.

Blood Bros. Elects New Directors. *The Automobile,* January 20, 1916, p. 158.

Maurice Blood's Obituary. *The Automobile,* May 17, 1917, p. 944.

Maurice Blood Taken by Death. *The Kalamazoo Gazette,* May 9, 1917.

C. C. Blood, 89, Pioneer Auto Builder, Dies. *The Kalamazoo Gazette,* March 1949.

James J. Green. *From Blood-Brothers Machine Company to Rockwell International,* 1978. Unpublished document on file at the Allegan Public Library, Allegan, Michigan.

Fig. 10-1. The track at the Kalamazoo County Fairgrounds, circa 1912. The track, built in 1902, was also known as Exposition Park and Recreation Park and was a major stop on the Grand Circuit for trotters and pacers, including many entries from the Kalamazoo area. It was also the site of dirt-track automobile racing from 1914 to 1935. The horse owners never liked the chloride that the race car promoters spread on the track to curtail the dust, and the two groups never accommodated one another very easily. Plans made in 1914 to build a two-mile track and a larger grandstand for automobile racing never materialized. (DOL)

Chapter 10

The Kalamazoo Race

1914

*"Kalamazoo doesn't realize the importance of the race
to be held here Saturday afternoon."*

—Charles Ireland

The Kalamazoo County Fair has always been a major event, but the celebration on September 21 through 26, 1914 was an historic occasion. There were the usual contests for the best fruit pies, jellies, and fancy work; poultry and livestock competitions—even a demonstration by the U.S. Post Office. But the greatest importance of the 1914 fair was that Kalamazoo played host to the first one hundred mile automobile race in Michigan. Horse racing was a way of life in the community and always drew a crowd to Recreation Park, but interest in the automobile race ran so high that additional trains were scheduled to carry the estimated 20,000 fans in and out of the city. In an interview with *The Gazette*, September 26, 1914, Charles Ireland of Chicago, a member of the American Automobile Association contest board, commented:

> Kalamazoo doesn't realize the importance of the race to be held here Saturday afternoon. Gauged from the standpoint of the purse that is offered, it isn't much, but when the field of starters is considered, it promises a wonderful race. Everything is ready for the biggest automobile race ever held in Michigan. The cars are tuned to the finest, the track is as good as a mile dirt track could be made, final instructions have been given the drivers, mechanicians, and pitmen. All that remains is the big noise which will be pulled this afternoon promptly at 3:00 o'clock.

The grand inaugural one hundred mile race, under the supervision of William Engleman and the American Automobile Association, was a major event on the racing circuit that year. Indeed, "the eyes of the racing world were centered on Kalamazoo because of the quality of the race cars and the reputation of the drivers." The race card read like an abbreviated Indianapolis 500 competition and included "Terrible" Teddy Tetzloff, the famous Ralph DePalma, and Michigan's own Bob Burman, as well as the Bergdoll brothers, and Eddie O'Donnell. The cars were of equal promi-

Fig. 10-2. Burman drove the French-built Peugeot in this photograph in the 1915 Indianapolis race and it is believed to be the same car he drove to victory in Kalamazoo. His average speed of 63.53 mph set a world's record for a one hundred mile race on an oval track. (IMS)

nence, including Delage, Duesenberg, Maxwell, Mercedes, and Peugeot. Truly, this race was an international event of considerable stature and was under close scrutiny by the racing fraternity.

Howard Blood had worked diligently over the past year building the Cornelian, a light car he hoped would find a permanent position in the marketplace and the automotive world. A friendly but fierce competition existed between Howard and his father Maurice as they each worked to develop a car that would meet the demands of a growing market for cars weighing less than 1,000 pounds, powered by engines under 100 cid, and selling for $400–$500. Young Howard had introduced such a car to Kalamazoo on September 21, 1913, and now on September 26, a year later nearly to the day, he had a rare opportunity to test his car against some of the finest racing machines in the world.

The promotional festivities began on Thursday of that week, when Teddy Tetzloff drove his massive Maxwell race car on the outside mile track against a tandem of horses running the inside half-mile oval. Teddy turned the mile in 58.75 seconds, but the horses galloped half the distance in 56.75 seconds to take the prize with two seconds to spare. The final preparations followed the next day when the world-famous drivers visited the track to inspect the site and conduct their practice runs. E. A. Moross, race promoter and former manager of the Indianapolis Speedway, was on hand to review the track. He commented in the September 24, 1914 *Gazette*, "I have never seen as careful

Fig. 10-3. Eddie O'Donnell, who had replaced Eddie Rickenbacker on the Duesenberg team for the Kalamazoo race, piloted this car to fifth place in the 1915 Indianapolis 500 where this photograph was taken. The car in this photograph is believed to be the same one that he drove to second place at Kalamazoo in 1914. (IMS)

a preparation undergone over any mile track, preparing it for a contest as has been done here." That preparation included steel fences to keep the cars on the track and extra wooden fences to keep the spectators off the track. The "pits," for changing tires and adding fuel, lined the infield and a coating of chloride was spread on the track to reduce the clouds of dust that swirled about the cars as the tall, narrow wheels churned into the dirt.

When Howard and Lawrence Blood rolled the diminutive Cornelian out onto the track for the Friday practice, interested onlookers and auto company experts from Sterling Engine, Zenith Carburetor, and Kent Ignition stood in the pits to watch the Cornelian's performance. One can only imagine the excitement and the thrill of the competition felt by the two young men from this small midwestern town as their car faced an array of Indianapolis race cars. On the first practice run, Lawrence Blood and his "mechanician," Vern Shobe, of the Zenith Carburetor Company, started about twelve lengths behind Ralph DePalma's giant Mercedes, pulled along side on the back stretch, and then easily swept past the big machine as the cars entered turn three. The Cornelian continued its impressive performance holding speed around the inside of the track while the larger cars, their massive engines booming and wheels spinning against the loose dirt, were slowed as they lost traction and slid to the outer edge on the turns.

The Cornelian's engine, with a displacement of only ninety-five cubic inches, was minuscule

Fig. 10-4. Rene Thomas drove this French-built Delage to victory in May of 1914 at Indianapolis. Interestingly, the car carries the same #16 as the Delage that Charlie Newhouse drove to third place in Kalamazoo in September of 1914. (IMS)

compared with the other racers, but the de Dion suspension provided a handling advantage at high speed that could not be matched by the large-displacement cars. The differential on the Cornelian was tied directly to the frame and then connected to the rear wheels by short shafts with universal joints at either end. This suspension geometry reduced the unsprung weight of the car and significantly increased its stability. The de Dion suspension was a remarkable achievement when it was developed at the turn of the twentieth century, and the longevity of the design concept is documented by its appearance on a Formula I Ferrari some fifty years later.

During that Friday session, "Terrible" Teddy Tetzloff, who was still smarting from his loss to the horses on Thursday, blew a tire and drove his Maxwell through the guard rail at seventy miles an hour. The car catapulted off the ten-foot embankment of the track, tumbled onto the spectators' wooden fence, and finally somersaulted over a rubbish heap, burying the nose of the car into the soft earth. Remarkably, the car appeared to need only a new radiator and some minor front end work, but Teddy and his mechanic, Dominic Basso, were whisked off to the hospital with lacerations of the head and shoulders.

Harry Scott was a local race enthusiast who, within the next five years, would build a Duesenberg-powered Wolverine in Kalamazoo. He owned the Kalamazoo Auto Sales Company on West Main Street and served as host to members of visiting race car teams, making his facility accessible as a storage area and meeting place. On Friday evening, the drivers and mechanics, possibly many of them still wearing their oil-stained racing coveralls, met at Scott's agency with the American Automobile Association officials to review the starting instructions, flag signals—red for clear, yellow for stop, green for one more lap to go, and checkered for finish—and the right-of-way for entering the pits. One can assume that the men were boisterous, the conversation heady, and that the air reeked of the smell of gasoline and cigar smoke.

Teddy Tetzloff was not there when the meeting opened, and E. A. Moross went to the hospital and literally pulled him from the hands of the physicians for delivery to the meeting. When he arrived, his head swathed in bandages, he was greeted with an enthusiastic standing ovation from the other drivers.

Initially, eighteen drivers applied to enter the race, but the number was reduced to sixteen when two drivers were proclaimed ineligible for participating in unsanctioned events, and then reduced again when four other drivers failed to qualify. "Wild" Bob Burman applied for a late entry and, given his reputation, a simple canvass of the drivers at that meeting was sufficient for approval, although there was no sympathy for awarding the appearance money that Bob had demanded. The final field included thirteen drivers. Howard and Lawrence Blood left the meeting believing that Lawrence was among those who had qualified, considering his successful driving demonstration that afternoon before the technical committee of the American Automobile Association.

The weather for the Saturday race was perfect. The sky was clear and the temperature hovered around sixty-five degrees. The little Cornelian was a local favorite and cheers greeted its entry, as Lawrence Blood, with Vern Shobe at his side, pushed the little car onto the track to take its place on the starting line just before the three o'clock post time. Both men were much surprised when Bill Engleman, the American Automobile Association track official, approached Lawrence to inform him that he was not certified and would not be allowed to race. Lawrence's driving skills the day before probably appeared competent enough, but the lack of experience of this young man became known to the officials in the interim and there is some evidence that other drivers expressed antagonism toward the little Cornelian. Given its size, it would not have been regarded as a legitimate race car. In addition, Lawrence had no personal history of auto racing and had not even served as a riding mechanic. The inherent dangers in allowing a novice to compete against such seasoned drivers was all too obvious to the officials. The final permission for Lawrence and the Cornelian to enter the Kalamazoo race was denied.

The situation appeared grim as Lawrence and Howard ran about the infield going from one pit crew to the next seeking a substitute driver who was registered with the American Automobile Association. Fortunately they found "Cap" Kennedy, a driver of some reputation who had been unsuccessful in his own bid to enter a Chalmers Six and was without a race car. He consented to pilot the Cornelian and in turn asked "Dutch" Kline from the Keeton team, who had experience as "mechanician" for Bob Burman at Indianapolis, to serve as his mechanic. Reluctantly, the race officials permitted the Cornelian to race. With nary a practice lap around the track, the two settled into the little car and were prepared for the start, which, under the circumstances, had been delayed until 3:12 p.m.

The final field for the day's one hundred mile race was published in the September 26, 1914 issue of *The Gazette*, and listed an impressive array of some of the finest race cars in the world. All

Fig. 10-5. The diminutive Cornelian powered by a 95 cid Sterling engine was dwarfed by the other cars that ran at Kalamazoo in 1914. The driver in this photograph is believed to be Lawrence Blood, "the home town boy," who qualified for, but was unable to gain entrance into, the Kalamazoo race. The car finished seventh with "Cap" Kennedy at the helm. (DOL)

but the Cornelian were considered as the best available. In spite of the setback created by Lawrence's removal, Howard Blood, at the age of twenty-eight and with only four years of automotive experience since his graduation from the University of Michigan, was prepared to face these internationally-renowned race cars and the famous drivers who were to guide them that day. The measure of Howard's accomplishment is difficult to gauge. He was not exactly an amateur "shade-tree" mechanic, but designing and building a car within a period of a year that proved competitive against Indianapolis-caliber race cars was a considerable achievement. Howard was a young man from a small auto parts manufacturer and was competing against some of the most renowned companies in the world including Delage, Duesenberg, Marmon, Maxwell, Mercedes, and Peugeot. September 26, 1914 was an extraordinary day in Kalamazoo, Michigan.

The race was advertised as an international competition featuring DePalma from Italy, Tetzloff from Russia, Callaghan from Ireland, Carlson from Norway, and the Bergdoll brothers from Germany. Tetzloff was born in the salt mines of Siberia, "that terror of all prisons"; his presence in Kalamazoo was billed as an example of Darwin's theory of the survival of the fittest.

A number of European-made race cars were evident on the American Automobile Association racing circuit, and the presence of the French-built Peugeot, with a 247 cid engine piloted by Bob Burman, was not a surprise to local enthusiasts. Burman was billed as a "product of Michigan" and was a veteran of the Vanderbilt Cup Races. In 1913, he had attempted to set a speed record for five miles at Recreation Park in Kalamazoo driving the "Blitzen Benz" with its massive 928 cid engine. His zest for speed and his daredevil exploits were legendary, including his surviving a spectacular flip in the 1912 Indianapolis race. The field also included a big German-built Mercedes with a 270 cid engine driven by the famous and fiercely competitive Ralph DePalma who had placed sixth at Indianapolis in 1911. DePalma had become a "folk hero" in 1912 at Indianapolis after his Mercedes was disabled just a few miles from the finish, and he pushed the car across the finish line.

America's automotive prowess was well represented and included two cars powered by Duesenberg engines. Fred and Augie Duesenberg already had an established reputation and their factory

THE FINAL RACE CARD

DRIVER	CAR	NO.	FINISH	SITE OF MANUFACTURE/ OWNER
Bob Burman	Peugeot	61	1	France/ Peugeot
Eddie O'Donnell	Duesenberg	3	2	St. Paul Minnesota/ Fred Duesenberg, St. Paul
Claude R. Newhouse	Delage	16	3	France/ W. E. Wilson, Rochester, New York
Jack Callaghan	Keeton	9	4	Detroit, Michigan/ Keeton Co.
Wilbur De Alene	Marmon	18	5	Indianapolis, Indiana/ Marmon
Grover C. Bergdoll*	Erwin	2	6	Philadelphia Pennsylvania/ G. C. Bergdoll
"Cap" Kennedy	Cornelian	7	7	Kalamazoo Michigan/ Howard Blood, Kalamazoo**
Erwin B. Bergdoll*	Benz***	8	8	Germany/ E. R. Bergdoll, Philadelphia, Pennsylvania
Tom Alley	Duesenberg	12	9	St. Paul, Minnesota/ Fred Duesenberg, St. Paul
W. H. Tidmarsh	Great Western	11	10	Peru, Indiana/ W.H. Tidmarsh, Elgin Illinois
Willie Carlson	Maxwell	na	11	New Castle, Indiana/ Maxwell Co.
Ralph DePalma	Mercedes***	10	12	Germany/ Mercedes Co.
Teddy Tetzloff	Maxwell	1	13	New Castle, Indiana/ Maxwell Co.

   *   Note that Erwin Bergdoll and Grover Bergdoll were brothers.
  **   Note that the Blood Brothers did not move to Allegan, Michigan until December, 1914.
***   Note that in 1914, Mercedes and Benz were independent and separate builders.

team, captained by Eddie Rickenbacker, dominated the dirt track circuit in 1914 with thirty-four wins in seventy-three starts. Early reports indicated that Rickenbacker would drive in Kalamazoo, but he was replaced by Eddie O'Donnell who had served as Rickenbacker's riding mechanic that season and would drive for the Duesenberg team at Indianapolis the following spring. The Maxwell, piloted by "Coal Oil" Willie Carlson, was powered by a 444 cid engine, and had just come from a recent victory at the Golden Potlatch in Tacoma, Washington. Wilbur De Alene was the Canadian Champion astride the same Indianapolis-built Marmon that he had driven to second place at the 1914 Grand Prix in Santa Monica. These were cars of considerable standing, and it was remarkable that the race that year was to be hosted in a small midwestern town.

The little Cornelian, piloted by the very competent "Cap" Kennedy, was powered by a unmodi-

Fig. 10-6. "Terrible" Teddy Tetzloff, the man from the Siberian salt mines, at the wheel of the Maxwell. This photograph was taken in May of 1914 at Indianapolis, and this car has the same engine displacement as the one he drove in Kalamazoo. It is also believed to be the same car he drove through the fence during the practice run in Kalamazoo prior to the September 1914 race. (IMS)

fied Sterling motor with a 2⅞" bore and 4" stroke, for a total displacement of only 95 cid. It was less than one fourth the size of the Maxwell engine and weighed 190 pounds. It was rated at only 12.1 hp with a Zenith carburetor and Kent ignition system.

The frustration caused by the Automobile Association's last-minute decision, the excitement of the race, and pride of accomplishment that Howard Blood felt that day are reflected in the letter he wrote to the editor of *Light Car* shortly after the race.

> To the Editor, the *Light Car*:
>
> In answer to your inquiry as to the details of the Cornelian car, which entered the recent race meet here, I am pleased to give you the following details.
>
> The Cornelian was equipped with a Sterling overhead valve motor, 2⅞ inches by 4 inches, a Zenith carburetor was fitted with an auxiliary oil tank hand pump to meet all possible demands for oil. A pressure feed was fitted to the gasoline tank although we do not believe that it was necessary. We fitted a condenser to the radiator to aid in our plan of making a 100-mile run without stopping. We used Michelin 28 x 3 inch clincher racing tires, and fastened them securely to the rims with 8 lugs in each wheel.
>
> We used a three-to-one gear ratio in place of our regular 4 to 1. This little car will run consistently 75 miles per hour on the straightaway at better than 2700 R.P.M. motor speed. The car is essentially, in its main features, a stock car.
>
> We had considerable difficulty in getting the little Cornelian entered in a race against such monsters as DePalma's Mercedes (275 cid), Burman's Peugeot (247 cid), Carlson's Maxwell (444 cid),

two Duesenbergs, a Benz, a Marmon, a Keeton, and a Delage. It was only by securing the services of an experienced driver, "Cap" Kennedy, at the last minute that we got around the obstacles that had been placed in our path. Kennedy and "Dutch" Kline, another regular driver who consented to act as mechanician, had never seen the Cornelian until 20 minutes before the race.

For the first twelve laps of the race they did not seem to get the hang of the thing and our car trailed in last position. It began to look as if our attempt to prove that the light car is a machine to be reckoned with in a free-for-all race was bound to fail, but suddenly the boys seemed to "find" her and from the twelfth lap to the fortieth, the car averaged 57 miles per hour which was equal to Bob Burman's average during the first half of the race.

Kline, however, was used to shoving oil into 100-horsepower motors instead of 13-horsepower motors, and at the 40-mile point he had used up the entire supply of oil, which necessitated a stop for which we had not prepared in the pit, as we had felt that our oil supply was ample. This stop took place in the forty-third lap at which time we were in sixth position and in another lap would have been in fifth position in this field of twelve of the finest racing machines in the world. The water in the radiator was not boiling at the time of this stop in the forty-third lap, but the crank shaft bearings had suffered somewhat from running dry.

Much vibration was set up in the otherwise smooth-running motor, after the oil mishap, which in the sixty-ninth lap caused a breakage in the gasoline line. Repairing it consumed 8 minutes and 25 seconds, as it was not only necessary to repair the line, but Kline had to carry two gallons of gasoline clear across the field, as the gasoline had been lost through the break. At the close of the race we were running in splendid shape in seventh position. Kennedy and Kline did remarkably well considering that they knew absolutely nothing about the car they were handling, but had our own boys been in the car, there is little doubt but we would have finished either third or fourth.

This remarkable demonstration of speed and endurance we attribute:

1 – To the wonderful little Sterling motor;

2 – To the wonderfully high mechanical efficiency of our transmission system. New departure ball bearings being used throughout;

3 – To the very low percent of unsprung weight which we have obtained by our special axle construction. This enabled us to maintain top speed on the turns while holding close to the inside fence, and prevented the bounding and jumping which would ordinarily take place in so light a machine. We were never passed on the turns.

Signed:

Howard E. Blood, Vice-President

Blood Bros. Machine Co.

The 1914 race was an historic event for Kalamazoo and the Cornelian's seventh place finish out of thirteen entries was most surprising to all except Howard Blood, who made the following comments to the *Gazette* in a September 27, 1914 post-race interview:

Of course I am disappointed in that Lawrence was not allowed to drive, for I am certain with him at the wheel the Cornelian would have made a nonstop trip for the hundred miles and we would have finished second or third. Lawrence has been with the car every day and knows every nut and bolt. Kennedy did well under the circumstances, but no man, no matter how experienced a driver, could take the Cornelian or any other strange car and drive it in a race like that without a little instruction in its mechanism. The only stops that were made were directly the cause of the crew's unfamiliarity with the car. Still I think the Cornelian made a remarkable showing when one considers that it is a stock car and not a heavily-powered racer. I am very much pleased indeed with its performance.

Many drivers who had expressed antagonism toward the Cornelian before the race subsequently expressed regret that Lawrence had not been allowed to drive the car and show its best performance. "Cap" Kennedy, who drove the Cornelian, was also much impressed and offered Howard a good sum of money for the car immediately after the race, announcing that he could clean up any of the big boys once he got better acquainted with it. Finally E. A. Moross invited Howard to add the car to the racing stable that he managed, but Howard declined, just as he had turned down the offer by "Cap" Kennedy. Howard had other plans for the little Cornelian.

The race put Kalamazoo in the limelight for the moment. Bob Burman, driving a Peugeot, broke the world record for seventy-five as well as one hundred miles, covering the distance in 90 minutes, 29⅗ seconds for an average speed of 63.53 miles an hour, and taking the first prize of $1,000. He would guide the big Peugeot to sixth place at Indianapolis the next spring, but die at Corona Speedway in California on April 8, 1916. Eddie O'Donnell placed second in a Duesenberg with an average speed of 62.8 miles an hour, and collected $750. He would drive a Duesenberg to fifth place the next spring at Indianapolis, but die on the wooden plank track at Beverly Hills, California in November of 1920. Claude R. Newhouse was third in the Delage with an average speed of 62.03 miles an hour and collected $500. He never did race at Indianapolis, and his eventual fate is unknown. Callaghan, the venerable Irishman, was fourth in the Keeton and collected $250; his fate is also unknown. When Burman crossed the finish line, "Cap" Kennedy and the Cornelian had completed seventy-seven laps which qualified him for seventh place. "Cap" never did qualify for Indianapolis, and his destiny is also unknown.

Billy Carlson's huge Maxwell with the 444 cid engine was twelfth. Carlson would die the next summer of injuries suffered on July 4th at the wooden plank Pacific Coast Speedway in Tacoma, Washington. Both Teddy Tetzloff and Ralph DePalma withdrew early. Tetzloff was unable to completely repair his Maxwell after the fence-crashing incident during Friday's practice run and the car was not really raceworthy. DePalma, refusing to don a protective mask, had gotten some of the calcium chloride from the track in his eyes and he withdrew after racing evenly with O'Donnell's Duesenberg for the first twenty-five miles.

DePalma's career spanned some twenty-seven years and 30,000 miles of treacherous racing track; he is considered one of the greatest drivers of all time. He entered 2,800 races and won on 2,000 occasions. He died of natural causes at the age of seventy-two in early 1956. He still holds the record for "leading laps" at Indianapolis with 613. His brief appearances in Kalamazoo in 1914 and 1915 remain small, but glorious, parts of the racing legacy at the Kalamazoo Fairgrounds.

The 1914 race was considered very successful, and William Engleman from the Automobile Association initiated a campaign to build a two-mile high-speed track in Kalamazoo that would serve as one of the major sites on the racing circuit; a $250,000 facility was envisioned with a half-mile grandstand to seat 50,000 people. The proposed track was described in *The Kalamazoo Gazette* on September 14, 1914:

Fig. 10-7. "Coal Oil" Willie Carlson drove the second big Maxwell at Kalamazoo. This photograph was taken at Indianapolis in May of 1914 and the car has the same engine displacement as the one he drove in Kalamazoo in September 1914. Photographs in the local Telegraph-Press *verify that this Indianapolis car is the same one he raced in Kalamazoo. (IMS)*

> Jack Prince, track builder, was a recent visitor to Kalamazoo and has been booming the proposition. His plans call for a two-mile plank track built of two by fours set on edge. The speedway will be banked forty degrees on the turns and ten degrees on the straight away sections. Prince is so optimistic over the speed possibilities that it is stated that he is willing to file a bond to the effect that properly equipped racing cars will make an average of 120 miles per hour. The speed attained by the De Lage at Indianapolis in the 500-mile race Memorial day was between eighty and 83 miles per hour.

The dream of construction never materialized. Kalamazoo was a "horse-race town," and the planned automobile race track would have used the entire horse track area, as well as the baseball fields and the adjacent land to the rear. The engine noise, track chloride, and the havoc created by high-speed accidents did not make automobile racing a welcome guest at a horse racing track. Automobile races did continue in Kalamazoo at Recreation Park until 1935, and these events involved some well-known drivers, but none came close to the excitement and the prestige of the 1914 race, with its cadre of famous drivers, national notoriety, and level of hometown enthusiasm created by the locally-built Cornelian.

The Blood Brothers Machine Company left Kalamazoo for Allegan after the holiday season in 1914 and soon afterward Howard began preparations to race the Cornelian at the Indianapolis 500 in May of 1915.

Fig. 10-8. This photograph of Ralph DePalma next to the big Mercedes was taken in 1913 at Indianapolis. The confidence and the swagger of the renown driver who raced on some 2,800 occasions, including Kalamazoo in 1914 and 1915, is embodied in this scene. (IMS)

REFERENCES

Scene to Be Duplicated Here Next Saturday. *Kalamazoo Telegraph-Press*, September 22, 1914.

Friday's Fair to Draw Crowd. *Kalamazoo Telegraph-Press*, September 24, 1914.

To Operate on Special Schedule. *Kalamazoo Telegraph-Press*, September 24, 1914.

Special Trains for Visitors for Races. *The Kalamazoo Gazette*, September 26, 1914.

On Special Schedule. *Kalamazoo Telegraph-Press*, September 24, 1914.

Eyes of Racing World Centered on Kazoo Today. *The Kalamazoo Gazette*, September 26, 1914.

Great Drivers to Race Here. *Kalamazoo Telegraph-Press*, September 18, 1914.

Ralph DePalma and Other Noted Pilots Will Make Big Race. *Kalamazoo Telegraph-Press*, September 19, 1914.

Five of America's Noted Auto Drivers Reach City. *Kalamazoo Telegraph-Press*, September 21, 1914.

Teddy Tetzloff Picked by Many Enthusiasts as Speed Demon to Give Ralph DePalma Race. *The Kalamazoo Gazette*, September 23, 1914.

World's Noted Pilots Start in Kalamazoo Race Next Saturday. *Kalamazoo Telegraph-Press*, September 24, 1914.

Rain Decreases Fair Crowd. *The Kalamazoo Gazette*, September 25, 1914.

Preparations Made at Recreation Park for 100 Mile Contest Are Highly Commended by Noted Drivers Here. *The Kalamazoo Gazette*, September 24, 1914.

Root and Flansburg Prepare Rules for Great 100 Mile Auto Race on Saturday. *Kalamazoo Telegraph-Press*, September 24, 1914.

The Cornelian Racer Shows Big Speed Veterans How to Take the Turns. Speed Creates Amazement. *The Kalamazoo Gazette*, September 25, 1914.

Two Escape Death When Car Blows Tire. *The Kalamazoo Gazette*, September 26, 1914.

Teddy Tetzloff Goes Through Fence, Comes Back Smiling. *The Kalamazoo Gazette*, September 26, 1914.

Drivers Will Meet Officials. *The Kalamazoo Gazette*, September 25, 1914.

Buzz Wagons and Speed are Chief Topics. *The Kalamazoo Gazette*, September 25, 1914.

State's First 100-mile Race Great Success. *The Kalamazoo Gazette*, September 27, 1914.

Bob Can Certainly Smile When He Wins Such a Race. *The Kalamazoo Gazette*, September 27, 1914.

Bob Burman: Life in the Fast Lane. *The Kalamazoo Gazette*, February 28, 1990.

Cornelian Makes Amazing Showing in 100 Mile Race. *The Kalamazoo Gazette*, September 27, 1914.

Light Car Made Great Speed in Kalamazoo 100-Mile race. *The Light Car*, 1914.

All Nationalities Are Represented in Great Race. *Kalamazoo Telegraph-Press*, September 25, 1914.

Two Auto Drivers Hurt in Try-Out. *Kalamazoo Telegraph-Press*, September 25, 1914.

Griffith Borgeson. *The Golden Age of the American Racing Car*. New York: Bonanza Books, 1966.

Jack C. Fox. *The Illustrated History of the Indianapolis 500*. Indianapolis, Indiana: Carl Hungness, 1994.

William F. Nolan. "Ralph DePalma." *Automobile Quarterly*, Vol. 2, No. 3, 1963, pp. 264–71.

Two Mile Auto Speedway, Plan of Capitalist. *The Kalamazoo Gazette*, September 25, 1914.

Cyril Posthumus. "Prophet Without Honor; The 1915 Indianapolis Cornelian." *Motor*, January 17, 1970.

Fig. 11-1. This photograph of the Cornelian race car, circa Spring 1915, may document the trial run on the streets of Allegan, Michigan, after final preparations were complete, although the exact time and location of this photograph is unknown. Louis Chevrolet is at the wheel, and Howard Blood, who designed and built the car, is in the mechanic's seat. This is a rare photograph of the two men together who were responsible for the Cornelian's entry in the 1915 Indianapolis 500. Note the traces of mud on the side of the car behind the front wheel, suggesting that they had taken the car for a test drive around the countryside. (BWC)

Chapter 11

The Cornelian at Indianapolis

1915

"This grasshopper among elephants has a motor of
a paltry 116 cid and yet can lap at over 80 mph."
—Motor World, 1915

The success of the Cornelian at Kalamazoo in the fall of 1914 was sufficient to convince Howard Blood and some of the factory representatives that the Cornelian had a chance at the big race on Memorial Day in Indianapolis the following spring. The Sterling engine that powered the Cornelian was built by a company within William Durant's empire and was managed by William H. Little, who had watched the performance of the Cornelian from track side in Kalamazoo in 1914. Both Louis Chevrolet and William Little had been involved with Durant's racing efforts with Buick, and it was Little who brought Louis Chevrolet and Howard Blood together. On February 25, 1915, Louis Chevrolet was named as the driver for the Cornelian, and shortly thereafter Joe Boyer signed on as Chevrolet's relief driver. Later that spring, "Dutch" Kline, who had served as the Cornelian's riding mechanic in Kalamazoo in 1914, also agreed to serve in the same manner for the 1915 Indianapolis race.

The association between the eminent Louis Chevrolet and the young and inexperienced Howard Blood, with a single dirt track race to his credit, seemed implausible. At first blush, the diminutive Cornelian had no chance for victory and only a slim chance to place among the top finishers against the monsters of the brickyard. One wonders why Louis Chevrolet would cast his lot with the Cornelian. In retrospect, the Cornelian's de Dion driveline, and four-wheel independent suspension, as well as its small stature, may have attracted Louis Chevrolet. Chevrolet's reputation in the racing community also may have affected his decision to drive the little car: "this grasshopper among elephants" according to *Motor World*, from a fledgling automobile company in tiny Allegan, Michigan. There is some conjecture that the car was allowed to run only because of Chevrolet's reputation and the lack of other qualified entrants for the 1915 race. In fact, there were seventeen other cars that failed to qualify for one reason or another, and any one of them might have displaced the little Cornelian that sat in twenty-third position, second to the last, at the start of the race. When four Peugeots qualified, the fourth car was not allowed to run because race rules allowed only three cars sponsored by a single manufacturer to compete. The same rule applied to the four Sunbeams and the Maxwells, since the Harroun Special was regarded as a Maxwell. There were three Mercers, including one driven by the famous Barney Oldfield that failed to qualify, and the Bergdoll, driven by Grover Bergdoll who had defeated the Cornelian at Kalamazoo, also did not qualify. A Buick, with a considerable race history also failed to make the final field, and the three cars prepared by Finlay R. Porter with the famous Knight sleeve-valve engines failed before the start of qualifying runs because of broken piston rings. The little Cornelian did qualify. On the one hand, there were a number of events of chance and favorable circumstance that disqualified other very competitive entries and allowed Howard Blood's car to reach the starting line. On the other hand, the Cornelian was very well prepared and competitive. Many other cars of greater reputation failed because of mechanical problems including broken connecting rods, holes in cylinder castings, and split piston rings.

In spite of his reputation, racing experience, and the success of the passenger car that carried his family name, Louis Chevrolet was struggling in 1915. He was a burly bear of a man and had a terrible temper, almost uncontrollable at times; during several of his outbursts he had behaved rashly, hurting both his reputation and his career opportunities in the automobile industry. In 1915, Chevrolet needed, and needed very badly, an opportunity to reestablish his reputation. In spite of his past victories, the premiere companies of Bugatti, Duesenberg, Mercedes and Stutz had not extended to him an invitation to pilot one of their cars and Chevrolet turned to the little Cornelian. Certainly, William H. Little, who was a close associate of Chevrolet, would have endorsed the Cornelian after watching its performance in Kalamazoo, but this was a car that had not yet completed a race of 100 miles, let alone the grueling ordeal of a 500 mile race against the toughest competition in the world. The impetus that led Chevrolet to agree to enter and drive a car powered by an engine with a displacement just over one hundred cubic inches was most likely desperation. The size of the closest competition was a lone Peugeot at 188 cid, and all of the remaining cars carried engines with a displacement of at least 277 cid. The power differential between the Cornelian and the other entries was substantial and a factor that would be difficult to overcome even by the experienced Louis Chevrolet.

Chevrolet was both knowledgeable and experienced, having served his apprenticeship in the best of the automobile houses and racing stables. He was born in Switzerland on December 25, 1873, and his family subsequently moved to Beaume, France. A self-taught mechanic, he served as an apprentice in a bicycle shop as a teenager, where he became familiar with the early de Dion-designed motorized tricycles. He emigrated to Canada in 1899, and quickly became associated with Henri Bourassa who built the first car in Montreal, Canada. Just after the turn of the twentieth century he moved from Montreal to New York City where he was employed first by the de Dion agency and then by Fiat. He so impressed the people at Fiat that in 1905 he was offered a position on the company's racing team. During this period he also associated himself with Carl Fisher who was one of the four men who founded the Indianapolis Motor Speedway. In 1908, he signed with Victor Hemery, a famous French driver, to serve as his riding "mechanician" and later joined Bill Pickens's Buick racing team where he served as mechanician for Bob Burman. He finally got the personal recognition he deserved when he was given the opportunity to race and then won the hill climb at Lookout Mountain. From that day onward his reputation grew with each race and each record of accomplishment. By 1909 he was considered one of the foremost drivers in the country. During this frenetic era, he found time to marry Suzanne Tyreyvoux and they settled in comfortable surroundings in New Orleans's French Quarter.

The venerable "Billy" Durant had acquired control of Buick in 1904 as a part of his plan to create General Motors and control the industry. When Louis and Arthur Chevrolet joined the Buick racing team around 1909, they, too, were absorbed into this great plan of expansion. Louis had a stormy reputation, and Durant, who tolerated Chevrolet's antics at the wheel of the Buick race cars, was intolerant of his behavior in other circumstances. He hired Arthur and not Louis as his personal chauffeur and, according to the history by Zavitz, Durant commented about the decision, "I would not take any chances with that crazy Louis."

Durant's empire expanded quickly, perhaps too quickly, and it outgrew its financial foundation. A group of New York bankers offered to shore up the emerging corporation with a $10 million loan, but demanded that the reserved and meticulous Henry LeLand and not Billy Durant be placed in control. Consequently, Billy Durant was given the title of vice-president and allowed to retreat to Flint, Michigan, to busy himself with other projects. Undaunted, Durant began forming a plan to regain control of the company. First, he was able to have William H. Little reassigned from Buick to his own projects in Flint, and when the conservative LeLand dismantled the Buick racing team, Durant also acquired the services of Louis Chevrolet.

Prior to Durant's ouster from the command of General Motors, he had tried to buy the Ford Motor Company on two different occasions, and would have been successful, had he had the ready cash that Henry Ford demanded on both occasions. His next tactic was competition, and he asked both Little and Chevrolet to design a four-cylinder automobile to compete with Henry Ford's famous Model T. In the process of building a new car company, Durant exchanged a majority of the stock in his company for the engine that Chevrolet built and the rights to use the Chevrolet family name.

Progress was slow, and Louis Chevrolet sought the assistance of Etienne Planche, a Swiss-born designer with experience at the Mercer Automobile Company. Planche was well respected, and had designed a marvelous air-cooled four-cylinder motorcycle engine in 1908. In spite of Planche's expertise, it was not until late 1912, almost eighteen months after Durant's initial announcement of his intent to build the Chevrolet car, that the first car was completed. The car that Louis and Etienne finally produced was big, ponderous, and at $2,200, very expensive, but with power from a 299 cid engine, it was also very fast. These characteristics, however, were hardly the optimum to compete with the small, inexpensive, and nimble Ford Model T, as Durant had intended.

In 1911, Durant established the Chevrolet Motor Car Company ("Car" was later dropped from the title) and the Little Motor Car Company. The latter built the inexpensive Little in Flint, Michigan, that sold well, but it was a low budget operation and the car was not very durable. Consequently, Durant decided to combine the best aspects of the inexpensive Little and the very expensive Chevrolet in a new car to be manufactured in Flint and sold under the Chevrolet name. In late 1913, the first two new Chevrolets were introduced to the public: "The Royal Mail," and the "Baby Grand," selling at a moderate cost of $750 to $875, although still twice the cost of the Model T.

Neither of these cars was envisioned by Louis Chevrolet, and he was so incensed with Durant's unilateral action that he stormed into Durant's office and slapped his Chevrolet stock certificates on Durant's desk. According to the legend surrounding this incident, Chevrolet also provided a graphic description of what Durant might do with the "worthless paper."

Immediately after this brouhaha in early 1914, Louis founded the Frontenac Motor Corporation, initially to build race cars but presumably with the intent of manufacturing passenger cars. Etienne Planche, who had designed the first "big" Chevrolet with Louis, moved on to work with Dallas Dort, and the Dort Motor Car Company would eventually manufacture closed car bodies in Kalamazoo. Albert Champion, founder of the Champion and the AC Spark Plug Companies, provided the financial backing for Chevrolet's enterprise, and Louis quite quickly completed designs for two new engines and a complete car. Disaster continued to haunt Chevrolet.

Following a disagreement, Louis reportedly "beat up" Albert Champion, who was almost as tough as Chevrolet. He had beaten him almost to death, and he left Champion's office with the warning that if their paths crossed again, he would finish the job. Reportedly, Champion followed the instruction without a challenge, but the incident not only cost Chevrolet a chance to share in the Champion fortune, but also delayed the introduction of his Frontenac-powered race cars until 1916. In a period of a few years, Chevrolet's violent temper had cost him two fortunes, one from the Chevrolet Motor Company and a second from the Champion Company.

Louis Chevrolet's reputation was founded initially on the success of the Buick racing team, and later grew with his daring exploits in his own Frontenac racers. His career was a stormy one. Between 1905 and 1920, he lost four riding mechanics to fatal injuries and spent three years recovering from race-related accidents, the worst of which occurred at the Indianapolis race in 1920. His temper was just as hazardous as his driving, and in 1911, he withdrew entirely from the racing circuit when he took great umbrage at the refusal by the other drivers to allow his last-minute post entry at the first Indianapolis 500 that year. In so doing, he had ostracized himself from the racing fraternity with his own bad temper.

Automobile racing and automobile development were his avocation and his livelihood and he needed to rejoin the automotive community. He first attempted to return to the circuit by entering a road race from Los Angeles to Phoenix that was held in the fall of 1914. This event did not seem to merit any special status and did not advance his career. The popularity of road racing was declining in the early teens and public interest in closed circuit racing was growing, particularly after the inaugural Indianapolis 500 race in 1911. Louis needed the public notoriety offered by the now-famous Indianapolis 500 event to promote himself and eventually the Frontenac Company. At the same time Howard Blood sought to enhance the reputation of his family name and the Cornelian. These curious circumstances, and perhaps William Little's convincing rhetoric, brought together an unlikely pair: the emotional and boisterous Louis Chevrolet and the quiet and reserved Howard Blood. Most writers believe that neither expected to win, although few people of their competitive caliber ever prepare to lose at such an endeavor. Surely, both recognized an opportunity for a memorable day.

Louis Chevrolet was named as the driver for the Cornelian in February 1915. Shortly after the announcement, he and his brothers, Gaston and Arthur, descended on the Blood brothers plant in Allegan, Michigan, to prepare the Cornelian light car for the torturous trials at Indianapolis. First,

Fig. 11-2. Ray Perrigo, the man who brought the Blood Brothers Machine Company to Allegan, Michigan, and who was subsequently appointed as sales manager for the Cornelian car, sits at the wheel of the Cornelian race car just before it was loaded on the train in Allegan bound for Indianapolis. The other man in the photograph is Dutch Kline. (KLL)

they replaced the leather-type universal joints with Hooke-type joints, and then they replaced the steering cables with steel rods. The steering mechanism was simple and reminiscent of a soap box derby car: a chain wrapped around a gear that pulled the steering rods one way or the other as the gear was rotated by moving the steering wheel. The rear section of the car body was cut off and a low-slung racing tail was welded aft of the seat. An attractive streamlined cowl, with built-in windscreen around the cockpit (a functional and attractive amenity that no other entrant could brag about) finished the final envelope for the car. After the car arrived in Indianapolis, the Rudge-type knock-off wire wheels, with 30 x 3½" tires were then mounted on the spring-type axles. The suspension did not include shock absorbers and vertical movement with this geometry is estimated at three inches.

The driveline configuration, with the de Dion-type differential and four-wheel independent suspension used for the stock Cornelian, was maintained, but the Chevrolet brothers made a number of changes in the engine. The 103 cid Sterling motor was bored out and reportedly reached 115 cid, although it was listed as 103 cid in the Indianapolis race publications. Aluminum alloy pistons were inserted in the block along with 1¼" diameter valves. The intake manifold and cylinder head were then reworked to accept two Master-Miller racing carburetors. These changes raised the power to thirty horsepower or maybe thirty-five horsepower at 3500 rpm. The Cornelian built for Indianapolis was not the same car that had raced in Kalamazoo the previous fall, but it was still grossly underpowered compared to the 274 cid engine that powered Ralph DePalma's Mercedes, and Dario

Fig. 11-3. This photograph of the Cornelian at Indianapolis shows the car as it was raced. The number 27 is painted on its side and the wheels are fitted with knock-off hubs. Louis Chevrolet is at the wheel and Dutch Kline is the riding "mechanician" in the foreground. Arthur and Gaston Chevrolet are the two men with mustaches, from left to right respectively, behind the front of the car. Howard Blood is in the trench coat and cap directly behind the car. Lawrence Blood, is in the middle with the bow tie. Wallace Blood, eventually of the Motor Age *staff, is believed to be the young man attired in hat and suit, on the left, just to the rear of the car. (IMS)*

Resta's Peugeot, and the 299 cid Duesenberg engines mounted in five other cars.

Several days before the track opened for practice, the Cornelian was loaded on a flatbed railway car in Allegan, Michigan, and transported to the Indianapolis raceway. Extant photographs of the Cornelian show a white car with either number 10 or 27 painted on its side. The assigned numbers in 1915 were based upon qualifying position and the number on the Cornelian was changed from 10 to 27 to designate its position after the qualification run was completed. The Cornelian actually started in position number twenty-three, but some numbers (*e.g.,* 11 and 13) were not used, perhaps for superstitious reasons. The part played by superstition in the race was interesting news. On May 27, 1915, *The Kalamazoo Gazette* , believing that the Cornelian would be assigned number 24, predicted a win for the Cornelian, because all past winners at Indianapolis carried the number 8 or its multiples:

> If ole Maw Superstition counts, the midget Cornelian racer, built by the Bloods of Allegan and
> driven by Louis Chevrolet, ought to cop the 500-mile spin over the Indianapolis oval Saturday.
> Why? Because every car that has ever finished the big grind minus dust in the driver's eyes has

Fig. 11-4. The Cornelian wearing the number 10. This photograph, published as the official photograph for the race, is believed to have been taken shortly after the Cornelian's arrival in Indianapolis. The number was later changed to 27 to correspond with its qualifying position. The Cornelian actually held position number 23, a discrepancy due to the fact that some numbers, such as 11 and 13, were not used; presumably this practice reflected a racetrack superstition. Note also that this car is not fitted with the knock-off hubs that were added before the race. (IMS)

carried the number eight or its multiple. Never has a car won than was other than eight or its multiple. Chevrolet's car will carry the number "24."

The superstition of "eight" was apparently overwhelmed by greater forces. The Cornelian was subsequently assigned the number 27 and Ralph DePalma eventually won the race in a Mercedes carrying the number 2.

There was considerable interest in the race among Kalamazoo sportsmen and the *Kalamazoo Telegraph-Press* published instructions for the driving trip to Indianapolis. The trip began on Main Street with detailed instructions to turn left at the blacksmiths, left at the Church, through Almena and so on to Plymouth, South Bend, Kokomo and on to Indianapolis, Indiana.

Many race cars were driven or towed to events, but the Cornelian arrived in Indianapolis by rail. Soon after arrival, the team was assigned garage number 17 in the preparation area, an area that even then was called "gasoline alley." Their garage location provided a grim reminder of the inherent dangers of the sport. Directly across from them was Eddie O'Donnell's Duesenberg. He had driven the same car to second place in Kalamazoo the previous fall, and would place fifth at

Indianapolis in 1915. Eddie would die at the wheel on November 25, 1920 on the board track in Beverly Hills, California. Joe Cooper's Sebring was also nearby and he would crash into the wall on the south chute after 154 laps of this race. Joe would survive this time, but not the crash in August of the same year in Des Moines, Iowa.

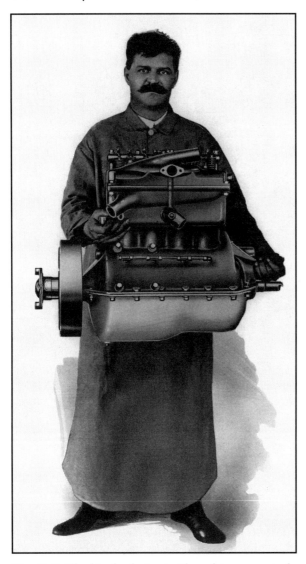

Fig. 11-5. The big, burly Louis Chevrolet appears to be holding the little Sterling engine that powered the Cornelian at Indianapolis in 1915. The actual stand that held the engine was painted out of the photograph. (IMS)

Louis Chevrolet had prepared the Cornelian in just three months. And, in an effort to gain every advantage, Joe Boyer, Chevrolet's relief driver, who was smaller than the burly Louis, drove the qualifying laps. As it turned out, the Cornelian was the only car to qualify on the first day with a respectable speed of 81.1 miles an hour, including a run of 94 miles an hour on the straightaway. The car's speed was just ahead of the required minimum of 80 miles an hour, and just behind George Hill's Bugatti, with its 300 cid engine, that qualified at 81.52 miles an hour the next day. The Cornelian's performance was impressive for a car weighing just under 1,000 pounds and powered by an engine just over 100 cid. Its performance was highly regarded, and it received more attention by track officials than any other car except DePalma's Mercedes. Forty-five entries eventually competed for a place among the twenty-four available starting positions. Joe Boyer's qualifying time placed Louis Chevrolet in position number twenty-three. The Cornelian was second to last, but they had qualified—an accomplishment that eluded many highly-respected race cars.

The competition in 1915 was impressive in terms of the size of the machines and the quality of the drivers. The displacement limit was set at 350 cid, down from the 450 cid limit of 1914, in an effort to attract some of the smaller European cars. The engines ranged from 188 cid in Babcock's French-built Peugeot to 300 cid in George Hill's Italian Bugatti, and then there was the little Cornelian with the 115 cid Sterling motor developing 30-35 hp.

The drivers included Ralph DePalma, Dario Resta, Ralph Mulford, Eddie Rickenbacker, Bob Burman, Billy Carlson, Willie Haupt, and "Howdy" Wilcox. "Howdy" Wilcox had been driving at Indy since the inaugural race. In 1915 he guided one of the three Stutz racers, with a 296 cid engine, to a qualifying speed of 98.9 miles an hour and the pole position. His qualifying speed was almost twenty miles an hour faster than that of the Cornelian. He qualified for eleven races between 1911 and 1923 at Indianapolis and took first place in 1919, but would die on a treacherous curve at Altoona, Pennsylvania, September 4, 1923.

Ralph DePalma, who had raced at Kalamazoo in the huge red, white, and black Mercedes powered by a 274 cid engine, turned in a 98.58 qualifying speed to capture the second position in the front row. Dario Resta in a Peugeot with a 274 cid engine finished the qualifying lap at 98.47 miles an hour, for the third position. Earl Cooper in a second Stutz completed the front row of four cars with a qualifying time of 96.77 miles an hour.

There was some initial jockeying for position during the first thirty-three laps, but after that point, the lead was held by either Ralph DePalma or Dario Resta. DePalma was able to maintain a speed of 89.84 mph over the last two hundred miles to win, almost four minutes in front of the second place Dario Resta. DePalma was probably the most famous driver in the race. He was national champion in 1912, and after the Indianapolis 500 that year, a folk hero among racing enthusiasts. He was leading Joe Dawson's National by four laps

Fig. 11-6. The Cornelian's drive train. The overhead valve Sterling engine is in the foreground and the de Dion-type transmission/differential combination is in the background. The transmission/differential was bolted to the chassis, reducing the amount of unsprung weight, and was connected to the rear wheels by short half-shafts with universal joints at either end. This drive train geometry, combined with a four-wheel independent suspension, offered a handling advantage over the larger and more powerful cars. This innovation was not "introduced" again on race cars for another 35 years. (DOL)

at Indianapolis until the 197th lap when a piston blew, eventually silencing the engine just a lap and a half from victory. Undaunted by the mechanical failure, a smile covering the terrible feelings of defeat, he and his riding mechanic got out and literally pushed the car around the track and across the finish line with the cheers of the crowd echoing off the grandstand. His gritty performance, of course, did not change his eleventh place finish, but won the hearts of racing fans. He suffered similar mechanical problems in 1915, breaking a connecting rod that punched two holes in the engine block, but the "intrepid DePalma" was able to guide the Mercedes to victory. He drove his crippled car directly to the garage and emerged only after the crowd of well-wishers caved in the door. According to the report in the June 3, 1915 *Motor Age*, DePalma turned to his mechanic, Louis Fountaine, after the race with the following comment: "Louis, you're an awful little runt, but believe me you're some mechanic."

The 1915 race had been postponed from Saturday, May 29, to Monday, May 31, because of rain, and the roads and walks inside the track were ankle-deep in mud when the spectators stormed the gates at 5 a.m. "The Beau Brummels who wore white silk hose wished they hadn't. After the comple-

Fig. 11-7. The photograph shows the start of the 1915 Indianapolis 500 race. Howdy Wilcox in a Stutz sits at the pole position, and Ralph DePalma is second in a Mercedes. Dario Resta is third, designated by the number 3, in a Peugeot, and Earl Copper in another Stutz is in fourth place with the number 4 painted on the radiator. The Cornelian, in position number 23 is not visible in the photograph. (IMS)

tion of the race, when the mud-spattered crowd finally got back to town, the bootblacks did a rushing business," commented J. C. Burton, the *Motor Age* reporter. The Cornelian was the first car in the pits, but neither the early arrival nor the rain delay helped the little race car. Chevrolet drove gallantly, moving quickly from twenty-third to nineteenth place. In spite of a stop for water and new spark plugs, he continued his assault and moved to twelfth position after 100 miles. He was competing evenly with Billy Carlson's Maxwell with its 298 cid engine, until he ran out of gasoline on the back stretch. The pit crew hurried across the infield hauling the needed fuel in buckets and Chevrolet returned to the race. In spite of two more stops for water, he was still competitive. Final disaster struck at 180 miles, when a valve broke and dropped onto the aluminum piston shutting down the engine. The Cornelian finished in twentieth position.

The little Cornelian offered a number of unique characteristics and, given better knowledge, improved metallurgy, and more horsepower, Howard's dream might have made an indelible influence on track racing in this country. First, the Cornelian cowling was finished with a built-in windshield, a concept that was "introduced" by Maserati on its Formula I car in 1954. Second, the Cornelian featured monocoque or uni-body construction, in which the body plates are welded together with bulkhead supports to serve as both body and frame. That concept was "introduced" into Formula I racing in 1962 by Colin Chapman, and the design set a standard for most racing cars that followed. Third, the four-wheel independent suspension found on the Cornelian predated the similar Mercedes design that was "introduced" some nineteen years later. Finally, the

Fig. 11-8. The official and dramatic photograph of Ralph DePalma, winner of the Indianapolis 500 race in 1915. DePalma is facing the camera, and his mechanic, is facing forward. (IMS)

drive train with a transmission and differential bolted to the frame was "introduced" some forty-seven years later by Lotus on its Formula I competition cars.

If it had had a bit more horsepower and tougher valves, resulting in a better showing at Indianapolis, the Cornelian, with neither the frame nor the axles of conventional cars, might have set a standard that would have moved racing toward a smaller engine and independent suspension. The Cornelian might have changed racing just as quickly and significantly as the rear engine Cooper Climax, that set a standard of design in 1961 from which few, if any, of the cars at Indianapolis now deviate.

In spite of the innovations and its popularity at the track in 1915, the Cornelian seemed to be forgotten immediately, although now it is a featured photograph for the 1915 race in almost every history of the Indianapolis Speedway. A report in the June 1915 issue of *Motor Age* recorded the disappointment: "Early elimination of the little Cornelian was, from a mechanical standpoint, one of the regretted results of the pace set, because of the remarkable speed shown for so small a motor—nearly 75 miles an hour for over 190 miles."

Howard Blood returned to Allegan, the Chevrolet family moved on, and Louis introduced the successful Frontenac race cars. The Cornelian car was sold to Roscoe Dunning, and some writers claim that Howard did so in despair just after the Memorial Day event. Dunning apparently en-

Fig. 11–9. The sterling silver Borg-Warner trophy in the background has been symbolic of victory at the Indianapolis 500 since 1936, and a silver likeness of each winner has been added to the trophy since that date. In front of the trophy from left to right are: E. A. "Roscoe" Turner, a well-respected pioneer aviator; Eddie Rickenbacker, who raced at Indianapolis from 1912 to 1916 and become a renowned flying ace in World War I, winning both the Distinguished Service Cross and the Congressional Medal of Honor; and Howard Blood, vice-president of Borg-Warner. Blood's involvement in the development of the trophy is unknown, but given his history in racing and flying, one can assume that it was a joint effort with Rickenbacker and that he was actively engaged in the project. Rickenbacker purchased the Indianapolis Speedway on August 15, 1927 and remained its president until he sold it to Tony Hulman on November 14, 1945. The raceway was closed during World War II, so this photograph must have been taken between 1936 and 1941; it is believed to be circa 1941.

tered the car in several dirt track events, "a waste of sophisticated design in unsophisticated events," according to Griffith Borgeson, and the little car faded quickly into obscurity. Reportedly, the Cornelian's engine and transmission were found in the northeast in 1965 and returned to the

Indianapolis Museum, but the body had found its way to the junk yard, perhaps to supply the voracious appetite of the scrap drives of World War II.

Louis Chevrolet continued to race at Indianapolis after 1915 and placed eighteenth in 1920, but that was to be his last appearance. He suffered severe injuries during a practice run that year and his brother, Gaston, was killed on November 20, 1920 on the wooden track at the Speedway in Beverly Hills. The same accident claimed the life of Eddie O'Donnell who had raced a Duesenberg at Kalamazoo in 1914. Louis withdrew from racing for good after the tragedy and concentrated on building race car engines under the Frontenac name plate. The "Fronty Fords" were successful at many tracks in the 1920s. In 1921, the Frontenac Company, with Allan A. Ryan and William N. Thompson, both associated with Stutz, began building passenger cars in Indianapolis. There in the former factory of the Empire Motor Car Company, they manufactured a car of advanced design created by Cornelius Van Ranst, who also made a major contribution to the development of the front-wheel drive L-29 Cord. The Cord would eventually become the subject of study when Checker Cab Manufacturing Company in Kalamazoo considered building a front-wheel drive automobile.

The Frontenac was introduced at the Indianapolis 500 in 1922, but the economic times were not conducive to success and bankruptcy followed in 1925. Louis Chevrolet engaged in a succession of manufacturing ideas, including the Chevrolair auto engine and a ten-cylinder radial aircraft engine. He seemed always to be on the edge of greatness and considerable wealth, but toward the end of his career, his livelihood was gained from work on the production line building the cars that bore his family name. Had he kept the Chevrolet stock certificates, he would have been a rich man and his story might have been quite different. However, he lived a life much fuller than most before he died on June 6, 1941 in Detroit of a cerebral hemorrhage at the age of sixty-eight.

Racing at Indianapolis and other major tracks was discontinued in 1917 and 1918 because of World War I. Howard's father died in May of 1917, and Howard turned his attention to other matters. His interests in mechanics and speed led him, as well as many drivers on the racing circuit, to a two-year stint in the Air Force, where he served as a test pilot and commander at McCook Field in Dayton, Ohio. After his discharge, his mechanical aptitude and management skills led to promotion within the executive ranks of Borg Warner and the Detroit-based Norge Company.

Massie reports that as late as 1966, Howard Blood spoke optimistically about the car: "Had I priced it at $500 it would have sold well and we would have made a go of it." The Cornelian was the "little car that could," but no one, not even Louis Chevrolet, seemed to notice. The major lessons learned from the Cornelian at the Indianapolis track in 1915 about suspension and drive train geometry were not "introduced" to the American racing circuit for another thirty-five years. It is interesting that a car that is written about now with such respect, was forgotten so quickly after an impressive showing at the grand Memorial Day event. Imagine a car with a 115 cid engine, built in Allegan, Michigan, by a twenty-eight year old engineer, remaining competitive with the most powerful racers, using the best technology and built by the most prestigious automobile manufacturers of the day. Unfortunately, there was a lesson in Howard Blood's accomplishment that remained dormant within the racing fraternity.

REFERENCES

Louis Chevrolet Accepts Mount at Indianapolis. *Motor Age*, February 25, 1915, p. 40.

Chevrolet to Drive in Indianapolis Race. *The Horseless Age*, March 10, 1915, p. 328.

Jack C. Fox. *Illustrated History of the Indianapolis 500, 1911–1984.* Speedway IN: Hungness, 1994.

Griffith Borgeson. *The Golden Age of the American Racing Car*, New York: W. W. Norton, 1966.

Arch Brown, Pat Chappell, and Bob Hall. *Chevrolet Chronicle, A Pictorial History from 1904,* Lincolnwood, IL: Publications International, 1991.

Timothy Jacobs. *A History of General Motors*, Greenwich, CN: Brompton Books, 1992.

R. Perry Zavitz. "Louis Joseph Chevrolet." *Old Cars Weekly News and Market Place*, June 11, 1992.

Chevrolet and Cornelian Light Car. Indianapolis 500 Race Program, May 1915, pp. 15, 21.

Cyril Posthumus. "Prophet Without Honour; The 1915 Indianapolis Cornelian." *Motor*, January 17, 1970.

Hooray for Cornelian and No. 24. *The Kalamazoo Gazette*, May 27, 1915.

Are You Going to Indianapolis? This Will Help. *Kalamazoo Telegraph-Press*, May 19, 1915.

Cars Will Cut Loose This Week. *The Kalamazoo Gazette*, May 19, 1915.

Bill Pittman. *The Indianapolis News 500-Mile Record Book.* Indianapolis: Indianapolis Newspapers, 1967.

Cornelian May Prove Big Sensation. *Kalamazoo Telegraph-Press*, May 19, 1915.

Cornelian Does 94 Miles an Hour in Elimination Trial; Proves Sensation. *The Kalamazoo Gazette*, May 21, 1915.

Little Cornelian Car Hangs Up New Record. *Kalamazoo Telegraph-Press*, May 26, 1915.

Cornelian Makes Sensation. *The Allegan Gazette*, May 15, 1915.

The First to Qualify. *The Allegan Gazette*, May 22, 1915.

Donald Davidson. *A Salute to the 75th Anniversary of the Indianapolis 500.* Indianapolis: Indianapolis Motor Speedway, 1986.

World's Greatest Racecourse Built in 1909 by Four Indianapolis Sportsmen. *Kalamazoo Telegraph-Press*, May 27, 1915.

Twenty-two Cars Qualify for Indianapolis 500 Mile Sweepstakes. *Motor World*, May 26, 1915, pp. 5–11.

Barney Oldfield Will Start in Hoosier Race. *Kalamazoo Telegraph-Press*, May 19, 1915.

Harry A. Tarantous. "Lap-by-Lap Story of Ralph de Palma's Spectacular Victory." *Motor Age*, June 3, 1915, pp. 12–16.

DePalma Wins Great Race and Smashes All Records. *The Kalamazoo Gazette*, June 1, 1915.

J. C. Burton. "Ralph DePalma Wins Indianapolis in Record Time." *Motor Age*, June 3, 1915, pp. 4–10.

Anthony J. Yanik. "The Cornelian and the Indianapolis 500." *Chronicle*, Vol 24, No. 1, May–June, 1988.

Darwin S. Hatch. "Mechanical Lessons Taught in Record Breaking Contest." *Motor Age*, June 3, 1915, pp. 17–20.

George Moore. "Worlds of Speed." *Unknown Source*, February 1965, pp. 6–7.

Pal's Death in Big Race Ends Career of Heir to World's Speed Crown. *The Kalamazoo Gazette*, December 17, 1920.

Beverly Rae Kimes and Henry Austin Clark Jr. *Standard Catalog of American Cars, 1805–1942, 3rd ed.* Iola WI: Krause Publications, 1996.

Obituary; Maurice E. Blood. *The Automobile*, March 17, 1917, p. 944.

History of Wright Air Base, Wright Air Museum brochure, Dayton, Ohio.

Herbert. S. Chase. *Who's Who in Michigan*. Munising, Michigan: Who's Who in Michigan, 1936.

Larry Massie. "Indy 500 Dashed Dreams of Allegan Carmakers." *Kalamazoo Hometown Gazette*, August 24, 1989.

Five-Hundred-Mile Race Echoes from the Resonant Saucer of Speed. *Motor Age*, June 3, 1915, p. 11.

Fig. 12-1. Artist's image of the Michigan Motor Car Company (Michigan Buggy) factory used in many advertisements and brochures. The factory was completed just after the turn of the twentieth century and another addition was made in 1912. This particular image is from the 1913 sales catalog and is an enhancement of the actual facility. Much of the building still exists in Kalamazoo and even though many changes have been made, it is clear that the facility was never as large as the one portrayed here. (DOL)

Chapter 12

The Mighty Michigan-40

1909–1913

"The vehicle of quality and refinement,
everything is strong and substantial,
everything is good, everything is simple,
everything is perfect, everything works."

—Company sales brochure

Manufacture of the Mighty Michigan was predated by the planned manufacture of the "Kalamazoo," a horseless carriage designed by the owners of Michigan Buggy and announced by Henry Lane in the *Kalamazoo Evening Telegraph* in February and again in July of 1903. Frank Burtt, another of the pioneer auto manufacturers in Kalamazoo just after the turn of the twentieth century, later reported that he, with Henry Lane, Frank Lay, and Walter Cannon, had traveled to Chicago in 1902 to inspect an automobile there. They had an example of that car shipped to Kalamazoo but later returned it because of perceived inadequacies. As a result of this venture, Burtt began production of the Cannon automobile, named after Walter Cannon who designed the car. The owners of Michigan Buggy also planned to build a car of their own, but the eventual production of the Cannon car was a joint venture of the two companies. Lay and Lane had experience and reputation in the horse-drawn vehicle trade, and they finished the wood bodies, paint, and upholstery work for the Cannon automobile from 1902 to 1905. Michigan Buggy also advertised the Cannon, including a picture and a list of specifications of this car in their 1904 catalog of horse-drawn vehicles. Because of the similarity between the Cannon and the Kalamazoo motorcar envisioned by Michigan Buggy, one is tempted to conjecture that the descriptions concerned the same car. Perhaps Henry Lane assumed Michigan Buggy would get credit for the Cannon car and it would be named the "Kalamazoo." Newspaper reports in 1903, however, were very clear that the addition of the Kalamazoo built by Michigan Buggy would bring the number of automobile manufacturers in the city to three; the other two were the Cannon built by Burtt Manu-

Fig. 12-2. "The Electric Lighted Line," the Michigan Model B, was first offered in 1909 and about fifty of these cars were built that year and another one hundred with the same open carriage-type body were built in 1910 on a 112" wheel base. The Model B sold for $1,750. This car was powered by a Hazard 36–40 horsepower engine. Production ended in the summer of 1911 when the Hazard Company, of Rochester, New York, ceased making engines. Note that the side lamps do not have the chimney typical of kerosene lamps. The Model B offered electric driving lamps long before other major American makes. This particular image appeared in the Kalamazoo Telegraph *in May of 1910 and also in the* Cycle and Automobile Trade Journal *for March, 1911. (PFL)*

facturing Company and the Michigan built by the Michigan Automobile Company Limited, owned by the Bloods and the Fullers. The identification of three companies by the newspaper made clear that the Kalamazoo was built and tested as Lane had reported, but that the car was never manufactured beyond three or four initial vehicles.

While there is no evidence that a car named the Kalamazoo was manufactured beyond the initial models announced by Henry Lane, Michigan Buggy's association with the Cannon led to additional planning for the manufacture of an automobile. In 1909, Michigan Buggy produced the first of the big Michigan cars, and in later years, forty-horsepower automobiles subsequently identified as the "Mighty Michigan." There is no relationship, except for the similarity of name, between the "Mighty Michigan" built by Lane and Lay, and the earlier "Little Michigan" car built by the Bloods and the Fullers. The Blood brothers subsequently left the Michigan Automobile Company in 1904 and after that the "Little Michigan" was built exclusively by the Fullers. The Mighty Michigan was a successor to the smaller Michigan only in name, as recorded in a personal letter from H. L. Fuller, a descendent of Charles B. Fuller. In that letter, as reported by Crews, he affirms that the name for the original Little Michigan was given by the Fuller family to M. Henry Lane, Frank Lay, and the Michigan Buggy Company in 1909. The extension of privilege was affirmed in Frank Fuller's notes, but beyond that, there was no relationship between the two companies.

Other aspects of the company's name may also create some confusion. Initially, the Michigan was identified as a product of the Michigan Buggy Company, but subsequent references refer to the Motor Car Department, since the company continued to manufacture horse-drawn vehicles. On September 24, 1912, the Michigan Motor Car Company was incorporated by the Lay family and is distinct from the Michigan Automobile Company founded on December 31, 1902, by Frank and Charles Fuller with the Blood brothers. In January of 1913, the Fullers also changed the name of the Michigan Automobile Company to Fuller and Sons Manufacturing Company in an effort to remove any confusion between the two concerns holding the Michigan name.

The Michigan Motor Car Company name appeared in many of the Michigan Buggy Company's publications and advertisements as "being owned by the owners of the Michigan Buggy Company." This company was an independent entity, and many of the national magazines identified the company as the Michigan Motor Car Company, rather than the Michigan Buggy Company after the publicized name change. In Kalamazoo, however, it was known simply as Michigan Buggy.

Founding the car company seemed to impact executive positions more than the manufacture and sale of automobiles. The annual report for the car company in 1912 listed capital stock of only $1,000 with total cash on hand of $250. The character of the business for that year was listed as "none," with no credits owed and no tangible property or real estate owned. The president of the Michigan Motor Car Company was Frank B. Lay. His two sons and Victor Palmer were listed as directors and the name Henry Lane was conspicuous in its absence from the list of directors, for by this time Lane had been deposed as president of Michigan Buggy. In 1912, most references in reports, some advertisements, and news releases simply cited the "Michigan Buggy Company" when referring to the auto manufacturer, probably because of its name recognition value. When the motor car manufacturing enterprise failed, however, both entities were identified, both were involved in the bankruptcy hearing, and both companies fell with the bankruptcy decision.

Manufacture of the first Michigan car occurred in late 1909, although the exact beginning of production is uncertain. According to a company brochure published in 1912, the company officials got together in September 1909 and decided that a high-class car offered at a reasonable price could deliver an eight percent profit. An advertisement by the company in *Automobile Topics*, March 30, 1912, describes the birth of the Michigan in 1909 and the logic of its price structure:

> In 1909 we started to build automobiles. A simple announcement to our agents disposed of all of the cars we could build. No expense.
>
> And thus it has been ever since. Our agents have absorbed our entire product. Thus for representation which has cost other manufacturers fortunes, we have paid not a cent. And that is why we undersell.

Testimony given by Victor Palmer, Michigan Buggy's secretary-treasurer, at the 1913 bankruptcy hearings corroborates this citation of the 1909 production date, and according to his testimony, the company produced about one hundred cars in 1909. Most were sold locally and only a small portion of those were ever shipped to dealers. This initial production was then followed by 500 cars in 1910, and the first major delivery that year was a carload of Michigan cars shipped April 8, 1910, to O. E. Short, the company's New York City agent. Palmer also reported that another 1,000 cars were built in 1911, 1,700 in 1912, and 4,000 in 1913 for a total of 7,200 cars. Vehicle identification numbers for 1913 exceed 7,200 thus verifying the total production for the company at around 7,200 cars. Finally these figures are corroborated by a *Kalamazoo Gazette* article that appeared on February 20, 1912, and reported the general health of the company. That statement read as follows:

> The manufacture of the well-known "Michigan" automobile by the Michigan Buggy Com-

pany constitutes Kalamazoo's chiefist *[sic]* automobile concern today. Three years ago *[1909]* this celebrated buggy-making firm began the manufacture of automobiles. The first year they turned out 700 cars *[note: this figure is the approximate sum of six hundred for 1909 and 1910 quoted by Palmer in his testimony]* which sold at about $1,750 apiece. The car was a success from the first and it was found that it could be manufactured at a handsome profit. Last year 1,000 Michigan cars were made, the price dropping to $1,400 and this year the Michigan Buggy Company will make 2,000 of these fine cars and could sell ten times that number if they had a plant large enough to manufacture them. The 1912 model is a beauty and sells for $1,400 and $1,500. At present a dozen of these cars are being turned out of the factory and shipped daily.

The 1910 Michigan was first advertised in the *Kalamazoo Telegraph* on May 28, 1910 by the Russell and Albrecht agency. The 1910 Model B was a five-passenger touring car, with a 112" wheel base and weighed 2,300 pounds. The Michigan had right-hand steering and the shift and brake levers were mounted outside of the driver's cockpit on the right side of the car, preventing ready access from that side. There were no entrance doors to the driver's compartment, a typical vehicle body configuration identified as "carriage-style." When both the front and the rear entrances were without doors, the style was known as "surrey."

The right-hand steering on early cars appears as an anomaly only in comparison to today's automobiles. Early motorcars were driven on the right-hand side of the road and from the right-hand side of the vehicle in the tradition of the horse-drawn vehicle. The most critical concern of the driver was the constant challenge of avoiding the right-hand ditch rather than the infrequent appearance of another car passing on the left from behind or in an oncoming lane. Most roads at the time were so ill-defined that there was no explicit lane of traffic. Due to the primitive roads, the need to pay attention to the ditch was essential, making a right-hand drive that allowed the driver to monitor roadside obstacles a convenience. Henry Ford introduced the Model T Ford in 1908 with left-hand drive, one of the few cars so designed. The steering controls of almost all cars migrated to the left by 1915, although some remained on the right into the 1920s.

The engine for the 1910 Michigan was built by Hazard Motor Manufacturing of Rochester, New York. The cylinders were cast in pairs and bolted to the cast-aluminum oil pan forming a four-cylinder unit. With a magneto ignition, it was initially rated at thirty horsepower, but subsequently raised to forty. The driving and side lamps were electric, a rarity in this period, making the Michigan one of the first to offer electric lighting. All other major makes, Buick, Cadillac, Oldsmobile, and Packard were equipped with acetylene gas driving lamps and kerosene oil side and tail lamps. Electric headlights were first manufactured in 1908 and provided twenty or so candlepower, but few auto makers offered them, and such lighting did not begin to become popular until 1912 when Cadillac introduced the electric starter and electric driving lamps. Electric driving lamps were dropped after the 1911 Model B was discontinued by Michigan Buggy; acetylene gas and oil lamps were used on the new 1911 models. Electric driving lamps returned on the 1913 Michigan.

The company was very proud of the Model B. Their sales brochure entitled "The Wonderful Michigan Electric Lighted Line" described it as:

> The vehicle of quality and refinement, everything is strong and substantial, everything is good, everything is simple, everything is perfect, everything works.

> A great country car. Well powered in proportion to weight. Goes anywhere that any car will go.
> All lights are electric, no bother, no dirt, no oil, push the button at any time and the car is
> lighted.

In an effort to substantiate its claims and to prove the capability of its Michigan, Edwin Gerber, Michigan Buggy's East Coast distributor, and Victor Palmer, its secretary-treasurer, set out for Pittsburgh—a distance of 437 miles—in a new Michigan Model B on May 27, 1910. The car was driven from the factory to the Rickman Hotel, and the party left the hotel the afternoon of May 27, with James Woodworth and Roy Moore sharing the driving chores. The first 115 miles were made without stopping, and the roads were described as "heavy," a polite description for the deplorable Michigan roads at the time. Running time for the trip was twenty-one hours and thirty-eight minutes and the car reached Pittsburgh on the evening of Saturday, May 28, having consumed thirty gallons of gasoline. According to the log, nine hours of driving were completed with electric lights.

The subsequent introduction of the Michigan at an endurance run in Kalamazoo, sponsored by *The Kalamazoo Gazette*, was tied to an unfortunate circumstance. The Michigan was one of thirty cars to be entered in the contest. The field included Brush, Buick, Cadillac, Carter Car, E. M. F., Flanders, Ford, Maxwell, Mitchell, Oldsmobile, Overland, Regal, and Reo. The contestants were scheduled to leave from South Burdick Street at regular intervals and the cars that day were described as having "roaring and muffled motors exploding impatiently." The cars proceeded from South Burdick Street to Exchange Place where they were officially registered and sent on their way from the offices of *The Kalamazoo Gazette*. It was a heralded affair. Towns along the way "were set on fire with the idea," promising services for the cars, and Marshall Mackey had made arrangements to welcome the participants in South Haven. The welcoming committee planned to meet the cars some twelve miles outside of town toward Bangor, and then escort them to the Hotel Johnson for a sumptuous banquet. David Reid's garage was secured for the storage of the automobiles, and, after a planned hour of bathing for the automobilists, the cars would return to Kalamazoo. The intent of the event was described in *The Kalamazoo Gazette* on June 18, 1910:

> The purpose of the run, as stated before, is to show to the pessimistic and the doubting the
> true ability of the modern automobile of today and emphasize the fact that any man with
> ordinary intelligence can successfully motor all kinds of roads without worry or fear of breaks
> or having mechanics accompanying. The run to South Haven, although short, is a true typical
> type of road, same as would be found in motoring the country over. Sand is one of the big
> worrying factors to the amateur automobilist and practically half of the road to South Haven
> lays [sic] over a route of sand.

The rules of the contest, explained in the June 16 *Gazette,* were as follows:

> An enthusiast for one make will ride in the machine of another. For example, a Buick booster
> will ride in a Mitchell and a Mitchell enthusiast will ride in a Buick and each will keep an eagle
> eye on the other. The idea is to demonstrate the greater reliability and dependence that can be
> put into a machine of today and disabuse the fallacy that automobiles go wrong unless driven
> by a mechanician.

The 1910 Michigan was one of the last cars to leave the city that day with Victor Palmer, representing the Michigan Buggy Company, and Frank Russell, representing the Russell and Albrecht

FIVE-PASSENGER TOURING CAR

Fig. 12-3. The Michigan five-passenger Model E was first introduced at the automobile shows in the winter of 1911. The carriage-type body was similar to the Model B, also with right hand steering, and mounted on a 112" wheel base; it sold for $1,500. The four-cylinder engine, with cylinders cast "en-bloc," was manufactured by the Falls Company of Sheboygan Falls, Wisconsin, and was rated at 30–33 hp. This model offered an electric trouble light, but in contrast to the 1909–10 Model B, the driving lamps and side lamps burned acetylene gas and kerosene respectively. Note the chimney on the side lamp and the large tank for lamp gas storage on the running board. The smaller tank is for compressed air and is sufficient to inflate twenty-two tires. This image was taken from a 1911 sales brochure distributed by Dewey and Company of Plano, Illinois. This image also shows an electric horn, although a preliminary company catalog for 1911 shows a bulb horn typical of the era. (DOL)

agency that sold the cars locally, seated comfortably in the back seat. The driver was James Woodworth, the same man who navigated the Michigan's reliability demonstration run to Pittsburgh just a month before. J. George Sharker, manager of the Cable-Nelson piano store in Kalamazoo, occupied the left front passenger seat, presumably serving as judge and enthusiast for another make of automobile, as dictated by the rules.

The car left the *Gazette* office as scheduled, and Woodworth drove west along Main Street. At the corner of West Main and Woodward Streets as James Woodworth pulled out to pass a street sprinkling machine, the tires slid on the wet pavement and then caught on the lip of the trolley track. The car skidded sideways out of control and slammed into a telephone pole. All of the occupants were thrown from the car, but Sharker, fulfilling a premonition of death he had expressed to Russell at the beginning of the trip, suffered massive head injuries when he hit the pavement. The twenty-year-old Woodworth was on his feet instantly, but became hysterical when he saw the bloodied form of Sharker lying lifeless on the street. Dr. Rush McNair, one of the first surgeons in Michigan and instrumental in founding Bronson Hospital in Kalamazoo, always seemed to be in attendance in emergencies. He tended to the minor bumps and bruises of Russell and Palmer, who were both badly shaken. He estimated that Sharker died instantly. The news reached the *Gazette* office almost immediately and word went out for the cancellation of the contest, and so ended the first endurance run from Kalamazoo.

ROADSTER

Fig. 12-4. The 1911 Michigan Model D had the same engine and mechanics as the Model E, but was offered with a two-seat roadster body and a 30-gallon rear-mounted gas tank. The roadster sold for $1,350. Note the attractive top arrangement. The top was tied to the front frame with leather straps and did not fasten to the windshield. The arrangement was typical of the period. The Prest-O-Lite acetylene tank to power the driving lamps was mounted on the running board. The second smaller tank on the running board holds sufficient air to inflate twenty-two tires. Note that the horn mounted next to the spare tire is electric. This image is also from the Dewey and Company brochure. (DOL)

William Neely reports in *The Jim Gilmore Story* that the 1909 Cadillac was driven that day by James Stanley Gilmore and Vern MacFee, although he casts the event as a race rather than the endurance run advertised by the *Gazette* and the event promoters. According to the saga that he relates, the two left Kalamazoo at 7:55 a.m. and covered the distance to South Haven in two and a half hours, in spite of eleven flat tires, for an average speed of twenty miles an hour.

(In a side note, James Stanley Gilmore and his brother John were founders of Kalamazoo's Gilmore Brothers Department Store. James married Ruth McNair, daughter of Dr. Rush McNair, and they had three sons: Stanley, Irving, and Donald. It was Donald who later founded the Gilmore Car Museum, a collection of Kalamazoo-built automobiles, and Jim Gilmore, James Stanley's grandson, became involved in racing at Indianapolis in the 1960s.)

In spite of the endurance run mishap, the Michigan Model B proved worthy, and in March 1911, the company displayed the Model B and three new models at the national shows. The 1911 Model B was the same as the 1909–10 model with a 112" wheel base and a carriage-type open body. This model was described as having a four-cylinder Hazard engine with a 4" bore and a 4.5" stroke forming a single unit with the multiple disc clutch. The engine was reported as thirty-six horsepower in the *Cycle and Automotive Trade Journal*, while the company claimed forty horsepower in their sales brochure. The Hazard Company went out of business in the summer of 1911 and Michigan Buggy discontinued the Model B at that time.

FIVE-PASSENGER FORE-DOOR CAR

Fig. 12-5. The 1911 Michigan Model H was a five-passenger touring car with the same wheel base, drive train, and mechanical components as Models D and E, but without the carriage-type body. The four door construction was identified as the "fore-door model," and sold for $1,600. This image is also from the Dewey and Company brochure. (DOL)

Three new models for 1911 included the Model E touring car (selling for $1,500), and the Model D, a two-passenger roadster with a thirty-gallon gas tank at the rear (selling for $1,350). Like the Model B, both the Model D and the Model E had a carriage-type body mounted on a 112" wheel base.

The 1911 "fore-door" Model H touring was the newest and most refined of the new models, offering four entry doors rather than the open carriage body of the other 1911 models. All hand levers were mounted inside the enclosed vehicle and the general design served as the basis for the 1912 models. The new 1911 models were powered by a thirty-horsepower Falls engine, made in Sheboygan Falls, Wisconsin. The engine make is verified by a surviving 1911 Michigan that has the Falls identification on the engine. The four-cylinder Falls engine for 1911 was cast "en bloc," meaning cast in a single engine block as in modern engines, rather than the standard practice of the time to cast separate one- or two-cylinder units and then bolt these together on a cast aluminum oil pan. The engine had a 4" bore and a 4.5" stroke. The carburetor was by Stromburg and the ignition by Splitdorf, with two spark plugs per cylinder. Dewey and Company, an agency in Plano, Illinois, advertised this model at $1,600.

The standard color for the 1911 cars was black, and the trim was nickel, replacing the brass used on the earlier Model B; other paint choices or brass trim were available upon request. The seating was of the finest black leather over curled hair. Standard equipment included an eight-day keyless clock, a compressed air tank with sufficient capacity to inflate twenty-two tires, and a full set of acetylene gas driving lamps. Curiously, the car was equipped with an electric trouble light and an electric horn, but the electric driving lamps used on the 1909–10 Model B were dropped in favor of the acetylene gas type and kerosene oil side lamps.

Fig. 12-6. The 1912 Michigan Model K was advertised nationally beginning in October 1911. It appears to be a refinement of the 1911 Model H, with a longer wheelbase. The Model K was a five-passenger "fore-door touring" on a 116" wheel base with right-hand steering, a Buda 40 hp engine, a three-speed transmission, and Prest-O-Lite acetylene gas starter not commonly found on most cars of that year. The Model K was supplied with acetylene gas driving lamps and three oil lamps of white nickel. The Model K sold for $1,500 with the option of a 60" tread for the "Southern trade." This image was taken from the 1912 company catalog. (PFL)

The promotion campaign for the 1912 models began in the fall of 1911 with a series of advertisements using an original painting of a four-door touring car, much like the 1911 Model H, showing two men in the front seat and three people in the back seat. Apparently they are not family members. This painting served as the basis for a variety of advertisements that were initially placed in over a dozen magazines, including *Saturday Evening Post, Colliers Weekly*, and *Life* as well as a host of farm-related publications and automotive trade journals. The company advertisements for 1912 were not hesitant in their claims.

> The Michigan is a big, handsome, powerful, dependable car that suffers none by comparison
> with Packard, Peerless and Lozier. Price $1,500. You can run it alongside a Packard, a Pierce, a
> Mercedes, or any of the high-priced machines and you won't feel ashamed of it. And there isn't
> a car—AT ANY PRICE—that has a more magnificent finish of body or better upholstery.

Michigan Buggy had a reputation for producing the finest horse-drawn vehicles and they intended to produce motorcars that rivaled the best in the industry. The company offered six cars in 1912, two with a forty-horsepower and four with a thirty-three horsepower four-cylinder engine, all with right-hand drive. These were "assembled cars" and, according to the testimony of the company accountants, eighty-five percent of the parts were manufactured elsewhere and brought to Kalamazoo for final assembly. Frank Fuller of Michigan Automobile Company had complained that automobile manufacture in 1903 was very difficult, because there were no parts suppliers. By 1910 there was an abundance of such suppliers, making possible the manufacture of automobiles in the manner used by Michigan Buggy. Much of their advertising, however, gives the impression that the components were built in-house since there was a general hesitancy among the buying public for "assembled vehicles." Given the company's past experience with the horseless carriage trade, Michigan Buggy probably concentrated on body construction, painting, and upholstery and did not manufacture the mechanical components.

The 1912 production year marked a major transition for Michigan Buggy with the added option of a self-starter mechanism, an array of six vehicles, and the first use of the forty-horsepower Buda engine for the "Mighty Michigan" line. Michigan Buggy actually offered two types of self-starters, a feature available on such luxury cars as Lozier, Locomobile, and Winton. The operation of these units is described in the 1914 *Dyke's Automobile Encyclopedia.* The air starter worked from a compressed air tank carried on the side of the car and replenished with a small compressor working off the car's engine, although the system on the Winton used stored-up exhaust gases for this purpose. Regulated through a distributor, the air, under pressure, was forced into the cylinders with the same timing as a running engine, thereby turning the engine over in the same manner as a running engine until it fired. The system was initiated with the depression of a pedal, and followed by a quiet whirr, the engine magically came to life.

Fig. 12-7. The distinctive Buda 40 hp motor that was used for the first time in the 1912 Michigan–40 and shown here as it appeared in the 1912 catalog. Note the sloping water jacket on the top of the engine and the casting above the engine with four holes to hold the spark plug wires. Note also the similarity of this engine to the engine from the 1913 catalog as shown in Fig. 12-14. (DOL)

The other option was a Prest-O-Starter acetylene gas system. In this case the acetylene gas was pumped into all cylinders simultaneously. Contact with the coil was then made by turning on the ignition switch and a spark from the coil ignited the gas, turning the engine over, so that the sequence of gas intake and igniting of the spark followed as with a running engine. In either case, these self-starting options were better than hand-cranking a forty-horsepower engine, although not as good as the electric starter that the company introduced in 1913.

When the 1912 show season opened in January of that year, Michigan Buggy displayed five models, including two, the Models D and E, that were essentially holdovers from the 1911 line. These two models were powered by the same Falls thirty-three horsepower engine that was used in all of the 1911 models, except the Model B that had a Hazard engine. The continuation of these two models in 1912 explains why a letter from Michigan Buggy to the Falls Engine Company appeared in the 1912 catalog, although the Falls engine was not installed in the new Michigan cars for 1912 and disappeared completely after Models D and E were discontinued.

The 1912 Model E five-passenger touring car was a refinement of the 1911 Model with four doors rather than the carriage body and was advertised as beautifully finished with construction similar to the big forty-horsepower models. "You cannot duplicate this value in any other make of automobile for less than $1,500," proclaimed the company's advertisement. The second Falls-pow-

Model "E"—Michigan "33"
5 Passenger Touring Car

Fig. 12-8. The 1912 Model E Michigan "33" was a continuation of the 1911 with a four-door touring body rather than the carriage body used the previous year. Note the construction of the body, as the front passenger section is separate from the rear tonneau that is bolted to the frame so that the rear doors latch on the front body section. This image is from the 1912 announcement distributed at the New York Automobile show by the Short and Hessner Agency in January 1912 and it also appears in The Motor World *that same year. (DOL)*

Model "D"—33 H. P.
Roadster

Fig. 12-9. The Model D Michigan "33" two-seat roadster was advertised as "…a marvel of power and speed. Even tho rated at but 33 hp, it will develop 55 miles an hour. It is the ideal type of modern business and suburban car." This image is also from the 1912 show announcement published before the 1912 Model D roadster was discontinued in the spring of 1912. (DOL)

ered vehicle, the 1912 Model D roadster, was offered essentially without modification of the 1911 model. These two models were discontinued in the spring of 1912 and did not appear in the more extensive second catalog published by the company for that year.

The 1912 Model K, "The Mighty Michigan," was a five-passenger touring car with right-hand drive, built on a 116" wheel base and powered by a forty-horsepower engine built by Buda Manu-

Fig. 12-10. The 1912 Model M had the same engine and mechanics as the 40 hp Model K, but with a roadster body. This car was intended for country driving and for that reason it was equipped with a forty-gallon gas tank. The company claimed that the car was capable of reaching speeds of seventy miles an hour. The Model M sold for $1,500. This image was taken from the 1912 company catalog. (PFL)

Fig. 12-11. The 1912 Model H was a five-passenger torpedo touring car for the average family, with the same self starter and materials used in the Michigan "40." The Model M was powered by a 33 hp Sandusky engine and mounted on a 112" wheelbase. Note the straight body line that is an integral structure and not composed of a forward compartment with a rear tonneau attached to it, as was noted for the Model E. This body style was initially called the "torpedo touring," although that nomenclature was later dropped in favor of just "touring." The Model H sold for $1,400. This image is also from the 1912 company catalog. (PFL)

Fig. 12-12. The 1912 Model G had the same mechanical characteristics and 33 horsepower Sandusky engine as the model H, but was offered with a roadster body. The image is from the same 1912 catalog. This roadster was introduced after Models D and E were discontinued. (PFL)

facturing, Harvey, Illinois. It was advertised as "absolutely silent," with a 4.25" bore and a 5.25" stroke, enclosed valves, a three-bearing crankshaft and a Stromberg carburetor. This vehicle included a gas-powered "Michigan" self starter and inside controls. The car rode on 34" x 4" tires with demountable rims. All trim was nickel, although surving examples of the Model K have brass lamps that were offered as an option. The Model K sold for $1,500 and included gas-burning driving lamps, gas generator for the lamps, and all tools, but other equipment was in addition to the base price. A speedometer cost $20, a windshield $25, top and side curtains $60, and an electric trouble light and horn could be obtained for $165.

The Model M—"The Michigan Flyer"—had a two-seat roadster body and the same quality of style and finish as the Model K. The Flyer had a forty gallon gas tank and an advertised speed of seventy miles an hour. The company was very aggressive in its sales promotion and offered the following challenge to prospective agents: "A man who couldn't sell this car couldn't sell gold dollars for eighty cents!"

The company built two models in 1912 powered by a thirty-three horsepower engine manufactured by the Sandusky Auto Parts and Motor Truck Company, Sandusky, Ohio. Note that there were ultimately six models after January 1912, but Models D and E for 1912 were powered by the thirty-three horsepower Falls engine and were discontinued that spring. This Sandusky-powered Series 33 was mounted on a 112" wheel base, again with right-hand drive, and was considered particularly appropriate for export. The Model H, a torpedo touring, and the Model G, a two-door roadster, both sold for $1,400. These cars were finished in black with gray or cream wheels. The engine was rated at thirty-three horsepower using a 4$\frac{1}{16}$" bore, a 4½" stroke, and a Stromberg carburetor. All models were sold with a magneto, two oil lamps and two driving lamps, a gas generator for the driving lamps, nickel trimmings on the lamps, and all tools. These cars carried a lifetime guarantee against breakage and defects, and the company asserted that sixty-two percent of the 1912 production total, or 1,054 cars, was already sold as early as September of 1911.

The rapid growth in the company between 1909 and 1912 convinced the directors to expand their manufacturing facility in July 1912 with a three-story addition, and to expand their manufacturing line to include blankets and robes in a new factory at Lane Blvd. and Factory Street. The addition of a million square feet to the manufacturing plant made Michigan Buggy the sixth largest among automobile factories in the country. The decision was also made to engage in a massive advertising campaign in late 1912, usually featuring the

Fig. 12-13. This image shows the interior of the "Mighty Michigan" with the steering wheel on the left and the shift controls in the center of the car as is found on modern automobiles. The circles on either side of the compartment are the nickel-plated doors that open to provide lighting for the interior of the car. (DOL)

1913 forty-horsepower models, and reportedly, the expenditure for that campaign approached $350,000. Advertisements appeared in all of the leading magazines, including *Life, Colliers Weekly,* and *Saturday Evening Post* as well as the leading automotive periodicals.

At the same time, the company enlarged its sales agencies. The Michigan Motor Car Company of California was founded that September for the specific purpose of distributing cars on the West Coast and in Hawaii. Victor Palmer was president, Frank Lay, Jr. was first vice-president, William Cameron was second vice-president, George Dougherty was third vice-president, and Charles Bobb was secretary. After the fall of Michigan Buggy, Charles Bobb subsequently opened the Automobile Top Company in Kalamazoo, but he should not be confused with James Bobb of the Limousine Top Company, also of this city and later part of the E. L. Cord conglomerate. In addition to Hawaii, the Michigan Buggy Company was expanding its export business to Europe, and the Michigan Series-33 sold well, particularly in Italy because it met the engine restrictions on the continent. Sales also extended into Russia, where R. Kewerkoff controlled Michigan Motor Car sales with a large agency and showroom in downtown Moscow.

Preparation for the 1913 production year began in the summer of 1912, with a newly designed body on a larger chassis for both the Series-33 and Series-40. The major news for 1913 was the change from right-hand to left-hand steering, an expensive modification that was introduced, according to the company, by Cameron and was accomplished against stubborn prejudice. In 1912 the controls for cars with right-hand steering were inside the car and mounted on the right, in deference to a right-handed population. Some manufacturers made no pretense of having a right-hand door, enclosing handbrake and gearshift lever where the door would be mounted. Since the right-hand door was inoperable, both passenger and driver were forced to enter and exit through the left-hand door, which was a considerable inconvenience. When the gearshift lever and other controls were moved to the center of the car to create four true doors, this arrangement naturally pushed the steering wheel to the left so that the controls were still operated with the driver's right hand. Michigan Buggy sales catalogs for 1913 noted that the change brought the driver to the high point of the crowned road, giving a more commanding view of the situation and allowing him to judge distances between his car and approaching vehicles to the left more easily than with the right-hand driver's position. The company also noted that other expensive cars—Packard, Peerless, Lozier, and National—had also made this change in their 1913 models.

Fig. 12-14. The Buda engine, rated at 40 hp and used in the Mighty Michigan, as it appeared in the 1913 sales brochure. Note the distinctive water jacket and fastener for the spark plug wires on top of the engine. (DOL)

After offering an array of vehicles in 1912, the company settled on two series of automobiles. The Series-33 automobile sat on a 114" wheel base, rode on 35" x 4" tires and weighed 2,850 pounds. It was offered as a four-door touring, designated as the Model L, and a two-door roadster designated as the Model O. These models were built with the same quality of finish, fine leather interior, and other options that were offered on the Michigan-40, but at $1,500, selling for $85 less than the larger car. The sporty torpedo touring designation that was offered in 1912 was dropped in favor of the term "touring." The thirty-three horsepower Sandusky engine had a 4.06" bore and a 4.5" stroke with a calculated displacement of 233 cubic inches. The engine was linked to a three-speed transmission.

The larger of the two series in 1913, the Mighty Michigan-40 sat on a wheel base of 118", with 35" x 4½" tires and weighed 3,100 lbs. The Buda engine had a 4.25" bore and a 5.25" stroke, with a calculated displacement of 300 cubic inches. The engine was linked to a four-speed transmission.

In spite of the claims of three hundred improvements in vehicle design, this period was not without its difficulties. A large number of Sandusky engines that had been purchased from the Sandusky Auto Parts and Motor Truck Company in Sandusky, Ohio were found to be faulty. The Buda engine used in the forty-horsepower models was unparalleled in quality of manufacture, and there is no evidence that these engines failed. The testimony and published reports indicate that after the 1912 Falls-powered Models D and E were discontinued, only the Sandusky engine was used in the 1912 and 1913 Series-33 Michigan and only this unit failed. The exact nature of the malfunction was not disclosed in testimony at the Michigan Buggy bankruptcy hearings, but, interestingly, none of the Series-33 Michigan cars appear to have survived, suggesting that the faulty motor may have been responsible for their gradual discard over the years. The larger forty-horsepower cars often survived because they were powerful enough to perform other work well after they were taken off the public roads.

Company officials testified at the criminal trial of Victor Palmer in 1914 that "after the first cars were made and sold by the company, in the spring of 1913... the company was forced to spend $100,000 to send men to all parts of the country and replace the motors." The $100,000 cost of this correction was cited as part of the financial problem that brought on the bankruptcy in late summer of 1913. The company's attention to this problem at least demonstrated their willingness to uphold their published product guarantee: "We will accord to every purchaser the same or better care than is given by any Motor Car Manufacturer—and to this the MICHIGAN will add the special liberality that has characterized its nationwide business for a third of a century."

The Sandusky Auto Parts and Motor Truck Company began manufacturing trucks and engines in 1911, but declared bankruptcy in November 1913, immediately following the bankruptcy of Michigan Buggy. Subsequently, the Sandusky company was sold in March of 1914. According to a report in the *Automobile Trade Journal* of October 1913, Sandusky Auto Parts went bankrupt "owing to the failure of Michigan Buggy." In November of 1913, *Motor World* reported that the Sandusky Company was "brought down by the failure of Michigan Buggy." The failure of Sandusky Auto Parts as a result of the Michigan Buggy failure makes clear that the survival of the Ohio firm was dependent upon production of Michigan cars.

The Michigan cars with the faulty Sandusky engines also created havoc for others as early as 1911. The National Motor Car Company in Oklahoma City, Oklahoma, ordered three 1912 Michigan cars in October of 1911. The cars were shipped from Kalamazoo on December 11, 1911, but National found them to be defective

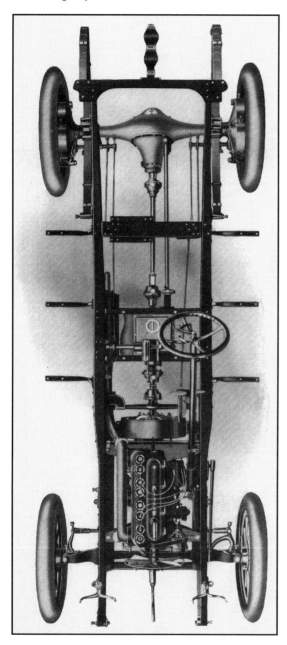

Fig. 12-15. The photograph of the chassis for the 1913 Mighty Michigan shows the four universal joints, two between the flywheel and the transmission and two between the transmission and the differential. The torque rod is to the right of the drive shaft connecting the rear axle to a double spring buffer on the frame just behind the transmission. (DOL)

and subsequently refused payment. A persistent representative of Michigan Buggy finally persuaded William Nation of the Oklahoma City firm to sign the drafts and accept the cars. These drafts were then discounted by Michigan Buggy to the Kalamazoo Savings Bank, a common practice of the company, and the bank in turn brought suit against Mr. Nation for non-payment. The issue was not resolved until October of 1913, when the courts ruled that Nation did not have to pay for the faulty cars, and these three cars were attached to the list of disputed property in the ongoing bankruptcy hearings of the Michigan Buggy Company.

In February 1914, after the fall of the Michigan Buggy Company, the Auto Parts Company of Chicago advertised the availability of a sufficient line of parts necessary to build a complete Michigan automobile, including the motor. The price was $585. The report does not differentiate between the Series-40 and the Series-33, so the advertised availability of parts does not substantiate any conjecture about the motor problems associated with the Sandusky-powered Michigan cars. In June 1914, Michigan parts were also sold by the Abbot Motor Company in Detroit and the Michigan Motor Parts Company of Kalamazoo, attesting once again to the demand for the car. In the latter case, however, the investor who had purchased the assets of the Michigan Motor Car Company brought suit against the parts company for alleged infringements.

The 1913 Mighty Michigan-40 was offered in two models: the Model R was a four-door phaeton and the Model S, a two-seat roadster. While Michigan Buggy liked to compare this car with the Packard, Peerless, and Pierce Arrow, all three of these manufacturers offered a car in their "smaller series," with an engine that was much larger than the Michigan's. The top of the line Peerless and Pierce Arrow in 1913 were powered by a whopping 824 cid powerplant. The Michigan was an impressive vehicle, larger than some, but not quite the size of these prestigious marques. The 1913 Michigan's reputation for size and power, however, is enhanced by stories of its performance, including that about an Illinois farmer who drove his newly-purchased machine home in second gear because he feared the potential speed of the car in high gear.

The Michigan Buggy Company did not identify the engine manufacturer for the 1913 cars, and in fact implied that it was designed by chief engineer, W. H. Cameron and built by the Michigan Buggy Company. This practice by automobile manufacturers of purchasing an engine from an independent company and then using their own company logo on the engine was not atypical at the time. The description of the Buda engine used in the 1913 catalog is as follows:

> One of Cameron's triumphs for the 1913 is found in the remarkable silence of the MICHIGAN motor. No motor on a car of any price is more free of noise. So smooth and silent is the MICHIGAN motor that it is almost impossible for any one standing a few feet away to tell whether it is running or not.

Writing in the *Horseless Carriage Gazette*, 1962, Howard Crews reported that the Michigan automobile was powered by a Buda engine, and present owners of surviving Michigan-40 motorcars agree, although nothing in the company's sales literature mentions Buda. The valve covers on these engines, and some are cast aluminum and others stamped, show an "M" enclosed in a circle, but have no identification other than engine casting numbers. The Buda motor is distinct in appearance, however, and the photographs of the engines appearing in the Michigan sales literature for 1912 and 1913 are the same as those appearing in the Buda parts book for 1913. Finally, one current owner of a 1912 Michigan found "Buda" stamped on the piston when he removed it for some mechanical repair.

The Buda Manufacturing Company, of Harvey, Illinois, began building stationary engines in

Fig. 12-16. The 1913 Mighty Michigan Model R Touring car was a big powerful car with a 40 hp Buda engine, four-speed transmission, and the finest exterior painting and interior leather seating, typically available only in higher priced automobiles. The driving and side lamps were electric. The car could be ordered with either a Prest-O-Lite gas starter for $20 or an electric starter for $125. The first automobile electric starter was offered on the 1912 Cadillac, making the 1913 Michigan a very up-to-date automobile. The image is from the 1913 company catalog. (DOL)

1892, but did not initially develop engines for automobiles. The forty-horsepower Buda, measuring 4.25" x 5.25", appeared in the 1912 and 1913 Michigan, as well as the 1913 Kalamazoo truck. Reportedly, the same four-cylinder Buda engine was later used in an early military tank, circa 1915. Both the 1923 Checker and the 1925 Bauer taxis were powered by Budas rated at 22.5 horsepower. These engines had a reputation for quality of manufacture and longevity of service unrivaled in the industry and are still respected among members of the hobby who collect and tour with the Mighty Michigan car.

The Buda engine installed in the Michigan was built with a 2½" crank shaft tied to a four-speed transmission with oversize gears, typical of a sixty horsepower engine, giving the Michigan added strength. An arrangement on the drive train added two universal joints between the engine and the transmission and two between the transmission and the rear end (for a total of four) that, according to the company, allowed full transmission of the engine's power unhampered by the typical torque strain in a rigid unit. The transmission was a four-speed with a direct drive in high gear, comparable to the transmission in much higher priced cars such as the Pierce Arrow at $5,000, the

Mighty Michigan Roadster, Model "S," 40 H. P.
$1,585 Fully Equipped

Fig. 12-17. The 1913 Model S roadster had the same mechanical details and forty-horsepower engine as the Model R, but with a roadster body. Note that the top is not held by leather straps as was used on the 1911 roadsters. This image is from the 1913 sales catalog. (DOL)

Peerless at $4,300, and the Locomobile at $3,600. All three of these cars, however, were powered by a six-cylinder engine that was much larger than the four-cylinder, three hundred cubic-inch engine in the Michigan.

The company's advertising agent portrayed the car with a sense of grandeur, and the power plant and drive train were advertised with much fanfare. The tires were touted as capable of supporting a much larger car, and the Michigan was cited as "over-tired" in company advertisements. The company always referred to the "War of the Forties" among leading car manufacturers in 1913, although there appeared to be no reciprocating reference from other manufacturers to the battle. Michigan Buggy's advertising copy described that war as "the fiercest rivalry this line has known. It is a war of giants, a lining up of masters whom all rivals must respect."

In entering the "War of the Forties," the company claimed that the thirty-horsepower machine was underpowered and therefore unreliable in hilly country, while those above forty-horsepower were overpowered as well as expensive to purchase and maintain. The company asserted that the Michigan-40, with an actual rating of forty-six horsepower, was the middle ground. The Michigan sold at $1,585, and the company claimed "Our War-time price" was the best bargain in its class. To be sure, most of the forty-horsepower automobiles with similar accoutrements were offered at

$2,200 to $6,000. Later testimony by company accountants, however, made clear that the car was too much of a bargain, for the actual production costs of the Michigan approximated the retail cost of the car and, given that dealers purchased cars at a discount, each car was sold at a loss. Michigan Buggy was on the road to bankruptcy in 1909 the day the first motorcar rolled out of the plant.

Fig. 12-18. The 1913 Michigan was W. H. Cameron's WONDER CAR according to the company's sales brochures. His name carried some notoriety, although Bill Cameron, writing in 1990, claims that Michigan Buggy used only the initals "W. H." to create a potential confusion with the notable automotive engineer Everett Scott Cameron, a confusion that could only serve to its advantage. (DOL)

W. H. Cameron was hired as the chief engineer and was given credit for the overall design of the 1913 Michigan-40. The company's advertisements announced the car as Cameron's, identifying it as "Cameron's Great Car," or "Cameron's Wonder Car" and simultaneously cited his past accomplishment of building over 100,000 cars. Cameron had worked at Willys-Overland and had spent a few months at E. M. F. and sometime in 1910 had spent several months in Europe studying automobile manufacturing. He is believed to have joined Michigan Buggy sometime in 1910 or early 1911 since the first 1913 Michigan cars were advertised as being ready for shipment in late fall of 1912. The time required to bring Cameron's design to production and therefore the date of his hire is difficult to estimate.

Interestingly, there was another Cameron in the automobile industry. Everett Scott Cameron was born in Nova Scotia in 1877 and at the age of twenty-two built a three-cylinder steam car. His was a life of accomplishment in the automobile industry before his death in 1965, including a six-cylinder air-cooled engine, a seven-cylinder radial aircraft engine, an inverted marine engine and an air boat, as well as a Cameron-powered tractor and a series of automobiles bearing his name. Cameron had built a considerable reputation during the first decade of the century, both in production of the Cameron car and successful competition at tracks in the United States and England, and there was every possibility that he had some name recognition value by 1912.

Bill Cameron, writing in 1990, suggests that Michigan Buggy did not clarify the Cameron name, and only the initials "W. H." were ever used, thus creating the possibility that Michigan Buggy sought to gain some value in the obvious confusion between the Cameron names by making statements such as "this is a Cameron car."

The body of the 1913 Mighty Michigan was styled by John A. Campbell who was touted by the company as, "the most famous designer in the United States." Reportedly, he had designed vehicle bodies for the King of England and the Sultan of Turkey. The company advertisements concluded that "many of the most distinguished families in Europe and America have long given preference to Mr. Campbell's designs." Campbell's resume is unavailable, but he lived with his wife, Josephine, at 432 Academy Street in Kalamazoo from 1908 through at least 1912 and was identified in the City

Directory as a draftsman at Michigan Buggy in 1911, and as a draftsman or designer in other years. The design of the first Michigan is thought to have begun in 1908 or early 1909. John Campbell was listed as a draftsman in the 1909 Kalamazoo directory; a second draftsman, Jesse Campbell, renting a room at 815 Egleston, was also identified as an employee of Michigan Buggy in that year. There is no assumption of family ties between the two, but the identification of two draftsman suggests design work at the plant increased during 1908 and 1909.

Fig. 12-19. The electric starter with silent chain was mounted next to the universal joint on the shaft between the flywheel, on the left, and the transmission, on the right. The view is from underneath the chassis. (DOL)

The interior finish of the Michigan substantiated the boasts about the quality of manufacture. The seating was the finest grade leather costing twenty-one cents a foot when many higher priced cars used materials costing eighteen cents a foot. The cushions were fourteen inches deep and filled with the finest grade of curled hair, costing fifty cents a pound, processed so that it did not "pack." The leather was finished in a diamond tuft and a "French roll" on the seat backs provided the type of seating available in cars costing $3,000 and higher.

Campbell made several styling improvements to the body from the previous year including an increase in the overall size of the vehicle. The wheelbase for the Michigan-40 was increased from 116" to 118", an attractive lip was added to the front fender, and a bit more sweep given to the trailing edge of the rear fender. A refinement to the hood, and a pronounced cowl with attached windshield, eliminated the conservative appearance of the 1912 model cars. Two large, round headlamps with nickel finish were complemented by large, round surface-mounted electric lamps on either side of the cowl, giving the car an integrated appearance. The cowl lights also featured doors of nickel on the back of the lamp that could be opened to illuminate the speedometer, control switches, and pedals in the interior of the car. A special foot rail and robe rail completed the rear tonneau. The optional dash ventilators at $5 and a clock and light attachment on the speedometer for another $15 were popular options. A complete set of tools was provided in a long tool chest integrated into the running board and included in the base price.

Fig 12-20. The 1913 Mighty Michigan Model L Touring car was powered by a 33 hp four-cylinder Sandusky motor and had all of the accoutrements and quality of construction as the bigger, more powerful 40 hp Model R. The image is from an advertisement extolling the Model L as "America's leading car for the export trade." (DOL)

The electric starter was offered first by Cadillac in 1912, and Michigan Buggy made one available on their cars in 1913 for an additional cost of $125. The starter spun the engine by a silent chain connected to the clutch shaft just behind the flywheel rather than being attached to a ring gear on the flywheel. This arrangement had two advantages. First, if the engine quit in an emergency situation, the car could be moved by using the starter as an electric motor. The company claimed that the starter was capable of turning the engine for two hours until the battery was dead but without harm, and when the battery was recharged the process could be repeated. Second, if the starter would not operate, the chain could be easily removed and the car started by hand-cranking the engine.

The wheels were mounted beneath the frame on four elliptical springs that were strong enough to provide solid support but soft enough to come together on very bumpy roads. In order to prevent the potential for steel striking on steel, a thick rubber bumper was placed between the springs to absorb the shock on the occasions when the spring was fully compressed. The two-wheel brakes were large and of the expanding type mounted on the inside of the hub. Many manufacturers in this era mounted the brakes external to the hub leaving the brake surfaces open to mud and water.

The steering wheel was mounted on the left and the controls were mounted in the center of the dash with full electrical power including the starter, side lamps, headlights, and horn. These electrical accoutrements were considerable achievements in comparison to much larger manufacturers—Buick and Ford for example—which were still offering acetylene gas lighting and oil side lamps. Of special interest were the adjustable steering column and foot pedals that the company touted as a convenience for women and girls. The fact that Frank Lay, Sr. and George Lay were both small men, while the younger son, Frank, Jr., was well over six feet tall, might also have had something to do with this convenience. Another advertised attraction for women drivers was the leather-faced cone clutch, which replaced the multiple disc unit of 1912 and was soft enough to be pushed by hand.

Fig 12-21. The 1913 Mighty Michigan Model O Roadster was powered by the same engine and was finished with the same quality as the 33 hp Model L. Photographs of the Model O are not easily available, and are not included in the 1913 sales brochure, suggesting that few were ever built. (DOL)

Standard finish for the 1913 Michigan was a black body, fenders and hood with white striping. The interior was black Spanish leather, and the top was a black silk mohair with matching boot and trimmings. Three other combinations were available for an additional $25. First was a Michigan Golden Auto-Brown on the body, fenders, and hood with a lighter brown striping edged with a fine line of gold. The brown paint, described as "a mellow golden brown," was first introduced on the 1912 automobiles and was claimed to be an "eye catcher." Seating for this option was brown Spanish leather with a brown silk mohair top, matching boot, and trimmings. A second option was silver gray paint on the body, fenders, and hood, with a dark gray stripe and a narrow edge of gold; seating was gray Spanish leather with a gray mohair top, matching boot, and trimmings. The final option was the Michigan deep olive green applied to the body and hood with black fenders and white striping. The seating was a dull black leather and the top a black mohair with matching boot and trimmings. The running gear for all color options was black.

The variety of color was a manufacturing extravagance for a car in this price range; most companies had a single color per model year. Baked enamel had been used for years by bicycle manufacturers, and many automobile manufacturers began experimenting with it around 1908. Metal parts could be sprayed or dipped and then baked, but only a black paint based on Gilsonite, a pigment derived from coal, could withstand the 450-degree curing process. Michigan bodies were steel over wood, common at the time, and wood would burn or split at the high drying temperature required for paint. These characteristics explain why the fenders, hoods, and other metal parts of early cars were usually painted black while the wood-formed body was painted another color: only the black could be baked for a durable finish. The 1915 all-steel-body Dodge was painted entirely with black enamel and then cured at 450 degrees without harm. Henry Ford's famous adage of the time—that a Model T was available in any color as long as it was black—reflected the limitations of the manufacturing process rather than a personal quirk or conservative aversion to color.

The alternative to black enamel was layer after layer of clearcoat varnish over a color coat. In 1913 this finish work was a long and tedious process performed by patient and meticulous men. The process is described in company documents, as well as by Lamm in his 1997 history on the subject. The body was first prepared with a thorough cleaning and sanding, then coated with a mixture of half lead and half body filler followed by a series of coatings and repeated sanding that were rubbed out progressively with finer and finer material—first pumice, then moss hair, and then felt. An additional secret three-step process was also used by Michigan Buggy to insure evenness and permanence of the finish. After the final sanding, twenty-two coats, including undercoating, color and varnish, were brushed carefully over the body, each at right angles to the previous coat, and finished with several coats of rubbing varnish that were polished at each step to the evenness of fine ivory. These final coats had the consistency of molasses, and each one took a week or two to air-dry, thus requiring the construction of massive facilities to provide large areas in which the bodies could be stored for long periods without disturbance. The transport of car bodies in various stages of painting about the building required the employ of gangs of men who did nothing more than move bodies from one place to another through these painstaking operations. The entire process took six weeks.

The quality of the final finish was a credit to the patience of craftsmen who worked with two badger hair brushes. The first brush was used to apply the paint or varnish and the second picked off bits of lint and dirt nicknamed "lice." Paint rooms were kept clean and illuminated, but there were always "lice" in the air. The painters usually wore no shirts and, even in the summer heat, covered their arms and chests with linseed oil to reduce the circulation of lint and dust. The finished product glowed spectacularly but, in spite of all the care and preparation, within a year the varnish would oxidize and begin to darken, and within two or three years the color clouded. For cars driven often, and in inclement weather, rain drops would magnify the sunlight, leaving small permanent spots on the finish. A bird dropping had a similar but even more destructive effect. Some wealthy owners would order two bodies for a car, and periodically return one to the coach builder for revarnishing. In spite of these difficulties, Michigan Buggy was proud of the vehicle's finish and asserted that their process, with all of its secret steps, "gave each MIGHTY MICHIGAN the famous finish which never fails to excite the pride of the owner and the admiration of everyone who sees it."

The 1913 Michigan was an impressive automobile: big, powerful, and reasonably fast. With its four-speed transmission, forty-horsepower engine, and high-quality finish, this car was competitive with Locomobile, Lozier, and Pierce Arrow. Featuring leather seating, the latest electrical conveniences, a chain-driven electric starter, and adjustable driving controls, all at a cost of only $1,585, it was more of a bargain than the company could afford to offer. Eventually unpaid creditors and a bit of fraud brought the company to its knees, but that, as they say, is another chapter.

Fig. 12-22. "Some Things to Consider" was a large 2' x 3' poster intended to be hung on the salesroom or garage wall so that potential customers might make essential comparisons between the Mighty Michigan Model R and other automobiles. It is an interesting and seldom-seen piece of early advertising. (DOL)

REFERENCES

The Factory Back of The Car. *Motor*, March 1912, p. 79.

Michigan Buggy Adding. *The Automobile*, December 26, 1912, p. 1338.

Horseless Carriages Will Be Made by Lane & Lay. *Kalamazoo Daily Telegraph*, February 16, 1903.

"Kalamazoo" Name of New Automobile. *Kalamazoo Daily Telegraph*, July 15, 1903.

The Michigan Buggy Company. *The Horseless Age*, August 1903, p. 12.

Kalamazoo High Grade Carriages. Michigan Buggy Catalog, 1904.

10,000 Michigan Agents. *Automobile Topics*, March 30, 1912, p. 346.

The Cannon Auto. *The Automobile*, February 12, 1904, pp. 190–191.

Howard Crews. "Evolution of the Michigan." *The Horseless Carriage Gazette*, January–February 1962, pp. 16–20.

Frank D. Fuller. *Board Minutes*, Michigan Automobile Co. Ltd. 1902–1914.

Michigan Changes Name. *The Automobile*, January 23, 1913, p. 275.

Michigan Motor Car Company. *Automobile Trade Journal*, October 1912, p. 94.

Names Cause Confusion. *The Accessory and Garage Journal*, March 1913, p. 32.

Fuller & Sons, Mfg. Co. Succeeds Michigan Automobile Co., Ltd. *Horseless Age*, January 22, 1913, p. 176.

Michigan Motor Car Company Annual Report for 1912, January 1913.

Michigan Automobiles for 1912. Michigan Buggy Catalog.

Michigan Buggy One of Kalamazoo's Largest Industrial Institutions. *The Kalamazoo Gazette*, July 20, 1913.

Palmer to Testify in Own Behalf. *Kalamazoo Telegraph-Press*, April 4, 1914.

Mighty Michigan "40"—$1500. *Automobile Topics*, March 30, 1912, p. 347.

Ship a Carload of "Michigans." *The Kalamazoo Gazette*, April 8, 1910.

Kalamazoo Pioneer in Automobile History. *The Kalamazoo Gazette*, February 20, 1912.

The Michigan. *Kalamazoo Evening Telegraph*, May 28, 1910.

Left Hand Control Adopted by Many. *The Automobile*, January 18, 1912, p. 218.

The Wonderful Michigan Electric Lighted Line. Michigan Sales Brochure, Spring 1910.

Jan P. Norbye and Michael Lamm. "Making Light of The Subject." *Automobile Quarterly*, Vol. 36, No. 3. May 1997, pp. 94–99.

Michigan Auto Runs to Pittsburgh in 21 Hrs. 28 min. *Kalamazoo Evening Telegraph*, circa May 27, 1910.

Michigan "30." 1911 Sales Catalog from Dewey & Company, Plano, Illinois.

To Hold Local Auto Contest. *The Kalamazoo Gazette*, June 16, 1910.

Out-of-Town Autos in Endurance Run. *The Kalamazoo Gazette*, June 17, 1910.

Machines to Start From Gazette Office. *The Kalamazoo Gazette*, June 18, 1910.

Cable-Nelson Mgr. Auto Run Victim Had Death Premonition. *The Kalamazoo Gazette*, June 30, 1910.

Endurance Run is Abandoned. *Kalamazoo Evening Telegraph*, June 30, 1910.

Automobile Judge Meets Death. *The Kalamazoo Gazette*, June 30, 1910.

Death Rides with Autoist. *The Kalamazoo Gazette*, July 1, 1910.

William Neely. *The Jim Gilmore Story*. Tucson, Arizona: Aztec Corporation, 1988.

Same Place, Same Men, Same Make Car. *Kalamazoo Gazette*. July 19, 1959.

Michigan Gasoline Cars. *Cycle and Automobile Trade Journal*, March 1911, pp. 168, 194.

Michigan Buggy Company's Flush Side Body. *The Horseless Age*, January 4, 1911, p. 49.

Michigan Buggy. *The Automobile*, January 5, 1911, pp. 95, 98.

Michigan. *Motor Age*, January 5, 1911, pp. 70–71.

Announcing the Dominant Star in the Automotive World; The Michigan.
    Michigan Buggy Company Catalog for 1911.

Michigan "40" $1,500. *The Motor World*, October 26, 1911, p. 337.

Save $600. *The Carriage Dealers Journal*, December 1911, p. 21.

Michigan Automobiles Announcement 1912. Michigan Buggy Catalog, New York Show,
    January 1912.

Creating New Business. Information brochure for the agents of Michigan Buggy Company,
    Kalamazoo, Michigan.

Michigan Cars for 1912 with Long Stroke Engines. *Automobile Trade Journal*, April 1912,
    pp. 210–213.

A. L. Dyke. *Dyke's Automobile Encyclopedia*, Third edition: St. Louis: A. L. Dyke Publisher,
    1913.

Michigan Has Two Chassis. *The Automobile*, February 1, 1912, p. 390.

Mighty Michigan Forty. *The Automobile*, August 8, 1912, p. 86.

Michigan Pleasure Cars. *Automobile Trade Journal,* February 1912, p. 220.

Michigan Roadster. *Motor Age*, January 25, 1912, pp. 20–24.

Michigan Line Is Thoroughly Reconstructed. *Motor World*, November 28, 1912, p. 19–20.

Michigan Gasoline Cars. *Automobile Trade Journal*, March 1912, p.190.

Mighty Michigan Forty. *The Automobile*, June 27, 1912, p. 86.

New Michigan Models. *The Horseless Age*, July 10, 1912, p. 64.

Michigan Motor Cars. *Automobile Dealer and Repairer*, July 1912, p. 66.

Embarrassment of the Sandusky Auto Parts and Motor Truck Company.
    Automobile Trade Journal, October 1913, p. 197.

Coast Representation for the Michigan. *The Horseless Age*, September 4, 1912, p. 366.

San Francisco, Cal. *Motor Age*, September 1912, p. 51.

Michigan Establishes Branch. *The Accessory and Garage Journal*, October, 1912, p. 9.

Removals and Trade Changes. *Automobile Trade Journal*, October 1912, p. 92A.

Now Europe, Too. *Automobile Dealer and Repairer*, December 1912.

Michigan Cars in Moscow. *Motor*, June 1913, p. 97.

American Cars in Italy. *Motor Age*, July 17, 1913, p. 27.

Michigan—Adopts Left Drive. *The Automobile*, January 9, 1913, p. 125.

The Mighty Michigan 40 for 1913. Michigan Motor Car Company Catalog.

The Mighty Michigan "33" Model L. Michigan Motor Car Company Sales Brochure for 1913.

Victor Palmer Believed 1913 Circular True. *The Kalamazoo Gazette*, April 4, 1914.

A Strong Guarantee. *The Automobile*, March 28, 1912.

Sandusky's Assets and Liabilities Almost Equal. *Motor World*, November 27, 1913, p. 10.

Dauch Buys Sandusky Truck Plant. *The Horseless Age*, March 11, 1914, p. 394.

Drafts for Faulty Cars Not Binding on Dealers. *Motor World*, September 4, 1913, p. 8.

Need Not Pay for Faulty Engines. *Automobile Topics*, October 25, 1913, p. 836.

Auto Parts Company Exhibits Michigan Car Parts. *Automobile Trade Journal*, February 1914, p. 97.

Dauch Incorporates for $1,000,000 to Take Sandusky Parts. *Automobile Topics*, April 11, 1914, p. 637.

The Mighty Michigan Factory Behind the Car. Company Sales Brochure for 1913.

Buda Motors Transmissions and Unit Power Plants. Bradenburg and Company catalog No. 172, circa 1913.

C. H. Wendel. *American Gasoline Engines Since 1872*. Osceola, WI: Motorbooks International, 1994.

The War of 1913. *The Automobile*, September 5, 1912, p. 132.

To Win the Fiercest War. *Automobile Dealer and Repairer*, October 1912, p. 66.

Cameron's Great Car—Find a "40" Like It. *The Automobile*, November 7, 1912, p. 137.

Lesser Forties Can't Compete With This. *Motor Age*, January 16, 1913, p. 118.

W. H. Cameron. *Automobile Trade Journal*, July 1912, p. 91.

William T. Cameron. *The Cameron Story*. Tucson, Arizona: International Society of Vehicle Preservation, 1990.

America's Leading Car for the Export Trade. Company Sales Brochure, 1913.

The Mighty Michigan for the Woman That Drives. Company Sales Brochure, 1913.

Michigan Gasoline Pleasure Cars. *Automobile Trade Journal*, March 1913, p. 216.

Mighty Michigan "40." *Automobile Trade Journal*, May 1913, p. 311.

New York Show. *The Horseless Age*, January 15, 1913, p. 123.

Michigan Pedals. *Motor World*, January 16, 1913.

Mighty Michigan "40." *The Automobile*, December 26, 1912, p. 94.

Adjustable Automobile Pedals. *The Automobile*, August 7, 1913, p. 237.

Series of New Models, Michigan "40." *Motor*, December 1912, p. 100.

Men Will Want These Things This Year in a "40." *Motor Car*, January 1913, p. 68.

Michigan Model R Touring Car. *Automobile Trade Journal*, January 1913, p. 138–138A.

Passenger Car Chassis List. *The Automobile*, January 9, 1913, pp. 142–143.

Michael Lamm. How Cars Got Colors. *Invention and Technology*, Spring 1997, pp. 62–63.

Arnie Dickson and Charles Fernandez. "Chronology of Automotive Paint," *Old Cars Weekly News and Market Place*, April 9, 1992.

The Mighty Michigan Painting. Company Brochure for 1913.

Michigan Motor Car Company. *Automobile Trade Journal*, April 1914, p. 86.

The Story Begins With the Kalamazoo River...

The Kalamazoo River was the primary route into the Kalamazoo valley when French traders arrived by canoe and the first fur trading post was built in 1824. The postcard at left is circa 1910—and the women in the canoes are not French traders. (DOL)

Michigan Central Bridge, Kalamazoo, Mich.

In 1846 the tracks of the Michigan Central Railroad connected Detroit and Kalamazoo, opening access to the east by train and eventually replacing the river as the primary means of commercial transportation. The postcard above is circa 1915. (DOL)

The river served as the means for early transportation, and the portage around its rapids and hospitable land on its banks defined the location of the first settlement that became Kalamazoo. The postcard at right, with its jaunty boating party, is circa 1911. (DOL)

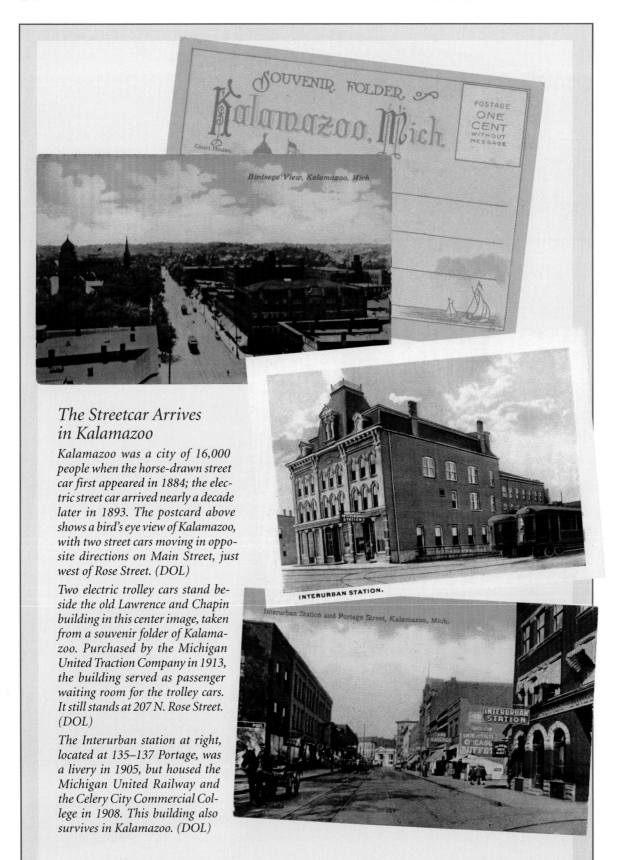

The Streetcar Arrives in Kalamazoo

Kalamazoo was a city of 16,000 people when the horse-drawn street car first appeared in 1884; the electric street car arrived nearly a decade later in 1893. The postcard above shows a bird's eye view of Kalamazoo, with two street cars moving in opposite directions on Main Street, just west of Rose Street. (DOL)

Two electric trolley cars stand beside the old Lawrence and Chapin building in this center image, taken from a souvenir folder of Kalamazoo. Purchased by the Michigan United Traction Company in 1913, the building served as passenger waiting room for the trolley cars. It still stands at 207 N. Rose Street. (DOL)

The Interurban station at right, located at 135–137 Portage, was a livery in 1905, but housed the Michigan United Railway and the Celery City Commercial College in 1908. This building also survives in Kalamazoo. (DOL)

Kalamazoo's First Auto

Kalamazoo's first automobile, a steam-powered Locomobile purchased by George W. Taylor, arrived in Kalamazoo in the spring of 1900. The car was subsequently sold to W. E. Upjohn, and is currently on display at the Gilmore Car Museum. (DOL)

The postcard shows Lovers Lane, a road often driven by W. E. Upjohn, just south of Kalamazoo. (DOL)

The Sport of Automobiling

In the spring of 1903, Archibald Campbell took delivery of an Orient Buckboard built in Waltham, Massachusetts. That Orient Buckboard, shown at top, is now on display at the Gilmore Car Museum. (GCA) Campbell was employed at the Upjohn Company and lived at 606 W. South Street, not too far distant from the scene depicted on the postcard at left. (DOL) In August 1903, he challenged other owners of light cars to a race at Recreation Park and on the broad avenue of Main Street, shown in the postcard at right. (DOL)

The Driving Season

The snowy scene on the postcard at right is Lovell Street in the winter of 1908. (DOL) During the first decade of the 20th century, the driving season was restricted to the months of good weather. When it snowed, people who owned a horseless carriage parked it in the barn and turned to horse-drawn sleighs for transportation along with the rest of the population. The Michigan Portland Cutter below is owned by Chris and Ann Garlitz, and is a beautiful example of a period sleigh, circa 1908. (CAG)

The Michigan Buggy Company built sleighs and horse-drawn vehicles in plants at Porter and Willard Streets before two fires forced them to build at Reed Avenue and Factory Street.

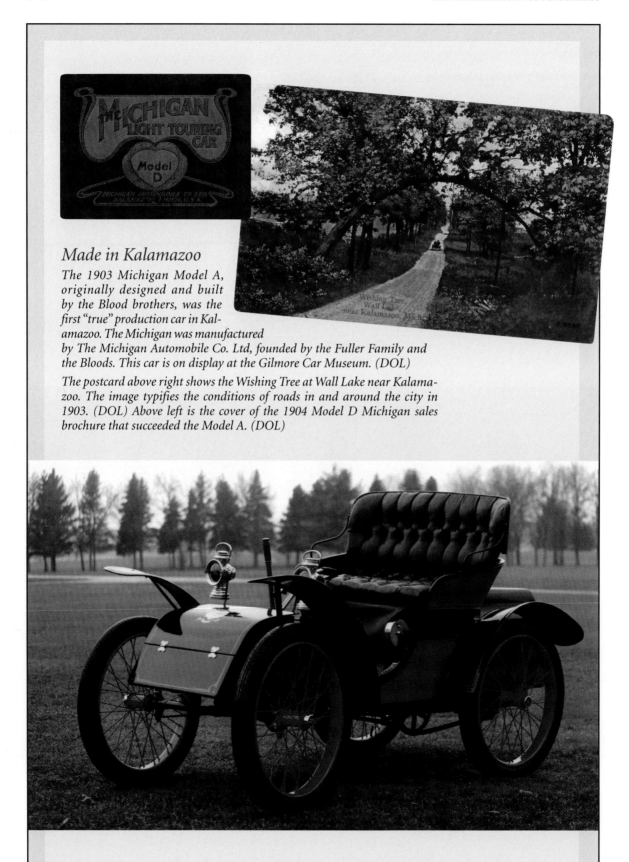

Made in Kalamazoo

The 1903 Michigan Model A, originally designed and built by the Blood brothers, was the first "true" production car in Kalamazoo. The Michigan was manufactured by The Michigan Automobile Co. Ltd, founded by the Fuller Family and the Bloods. This car is on display at the Gilmore Car Museum. (DOL)

The postcard above right shows the Wishing Tree at Wall Lake near Kalamazoo. The image typifies the conditions of roads in and around the city in 1903. (DOL) Above left is the cover of the 1904 Model D Michigan sales brochure that succeeded the Model A. (DOL)

Kalamazoo's First Dealership

The Cadillac rear-entrance tonneau in the photograph above cost $850 in 1903, and by 1905 there were five Cadillac automobiles in Kalamazoo. (DOL)

William O. Harlow sold Cadillacs from his sporting goods store on South Burdick. (Note the Cadillac sign in the postcard above, circa 1912.) Repairs were made in the alley in the back of the store. (DOL)

The Allendale Hotel, Gull Lake, Mich.   12650

The King of Sports, The Queen of Amusements

The Model T Ford first appeared in late 1908, and the 1910 models decked out in red paint and sparkling brass made quite an impression at the inaugural automobile show in Kalamazoo in the winter of 1910. The Philip Glass agency sold six 1910 Model T Fords during that show. (DOL)

By the summer of 1910, the Gull Lake area was a popular vacation and recreational spot and an enjoyable destination for automobilists. This postcard shows the Allendale Hotel, one of the popular attractions at the lake. (DOL)

Eyes on Kalamazoo, 1914

Two identical Delage race cars, with Grand Prix specification, were built in Europe in 1913. After competing in several races on the continent, they were shipped to the U.S. to compete in the 1914 Indianapolis 500 race. René Thomas drove the number "16" car to first place and Albert Guyot placed third in the number "10" Delage. The cars were then shipped back to New York City in preparation for return to Europe. Billy Knipper, a well-known race car driver at the time, found both cars on the docks in a New York harbor and purchased one—presumably the car that had finished first. In the fall of 1914, this Delage was driven to third place in Kalamazoo with Claude (Jack) Newhouse at the wheel; the trophy is shown at right. (DOL)

The Delage appeared again at the Indianapolis race in 1915 and, based on starting position, was renumbered "17," racing against the Cornelian for a second time. This time John DePalma was at the wheel, but the car was withdrawn after forty-one laps because of a loose flywheel. The DeLage disappeared following the race, but surfaced again after World War II and is now on display at the Indianapolis Motor Speedway Hall of Fame Museum. (IMS)

Recreation Park, in Kalamazoo, was the site of the Grand Circuit for trotting horses and the first 100-mile automobile race in 1914. That race included Howard Blood's Cornelian. The postcard at left depicts the horse race and is dated 1912. (DOL)

On to the Indianapolis 500

The 1913 Model L45 was one of three race cars built by Peugeot in France and shipped to the United States in 1914. Bob Burman drove one of the three to first place at Kalamazoo in September 1914. Dario Resta, who drove the car shown here, placed second at the Indianapolis 500 in 1915 and subsequently won the grand event in 1916. The car is owned presently by the Bothwell family and is the only surviving member of the three original 1913 Peugeot race cars. Its 274 cid engine and qualifying speed of 98.58 mph made it one of the "elephants" that dwarfed the small Cornelian in 1915. (BRC)

The image on the postcard above is an early depiction of the Indianapolis race course where the grand 500 mile race was first run in 1911. In 1915, Louis Chevrolet drove Howard Blood's Cornelian to a twentieth place finish, and the programme is from that year. (DOL)

The Cornelian: A Grasshopper Among Elephants

The 1915 Cornelian race car did not survive; the car above is a "re-creation" of the original. Al Rohrstaff of Kalamazoo started with a Sterling engine, and a Cornelian radiator, cap, badge, and steering wheel. He reproduced every construction detail, installing each bolt and rivet to re-create the original monocoque body. In the photo above, the car sits in front of the old Blood Brothers factory at 633 W. Ransom where the Cornelian was built until December 1914. (DOL)

The postcard depicts the beginning of the Indianapolis race and is dated 1913. (DOL)

The Gold Miner's Deposit

This 1911 Michigan, Model H, number 1001, with 33 hp Falls engine, is owned by William Cuthbert. This car was impounded by a hotel in San Francisco, circa 1914, when an erstwhile gold miner couldn't pay his bill for food and lodging. It was found by Bill's father in the 1950s, when he was approached by a man seeking a "dima fer a cuppa caffee." He agreed to provide money in exchange for information about the location of an antique car. Much to his surprise, the man led him into the basement of the hotel where the car was hidden behind many decades of accumulated junk. His successful negotiation with the hotel management saved the car from the ravages of time. (BCC)

The accompanying postcard shows the Rickman Hotel on North Burdick Street, the departure point for the trip from Kalamazoo to Pittsburgh with the 1910 Model B Michigan. (DOL)

HOTEL RICKMAN
ABSOLUTELY FIRE PROOF
KALAMAZOO,   MICHIGAN.
UNDER NEW MANAGEMENT
WALTER BARNES   -:-   R. LEE PFEIFFER

Frank's Dream: The Michigan

This 1912 Model K Michigan, owned by Bill McCleary, is shown with the nickel lamps and trimmings that were standard in that year. (DOL)

Frank Lay purchased the stately conservative residence at 523 West South Street, circa 1909, and lived there until his death. The home still stands in Kalamazoo. (DOL)

Victor Palmer and the 1912 Michigan

This 1912 Model K Michigan, owned by Jim and Loretta Cesari, is shown with brass lights and trimmings. Nickel trim was standard in 1912, and the company boasted about its superiority over brass, but brass fittings were still an advertised option. (JLC)

The postcard depicts the famed Burdick Hotel and the Hanselman building at the corner of Main and Burdick Streets. A city center in its day, the Burdick was the site of the argument that almost came to blows between Victor Palmer and M. Henry Lane following Palmer's testimony at the bankruptcy hearing. (DOL)

A Mighty Survivor

This 1913 Michigan with Buda engine was found in Iowa with fewer than 6,000 miles on the odometer. According to legend, the teenage son who was assigned driving chores always had an excuse—tires low, gas near empty, weather too hot—for not taking his grandmother (the car owner) where she wished to go. In a fit of anger, she told the young man to put the car up on blocks in the barn as it would not be driven again, and that instruction was never revoked by any successive generation. The car was found in 1992 and shown at the Hershey Meet in 1993. It was subsequently purchased by John McMullen, who restored it to its original specifications. (JMC)

The postcard on the left shows Burdick Street looking north from Main Street, circa 1913. The car on the left has the general characteristic of the 1913 Michigan, except the distinctive cowl lights are missing. (DOL) The postcard on the right shows West Main Street in Kalamazoo; the stone home on the left is the "Lane Castle" at 507 West Main, residence of Henry Lane, original founder of the Michigan Buggy Company. The home was demolished after World War II. (DOL)

At the Station

This 1913 Michigan Model R, finished in silver with red trimming, is owned by Jonathan Weiner. (DOL)

During the 1914 bankruptcy hearings, Victor and Mary Palmer attempted to escape from Kalamazoo to New York City. The early arrival of their luggage at the Michigan Central Station sent a warning to the court officials, and their plan was foiled before the train arrived. The station in Kalamazoo (shown at right on a souvenir postcard folder, circa 1914) has been historically renovated and looks much the same today. (DOL)

The Beauties of Limousine Body

In 1928, E. L. Cord announced the purchase of a majority of stock in Limousine Body; after that, most of Limousine's production was dedicated to Auburn and Cord automobiles. The Auburn convertible sedan, the seven-passenger sedan and the cabriolet, and the Cord cabriolet and the convertible sedan were built in Kalamazoo. The 1930 L-29 Cord convertible sedan with front-wheel drive (above) is owned by Richard and Janet Saddler. (DOL) The 1931 Auburn phaeton with rear-wheel drive (below) is owned by Wes Myrick. (DOL)

The Luxurious Kalamazoo "55-12"

The Luxurious Kalamazoo

The sales brochure for the Kalamazoo Series 55 rail bus manufactured by the Kalamazoo Railway Supply Company, circa 1922–29, shows a variety of vehicles, including the Officials' Inspection car, "especially designed for comfort, safety and speed." At top is the company's letterhead used before 1896. (DOL)

KALAMAZOO MANUFACTURING COMPANY
FORMER NAME—KALAMAZOO RAILWAY SUPPLY COMPANY
Railway Motor Cars and Equipment
KALAMAZOO RAILWAY
SUPPLY DIVISION   CABLE ADDRESS: VELOCIPEDE
                                                        GENERAL OFFICES and FACTORY
                                                        KALAMAZOO 24E, MICHIGAN, U.S.A.

GREYHOUND

The Exciting Escorter

The "Greyhound Escorter" (top) is believed to be an experimental model developed by Kalamazoo Manufacturing in 1963. The purpose, or extent of the competition, for which this vehicle was designed is unknown. (DOL)

The K-series platform truck was a rugged workhorse for "lateral material handling" inside and outside the plant. The truck was powered by a Chrysler slant-six 225 cid engine, rated at 132 horsepower. (DOL)

At the Country Club

*This beautiful 1920 Roamer roadster is finished in yellow with black fenders and yellow
leather upholstery. It is similar to the first Roamer sold in Kalamazoo in 1917. (GCA)
The postcard depicts the Kalamazoo Country Club, with perhaps a Roamer in the drive,
circa 1918. (DOL)*

Roamer: Beautiful, Striking and Speedy

"We are the originators of the Sport Model, and made it popular. This model is beautiful, striking and speedy," read the advertisement copy in this 1921 Roamer brochure. (DOL) The 1921 L-88, with all of the appearance of a Rolls Royce, sold well to people of reputation in this country and on the European continent as well. The example below is owned by Ivan Richards. (DOL)

The Elegant
Roamer Landaulet

The 1920 Roamer Landaulet was intended to be chauffeur-driven and is believed to have been bodied by Rubay. This Roamer is on display at the Gilmore Car Museum. (GCA)

Roamer advertisements always placed the cars in elegant settings. The cover of the 1921 sales brochure, distributed at the January 15, 1921 National Automobile Show in New York, shows a chauffeur-driven touring car with Victoria top, somewhere in southern California. (DOL)

Barley: It's Roamer-Built

The Barley was introduced in 1923 by the Roamer Motor Car Company in an effort to attract additional sales. This was a lower-priced car, but had all the quality of construction as the more expensive Roamer. (DOL) Five hundred shares of Roamer Motor Car Company stock were issued on March 6, 1923 following a company reorganization and a change in name from The Barley Motor Car Company. The stock is signed by A. C. Barley as president. (DOL)

ROAMER
America's Smartest Car

THE crowning touch, the indispensable link, that unites city and country, is the motor car. And thrice blessed is he whose equipage combines unfailing power, individuality of line and moderate maintenance, to the exceptional degree which characterizes every Handley-Knight.

Touring in the Handley-Knight.

A beautiful example of advertising for the Handley-Knight touring car from a company sales brochure, circa 1921–22. (DOL)

THE ideal car for theater party, social driving, cross-country tours—all-round, all-season comfort and dependability for every motoring occasion—is this Handley-Knight Sedan. Lacking no least essential of luxury, its performance is equally distinguished for everyday economy.

Stepping Out in the Handley-Knight

An elegantly illustrated advertisement for the Handley-Knight sedan in a company sales brochure, circa 1921–22. (DOL)

Handley-Knight: America's Finest

This 1921 Handley-Knight, with sleeve valve engine, is on display at the Gilmore Car Museum. (DOL) The stock certificate above was issued in May 1920 at $32.50. The company was incorporated with $1 million in capital, but it is worth recalling that Walter P. Chrysler's annual salary at Willys-Overland in 1921 was $1 million. The stock was purchased by C. S. Campbell, who signed the certificate as vice-president. (DOL) The knight on the 1921 company sales brochure was an image used extensively in Handley-Knight advertising. (DOL)

Hey, Taxi!

The Pennant cab (inset) was manufactured by the Roamer Motor Car Company in 1923–24, using the Barley chassis. The Pennant is not well known, although, when first introduced, some assumed Roamer would give up its passenger car production to concentrate on taxi cabs. (DOL) The similarity between the 1923 Pennant cab and the 1923 Checker cab (top) is striking, but their histories are vastly different. The Pennant was gone by 1925 and the Checker survived for almost sixty years. (DOL)

Checker: Strength and Beauty

The 1923 Checker (top) is believed to be one of the first built in Kalamazoo. It was retained for many years at the Checker plant and eventually placed on display at the Gilmore Car Museum. (DOL) The 1936 Checker Model Y (below) had the same body lines as the 1933 Checker Model T, but the front end treatment is distinctively different with its massive radiator shell and simple stainless steel strips attached to the wire mesh grill. (DOL)

Art Deco Cabs

The 1933 Checker Model T was noted for its art deco design, with sculptured fenders cut back at the top and a low silhouette windshield. This car is on display at the ACD Museum in Auburn, Indiana. (ACD) The logo is from the 1930 Checker Parts Book. (DOL)

The Checker Legacy

The slab-sided A-8 first appeared in 1956, a style that continued with minimal change until the end of production in 1982. The yellow and green cab above is circa 1958. (DOL) Checker began manufacturing for the consumer market in 1960 as "an uncomplicated approach to what you want most in a car." The Marathon 4-door sedan was typical of their offerings. (DOL) The Checker Aerobus below was a popular mode of transportation to and from the major airports in America. This image is from a 1969 company sales brochure. (DOL)

CHECKER *Marathon 4 door Sedan*

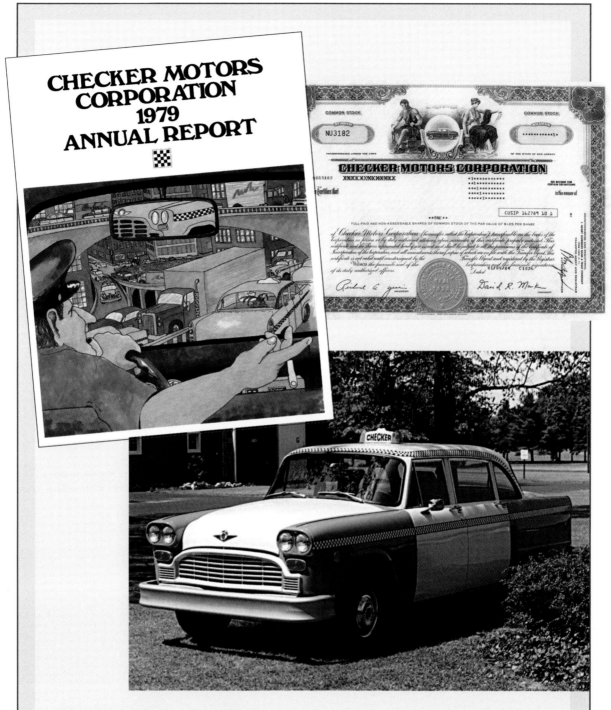

The Dawn Before the Fall

The cover of the 1979 Checker Motors Corporation annual report, with its humorous illustration by artist Steve Hansen, shows a city full of the ubiquitous Checker. The corporate mood was good, although disaster was just around the corner. The last Checker, produced in July 1982, was finished in green and cream with the traditional checkerboard trim. This car is on display at the Gilmore Car Musuem. By 1984, manufacture of the famed Checker was just company history. The Checker stock certificate for a single share is from that year and signed by David Markin as president. (DOL)

"People Gawked and Pointed..."

The 1991 edition of the Sunseeker, built by students in the mechanical engineering program at Western Michigan University, gives a futuristic peek at the possible car models of tomorrow. (WMU) At top, the Sunseeker team races after Western Michigan University's entry in the '91 race for solar-powered cars. Time *magazine reported "...along the way, people gawked and pointed, squinted and saluted, did double takes, took snapshots and lifted small children to give them a better look at what their future might be." (WMU)*

Part III

MICHIGAN BUGGY DOOMED

1913–1917

∾

The streets of Kalamazoo appear quiet in the summer of 1913, just before the Michigan Buggy Company closed its doors. The trolley cars provided public conveyance, and several cars are parked along the curb, although bicycles remained a popular means of transportation. (WMU)

Chapter 13

The Ledger

July and August 1913

*In view of the company's rather peculiar
and incomplete method of accounting,
we have been only partially successful in securing answers.*
                                —Summary of auditors

The financial transactions of the Michigan Buggy Company were entered into large ledgers trimmed in leather and canvas. The flair of the quill pen, the accompanying initial of the bookkeeper, and the dctail of the entries suggested a precision of accounting that proved to be an unfortunate illusion. A sample of entries from the company ledger follows.

∽ ACCOUNTS RECEIVABLE ∽

Dec 4, 1911	Sale of Colt to F.B. Lay	– ck	60.00
April 20, 1912	Sam Folz Auto	– ck	50.00
May 4, 1912	Penna Sales Corp.	– ck	33,975.00

∽ EXPENDITURES ∽

May 4, 1912	C.E. Johnson	– 3# Grease	.12
	S.A. Morrison	– Cleaning cesspool	10.00
	Henderson Ames Co.	1½ yards Moleskin	2.25

∽ DEPOSITS ∽

May 8, 1912	C.C. Nat Bank	5,144.78
	Kal Save	2,363.20
	Kal Nat Bank	14,484.55

Once it became public that its apparent financial stability was an illusion, the demise of the Michigan Buggy Company was rapid. Although the exact moment of the onset of the crisis is unknown, most probably, like a spring storm, it gathered slowly. The first evidence of the company's financial trouble began to appear in the spring of 1913. Various suppliers had difficulty obtaining payment for delivered goods, and rumors that the company was $1 million in debt circulated about Cleveland, Ohio. One supplier from that city appeared at the Michigan Buggy factory with his attorney and a simple demand: "I am either going to have cars, money or trouble."

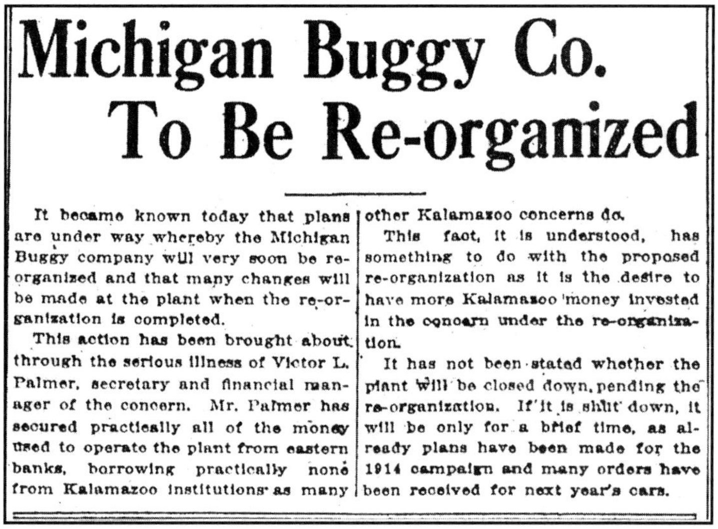

An accommodation was quickly negotiated. Thirteen Mighty Michigan cars were delivered to his Cleveland plant between July 22 and July 24, 1913, and a credit of $17,225 was applied against his claim. Reportedly, a Detroit firm used a similar tactic and also received several vehicles before the

Michigan Buggy Co. To Be Re-organized

It became known today that plans are under way whereby the Michigan Buggy company will very soon be re-organized and that many changes will be made at the plant when the re-organization is completed.

This action has been brought about through the serious illness of Victor L. Palmer, secretary and financial manager of the concern. Mr. Palmer has secured practically all of the money used to operate the plant from eastern banks, borrowing practically none from Kalamazoo institutions as many

other Kalamazoo concerns do.

This fact, it is understood, has something to do with the proposed re-organization as it is the desire to have more Kalamazoo money invested in the concern under the re-organization.

It has not been stated whether the plant will be closed down, pending the re-organization. If it is shut down, it will be only for a brief time, as already plans have been made for the 1914 campaign and many orders have been received for next year's cars.

Fig 13-2. Kalamazoo Telegraph-Press *headline from July 31, 1913.*

month was out. The rest of the creditors were not so lucky and some months later George B. Lay, Jr. admitted that the Michigan Buggy Company creditors "had been buffaloed" in the spring and summer of 1913.

The financial crises worsened during the summer and toward the middle of July 1913, numerous reorganization meetings were held at the factory, at Victor Palmer's home, and at the Lane Castle. The participants included M. Henry Lane and Frank Lay, Sr., the company directors; Victor Palmer, company treasurer; and Stephen B. Monroe, then president of the Kalamazoo City Savings Bank. Charles E. Johnson, assistant secretary of the company, and Morris S. Arnold, head of the auditing department, also attended on occasion.

At one meeting, Henry Lane presented a financial statement to the group that showed an indebtedness of $3 million, although he also estimated that the payment of pending notes from dealers would be almost sufficient to raise this amount. Working capital was limited and a plan to raise $200,000 was proposed, calling for Lay and Lane to mortgage all of their personal property and financial holdings. A dispute between the two about financial withdrawals from the company and the Lay family's removal of Henry Lane as president of the company had chilled the relationship between the brothers-in-law. Lay and Lane had exchanged only pleasantries for the past several years, and the ill-conceived plan requiring cooperation between the two estranged directors never materialized.

At a second meeting Stephen Monroe recommended that Edwin Gerber, president of the Pennsylvania Sales Company and director of sales for Michigan Buggy on the east coast, be asked for monetary help. Unfortunately, there was considerable disagreement between Gerber and the company about the receipts for three hundred cars which had been delivered to his Pittsburgh agency and also a loan to Gerber for $396,000 which was backed solely by undated promissory notes held in the Michigan Buggy Company's vault.

When these various schemes to raise cash failed, the company was closed on July 31, 1913, with the public announcement that the concern was being reorganized due to Victor Palmer's illness. At the same time, Stephen Monroe abandoned all hope of refinancing the company and the very same day made arrangements to sell to Edwin Gerber, the company's Pittsburgh distributor, at twenty cents on the dollar, over $145,000 in Michigan Buggy notes held by the Kalamazoo City Savings Bank. Gerber's purchase of these notes at a discount price made him the banker for Michigan Buggy, transferring the company's obligation from the bank to him. In other words, he had spent $29,000 to gain an equity of $145,000 in company goods, and he could now use the same notes to erase any pending obligations he had with Michigan Buggy or to purchase cars. Monroe's decision was not a bad one, since the average return to a creditor from a bankrupt firm was twenty cents for each dollar of credit.

NOTED AUTOMOBILE EXPERT HERE TO TAKE CHARGE OF MICHIGAN CO. AFFAIRS

If Present Plans Carry, Kalamazoo Will Have One of Biggest Auto Plants in the State.

If present plans carry, Kalamazoo will have one of the biggest automobile plants in the state. Creditors have taken over the affairs of the Michigan Buggy company and have secured the services of W. A. McGuire, the best organization man in the automobile world, to come here and set things right at the plant of

Fig 13-3. Headline from The Kalamazoo Gazette, *August 4, 1913.*

Edwin Gerber was a crafty business man, and his scheme was telling. His attorney once described him as "a real commercial artist and a salesman of no mean ability," and his purchase of the notes was the first hint of his intent to assume control of the company. He had the opportunity to loan money to the directors, but he had refused. Instead, he purchased company notes and sought to garner support from the Kalamazoo Commercial Club. The true intent of his involvement would be made public when the summer turned to autumn.

The news in the local press remained encouraging throughout the first week of August, particularly when W. A. McGuire, touted as the best organizational man in the automotive world, arrived in town to take charge in the midst of the crises. McGuire had been vice-president of the Maxwell Motor Company, had been previously employed by the Hudson Motor Company, and had served as the general manager at the Ford Motor Company for several years. It was rumored that Henry Ford paid him $1 for each car produced as compensation for his organizational talents, an amount that was not inconsequential since Ford production exceeded 100,000 vehicles in 1912. McGuire was certainly knowledgeable about automobile manufacture, but his sole function in Kalamazoo over the next two days was to assist the auditors in their review of the automobile and blanket merchandise of Michigan Buggy and not to reorganize the company.

The complete audit took almost a month, but the severity of the situation was clear almost immediately. Within one day of McGuire's departure, the Detroit Trust Company was named as receiver and their representative, Joseph A. Bower, arrived in Kalamazoo to protect the interests of the many banking houses. In spite of the financial difficulties, the press release by the *Telegraph-*

Press on August 2, 1913 was very optimistic:

> It is claimed that there is a steady growing demand for Michigan automobiles and there is no
> trouble experienced in selling this machine both in this country and abroad.
>
> The new 1914 models have been built and agents throughout the United States state that the
> new machine is a winner in every way and that the Michigan will sell better than ever.

The predictions were unfounded. There were no 1914 models. The plant closed on August 6, 1913 and public optimism quickly dwindled. A small crew of about two hundred men continued to work, cleaning up the stock and completing the manufacture of some 1913 models, but the major work accomplished in the plant during this period was performed by the auditors from the Detroit Trust Company.

MICHIGAN BUGGY CO. WILL RESUME OPERATIONS FULL BLAST IN A FEW DAYS

Official Announcment by Detroit Trust Company Today Sets Aside All Exaggerated Reports Regarding Losses of the Big Concern—Business One of the Best in Michigan.

Eastern Banks' Hold Greatest Share of Direct Obligations and Are Looking Forward to Speedy Adjustment in Way of Re-organization.

Local Bankers and Business men Confident That There Will be Practically No Loss Because of First Class Outstanding Paper Made by Firms of the Highest Financial Standing.

Fig 13-4. Headline from Kalamazoo Telegraph-Press, *August 7, 1913.*

On August 13, the W. T. Richards Company, the Jefferson Park National Bank, and Walter F. Lewis, of Lewis Spring and Axle Company, filed a petition in federal court in Grand Rapids. On the basis of this petition, Judge Clarence W. Sessions pronounced the firm "bankrupt" and warned all creditors that they would not realize the full amount of their pending accounts. In spite of this news, the August 15 *Telegraph-Press* predicted the continuation of the horse-drawn vehicle portion of the plant, and so certain were reports that the paper "authoritatively announced" that buggy manufacture would resume on the following Monday, August 17. The effect of the pronouncement is uncertain, but one can imagine the explosive situation when eager workers appeared at the locked doors of the big plant early Monday morning after two weeks without a paycheck. The optimism in the press seemed to dissipate entirely after that incident. A meeting of all of the creditors was called in Grand Rapids on September 24, 1913.

Subsequently, the accounting published in the *Kalamazoo Telegraph-Press* on September 17, 1913, verified the earlier rumors. The total liabilities for Michigan Buggy were $2,951,010.52 and the company's assets were only $1,261,387.92, leaving a liability of $1,689,622.60 owed to the creditors. The most important aspect of the balance sheet was the discrepancy between the company's appraisal of the inventory using a retail market value, and the receiver's estimate of the wholesale cost of that same inventory. The wholesale cost of the assets was much lower than the appraised retail market value, and, with that change alone, the company's deficit increased from $169,000 to one exceeding $1.6 million. In light of the different approach to the estimates, the attempts by the company directors to raise only $200,000 in July

1913 become understandable. The directors had used the higher retail market value of the inventory yielding only a $169,000 deficit and were not cognizant of the true size of the debt.

Michigan Buggy was doomed, the company now identified in the press as "defunct," and the prior optimism replaced with the query: "What is Kalamazoo going to do with this great plant?"

The Detroit Trust Company's audit was published in the *Kalamazoo Telegraph-Press* on September 17, 1913 with the following ominous statement:

In view of the company's rather peculiar and incomplete method of accounting, the absence of complete cost or inventory data and the volume and the varied nature of the financial transactions, the compiling of such a statement of assets has been rather an unusual and difficult task. Verifications of accounts have been requested from all creditors and debtors records, but we have been only partially successful in securing answers.

GRANT LEAVES ON SECRET MISSION----BELIEVED TO BE IN EAST WITH GERBER

Fig 13-5. Headline from September 7, 1913 Kalamazoo Telegraph-Press.

Edwin Gerber had been summoned early in this affair as a financial advisor and trusted confidante, but he was an opportunist who sought to take advantage with every turn. On September 7, 1913, James Grant, president of the Commercial Club, went to Pittsburgh to speak with Gerber, perhaps at his beck and call, but most certainly under secrecy and suspicion. The concern of the *Telegraph-Press* was such that it publicly disclosed the trip by Grant and published a warning at the end of the article: "Kalamazoo is watching the Commercial Club." Just four days prior to Grant's departure, a business note appeared in the September 11 issue of the national publication *Motor Age*, stating that the Edward F. Gerber Company of Pittsburgh had made arrangements to take over the business of the Michigan Motor Car Company, the Michigan Buggy Company, and the Kalamazoo Blanket Company. This preemptive move by Gerber was most likely intended to fend off potential bids for the company by other entrepreneurs, and public statements some weeks later indicated that the strategy was effective. The early association between Grant and Gerber, however, would weaken the Commercial Club's ability to influence the outcome of the bankruptcy hearings.

As the summer of 1913 ended, the Michigan Buggy Company was proclaimed defunct, with its affairs in disarray and, in spite of early optimism, there would be no Mighty Michigan for 1914. The doors at Michigan Buggy were closed for business on August 6, 1913 and reopened on September 10, 1913 to begin the bankruptcy hearings. Edwin F. Gerber of the Pennsylvania Sales Company was the first person to testify before Bankruptcy Referee Banyon in the administrative offices at the local plant.

At the end of the first week of the hearings, Edward Dingley, writing in *The Progressive Herald* on September 13, placed the events in perspective with his own choice commentary, foretelling the debacle that would follow during the fall of 1913. His writings describe the atmosphere in the hearing room in a style not found in any other paper:

It is a sordid affair—a sort of autopsy over a corpse—with a lot of hungry and technical lawyers growling at each other and bulldozing the witnesses, for which they receive from one hundred to twenty-five dollars a day. Lawyers live off the troubles and misfortunes of others; and when all the fat fees are paid to the attorneys, there will be little left for the creditors.

What a feast for a dozen or more lawyers! They sit around the tables in the improvised court room in the Michigan Buggy Company building and watch each other with lynx eyes.

Sanford Ladd the attorney of the receiver is pugnacious and pointed. He has a sneering way about him....Joseph Hamlin Jr., and Steward Knappen of Grand Rapids are also attorneys for the receivers. They sit at the center table with Ladd and the three hold whispered conversations.

George J. Reynolds of Pittsburgh is E. R. Gerber's attorney. Reynolds is a smooth proposition, rather quiet, but clear headed. ...[H]e smells of a pink in his button-hole to conceal his mirth.

At the left sits Victor L. Palmer and his attorney Burritt Hamilton of Battle Creek—a severe looking man with a smooth face and scholarly expression.

Next comes Claude Carney, attorney for Frank Lay Jr. and George Lay.

The fight is over dollars; and the alleged process of determining justice is merely a contest of lawyer's wits.

The stage was set for the turmoil that would fill the local papers for the next four months.

REFERENCES

Michigan Buggy Accounts Ledger, 1912. Western Michigan University Archives, Kalamazoo MI.

Michigan Buggy Co. to Be Reorganized. *Kalamazoo Telegraph-Press,* July 31, 1913.

Witness Tells of Protest He Made to Palmer Against Fixing Up Report. *Kalamazoo Telegraph-Press,* October 13, 1913.

Eastern Bankers Here in Effort to Re-organize Michigan Buggy. *Kalamazoo Telegraph-Press,* August 1, 1913.

Future of Michigan Buggy Now Appears to Be Safe. *The Kalamazoo Gazette,* August 8, 1913.

Michigan Buggy Outlook Hopeful. *The Automobile,* August 14, 1913, p. 305.

Plant Will be Put in Operation Soon. *The Kalamazoo Gazette,* August 17, 1913.

Experts Will Decide How to Run Factory. *Kalamazoo Telegraph-Press,* August 2, 1913.

Inventorying Michigan Assets. *Motor Age,* August 21, 1913, p. 15.

Receiver Tells of Plans of Future. *The Kalamazoo Gazette,* August 26, 1913.

Noted Automobile Expert Here to Take Charge of Michigan Co. Affairs. *The Kalamazoo Gazette,* August 4, 1913.

Kalamazoo Has Up-to-Date Equipment. *Motor,* August 1913, p. 85, 87.

Work is Halted by Michigan Buggy. *The Kalamazoo Gazette,* August 5, 1913.

Michigan Buggy Plant Closed. *The Automobile,* August 7, 1913, p. 362.

Receivership for the Mighty Michigan. *Motor World,* August 7, 1913, p. 7.

Michigan Buggy Co. Will Resume Operations Full Blast in a Few Days. *Kalamazoo Telegraph-Press*, August 7, 1913.

Michigan Officers Sued. *Motor Age*, August 21, 1913, p. 15.

Statements Made by Michigan Buggy Company Receivers. *The Kalamazoo Gazette*, September 9, 1913.

Name Receiver for Buggy Co. *The Kalamazoo Gazette*, August 7, 1913.

Portion of Buggy Plant Will Be Put in Operation Soon. *Kalamazoo Telegraph-Press*, August 15, 1913.

Much Interest in Announcement About Buggy Co. *Kalamazoo Telegraph-Press*, August 16, 1913.

What Is Kalamazoo Going to Do With This Great Plant? *Kalamazoo Telegraph-Press*, October 30, 1913.

Financial Statement Is Unraveled. *The Kalamazoo Gazette*, September 18, 1913.

Michigan Failure Reveals Wonderful Finance System. *Motor World*, August 14, 1913, p. 5.

Statement of Affairs of Michigan Buggy. *Kalamazoo Telegraph-Press*, September 17, 1913.

Grant Leaves on Secret Mission — Believed in East with Gerber. *Kalamazoo Telegraph-Press*, September 7, 1913.

Takes Over Michigan Business. *Motor Age*, September 11, 1913, p. 42.

Special Telegram. *The Automobile*, September 4, 1913, p. 441.

Michigan Sale Is Deferred. *Motor Age*, September 4, 1913, p. 21.

Buggy Company Is Adjudged Bankrupt. *The Kalamazoo Gazette*, August 28, 1913.

Michigan Buggy Inquiry Begins. *Kalamazoo Telegraph-Press*, September 10, 1913.

Gerber First Witness Called in Hearing. *Kalamazoo Telegraph-Press*, September 10, 1913.

Michigan Buggy Co. *Automobile Trade Journal*, September 1913, p. 67, 80.

Affairs of Michigan Bankruptcy Proceedings. *The Progressive Herald*, September 13, 1913.

Fig 14-1. The scene is Main Street in Kalamazoo, facing east. Burdick Street is to the left, and Portage Street is to the right just before the FOLZ sign. The scene is typical of the street activity during the fall of 1913 when news of the bankruptcy was being published. Perhaps the boy on the left is selling that day's edition of the Kalamazoo Telegraph-Press. *(WMU)*

Chapter 14

The Bankruptcy Hearing

September and October 1913

The name Kalamazoo has been soiled with gossip and scandal.
Kalamazoo is being injured beyond repair.
—*The Progressive Herald*

It was September 11, 1913 and the bankruptcy hearings had opened the day before in the crowded, stuffy offices of the Michigan Buggy Company with Edwin E. Gerber, president of the Pennsylvania Sales Company, on the stand for most of the day.

"You're a shyster lawyer!" shouted Gerber, pointing his finger at Sanford Ladd, counsel for the Detroit Trust Company.

This heated exchange was typical of the squabbles and emotional discord that characterized the series of hearings following the closing of Michigan Buggy.

The doors of the great plant closed on August 30, 1913, and the company was placed into receivership with the Detroit Trust Company. From the end of that summer through the late spring of 1914, Michigan Buggy and its board of directors were under close scrutiny by several investigatory bodies in both public and private forums. Although most of these hearings were held from the beginning of September through the middle of November 1913, the most important was the bankruptcy hearing that opened in September 1913 and lasted through the following spring. From the evidence disclosed in these hearings came the Federal Grand Jury investigation of Michigan Buggy in the winter of 1914, and, ultimately, the criminal proceedings in the spring of that year against Victor L. Palmer, secretary-treasurer of the magnificent manufacturing concern.

W. John Banyon served as bankruptcy referee, and the feisty, combative attorney Sanford Ladd, of Warren, Cady and Ladd, represented the interests of the Detroit Trust Company. In doing so, he also represented the eastern financial houses and the automotive parts suppliers who provided the capital and material for the construction of the Mighty Michigan. Claude S. Carney, although still involved in the contested seat for Michigan's third congressional district, represented Victor L. Palmer with the assistance of Burritt Hamilton of Battle Creek. Carney alone represented Frank B.

Lay, Jr. and George Lay. George Reynolds represented Edwin F. Gerber and the Pennsylvania Sales Company, although he did so with considerable difficulty since he was licensed to practice in Pennsylvania and the hearing officer refused to extend any courtesy to him.

The bankruptcy hearing opened under the auspices of the district court of the United States. The sole purpose was to review the financial transactions of the company and to identify the responsibility and the liability for the extraordinary debt that engulfed the firm. Michigan Buggy had a long and respected tradition of manufacturing quality horse-drawn vehicles when they began producing a motorcar in 1909, a decision that eventually proved to be the company's downfall. The angry creditors working through the courts sought answers to the sudden financial downturn and the whereabouts of their money.

E. F. Gerber First Witness Called In Hearing Being Conducted Today At the Plant of the Concern

Claims He Does Not Owe Local Company a Cent---The Hearing Will Be Continued For Many Days

Fig 14-2. From the Kalamazoo Telegraph-Press, *September 10, 1913.*

During the first few sessions, much of Sanford Ladd's attention was directed to the last few days of July 1913 just before the "crash" that closed the company doors. Ladd spoke of July 27, 1913 as though it was "Memorial Sunday" in the history of the company. "Somebody must have known that the money was not available and that the crash would come on July 28," he charged, referring to the deal that Gerber cut with the directors. The deal that was cut that day wiped out all of Gerber's debt with the company and simultaneously allowed him to acquire over four hundred Michigan cars at bargain prices.

Edwin F. Gerber, whose company served as the eastern distributor for Michigan Buggy, was one of the primary witnesses throughout the proceedings. During the initial session, reported by the *Telegraph-Press*, on September 11, Gerber spoke for nearly thirty minutes recounting the history of the relationship between the Pennsylvania Sales Company and Michigan Buggy. Their association began in 1903 with Gerber's purchase of five hundred sleighs and grew from a $100,000 transaction that year to more than $1 million in annual sales by 1912.

After Gerber's historical account, Ladd declared that the "Pittsburgh man" owed Michigan Buggy over $380,000, a charge that brought a burst of laughter from Gerber who was a frustrating antagonist for Ladd throughout the hearings. Gerber contended that settlement on all accounts was made with Michigan Buggy at the end of each month, and that all his accounts were paid in cash and promissory notes. Gerber also argued that a review of the accounts by his own auditing department in June of 1913 revealed that Michigan Buggy had been overpaid, not only in 1913, but in 1909 and 1910 as well. "Michigan Buggy owed me and not the other way around," he laughed, taunting Ladd at every opportunity.

Gerber had brought with him a card on which he had recorded the annual sales for Michigan

Buggy and the Pennsylvania Sales Company with the intent of showing that the sales of horse-drawn vehicles and motorcars through his company was the major source of growth for the Kalamazoo-based concern. According to Gerber, these dollar amounts were reported by January 31 each year. He argued that the table showed that as total sales for his company grew, so did the total for Michigan Buggy.

DATE	PENNSYLVANIA SALES	MICHIGAN BUGGY
Jan 31, 1906	40,000	60,000
Jan 31, 1907	120,000	160,000
Jan 31, 1908	210,000	200,000
Jan 31, 1909	370,000	400,000
Jan 31, 1910	600,000	400,000
Jan 31, 1911	800,000	800,000
Jan 31, 1912	950,000	1,400,000
Jan 31, 1913	1,250,000	3,300,000

Although the productivity of Michigan Buggy was not solely dependent upon the success of the Pittsburgh concern, Gerber summed up the relationship proudly and almost arrogantly: "When the company fell on hard times, it was *me* that the directors summoned to Kalamazoo for counsel and financial help," he declared.

The Pittsburgh firm was not the largest dealer for Michigan Buggy, according to the record of holdings that was sent to the creditors and later published in the January 19, 1914 *Telegraph-Press*. That list, presented here in order of dollar amount held, showed Dewey and Company in Plano, Illinois, with well over $1 million worth of Michigan cars in the summer of 1913:

OUTSTANDING ACCOUNTS IN SUMMER 1913

Dewey and Company	Plano, IL	1,063,944.16
Penna Sales Company,	Pittsburgh, PA	325,409.41
Michigan Auto and Buggy	Portland, OR	244,962.51
Emil Theno	Charles City, IA	232,386.75
C. L. Perrin	Los Angeles, CA	134,000.00
A. C. Thompson Cage Company	St Paul, MN	118,143.20
Kiel and Evans	Oakland, CA	92,592.67
Western Implement Company	Sioux City, IA	80,557.67
O. E. Short	New York, NY	44,802.92
T. O. Probey	Washington, D.C.	34,685.48
Ford Bros Auto Sales Company	Toledo, OH	33,778.80
A. J. Jones	Fresno, CA	25,722.82
King McDonnell Company	Sacramento, CA	22,428.75
George Seeley	Saginaw, MI	18,187.50
P. J. Tierney	Ft. Dodge, IA	17,403.53
L. Whitney Company	Kansas, MO	6,296.55

The list makes three interesting points. First, since Gerber was not the major dealer, it strengthens Ladd's assertion that the "Man from Pittsburgh" received special treatment by the directors. Second, since this list summarized the unpaid and undated notes totaling $2,426,302.72 found in the company safe, it strengthen Ladd's assertion of the financial mismanagement by the accounts receivable department that reported to Palmer. Third, since the entire list of creditors was a much sought after item by Gerber three days before the creditors' first meeting, it strengthened Ladd's assertion that Gerber intended to "take over" the company to the detriment of the creditors. Earl J. McCone, a Michigan Buggy Company bookkeeper, testified in mid-October that first George Lay and then Thomas Orrell asked for a list of creditors. Both Lay and Orrell were close to Gerber; both had been in his employ; and both men told McCone that he could name his own price for such a list.

EDWIN GERBER ON STAND IN AUTO COMPANY PROBE

Man Who Posed as Savior of Local Concern Vigorously Denies That He Owes Red Penny to Bankrupt Firm

Fig 14-3. From The Kalamazoo Gazette. *September 11, 1913.*

The story of the last days of the company was a complex one. Gerber arrived in Kalamazoo on Sunday, July 27, 1913 and Frank Lay, Sr. and his two sons went to visit him at his room in the new Burdick Hotel. Lay asked how much Gerber could raise and estimated that Michigan Buggy needed $400,000 to continue its operations. Gerber suggested that Frank Lay, Sr., and M. Henry Lane mortgage their personal estates and perhaps Palmer could offer another $100,000 to raise the needed cash. Lay emphasized that such a plan was not feasible since it would require him to bring in all outstanding personal accounts.

Michigan Buggy had been started by George T. Lay, Frank Lay's father, and the company had been in business for over twenty years. Lay's appeal to the flashy salesman from Pittsburgh for financial help had to be difficult. He and his sons left the Burdick without bringing the matter to a resolution and Gerber arrived at the factory on Monday morning with a different plan that involved selling him three groups of cars. He later testified that he contracted for twelve hundred cars with Frank Lay, Jr.

Those Michigan cars (and Gerber testified that he had seen a list of the cars held by Frank Lay, Jr.) represented a major asset of the company from which the creditors could obtain a return on their investment, and Ladd was very interested in the final disposition of these vehicles. Gerber had moved quickly and assuredly, sweeping the assets from the company ledgers before anyone outside of the company knew the financial condition of the concern.

The first of the summer sale was a group of thirty-eight cars with fine upholstery and expensive paint options. The contract for this sale was completed on July 28, 1913 and these cars were sold COD, with a balance due five days after delivery. Gerber paid $525 for the thirty-three horsepower Model L without a starter, and $675 for the forty-horsepower Model R with an electric starter. Attorney Ladd sought to determine why the company would deliver custom-finished cars with a retail price of $1,585 to the Pittsburgh agency for about one-third the price without either a cash settlement or a promissory note, but he could not break Gerber's testimony. The exchange between the two men was recorded in the *Telegraph* on September 11, 1913.

Attorney Ladd: "Why did Mr. Palmer or Mr. Lay, Jr. sell you these cars so cheaply?"

Gerber: "Palmer gave me a special price, because he knew I would pay cash."

Ladd: "Isn't it a fact that you were trying to buy up all of the Michigan automobiles in the United States of America?"

Gerber: "No, I only bought 400."

Ladd: "How many did you get?"

Gerber: "I didn't get any."

Ladd: "Did you try to attach them?"

Gerber: "I did attach some of them."

Ladd: "When you made the purchase you had the cars headed for Pittsburgh?"

Gerber: "Mr. Lay, Jr. might have ordered them shipped from different points where they were located."

Ladd: "And you had under control practically all of the Michigan automobiles in the country?"

Gerber: "No, I paid for 400…"

The arrangements for the second of the special summer sales were completed on July 29, 1913 and included four hundred cars that were spread across the country from Chicago, Illinois, to Sacramento, California. These cars were to be shipped to Gerber's sales office in Pittsburgh. Interestingly, the minutes of the meeting in which this decision was made were written prior to that meeting and apparently the details were penciled in later. These minutes did not include either the cost of the cars or the manner of payment, although later testimony established the cost at approximately $400 per unit. The contract was signed in pencil by George Lay as temporary secretary. George was the primary negotiator for the deal and a former employee of the Pennsylvania Sales Company, so Ladd regarded this arrangement with suspicion. The arrangements for this sale were also made with the approval of Palmer, but later, when the bargain was discovered, Frank Lay, Sr. demanded that his son issue a stop order for all shipments. The resolution of this matter was never made clear in the transcripts of the hearing, and how many of these cars were eventually delivered to Gerber or how much money actually exchanged hands is unknown.

Ladd pursued the details of this second sale relentlessly to show at least the poor judgment and potentially the malfeasance of George Lay. The shipping cost, as high as $200 in some cases, was paid by Michigan Buggy Company and had to be subtracted from the $400 sale price for the car. Clearly, a return of approximately $200 on a car with a potential retail price of $1,585 was difficult to justify to the creditors with outstanding claims against the company.

The final transaction of the July sales to Gerber was for 278 automobiles and was completed on July 28, 1913. The total price was $143,300. The contract subsequently reduced this amount by $47,500, an amount cited as comprising a previous advance from Gerber, and another credit of $8,785.76, an amount that was cited as part of the E. F. Gerber Agent Account. These two adjustments, which Ladd was never able to document to his satisfaction throughout the hearing, reduced the final settlement to $92,014.24 for an average cost of approximately $330.00 per car.

Gerber paid for these cars with a cash payment of $32,743.27, several promissory notes that matured between August 1 and November 21, and two notes from the Michigan Buggy Company for $7,500 that he had purchased at a discount price from the local bank. This contract also provided for full settlement of the Pennsylvania Sales Company's consignment account and the vehicle account, leaving only the repair account showing a balance due.

Gerber defended the open repair account, claiming there were faulty engines, poor universal joints, and inoperative magnetos on many of the delivered cars. Ladd pursued this last exchange extensively, but unsuccessfully, in an effort to expose the arrangements in which the purchase of additional cars by Gerber could remove indebtedness for prior deliveries. The final exasperating disclosure for Ladd was that Gerber was unable to produce this final contract. He claimed that it had been either lost or misplaced when detectives from the Kalamazoo police department had searched his Pittsburgh office.

The losers in this arrangement were the creditors and, with few exceptions, these individuals never had the opportunity to receive automobiles in lieu of payment for materials delivered. The sale of the cars at reduced prices to Gerber meant no profit for Michigan Buggy and no opportunity for the company to trade vehicles with the parts manufacturers for the goods that were used to build the cars that Gerber bought. Gerber had always been treated well by the company including a confidential contract, written by Palmer, authorizing a five percent discount on the price of cars over and above the usual agency discount. Now, in the summer of 1913, he took additional advantage of the company's financial disarray.

The final manipulation by Gerber concerned the sales commission. This commission was paid in cash by Michigan Buggy to Gerber at the time that the cars were sold and shipped by Gerber to other dealers in his territory. The unpaid commission, cited as part of the E. F. Gerber Agent Accounts in the series of transactions in July, did not represent ready cash to the company, but a cancellation of Michigan Buggy's indebtedness to Gerber for the sales commission for cars sold by Gerber to other agencies in his territory. In essence, Gerber used the Michigan Buggy Company money to pay the debt that he incurred with Michigan Buggy when he took delivery of the cars in the summer of 1913. The evaluation by Gerber's attorney that Gerber was "a real commercial artist and a salesman of no mean ability" was certainly affirmed by this incident.

Exposure of these deals with Gerber infuriated the creditors, and when the time came, they would deny him the right to purchase the Michigan Buggy plant even though he appeared to be the only one with sufficient financial backing and interest to continue manufacture of the Mighty Michigan and horse-drawn vehicles. So great was their anger that they scuttled the only possibility of manufacturing the 1914 Michigan and the eventual payment for the goods they had delivered.

Gerber's purchase of discounted Michigan Buggy notes from the Kalamazoo City Savings Bank appears to be the action of an astute business man, but recall that Victor L. Palmer was also on the board of that bank. That raises questions about collusion. Why would the bank sell the promissory notes from Michigan Buggy to Gerber, who paid for them with another promissory note from the Pennsylvania Sales Company, and do so at a loss to the bank of eighty cents on the dollar? Returns to creditors from bankrupt companies usually averaged twenty to twenty-five cents on the dollar, and, after the plant closure was complete some nine months later, Michigan Buggy creditors did receive twenty-five cents on the dollar. The final resolution of the company's affairs showed that the bank's deal with Gerber in the summer of 1913 was a relatively good one and was completed without involvement in the legal process. In retrospect, however, the transaction in the summer of

1913 also showed that the principals, Palmer, Monroe, and Gerber, knew full well that the company was about to fail and they showed little responsibility for resolving the company's debt with its creditors.

Victor L. Palmer was also called to the stand during this period, and in spite of his claims of ill health, he was made to testify on the advice of a physician that Ladd brought to the hearing. Sanford Ladd was an effective interrogator who forced considerable information from Palmer and other officers of the company who were neither willing nor cooperative witnesses. His shouting and relentless questioning often led to emotional outbursts by witnesses and strong objections by their attorneys.

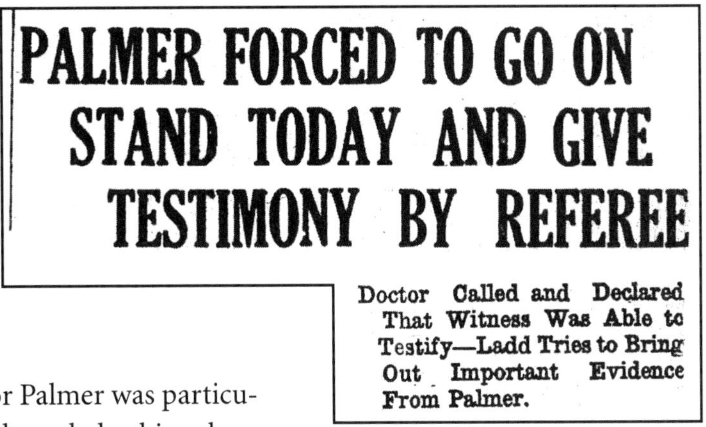

PALMER FORCED TO GO ON STAND TODAY AND GIVE TESTIMONY BY REFEREE

Doctor Called and Declared That Witness Was Able to Testify—Ladd Tries to Bring Out Important Evidence From Palmer.

Fig 14-4. From The Kalamazoo Gazette, *September 12, 1913.*

At times during the hearing, Victor Palmer was particularly intransigent, refusing to even acknowledge his role as financial officer. The following exchange between Palmer and Ladd was reported in the *Telegraph-Press* on September 11, 1913. When Palmer confessed that he did not know whether the department superintendents kept stock records, Ladd screamed at him, "Do you mean to say that you have never seen such a report during the 21 years you have worked here?" Ladd then sought additional information on his duties as treasurer. After Ladd asked what Palmer did for the company, "I worked hard for the company's interests" was the vague reply. Ladd was incensed by the ambiguity: "Your refusing to answer my questions or not understanding what I mean is all bunk," he shouted. Palmer sat unresponsive and passive on the stand, a newspaper clutched under his arm that he occasionally used to swat at pesky flies, a practice that irritated Ladd immensely. Eventually, under a barrage of questions, Palmer finally admitted that he was responsible for writing the checks and negotiating bank loans. "Yes," came the admission, "I was the principal financial officer of Michigan Buggy."

Subsequent testimony on October 10 from Monroe identified Palmer as the company's primary representative with full rights to make financial deals.

"Palmer was really the Michigan Buggy Company then," said Ladd.

"Practically so," was the reply.

Even with his admission that he served as the principal financial officer, Palmer continued to feign ignorance and denied knowing about several transactions as reported in the *Telegraph* on September 16, 1913. The Western Implement Company of Sioux City, Iowa, for example, was capitalized for a mere $5,000, and yet had been sent a large consignment of Mighty Michigan cars with a value of $150,000. The delivery was paid with a promissory note and the note was peddled immediately to the local bank at a discount. In another instance, the A. C. Thompson Carriage Company of St. Paul, Minnesota, had been sent about thirty-four Mighty Michigan cars with an approximate value of $50,000. In error, Michigan Buggy was sent a $200,000 promissory note for the shipment, and, curiously, that note was immediately discounted to a bank. Much of Ladd's probing with Palmer uncovered these and other questionable business practices including a reported reduction of company earnings by $500,000 in an effort to avoid federal taxes.

On September 18, Ladd began his assault on Palmer about the company's financial statement:

"There were $3,000,000 in assets according to the statement of Jan. 31," said Ladd.

"The statement shows that," replied Palmer

Figure 14-5. Victor Palmer, from a 1914 newspaper photograph.

Ladd: "What has become of the assets?"

Palmer: "The books will show."

Ladd: "The books show only $1,500,000 assets."

Palmer: "The books will show."

Ladd: "How do you explain the shrinkage in the assets?"

Palmer: "I don't explain it."

Ladd: "How do you account for the shrinkage?"

Palmer: "I don't know. I question your statement."

Ladd: "Can you be of any assistance?"

Palmer: "The books will show to the best of my knowledge."

Ladd: "The books show that the Pennsylvania Sales Company owes the Michigan Buggy Company $380,000, is that right?"

Palmer: "I don't know what the books show. I haven't seen them in over two months."

The hearing was adjourned due to Palmer's health, and when it reconvened, Ladd exposed Palmer's conflict of interest as a member of the board of directors of the Kalamazoo City Savings Bank and the Michigan Buggy Company. Ladd charged that Palmer knew quite well that the company was about to go under when he notified the *Kalamazoo Telegraph-Press* on July 30, 1913 that the company was to be reorganized and might be closed temporarily. Ladd also discovered during this testimony that in the last few days of July 1913, Palmer sold all of his shares in the company except one, so that when the company folded, Palmer's loss was negligible.

The first part of the bankruptcy hearings closed on September 20, 1913 and served only as the preliminary exposure of the intense cross examination that was to follow. Referee Banyan adjourned the case until September 24 and ordered Frank B. Lay, Sr.; his sons, Frank B. Lay, Jr., and George Lay; as well as M. Henry Lane, Victor Palmer, and others to appear before Judge Clarence Sessions in the federal court in Grand Rapids on that date.

While Gerber was being questioned about his financial dealings with the officers of Michigan Buggy, he continued to maneuver a buy-out of the company. He had informed *Motor Age* that he had arranged to take over the business of the Michigan Motor Car Company, the Michigan Buggy Company, and the Kalamazoo Blanket Company, a news release surely intended to discourage other potential buyers. At the same time, George Reynolds, Gerber's attorney, tried to influence the Kalamazoo Commercial Club. He pleaded Gerber's case at a luncheon meeting on September 11,

1913 and the next day *The Kalamazoo Gazette* described the negotiations and Gerber's offer to buy the company in the following manner:

> When the sun set the day the Michigan company closed, $1,000,000 in good will vanished and it has been vanishing with every sunset at the rate of $3,000.
>
> …[T]he motive back of the purchase by Gerber was prompted by a desire to conserve a sales corporation whose business it had taken years to develop.
>
> We went to see the receiver like two dogs off the street to say that we were here to offer him $375,000 for the stock not including the real estate. We were waved off as though it were 30 cents and we went home.

Attorney Reynolds attempted to create an image of Gerber as a savior who wanted nothing more than to purchase the company and begin production of the Mighty Michigan once again. He claimed that Gerber had already sold twelve hundred Michigan cars in 1913, and had excellent markets in some fourteen states. He also claimed that Gerber came here in July when the company needed money and tried to do his part to pay for automobiles, but he said, "the matters dropped through."

GERBER LAYS HIS PLANS BEFORE COMMERCIAL CLUB

Local Financiers Meet Following Decision at Luncheon Held at Noon on Thursday

Pittsburger Demonstrates His Earnestness to Start Wheels Turning in Big Factory of Buggy Company at Once.

To Make Bid Today.

Gerber made his original bid for the personal effects of the company not including the real estate, so that the production department could be placed in immediate operation. No offer was made for the real estate because the receiver alone could give title to real estate.

Gerber has intended from the first

Figure 14-6. Gerber plan makes headlines in the September 12, 1913 issue of The Kalamazoo Gazette.

The creditors met with Judge Sessions, and Gerber did make an offer to purchase the company and all assets for $350,000—a price that was attractive to many of the creditors at the time. Sanford Ladd was also present and spoke in his usual blunt manner: he had had enough of Gerber's obfuscation during the hearings. After reporting the testimony from Gerber and Palmer about their various financial dealings, he convinced the creditors to vote against the sale. Undaunted, Gerber followed his first offer with a second of $280,000 for the real estate, physical plant, and material on hand, but given the creditors' attitude after Ladd spoke, the second offer was also refused.

The Michigan Buggy officers were not required to testify at the hearing in Grand Rapids, but officials of the state Attorney General's office had heard enough from Sanford Ladd about the testimony and the discrepancies between the financial statements. Rumors of pending prosecutions circulated in the city when the bankruptcy hearings returned to Referee Banyon at the Michigan Buggy Plant where testimony resumed on October 8, 1913.

REFERENCES

Editorial. *The Progressive Herald*, October 25, 1913.

Michigan Buggy Company to Be Reorganized. *Kalamazoo Telegraph-Press*, July 31, 1913.

Michigan Buggy Inquiry Begins. *Kalamazoo Telegraph-Press*, September 10, 1913.

Palmer Tells Bankruptcy Referee About Dealings. *Kalamazoo Telegraph-Press*,
     September 11, 1913.

Report Shows How Money Was Divided at Factory. *Kalamazoo Telegraph-Press*,
     January 19, 1914.

Financial Statement Is Unraveled. *The Kalamazoo Gazette*, September 18, 1913.

Grilled by Trust Attorney. *Kalamazoo Telegraph-Press*, September 18, 1913.

Admits Contracting for 400 Autos. *The Kalamazoo Gazette*, September 11, 1913.

Could Name "His Own Price" for List of Buggy Company Creditors Testifies Witness at
     Hearing. *Kalamazoo Telegraph-Press*, October 15, 1913.

Gerber Must Explain Michigan Debt. *Motor World*, September 11, 1913, p. 6.

Monroe Tells of His Efforts to Save Buggy Company From Failure Last Summer.
     Kalamazoo Telegraph-Press, October 9, 1913.

Witness Tells of Protest He Made to Palmer Against "Fixing" Up Report.
     Kalamazoo Telegraph-Press, October 14, 1913.

Edwin Gerber on Stand in Auto Company Probe. *The Kalamazoo Gazette*,
     September 11, 1913.

*Transcript: The District Court of the United States for the Western District of Michigan.
     In the Matter of the Michigan Buggy Company Bankrupt, Fall 1913.*
     Western Michigan University Archives, Kalamazoo MI.

Michigan Buggy Company Creditors. *Automobile Trade Journal*, September 1913, p. 197.

Gerber Lays His Plans Before Commercial Club. *The Kalamazoo Gazette*,
     September 12, 1913.

To Hold on to Business. *Kalamazoo Telegraph-Press*, September 12, 1913.

Buys Autos to Hold Onto Business. *Kalamazoo Telegraph-Press*, September 12, 1913.

Palmer Forced to Go on Stand Today and Give Testimony by Referee.
     Kalamazoo Telegraph-Press, September 12, 1913.

Victor Palmer Is Near Collapse Under Charge. *The Kalamazoo Gazette*, September 13, 1913.

Lane Testifies Before Referee in Bankruptcy. *The Kalamazoo Gazette*, October 10, 1913.

Testify—Ladd Tries to Bring Out Important Evidence From Palmer.
     Kalamazoo Telegraph-Press, September 16, 1913.

Ask Palmer About His Sworn Statements. *Kalamazoo Telegraph-Press*, September 17, 1913.

Palmer Defendant in Suit for Bankruptcy. *The Kalamazoo Gazette*, September 23, 1913.

Palmer Will Be Called to Stand. *Kalamazoo Telegraph-Press*, September 13, 1913.

Michigan Buggy Company to Be Re-Organized. *Kalamazoo Telegraph-Press*, July 31, 1913.

Buggy Probe to Shift to Grand Rapids. *The Kalamazoo Gazette*, September 21, 1913.

Gerber Bids for Michigan Auto Company. *The Kalamazoo Gazette*, September 13, 1913.

Gerber May Buy Factory Right Away. *Kalamazoo Telegraph-Press*, September 17, 1913.

Big Mass Meeting to Be Held. *Kalamazoo Telegraph-Press*, September 17, 1913.

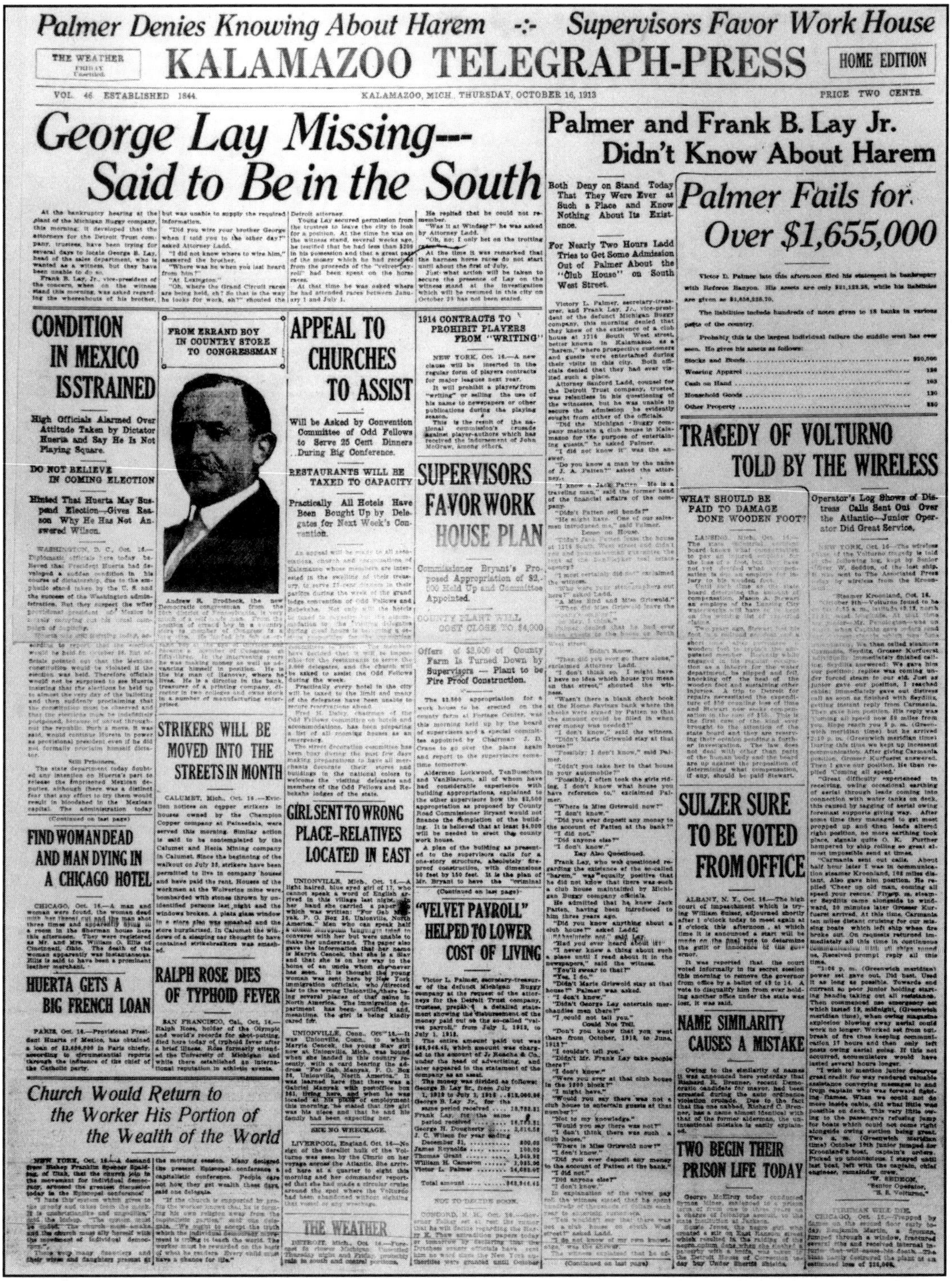

Palmer Denies Knowing About Harem -:- Supervisors Favor Work House

THE WEATHER FRIDAY Unsettled.

KALAMAZOO TELEGRAPH-PRESS

HOME EDITION

VOL. 46 ESTABLISHED 1844. KALAMAZOO, MICH., THURSDAY, OCTOBER 16, 1913 PRICE TWO CENTS.

George Lay Missing— Said to Be in the South

Palmer and Frank B. Lay Jr. Didn't Know About Harem

Both Deny on Stand Today That They Were Ever at Such a Place and Know Nothing About Its Existence.

For Nearly Two Hours Ladd Tries to Get Some Admission Out of Palmer About the "Club House" on South West Street.

Palmer Fails for Over $1,655,000

Victor D. Palmer late this afternoon filed his statement in bankruptcy with Referee Banyon. His assets are only $21,128.28, while his liabilities are given as $1,656,226.70.

The liabilities include hundreds of notes given to 18 banks in various parts of the country.

Probably this is the largest individual failure the middle west has ever seen. He gives his assets as follows:

Stocks and Bonds	$20,500
Wearing Apparel	100
Cash on Hand	103
Household Goods	130
Other Property	290

CONDITION IN MEXICO IS STRAINED

High Officials Alarmed Over Attitude Taken by Dictator Huerta and Say He Is Not Playing Square.

DO NOT BELIEVE IN COMING ELECTION

Hinted That Huerta May Suspend Election—Gives Reason Why He Has Not Answered Wilson.

FROM ERRAND BOY IN COUNTRY STORE TO CONGRESSMAN

Andrew B. Brodbeck, the new Democratic congressman

APPEAL TO CHURCHES TO ASSIST

Will be Asked by Convention Committee of Odd Fellows to Serve 25 Cent Dinners During Big Conference.

RESTAURANTS WILL BE TAXED TO CAPACITY

Practically All Hotels Have Been Bought Up by Delegates for Next Week's Convention.

1914 CONTRACTS TO PROHIBIT PLAYERS FROM "WRITING"

SUPERVISORS FAVOR WORK HOUSE PLAN

Commissioner Bryant's Proposed Appropriation of $2,500 Held Up and Committee Appointed.

COUNTY PLANT WILL COST CLOSE TO $4,000

Offers of $2,500 of County Farm Is Turned Down by Supervisors — Plant to be Fire Proof Construction.

TRAGEDY OF VOLTURNO TOLD BY THE WIRELESS

WHAT SHOULD BE PAID TO DAMAGE DONE WOODEN FOOT?

Operator's Log Shows of Distress Calls Sent Out Over the Atlantic—Junior Operator Did Great Service.

STRIKERS WILL BE MOVED INTO THE STREETS IN MONTH

GIRL SENT TO WRONG PLACE—RELATIVES LOCATED IN EAST

FIND WOMAN DEAD AND MAN DYING IN A CHICAGO HOTEL

HUERTA GETS A BIG FRENCH LOAN

RALPH ROSE DIES OF TYPHOID FEVER

"VELVET PAYROLL" HELPED TO LOWER COST OF LIVING

SULZER SURE TO BE VOTED FROM OFFICE

NAME SIMILARITY CAUSES A MISTAKE

TWO BEGIN THEIR PRISON LIFE TODAY

Church Would Return to the Worker His Portion of the Wealth of the World

SEE NO WRECKAGE.

THE WEATHER

Fig 15-1. During the month of October 1913, the papers were filled with stories of intrigue and rumors about the grand jury and the final collapse of Michigan Buggy. The extent of the difficulty was presented almost in its entirety in articles in the Kalamazoo Telegraph-Press *on October 16. Included were: "Wanted to 'Split' Money Secretly Deposited in Bank Early in Summer"; "George Lay Missing—Said to Be in the South"; "Palmer and Frank B. Lay Jr. Didn't Know About Harem"; "Palmer Fails for Over $1,655,000"; and "'Velvet Payroll' Helped to Lower Cost of Living." (DOL)*

Chapter 15

The Days of October

1913

"George Lay Missing; Palmer Denies Knowing About Harem"
"Velvet Payroll Helped Lower Cost Of Living"
"Palmer Fails For Over $1,655,000"
—*Telegraph-Press* headlines, October 16, 1913

I f there was a time of infamy in Kalamazoo during the Michigan Buggy Company hearings, the days of October 1913 created some of the most memorable moments. The major circumstances leading to the demise of Michigan Buggy, and which simultaneously vilified the primary participants, were exposed in the press that month, with a notable array of damaging disclosures coming forth on October 16, 1913. The front page of that day's *Kalamazoo Telegraph-Press* featured many of those damaging problems and provided the foundation for a story that would plague the city and shadow its citizenry over the next several months and have repercussions for years to come.

Victor Palmer had already been accused of falsifying the company's financial report to the creditors, and on October 16 he filed for bankruptcy with debts exceeding $1.6 million. The truculent Lay sons and their often frivolous manner became easy targets for the press. One report claimed that George Lay had run off to the south to avoid the legal process, and both Frank B. Lay, Jr. and Victor Palmer were questioned about the "velvet payroll," outrageous entertainment expenses, and the infamous harem on South West Street. Even the respected patriarchs Frank B. Lay, Sr., and M. Henry Lane were challenged, although the accusations against these two were never as substantial as those against Palmer and the "Lay Boys," as the latter were identified in an unsympathetic press.

George Lay had complained that he had only $200 to support himself and had been granted permission from some unidentified source to leave Kalamazoo to seek employment. He did so without a trace and remained absent from the city for much of October. His absence, coupled with the publicized accusations about gambling on the horses and the private sale of several cars in Dayton, Ohio, for a $1,200 profit, exacerbated the appearance of guilt and the public mistrust of the company and its high-ranking officers.

Frank B. Lay, Jr. was called to the stand periodically and grilled unmercifully by attorney Sanford Ladd about his conduct, the company's business, and his dealings with Gerber. Much of the story was reported by the *Telegraph-Press* on October 10, 1913. Ladd asked a number of pointed questions in rapid succession to which Lay often responded with tedious detail, and Ladd would shout admonishment: "We don't want any sermons here." When asked about inside deals with Gerber,

Figure 15-2. Claude Carney, from a 1913 newspaper photograph.

Lay sprang from his chair, his face white with rage, shouting, "I consider that an insult." These outbursts were not uncommon and were often followed by heated personal exchanges between Ladd and attorney Claude S. Carney, who represented Lay. Carney accused Prosecutor Ladd of "grandstanding," and called Ladd a "peevish puppy." Undaunted by the verbal attack, Ladd replied that he would take care of the case and then take care of Carney later. Referee Banyon attempted to quiet the atmosphere with humor. "My, my, how you fellows do talk," he exclaimed, but he was unsuccessful in quelling the animosity or the shouting matches between Ladd and Frank Lay, Jr. with the occasional interjection by the feisty Carney.

News reports of the charges facing the company's officers and the members of the Lay family appeared almost daily throughout the month to the detriment of the company, the city, and the citizenry. These hearings during the month of October exposed five major problems:

1. DISCREPANT REPORTS: Victor Palmer was in the worst position of all of the defendants when Ladd uncovered a discrepancy between the sworn statement of the financial condition of the company Palmer had submitted to the Michigan Department of Treasury on December 31, 1912 and the glowing report that he distributed on January 31, 1913 to several banks from which he would later obtain loans. The discrepancy in the assets was nearly $2 million, a revelation that would later bring Palmer to the criminal courts. During the cross examination Palmer also admitted that on June 30, 1913 he had prepared another statement showing total assets of the company to be $2,689,953.59 and liabilities of $881,441.11, a report he gave to the Chicago broker of Bond and Goodman early in July as collateral for planned loans to finance continued production of the 1913 automobiles.

There was little question that Palmer's annual report issued on January 31, 1912 was intended to create the impression of a company on a solid financial base. The following passage from that report was published in the September 29, 1913 *Telegraph-Press*:

> The motor car sales and demand for the product reasonably far exceeded our expectations, and it has met with public approval, and the demand for it is several times in excess of the production, and as a result that particular branch of the business is in a gratifying condition; at the same time we are not trying to meet or overmeet the demand with production, preferring to have a substantial waiting list. It is not the intention of the corporation to supplant the horse-drawn vehicle business with the motor car; neither is it the intention to build more of any product than can be safely marketed.

Palmer attempted to absolve himself of blame by denying that he controlled the finances and protested that he reported figures to both Lay, Sr. and Lane. His testimony was not well received by Lane, who challenged him in the arcade of the Burdick Hotel that evening, and the two engaged in heated debate. According to Palmer, he had just addressed a pleasant "good evening" to Mr. Lane "when the latter turned upon him in a fury and roundly berated him." Lane was quick to anger and, according to bystanders, Lane invited Palmer to "come outside." The incident was reminiscent of Lane's confrontation with the railroad men some fifteen years before. According to the newspaper report, if others had not intervened, there surely would have been a fight. Palmer spoke to a reporter that evening and the entire affair was described by the *Gazette* on September 18:

> Up to this time I have preferred not to be quoted in the newspaper for I desire none of that kind of publicity, wishing rather to have the real facts come out in the evidence. The evidence, however, seems to be leading in a direction that is not particularly relished by Mr. Lane and hence the threat to my life.

Furthermore, Palmer claimed that the members of the Lay family had removed Henry Lane from the presidency of the company in 1912 because of his attitude and to prevent ruin by keeping him from "milking the company" further. "I will not be the goat any longer," he told the reporter, and left the Burdick Hotel.

Palmer's bravado in the Burdick Hotel that evening quickly disappeared the next day in the hearing room where he complained of undue stress and ill health. His answers under questioning were those of a defeated man. Transcripts of the bankruptcy hearing are most telling. When asked if the company's liabilities on August 1, 1913 were shown to be over $3 million, almost four times the amount in his report, his noncommittal answer was, "So it has been shown."

When asked if he had borrowed money on the basis of the June statement, he again equivocated, replying "I think so."

The case against Palmer was growing, and by the middle of October he was desperate enough to attempt to leave the city. The discrepancy between his annual report to the state and his embellished reports to the banks was discovered on Tuesday, October 14, and the news appeared in the local papers on Thursday, October 16. That Friday two trunks appeared at the railway station from Palmer's residence and were checked through to New York City. Palmer and his wife arrived at the railway station around 5:30 that evening, but the trunks were held up by officials and the trip was squelched. The entire incident was surrounded by rumor that Palmer had traveled east the past June to secure loans that he then deposited in a Canadian bank. This story was substantiated in part by the disclosure of a slip of paper found beneath an officer's desk at a Detroit bank showing a transaction for $25,000 and signed by Palmer. Supposedly, a trusted chauffeur accompanied Palmer on that eastern trip and was given six month's salary and told not to return to Kalamazoo. It was believed that the chauffeur was residing in Peoria, Illinois, at the time of the hearing.

Palmer subsequently declared bankruptcy, citing assets of only $21,122.28, including $103 in cash, $130 in clothing, $120 in household goods, $330 in other property, and $20,000 in stocks and bonds. He asserted that his personal liabilities to eighteen banks amounted to $1,657,228.70, although there was no hint of the probable expenditures associated with such indebtedness. He withdrew to his residence for the next several weeks claiming illness caused by the stress from the hearings and his public humiliation.

2. SHODDY ACCOUNTING: Several other witnesses were called to the stand, including Everett E. Jacobus, head bookkeeper, and Earl J. McCone. McCone had many years of experience in the vehicle business, although he had just joined the company in November of 1912. Soon after he started work at Michigan Buggy, he discovered that the company was unable to determine the cost of producing a single car and that the company's inventory was figured at "retail market value" rather than the actual cost of the merchandise. Since the supposed "market value" of the goods was always the greater of the two, this style of accounting inflated the assets. McCone also discovered outstanding unpaid accounts of $300,000–$325,000, but he testified that he was surprised to find that Palmer had little interest in these figures. According to McCone, as recorded in the *Telegraph-Press* on October 14, 1913, the annual report that Palmer prepared did not reflect the actual figures of unpaid accounts or notes receivable that were in his department:

> I knew that the list of bills receivable which I had prepared had not been turned over to Palmer.
> When I saw the annual statement with the list of bills receivable there, I made up my mind not
> to move my household goods to Kalamazoo.

The advertised price of a Michigan touring car in 1913 was $1,585 and McCone had estimated the cost of producing a single Model R touring car at $1,445. He used the blueprints to determine the cost of materials at $710 and then added the general labor expense, which brought the cost to $945. He added another $500 for all overhead costs, such as plant maintenance, foreman's salary, advertising, and interest on the notes, but even that figure did not include any irregularities, such as the $100,000 expense to replace the faulty Sandusky engines in some of the cars in late 1912 and early 1913. During the period of production from late 1909 through the summer of 1913, he figured that the company lost about $200 on each car manufactured. Only the continued profits of the horse-drawn vehicle department allowed the company to last as long as it did. Earl McCone was articulate, self assured, and forthright. His testimony, as recorded by the *Telegraph-Press* on October 14, 1913, was devastating.

> I asked some one if these people realized the condition the factory was in. The party told me
> that the failure was not going to hurt Mr. Palmer, as he was protected. He said that he knew
> that Palmer had been fixing himself for this for two years but no one could convince the other
> officials. …Certain officials did not want to know the actual cost of the cars as they might lose
> their soft jobs.…
> I objected to the way the inventory was figured from start to finish. There was a great army of
> well-paid employees who were non-producers. …I went to Mr. Lay [George Lay] and told him
> that there was not a nickel being made on the cars manufactured.
> Mr. Lay said; " Well we made money last year."…
> I told Mr. Lay that this accounting system would break the business. I explained that the bank
> of England could not stand up under these losses.

According to McCone, the sale of the cars actually exacerbated the revenue loss. Gerber demanded cars at discount prices and the officials complied, reasoning that the loss on these sales could be made up by increased production and sales to other companies. The sales to other dealers, however, could not take up the slack, particularly if Gerber sold most of the cars and was also paid a commission by the company for cars sold to dealers in his territory. Finally, many of the other dealers were not financially secure enough to purchase large numbers of cars and even then, most dealers purchased cars with promissory notes. The notes in turn were sold to banks at a 6 percent discount, and some were even sold a second time at another 6 percent discount thus substantially reducing the potential for any profit to the company.

Jacobus was the senior of the two bookkeepers and had been in the employ of the company for six years. He was familiar with the endless chain of financial paper and the undated promissory notes in the vault. The notes would come from the dealers to Palmer, he testified, then to Mr. Johnson, head of the bookkeeping department, who would date them and turn them over to Jacobus, who gave them to Mr. Arnold for deposit in the bank. Jacobus testified that as far as he knew no one kept track of these dealers' notes. He also estimated that the notes had a face value of up to $7.2 million, and that many had been sold to banks or were "just floating around the country." He claimed, for example, that the notes for the first load of 1910 vehicles sent to O. E. Short in New York City in the spring of 1910 were never paid and that the notes remained in the vault and had not been sold to any banks.

During the testimony from Jacobus, as reported by the *Telegraph* on October 13, 1913, Sanford Ladd summarized the situation in his typical direct style.

"This was a clear blue sky business," exclaimed Attorney Ladd in disgust, and the witness admitted, "that it did look that way."

"In other words," concluded Ladd, "the very day that the company decided to get away from the vehicle business with its slow but sure profits, right then, the company was doomed."

3. PRIVATE AUTO SALES: Another major point of irritation for the creditors was the distribution of cars among the officers who were found to possess one or more Michigan cars, as well as the distribution of cars to Kalamazoo city officials. Apparently this give-away program was entirely at the expense of the creditors. Interestingly, some of these auto assignments were not charged on the books until just after the company's closing and prior to the arrival of the auditors. The list of assignments included: M. Henry Lane, car #5781; Frank Lay, Sr. car #4347 and car #7230; Victor Palmer, car #5314 and car #7211; Frank B. Lay, Jr. car #5644, car #7219, car #3628 and car #6032; George Lay, car #5875 and car #5928; William Cameron, car #5464; and George Daugherty, car #6151. Owning a $1,500 car in 1913 was indicative of considerable wealth, but for Frank B. Lay, Jr. to own four cars was a considerable extravagance. These disclosures raised the ire of the creditors who demanded to know if company officers had the right to "loot" the assets of a corporation without the knowledge of the stockholders and creditors.

The bankruptcy hearing transcripts and the *Telegraph* of October 10, 1913 provide the record of the testimony. Ladd turned his attention directly to Frank Lay, Jr.'s private sale of company cars and then launched an attack on Lay concerning the sale of the cars to Gerber in late July of 1913. He opened the questioning by asking Lay about sending a former physician, Dr. Lawton, to Toledo, Ohio, to sell a car for $1,000:

Ladd: "What did you do with the money?"
Lay: "I spent it."
Ladd: "Tell where any part of the $1,000 cash you received for the car went for?"
Lay: "Grocery and meats."
Ladd: "Did you use it to pay any debts?"
Lay: "I don't remember that I owed anything. Spent some for street car tickets, groceries and

meats, a suit of clothes, golf sticks, golf balls, and looking for a job."

Ladd: "You went to Atlantic City with Mr. Gerber?"

Lay: "I saw him in Pittsburgh."

Ladd: "You are the man that sent all of the cars from all parts of the country to Pittsburgh?"

Lay: "Yes."

Ladd: "Didn't you send a message to Portland telling them to send cars to Pittsburgh?"

VICTOR PALMER IN NEAR COLLAPSE UNDER CHARGE

Physician Orders Him Taken From Stand when Accused of Covering Up $1,250,000 in Dealer's Notes

Fig. 15-3. Palmer was besieged on the stand. The Kalamazoo Gazette, September 13, 1913.

Lay: "I might have sent it."

Ladd: "Telegrams which were sent to Portland in July told agents there to go to all points along the Pacific coast from Portland to Sacramento to send cars to Pittsburgh. 'Work night and day and telegraph me daily in Pittsburgh,' the message said. You flooded the country with telegrams to dealers all over the country just like that, didn't you?"

Lay: "I made a sale of certain cars to Mr. Gerber so that we could realize cash for them. I wanted to get cash on them."

Ladd: "How much was Gerber going to pay you personally?"

Lay: "I consider that an insult. Not one cent have I ever received. I did it for the best interests of the concern."

Ladd: "So you thought it good judgment to send cars across the continent to Pittsburgh at a freight cost of $200 and sell them in Pittsburgh and net $300, didn't you?"

Lay: "I don't remember the figures."

Ladd: "How much were you going to get for those cars. Five hundred and fifty dollars?"

The witness appealed to the court asking whether he should answer.

Ladd (pointing a finger at Lay): "You can answer, but not preach a sermon."

Ladd: "When did you get the $1,000 at Toledo, before or after you sent the telegrams?"

Lay: "Before."

Ladd continued to probe the sale of a car with a retail value of over $1,500.

Ladd: "Oh, you took an automobile, charged yourself $900, and sent it to Toledo and sold it for $1,000?"

Lay: "I needed the money, the company owed me."

Ladd: "Oh, the velvet payroll, eh? As sales manager of the Michigan Buggy Company, it was your practice to sell machines for whatever you could get?"

Lay: "I thought that deal I made with Gerber was a good one. I will explain if Mr. Ladd will allow me."

Ladd: "You are not running the show here… I object. Your father, when he learned of the Gerber deal, he tried to stop it?"

Lay: "Circumstances changed."

Ladd: "You knew Gerber had an account of $800,000 here, didn't you?"

Lay: "I didn't know."

Ladd: "Was the contract with Gerber ever delivered to him?"

Lay: "Yes sir."

Ladd: "When?"

Lay: "On the Tuesday following Gerber's arrival on July 28."

Ladd: "Wasn't it on Monday, the day before the directors meeting on Tuesday?"

Lay: "I don't remember a meeting on Tuesday."

Edwin Gerber claimed that the contract, absolving him of all debt with the Michigan Buggy Company, had been misplaced by the Kalamazoo detectives who

LANE TESTIFIES BEFORE REFEREE IN BANKRUPTCY

Chairman of Board of Directors of Defunct Michigan Buggy Co. Gives Evidence

Fig. 15-4. Headline from The Kalamazoo Gazette, *October 13, 1913.*

searched his Pittsburgh office. Ladd charged that the minutes of the meeting in which the Gerber contract was drafted had been prepared suspiciously prior to the meeting by Frank Lay, Jr. Therefore, the time of the delivery of the contract became an important point of the hearing.

Ladd: "So you don't remember the meeting on Tuesday, when you and your brother bolted—when your father and Mr. Lane said the contract was void?"

Lay: "I can't remember the exact day."

When Victor Palmer returned to the stand, Ladd turned his questioning to the apparent partiality shown to Gerber in his dealings with the Michigan Buggy Company.

Ladd: "Now why did you extend the amount of credit that you did to Mr. Gerber?"

Palmer: "I didn't know that he had such an account."

Ladd: "Why did you allow him to have an account of from $300,000 to $400,00?"

Palmer: "To the best of my recollection, we had notes here covering that amount."

Ladd: "You know that he came here in the last part of July and took those notes?"

Palmer: "So I have heard."

Ladd: "Did Mr. Gerber have a special dispensation around here?"

Palmer: "No!"

Ladd: "Didn't Gerber get five percent more [referring to the discounted price of the cars] than any of the agents?"

Palmer: "Not that I know of."

Ladd: "Wasn't George Lay a director in Gerber's company?"

Palmer: "Not that I know of."

Ladd: "Gerber was in very close touch with you, wasn't he?"

Palmer: "He was here from time to time; I introduced him to the local banks."

Charles B. Hays, former mayor of the city and noted real estate developer, was implicated in the financial mess a second time during the questioning of Palmer concerning the shoddy practices of the company. In 1909, Hays had helped sell stock to raise money for developing the Mighty Michigan, and on this day he was implicated by his ownership of an automobile given to him by the company. Testimony by Palmer concluded that the car had been given to Charles B. Hays in compensation for some service rendered, but a description of the exact nature of the service was not forthcoming. According to Palmer, officials of the city of Kalamazoo, as well as Cameron, the chief engineer, and Dougherty, another manager, also had cars because the company owed them money.

VELVET PAYROLL OF BUGGY COMPANY IS UNCOVERED ON WITNESS STAND

Testimony Before Referee Full of Sensations; Huge Amounts Charged to Fictitious Account and Handed to Officers

FINANCIAL STATEMENT IS UNRAVELLED

Attorney for Receiver Declares Half Million Dollars Is Entered Twice in General Inventory, Other Queer Features Appear

Fig. 15-5. "Velvet Payroll" makes its public appearance in The Kalamazoo Gazette, September 18, 1913.

Ladd continued to probe the sale of cars at reduced prices to Gerber, and to implicate Frank Lay, Jr. as the perpetrator of a scheme to defraud Michigan Buggy to his and Gerber's benefit. The private sale of the cars, the special sales at discount prices to Gerber, and the status of the financial accounts between Gerber and the Michigan Buggy Company would prove to be lingering points of contention between the creditors and Gerber. That conflict would dictate the final dissolution of the magnificent plant and the Mighty Michigan.

4. THE VELVET PAYROLL: The arrangements for special salary payments were also disclosed in October under Ladd's incessant questioning. His combative style of cross examination changed little and he pursued this line of questioning with a vengeance. The "velvet payroll" was purportedly conceived at the new Burdick Hotel in January of 1913, by Victor L. Palmer, George Lay, and Frank B. Lay, Jr., although these men held only ten percent of the shares of the now-defunct company. Frank Lay, Sr. testified that as president of the company he was unable to obtain the minutes of that January meeting, and Lane in turn claimed that he never did receive the $6,000 that was his reported share. Palmer attempted to blame the special payroll on the elder Henry Lane, but the former company president vigorously denied the existence of the velvet payroll with this curious statement in an interview with a Gazette reporter on September 19, 1913:

> It was never heard of in the history of the company until July 1913. The statements of Mr. Palmer were maliciously and absolutely false and he knew they were when he made them…
>
> [T]here never was any such thing as a velvet payroll.

Lane suggested that several years ago one of the department heads had been given a contract in which he would receive $300 at the end of the year, but that was not "velvet" and there was nothing secret about the arrangement. Both Frank Lay, Sr. and Henry Lane successfully distanced themselves from the "velvet payroll," a move that was to their benefit when the criminal proceedings began in the spring of 1914.

The distribution of the money to the "velveteers" was reported in the Telegraph-Press on two occasions: September 18 and October 16, 1913. The first account resulted from testimony by Victor Palmer, while the second was taken from a detailed statement prepared by Palmer for the period July 1, 1912 to July 1, 1913 at the request of the Detroit Trust Company. The discrepancy of $68,946.45 between the October report and the September report suggests that after his testimony, Palmer attempted to diminish the size of the special payroll in the latter report and distribute the blame among other officials. When the report was issued, it was the smaller of the two figures that the Detroit Trust Company reported to the creditors of the company. There was no disagreement that the funds were charged to a bogus account for J. Roach and Company, listed under the heading of advertising and further disguised on the company's books as an asset.

THE VELVET PAYROLL

EMPLOYEE'S NAME	COMPANY POSITION	REPORTED 9-18-13	REPORTED 10-16-13
Henry Lane	Board Chairman	6,000.00	N/R
Frank B. Lay, Sr.	President	35,000.00	12,000.00
Frank B. Lay, Jr.	Vice-president	25,000.00	18,783.31
George T. Lay	Vice-president	25,000.00	18,783.31
George Dougherty		N/R	2,816.53
J. C. Wilson	Production Manager	N/R	300.00
James Reynolds	Order Dept. Head	N/R	100.00
Thomas Grant	Assembly Manager	N/R	1,049.98
William H. Cameron	Chief Engineer	16,000.00	1,035.00
Victor Palmer	Secretary/Treasurer	25,000.00	14,083.07
TOTAL		$132,000.00	$68,946.45

In addition to this distribution of funds, additional money had been set aside in a bank in nearby Marshall, Michigan, late in the summer when it appeared that the Hydraulic Press Steel Company of Cleveland, Ohio, would place a lien on company funds. Ladd made claims of mismanagement of these funds, but Frank Lay, Jr. contended that the money had been set aside to meet payroll obligations at the end of the summer. On August 5, Frank Lay, Sr. and Henry Lane were placed on the factory payroll and, by Judge Mills' order, each received a $500 draft in payment for their July work. This disclosure of additional funds that might have been used to meet some of the company's outstanding promissory notes only served to fuel the existing anger of the creditors.

In a vain attempt to protect himself, Palmer accused Henry Lane of taking $35,000 to $60,000 and Frank B. Lay, Sr. of taking approximately $35,000 out of the business. According to Palmer, all of the real estate owned by the two men was once listed as a company asset and both the property and the taxes were charged off to the company, including a portion of the construction funds for Lane's expensive residence, known because of its grandeur as "The Lane Castle." On a second occasion, when a bond issue was authorized by the directors, Lane mortgaged the house for $40,000 and pocketed the money. When the bonds were sold, $40,000 was paid back to Lane to release the lien. In his testimony, reported in the *Telegraph-Press* on September 18, 1913, Palmer asserted:

> I estimate that since 1907 M. H. Lane and F. B. Lay, Sr. have taken out of the company in the
> neighborhood of $750,000. In 1911 alone, on the dividend declared on the stock, $150,000

was drawn out of the company and disbursed. There was constant friction between the two owners, as a result of each being fearful that one would secure more money from the company than the other.

5. THE HAREM: The disclosure of the so-called "harem" at 1216 South West Street (South Westnedge Avenue) where company officials were said to have taken potential customers for entertainment was a major exposé. The report, written by a Detroit journalist, appeared in *The Kalamazoo Gazette* on October 8, 1913:

> Kalamazoo is a city with a headache, awaking from a financial jag which had gripped it for many months, with the feelings of the cold gray dawn of the morning-after now prevalent.
>
> The existence of this so-called harem was widely known in Kalamazoo. During the delirium of the financial jag on which the town has been there even was a little hysterical sort of fancy for this harem. Just as some men will brag of their ability to drink every one else under the table, so there was an exalted feeling in deleterious spendthrift circles that Kalamazoo was sort of "going everyone else one better," by having in its midst a coterie of grotesque spenders who maintained their own private harem for the entertainment of themselves and their friends.
>
> This alleged harem was in reality a house of debauchery, drinking and gambling containing several women and having for its habitues an exclusive circle of men. It was located on South West Street.

Ladd was relentless in his questioning of Victor Palmer about the existence of the house, but as the testimony was reported in hearing transcripts and in the *Gazette* on October 16, 1913, he got nothing but elusive answers.

Ladd: "Did the Michigan Buggy company maintain a clubhouse in Kalamazoo for the purpose of entertaining guests?"

Palmer: "I did not know it."

Ladd: "Do you know a man by the name of J. A. Patten?"

Palmer: "I know a Jack Patten, he is a traveling man."

Ladd: "Didn't Jack lease the house at 1216 South West Street and didn't you and your salesman guarantee the rent at the DenBleyker real estate agency?"

Palmer: "I most certainly did not."

Ladd: "Who are your stenographers out here?"

Palmer: "A Miss Bird and Miss Griswold."

Ladd: "When did Miss Griswold leave the company's employ?"

Palmer: "In May I think."

When Palmer denied that he had ever taken guests to the house, Ladd continued to press the point, often repeating the same question, or a variation thereof, in an attempt to break his testimony. Palmer remained noncommittal, often shouting his answers at Ladd and continued to claim no memory of the circumstances about which Ladd so artfully probed. In spite of the intense questioning the issue ended unresolved.

Ladd: "Did you ever go there (to the house) alone?"

Palmer: "I don't think so, I might have, I have no idea which house you mean on the street."

Ladd: "Did not Miss Griswold stay at the house?"

Palmer: "Possibly, I don't know."

Fig. 15-6. The headline "Some Michigan Buggy Beauties" and these four images appeared in the August 21, 1909 issue of the Michigan Buggy News *with the caption "These young women write our letters—and sometimes wait on dealers! Come see them." Could these photographs be of Miss Bird or Miss Griswold?*

Ladd: "Didn't you take her to that house in your automobile?"

Palmer: "Possibly, I often took the girls riding, I don't know what house you have reference to."

Ladd: "Where is Miss Griswold now?"

Palmer: "I don't know."

Ladd: "Don't you know that you went there from October 1912 to June 1913?"

Palmer: "I couldn't tell you."

Ladd: "Didn't George Lay entertain merchandise men there?"

Palmer: "I could not tell you."

Ladd: "Were you ever at the clubhouse in the 1200 block?"

Palmer: "I might have."

Ladd: "Would you say that there was not a clubhouse to entertain guests at that number?"

Palmer: "Not to my knowledge."

Ladd: "Would you say there was not?"

Palmer: "I don't think there was such a clubhouse."

Ladd: "Where is Miss Griswold now?"

Palmer: "I don't know."

Ladd: "Did you ever deposit any money to the account of Patten at the bank?"

Palmer: "I did not."

Ladd: "Did anyone else?"

Palmer: "I don't know."

Ladd: "You wouldn't say that there was not a clubhouse on South West Street?"

Palmer: "I do not know of my knowledge."

The witness claimed that he spent hundreds of thousands of dollars to entertain potential customers and often took them to local hotels or the Post Tavern in Battle Creek, but Ladd was unable to break his testimony or his denial that the company maintained a house of prostitution and gaming. The faulty memory that Palmer revealed in this testimony was typical and evident throughout the hearings. Eventually, his evasiveness would prove to be his downfall. The questions continued:

Ladd: "You were at this house at times yourself, Mr. Palmer?"

Palmer: "I couldn't say that."

Ladd: "You wouldn't deny it would you?"

Palmer: "I couldn't say that."

Ladd: "Didn't you take guests there?"

MAINTAIN GAY HAREM ON CASH OF STOCKHOLDERS

Cyclonic Sensation Created Through State by Revelations of Scandal in Buggy Company Investigation

During Delirium of Power Auto Company Officials Carouse and Make Merry in House on West Street

DUPED INVESTORS MUST PAY BILL

Fig. 15-7. This headline appeared in The Kalamazoo Gazette *on October 8, 1913 and raised the ire of the "duped investors."*

Palmer: "I did not."

Ladd: "Did you ever see any gambling there?"

Palmer: "I don't know."

Ladd: "Was there a roulette wheel there?"

Palmer: "I don't know."

Ladd: "Wasn't that place in charge of Miss Beasley?"

Palmer: "I don't know."

Ladd: "You say that you didn't guarantee the rent of that place—or that anyone else didn't?"

Palmer: "To the best of my knowledge and belief."

Ladd: "You don't recall anything about the house?"

Palmer: "I don't know."

Ladd: "Wasn't the place rented until July and closed in June?"

Palmer: "I don't know."

Ladd: "Didn't Miss Griswold have the key?"

Palmer: "I don't know."

Ladd: "She left the company in May, didn't she?"

Palmer: "I couldn't say exactly."

Ladd was relentless in pursuing the details and Palmer, responding in angry tones, often shouted his denials at the attorney, but Ladd was never able to get an answer of any substance from Palmer about the "harem."

Ladd subsequently pursued a similar line of questioning with Frank Lay, Jr., but again without success. While all of the company officials seemed to accept the existence of the "clubhouse," none had any recollection of how the house came into being nor, according to their testimony, had they ever visited the residence. Ladd's cross examination, that quickly turned into a shouting match with Frank Lay, Jr. was no more productive than his questioning of Palmer.

Ladd: "Did you know anything about a Club house?"

F. Lay, Jr.: "Absolutely not. I never knew a thing about such a place until I read about it in the newspapers."

Ladd: "You'll swear to that?"

Lay: "I will."

"You are excused," said Ladd, laughing at Lay as he left the stand. Clearly, Sanford Ladd had a number of facts, some circumstantial evidence, and a number of accusations about the "harem" on

South West Street, but in spite of his relentless and often leading questioning, he could not get either Victor Palmer or Frank B. Lay, Jr. to admit to the existence of such a place.

Ladd attempted to establish that the Michigan Buggy's "Patten account" was the "harem" and that the "J. Roach account" was the "velvet payroll." Reluctantly, Ladd turned to questioning about

the financial affairs of the company to prove the real intent of the two Michigan Buggy Company accounts. Palmer continued to be evasive and, because of an alleged poor memory, his answers provided neither credible substance nor worthwhile content.

The events of October caused great stir among the citizenry, but the major issue was undeniable. Palmer did admit that he distributed discrepant annual reports to the state and to the banks, and that he had prepared a statement dated June 30, 1913 showing that the company's assets were $2,689,953.59 and the liabilities were only $881,441.11. He presented this statement, compiled just one month before the failure of the company, to the Chicago bond brokers of Bond & Goodman in early July. Palmer attempted to protect himself, claiming that he had obtained the figures from the department heads. Although he

Fig. 15-8. This photo ran under a headline "House Known as 'The Harem'" in the October 18, 1913 issue of The Kalamazoo Gazette.

continued to be evasive in his answers, this record of falsifying assets of well over $1 million would eventually prove to be his downfall.

REFERENCES

Wanted to "Split" Money Secretly Deposited in Bank Early in Summer. *Kalamazoo Telegraph-Press*, October 16, 1913.
George Lay Missing, Said to Be in South. *Kalamazoo Telegraph-Press*, October 16, 1913.
Grand Jury to Probe Michigan Buggy. *The Horseless Age*, October 8, 1913, pp. 563–64.
Palmer Fails for Over $1,655,000. *Kalamazoo Telegraph-Press*, October 16, 1913.
Trust Company Attorney Grills Frank B. Lay. *Kalamazoo Telegraph-Press*, October 10, 1913.

Michigan Buggy Liabilities Eighty Times Greater Than Assets. *The Horseless Age*,
    October 22, 1913, p. 14.

Hearing to Start Again on Tuesday. *Kalamazoo Telegraph-Press*, October 25, 1913.

Lay Denies Brother Has Fled From Quiz. *The Kalamazoo Gazette*, October 18, 1913.

Blame for Statement Put on Victor Palmer. *The Kalamazoo Gazette*, October 9, 1913.

Creditors Want Goods They Sold. *Kalamazoo Telegraph-Press*, November 12, 1913.

Rumored Attorney General Will Force Prosecutions. *Kalamazoo Telegraph-Press*,
    September 29, 1913.

Directors Near Fisticuffs in Hotel Lobby. *The Kalamazoo Gazette*, September 18, 1913.

*Transcript: The District Court of the United States for the Western District of Michigan.
    In the Matter of the Michigan Buggy Company Bankrupt, Fall 1913*. Western Michigan
    University Archives, Kalamazoo MI.

Trunks Mysteriously Shipped From Palmer Home. *Kalamazoo Telegraph-Press*,
    October 18, 1913.

Figures in Annual Report of Buggy Company Were Padded. *Kalamazoo Telegraph-Press*,
    October 14, 1913.

Selling Price of Cars Less Than Their Cost. The Kalamazoo Gazette, October 15, 1913.

Michigan Motor Car Company Failure a Bad One. *Automobile Trade Journal*, November
    1913, p. 76.

Probing Adds to Odor From Michigan Buggy's Failure. *Motor World*, October 14, 1913, p. 7.

Disclose High Finance of the Michigan Buggy Co. *The Horseless Age*, October 15, 1913,
    p. 607.

Chicago Mail Order House and Kalamazoo Man May Bid for Michigan Buggy Co.
    Kalamazoo Telegraph-Press, October 13, 1913.

Trust Company Wants to Know About Sale of Cars. *Kalamazoo Telegraph-Press*,
    November 11, 1913.

Report Shows How Money Was Divided at Factory—Many Notes Ready to Go.
    Kalamazoo Telegraph-Press, January 19, 1914.

Sales Manager Pleads Complete Innocence. *The Kalamazoo Gazette*, October 11, 1913.

Velvet Payroll of Buggy Company Is Uncovered. *The Kalamazoo Gazette*,
    September 18, 1913.

M. H. Lane Denies He Was Author of Velvet Payroll at Michigan Buggy Co.
    The Kalamazoo Gazette, September 19, 1913.

Lane Testifies Before Referee in Bankruptcy Hearing. *The Kalamazoo Gazette*,
    October 10, 1913.

Lay Sr. Didn't Know Anything About Crooked Work Around Factory.
    Kalamazoo Telegraph-Press, October 15, 1913.

Grilled by Trust Attorney. *Kalamazoo Telegraph-Press*, September 18, 1913.

"Velvet Payroll" Helped Lower Cost of Living. *Kalamazoo Telegraph-Press*,
    October 16, 1913.

Maintain Gay Harem on Cash of Stockholders. *The Kalamazoo Gazette*, October 8, 1913.

Palmer and Frank B. Lay Jr. Didn't Know About Harem. *Kalamazoo Telegraph-Press*, October 16, 1913.

Some Michigan Buggy Beauties. *Michigan Buggy News*, August 21, 1909.

Officials Knew Failure of Co. Was Sure to Come. *Kalamazoo Telegraph-Press*, October 8, 1913.

FIGHTING TO KEEP AUTO COMPANY IN KALAMAZOO

Commercial Club Sends Committee to Grand Rapids to Urge Any Favorable Bid for Buggy Plant.

At a special meeting of the board of directors of the Commercial club held last night the special committee appointed to represent the organization at the Grand Rapids hearing were instructed to fight strongly for any bid which would permit the Michigan Motor Car company to start active operations without delay.

The much mooted bid of E. F. Gerber of Pittsburgh, which was withdrawn at the first hearing September 24, was strongly favored by the board of directors.

The club has declared itself ready to favor any bid which will bring about the immediate operation of the factory, thereby saving the city from losing a large number of valuable citizens. For this reason the Gerber bid is considered by them to be valuable.

Gerber has behind him a strong selling combine. He has agents throughout the country waiting for shipments of cars. A strong organization of this kind, if properly managed, would mean much to the city, they say.

President Grant, in speaking to the directors, said: "What if we few men here were to raise enough capital to purchase the Michigan plant? We would have a white elephant on our hands with no organization to promote the sale of cars." This was the concensus of opinion of the men present.

The committee, composed of James Grant, O. K. Buckhout and J. H. Burke, was instructed to use every effort in their power, after hearing all bids, to bring about the acceptance of the one which would result in the quickest resumption of work, whether that bid was made by local or out of town parties. The committee will fight any proposal looking to the dissolution of the enterprise.

Fig. 16-1. Members of the Commercial Club made speeches, but without financial backing their efforts were ineffective. This headline appeared in The Kalamazoo Gazette, *October 13, 1913.*

Chapter 16

Michigan Buggy Sold

November and December 1913

Think of a concern that was doing a three million dollar business in 1913, that
had a payroll of $75,000 per month being sold off as junk.

—*The Progressive Herald*

The autumn of 1913 and its following holiday season were not festive times in Kalamazoo. The gloom of the collapse of Michigan Buggy hung over the city like a dark cloud, and the eventual sale of the great plant brought a grim finality to the situation. Many Michigan Buggy employees had already left the city and those who remained faced the coming winter storms with uncertainty. Michigan Buggy was placed on the auction block like an old house and with it, the jobs of the men who had made it hum were hammered down by the auctioneer.

The citizens who had purchased common stock in the company as a good faith gesture to support a local enterprise also were informed that they would not get a penny in return. The long and intricate legal battles; the exposure of the self-serving decisions by Gerber, Monroe, Palmer and other company officers; and the financial collapse of the local groups that attempted to purchase the plant had sucked much of the strength from the community and its inhabitants. News of the company's closure had filled the papers almost daily for the past three months and the community was tired of the drama, the uncertainty, and the negative publicity. The Federal Grand Jury was convened in early December to investigate a number of issues, including published reports in the *Weekly Advocate* of graft on the city council in connection with the purchase of ornamental light poles, bribery in the purchase of land for Michigan United Traction, and political favoritism in using expensive paving brick in certain building construction projects, as well as the questionable financial affairs of Michigan Buggy. Many of these events raised suspicions among neighbors, adding to the personal strife within the community, but more turbulence was to follow in 1914.

Soon after the plant closure and the beginning of the bankruptcy hearings, the creditors began to entertain the notion of selling the Michigan Buggy plant, its manufacturing machinery, products, and property. There were three major contestants in the battle to gain control of the once thriving concern: Edward F. Gerber of the Pittsburgh-based Pennsylvania Sales Company; Samuel Winternitz, a Chicago-based auctioneer and wrecker; and various groups of Kalamazoo residents, including the Commercial Club and former employees of the company.

Edward Gerber mounted an aggressive campaign to wrest control of the concern from the receiver, and at one time bragged that he was willing to wager $10,000 that he would be successful in purchasing the company. He had submitted a statement to the national periodical *Motor Age* magazine that he planned to "Take Over Michigan Business." That public notice seemed sufficient to persuade other potential buyers that a deal for the company had been struck and other offers would not be considered. On the morning of September 24, 1913 he submitted a bid of $350,000 at a creditors' meeting in Grand Rapids, Michigan, for all assets, the plant, and all related property and product of the Michigan Buggy Company. A number of creditors were favorably inclined to accept while others were very reluctant to allow Gerber to control all assets including the accounts receivable. The bid was summarily denied. Gerber submitted a second bid later the same day of $280,000 for the real estate, the plant, and material, but did not include accounts due the company. He also promised that if his bid was successful, he would start up the company's manufacturing work by October 1 of that year.

The thought of an operational plant was tempting, and some of the creditors were receptive to the bid. Sanford Ladd, representing the Detroit-based receiver, however, spoke vehemently against the transfer to Gerber, citing evidence of bad management and arguing that Gerber's control of the concern was detrimental to the interests of the creditors. Ladd spoke directly and without compromise on the issue as recorded in the *Telegraph* on September 24, 1913:

> We claim that Mr. Gerber owes the Michigan Buggy Company $380,000. "This looks to us like an attempt made to scuttle the company after the business has been wrecked," said Mr. Ladd.
> "The acceptance of this bid would seriously jeopardize the interests of the creditors," he added.

President Bowers of the Detroit Trust Company sided with Ladd by describing the proceedings of the bankruptcy hearing that had uncovered the "velvet payroll," the "harem" on West Street, and finally, the consignment of over seven hundred Michigan cars to Gerber at bargain prices in July, 1913 before the financial difficulties of the company were made public. There was much distrust of Gerber among the creditors and both bids were firmly defeated, while at the same meeting the Detroit Trust Company was given a vote of confidence as trustee for the concern.

The attorney for one of the creditors summed up the vengeful feeling of the group: "We can only get about fifteen percent of what is coming to us and we are willing to let the tail go with the hide… [W]e want to know where our money went."

Three groups within the community also sought to purchase the company. The Commercial Club of Kalamazoo seemed to provide the most potential on the one hand, but appeared the most inept on the other. In early September, Fred C. Butler, secretary of the club, admitted to a *Telegraph-Press* reporter, "Presently we do not know where to begin." The club's membership consisted of six hundred of the leading businessmen in the city, and an editorial in the *Kalamazoo Telegraph-Press* on September 12, 1913 claimed that the opportunity for action was here. "Any HONEST plan could be carried through successfully," claimed the editor, citing the potential and tremendous power of the club. There were rumors in the community that the manufacturing enterprise might be moved to Connersville, Indiana; Hamilton, Ohio; or Greenville, Pennsylvania, to produce the

"Pittsburgh-Michigan," and, finally, that Michigan Buggy employees had already been contacted about their willingness to move. While these rumors exacerbated the ever-present fear of losing Michigan Buggy and, in spite of the editor's call to action—"Kalamazoo is watching the Commercial Club to grasp the opportunity"—the Commercial Club's response to the challenge was less than forthright.

Members of the Club met with George A. Reynolds, Gerber's attorney, at a luncheon on September 12, and then held a mass meeting of the Commercial Club on September 17, 1913. The Buggy Company case, however, was buried in an agenda for that meeting that included new bylaws, the convention policy, and the formation of the committee of one hundred. The Commercial Club of Kalamazoo did send out

Employes of the Michigan Buggy Company Anxious To Purchase the Vehicle Plant

While Commercial Club Officials Are Busy With "Outside" Matters, Men Here Are Raising Money—May Call Big Mass Meeting to Take Up Offers.

Fig. 16-2. The employees tried in vain to raise fnds followingthese headlines from the October 7, 1913 Kalamazoo Telegraph-Press.

letters to over five hundred creditors, called numerous meetings, and presented their case at every opportunity, but seemed unable to devise a reorganization plan or a funding program acceptable to the creditors. When James Grant, the Club president, and Dallas Boudeman, local attorney and spokesman, spoke at a major meeting of the creditors, they spoke only of the terrible financial loss to Kalamazoo, but offered no alternative plan. On September 23, a booster committee was appointed in an effort to initiate some action. By early October, the possible sale of the plant was being discussed in earnest and was reported in the *Telegraph* and the *Gazette* on October 4. Dallas Boudeman asked that the company and the property remain intact:

> Representing the citizenship of Kalamazoo, I am most certainly against the acceptance of the bid offered by the wrecking company. In the best interests of Kalamazoo, and I believe the creditors as well, it should not be considered for a moment. The dismantling of the magnificent plant is, to my mind, a monstrous proposition. It should be opposed by all creditors.

Judge Sessions responded with his customary humor, to the entertainment of the assembled creditors, when he remarked, "Then you are in favor of cutting the dog's tail off by inches instead of all in one operation."

The creditors did not respond well to the club's presentation that included the goodwill of the people of Kalamazoo, but no financial support. The creditors' position was made clear at the close of the meeting and the curt answer was given by Attorney McKeever of Chicago: "We had expected that as a result of the agitation in Kalamazoo that we would receive an offer from there.This is a matter of dollar and cents and not of sentiment."

A major attempt was also made by an employee group during late September and early October of 1913 to raise sufficient funds to buy at least the horse-drawn vehicle department of the company. Unfortunately, they were able to obtain pledges from one hundred stock holders for only $40,000 of the $100,000 required to reopen that portion of the company. Some conversation transpired between the employees and the creditors, but the Detroit Trust Company made clear that a bankruptcy review would continue no matter what the employees were able to arrange.

Charles B. Hays published a large advertisement in the October 4, 1913 issue of *The Kalamazoo Gazette*, extolling the virtues of the plant and calling for support from the citizenry:

> Inexperienced local men have not unwisely bought the plant—that helps.
>
> Let us all forget Gerber and the creditors;
>
> Let us all do what we can to get a new, sound, solid profit-making plant on the site.
>
> Possibly it would be as well to forget autos and remember buggies. There are real profits in buggies.

The Hays' campaign spoke against the Commercial Club and Gerber and echoed an often heard claim that other buggy plants, the Page Brothers Company in Marshall, Michigan, for example, were turning a profit while the automobile business was profitable only if high production capabilities were possible. It is worth noting that in the fall of 1913 Henry Ford was developing the production line at the Highland Park plant and simultaneously increasing employee salaries to $5 per day. In spite of the public calls for support and attempts at fund-raising by groups of employees, including a personal attempt by M. Henry Lane, the future of Michigan Buggy remained in the hands of the courts. Formal bids for purchase of the plant were entertained by Judge Sessions in Grand Rapids, Michigan.

On October 3, 1913 Gerber submitted to Judge Sessions the following bids:

1) $325,000 for the property and all accounts receivable;
2) $350,000 for the same property as in number 1, but with deferred payments over the next year;
3) $240,000 for the same property, excluding the accounts receivable;
4) $265,000 for the same property, excluding accounts receivable and with deferred payments for one year.

In contrast, Samuel Winternitz offered a $200,000 guarantee for an auction of the company holdings exclusive of the real estate.

In the afternoon session, Gerber offered a final bid of $265,000 in cash for all of the personal effects of the company including all real estate and manufacturing equipment in the buildings. Winternitz countered with $225,000 net cash for an auction sale of the vehicle and automotive plants. Three separate bids were also received for the blanket department, and two separate bids were received for the dwelling houses and real estate adjacent to the factory.

In spite of the larger bid from Gerber and his promise to reopen the factory and the emotional pleas by James Grant and Dallas Boudeman on behalf of the citizens of Kalamazoo, the creditors unanimously accepted Winternitz's final bid. There was strong prejudice among the creditors against Gerber because of his purchase of a large number of cars at bargain prices. The creditors considered that sale of automobiles at the end of July as money from their pockets and, because of it, they were reluctant to trust Gerber and his promises.

The law required a fifteen-day waiting period following the final bid during which any dissatisfied creditor could object to the offer. On October 21, 1913 the final offer by the Winternitz Company was reaffirmed in the United States District Court of Judge Clarence W. Sessions, in spite of the continued bids from Gerber and the fervent pleas from local employee groups. At the same time, rumors of other interests in the company filled the papers. Much of the worry and concern over the destruction of the plant was dispelled when Winternitz promised to attempt to sell the property as an entity during the next twenty days. If that sale proved unsuccessful, however, the entire enterprise would be sold in parcels at auction. "We are not wreckers," said Winternitz. "We are commercial business people. We expect to do good for Kalamazoo if our bid was accepted."

These statements seemed to assuage the objections of Edward Gerber, Attorney Boudeman, and President Grant. The court adjourned.

The decision of the court was final, however, and Michigan Buggy was doomed. The grand plant, the machines, the partially finished products, the raw materials, and the adjacent real estate were placed on the auction block by the

AUTO COMPANY DOOMED; WILL DISMANTLE PLANT

While Attorney General Starts Grand Jury Investigation Here, Creditors Sign Death Warrant of Factory

Fig. 16-3. *"Death Warrant" headline for Michigan Buggy factory from the October 4, 1913* Kalamazoo Gazette.

Winternitz Company of Chicago on Tuesday, December 9, 1913. In spite of the promise by Winternitz, the sale notices that were distributed by the Detroit Trust Company just before the auction date stated that the personal property of the Michigan Buggy Company would be sold in lots and parcels and not as a whole. The real estate would be sold first, followed by the automobile department, the iron working machinery, the trimming department machinery, the buggy department, the blanket department, all remaining automobiles, woodworking machinery, the sleigh department, paints, oils, and fixtures in that order. In spite of his original promise for sale of the company as an intact whole, Winternitz declared that the auction had to be conducted as advertised.

The Winternitz Company planned to offer the goodwill that included customer accounts, patents, blue prints, and customer correspondence with the understanding that the purchaser of the correspondence would turn over all letters pertaining to the manufacture of automobiles and accessories to the purchaser of the Michigan Motor Car Company. Under these circumstances, however, purchasing the Motor Car Company would not guarantee purchase of the iron working or the trimming machinery upon which the manufacture of automobiles depended. The final sales strategy was an optimal one for a financial return to the creditors, but a minimal one for reestablishing the company as a going concern.

Representatives from various industries began to arrive in Kalamazoo on December 3, 1913 to inspect the plant and the items that would be sold. Among the prospective buyers was C. A. Finnegan, president of the Empire Smelting Company in Depew, New York. Earlier that year he had paid $51,000 for the Thomas Automobile Company in Buffalo, New York, that manufactured the famed Thomas Flyer, winner of the New York to Paris race in 1907. On April 21 of the same year, he had purchased the well-known Matheson Automobile Company (William Randolph Hearst owned two Matheson automobiles) in Wilkes-Barre, Pennsylvania. Finnegan was a legitimate contender for Michigan Buggy ownership, but Gerber's notice in *Motor Age* that he had purchased the company and his announced wager that he would buy the company caused Finnegan to withhold his bid of $265,000 to purchase the company intact. That offer was $40,000 in excess of the amount required under the terms of the sale and might have meant the continuance of the Mighty Michigan. By the time Finnegan had discovered Gerber's ruse, Winternitz had already made an advertised commitment to sell the company as component parts and it was too late for Finnegan to make a bid for the entire operation.

Finnegan did submit a bid to the Winternitz Company of $175,000 to purchase the vehicle and automobile departments of the company, a bid that did not include the real estate, the blanket factory, or the lumber at the mill. His plans appeared to entail the completion of an estimated five hundred cars from the remaining stock and then to use the factory as an automobile parts supplier for Michigan cars.

The purchase of bankrupt companies was Finnegan's business. At the same time he was bidding on Michigan Buggy, he was negotiating with the American Locomotive Company in an effort to purchase the service department of the discontinued Alco Motor Car. He had converted two other companies he had purchased into auto supply operations, so a similar automobile parts operation probably would have been profitable in Kalamazoo for three to five years. Finnegan showed no interest in the bonus offered by the Kalamazoo Commercial Club for the continued operation of the plant for a five-year period. He wanted to conduct the business as he saw fit, and, as he commented to the press, he had no intention of being "bound by a contract to operate a plant in this city for a number of years." Officers of the Detroit Trust Company considered his bid up until the auction opened, but ultimately found it unacceptable.

The week the sale opened, a raging blizzard broke early Sunday morning and continued just past dawn on Monday. The storm seemed most severe in Kalamazoo, which was buried under a foot of snow. The factory was well south of town, and though the storm hindered travel in and around the city, the auction took place as scheduled. The papers reported that few buyers were in the city to attend the disposal sale. Many of the two hundred people that did show were local curiosity seekers or simply there to enjoy the complementary lunch. The *Progressive-Herald* reported that, "Henry Lane, once proud and domineering, wandered about unnoticed in the crowd like a lost soul."

The real estate sale did not go well. Winternitz opened the bidding at 9:00 a.m. Tuesday, December 9, 1913 with the usual call:

"How much am I bid for the real estate?"

"Ten thousand dollars," was the lone bid from the back of the room.

Winternitz scornfully replied, "I am selling the property itself, not a photograph of it."

"Rip the building to pieces and you can get more than $100,000 for it," yelled another man endeavoring to inspire the bidders and push the sale of the property.

Even after much cajoling, the best the auctioneer could wrangle from the crowd was a modest $15,000, an amount well under the $50,000 that was demanded by the courts. Winternitz brought down his hammer; the real estate was considered a "no sale," and it was turned over to the Detroit Trust Company for disposal.

The remaining effects of the company were auctioned off during the latter part of the week and all reports indicated that everything other than the real estate sold without incident. The first sale was knocked down to Nathan Gumbinsky, a member of the salvage company of Oscar Gumbinsky and Brothers in Kalamazoo. For $10,500, he purchased the good will of the Michigan Motor Car Company (the motorized vehicle part of the company) that included the correspondence, list of agents, blue prints, and the Michigan's repair schedule, and manuals.

The auction continued through the week, and on Thursday, E. P. D'Arcy, owner of the D'Arcy Spring Company in Kalamazoo, purchased for $1,200 the good will, patents, trademarks, and the correspondence of the Michigan Buggy Company (the horse-drawn vehicle part of the company), including the right to use the trade name. He also purchased a considerable portion of the buggy supply department with the intent of filling accumulated supply orders and to service the 35,000 existing Michigan Buggy customers across the United States and Canada. He then announced his intent to reorganize the vehicle department with the aid of local capital in order to begin the manufacture of buggies and sleighs to fill the four hundred orders for horse-drawn vehicles that had been received at the company since August. There is no evidence of a revival of the Michigan Buggy Company, although some of the supplies may have been incorporated into the very successful D'Arcy Spring Company's product line.

A. C. Finnegan had been unsuccessful in his prior bid for the automobile and buggy departments and, except for the purchase of a few sets of tires and other standard parts and parcels, he did very little bidding. He had lost interest, and the other men involved in the venture with him left the evening prior to the sale. Toward the end of the week, the Winternitz Company was able to hurry matters along and sold all of the stock and personal effects of the company, including $30,000 worth of leather for trimming and upholstery that was hammered down at fifty cents on the dollar. The final sales total did not come within $50,000 of the amount predicted by the Chicago-based auction, but even at that, Winternitz reportedly made a profit of $100,000.

The sale of the second-hand Michigan automobiles—and there was no indication that new cars were available at auction—brought many surprises and, once again raised the ire of the creditors. All of the used Michigan cars sold at auction for at least $500, while Gerber had purchased new cars from the company for $450 just three months prior to the auction sale. The small discrepancy between the used and new car price reinforced once again the creditors' belief that Gerber had conspired with members of Michigan Buggy for his own profit and had done so at their expense. The creditors anticipated a mere fifteen percent of the value of their bills receivable from Michigan Buggy and Gerber's business practices did not please them.

The sale continued through the end of the week, and on Friday, William Maxwell, a Kalamazoo grocer residing at 122 West Water Street offered $40,000 for the factory and real estate holdings. The property included the seventeen acres of land, several factory buildings, the heating and lighting, power plants, sprinkler system, and line shafting all valued at $250,000. Maxwell's offer was the first to come close to the minimum acceptable bid of $50,000 that had been set by Judge Sessions of the circuit court, but the deal was not acceptable and the buildings and land lay idle for another year.

During and following the auction, there were several published rumors of companies that might purchase and occupy the plant. On December 9, the day the auction opened, S. F. Dobbins, president of the Marshall Furnace Company, entered into negotiations with the Kalamazoo Commercial Club to move his company to the city, following his failure to win a tax rebate from the Marshall council. Either the Kalamazoo negotiation was unsuccessful or his approach to Kalamazoo convinced the Marshall council to reconsider, for the furnace company remained at its original site.

The rumors began with headlines in the *Telegraph-Press* on December 11:

> GREAT PLANT MAY SOON BE HIVE OF INDUSTRY, WITH A GREATER NUMBER OF MEN EMPLOYED THAN EVER BEFORE… WILL NOT MAKE AUTOMOBILES IN THE FUTURE, BUT THE BUGGY AND BLANKET DEPARTMENTS TO BE ENLARGED… PUBLISHING DEPARTMENT EMPLOYING 250 MEN TO BE PLACED WHERE AUTOS WERE FORMERLY PRODUCED… COMMERCIAL CLUB RAISES $5,000 IN FIVE MINUTES TODAY TO BIND DEAL… PLANT MAY BE RUNNING BY JANUARY 1, 1914."

This abortive sale was followed by a rumor that appeared in January of 1914 when the headlines reported that a large, but unnamed furniture manufacturer from Grand Rapids, Michigan, planned to consolidate its three manufacturing operations in the Michigan Buggy plant.

None of these negotiations or rumors ever materialized and the Michigan Buggy facility remained vacant for almost a year. The building was finally sold for $45,000 on August 11, 1914 to Charles B. Hays, former city major and one of the city's best-known real estate developers, who had not escaped the personal vicissitudes of the bankruptcy hearing. This sale was not without conflict. Hays apparently purchased the property at the very last minute for just $5,000 more than an earlier bid submitted by W. E. Ready of Niles, Michigan. Ready had offered $40,000 for the property and had deposited earnest money, but was never given an opportunity to raise his bid after Hays made his offer. Ready issued a public complaint, but his claims fell on deaf ears. After Hays' purchase, the building remained empty for almost another year. It was not until the summer of 1915 that W. B. Smith purchased the property from Hays in a very private sale for an undisclosed amount of money. Smith was the agent for the recently founded States Motor Car Manufacturing Company. Manufacture of the States automobile, however, did not begin until the winter of 1916, almost two and a half years after the manufacture of the last Mighty Michigan.

REFERENCES

Kalamazoo Has Probably Lost Michigan Buggy Company. *The Progressive Herald*, November 8, 1913

What Is Kalamazoo Going to Do With This Great Plant? *Kalamazoo Telegraph-Press*, October 30, 1913.

Gerber's Bid Rejected by Unanimous Decisions. *The Kalamazoo Gazette*, September 25, 1913.

Buys Autos to Hold on to Business. *Kalamazoo Telegraph-Press*, September 12, 1913.

Takes Over Michigan Business. *Motor Age*, September 11, 1913, p. 42.

$100,000 Is Now Raised to Purchase Plant Here. *The Kalamazoo Gazette*, October 22, 1913.

Will Kalamazoo Save Michigan Buggy Co.? *Kalamazoo Telegraph-Press*, October 24, 1913.

Buggy Plant Up Today. *Kalamazoo Telegraph-Press*, September 24, 1913.

Michigan Buggy Affair. *Kalamazoo Telegraph-Press*, September 25, 1913.

The Opportunity Is Here. *Kalamazoo Telegraph-Press*, September 12, 1913.

Michigan Buggy Plant to Stay in Kalamazoo. *The Kalamazoo Gazette*, October 2, 1913.

Must Wait Ten Days for Buggy Sale. *Kalamazoo Telegraph-Press*, October 2, 1913.

Commercial Club Hears New Plans. *Kalamazoo Telegraph-Press*, October 10, 1913.

Gerber Lays Plans Before Commercial Club. *The Kalamazoo Gazette*, September 12, 1913.

Big Mass Meeting Is to Be Held. *Kalamazoo Telegraph-Press*, September 17, 1913.

Excellent Committee Is Named to Perfect a New Kalamazoo Booster Club. *Kalamazoo Telegraph-Press*, September 23, 1914.

Commercial Club Backed Offer of Gerber Before Last Meeting of Creditors. *Kalamazoo Telegraph-Press*, October 4, 1913.

Many Facts Kalamazoo Citizens Should Know. *The Kalamazoo Gazette*, October 4, 1913.

Auto Company Doomed, Will Dismantle Plant. *The Kalamazoo Gazette*, October 4, 1913.

Employees of the Michigan Buggy Company Anxious to Purchase Vehicle Plant. *Kalamazoo Telegraph-Press*, October 7, 1913.

Commercial Club Plans to Save Buggy Company. *The Kalamazoo Gazette*, October 18, 1913.

Declare Plant Will Pay Out in Two Years. *The Kalamazoo Gazette*, October 24, 1913.

Factories For Busy Kalamazoo. *The Kalamazoo Gazette*. October 30, 1913.

Michigan Buggy, Things to Consider. *The Kalamazoo Gazette*, October 4, 1913.

Buggy Co. Plant Is Sold Today. *Kalamazoo Telegraph-Press*, October 3, 1913.

Sale of The Michigan Buggy Company Plant Will be Made Within 24 Hours. *Kalamazoo Telegraph-Press*, November 11, 1913.

May Yet Save Kazoo Capital Auto Co. *The Kalamazoo Gazette*, October 5, 1913.

Fighting to Keep Auto Company in Kalamazoo. *The Kalamazoo Gazette*, October 3, 1913.

Chicago Mail Order House and Kalamazoo Man May Bid for Buggy Co. Plant. *Kalamazoo Telegraph-Press*, October 13, 1913.

Winternitz Gets Plant of Michigan Buggy Co. *The Kalamazoo Gazette*, October 22, 1913.

Will Offer Big Price for Michigan Buggy Co. *The Kalamazoo Gazette*, October 29, 1913.

Movable Assets of Michigan Buggy Co. *The Automobile*, October 9, 1913, p. 675.

Michigan Plant Sold for $225,000. *Automobile Topics*, October 25, 1913, p. 829.

Creditors Again Turn Down Gerber. *Kalamazoo Telegraph-Press*, October 22, 1913.

Michigan Buggy Creditors Turn Down Best Offer. *The Progressive Herald*, October 25, 1913.

Gerber and Local Men to Hold Meeting With Commercial Club in Regard to Factory Tonight. *The Kalamazoo Gazette*, October 30, 1913.

Gerber Gives Kazoo Buggy Company Slip. *The Kalamazoo Gazette*, November 8, 1913.

Few Hours Left Sale of Buggy Plant. *Kalamazoo Telegraph-Press*, November 10, 1913.

Chicago Bidder Declares That He Does Not Mean to Wreck Plant as Reported. *Kalamazoo Telegraph-Press*, October 21, 1913.

Michigan Buggy to Be Sold. *Kalamazoo Telegraph-Press*, December 8, 1913.

Piecemeal Sale of Factory Advertised. *The Kalamazoo Gazette*, November 25, 1913.

Buggy Plant Under Hammer Next Week. *The Kalamazoo Gazette*, December 2, 1913.

Buyers Coming to Look Over Material for Sale at Michigan Buggy. *Kalamazoo Telegraph-Press*, December 2, 1913.

Beverly Rae Kimes and Henry Austin Clark Jr. *Standard Catalog of American Cars, 1805–1942, 3rd ed.* Iola, WI: Krause Publications, 1996.

Deal for Michigan Buggy Plant Is Off. *The Kalamazoo Gazette*, November 21, 1913.

Gerber Was Reason for Close Down. *Kalamazoo Telegraph-Press*, December 16, 1913.

Firm Bidding for Plant of Auto Company. *The Kalamazoo Gazette*, December 6, 1913.

Auction Will Start Tuesday. *Kalamazoo Telegraph-Press*, December 6, 1913.

City Buried Under a Foot of Snow. *Kalamazoo Telegraph-Press*, December 8, 1913.

Buggy Plant Auction Sale Starts Today. *Kalamazoo Telegraph-Press*, December 9, 1913.

Sale of Michigan Buggy Material Attracts Crowd. *The Progressive Herald*, December 11, 1913.

Real Estate Not Sold by Auction. *Kalamazoo Telegraph-Press*, December 9, 1913.

$40,000 is Highest Bid for Factory. *Kalamazoo Telegraph-Press*, December 13, 1913.

Michigan Buggy Property Goes to Junk Dealer. *The Horseless Age*, December 17, 1913, p. 1023.

Sales of Michigan Assets. *The Horseless Age*, December 10, 1913, p. 984.

Plant of Auto Company Goes Under Hammer. *The Kalamazoo Gazette*, December 10, 1913.

Offers Bid for Real Estate of Auto Company. *The Kalamazoo Gazette*, December 14, 1913.

Gumbinsky New Owner of Company. *Kalamazoo Telegraph-Press*, December 9, 1913.

Kazoo Men to Secure Buggy Co.? *Kalamazoo Telegraph-Press*, December 9, 1913.

Saves Michigan Buggy Company to Kalamazoo. *The Kalamazoo Gazette*, December 11, 1913.

Sell Old Autos for Big Prices—New Ones Cheap. *Kalamazoo Telegraph-Press*, December 11, 1913.

May Close Michigan Buggy Sale Today. *The Kalamazoo Gazette*, December 11, 1913.

Buggy Company Sale Brings Big Surprise. *The Kalamazoo Gazette*, December 12, 1913.

Sale of Michigan Buggy within 24 Hours. *Kalamazoo Telegraph-Press*, December 11, 1913.

Kazoo May Get Marshall Industry. *The Kalamazoo Gazette*, December 9, 1913.

Will Kalamazoo Let This Chance Slip By? *Kalamazoo Telegraph-Press*, December 9, 1913.

Niles Man Purchases Property of Michigan Buggy. *Kalamazoo Telegraph-Press*, July 21, 1914.

Charles B. Hays Buys Factory From Receiver. *The Kalamazoo Gazette*, August, 11, 1914.

States Motor Company Soon to Appear. *Motor World*, December 16, 1914, p. 9.

Chapter 17

The Grand Jury Investigation

December 1913 – February 1914

*For many weeks, many have been maligned and good businessmen
of the highest grade of integrity have been questioned
because of the failure of the Michigan Buggy Company.*
—Square Man's Convention

Announcements of a Grand Jury investigation concerning the Michigan Buggy Company began to appear in the local press as early as October 3, 1913, just two short months after the company's closure. The improper dealings by the officers of the Michigan Buggy Company were at the forefront of the hearings, but other issues were also raised by the local citizenry in a horde of letters sent to the circuit court. There were charges of graft associated with the heating and telephone franchises authorized by the county board of supervisors, as well as questions about the exorbitant prices paid for ornamental light poles in the city. Several charges of graft were also made concerning paving contracts, the extension of the streetcar line on Portage Street, and the use of expensive paving brick, rather than construction brick, for public buildings.

Citizens from nearby villages also expressed concern about the free automobiles distributed by Michigan Buggy and the effects of those gifts on local business and politics. Kalamazoo County Sheriff Ralph W. Chapman had received a used car as a gift from Victor Palmer and, prior to any Grand Jury investigation, found himself explaining that gift before a session of the county supervisors. Only when he was able to list the cost of repairs for which he had paid the bill was the board satisfied.

Attorney General Grant Fellows arrived in Kalamazoo on September 30, 1913 to secure a copy of the testimony taken from Michigan Buggy officers at the bankruptcy hearings. Fellows was so impressed with the content of that testimony that he appeared before Judge Nathaniel H. Steward in circuit court just three days later with the following statement that appeared in the October 3rd issue of the *Kalamazoo Telegraph-Press*:

> It is my duty as an officer of the state to ask for this investigation. This city has been in the
> hands of a coterie of men who sought to make money too rapidly. The city and county owe it

to themselves and to the state to have this investigation. Kalamazoo must purge itself of existing conditions. It seems wise that we should have a special prosecutor. I have read the evidence
in the bankruptcy proceedings before asking for this jury. I have also talked matters over with
men in close touch with the situation.

The *Kalamazoo Telegraph-Press* was very supportive of Grant Fellows, Judge Stewart, and the
"Square Man's Convention," as the Grand Jury was identified in the October 3, issue.

> For many weeks, many have been maligned and good businessmen of the highest grade of
> integrity have been questioned because of the failure of the Michigan Buggy Company....
> The innuendo, false reports and malicious lies shall be opened up and exposed, and the scan-
> dal mongers and gossipers come to their just court and answer....
> No man or woman need have the slightest fear of the grand jury investigation save they that
> are guilty of an offense.... It will be a legal audit of the accounts of things as they exist and a
> true report handed out.

Note at this time that the rhetoric implied rumor on the part of the citizenry rather than wrong-
doing on the part of the company directors. Soon after this issue of the *Telegraph-Press,* the spirit
of the paper's reporting took a decided turn.

Turmoil and controversy, however, followed even this time-tested procedure of law. Nathaniel
H. Stewart was appointed judge of the Ninth Judicial Circuit by Governor W. N. Ferris to fill the
county's highest office after the death of Judge Frank E. Knappen. Stewart, who had been president
of the Kalamazoo County Bar Association, made the following statement to the *Telegraph-Press* on
August 7, 1913.

> I want to thank my friends who have not only wished me well, but thought me well. I have
> asked no one for this office that has come to me, nor have I asked anyone to intercede on my
> behalf. My friends I always thank. For my enemies who have in secret and in stealth, with lies
> and misstatements sought to defeat the wishes of my friends, I have nothing but compassion
> mingled with pity.

Neither the nature of the controversy of this appointment nor the identification of the "en-
emies" is known. Clearly the statement in August that year predicted some of the conflict in the
selection of the Grand Jury the following October. The Grand Jury was the first such investigation
in the county since 1871 and the first ever called by the head of the state legal system. The following
months would prove to be momentous and difficult times for Kalamazoo.

The first group of twenty-three men selected to serve on the Grand Jury was published in the
October 23, 1913 issue of the *Kalamazoo Telegraph-Press.* Unfortunately, the first jury had not been
appointed according to protocol, because one of its members, W. N. Pomeroy, was a stockholder in
the Michigan Buggy Company. A second jury was selected, although this process would also entail
conflict. The final group of twenty-two men consisted mostly of farmers. The paper was quick to
note, however, that the men from the city were from various lines of business and that there was no
question that all were above average intelligence. The Grand Jury was sworn in on November 19,
1913 "to fear or favor no one," and then convened on November 26, 1913, the day before Thanks-
giving, to elect a foreman and a secretary. Subsequently, the jury was adjourned until December 1,
1913 when the actual work of the investigation was scheduled to begin. Byron Carnes served as the
jury foreman and Henry Piper was named stenographer, but when Piper became ill, Joseph W.

Stockwell replaced him in that role and he would later become the central figure in the lawsuit against the jury.

The proceedings were supervised by attorney Grant Fellows and the actual trial was held in circuit court before Judge Steward. Fellows considered the Grand Jury to be of such importance that he recommended the appointment of a special prosecutor to replace prosecuting attorney Milo Bennett. On November 14, 1913 he appointed Charles W. Nichols, a prominent Lansing attorney, although this appointment would subsequently lead to another conflict. Nichols had a reputation as a fearless lawyer, had served as legal counsel to the State of Michigan for the previous eighteen years, and had gained notoriety in the case against the International Harvester Company. Milo Bennett was an elected official and a "small town lawyer" who was pushed aside by the more aggressive and more experienced attorney from Lansing. Curiously, when Judge Stewart went searching locally for a prosecutor, he approached the most competent attorneys in the Kalamazoo area: William Potter, Claude S. Carney, Alfred Mills, and Harry Howard, and all gave the same response; "We have already been retained by Mr. Palmer." Almost by the process of elimination, Stewart was forced to seek assistance in Lansing.

Fig. 17-1. Harlan Babcock, editor of the Advocate, *a weekly paper owned by M. Henry Lane.*

The professional jealousy and public controversy between Milo Bennett and Charles Nichols began to appear in the press in November 1913, and was exploited more than usual, perhaps due to the absence of news from the Grand Jury hearings.

Only occasional reports filtered down to the press and those were mostly the names of members in the community who testified before the court. The first witness called was Harlan E. Babcock, editor of the *Advocate*, who had reported in his weekly paper a number of questionable transactions in the city. The second was Fred C. Eldred who had assisted in the preparation and the sale of Michigan Buggy stock; he was followed by Frank C. Clay, a salesman for Michigan Buggy. Alfred I. Noble, superintendent of the Kalamazoo State Hospital; Mrs. Mary C. Hovey, and Mrs. Betsy Richardson were also called as each had purchased Michigan Buggy stock and the courts sought information about the promises made at the time of the stock sale. Just before the new year, Palmer, Lay, Lane, and Monroe were identified as witnesses before the jury, but the findings remained undisclosed. The bankruptcy, the auction sale, and the secretiveness of the Grand Jury seemed to flow into every corner, casting a malaise across the community at the end of 1913.

The year 1913 was difficult for the entire country due the uncertainty in currency legislation and was particularly difficult for Kalamazoo due to the failure of Michigan Buggy. Even the financial affairs of the courts were in an upheaval. After much cajoling, the Grand Jury members finally received their salary just before Christmas. They were paid $3.00 per diem plus mileage, and their pleas were published in the local press. "We need the money with Christmas coming," exclaimed one, while another complained: "I have got just enough to get me back home right now." Kalamazoo attempted to celebrate the New Year in good spirits and a holiday vaudeville was advertised at

Fig. 17-2. The Majestic Theater was the site of the New Year's Eve entertainment in 1913, but the gaiety seemed to do little to assuage the pain that had been heaped upon the city by the failure of the Michigan Buggy Company and the continuance of the Grand Jury investigation. (DOL)

the Majestic theater, featuring performing seals, Clara Ballerini, and the Dancing Beau Brummells. Free dancing on stage followed the second performance from eleven until midnight, but the planned entertainment did not relieve the pain of the community.

The New Year's Eve edition of the *Kalamazoo Telegraph-Press* carried a series of optimistic predictions by local businessmen and city notables who sought to soothe the situation. Attorney John Adams was most eloquent in his summary:

> During the past two months certain financial conditions of industries have thrown people into a "scare." Now this "scare" is over and the business of this city is to progress as never before. A failure of any institution is not necessarily disastrous to a city. It has been the subsequent flurry and talk which created a partial dissatisfaction for the time being. But the people are rapidly coming to see that knocks do not count at all. We are just about to be launched on the coming of a Golden Age.
>
> Just as truly as the world loves a booster, it abhors a knocker. There is no place for the latter except on the scrap heap. I believe that we have weathered a storm and weathered it well.

So it went from one man to the other, each man hoping to boost the city and command success by public statement, but the disgrace that would befall the city was not yet complete.

In spite of the celebration and the optimism, the new year would not be kind to Kalamazoo. When the year 1914 opened, the community was not only trying to deal with the loss of one of its largest manufacturers, but it was immersed in the Grand Jury investigation and those responsible for the conduct of the Grand Jury process were waging a public contest regarding their authority. The year began with a public debate when Prosecutor Milo Bennett presented a number of complaints to the Kalamazoo County Board of Supervisors concerning his mistreatment. First, he attacked State Attorney Grant Fellows for calling the Grand Jury, and then he attacked Judge Stewart for appointing Charles W. Nichols as prosecutor without consulting him. Bennett's plea to the Board was emotional and was recorded in the *Telegraph-Press*, on January 7, 1914:

> I have done every blessed thing that any human could do to make the Grand Jury a success.
> My dignity and the dignity of my office has been trampled on. I have been so mad that I
> believe that I could have done murder if I had the right individual to work on.

The board was sympathetic to Bennett's complaints and commended his actions by resolution in the board minutes. The political turmoil was substantial and quickly reached the State Attorney's office. Governor Ferris thought it important enough that he sent a representative from his office to investigate the discord in the city. The Grand Jury was then reconvened and Prosecutor Bennett was called before that body, not as an officer of the court, but as a witness to give testimony.

The Grand Jury was finally closed on January 14, 1914 after twenty-eight days of service and a cost to the taxpayers of approximately $7,000. The initial work ended with a flurry of indictments that figuratively shook the foundations of the community just as an earthquake might rock its physical structure. The indictments were published by *The Kalamazoo Gazette* and the *Telegraph-Press* on January 16, 1914. The jury was formally dismissed on February 5, 1914.

M. Henry Lane, one of the original founders of Michigan Buggy, former president of the firm, and a recognized financial power in the city was charged with the fraudulent issue of stock to thirty-one individuals. The charge stemmed from the circulation of a stock prospectus that cited a lien on the company as collateral for the stock and thereby inferred the investment was without financial risk. In spite of the statement, those who purchased the stock found it to be worthless after the bankruptcy declaration.

Henry Lane was in Montreal conferring with officials of the Grand Trunk Railroad trying to persuade them to move their car shops to Kalamazoo at the time the news of the indictment was released. He returned to Kalamazoo on Monday, January 19, and went directly to the courthouse. He was met there by millionaire George Bardeen, head of the Otsego Paper Mill and Sam Folz, owner of the Folz Department Store in Kalamazoo. Both men were prepared to serve as bondsmen. Lane was in good spirits and joked with the reporters as he entered the building: "You fellows have been raising the devil while I was away," he said with a smile and turned to his attorney, Harry Howard, to confer about the issues at hand. The reading of the indictment was waived and Bardeen swore he was worth $5,000, and considering Bardeen's renown wealth, the affirmation was followed by quiet laughter that slowly circled the room. The entire affair did not last more than ten minutes after which the four men left the courthouse.

Frank B. Lay, Sr., patriarch of the family since his father's death, president of Michigan Buggy and the Michigan Motor Car Company, was charged with fraudulent issue of stock. The charge arose out of the same circumstance that formed the basis of the charge against Lane. Frank Lay also was out of town at the time the indictments were released, and he went directly to the county building when he returned to Kalamazoo. He furnished the $5,000 bail, with M. J. Bigelow, president of Phelps-Bigelow Windmill Company and J. B. Balch, president of Kalamazoo Cold Storage, serving as bondsmen.

Frank Lay's mood at the court differed from that of Lane, and the news reporters that day were struck by the very apparent disappointment in his face. He was a highly respected citizen of the community, past president of the school board, and past president of the Commercial Club with a strong record of involvement in community affairs. No one had expected that he would be indicted. His one ambition was to groom his sons to assume the directorship of the company. He had brought them into the company and had guided them through the various positions in the factory until they had risen to the level of vice-president. All of that was now destroyed and it was his "blasted hopes," as he expressed his sentiment to his friends, that had brought him the greatest grief.

Fig. 17-3. Frank Lay, Sr. The photo accompanied his 1933 death notice in the The Kalamazoo Gazette.

Frank B. Lay, Jr., the youngest son and vice-president of the Michigan Buggy Company and a director of the Michigan Motor Car Company, was charged with perjury and embezzlement. Frank Lay had inherited his grandfather's physical stature and, standing over six feet tall, was a formidable sight among men of lesser countenance. He was the first of the two brothers to appear in court, and when George arrived Frank placed his arm around the elder and much smaller sibling as they joked privately about the turn of events. They were young, well-heeled, and accustomed to convenience and social advantage. Few circumstances disrupted their life style and the current indictments seemed to pose little threat to them. Frank entered a plea of not guilty and the bond of $15,000 was posted by Harry Gumbinsky, a partner in the local scrap company who had purchased the good will of the Michigan Motor Car Company.

The charge of embezzlement stemmed from Frank, Jr.'s part in devising and accepting money through the "velvet payroll" on July 1, 1912 in the amount of $26,399.92, another payment of "velvet" on January 2, 1913 in the amount of $42,446.52, and for stealing $2,100 from the company on July 1, 1912. The charge of perjury was based on the jury's belief that he had lied under oath about his involvement in these affairs of the Michigan Buggy Company.

George Lay, the eldest son, vice-president of the Michigan Buggy Company and a director of the Michigan Motor Car Company, was charged with embezzlement and larceny. George was charged with the same offenses as those cited for brother Frank, except the incident of theft of $2,100 on July 1, 1912 was listed as a part of the "velvet payroll" scam. He stood with an air of confidence and perhaps a bit of defiance, as his $15,000 bond was quickly raised with John B. Doyle and E. J. Dayton serving as bondsmen.

Victor L. Palmer, secretary-treasurer of both the Michigan Buggy Company and the Michigan Motor Car Company, was charged with perjury and embezzlement. His bail, set at $25,500, was provided by his father, George W. Palmer from St. Joseph, Michigan. Victor Palmer had appeared in court around six o'clock on the evening the indictments were issued. In contrast to the confidence of Henry Lane, the disappointment of Frank Lay, Sr., and the jovial mood of the Lay sons, his demeanor was that of a downtrodden man. He was described by reporters as being a "wreck." He returned the next day on the arm of his aged father to face a second charge and, according to reports, his pitiful appearance almost brought the court officers to tears. Palmer presented a second $15,000 bond and in a trembling voice asked to be excused.

Palmer was charged with issuing, or causing to be issued, preferred Michigan Buggy stock on the same fraudulent basis as that on which M. Henry Lane and Frank Lay, Sr. had been charged. He was also charged with embezzlement for devising the "velvet payroll" and approving the account-ing entry for that payment to the fictitious J. Roach and Com-pany, as well as accepting $26,399.92 from the "velvet payroll" on July 1, 1912 and another $42,446.52 in "velvet" on January 2, 1913. Finally, he was charged with perjury for issuing a false set of annual reports to the Secretary of State in 1909 and 1910 and for distributing a financial report to banks on January 31, 1913 that falsely stated the amount of the company's debt. Palmer was represented by Claude Carney of Kalamazoo and Burritt Hamilton of Battle Creek.

Charles B. Hays, former mayor of the city and energetic real estate broker, was not indicted until January 28, 1914. At that time he was charged with issuing a misleading statement rela-tive to the Michigan Buggy Company preferred stock—the same issue that formed the basis of the indictments of Henry Lane and Frank B. Lay, Sr. The issue in Hays' indictment was the preparation of a prospectus for the sale by Michigan Buggy stock through his office. That prospectus assured the purchaser that the stock was protected by a lien against the Michigan Buggy Company, and for that reason there was no chance that the in-vestors would lose their money. Many people testified that they

Fig. 17-4. Charles B. Hays, former Kalamazoo mayor and well-known real estate broker, whose indictment on charges in the Michigan Buggy case came as something of a surprise to the community.

had invested in Michigan Buggy because of that assurance and then found that the stock was worthless after the company went bankrupt. Hays claimed that he was in Europe at the time the prospectus was prepared and knew nothing about the distribution of these documents. In his typical eloquent fashion, Hays made a public statement at the time he was charged that appeared in the *Telegraph-Press*, January 28, 1914:

> I have no fear as to the results of this case at the bar of public justice when the searchlight is thrown on my personal and business career. My friends will be proud of my record when filed in the archives of the court.

Considering Hay's reputation as a conscientious public official, the indictment was a surprise to the community. Two respected community leaders, F. M. Hedge, president of the Kalamazoo Paper Company, and E. S. Rankin, a well-known Kalamazoo insurance man, served as bondsmen.

Fred C. Eldred worked in Illinois as a stock salesman promoting stock in a paper mill being developed there by the Gumbinsky brothers of Kalamazoo, partners with the scrap company that had purchased the "goodwill" of the Michigan Motor Company. Eldred was a former stock and bond salesman for the Charles B. Hays Stock and Bond Company, and was accused in the indict-ment of preparing the alluring prospectus that purportedly assured that the stock was protected by a lien on the Michigan Buggy Company and therefore was without risk of financial loss.

Eldred did not reside in Kalamazoo but in Morris, Illinois, at the time of the indictments. After his arrest he was hauled back to the city by undersheriff John Shields and, because he had not lived in Kalamazoo for some time, he had difficulty raising bail. His situation was reported in the January 14 issue of the *Telegraph-Press*, when he pleaded his case before the judge:

> I had friends here whom I thought would not hesitate in going on my bail. Some of these were
>
> quick to turn me down when they found I was in trouble.

Eventually M. J. Bigelow and J. B. Balch, who had served as bondsmen for Frank Lay, Sr., consented to serve as bondsmen for Eldred, but they were later replaced by the Gumbinsky brothers, Eldred's employers. However, when news of the indictment reached Morris, Illinois, Eldred was given notice that his services were no longer needed there, and the Gumbinsky brothers relinquished their bail commitment. Eldred once again surrendered to the Sheriff. Judge Stewart, who was familiar with Eldred's difficulties, released him on his own recognizance so that he might attempt to find employment in this area. The Eldred story is a pitiful one, for he was involved only tangentially, but the bankruptcy and the legal process disrupted his life and endangered his future.

Stephen B. Monroe, former financier and president of the Kalamazoo City Savings Bank, was charged on February 5, 1914, the final day of the Grand Jury hearings, with fraudulent issue of stock. The charge was that he falsely made, altered, and counterfeited certain stock certificates of the Michigan Buggy Company. Furthermore, these stocks were never issued to the individuals whose names appeared on the face and the documents remained in the company's stock book where they were found at the time of the company's failure.

Monroe was represented by Harry Howard and the $5,000 bail furnished by Charles A. Peck. Monroe was the last to be indicted, and by the time the jury had reached the final stage of the indictments, the process had become very personal, pitting one citizen against another. After the proceedings, Monroe made the following comments to a reporter in the February 6, 1914 issue of *The Kalamazoo Gazette:*

> It is charged that I falsely forged and counterfeited certain preferred stock certificates of the
>
> Michigan Buggy Company, which were never issued and were in the company's stock book at
>
> the time of its failure.... The charges are wholly groundless. Nevertheless, I feel deeply the
>
> disgrace sought to be forced upon my family and all I can say is that I have not enough malice
>
> in my heart to wish the same fate to the families of those who are responsible for this.

The Grand Jury then concluded its service with a scathing report of the conduct of Prosecutor Milo Bennett in which it charged that he refused to attend Grand Jury sessions and to perform the appropriate duties for which he was elected. It also charged that he sought to discredit the Grand Jury through statements to the public press and that he had withdrawn $245 from the county treasury improperly. The public statement vilified the prosecutor in no uncertain terms with the following entry in that report published by the *Telegraph-Press* on February 5, 1914:

> He had not hesitated to apply the most vile, profane, obscene and vulgar epithets to the chief
>
> executive of the state and… he is utterly incompetent to discharge the duties of office to which
>
> he was elected.

Bennett, of course, denied the charges, contending that he had never been asked to attend any sessions of the Grand Jury and that payment of fees was well within the prerogative of his office. Eventually he filed a petition with Judge Stewart asking that the Grand Jury report be expunged.

PROSECUTOR BENNETT IN HIS REPLY

Special Investigator Nichols Declares Report Was Drawn Up In Secret And He Knew Nothing Of It

Accused Official Says Court, Clerk and Supervisors Passed Upon Bills Against County and Points Out Law Providing Fee.

HAS BRIEF NOW BEFORE STEWART

Regrets Injustice of Not Being Able to Face Accuser in Public to Refute Charges Made Against Administration of His Office. ~

The grand jury yesterday morning filed a report with Judge N. H. Stewart, which, on the face of it, reflects somewhat upon the administration of the prosecuting attorney's department. In the document the gravest charges are leveled against Prosecutor Bennett. He in a dignified communication to The Gazette, states openly and freely to the public his

Replies to Charges

Jury Feels Duty Bound to Call Attention of Court to State of Affairs Said to be Existing in County Prosecutor's Office.

DECLARES BENNETT'S FEES ILLEGAL

Raps Prosecutor for Not Taking Charge of Investigations Made by Grand Jury and Making Special Attorney Necessary for Probe.

FOLLOWING IS THE REPORT SUBMITTED BY THE GRAND JURY.

State of Michigan—To the Circuit Court for the County of Kalamazoo—We, the members of the Grand Jury now in session, beg leave to report, in addition to the reports already made, that our investigations have disclosed the existence of a state of af-

Fig. 17-5. The criticism of prosecutor Milo Bennett's conduct was just one of many side dramas marking the Michigan Buggy Grand Jury hearings in The Kalamazoo Gazette, *February 4, 1914.*

The turmoil and conflict between Milo Bennett and the Grand Jury continued to spread and because of it Edward N. Dingley, editor of *The Progressive Herald*, a local weekly newspaper, was charged with contempt of court on February 15, 1914. Dingley had written an article charging that Judge Stewart had prepared the report published by the Grand Jury in which Milo Bennett was censured. Although members of the Grand Jury prepared affidavits attesting to the fact that the judge did not know about the report before it was released, Dingley still refused to withdraw his complaints and apologize to the court. A trial followed and Dingley later published a stenographic report of it, asserting that he, too, had been denied fair treatment. Crowds filled the courtroom and there was much to-do in the papers about Dingley's willingness to go to jail rather than pay a fine or apologize for a report that he considered a factual account of the event. When the final sentence—a $200 fine—was handed down, the message of Judge Stewart, as reported in the *Gazette* on February 26, 1914, contained no ambiguity:

> You have violated every principle of good citizenship in your attacks on this court, under your own confession, and now it becomes the duty of the court to administer such mild punishment as must meet with the approval of all good citizens, stripped absolutely and complete of any malice or hatred.
> The judgment of the court is that you pay a fine of two hundred dollars—and the court will

Judge Again Delays the Sentencing of E.N.Dingley

E. N. DINGLEY STILL REFUSES TO RETRACT CHARGES HE MADE AGAINST JUDGE N. H. STEWART

JUDGE N. H. STEWART
He has found Dingley guilty of contempt of court, but twice has put off sentencing defendant.

E. N. DINGLEY
Knowing that he probably faces a jail sentence, editor refuses to retract statements.

JUDGE DELAYS SENTENCE

(Continued from page one.)

In the supervisors' room at the court house. Following this meeting behind closed doors, Attorney Hooper announced that there was nothing to be given out in any information way until tomorrow morning.

"We feel, out of respect to Judge Severens, that it is proper, we consider the proposition made us. We will announce our decision tomorrow morning," said Hooper.

It is understood that Judge Severens also had a conference with Judge Stewart prior to the time that he conferred with Dingley regarding the retraction. As a member of the bar and a friend of both men, Judge Severens is said to be anxious to bring about peace between them.

After the conference with Judge Severens, Dingley was surrounded by friends. He seemed to be in the best of spirits and joked with his acquaintances.

No Hunger Strike.

When asked if he intended to go on a hunger strike if sent to the county jail, he stated that Sheriff Chapman had informed him that there was a particularly good bill of fare at the jail this week. This brought a laugh from the crowd.

The big feature of the court proceedings was the large crowd. Even standing room was at a premium. A half hour before court convened the room was crowded. At 10 o'clock, the time set for court to convene, people anxious to witness the proceedings completely filled the court room and the corridors of the county building.

Lawyers Present.

The Kalamazoo attorneys who arrived early took the chairs usually occupied by members of the jury. They joked about the "ringside seats" and asked each other when the bout was going to start. With the exception of the members of the bar, the big crowd was tense with expectation. The peo-

Great Crowd in Court Room This Forenoon When Case Was Called—Dingley Absolutely Refuses to Retract Charges He Made Against Judge—Former Judge Severens Appears in An Effort to Settle Trouble.

Ask Explanation.

Immediately after it was announced that the case would go over until tomorrow morning, Dingley was surrounded by friends who asked for an explanation of the matter.

"Judge Severens came to me this morning and asked if I would retract. I informed him that I would not. He then had a talk with my attorney. I was ready to go ahead with the case this morning," explained the local

Fig. 17-6. No one was immune from the judicial proceedings. This article from the February 24, 1914 Telegraph *describes the turmoil between the press and the courts as Judge Stewart hands down a sentence against publisher Dingley.*

give you 48 hours within which to pay it—or stand committed to the county jail until such fine is paid, not to exceed thirty days.

The conflict between the courts and the editor of *The Progressive Herald* added to the bizarre ending of the Grand Jury, and, in turn, disrupted existing social standards in the community. The sense of what was right and what was wrong seemed to flutter with the winter storms. In spite of the noble intention of the process, the substance of the indictments handed down by the Grand Jury were questioned as Dingley attacked both the veracity and the integrity of the courts. Those indicted were men of means and social standing in the community and soon after the indictments were published, they began to mount a defense. Their attorneys appeared in circuit court on February 17, 1914 with pleas for abatement of all charges against Frank Lay, Sr., M. Henry Lane, Charles Hays, and Stephen Monroe. While Victor Palmer had been named in the same indictments, pleas for abatement on his behalf were not brought forward at this time.

The attorneys made five arguments. First, Joseph Stockwell, an officer of the court and official stenographer for the Ninth District Court, was an illegal member of the Grand Jury. The attorneys charged that the problem began when W. N. Pomeroy was seated. They asserted that the sheriff knew very well that Pomeroy owned preferred stock in the Michigan Buggy Company and was not qualified to sit on the jury. When Pomeroy was subsequently disqualified, Stockwell was drawn from among the bystanders at the courthouse and was placed on the jury. His name never appeared in the pool of potential jurors, and he, also, should have been disqualified.

Second, the attorneys argued that Prosecutor Nichols had not been legally appointed as the prosecutor. Nichols was named before Milo Bennett, the elected prosecuting attorney for the county, had filed a petition for either a special assistant or a special prosecuting attorney. Therefore, they argued, Charles W. Nichols had no authority in the case.

Third, the attorneys argued that Judge Stewart was the father of Donald Stewart, a stockholder in the Kalamazoo Railway Supply Company that was a creditor of the Michigan Buggy Company and that Stewart's former clients, W. H. Cameron and George Dougherty, were also employees and creditors of the company. The circumstance created a conflict of interest for the judge.

Fourth, they argued that the judge and three of the jurors were stockholders in the First National Bank and the Farmers National Bank, both of which were also creditors of Michigan Buggy, thus making these four individuals biased participants.

Fifth, and finally, they argued that the indictments charged no crime under Michigan statutes.

The cold winter winds seemed more bitter than usual in Kalamazoo toward the end of February 1914, and the local press was filled with legal assaults on a number of community leaders. The directors of one of the largest manufacturing concerns in the city as well as other respected citizens, including the former mayor, had been indicted for fraud, perjury, and embezzlement, and a number of real estate brokers in the area had been charged with dishonest practices. Milo Bennett, the elected county prosecutor, had been assailed as incompetent by the Grand Jury and now sought to have his record expunged. Edward Dingley, editor of *The Progressive Herald*, had charged that the Grand Jury report was either prepared by or released to the public by Judge Stewart. Dingley was now facing legal action defending his right to publish what he considered a fair evaluation of the conduct of the court. In addition, his article also accused state attorney general, Grant Fellows, of influencing the Grand Jury.

Kalamazoo was in an uproar and Judge Stewart publicly lamented the constant turmoil and strife within the community, but before the city could begin to adjust to the array of Grand Jury indictments, on February 3, 1914, Sanford Ladd of the Detroit Trust Company convinced Referee J. W. Banyon to reopen the bankruptcy hearings. Victor Palmer had produced copies of the 1889 and 1890 annual reports of the Michigan Buggy Company showing that the real estate owned by Frank B. Lay, Sr. and M. Henry Lane should be considered an asset of the company. The hearings were delayed until May to avoid a conflict with Palmer's criminal trial. When Palmer was questioned about the matter, his response appeared in the *Kalamazoo-Telegraph* on May 14, 1914:

> It was my understanding that Lay and Lane properties were owned by the Michigan Buggy Company. The company bought up the property and kept up the taxes. About half the property of the company at one time was the real estate.

The testimony was important, for these statements provided the basis for reopening the bankruptcy hearings. The intent of Sanford Ladd was to show that Lay and Lane had purchased land using money drawn from Michigan Buggy thus making those properties an asset of the company that could then be recovered from the personal assets of Lay and Lane for distribution to the creditors. The first issue concerned the payment for some company stock that matured in 1913. Reportedly, Lane received $20,000 and Lay $14,000 from this transaction. Ladd argued that, since the stock sale was for property owned by the company, these proceeds should not be considered personal payments to the two directors.

The bankruptcy hearing was convened and Sanford Ladd grilled Henry Lane relentlessly concerning the issue. Lane, controlling his temper with apparent difficulty, was defiant in his response, as recorded in the *Telegraph-Press*, May 14, 1914:

> "This sharp is trying to catch something," Lane bellowed in response to Ladd's questioning. Lane rose from the witness chair, and pointing his finger at Ladd, he began pacing directly in front of the court stenographer. "Why don't you put on Palmer, Lay or the array of bookkeepers, instead of the most ignorant one? I don't know anything about books. I worked in the factory for twenty years and got nothing for it. I did not purchase any private property with money from the Michigan Buggy Company save that which rightfully belonged to me either as profits or original capital."

Lane was self-assured and assertive, and his outburst in this instance was typical of his character. Ladd knew better than to tangle with him, and he gently reminded the former company president that he was on the stand and asked him to return to the witness chair. Lane took his seat, but in spite of further testimony there was no subsequent progress on this issue.

The testimony did reveal that Lane had withdrawn $40,000 from the company to build his residence, but, given this admission, he then assailed Frank Lay, accusing his brother-in-law of cavorting about the countryside, showing off his fast horses, spending company money, and making a profit for himself on the side. Lane also charged that Frank B. Lay, Sr. had withdrawn more money from the company than he had withdrawn, revealing once again the terrible rift between the family members.

Palmer had initiated the disclosure of the discord between the Lay and Lane families to draw attention away from himself. He seemed to take every opportunity to reveal the friction and the personal animosity between the two because of the perceived discrepancy in the distribution of funds.

The second issue that Ladd wanted to unravel at the hearing concerned the so-called "terminal property." In 1892, Frank Lay, Sr. and Henry Lane had purchased some railroad property and with it the "terminal franchise" that granted the right-of-way to lay railroad track through the city streets. Lay and Lane had formed the Belt Line Railway to build a connecting line through the city and the company had, in fact, laid some track on Porter and Pitcher Streets one Sunday afternoon before the turn of the twentieth century. Little seemed to follow this initial step. In 1908, Lane and Lay sold the property and the franchise to the Grand Trunk Railroad for $100,000, and Lane admitted that he received around $50,000 in that transaction. The franchise sale was later approved by the City Council on December 14, 1908, and in spite of Mayor Frank H. Milham's emotional plea to the contrary, only a single dissenting vote was cast. Milham argued that the Grand Trunk already had three access routes into Kalamazoo and the city did not have to disrupt street traffic by using the tracks on Porter and Pitcher Streets. Furthermore he charged that Lay and Lane had been granted the franchise and had done nothing but encumber the streets with useless rails. They then sold the franchise and the right to build on city property, a sale that amounted to transferring city property to the Grand Trunk for their personal profit. It was Charles Hays who drafted the ordinance approving the franchise sale agreement that was brought before the Council and Frank Burtt cast one of the supporting ballots as a member of the Council, suggesting a certain cohesiveness among the automobile men of the city.

Ladd pressed the stock sale as well as the franchise sale, trying in vain to show some connection between the properties and the assets of the Michigan Buggy Company. Palmer was returned to the stand for further questioning, but this time he resisted and refused to answer any more questions on the advice of his counsel. He had divulged much about the company in his testimony at the bankruptcy hearings in the fall and again in early January to the Grand Jury. His testimony led to his own indictment and criminal trial. He feared that further testimony would be self-incriminating. These attempts by Ladd and the Detroit Trust Company to extract additional information from Victor Palmer were unsuccessful.

Henry Lane admitted to the sale of the franchise and openly admitted to the receipt of large sums of money, but would not admit to either wrong doing or the inadvertent use of company funds in the purchase of this property. The disclosure of the terminal property sale and the personal conflicts over money between Lay and Lane made sensational news, but without any legal culpability. Interest in the issue quickly waned, and the second series of bankruptcy hearings was brought to a close without further charges. In essence, these matters died for lack of evidence.

In addition to the legal tensions, there were social and economic problems in Kalamazoo. The Michigan Secretary of Labor had estimated the unemployment rate in the winter of 1914 at about 40 percent of an estimated 4,000 potential workers in the city, while the Municipal Charities reported that 3,000 families were just on the poverty borderline. Many families hauled coal by the basketful as they struggled to heat their homes against the bitter winter weather. These were families in trouble, however, not roving professional tramps. The Commercial Club was certain that these men were willing to work for their bread and on this premise the club sought to increase the number of workers needed to install the new sewer line along Pitcher Street by reducing the length of the work day for each work gang. It was a difficult winter in 1914, and almost all of these local tribulations were rooted in the aftermath of the Michigan Buggy closure.

The final resolution, however, had not yet been reached.

REFERENCES

Salient Features About Calling Grand Jury. *Kalamazoo Telegraph-Press*, October 3, 1913.
First Time in State's History Grand Jury Is Demanded by Atty. General.
    Kalamazoo Telegraph-Press, October 3, 1913.
Square Man's Convention. *Kalamazoo Telegraph-Press*, October 3, 1913.
Many Facts Kalamazoo Citizens Should Know. *The Kalamazoo Gazette*, October 4, 1913.
Will Accept Highest Office in the County. *Kalamazoo Telegraph-Press*, August 7, 1913.

Hon. N. H. Stewart Receives Word of His Appointment. *Kalamazoo Telegraph-Press*,
    August 8, 1913.

New Official Today Takes Over Office. *Kalamazoo Telegraph-Press*, August 16, 1913.

Farmers Predominate on This Grand Jury. *Kalamazoo Telegraph-Press*, October 23, 1913.

Grand Jury Will Go Deep for Facts. *Kalamazoo Telegraph-Press*, October 23, 1913.

Grand Jury List Void; To Draw Another Panel. *The Kalamazoo Gazette*, October 28, 1913.

Find New Twist in Law Governing Grand Jury. *The Kalamazoo Gazette*, October 29, 1913.

Grand Jury to Convene on November 24. *Kalamazoo Telegraph-Press*, November 3, 1913.

Stewart's Charge to Grand Jury Devoted Mostly to Attack on Newspapers.
    Kalamazoo Telegraph-Press, November 11, 1913.

All Prepared to Draw Jury. *Kalamazoo Telegraph-Press*, November 11, 1913.

New Grand Jury Drawn, Farmers in Majority. *Kalamazoo Telegraph-Press*,
    November 15, 1913.

Grand Jurors Must Take Oath to Fear or Favor No One in Their Work.
    Kalamazoo Telegraph-Press, November 19, 1913.

Alamo Farmer, Who Is Secretary of Grand Jury, Will Be Busy Man During County
    Investigation. *Kalamazoo Telegraph-Press*, December 1, 1913.

Some of the Members of Kazoo Grand Jury. *Kalamazoo Telegraph-Press*,
    November 16, 1913.

Special Prosecutor Is Named, Draw Jury Today. *The Kalamazoo Gazette*,
    November 15, 1913.

Governor Ferris Order to Officials of County Regarding Grand Jury.
    The Kalamazoo Gazette, November 21, 1913.

Chapman Now Serving Papers on Grand Jurors. *The Kalamazoo Gazette*,
    November 16, 1913.

Nichols Will Give His Time to Probe Here. *The Kalamazoo Gazette*, November 16, 1913.

County Officials Find Palmer Has Retained Attorneys Sought as Prosecutors For
    Grand Jury. *The Kalamazoo Gazette*, October 28, 1913.

Bennett Washes Hands of Grand Jury Inquiry. *Kalamazoo Telegraph-Press*,
    November 18, 1913.

Scathing Reprimand from Judge. *The Kalamazoo Gazette*, November, 21, 1913.

Prosecutor Bennett Shies at Grand Jury. *The Kalamazoo Gazette*, November 19, 1913.

Grand Jurors to Start on Labors Today. *The Kalamazoo Gazette*, December 2, 1913.

Grand Jury Begins Work, One Excused, H. E. Babcock Witness. *Kalamazoo Telegraph-Press*,
    December 2, 1913.

Ike Bloem Summoned Before The Body Today. *Kalamazoo Telegraph-Press*,
    December 3, 1913.

Grand Jury in Probe of Buggy Firm. *The Kalamazoo Gazette*, December 3, 1913.

Members of The Grand Jury. *Kalamazoo Telegraph-Press*, December 4, 1913.

Grand Jury Questions Buggy Men. *Kalamazoo Telegraph-Press*, December 4, 1913.

Man Who Rented House on West St. Before Grand Jury Yesterday Afternoon.
    Kalamazoo Telegraph-Press, December 5, 1913.

Grand Jury Quits Till Next Monday. *The Kalamazoo Gazette*, December 5, 1913.

Eldred Witness Before Grand Jury. *Kalamazoo Telegraph-Press*, December 11, 1913.

Buggy Salesman Before Grand Jury. *Kalamazoo Telegraph-Press*, December 11, 1913.

Testimony of Women Is Given to Jurors. *The Kalamazoo Gazette*, December 11, 1913.

No Indictments Until Jury Finishes Work. *Kalamazoo Telegraph-Press*, December 20, 1913.

V. L. Palmer May Soon Go Before Grand Jury. *Kalamazoo Telegraph-Press*,
    December 30, 1913.

Grand Jury Appeals to County Clerk Asking for Pay for Services.
    Kalamazoo Telegraph-Press, December 23, 1913.

Jurors to Draw Pay Only for Actual Time Served. *Kalamazoo Telegraph-Press*,
    December 24, 1913.

Grand Jury to Convene Tomorrow. *Kalamazoo Telegraph-Press*, December 25, 1913.

Grand Jury Gets Money. *Kalamazoo Telegraph-Press*, December 26, 1913.

Before Grand Jurors. *The Kalamazoo Gazette*, December 31, 1913.

What the New Year Holds For Kalamazoo. *Kalamazoo Telegraph-Press*, December 31, 1913.

At The Majestic. *Kalamazoo Telegraph-Press*, December 31, 1913.

Grand Jury Will Have to Remove. *Kalamazoo Telegraph-Press*, January 1, 1914.

Bennett States Position to Board. *The Kalamazoo Gazette*, January 1, 1914.

Questions Validity of Grand Jury. *Kalamazoo Telegraph-Press*, January 5, 1914.

Prosecutor to Block The Payment of Jury Work. *Kalamazoo Telegraph-Press*,
    January 5, 1914.

Attorney General Says Pay Stockwell's Bill, Prosecutor Says Not To.
    Kalamazoo Telegraph-Press, January 8, 1914.

Supervisors Pay Bill. *Kalamazoo Telegraph-Press*, January 8, 1914.

Prosecutor Bennett in Tirade Against Judge and Nichols. *Kalamazoo Telegraph-Press*,
    January 7, 1914.

Bennett's Action Toward Grand Jury Is Endorsed. *Kalamazoo Telegraph-Press*,
    January 8, 1914.

Governor Orders Probe of Official Row Here. *The Kalamazoo Gazette*, January 13, 1914.

Grand Jury to Re-Convene on Wednesday. *The Kalamazoo Gazette*, January 13, 1914.

Grand Jury Ends Probe Tuesday at Noon: Will Report Findings Today.
    The Kalamazoo Gazette, January 14, 1914.

Grand Jurors Work Hard on The True Bills. *Kalamazoo Telegraph-Press*, January 14, 1914.

Mass of Indictments Blocks Jury Report: Plan to Close Today. *The Kalamazoo Gazette*,
    January 15, 1914.

Members of The Kalamazoo County's Grand Jury. *The Kalamazoo Gazette*,
    January 15, 1914.

Investigating Body Takes Recess Until January 26. *The Kalamazoo Gazette*, January 16, 1914.

Michigan Buggy Men Indicted. *The Horseless Age*, January 21, 1914, p. 101.

Lane and Lay Indicted. *Kalamazoo Telegraph-Press*, January 16, 1914.

Complete List of Those Indicted by Jury. *Kalamazoo Telegraph-Press*, January 19, 1914.

Charges Released, Expect Second Report Today. *The Kalamazoo Gazette*, January 16, 1914.

M. H. Lane Is Hurrying to Face Charges. *Kalamazoo Telegraph-Press*, January 17, 1914.

M. H. Lane in Montreal When Indictment Voted. *Kalamazoo Telegraph-Press*,
    January 17, 1914.

M. H. Lane Goes Direct From Train to Court. *Kalamazoo Telegraph-Press*, January 19, 1914.

Father and Two Sons Must Fight for Liberty. *Kalamazoo Telegraph-Press*, January 17, 1914.

Can Officers of Corporation Loot It? *Kalamazoo Telegraph-Press*, January 16, 1914.

Indicted For Grave Charges, $15,000 Bond, Expect More Arrests to Come Today.
    The Kalamazoo Gazette, January 16, 1914.

Victor Palmer Passes Up $15,000 Position. *Kalamazoo Telegraph-Press*, January 17, 1914.

Palmer—Appears on Verge of Collapse When Brought Into Court; Aged Father Walks at
    His Side. *The Kalamazoo Gazette*, January 14, 1914.

Lay Boys First Served. *Kalamazoo Telegraph-Press*, January 15, 1914.

Lays' Plan to Fight Suit in Bankruptcy. *The Kalamazoo Gazette*, January 21, 1914.

What Former Mayor Says of Indictment. *Kalamazoo Telegraph-Press*, January 28, 1914.

Hays Gives Bail—Jury Adjourns to Thursday. *Kalamazoo Telegraph-Press*, January 29, 1914.

Indictment Mere Revenge States Hays. *The Kalamazoo Gazette*, January 29, 1914.

Eldred Is Now After a Bondsman. *Kalamazoo Telegraph-Press*, January 17, 1914.

Indictment of Eldred Loses Him a Position. *Kalamazoo Telegraph-Press*, January 17, 1914.

While Eldred Is Before Grand Jury He Is Given Up by Bondsmen.
    Kalamazoo Telegraph-Press, January 26, 1914.

Court Lets Eldred Go on Honor. *Kalamazoo Telegraph-Press*, January 27, 1914.

Indictment Is Voted Against S. B. Monroe. *The Kalamazoo Gazette*, February 6, 1914.

Grand Jury in Special Report Assails Operations. *Kalamazoo Telegraph-Press*,
    January 29, 1914.

Fellows Denies Charge. *Kalamazoo Telegraph-Press*, February 2, 1914.

Scathing Report Is Made by Grand Jury About Official. *Kalamazoo Telegraph-Press*,
    February 5, 1914.

Jury Feels Duty Bound to Call Attention of Court. *The Kalamazoo Gazette*,
    February 6, 1914.

Prosecutor Bennett in His Reply. *The Kalamazoo Gazette*, February 6, 1914.

Bennett Wants Charges Expunged From Records. *The Kalamazoo Gazette*,
    February 19, 1914.

Deplores Constant Stirring Up of Strife in Kalamazoo County. *Kalamazoo Telegraph-Press*,
    February 19, 1914.

Threats Are Made to Get Judge in Anonymous Note. *The Kalamazoo Gazette*,
    February 17, 1914.

Dingley Is Held Guilty; Stewart Defers Sentence. *The Kalamazoo Gazette*, February 17,
    1914.

E. N. Dingley Refuses to Make Apology to Court. *The Kalamazoo Gazette*,
    February 21, 1914.

Judge Again Delays The Sentencing of E. N. Dingley. *Kalamazoo Telegraph-Press*,
    February 24, 1914.

Dingley Will Be Sentenced This Morning. *The Kalamazoo Gazette*, February 24, 1914.

Dingley Fined $200, Must Pay It in Two Days or Serve Jail Term. *The Kalamazoo Gazette*, February 26, 1914.

Dingley Will Do Time Rather Than Pay Fine. *The Kalamazoo Gazette*, February 27, 1913.

Defense Opens War on Grand Jury. *The Kalamazoo Gazette*, February 17, 1914.

Hearings to Be Resumed in Buggy Case Feb. 18. *Kalamazoo Telegraph-Press*, February 3, 1914.

Terminal Property Brought $150,000 Admits M. Henry Lane. *Kalamazoo Telegraph-Press*, May 14, 1914.

Milham Gives Reasons in Veto Message in 1908 Why He Opposed Giving Permission to Lane and Lay to Sell Property Rights to City. *Kalamazoo Telegraph-Press*, May 14, 1914.

Lay on Stand Today, Gives New Facts. *Kalamazoo Telegraph-Press*, May 14, 1914.

Used Buggy Co. Money to Make Deals. *Kalamazoo Telegraph-Press*, May 14, 1914.

Palmer Refuses to Answer Questions, Is It Contempt? *Kalamazoo Telegraph-Press*, May 15, 1914.

Milham Said Someone Would Get Cash, Lane Admits He Got It. *Kalamazoo Telegraph-Press*, May 15, 1914.

Poverty and Suffering Touches Hearts of Kalamazoo's Citizens. *The Kalamazoo Gazette*, February 15, 1914.

How to Care for 2,000 Unemployed Is Problem. *Kalamazoo Telegraph-Press*, February 16, 1914.

Ask Manufacturers to Aid Jobless. *The Kalamazoo Gazette*, February 17, 1914.

City Council Provides Work for Unemployed. *The Kalamazoo Gazette*, February 17, 1914.

$1,585

With Electric Lights—Four Forward Speeds
Tires 35 x 4½ — Cushions 14 Inches Deep

To Win This War of "40's"

There are 72 makers building cars this year in the 40-horsepower class.

They have brought to their aid an army of the ablest engineers.

They are offering costly features—giving wonderful equipment—building splendid cars. Some of these cars, in luxury and comfort, break all records in extravagance.

Yet prices are cut to what small "30's", unequipped, cost but a short time back.

All because legions of buyers are now coming to Forties. And 72 makers, in a fight for supremacy, are trying to outdo rivals.

Cameron's Greatest Car

We saw this fight coming, and four years ago we started in to get ready.

By outbidding others, we secured W. H. Cameron for our chief engineer. He has built over 100,000 cars.

We secured John A. Campbell—who has been designer for kings—to create for the Michigan his masterpiece body. And we placed in charge of every part and detail the ablest experts obtainable.

We built in those four years about 5,000 cars, and watched every car's performance. Year after year we worked out improvements, until more than 300 were added.

We watched every rival, to let no one outdo us. And we kept cutting the price, as we increased our facilities, despite all the costly additions.

And now, with the best car Cameron can build—with the last word in luxury—with every up-to-date feature—we come to claim leadership among all cars of this class. To gain that place quickly, we have fixed our price for the coming year at $1,585, all equipment included.

4,275 Cars Sold Before the Formal Announcement Was Made

The better dealers have known, for two or three years, that this matchless car was coming. Year after year they have watched it grow better, more luxurious, more complete. Last year they ordered from us twice what we could make.

This year they flocked to our factory. Even before the new car was formally announced they had placed with us orders for 4,275 cars. And orders for hundreds are now coming in daily.

When you make comparisons such as dealers make, you will say with them that the Michigan "40" outbids all rivals in the points which you prize most.

Your Verdict Wanted Now

Now we want your verdict. The Michigan "40" is now on show in nearly every city. Compare it with all other cars in the features that you seek.

Compare its length, its width of seat, its room. Compare its body design, its finish, its trimmings. Compare the depth of upholstering.

Compare the size of vital parts—the margins of safety—the power of the brakes. Compare the spring dimensions. Compare the tire width, for there lies the secret of small tire upkeep. Note our four-forward-speed transmission.

Compare the equipment. The electric lights as an extra, on other cars, would cost $125. Note what our price includes. Then compare the price.

Do this in justice to yourself. If the Michigan "40" stands unapproached in the Forty class, you want to find it out. And this is the way.

Start by sending for our new catalog. It gives every detail, pictures every part, shows the various bodies. Then we'll tell you where to see the car.

MICHIGAN MOTOR CAR COMPANY, Kalamazoo, Michigan
Owned by the Owners of the Michigan Buggy Company

Fig. 18-1. In the fall of 1912, Michigan Buggy began an advertisement campaign, that according to their own statement, cost $650,000. Interestingly, this expenditure was made at the same time they boasted that 62 percent of the planned production of Mighty Michigan cars was already sold. The company advertised in all of the national publications and automotive magazines. There were over 300 exhibits at Palmer's trial; one of those was a notebook filled with these advertisements that became a major source of evidence. The advertisement shown here was typical of the national campaign.

Chapter 18

The Trial of Victor L. Palmer in Federal Court

March – June, 1914

*It is true that certain large financial institutions
have suffered heavy losses through the failure
of the Michigan Buggy Company, and for these losses
I accept a share of the responsibility.*

—Victor Palmer

At nine o'clock on Monday evening, March 2, 1914, Deputy United States Marshal E. J. Robinson arrived without warning at Victor Palmer's residence at 320 South West Street (Westnedge) with a warrant for his arrest. He was immediately taken before United States Commissioner Joseph W. Stockwell. Bail was set at $10,000, and was provided by his father, George W. Palmer, and his uncle, Charles A. Palmer, both of St. Joseph, Michigan. Ironically, Stockwell was the same individual who had served as the stenographer on the Grand Jury that had handed down the injunctions against Palmer, and whose presence on the jury was at issue when Palmer's lawyer had sought, rather unsuccessfully, the abatement of the charges made by the Grand Jury against Palmer and the others.

Victor Palmer was bound over for trial in federal court before Judge Clarence Sessions by the Federal Grand Jury at Grand Rapids on March 3, 1914. He was defended by Claude Carney, who had represented the Buggy Company officials at the bankruptcy hearing the previous fall; Burritt Hamilton, who also was involved in the bankruptcy hearings; and William Potter of Hastings, Michigan. Carney was still stinging from the failure to win the contested seat in Michigan's Third Congressional District. Not only had he failed to gain that disputed seat, he had been publicly admonished and charged with "partisan politics" when he appealed to the Democratic members of Congress "to make a decision that was good for the party."

By this time, Victor Palmer was acknowledged as "the financial brains" behind Michigan Buggy and had been charged with fraudulent use of the mails by sending false financial statements to banks on three different occasions, March 1, 1912, March 1, 1913, and June 1, 1913, for the purpose of obtaining loans and an increase in the company's line of credit. In the last two statements he had set the assets at $1 million more than actual and the liabilities at $1 million less than actual, creating a $2 million differential between his statements and the actual financial condition of the company. The three alleged offenses were all misdemeanors, but each carried a penalty of $1,000,

Figure 18-2. Victor Palmer, by now a notorious figure in Kalamazoo, circa 1914.

or up to one year in prison, or both. The circumstances were most serious for a man of his financial reputation and social standing in the community, and the emotional strain and deepening depression were evident on his face as he entered the commissioner's office. "The persecution still keeps up" was his only response when bail was set that evening.

The trial opened on March 24, 1914 and the jury was sworn in at 10:10 that morning. The case for the prosecution was presented by District Attorney Bowman in a meticulous and devastating manner. Bowman showed that the fraudulent financial statements had been prepared by or approved by Palmer, that the statements had been distributed to and received by various banks, and that the content of those statements had determined the amount of credit extended to Michigan Buggy by those banks.

Miss Mabel Bird, Palmer's private stenographer, was first to testify that the financial statement that resulted in the indictment had been dictated to her by Palmer. Carney also established during cross examination that Miss Bird was now employed at the Detroit Trust Company, the receiver for the defunct Michigan Buggy Company.

President Chandler of the Wichita National Bank of Kansas was then called to the stand by the prosecution. He testified that Palmer's statement had been delivered to him and that it had been used in his decision to loan money to Michigan Buggy. He considered the report to be a model in clarity of presentation and style, and had called one of the local paper mills to ask why their reports were not as good.

G. J. Haines, assistant cashier of the Citizens National Bank of New York, followed Chandler. He had visited with Palmer in December of 1911 and, on the basis of that visit, had extended a $125,000 line of credit to Michigan Buggy. At the time Michigan Buggy went into receivership, there was an outstanding balance of $80,000 with Citizens. Palmer's attorney, Claude Carney, attempted to show that the line of credit already existed and that the fraudulent statements released by Palmer did not result in the extension of additional credit to Michigan Buggy. Haines was resolute in his testimony that the line of credit extended by the bank followed the receipt of the fraudulent statement.

L. H. Gethoefer was a cashier at the Columbia National Bank in Grand Rapids, Michigan, at the time of the transactions and was, at the time of the trial, vice-president of the Marine National Bank in Buffalo, New York. Carney attempted to distract the witness with his cross examination by references to the payments made to the bank during the period in question. The witness conceded that Michigan Buggy had liquidated a considerable amount of its indebtedness between March 17, 1913, the date of the receipt of the false statement, and August 2, 1913, the date the company was closed. The witness also made clear, however, that during the same interval the company increased its indebtedness with the bank by $11,000. His testimony verified that credit was extended based upon the fraudulent statement, and that, at the time of the failure, the company owed the bank $117,000. Finally, the witness testified that his correspondence with the company was with Palmer and Palmer alone, and not Henry Lane or Frank Lay, Sr., confirming that Palmer was regarded as the primary financial officer for Michigan Buggy. Gethoefer confessed that he was much impressed with Palmer when they first met in the spring of 1911, and that he was particularly impressed with Palmer's expressed intent to limit the manufacture of cars to the number for which the company had orders. His testimony emphasized, once again, that Palmer was the primary source of company financial policy and that his word carried great weight among the bankers in evaluating the company's standing.

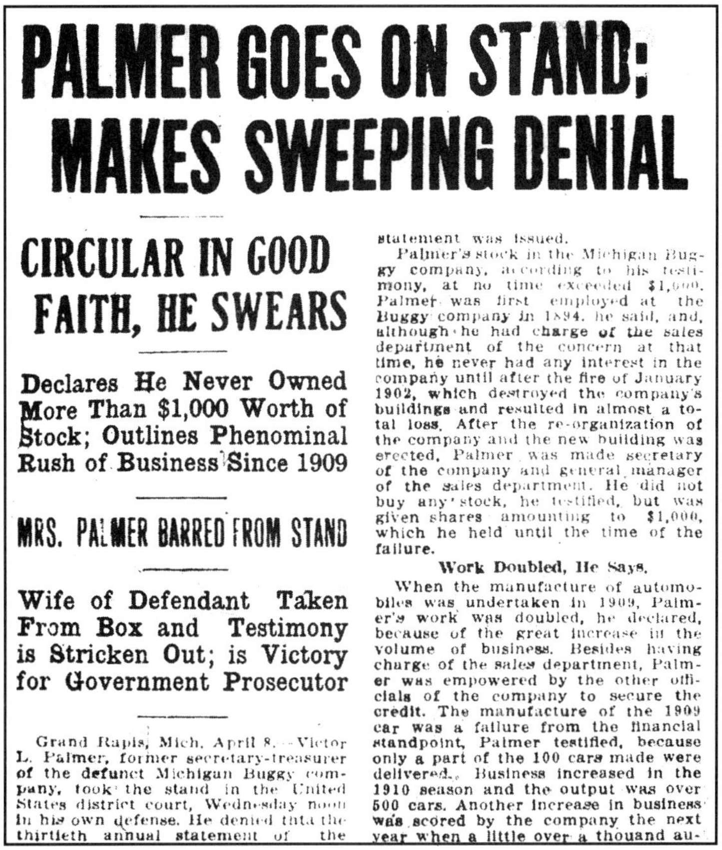

PALMER GOES ON STAND; MAKES SWEEPING DENIAL

CIRCULAR IN GOOD FAITH, HE SWEARS

Declares He Never Owned More Than $1,000 Worth of Stock; Outlines Phenominal Rush of Business Since 1909

MRS. PALMER BARRED FROM STAND

Wife of Defendant Taken From Box and Testimony is Stricken Out; is Victory for Government Prosecutor

Grand Rapis, Mich. April 8.—Victor L. Palmer, former secretary-treasurer of the defunct Michigan Buggy company, took the stand in the United States district court, Wednesday noon in his own defense. He denied that the thirtieth annual statement of the statement was issued.

Palmer's stock in the Michigan Buggy company, according to his testimony, at no time exceeded $1,000. Palmer was first employed at the Buggy company in 1894, he said, and, although he had charge of the sales department of the concern at that time, he never had any interest in the company until after the fire of January 1902, which destroyed the company's buildings and resulted in almost a total loss. After the re-organization of the company and the new building was erected, Palmer was made secretary of the company and general manager of the sales department. He did not buy any stock, he testified, but was given shares amounting to $1,000, which he held until the time of the failure.

Work Doubled, He Says.

When the manufacture of automobiles was undertaken in 1909, Palmer's work was doubled, he declared, because of the great increase in the volume of business. Besides having charge of the sales department, Palmer was empowered by the other officials of the company to secure the credit. The manufacture of the 1909 car was a failure from the financial standpoint, Palmer testified, because only a part of the 100 cars made were delivered. Business increased in the 1910 season and the output was over 500 cars. Another increase in business was scored by the company the next year when a little over a thousand au-

Figure 18-3. News of Palmer's trial continued to make headlines in the local press. This clipping is from the April 9, 1914 issue of The Kalamazoo Gazette.

These primary witnesses were followed by a series of statements by several accountants, J. J. Jerome from the Detroit Trust Company, and Maurice S. Arnold and E. E. Jacobus from Michigan Buggy. Jerome identified expenditures that were improperly recorded as accounts receivable, and the latter two accountants testified to Palmer's review of the books, including the identification of his personal marks that effectively countered Palmer's testimony that he had never seen the books. Finally, both Buggy Company accountants stated that the figures in the statements sent to the various banks were prepared at the instruction of Palmer.

Palmer attempted to defend himself by pleading ignorance of the specific aspects of these reports. He also confessed that the increase in the complexity of business as a result of the decision to manufacture gasoline-powered automobiles had made the financial aspects of the concern very difficult. In essence, he argued that the job was more than he could handle, that he was distracted by additional work in sales, and that mistakes were made due to the ever increasing demands on his time. He tried to place his wife, Mary, on the stand to testify about the personal strain incurred by the overwhelming press of work following the company's decision to manufacture cars. Judge Sessions seemed unimpressed with his argument and did not allow the testimony.

More than three hundred exhibits, including financial statements and books from the insolvent firm, had been presented, but the issue finally turned on the false financial statement distributed on March 1, 1913. The question was whether Palmer was culpable in the preparation of the fraudulent statement.

District Attorney Bowman, declared in his closing argument that the statement was not only deceptive, but fraudulent and "admittedly so." Bowman insisted that the entries were made for a purpose and that Palmer had worked out the details of the scheme. Part of that closing argument was reported in the *Gazette* on April 11, 1914:

> Items entered as accounts receivable and cash items in transit C.O.D. entered on the statement as $800,000 included hundreds of thousands of dollars worth of items which were not accounts receivable. Included in this statement was money spent for advertising, printing, the construction of a new auto building and power plant equipment and auto expense.

The exact violation, as reported in the same issue of the *Gazette*, involving eleven counts and a possible sentence of fifty-five years in prison, was "…devising a scheme to defraud or with intent to defraud, and using the United States mail toward the furtherance of that purpose."

The report of the courtroom drama in that issue on April 11 was as follows:

> Grand Rapids Mich., April 10, 1914—H. C. Murray of Sparta and spokesman for the twelve-man jury delivered the verdict without preamble; guilty as charged, which covered all eleven counts. These fateful words, cut like a sharp knife thorough the silence of Judge Sessions' courtroom in the federal building at 4:45 o'clock in the afternoon, as the jury that had sat in judgment in the trial of Victor L. Palmer of Kalamazoo, former secretary-treasurer of the defunct Michigan Buggy Company, since March 23, rendered its verdict.

When the verdict was read, Palmer showed little emotion. Only a slight grimace and a heightened touch of color in his face were evident as he silently assisted his father with his overcoat. He spoke not a word, either to his father or his wife, as the three left the courtroom.

The defense attorneys were devastated. The maximum penalty was five years in prison and a $1,000 fine for each of the 11 counts. Burritt Hamilton was the first to recover from the shock. He made a perfunctory motion for a stay, and subsequently Claude Carney raised the issue of bonds, but the matter was done. Sentencing was set for April 20, 1914.

A large crowd of friends and well wishers as well as the curious from Kalamazoo gathered in the court on April 20, 1914 to listen to the conclusion of the affair. Many of Palmer's friends thought that he had capitulated to the circumstance and were much surprised when his attorneys entered a plea for a new trial when the court resumed that day. This time, the attorneys charged that the judge's direction to the jury, that had lasted over an hour, during which he had instructed the jurors not to pay attention to any evidence concerning Palmer's honesty or intent in distributing the statements, constituted a direction to the jury to find a verdict of "guilty." In sum, the influence exerted by the judge denied their client a fair trial and they demanded a retrial. For the moment, sentencing was delayed until April 24.

Only the defendant, his family, the attorneys, and members of the press were in court when it was reconvened on April 24, 1914. Judge Sessions heard the arguments of the defense concerning Palmer's state of mind. Claude S. Carney argued well and at length before Judge Sessions seeking to establish a difference between "a scheme to defraud" and "a scheme to deceive," and by assumption then, that Palmer's intent was only to deceive. The law used the word "defraud," and Carney as-

serted that Palmer may have intended to deceive, but "had not devised a scheme to defraud or with intent to defraud." Therefore Palmer was entitled to a new trial. Carney was articulate and forceful in making this very technical argument. The judge's curt denial, that appeared in the *Telegraph-Press*, April 24, 1914, granted no substance to the technicality: "The motive had nothing to do with the issue.… Palmer had no right to resort to such an artifice to obtain money which he could not have obtained had he told the truth."

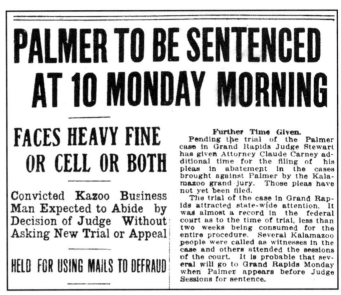

Figure 18-4. Headline from the April 9, 1914 issue of The Kalamazoo Gazette.

Judge Sessions pronounced Palmer's sentence: two years in prison at Leavenworth, Kansas. In conclusion, the judge allowed sixty days for Palmer to make an appeal and released him on a $10,000 bond. The financial and emotional cost of the continued court battle was too much, however, and on June 5, 1914, Victor L. Palmer accepted the sentence that would begin after the sixty days had elapsed on June 26, 1914. Sadly, on June 17, Victor Palmer was surrendered to the court by his father who wanted to be relieved of the responsibility of the bond he had posted. Palmer was then released on his own recognizance.

On June 18, 1914, Palmer turned himself in to the courts in Grand Rapids, Michigan, for transport to Leavenworth, Kansas, to begin serving his sentence on June 26. He left at noon the next day in the custody of United States Marshal Nicholas Whelan and was accompanied by his wife. Palmer was a pragmatic man, and he and his wife planned for her to make the trip with him and to secure housing near the prison so that she might visit as often as the rules allowed. Incarceration would not be pleasant, but prison officials could reduce the sentence to twenty months for good behavior. The government was building a new prison in Kansas City, Kansas, and special arrangements were made at Leavenworth for bankers and financiers to assist in the project. Palmer anticipated an assignment in the bookkeeping department.

Victor Palmer vowed to return to Kalamazoo after serving his sentence. He submitted a written statement of his innocence to the *Telegraph-Press* that was published on June 18, 1914, just prior to his departure. His statement read in part as follows:

> I am about to go to Leavenworth to serve the sentence imposed upon me by the United States
> District Court for a technical offense of which I believe myself to be guiltless. I know my own

intentions and I know that I have never intended to wrong any person out of a single dollar...
I am a victim of circumstance. Because I was a hard worker many duties came to me... I am
unable to prosecute my contest for vindication further.... I am sustained by the thought that
I have done my best for the protection of all interests.... I have not been personally instrumental in the loss of a single dollar to any man, woman or child.

A measure of the effect of his final plea is difficult to assess. Perhaps his friends found some
comfort in his words, while others considered it a vain attempt to regain a bit of his honor. His
name would be in the headlines once more a year later, but his subsequent return to the city was
without public notoriety.

The demise and financial ruin of the Michigan Buggy Company had been rapid, and Victor L.
Palmer, secretary-treasurer of the company, bore the brunt of the legal actions. His criminal trial,
which grew out of the bankruptcy investigations and testimony before the Grand Jury, set a record
for speed in federal courts. The chronology for the entire episode, from the date of the infraction
to the date of incarceration, lasted just over one year and proceeded as follows:

- March 5, 1913: Palmer issues the fateful financial statement for Michigan Buggy.
- August 5, 1913: the Detroit Trust Company is named receiver for Michigan Buggy.
- September 17, 1913: the bankruptcy hearing begins; Palmer testifies on September 19.
- November 26, 1913: the Grand Jury is sworn following the petition by the Attorney General.
- December 12, 1913: Palmer testimony begins and continues through December 15.
- February 28, 1914: Federal Grand Jury indicts Palmer for mail fraud.
- March 24, 1914: the criminal trial begins in Grand Rapids.
- April 24, 1914: Palmer is sentenced to two years in prison.
- June 19, 1914: Palmer departs for Leavenworth; his sentence begins June 26, 1914.

The incarceration did not bring an end to the episode for Palmer. On March 20, 1915, almost a
year to the day after his own trial began, he was brought back from Leavenworth to testify in the
criminal case against Frank Lay, Jr. and George Lay. He stepped from the train, stylishly dressed,
the old familiar smile in evidence, and appearing in better health than ever before. Friends had
packed the courtroom during the final days of his trial, but his return to the city was quiet. None of
their acquaintances from former days appeared at the railway station to greet the Palmers.

When called to the stand five days later, and much to the chagrin and frustration of prosecutor
Charles Nichols, Palmer refused to testify. The story was reported in the *Gazette* on March 25 and
26, 1915. The prosecutor was under the impression that Palmer had agreed to testify before leaving
Kansas. "Didn't you cause a telegram to be sent to me from Leavenworth saying that you would
testify," queried prosecutor Nichols. Palmer, perhaps feeling a bit smug in the apparent ruse and
manipulation of the prosecutor, was very curt in his reply: "I did not." Since there were charges still
pending against Palmer, he refused to testify under the Fifth Amendment of the Constitution,
asserting a danger of self-incrimination.

Livid with frustration at the turn of events, Prosecutor Nichols turned immediately to the court
officials, and ordered Palmer back to Leavenworth, making sure that his departure would be before
the start of the weekend. He had counted on Palmer's testimony in his case against the "Lay boys";
now he would take whatever small revenge he could. "We have no further use for Palmer," he said.

PALMER TO SERVE OUT HIS SENTENCE

GRAND RAPIDS, Mich., June 5.— According to United States Judge Clarence W. Sessions, presiding in the case, Victor L. Palmer of Kalamazoo, recently convicted of using the mails to defraud, has decided not to appeal his case and will serve his sentence of two years in the federal penitentiary at Fort Leavenworth, Kansas.

Palmer, who was secretary of the Kalamazoo Buggy company, now in the hands of a receiver, was convicted of having sent a false statement of the assets and liabilities of the company through the mail, in order to obtain credit. He was convicted in the United States court here and was sentenced by Judge Sessions to two years at Fort Leavenworth. He was granted a stay of 60 days for appeal.

Judge Sessions today announced that at the end of the 60 days Palmer has decided to begin his term in the penitentiary.

VICTOR D. PALMER.

Figure 18-5. Palmer submits to the inevitable; this clipping is from the June 5, 1914 issue of the Kalamazoo Telegraph-Press.

"Under no circumstances will Palmer be allowed to remain in Kalamazoo over Sunday."

The deputy warden from Leavenworth made the arrangements for Palmer's return and informed Nichols that a bill for the transportation expenses would be presented to the county the next day. The trials of Frank Lay, Jr. and George Lay were scheduled to continue without Palmer's testimony, although without his help, the trials of the two young men were mired in the courts for another eighteen months.

REFERENCES

Federal Grand Jurors Indict Victor Palmer. *The Kalamazoo Gazette*, March 3, 1914.

Palmer Pleads Not Guilty to Charge. *Kalamazoo Telegraph-Press*, March 3, 1914.

Carney Defeated in Congress Fight. *Kalamazoo Telegraph-Press*, January 14, 1914.

Palmer Trial Will Be March 17. *The Kalamazoo Gazette*, March 4, 1914.

Palmer Indicted by Federal Jury. *Automobile Topics*, March 7, 1914, p. 242.

Another Indictment Against Palmer. *The Horseless Age*, March 11, 1914, p. 394.

Palmer To Take Stand at Hearing. *Kalamazoo Telegraph-Press*, March 14, 1914.

Prosecutor Defends Grand Jury. *Kalamazoo Telegraph-Press*, March 16, 1914.

Palmer Ready for Trial on Tuesday. *Kalamazoo Telegraph-Press*, March 21, 1914.

Palmer Begins Fight Against Charge Made in Federal Court. *Kalamazoo Telegraph-Press*, March 24, 1914.

Victor Palmer Trial Is Resumed Today. *The Kalamazoo Gazette*, April 1, 1914

Auto Cases Up Again Next Week. *The Kalamazoo Gazette*, April 3, 1914

Palmer Is Said to be Real Head. *Kalamazoo Telegraph-Press*, April 3, 1914.

Palmer Scores Over Federal Prosecutor. *The Kalamazoo Gazette*, April 3, 1914.

Palmer to Testify on Own Behalf. *Kalamazoo Telegraph-Press*, April 4, 1914.

Victor Palmer Believed 1913 Circular True. *The Kalamazoo Gazette*, April 4, 1914.

Victor Palmer Trial to Close Next Saturday. *The Kalamazoo Gazette*, April 8, 1914.

Witnesses Defending Palmer Act. *Kalamazoo Telegraph-Press*, April 8, 1914.

Palmer Claims He Did Not Know Inventory of Buggy Plant. *Kalamazoo Telegraph-Press*, April 9, 1914.

Palmer Goes on Stand: Makes Sweeping Denial. *The Kalamazoo Gazette*, April 9, 1914.

Michigan Buggy Trial Notebook. Western Michigan University Archives.

Palmer's Fate Now Up to Federal Court Jury. *Kalamazoo Telegraph-Press*, April 10, 1914.

Palmer Case Goes into Hands of Jurors Today. *The Kalamazoo Gazette*, April 10, 1914.

Palmer to Fight Penalty Payment. *Kalamazoo Telegraph-Press*, April 11, 1914.

Guilty of Using Mails to Defraud Is Verdict. *The Kalamazoo Gazette*, April 11, 1914.

Palmer to Be Sentenced at Ten Monday Morning. *The Kalamazoo Gazette*, April 14, 1914.

Rumored Palmer Will Not Seek New Trial. *Kalamazoo Telegraph-Press*, April 17, 1914.

Want Trial Before Some Other Judge. *Kalamazoo Telegraph-Press*, April 18, 1914.

Palmer Seeks New Trial. *Kalamazoo Telegraph-Press*, April 20, 1914.

New Trial Is Sought by Victor L. Palmer. *The Kalamazoo Gazette*, April 21, 1914.

V. L. Palmer Granted Sixty Days to Make His Appeal. *Kalamazoo Telegraph-Press*, April 24, 1914.

Michigan Motor Car Company. *Automobile Trade Journal*, April 1914, p. 86.

Palmer Refuses to Answer Questions - Is It Contempt? *Kalamazoo Telegraph-Press*, May 15, 1914.

Palmer to Serve Out His Sentence. *Kalamazoo Telegraph-Press*, June 5, 1914.

Palmer Bill Withdrawn. *Kalamazoo Telegraph-Press*, June 17, 1914.

Palmer With Denial on Lips Goes to Prison. *Kalamazoo Telegraph-Press*, June 18, 1914.

Palmer With Officer, Is On Way to Prison. *Kalamazoo Telegraph-Press*, June 19, 1914.

Victor Palmer Back to Give Testimony in Frank Lay Case. *Kalamazoo Telegraph-Press*, March 20, 1915.

Victor Palmer Refuses to Testify in Lay Case. *Kalamazoo Telegraph-Press*, March 25, 1915.

Palmer Back to Prison. *Kalamazoo Telegraph-Press*, March 26, 1915.

Fig. 19-1. In the aftermath, Frank Lay, Sr., on the left, sits in the lobby of a local hotel, circa 1913. One might imagine that he has come to be with acquaintances in an effort to distract himself from the torment created by the indictment of his two sons.(WMU)

Chapter 19

Closure and Aftermath

*Kalamazoo Citizens must not forget
that the thing we are interested in now
is to put our shoulders to the wheel and push on.*

—Charles B. Hays

Closure of the Michigan Buggy Company on July 30, 1913 was followed by the bankruptcy hearings during September and October of 1913, and in turn by the sale and disposal of the company property in December of that year. Information from the bankruptcy hearing formed the basis of a Federal Grand Jury investigation that handed down indictments against the company directors in January 1914; those in turn led to the eventual criminal proceedings against Victor Palmer and the "Lay boys" in the spring of 1914. The plant's closure created severe economic hardship within the community, and by the winter of 1914, the estimate of the unemployed had reached 2,000 persons. The Commercial Club, Charity Officials, and the Michigan Federation of Labor sought to devise a plan to resolve the issues, but the best they could offer was city-sponsored work trimming trees and digging sewer lines in four-hour shifts in order to spread the work among the available men. According to city officials, the unemployed were not "roving professional tramps," and the call went out to all local manufacturers to provide access to jobs. The Michigan Buggy closure was not cited as the cause of the labor situation, but the loss of eight hundred jobs had to affect both its employees and those who provided support services to it.

The two local newspapers were also affected by the events that surrounded the Michigan Buggy affair. The story of the company's demise was reported almost daily from August 30, 1913 through the spring of 1914 in *The Kalamazoo Gazette* and the *Kalamazoo Telegraph-Press* with the latter as the more aggressive of the two. The *Gazette* was very conservative, almost protective on some occasions, in its reporting of the personal affairs of the officers of Michigan Buggy. The *Kalamazoo-Telegraph* published more news about the events than did *The Kalamazoo Gazette*, and the *Telegraph* emphasized the personal aspects of the conflict between the various parties, often with pejorative headlines. Typically, "the witnesses were questioned" in *Gazette* articles, but "the witnesses were grilled" when the *Telegraph-Press* reported the same story.

There was much public banter between the two papers, with the *Telegraph-Press* boasting about its superiority, claiming that it had published eight editions to the one by the opposing *Gazette*. On October 19, 1913 *The Gazette* made its counter claims, charging that the *Telegraph* was publishing fiction:

> Despite the broadsides of the ethereal fiction fired off at half cock through the medium of comic supplement "extras" by other Kalamazoo newspapers in which it was positively stated that warrants had been issued for Victor Palmer and Frank B. Lay, Jr....

The matter of these reports was a serious one. Claude Carney, attorney for Lay and Palmer, protested to the Booth newspapers about reports that appeared in Grand Rapids and Detroit concerning the anticipated charges and the arrest of his client, but his efforts were futile.

Eventually, the two papers were joined. The reports about the Michigan Buggy Company declined over the next few years, as did the apparent need for two newspapers in Kalamazoo. Although unrelated to the Michigan Buggy ordeal, *The Kalamazoo Gazette* bought the *Kalamazoo Telegraph-Press* in the spring of 1916.

The effects of the Michigan Buggy situation were widely felt, and the courts in the spring of 1914 resembled a three-ring circus. Following the public indictments from the Grand Jury, Victor Palmer was charged in criminal court, and then the Detroit Trust Company reopened the bankruptcy hearings, hoping to add the personal assets of Frank Lay, Sr. and M. Henry Lane to the financial pot from which to pay the creditors. Palmer had offered damaging testimony concerning the rift between Frank Lay, Sr. and Henry Lane, and at first was cooperative, but as his own trial unfolded, he refused to testify in the newly reopened bankruptcy hearing. He in turn was threatened with contempt of court by Judge A. F. Mills. In the midst of these two hearings, Edward N. Dingley, editor of *The Progressive Herald*, challenged the integrity of Judge Stewart, officer of the court responsible for the Grand Jury. Prosecutor Milo Bennett also made vehement charges against the grand jury. The entire legal system appeared "out of order."

The lives of seven leaders in Kalamazoo were forever changed: Frank Lay, Sr. and M. Henry Lane, directors of Michigan Buggy; Frank Lay, Jr. and George Lay, company vice-presidents; Victor L. Palmer, company secretary-treasurer; Charles Hays, business leader and former major of Kalamazoo; Stephen B. Monroe, president of the Kalamazoo City Savings; and finally Prosecutor Milo Bennett. The effects of the hearings and the trials in late 1913 and early 1914 reverberated through the community, challenging the legal core, the social strength, and the economic integrity of the city, leaving a legacy in Kalamazoo that was still discussed in the community after the end of World War II. Many people of lesser standing in Kalamazoo were also caught up in a frenzy of activity, particularly Fred C. Eldred, former employee of Charles B. Hays, who was indicted, arrested, and questioned before the court.

Victor Palmer felt the brunt of Michigan Buggy's failure more deeply than any of the others. His arrest in April 1914 was followed by a speedy trial in Federal Court in Grand Rapids and a two-year sentence in the federal penitentiary at Leavenworth, Kansas, beginning in June of that year. The rigorous grilling by Sanford Ladd during the bankruptcy hearing, the stress of the Federal Grand Jury indictments, and finally the cross examination during the criminal proceedings led to a nervous breakdown, bouts of severe depression, and general ill health during this trying period. It was only during the final stages of the trial and the final sentencing that Palmer appeared calm and resolute. His sentence was subsequently reduced for good behavior and he was released from prison and returned to Kalamazoo on January 17, 1916 to answer a charge of embezzlement in circuit court. His father, as before, posted the $5,000 bail.

Victor Palmer died on January 14, 1924 at the age of 53. He had joined Michigan Buggy as a bookkeeper and had spent almost twenty years with the company from 1894 through 1913, rising to the position of secretary-treasurer. He was prominently identified with business interests, serving on the board of directors of several banks in the city. He was survived by immediate family: his wife Mary Barnard Palmer, his parents, his sister, Mrs. F. A. Leach, and his brother, Frank Palmer.

M. Henry Lane, one of the original founders of the company, was deposed as president of the company by the Lay family in 1912. Because of that removal he emerged from the bankruptcy affair without being prosecuted and without a major financial penalty. Henry Lane was still being charged with the fraudulent issue of stock and the implication that the stock was a lien on the company as late as September 15, 1915, two years after the initial bankruptcy. Finally, the indictment was quashed by Judge Walter North of Battle Creek, Michigan. The judge ruled that even if the facts in the case were found to be true and Lane had approved the language in the stock prospectus implying the stock was a lien against the company, such facts did not constitute the commission of a crime. From the fall of 1913 through the fall of 1915, many of Lane's days were filled with attorney conferences and court appearances, but Henry Lane was an entrepreneur and even during the crisis of the bankruptcy and the Grand Jury he was out of town engaged in other financial deals that sought to bring new industry to Kalamazoo.

M. Henry Lane was not forced into bankruptcy, and within two years he was able to arrange his financial affairs to incorporate the Lane Truck Company. Manufacture of a line of vehicles began in the fall of 1917 in a building that was within a stone's throw of the Michigan Buggy plant. Due to failing health, he sold the company and the plant in 1918 to H. A. Crawford, formerly president of Lull Carriage, who began manufacture of the Kalamazoo truck in the same facility.

The Lane and the Lay family members had endured a strained relationship for many years and, according to family descendents, much of the difficulty was resolved in the aftermath of the trial. Ida Lay, Henry Lane's wife, and Mary Lay, Frank Lay, Sr.'s wife, were the best of friends, and no doubt it was their relationship that was at the bottom of the reconciliation. Henry Lane eventually retired to Florida and the local papers apparently lost track of his activities until the report of his burial on April 19, 1930.

Frank B. Lay, Sr. continued to reside in Kalamazoo living in the "Lay Mansion" at 523 West South Street. While he escaped criminal prosecution under the same circumstances that freed Henry Lane when Judge North quashed the indictments, Lay did not escape the financial consequences of the bankruptcy. He and his sons had removed Henry Lane as president in 1912, a move they believed was good for the company, but as president, Lay was responsible to the creditors as his name appeared on the notes issued by Michigan Buggy. Much to his chagrin, he was forced to declare bankruptcy on July 11, 1914. Although there was no public accounting of the cost, family descendants recall that he was very bitter about the personal financial burden that he was required to carry. They also remember Frank B. Lay, Sr. as an honorable man and a "workaholic" who was easily approached and who completed a deal with a handshake. The financial ruin of the company his father had founded with M. Henry Lane was personally difficult. All he ever wanted was to bring his sons into the business so that they might prosper and he was severely disappointed in the turn of events.

Frank Lay, Sr., had a long history of raising cattle and thoroughbred horses and had invested in the Tony Pony Line with Henry Lane around the turn of the twentieth century. After the bank-ruptcy, he purchased the Hillcrest Farms in Allegan County and, as his personal affairs settled, he turned to raising pedigreed cattle and race horses. Family descendants still recall that above his rolltop desk in the South Street mansion were hung photographs of the prize animals that consumed much of his time and energy. Frank Lay, Sr. died in Bronson Hospital on Friday, October 6, 1933 at the age of 77. He was survived by his wife, his three sons and two daugh-ters.

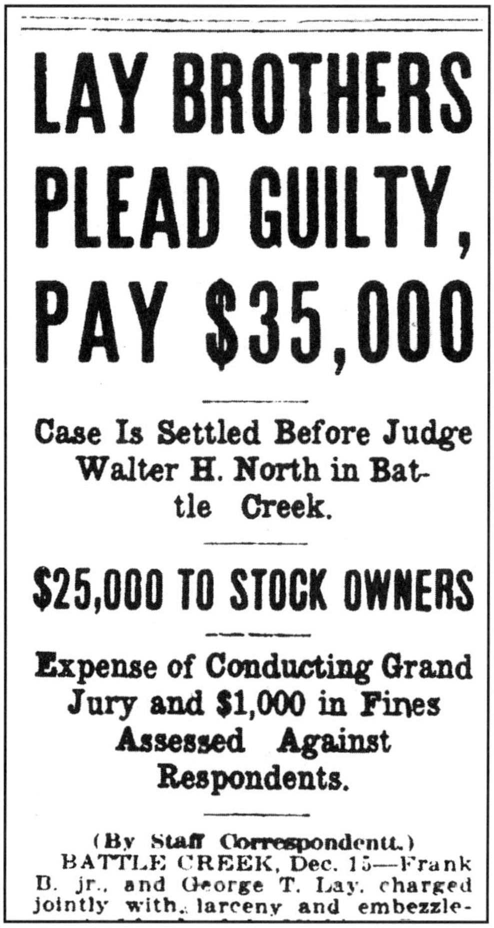

LAY BROTHERS PLEAD GUILTY, PAY $35,000

Case Is Settled Before Judge Walter H. North in Bat-tle Creek.

$25,000 TO STOCK OWNERS

Expense of Conducting Grand Jury and $1,000 in Fines Assessed Against Respondents.

(By Staff Correspondent.)
BATTLE CREEK, Dec. 15—Frank B. jr., and George T. Lay, charged jointly with larceny and embezzle-

Fig. 19-2. Clipping from the December 16, 1917 Kalamazoo Gazette.

Frank, Jr. and George Lay continued to fight the criminal charges against them throughout the sum-mer of 1914, but the entire affair was not finally settled until December of 1917, almost four years after the bankruptcy hearings began. Initially, the two sons were tried separately and Frank B. Lay was found guilty on April 3, 1915 and George Lay on April 14, 1915, both of embezzlement that resulted from the "velvet payroll." While the outcomes were the same, the drama of the trials was dissimilar. Frank, Jr. was stunned at the guilty verdict. He stood motionless before the court, towering above his wife and mother who stood by him, each one on the verge of a nervous breakdown. His father was nota-bly depressed by the verdict and sat silently in the rear of the courtroom.

George's trial followed and, given the verdict against Frank, the attorneys could predict the outcome. In an effort to protect the elder Lay from the resulting grief of the trial with George, Frank Sr. was conveniently detained in Fort Wayne and was unavailable to testify in court as a prosecution witness. Knowing the case was lost, the attor-neys tried to soften the consequence of the verdict. Several residents, including Dwight R. Curtenius and Addison Pengelly, were called as character witnesses. The two attorneys also wrote letters of support to the court expressing their belief that George Lay was not guilty. Their efforts did not alter the predictable outcome, and George, too, was found guilty.

The Lay boys appealed the decision to the Supreme Court and the case was eventually placed on the May term for the circuit court in 1917. Their attorneys also requested, and were granted, a change of venue from Kalamazoo County to Calhoun County because of irregularities in the se-lection of the jury. The trial was then scheduled for November, 1917 in Battle Creek, Michigan.

When the final trial came, the Lay brothers pleaded guilty to charges of larceny and embezzlement of the funds of the Michigan Buggy Company before Judge Walter H. North in Battle Creek on December 16, 1917. The prolonged legal battle had consumed much of their energy for the past four years, and the guilty plea appeared to be one of resignation in an effort to end this unfortunate aspect of their lives, although the final judgment also suggests a successful plea bargain. While they pleaded guilty to charges that carried a potential prison sentence, unlike Palmer neither of the Lay brothers was incarcerated. The final sentence included fines of $500 each, court costs of $9,000, and restitution to the stockholders, other than Lay family members and M. Henry Lane, of $25,000. The total penalty for the Lays was $35,000. In March of 1918, $24,950 was distributed to the stockholders, bringing the total return to the creditors of about thirty-three cents on the dollar. The remaining $50 of the repayment was turned over to the treasurer of Calhoun County. The $9,000 in court costs was credited to the general fund of Kalamazoo County, and the final $1,000 was allocated to the library fund. The payment to the library was wholly unrelated to the bankruptcy matter, and it suggests a bargain with various community constituents in lieu of community service.

The stockholders received a final payment from Frank and George Lay that was considered novel in the history of the Michigan courts and most likely was central to the plea bargain that is believed to have taken place. The Detroit Trust Company had worked diligently to restore the lost funds to the creditors, and a prison sentence for the Lay sons would have brought no return to those who had been wronged by the bankruptcy. The resolution of a cash settlement in lieu of a prison sentence seemed obvious, although probably not easily accomplished through the courts. The completion of these two cases ended the criminal court action against the two families in connection with the defunct concern. Both young men returned to Detroit where they were involved in the auto parts business and where Frank apparently remained. George Lay returned to Kalamazoo and reportedly spent much of his life attempting to assuage the hurt he had brought upon his family.

Charles B. Hays, former mayor of Kalamazoo, was indicted on January 29, 1914 by the Grand Jury, much to the chagrin of his business associates. Hays' comments in the court, as published in *The Kalamazoo Gazette*, January 29, 1914, reflect his manner of bearing as an articulate leader within the community:

> Every successful man must have his friends and his enemies and I am no exception. I am proud of both my friends and my enemies, the former because of their loyalty and their confidence and the latter because though bitter they are usually fair. While my enemies at this time have brought grief and humiliation upon my family, without excuse or reason, I feel sure that on the final judgment day those responsible for the indictment, which cannot be sustained in law or fact, will be held personally responsible before a Judge who knows no fear or favor and who has no enemies to revenge.

Charles Hays was charged with fraud based on two circumstances. First, the sale of $90,000 worth of preferred stock of Michigan Buggy at the time of the reorganization of the company in 1903. Second, the preparation of the prospectus for the stock by Fred C. Eldred, who was in his employ, just prior to the closure of the company, The changes were denied by the court in late April of 1914. The point of contention was the single statement in the prospectus that "the sale of the

Kalamazoo Honors Charles B. Hays Noted City Booster

Striking Sentiments Delivered at Banquet in Honor of Chas. B. Hays

Nothing can fail if we have co-operation.

Kalamazoo wants people who are looking on the bright side of things.

It is easy to find fault, but let us write those faults upon tablets which will disappear.

Kalamazoo likes a man who can start things, can mix and deal with people.

A man who does things is one who forgets himself.

Friendship of true and noble men comes from forgetting self.

Kalamazoo citizens must not forget that the thing we are interested in now is to put our shoulders to the wheels and push on.

CHARLES B. HAYS.

Glowing Tribute Paid to Man Who Has Done Much to Make City One of the Ideal Places of the Country. Those Who Are Trying to Tear Down have No Place in Kalamazoo", theme of Many Addresses—Affair one of Most Pleasing Ever Held Here.

"My hands are still gripping the handles of the plow and the end of the furrow is not yet in sight. I hope to accomplish much more for the good of Kalamazoo before I am called beyond."—Charles B. Hays.

With voice filled with emotion at the honor done him and the many words of appreciation spoken, Charles B. Hays, one of Kalamazoo's most prominent business men, last night closed his speech with a prayer to the Almighty for the many blessings given him during his lifetime.

In beginning Mr. Hays said: "I was not announced as one of the speakers for this evening. As guest of honor on this occasion, I am greatly honored by your presence.

Fig. 19-3. Charles Hays, indicted by the Grand Jury, emerged from the Michigan Buggy experience stronger than ever and was feted by the community at the grand opening of the Park-American Hotel.

stock was protected by a lien against the company and that there was no chance for the investors to lose." It was clear that Hays' office had served only as the fiscal agents for the sale of the stock, and that Hays was confused about the difference between owning stock and a property lien. Therefore nothing in the prospectus could support a charge of intent to defraud. Colonel Iris served as his attorney and made an eloquent and articulate argument that Hays was a businessman and not an attorney and that he had made a mistaken assumption that stock ownership was essentially a lien on the company. Judge Stewart agreed that there was no evidence of a crime under Michigan statutes, and the indictment was set aside.

On May 23, 1914 the *Telegraph-Press* announced the grand banquet at the Park-American Hotel to mark the opening of the hotel and to celebrate Charles Hays' reputation and leadership within the community. The guest list appeared in the *Telegraph-Press* on June 24, 1914, and read like a "who's who" in early Kalamazoo. C. A. Blaney, C. C. Bobb, O. K. Buckhout, H. A. Crawford, F. P. D'Arcy, Harry den Bleyker, Edward N. Dingley, G. E. Dunbar, Sam Folz, H. J. Fuller, James Grant, Harry Howard, George Hanselman, Otto Ihling, E. M. Irish, John McKinnon, S. B. Monroe, H. W. Parker, Goddie Rosenbaum, W. R. Taylor, and W. E. Upjohn were among the guests that evening.

Members of the Lay family and Henry Lane were not among the invited participants. W. R. Taylor, the toastmaster, opened the evening saying, "This gathering is not to celebrate the formal opening of a first-class hotel. We are here to do honor to a man who was born in Kalamazoo and through whose efforts Kalamazoo owes much of its progress."

Charles Hays' involvement in the bankruptcy of Michigan Buggy did not impede his business interests, and in December of 1919, he announced the organization of the Kalamazoo Land Company with a capital stock of $400,000 for the purpose of constructing homes in various sub-divisions to the south of Kalamazoo. A. C. Barley, president of Barley Motor Car Company, and Dr. W. E. Upjohn, president of the Upjohn Company, were named to the board of directors.

Fred C. Eldred, who was indicted for drafting the alluring prose in the text for the Michigan Buggy stock prospectus, was arrested by Sheriff John Shields in Morris, Illinois and hauled back to Kalamazoo in the morning of January 16, 1914. Essentially, he had been pulled into court on the coattails of Charles Hays. When the indictment against Hays was thrown out, so was the one against Eldred, but his life had already been damaged. Little was said about Eldred after the charges were thrown out, but he had lost his job as a result of the indictments and his eventual fate is unknown.

Stephen B. Monroe was president of the Kalamazoo City Savings Bank and a close friend of Victor Palmer when Michigan Buggy closed in August of 1913. In the winter of 1914, he was indicted for forgery and counterfeiting stock certificates, but escaped these charges when Judge North quashed the indictments against Frank Lay, Sr., and Henry Lane, as well as Monroe, in the fall of 1915. He appeared not to suffer any financial consequence, although he was forced to resign his position at Kalamazoo Savings and the *Kalamazoo Telegraph-Press*. He purchased the old Crane estate, described as a palatial residence in the Westnedge Hill area, with an estimated value of $35,000, in late April 1914. That house burned to the ground in early June of 1914 with an estimated loss of $20,000.

Edward F. Gerber got nothing more from the sale of Michigan Buggy after his bargain purchases in the summer of 1913. He left Kalamazoo after the hearings in search of other companies in financial difficulty. During the bankruptcy hearings, Sanford Ladd had argued vehemently that Gerber owed the Michigan Buggy creditors $380,000. Gerber scoffed at such claims, but that debt apparently stymied his subsequent attempts to purchase the Abbott-Detroit Motor Car Company. On February 16, 1914, Gerber was called back to Kalamazoo and his accounts with the defunct Michigan Buggy Company were reviewed once again. That audit showed some indebtedness to Michigan Buggy by Gerber's Pennsylvania Sales Company, and eventually Gerber paid a cash settlement to the Detroit Trust Company of between $50,000 to $75,000 to end the matter. After the debt with Detroit Trust was resolved, he purchased the plant and good will of the Abbott-Detroit Company for $237,500. He immediately wired George Reynolds, his attorney, who was waiting in Lansing to file the articles of incorporation for the newly-acquired company with a capital stock of $150,000. Gerber paid off the Abbott-Detroit creditors at fifteen cents on the dollar and vowed to continue manufacture of the automobile, just as he had promised to do with the Michigan in Kalamazoo. Gerber was out of the company within two years and R. A. Palmer, who had been with Cartercar in Jackson, Michigan, replaced him. Under R. A. Palmer, the company initiated an aggressive sales campaign, but after a move from Detroit to Cleveland, the Abbott-Detroit Company failed in October of 1917.

Milo Bennett was the prosecuting attorney for Kalamazoo County when the Grand Jury convened, but any authority that he might have had before that trial was superseded by the appointment of Lansing attorney Nichols. He subsequently lost his position. The scathing report about Bennett's conduct during the Grand Jury process, signed by Byron J. Carnes, jury foreman, was inadvertently released to the press apparently through Judge Stewart's office. Bennett brought a $50,000 libel suit against Joseph W. Stockwell, court stenographer, and other members of the jury. That case was decided in Judge Walter B. North's Calhoun County court in February 1916, and was found in favor of Stockwell and the defendant jurors. The verdict was subsequently reversed by the Supreme Court in June of 1917, and the $50,000 libel suit was rescheduled for hearing during the September term. Judge North of Calhoun County dismissed the case deciding that there was no way to place responsibility on individual jury members. The matter was finally settled out of court on December 9, 1917, for a sum "in the neighborhood of $1,200," as reported by the *Gazette*.

Edward N. Dingley, editor of *The Progressive Herald*, was a man of principle and had assumed a very aggressive publishing style during the period of the Grand Jury. He was found guilty of contempt of court for his unrelenting attacks on Judge Stewart, who was also a man of principle. The date for Dingley's sentencing was set and then postponed on at least two occasions because of the conflict between the two men. Even former United States Judge Henry F. Stevens, a friend of both men, tried to mediate the differences between the two. A group of Kalamazoo attorneys sat in the jury box and laughed about the ringside seats for the upcoming bout, while Dingley joked with onlookers about his planned hunger strike in jail. The sentence was eventually reduced to a $200 fine, but Dingley was resolute and vowed that "he would serve time before he would pay the fine." Subsequently, his attorney obtained a writ of *certiorari*, moving the review of the issue to the Michigan Supreme Court. In the meantime, however, the publisher of *The Progressive Herald* secured funds from the Progressive Party, and was prepared to pay Dingley's fine when the time came. The outcome of this conflict was not front page news during the next few months, suggesting that the fine was quietly paid and the matter brought to a close. Dingley left Kalamazoo. He died March 20, 1930 in Washington, D.C.

The Grand Jury members appeared in a half-page photograph in *The Kalamazoo Gazette* on January 15, 1914, all formally attired with solemn expressions. J. W. Stockwell, the most notable of the group, endured public accusations and condemnations through the complaints of Milo Bennett. Presumably, the lives of many others were affected in one way or another by the notoriety that followed and the continued public accusations made by Milo Bennett. Byron Carney, a resident of Vicksburg who served as the foreman, used the notoriety to his own advantage, becoming a Republican candidate for state representative from the second legislative district in Michigan.

The Michigan Buggy plant and the surrounding land did not sell at the auction and remained for only a brief period on the real estate market. In July of 1914, T. Willard Ready of Niles thought that he had purchased the property for $40,000, including nine buildings with over 1.3 million square feet of space for manufacturing purposes, four dwelling houses, nineteen acres of land, and a power plant. The buildings on the Michigan Buggy property were described as being in good shape and ready for occupancy and were appraised at $250,000. The minimum acceptable bid at the bankruptcy hearing had been declared as $45,000.

Willard Ready did not plan to move his own company to Kalamazoo but anticipated that at

NILES MAN PURCHASES MICHIGAN BUGGY

THIS GREAT PLANT WILL SOON BE HIVE OF INDUSTRY AGAIN.

Fig. 19-4. Hopeful headlines greet the news that the Michigan Buggy plant found a buyer. This article appeared in the July 21, 1914 Kalamazoo Telegraph-Press.

least two good-sized concerns from out-of-state would be likely tenants. One of the concerns rumored to be moving to Kalamazoo was the Havers Motor Car Company of Port Huron, Michigan. A strong bid was made by the Commercial Club in a lengthy telegram to the owners of the Havers Company after a fire destroyed the Port Huron plant on July 8, 1914. The fire was too much and Havers did not have sufficient financial resources to recoil from the disaster. A bankruptcy suit followed in November of 1914, ending any possible move to Kalamazoo.

The buildings and real estate of the Michigan Buggy Company were secured from the Detroit Trust Company for $45,000 by Charles Hays in the court of Clarence Sessions of Grand Rapids, Michigan within a month after Ready's bid. Ready was incensed over the turn of events. Not only was his original deal denied, but he was never given the opportunity to increase his bid, which he was willing to do. Hays, on the other hand, had a major investment in the area. In 1895 he began to remove the ponds and the mill races in the area south of the city—now known as Hays Park—and promised to construct boulevards in the area without cost to the city. Two of these streets were named Lane and Lay Boulevard. He was successful in his venture, although the city later paid $5,500 for the development of the park. The area was served by the Pennsylvania, New York Central, and Grand Trunk railways, and there was substantial support from the paper mills as well as the Commercial Club for Hays to gain control of the Michigan Buggy property. From all reports, Ready, who had few ties to the city, was "snookered" in the deal.

The Michigan Buggy property remained idle until 1916 when Hays was able to sell both the land and the buildings to W. B. Smith who planned to manufacture the States motorcar in the facility. The States venture was not successful, and in 1917, the property was sold again to A. C. Barley for the purpose of manufacturing the Roamer, "America's Smartest Car." The Sun Motor Car Company also attempted to purchase the plant in the summer of 1915, but R. Crawford, formerly of the Haynes Company, was unable to strike a deal with Hays. The Sun Company was then incorporated in Buffalo, New York, but subsequently moved to Elkhart, Indiana. The Sun Company, with the slogan "The Sun Outshines Them All," produced 337 cars in 1916 and 698 in 1917 before declaring bankruptcy. The Sun never approached the success of the Roamer and was not a loss for Kalamazoo.

Michigan Buggy was one of the largest and most successful manufacturing plants in Kalamazoo during the early part of the twentieth century. The seriousness of the situation was captured in an editorial by Edward Dingley entitled "What's the Matter with Kalamazoo?":

> The name Kalamazoo has been dragged through the Federal Courts, has been soiled with gossip and scandal, has been the synonym of frenzied finance and dishonest business and questionable conduct.... Back of all this snarl and mess is the prevailing desire for money— more money and the power that goes with it. [A] withering blast has swept over the city... a general air of depression and mistrust is abroad... Kalamazoo is badly wounded.
>
> [T]he greatest menace to Kalamazoo is the sensational and reckless afternoon daily... edited from Battle Creek, and Battle Creek chuckles over Kalamazoo's discomfort. The other "certain publication" (The Advocate) is used by the deposed president and former chairman of the board, to cudgel another officer of the company. And thus the war continues.
>
> The fact is Kalamazoo has been hit a hard blow, from which it will take years to recover.
>
> Kalamazoo is NOT the rotten city these publications would have the outside world believe. Kalamazoo is NOT an undesirable place in which to live. Kalamazoo's majority citizenship is NOT the Michigan Buggy Company type or the Lane type.
>
> What is the matter with Kalamazoo? Nothing if she is given the chance to rise above petty scandal, unfounded gossip and printed slander.... Kalamazoo is all right if the people want it so.

After the purchase of Michigan Buggy by Albert C. Barley, machines whirred and hummed once again in the great factory. The importance of the story, however, is not the Roamer, but that the social fabric of Kalamazoo survived the most tenacious attacks in its history upon the institutions of finance, government, and law.

Dingley aptly commented, "If from the ashes of a disaster comes a cleaner and saner business life, and a better citizenship, the catastrophe will not have been in vain."

REFERENCES

Buggy Plant Is Sold. *Kalamazoo Telegraph-Press*, October 3, 1913.

How to Care for 2,000 Unemployed Is Problem to Be Taken Up Today. *Kalamazoo Telegraph Press*, February 16, 1914.

Ask Manufacturers to Aid Jobless. *The Kalamazoo Gazette*, February 17, 1914.

Telegraph-Press Puts It All Over The "Opposition." *Kalamazoo Telegraph-Press*, October 19, 1913.

Attorney for Palmer and Lay Starts Action Against Papers Which Carried False Reports. *The Kalamazoo Gazette*, October 19, 1913.

Attorneys Appeal to High Court for Order to Get a New Trial Judge. *The Kalamazoo Gazette*, April 23, 1914.

In Decision Given Yesterday High Court Says Stewart Must Hear Cases. *Kalamazoo Telegraph-Press*, April 25, 1914.

Palmer Refuses to Answer Questions—Is It Contempt? *Kalamazoo Telegraph-Press*, May 15, 1914.

Palmer to Serve Out Sentence. *Kalamazoo Telegraph-Press*, June 5, 1914.

Palmer Bill Withdrawn. *Kalamazoo Telegraph-Press*, June 17, 1914.

Palmer With Denial on Lips Goes to Prison. *Kalamazoo Telegraph-Press*, June 18, 1914.

Palmer with Officer On Way to Prison. *Kalamazoo Telegraph-Press*, June 19, 1914.

Ask Parole for Victor Palmer. *Automobile Topics*, December 19, 1914, p. 413.

Victor Palmer Hearing. *The Automobile*, January 7, 1915, pp. 42-43.

Palmer Will Be Witness in Case. *Kalamazoo Telegraph-Press*, March 13, 1915.

Palmer Must Face Trial Here When His Sentence Ends. *Kalamazoo Telegraph-Press*, March 17, 1915.

Victor Palmer Back to Give Testimony in Frank Lay Case. *Kalamazoo Telegraph-Press*, March 20, 1915.

Victor Palmer Refuses to Testify in Lay Case. *Kalamazoo Telegraph-Press*, March 25, 1915.

Palmer Back to Prison. *Kalamazoo Telegraph-Press*, March 26, 1915.

No Liberty for Victor L. Palmer. *Kalamazoo Telegraph-Press*, December 17, 1915.

Victor Palmer Back, Is Released Late Today on $5,000 Bail. *Kalamazoo Telegraph-Press*, January 27, 1916.

Death Claims Victor Palmer at Home Here. *The Kalamazoo Gazette*, January 24, 1924.

Delay Case So M. H. Lane May Testify. *Kalamazoo Telegraph-Press*, March 29, 1915.

Fate of Lay and Lane Up to Judge North. *Kalamazoo Telegraph-Press*, November 23, 1915.

Lane and Lay Cases to High Court. *Kalamazoo Telegraph-Press*, November 27, 1915.

Ross Collier. *Ross Collier Collection*. Regional History Collections, Western Michigan University, A-1911.

Frank B. Lay Is Found Guilty. *Automobile Topics*, April 10, 1915, p. 707.

F. B. Lay Declared Bankrupt. *Kalamazoo Telegraph-Press*, July 11, 1914.

President Lay Fails to Appear as Witness. *Kalamazoo Telegraph-Press*, April 12, 1915.

Frank B. Lay, Old Resident of City Dies. *The Kalamazoo Gazette*, October 6, 1933.

Michigan Buggy Officials On Trial This Month. *The Horseless Age*, November 11, 1914, p. 742.

Lay Guilty Finds Jury. *Kalamazoo Telegraph-Press*, April 3, 1915.

"Velvet Payroll" Convicts F. B. Lay Jr. *The Horseless Age*, April 7, 1915, p. 455.

Denies Request That Case Be Dismissed Against George Lay. *Kalamazoo Telegraph-Press*, April 9, 1915.

George Lay Is Found Guilty. *Kalamazoo Telegraph-Press*, April 14, 1915.

F. B. Lay Case to Jury Today. *The Kalamazoo Gazette*, May 18, 1917.

To Try Lays in Calhoun Court. *The Kalamazoo Gazette*, June 19, 1917.

Lay Cases Go to Trial on Dec. 4. *The Kalamazoo Gazette*, November 25, 1917.

Lay Brothers in Court Today. *The Kalamazoo Gazette*, December 15, 1917.

Lay Brothers Plead Guilty, Pay $35,000. *The Kalamazoo Gazette,* December 16, 1917.

Lay Creditors To Get $25,000. *The Kalamazoo Gazette,* March 10, 1918.

What Former Mayor Says of Indictment by Jury. *Kalamazoo Telegraph-Press*,
    January 28, 1914.

Hays Gives Bail—Jury Adjourns Until Thursday. *Kalamazoo Telegraph-Press*,
    January 29, 1914.

Indictment Is Mere Revenge States Hays. *The Kalamazoo Gazette*, January 29, 1914.

Kalamazoo to Honor One of Its Chief Boosters and Builder of Park-American.
    Kalamazoo Telegraph-Press, May 23, 1914.

What Mr. Hays Says About Court Action. *Kalamazoo Telegraph-Press*, May 27, 1914.

Indictments Against Hays and Eldrid Are Thrown Out. *Kalamazoo Telegraph-Press*,
    May 27, 1914.

Indictment of Charles B. Hays Is Set Aside. *The Kalamazoo Gazette*, May 28, 1914.

Civic Boosters to Hold "Kalamazoo Dinner" at Park-American Sept. 18.
    Kalamazoo Telegraph-Press, September 11, 1914.

Company to Build 200 Homes Here Organized. *The Kalamazoo Gazette*, December 3, 1919.

Get Permits for 53 Homes. *The Kalamazoo Gazette*, April 2, 1920.

While Eldred Is Before Grand Jury He Is Given Up by His Bondsmen.
    Kalamazoo Telegraph-Press, January 26, 1914.

S. B. Monroe Resigns. *The Progressive Herald*, October 11, 1913.

Monroe Home Burns; Loss is Near $30,000. *The Kalamazoo Gazette*, June 7, 1914.

Indictment Against S. B. Monroe Dismissed Today in Circuit Court.
    Kalamazoo Telegraph-Press, September 24, 1915.

Grants Injunction Against E. F. Gerber. *The Kalamazoo Gazette*, November 22, 1913.

Gerber Settles With Detroit Trust Company. *Kalamazoo Telegraph-Press*, February 18, 1914.

Abbott to Build Nothing But Sixes for 1915. *Motor Field*, November 1914, p. 43.

Grand Jury in Special Report Assails Operations. *Kalamazoo Telegraph-Press*,
    January 29, 1914.

Bennett Wants Charges Expunged. *The Kalamazoo Gazette*, February 19, 1914.

Deplores the Constant Stirring Up of Strife. *Kalamazoo Telegraph-Press*, February 19, 1914.

Bennett Sues The Grand Jury Today for $50,000.00 Damages. *Kalamazoo Telegraph-Press*,
    February 4, 1915.

Grand Jury Cases May Not be Tried Next Week. *Kalamazoo Telegraph-Press*,
    February 15, 1915.

Calls Grand Jury Affair Disgrace to the County. *Kalamazoo Telegraph-Press*,
    February 19, 1915.

Grand Jury Cases May Go to Trial. *Kalamazoo Telegraph-Press*, September 14, 1914.

Judge North to Hear Trial of $50,000 Suit. *Kalamazoo Telegraph-Press*, November 27, 1915.

Was Bennett's Defeat Due to Grand Jury Act? *Kalamazoo Telegraph-Press*,
    November 29, 1915.

Bennett's Suit Against Grand Jury on Trial. *Kalamazoo Telegraph-Press*, November 30, 1915.

Throws Out Bennett Suit. *Kalamazoo Telegraph-Press*, December 2, 1915.

New Trial in Grand Jury-Bennett Suit. *The Kalamazoo Gazette*, June 29, 1917.

$50,000 Bennett Suit Is Settled. *The Kalamazoo Gazette*, December 9, 1917.

Dingley Is Held Guilty; Steward Defers Sentence. *The Kalamazoo Gazette*,
    February 17, 1914.

Supreme Court Not to Aid E. N. Dingley. *Kalamazoo Telegraph-Press*, February 21, 1914.

E. N. Dingley Refuses to Make Apology to Court. *The Kalamazoo Gazette*,
    February 21, 1914.

Dingley Awaits Action Tuesday to Make Appeal. *The Kalamazoo Gazette*, February 22, 1914.

Judge Again Delays Sentencing of Dingley. *Kalamazoo Telegraph-Press*, February 24, 1914.

Dingley Will Be Sentenced This Morning. *The Kalamazoo Gazette*, February 24, 1914.

Says Kalamazoo Grand Jury Fixed. *The Horseless Age*, February 25, 1914, p. 312.

Dingley Gets Writ From Supreme Court. *Kalamazoo Telegraph-Press*, February 26, 1914.

Dingley Fined $200. *The Kalamazoo Gazette*, February 26, 1914.

Dingley Will Do Time Rather Than Pay Fine. *The Kalamazoo Gazette*, February 27, 1914.

Many Tilts Between Judge and Attorneys. *Kalamazoo Telegraph-Press*, April 14, 1914.

Contempt Case Will Be Up Soon. *Kalamazoo Telegraph-Press*, June 11, 1914.

Niles Man Purchases Property of Michigan Buggy. *Kalamazoo Telegraph-Press*,
    July 21, 1914.

The $250,000 Michigan Buggy Plant Goes For $40,000. *The Horseless Age*, July 29, 1914.

Charles B. Hays Buys Factory From Receiver. *The Kalamazoo Gazette*, August, 11, 1914.

Michigan Buggy to Become Property of Hays Tuesday Morning.
    Kalamazoo Telegraph-Press, August 17, 1914.

Hays Buys Michigan Buggy for $45,000. *The Automobile*, August 20, 1914, p. 381.

Commercial Club Will Cooperate with Hays. *Kalamazoo Telegraph-Press*, August 31, 1914.

To Build Greyhound at $600. *Motor World*, July 14, 1915, p. 39.

Michigan Buggy Plant Sold—To Build $600 Car. *The Automobile*, July 15, 1915, p. 130.

Sun Motor Car Company Goes to Buffalo N. Y. *Kalamazoo Telegraph-Press*, August 6, 1915.

Editorial; What's the Matter with Kalamazoo? *The Progressive Herald*, October 25, 1913.

Part IV

COMMERCIAL VENTURES AND DREAMS OF GLORY

1900–1988

Chapter 20

The Kalamazoo Motor Vehicle Company

1913–1915

The "car" is said to show exceptional power in sand and on hills.

—The Kalamazoo Gazette

The story of the Kalamazoo Motor Vehicle Company begins with a newspaper report in *The Kalamazoo Gazette* on August 19, 1913 of a mysterious visitor, a group of promoters seeking stock subscriptions, and a search for an appropriate plant to build two-, five-, and ten-ton trucks. The demonstration model that was brought to the city purportedly was designed by a well-known automobile man with considerable experience.

Within a month, official word was disclosed in the *Gazette* on September 3, 1913 that Frank G. Clark, who was well known in Kalamazoo and was then living in Lansing, Michigan, had founded the Kalamazoo Motor Vehicle Company and would begin construction of a new line of trucks in the city to be known as the Kalamazoo. The manufacturing facility would be housed in the old Clarage Fan foundry building on North Church Street until a suitable plant could be found.

Frank G. Clark was a pioneer automobilist and it is unfortunate that his arrival coincided with the public announcement of the financial difficulties at Michigan Buggy, although the effect of the Michigan Buggy situation upon Clark is not known. Certainly, the bankruptcy hearings did not create a positive atmosphere for business in the city and his stay in Kalamazoo was brief. Before the turn of the twentieth century, Clark had been aligned with the horse-drawn buggy business, building carriages with his father, Albert Clark, who had founded Clark and Company of Lansing, Michigan, in 1865. Reportedly, in 1896, Frank Clark built the carriage body for the first experimental horseless carriage built by Ransom E. Olds. His father, Albert Clark, was not an automobile enthusiast and was hesitant about the emerging industry, so it was not until after his father's death in 1901 that Frank ventured into the industry by designing an automobile of his own. Frank spent almost eighteen months building a seven-horsepower runabout and in the spring of 1902, he founded the Clarkmobile Company to manufacture this vehicle. "They Go and Go Right" was the slogan, but it was Frank who went, and the company was sold to the Newway Company in 1905.

Frank subsequently joined with Claude E. Furgason, owner of a local machine shop, and together they founded the Furgason Motor Company in Lansing, Michigan, for the purpose of building the Clark. This car was twice the size and power of the Clarkmobile, but in spite of its apparent success Frank Clark decided to move into the expanding commercial vehicle field and, in 1911,

Kalamazoo Model B, 3000-lb. Stake, $1715.

Fig. 20-1. The Kalamazoo Model B, flare board style with a stake body, was powered by a twenty-three horsepower engine and sold for $1,715 in 1914 and 1915. This model is similar to the Superior truck that Frank G. Clark built in Lansing, Michigan, the previous year. This image is from the December 1914 issue of the Automobile Trade Journal. *(NAC)*

founded the Clark Power Wagon Company in Lansing, Michigan, to build commercial vehicles.

The story becomes a bit murky at this point. Some writers claim that Clark built commercial vehicles in Lansing for two years, founded the Columbia Truck and Trailer Company in 1913, and then moved to Pontiac, Michigan. His brief efforts to build the Kalamazoo truck in this city appear to have been lost in the sequence of history. There is agreement that he did direct the Columbia organization in Pontiac from

1915 until his retirement in 1927 and that he died some thirty years later in 1957 at the age of eighty-seven, but his brief sojourn in Kalamazoo is not well recorded.

The move from Lansing to Kalamazoo in the fall of 1913 by Frank G. Clark to found the Kalamazoo Motor Vehicle Company is well documented in *The Kalamazoo Gazette*. The ensuing manufacture of the Kalamazoo truck from 1913 through 1915, and the change in the name of that firm to Columbia Motor Truck and Trailer on July 3, 1915 is also well documented in the local press and national automotive periodicals. The known existence of the Columbia Motor Truck and Trailer Company in Kalamazoo and a company of the same name in Pontiac, Michigan, under Clark's direction, all documented in periodicals of the era, provides ample evidence of Clark's brief stay in Kalamazoo. Interestingly, the Columbia Company was founded in Kalamazoo in October 1912, a year before the *Gazette* documented the arrival of F. G. Clark's firm, suggesting that the Kalamazoo Motor Vehicle Company was absorbed into the Columbia Company. The Columbia Company was a family-owned business incorporated with a stock investment of $35,000. Frank G. Clark was named president; Hannah Clark, Frank's mother, was named vice-president; and Harriet E. Clark, Frank's wife, was named secretary-treasurer.

There was another Clark family company in Kalamazoo at the time, the Clark Engine and Boiler Company, but in spite of the *Gazette's* report that Frank was well-known in Kalamazoo, no evidence is found of a tie between Clark Engine and the Columbia Truck Company. Finally, the *Kalamazoo Directory* for 1916 recorded Frank Clark's move with the Columbia Truck and Trailer Company from Kalamazoo to Pontiac with a simple entry: "Removed to Pontiac."

Fig. 20-2. Two men unload farm products from a 1914 Kalamazoo truck onto a loading dock for shipment by rail. As early as 1914 the Canadian Pacific railroad recognized the motor truck as a potential vehicle for creating a feeder line between farmers and the railroads. Initially, the trolley car was thought to be the means to perform this function of supplementary transport, but only the motor truck was capable of running from the barn door to the railroad loading dock. This image is from a company sales brochure, circa 1914. (DOL)

On Sunday, September 15, 1913, Clark and an associate drove two trucks to Kalamazoo and in the process changed the name of the Lansing-built vehicles from "Superior" to "Kalamazoo." The Superior Model A was a one-ton express truck with a four-cylinder engine, three-speed transmission, double chain drive and solid rubber tires. Cost of the Superior was listed at $1,700.

The first Kalamazoo motor truck built in Kalamazoo appeared on the streets of the city on November 21, 1913, with O. S. Clark, presumably Frank's son, at the controls. This particular vehicle lacked a full seat back, was not equipped with lamps, and did not show the final decorative painting on the body that appeared on later vehicles. The description of this "car," as it was identified by the local press, suggests a vehicle similar to the Superior in construction and cost. After the introduction of perhaps one or two machines in late 1913, the Kalamazoo Motor Vehicle Company manufactured twenty-five trucks during 1914, their first complete year of production, and Clark was quoted as planning to manufacture two hundred trucks in 1915, using essentially the same design as in 1914 with a few minor improvements.

The Kalamazoo standard truck was built on a 110" wheel base, weighed 2,500 pounds and had a load capacity of 1½ tons. For those interested in additional load capacity, the Kalamazoo could be ordered with a trailer having a three-ton capacity, providing an overall capacity of 4½ tons in a single haul. The success of this truck and trailer combination no doubt gave way to the Columbia Truck and Trailer name.

The ground clearance for the Kalamazoo chassis was only 29½", considered very low for a truck, and a feature that contributed to the advertised low center of gravity. The Kalamazoo truck offered a thirty-horsepower Rutenber engine, Bosch magneto, Spicer universal joints, Sheldon axles, Hyatt sliding gear transmission, and Firestone tires. The availability of well-engineered components from

Fig. 20-3. The Kalamazoo Motor Vehicle Company sold a truck and trailer combination with the following appeal in their sales literature: "The guaranteed capacity of the 'Kalamazoo' Motor Truck is 3,000 pounds and the chassis price is $1,590. The combined capacity of the truck and the trailer is 9,000 pounds. The cost of the two is $2,265, a saving to you of $1,735 over an equally reliable 4½ ton truck." This image is from a sales brochure, circa 1914. (DOL)

independent manufacturers, a problem that Fuller had cited as an impediment to vehicle manufacture in the early part of the century, made possible the construction of a truck of this quality. This model sold for $1,800 in 1913 and received much favorable comment from local automobile men for its exceptional power on hills and in the sand, a predominant road surface in the area at that time. Gary Peters of 712 North Street was the second local drayman to purchase one of the early models in the spring of 1914, at a time when many local freight haulers were just beginning to replace horse-drawn vehicles with gasoline-powered trucks.

Improvements in the Kalamazoo were made for 1915, and the model shown at the Michigan Fair in the fall of 1914 had a two-ton capacity and was powered by a Buda engine, with a Kalamazoo-made Shakespeare carburetor, Bosch ignition, and Timken front end. The truck was capable of speeds up to fifteen miles an hour, and the chassis sold for $1,650. The cost increased to $1,775 with a mounted body, a decrease of $25 from the year before.

Most of the components for both the 1914 and the 1915 Kalamazoo models were standards within the industry at the time and were often mentioned in the description of other motor vehicles. Interestingly, the Rutenber engine was produced in Logansport, Indiana, under the supervision of the A. C. Barley family who some years later produced the Roamer in Kalamazoo, Michigan. The Buda engine was later used in the Kalamazoo-built Checker cab and by Kalamazoo Rail. The Shakespeare Company of Kalamazoo, builders of the carburetor for the truck, eventually became known for fishing reels and casting rods.

Clark had informed the local press that he was laying the foundation for a large, strong manufacturing firm with a permanent future in Kalamazoo. To that end, he planned to concentrate sales of the Kalamazoo in southwest Michigan and had not pursued the many requests for the product from dealers as far west as California. One can only speculate as to why Clark left Kalamazoo, but

Fig. 20-4. The Kalamzoo trailer was built on a sturdy frame with heavy-duty springs and solid rubber tires. The load capacity was rated at three tons. This image is from a sales brochure, circa 1914. (DOL)

it is known that he regarded the Clarage Foundry building in Kalamazoo as a temporary plant, although the Michigan Buggy plant was available in the late fall of 1913. Perhaps his success in finding a better facility in Pontiac led to his departure in late 1915.

The Kalamazoo truck of this manufacture did not appear at the annual auto shows in Kalamazoo nor were there *Gazette* advertisements exalting the strengths of the vehicle, although later commercial vehicles, the Lane and Kalamazoo, were conspicuous in both regards. Finally, the Kalamazoo name identification of two separate commercial vehicles has led to some confusion in the citation of these vehicles in historical encyclopedias. The Kalamazoo Motors Corporation that grew out of the Lane Motor Truck Company was founded by H. A. Crawford in 1919. It should not be mistaken for an outgrowth of the Kalamazoo Motor Vehicle Company. The latter company evolved into the Columbia Truck and Trailer Company that built vehicles in this city from 1913 to 1915 under Frank Clark's direction prior to his move to Pontiac, Michigan.

REFERENCES

Company Will Make Automobile Trucks. *The Kalamazoo Gazette*, August 19, 1913.

Company Organized and Plant Secured for Manufacturing the Up-to-Date Auto Truck in Kazoo. *The Kalamazoo Gazette*, September 3, 1913.

Albert Mroz. *The Illustrated Encyclopedia of American Trucks and Commercial Vehicles.* Iola, WI: Krause Publications, 1996.

Beverly Rae Kimes and Henry Austin Clark, Jr. *Standard Catalog of American Cars, 1805–1942*, 3d ed. Iola, WI: Krause Publications, 1996.

Vehicle Company Is Now Moving to City. *The Kalamazoo Gazette*, September 16, 1913.

New Columbia Truck & Trailer. *Motor World*, July 7, 1915, p. 55.

Kalamazoo Co. Changes Name. *The Automobile*, July 8, 1915, p. 80.

John Gunnell, ed. *Standard Catalog of Light Duty Trucks*, Iola, WI: Krause Publications, 1987.

R. L. Polk. *Kalamazoo Directory*, Detroit: Polk and Company, 1912.

_____. *Kalamazoo Directory*, Detroit: Polk and Company, 1915.

_____. *Kalamazoo Directory*, Detroit: Polk and Company, 1916.

First "Made in Kalamazoo" Motor Truck Appears on Local Streets. *The Kalamazoo Gazette*, November 22, 1913.

Kalamazoo Motor Trucks and Trailers. Sales brochure, Kalamazoo Motor Vehicle Company, circa 1914.

F. G. Clark President of Kalamazoo Vehicle Co. *The Horseless Age*, December 16, 1914, p. 868.

Kalamazoo Company to Build 200 Trucks. *The Automobile*, December 17, 1914, p. 1132.

Truck Specifications. *Automobile Trade Journal*, December 1914, pp. 210–11.

Kalamazoo Motor Trucks and Trailers. Company Sales Brochure, circa 1914.

Drayman Will Drive Kazoo Motor Truck. *The Kalamazoo Gazette*, March 6, 1914.

Building 3,000-Pound Truck. *Motor Age*, July 2, 1914, p. 44.

Michigan Fair Show Opens. *The Automobile*, September 9, 1915, p. 490.

Kalamazoo Motor Vehicle Co., Kalamazoo Michigan. *Horseless Age*, October 14, 1914, p. 575.

Truck Specifications. *Automobile Trade Journal*, December 1913, pp. 235–35A.

Chapter 21

The Lane Motor Truck Company

1916–1918

These trucks will put ginger in your business.

—Company advertisement

The trials of the Michigan Buggy Company had almost drawn to a close by the winter of 1916, although the old plant, now owned by William Smith of Toledo, Ohio, lay fallow, waiting for the influx of activity of a new industry. M. Henry Lane, former president of the defunct concern, seemed to have survived the bankruptcy and subsequent legal entanglements with only a tarnished image. His ability to raise investment capital remained intact, and on February 29, 1916, just two years after the Grand Jury indictments had been handed down, the Lane

Motor Truck Company was incorporated with a capital stock of $25,000. Lane was named president, W. A. Cook was named vice-president, and George Bardeen, Jr. secretary-treasurer. The plant was located at the southeast corner of Reed and Fulford Streets just west of and within view of Lane's former office at Michigan Buggy.

M. Henry Lane had not lost his zest for the industry after the Michigan Buggy closure, and his comments a year after the Lane Motor Truck Company was founded reflected his usual optimistic business manner. He com-

Fig. 21-1. *"These trucks will put ginger in your business," one of the more quaint slogans of the industry, was perhaps a statement that reflected Lane's own robust personality. (NAC)*

271

Fig. 21-2. "Profits—Deliveries and a Truck that Sells" was the sales pitch of this advertisement to potential truck dealers when it appeared in several issues of the Horseless Age *and the* Automotive Trade Journal *in 1918. The artwork is interesting—its image of a faraway city and a man carrying a bundle on his head struggling against the wind may depict the war in Europe. (ACA)*

mented to *The Kalamazoo Gazette* on January 25, 1917:

> *Our only hinderance to date has been obtaining an adequate supply of material. We are getting that trouble ironed out and expect to have plenty of material in the future. We have been running along very easily to date, and working out all of the details carefully so that when we do start there will be no delays.*

W. A. Cook, vice-president of the new firm, was also optimistic and spoke with exceptional pride about the trucks then on the factory floor. Kalamazoo seemed destined once again to take its place among the leading manufacturers of the industry.

Lane began production with a twelve-passenger car rather than a truck. The photograph in the *Gazette* on April 8, 1917, shows that the Lane Motor Truck Company built a very attractive touring car with seating for twelve passengers. The car was intended for use by the Riverside Transportation Company of Fort Myers, Florida, to be used for sight-seeing excursions between Fort Myers and Punta Gorda. The Lane automobile was built on a 120" wheel base using the same three-quarter ton chassis that was planned for the Lane Model A motor truck. The car was powered by a twenty-five horsepower Wisconsin four-cylinder engine. The handsome metal body for this car, with a design typical of the era, was the work of C. B. McDole, owner of a small sheet metal manufacturing firm at 218 East Water Street in Kalamazoo. The distinctive radiator with "LANE" embossed across the top of the shell was a prominent feature of the vehicle. The long, beautiful top with three rectangular rear windows was furnished locally by Limousine Top Company, and overall the design and finish of the car made a very handsome appearance. This particular car was the first of a large order to be furnished to the Riverside Company once the state highway was completed in southern Florida. The total production run for the twelve-passenger vehicle is unknown.

Initial manufacturing plans called for production of a light delivery truck, designated as the Model A. Apparently these plans were diverted to the twelve-passenger car that was built on the Model A chassis. The company subsequently dropped the light truck and concentrated on larger vehicles. The periodicals for the industry in that era carried numerous reports of manufacturing plans and impending production of various vehicles during 1916 and 1917, but the *Gazette* report on June 7, 1917, indicated that the first truck, a three-ton unit with a moving van body, was delivered to the Belmont Moving Company of Evansville, Indiana, in early June of 1917. Another unit was delivered to Bert Lee of Fort Wayne, Indiana, around June 17, 1917, and was closely followed by delivery of a beautifully finished, bright red truck with a 2½ ton capacity to Hawthorne Paper Company of Kalamazoo. Other deliveries during that summer went to Kalamazoo Ice and Fuel Company and William Traver of Hartford, Michigan. The extent of the Lane truck production is unknown.

The Lane Motor Truck Company eventually settled on a series of three trucks. The product line extended from the 1½ ton Model F at $2,250, to the 2½ ton Model B at $2,975, and the 3½ ton Model C at $3,700 f.o.b. Kalamazoo in 1918. The Model C chassis was equipped with electric lights and electric starter. The tail lights were set in a recess in the rear cross member of the frame, rather than being hung as an appendage to the vehicle, adding a bit of Henry Lane's style to the industry. A big five-ton model was also planned, but was not routinely available. All models were mounted on a 160" wheel base with an option of a 180" wheel base chassis for special applications. The Model F, the smallest of the three vehicles, was powered by a four-cylinder Wisconsin engine rated at twenty horsepower, while Models B and C, the larger two models of the offerings, were powered by a six-cylinder Continental engine, built in nearby Muskegon, Michigan. The Model C Continental engine was rated at thirty-four horsepower and the Model B at slightly less.

Production of the Lane truck reflected Henry Lane's experience with the Michigan car as both were built from standard components in the industry. The truck components, in addition to the Wisconsin and Continental engines, included Timken axles, Ross steering gear, Stromburg carburetor, Kalamazoo springs, and Willard battery. The wheels were artillery-type 36" x 5" and mounted with the finest Goodrich De Luxe tires in either a solid or pneumatic design. The body for each chassis was available in four styles: express, open flare, stake, or stationary top flare. Seating for the driver included full side curtains, cut and sewn at the Lane factory, and a low solid sliding door to protect the driver's feet in inclement weather. The door could be pushed out of the way in the seat box when weather permitted. A large radiator dominated the front of the vehicle with the name "LANE" prominently cast at the top. The radiator fin and tube cases were bolted together, allowing for easy removal for repair. Cooling was by a centrifugal pump.

Fig. 21-3. This advertisement, with the slogan, "Ask the Man Who Owns One," appeared in The Kalamazoo Gazette *on February 7, 1918. The slogan is associated with the famous Packard and appeared in an advertisement for that motorcar in the October 31, 1901 issue of* Motor Age. *The use of the slogan may have been the doing of the Thomas M. Orrell Agency in Kalamazoo and not the Lane Motor Truck Company, for the slogan was never repeated by Lane in national publications. (DOL)*

The war in Europe had slowed the production of automobiles in the U.S. and by the middle of 1918 a large proportion of almost every company's production was related to government contracts. These contracts determined truck production, and in some cases the lucrative contracts caused companies to eventually drop automobile production altogether to concentrate on commercial vehicles. Almost all of the Dodge Brothers' production, for example, was limited to automobiles with an army issue finish, while the Ford Motor Company discontinued the manufacture of automobiles for the duration of the war using the huge River Rouge plant for the production of Eagle submarine chasers, Liberty engines, and small tanks.

While the war effort was an impediment to automobile manufacture, it was a stimulant for truck production. In November of 1917, Lane obtained the first order from the war department for eight hundred trucks to be delivered over a three-year period. Henry Lane hoped that production would reach fifty trucks per month and even predicted that production might rise to twice that number before the year's end, but such optimism was never fulfilled.

On March 19, 1918, Henry Lane retired from the company because of poor health with plans for an extended southern trip. Although Lane sold his interest in the company, he intended to establish Lane truck agencies in Florida and other southern states. About the same time, additional truck agencies were established in Japan and others were planned for Europe, Australia, and several South American countries as well, attesting to Lane's international business interest. The Lane truck was sold locally through the Thomas M. Orrell Agency, at 434–440 West Main Street, one of the oldest automotive agencies in the city. Orrell had been associated with Michigan Buggy in its Pittsburgh agency and his association with Lane was most natural.

Following Lane's departure, the affairs of the company were placed in the hands of a committee headed by W. A. Cook, the former vice-president, and Dr. W. W. Lang, vice-president. L. W. Hamilton of Grand Rapids was appointed secretary-treasurer and director of the company. Amidst optimistic reports of the future for the manufacture of trucks in Kalamazoo, an optimism fueled in part by the war effort, Hamilton moved to Kalamazoo, taking up residence initially at the Park-American Hotel with his wife and son. At the initial press interviews Hamilton expressed his enthusiasm to the reporter from *The Kalamazoo Gazette* on March 18, 1918:

> *The future of the truck business is extremely bright, and we intend to make this concern one of the largest and most prosperous in Kalamazoo. We are able to buy springs, transmissions, universal joints, castings, and many other parts needed in the manufacture of our products. Our list of distributors is being added to regularly. Some of the best truck salesmen in America are now handling the Lane truck and find it a ready seller.*

Hamilton was complimentary about the many positive features of manufacturing in Kalamazoo, referring particularly to the other industries in the city supporting automobile manufacturing. At the same time, he revealed that the company intended to increase its capital stock to $250,000—ten times its original funding—and to improve the plant layout in order to increase production from twenty units a month to about thirty-five.

His optimism was short lived. The company was sold to H. M. Crawford, president of Lull Carriage Company, on March 9, 1919, almost a year to the day after Hamilton's arrival. Hamilton's report to the press of an estimated production of twenty trucks a month provides a calculated total production run of about 450 Lane trucks during the twenty-two months the company enjoyed active manufacturing, June 1917 through March of 1919.

Crawford proceeded to close the Lull Carriage Company in Kalamazoo, selling the plant to J. Dallas Dort for the manufacture of the Princeton and Harvard bodies for the Dort motorcar. In turn, Crawford moved his horse-drawn vehicle business closer to the primary market in the southern states. The change in markets for vehicles manufactured by Lull and the demise of the Lane Motor Truck Company gave birth to the Kalamazoo Motors Corporation under Crawford's leadership.

Fig. 21-4. The Model B 2½ ton Lane truck is shown fitted with a high-stake body. The name on the side of the truck is "Bert Lee." This image is from the Automobile Trade Journal, *November 1917. Note the light paint and fancy trim work on the wheels. (NAM)*

REFERENCES

To Make Light Truck. *Motor Age*, February 24, 1916, p. 47.

Albert Mroz. *The Illustrated Encyclopedia of American Trucks and Commercial Vehicles.* Iola, WI: Krause Publications, 1996.

Lane Truck Co. Formed. *Motor World*, March 1, 1916, p. 42.

New Lane Truck Ready. *Motor Age*, March 16, 1916, p. 46.

Lane Motor Truck Developing. *Motor Age*, March 30, 1916, p. 16.

To Build Lane Worm Driven Light Truck. *The Automobile*, March 30, 1916, p. 606.

Lane Trucks Out Soon. *The Automobile*, September 21, 1916, p. 502.

These Trucks Will Put Ginger in Your Business. *Motor Age*, June 27, 1918, p. 71.

Profits—Deliveries. *The Horseless Age*, May 1, 1918, p. 75.

Profits—Deliveries. *Automotive Trade Journal*, August, 1918, p. 252.

Will Make 300 Trucks Yearly. *The Kalamazoo Gazette*, January 25, 1917.

Lane Truck Co. Builds 12 Passenger Automobile. *The Kalamazoo Gazette*, April 8, 1917.

Lane Company Is Making New Truck. *The Kalamazoo Gazette*, June 7, 1917.

The Lane Truck Co. *The Automobile*, June 14, 1917, p. 1118.

Lane Makes New Truck. *Motor Age*, July 5, 1917, p. 53.

Lane's First Truck Built. *The Automobile and Automotive Industries*, October 4, 1917, p. 610.

Lane in One-to Five-Ton Capacities. *Automobile Trade Journal*, November 1917, pp. 246–47.

Eight Hundred Lane Trucks, Advertisement. *The Kalamazoo Gazette*, February 7, 1918.

Beverly R. Kimes, ed. *Packard, A History of the Motorcar and the Company*. Kurtztown, PA: Automobile Quarterly Publications, 1978.

Thomas M. Orrell Co. Advertisement. *The Kalamazoo Gazette*, March 17, 1918.

800 Lane Trucks Ordered. *Automotive Industries*, November 29, 1917, p. 985.

Lane Motor Trucks Meet All Demands. *Motor Age*, June 6, 1918, p. 93.

Profits—Deliveries. *Automobile Trade Journal*, May 1918, p. 423.

Three Lane Truck Models Offered. *Motor Age*, June 13, 1918, pp. 40–41.

Lane Motor Truck Co. *Automobile Trade Journal*, June 1918, p. 141.

Complete Equipment and Six Cylinder Engine Feature The Lane Line. *Automobile Trade Journal*, July 1918, pp. 241–42.

M. H. Lane Quits Truck Company. *The Kalamazoo Gazette*, March 19, 1918.

Lane Trucks for U.S. *Motor Age*, September 12, 1918, p. 19.

Three New Lane Trucks. *Motor Age*, February 6, 1919, p. 16.

2 Ton Gasoline Commercial Cars. *Automobile Trade Journal*, December 1918, p. 197.

3½ Ton Gasoline Commercial Cars. *Automobile Trade Journal*, December 1918, p. 209.

Kalamazoo to Take Lane. *Motor Age*, March 20, 1919.

$250,000 Auto Co. to Start in Kalamazoo. *The Kalamazoo Gazette*, March 9, 1919.

Fig. 22-1. An ornately painted Kalamazoo truck owned by the Upjohn Company is shown in front of the downtown plant. (UPJ)

Chapter 22

The Kalamazoo Motors Corporation

1919–1924

*Don't delay your purchase of your "Kalamazoo" too long
or you may be in the class of the "Foolish Virgin" of biblical fame.
YOU CAN'T LOSE IF YOU USE KALAMAZOOS.*
—The Four Runner

The skilled tradesmen and the industrious work force in Kalamazoo fueled the growth of a variety of manufacturing concerns in the city after the turn of the twentieth century. The transportation demands for moving raw material and manufactured goods in and out of the city were well provided by several railroads, but the local delivery of both raw material and manufactured goods still depended upon road-worthy vehicles. Prior to World War I, most cartage firms relied upon horse-drawn vehicles and light trucks. The latter were often converted from a standard automotive chassis as many independent concerns offered a kit—such as the Form-a-Truck, available through Kalamazoo Implement for $350—to convert the Ford Model T, Maxwell, Buick, and similar cars into a light-delivery vehicle. The transportation demands and government contracts of World War I, however, created a clear need for trucks designed to carry heavy bulk over primitive roads. Most commercial trucks were built after 1910, and while some trucks rated over one-ton capacity were available in those early years, the majority of the heavy-duty vehicles with a rating over 1½ tons were manufactured and marketed just before, and concurrently with, World War I.

Frank Burtt of Kalamazoo expressed his intent to build commercial vehicles as early as 1910, but it is doubtful that they were actually built. It seems that manufacturing in Kalamazoo did not enter the truck market until 1913 with the founding of the Kalamazoo Motor Vehicle Company, that was subsequently identified as the Columbia Truck and Trailer Company. The Lane Motor Truck company was founded in 1916, and Lane vehicles were manufactured in the city until 1919. Reportedly in 1917 another line of light trucks was built by the States Company in Kalamazoo,

Fig. 22-2. The Kalamazoo Truck factory near the end of the renovation in 1919. Note the piles of crates on the right. The old Michigan Buggy Company—the Roamer Motor Car Company at the time of the photograph—is just visible at the top left of the photograph. This image is from a company sales brochure. (DOL)

although production was limited. Commercial vehicle manufacture did not begin in earnest until the Kalamazoo Motors Corporation was founded in the spring of 1919.

On the first day of April 1919, the Kalamazoo Motors Corporation began building trucks ranging from 1½ to 3½ ton capacity. The corporation also held the patent rights to a semi-floating type truck axle and planned to manufacture axles and also to secure for the city an automotive radiator plant that would be located within the manufacturing enclave in the Hays Park area east of Lane and Lay Boulevards.

Truck production, with a goal set at five vehicles a day, continued while the company remodeled the former Lane truck plant at the southeast corner of Reed and Fulford Streets. The building renovations included the addition of sales and show rooms and some changes in the manufacturing areas intended to increase general productivity and efficiency. The company was originally incorporated with a stock value of $250,000 with a subsequent increase to $1 million, a sum that was substantially more than other automotive industries in the area. Such financial strength seemed to predict success.

The company board of directors was experienced in manufacturing and sales. H. A. Crawford, former president of the Lull Carriage Company, was named president; Joseph E. Brown of Bryant Paper was vice-president; W. B. Milham, also of Bryant Paper, was named treasurer; and R. M. Gregory was named secretary. The company grew out of the Lane Motor Truck Company that was incorporated in 1916 under the directorship of M. Henry Lane with a stock value of only $30,000. While president of the Michigan Buggy Company, Lane toyed with the idea of making commercial vehicles, but after the bankruptcy and sale of Michigan Buggy in 1913, Lane sought other avenues for his entrepreneurial instincts. The lingering legacy from the Grand Jury indictment, insufficient financial backing, or the disruption of parts suppliers created by the war in Europe as well as his own poor health all may have contributed to his decision to sell the Lane Motor Truck Company to Crawford and his associates in March of 1919.

The Kalamazoo Motors Corporation produced three standard size trucks, a 1½ ton selling for $2,800, a 2½ ton selling for $3,100, and a 3½ ton chassis for $4,300. The big five-ton road builder's special could be had for $4,800. The company used the four-cylinder Continental and the six-cylinder Wisconsin power plants as the two engine options, for each provided the best combination of economy, power, and durability. A choice of pneumatic or solid rubber tires was offered while standard equipment included electric lights, starter, horn, motometer, hubodometer (an odometer mounted on the wheel hub), radiator, and towing hooks.

Several extant testimonials indicate that the vehicles were well regarded for quality of construction and durability of service. "We are using a number of Kalamazoo trucks; they are giving excellent service and it is our intention to standardize on these trucks," wrote the president of Shawnee Milling Company, Shawnee, Oklahoma, in May of 1920. A demonstration of the truck's capability took place locally when a 3½ ton

Fig. 22-3. The Shawnee Milling Company vehicle reflects the rugged nature of the 3½ ton Kalamazoo. Note the big radiator with "Kalamazoo" inscribed at the top. (DOL)

Kalamazoo was credited with carrying the heaviest load ever on Kalamazoo streets. A local scrap dealer moved 16,600 pounds of scrap iron across town without mishap, a load fully 9,600 pounds above the capacity for the vehicle.

The Kalamazoo truck was sold locally in large numbers, and with great advantage to local companies, by the Thomas M. Orrell agency at West Main and Water Street. Orders were received from construction, cartage, and industrial companies in the Kalamazoo area, including Coca-Cola, Kalamazoo Hack and Bus, Kalamazoo Storage, Kalamazoo Stove, National Storage, Southside Lumber, the Upjohn Company, Wolverine Construction, and the Kalamazoo Fire Department. A ton and a half bus was sold to James F. Johnson for operation on the Long Lake and West Lake routes. The rolling chassis and engine were also sold to the Kalamazoo Railway Supply Company, with offices just a block east of the Kalamazoo Motors Company, for conversion to a gasoline-powered railway bus. Nationally, Kalamazoo truck sales extended as far west as Shawnee, Oklahoma, east to Baltimore, Maryland, and south to Fort Myers, Florida.

Shortly after its incorporation in the spring of 1919, Kalamazoo Motors sought to establish a distributorship in the eastern United States and contracted with Major Ralph Evans to found an agency in Baltimore, Maryland. Reportedly, the major had had some association with the automotive industry for twelve years, had been recently discharged from the armed services, and had supervised the army motorpool during World War I. Evans founded the Kalamazoo Truck Distributing Corporation of Baltimore, and in the spring of 1920 he took delivery of four trucks in Kalamazoo that he and a crew drove overland to Baltimore.

Fig. 22-4. Firemen pose by the new Kalamazoo truck that was delivered to the Kalamazoo Fire Department, circa 1921. While most fire engines were painted red, other options included black, green or white and the last was preferred in Kalamazoo. Some decoration was standard on trucks in this era, including red pinstriping, gold-leaf lettering and other gold ornamentation. Note the beautiful radiator that is finished in nickel rather than the heavy cast iron used on commercial Kalamazoo trucks. A similar image appears in the Kalamazoo Company sales brochure. (DOL)

Fig. 22-5. The Kalamazoo truck sits in front of Station No. 5 at 625 Douglas Avenue, where it was assigned, circa 1921. The conversion of a truck chassis for fire fighting was usually provided by an independent manufacturer, such as the Howe Company in nearby Anderson, Indiana or Seagrave in Columbus, Ohio. Both of these companies are known to have converted commercial truck chassis for fire fighting duties. The conversion company for the Kalamazoo truck is unknown; however, the annual reports for the fire department in 1921 and 1922 congratulate the city commission for purchasing Seagrave fire apparatus. In all likelihood, only the chassis was built by Kalamazoo Motor Trucks and all modifications and equipment to the rear of the cowl were furnished by Seagrave. (DOL)

Fig. 22-6. A number of Kalamazoo trucks were sold to local firms including the Home Furnishing Company (top enlargement), King Paper Company (top left), National Storage (middle left), Southside Lumber Company (middle right) and North Lumber Company (lower right). This composite image is from a company sales brochure, circa 1920. (DOL)

Major Evans' chronicle of the trip subsequently appeared in a sales booklet *Kalamazoo Motor Trucks: The Hand Made Truck*, published by the company, circa fall of 1920. The details of the trip followed his cryptic telegram of May 14, 1920, to H. G. Stiles who was the general sales manager at the Kalamazoo Motors Corporation.

> *FY-BALTIMORE MAY 14*
>
> *H G STILES*
>
> *KALAMAZOO MOTORS CORP KALAMAZOO MICH*
>
> *ARRIVED BALTIMORE EIGHT FIFTEEN PM THIS DATE TOTAL MILEAGE SIX HUN-*
> *DRED AND SEVENTY FOUR MILES ALL TRUCKS RUNNING PERFECT. LETTER AND*
> *FULL REPORT IN A FEW DAYS.*
>
> *EVANS*

Evans' report provides a wonderful history of the tribulations of travel in 1920 and the hardships of trucking during those early days. The story, as written by the major who seemed to delight in long intricate sentences, is reproduced here without correction and only minor modifications for the sake of clarity.

～

A DRIVE FROM KALAMAZOO TO BALTIMORE

Leaving Kalamazoo with two 3½-ton dump trucks, one 2½-ton chassis and one ½-ton truck on the afternoon of May 8th, at 4:45, a drive of 37½ miles was made to the town of Marshall, Michigan, which was the first overnight stop.

Leaving Marshall the next morning at 6:45, a direct easterly drive was made to Hillsdale, a distance of 34²/₁₀ miles, where we stopped for luncheon, and in the afternoon the drive eastward was continued to the town of Blissfield, Michigan where our second night was spent. The total mileage on this second day's drive being 46²/₁₀ miles, which was most discouraging when one stopped to think that our point of destination was some 650 miles distant and at that rate of travel it looked as though our trip would extend over a period of nearly fifteen days, but due to long and varied experience in overland trucking, we figured that we would arrive with the trucks in Baltimore on Friday, May 14, which meant only five days of driving and this to the rest of the crew seemed almost impossible and led them to believe that it was anticipated keeping the trucks on the road for twenty out of every twenty-four, but the final analysis showed that previous experience had taught that the cow trails of Michigan could not be compared with the roads of Ohio and the highways of the state of Maryland.

Leaving Blissfield on Monday, May 10th, at 7:30 in the morning, after spending three quarters of an hour greasing and oiling all of the trucks, our easterly drive was continued to Maumee, Ohio where we turned our noses south for Columbus and stopped for luncheon at a town called Findlay, Ohio. Having made a run during the morning of 63 miles, which gave all hands the grand and glorious spirit to have been traveling overland and pushing forward, and during that afternoon a distance of 68¹/₁₀ miles was covered, which landed us in Delaware, Ohio, where we spent our third night. Our total mileage for the day's drive being 131¹/₁₀ miles in the actual running time of ten hours and fifty minutes, although we had been at work for a total of sixteen and a quarter hours.

Leaving Delaware on Tuesday morning, May 11th, we continued southerly to Columbus and

Fig. 22-7. The Kalamazoo truck caravan led by Major Evans prepares to leave the factory. The sign at the top of the truck reads "Kalamazoo to Baltimore." (DOL)

turned our heads for the straight run east to Baltimore, stopping at Zanesville, Ohio, for luncheon and finishing the day at Cambridge, Ohio, at 7:20 in the evening, having covered a total mileage for the day of 103^{1}/$_{10}$ miles in nine hours and fifteen minutes over the best roads that we had so far encountered, although during the three-quarters of the day's run, we had been driving in a heavy downpour of rain.

Zanesville being 352^{2}/$_{10}$ miles from Kalamazoo, we decided that a general tightening up and thorough inspection of all the trucks should be made and an additional stop of two and half hours besides the luncheon period was made and each truck was thoroughly gone over and tightened up, as it is a well known fact that new vehicles should never be driven over 350 to 500 miles without being thoroughly looked over, and although a great many nuts and bolts were found to be loose, joy and satisfaction were expressed with the wonderful condition in which all the trucks were found.

Leaving Cambridge on Wednesday May 12th, we continued our drive passing through Wheeling W. Va., and stopped for luncheon at a little place called Morgan, which consisted of a railroad siding and a large hotel. This gave evidence of being a very prosperous place during the days gone by, but due to the 18th amendment to the Constitution (prohibition) is now only a place where meals can be served. But let it be said right here that should you ever pass that way around mealtime, as we did, don't hesitate to stop, for after the abundant chicken dinner which we had everyone felt as though new life had been injected and they were equal to face the driving rain for the rest of our journey. During the afternoon our drive to Uniontown, where we stopped on the fifth night of our journey, was made through what seemed to us a sheet of water and it was necessary for all hands to seek out the engineer of our hotel and bribe him to allow us to transform the boiler room into a clothes-drying establishment, as everyone had nothing but wringing wet wearing apparel. May it always be said that some of the people of Uniontown, Penna., are most hospitable and know exactly what a man needs when he is cold and chilled to the bone. Our total mileage from Cambridge, Ohio, to Uniontown, Penna., was 114⁸/₁₀ miles, which distance was covered in ten hours and twenty minutes of actual running time, although we were fourteen hours on the road, due to the terrific rain and slippery conditions in which the roads were found.

Leaving Uniontown on Thursday morning, May 13th, with our point of destination seeming near at hand, the sixth day of our journey was undertaken. Immediately upon passing the limits of the city the three and a half-mile 14% grade hill was encountered and our Kalamazoo trucks, true to their past records, climbed to the top of this mountain in third speed through fog which prevented a vision of more than 25 to 30 feet ahead of the truck. Emerging from the fog about a half mile from the top, and meeting a bitter wind which made one's nose and ears tingle as though it were the dead of winter, we stopped and put on more clothing, such as sweaters and raincoats, and stood for a few moments looking back over the fog bank which completely covered the valley lying a thousand and some feet below.

After this remarkable performance of hill climbing, all hands felt as though we could travel to the North Pole with the Kalamazoo trucks which we were driving. Continuing our drive this day, which let me call to your attention was the 13th of May, true to all days of that unlucky number, we drove over mountain after mountain meeting fog, wind and rain until we reached Cumberland, Maryland, where we once again began to realize that we were approaching some of the sunshine and warmth which we felt sure were awaiting us in our home state. Passing Cumberland we proceeded to a little town called Flintstone, where we spent the night, after having covered a total mileage on this most unlucky day of only 81¹/₁₀ miles in ten hours and ten minutes of actual running time which consumed fifteen and a half hours of the hardest driving that we had so far on the trip.

Leaving Flintstone Friday morning, May 14th, everyone was eager to make the final run of 121 miles to Baltimore that day, and let me impress upon you that our success in this last day of our journey was due to the wonderful performance of our Kalamazoo trucks and the fine highways of Maryland over which we drove them, and when we arrived in Baltimore that evening at 8:30, everyone felt as though they could continue for another hundred miles, as our driving had been so easy during that last day's run.

Computing our mileage in the six and a quarter days which we had been on the road and the actual running time which was kept in a log book, showed that we had covered 674 miles at an average running speed of 12¹/₂ miles per hour.

The gasoline consumption of the three different types of trucks which we brought, we considered remarkable after having driven them four of the six days in rain and fog. The model "G", or the 1¹/₂ ton truck made an average of 11³/₄ miles per gallon. The model "H", or 2¹/₂ ton truck, made an average speed of 8²/₁₀ miles per gallon and the Model "K", or 3¹/₂ ton dump trucks, made an average of 6 miles per gallon.

Our expenses for repairs were nothing and the consumption of oil and grease was very low, although both of these commodities were used lavishly to assure the perfect running and working of the new vehicles. The day following our arrival in Baltimore, the crank cases of all of the vehicles were drained and replenished with fresh oil; the trucks cleaned, and with the exception of a few bruises on the tires, due to the fierce condition of the roads in Michigan, one could not tell but what the vehicles had been shipped from Kalamazoo to Baltimore by rail.

For the information of those who may be driving vehicles overland in the future, I would suggest that all over-night stops be made in small towns and not the large cities, thereby avoiding all heavy charges which are made by garages for storage in large cities where vehicles can not be parked in the street. It was also found that far more satisfying meals at greatly reduced prices could be secured in the small towns.

It is also recommended to those who drive trucks overland that at least one-half hour be spent each morning in thorough greasing, oiling and examining the trucks to see that parts are not shaken loose, as

Fig. 22-8. Major Evans, on the right, surveys the situation as the truck caravan stops for gas and oil somewhere on the road to Baltimore, Maryland. (DOL)

the steady driving for ten to fourteen hours a day is bound to shake something loose.

It is also recommended that special attention be paid to the greasing of the steering apparatus, and by thoroughly greasing and oiling the steering mechanism on the first two days out, it will be found that trucks will steer very easily and obviate great strain and tire to the operator.

A few pictures taken while enroute are herewith submitted. It is, however, regretted that more satisfying views could not have been obtained, this being due to the inclement weather which seemed to haunt us.

After its incorporation in 1919, the company seemed to grow in strength and influence. The product was well-received in the industry and other purchasers sent letters of appreciation to the factory, although none as extensive as the Evans' chronicle. The company, however, survived the rigors of the industry for only four years. The precise reasons for the failure are not known, although product price fluctuations as high as 30 percent during the period of manufacture suggest that the economic pressures following World War I had a substantial impact on the firm. At the end of 1921 the company issued $250,000 worth of bonds to finance its manufacturing plans for 1922, that included an attractive passenger bus as well as the current line of trucks. Crawford looked forward to 1922 with anticipation, and his forecast of the 1922 business year that appeared in the *Kalamazoo Gazette*, December 30, 1921, was very optimistic:

Fig. 22-9. The coat and tie worn by the man on the left suggests that he is the proud owner of the Celery City Moving Company and a new Kalamazoo truck. (DOL)

> *The good times are just around the corner. We are beginning to get the breaks in our favor. We have come through the hardest period of depression, taken our losses to the fullest extent and cut everything to the bone. Better times are ahead.*

In spite of Crawford's optimism, truck sales were notoriously difficult for several years during the postwar period, as many banks were unwilling to carry the financial paper on the vehicles. A national report in 1923 claimed that financial institutions absorbed $250 million in truck paper annually as a result of deferred payments. Truck sales were still a growing part of the industry and many struggling dealers patched together poorly conceived and poorly funded vehicle sales that eventually led to the demise of their own business. The financial stability of the dealerships was weak and the salesmen relied on extended contracts from six to twenty-four months only to find the trucking firms often went bankrupt before the loan was paid. Many of the draymen purchasing the vehicles had little net worth beyond the down payment and had a reputation for poor financial responsibility. The effect was a growing number of repossessions, a weak second-hand truck market, and the refusal of many banking institutions to provide the necessary financial backing to sales agencies. A large number of well-established truck companies, and well-known automotive firms, succumbed to the business downturn and other financial pressures following World War I. The demise of a small, low-production firm in the midwest at this time is not surprising.

On May 12, 1923, John L. Carey was appointed receiver for the Kalamazoo company, and on March 31, 1924, he sold the entire assets and the goodwill of the company to the Sandow Motor Truck Company of Chicago Heights, Illinois. Sandow continued to provide service and parts for the Kalamazoo truck, but the onset of the Great Depression in 1929 brought Sandow's demise along with the demise of scores of other manufacturers.

REFERENCES

The Four Runner, Kalamazoo Motors Corporation, August 1920.

Motor Truck Revolutionizes U. S. Commerce. *The Kalamazoo Gazette*, September 9, 1923.

$250,000 Auto Company to Start in Kalamazoo. *The Kalamazoo Gazette*, March 9, 1919.

Albert Mroz. *Illustrated Encyclopedia of American Trucks and Commercial Vehicles.*
    Iola, WI: Krause Publications, 1996.

Kalamazoo to Take Lane. *Motor Age*, March 20, 1919, p. 21

Remodeling Motor Plant. *The Kalamazoo Gazette*, June 1, 1919.

To Make New Truck. *Motor Age*, May 22, 1919, p. 16.

Owners of Kalamazoo Motors Puts Capital at $1,000,000. *The Kalamazoo Gazette*,
    January 20, 1920.

Kalamazoo Truck. *Motor Age*, January 1920.

"Kalamazoo" Trucks Enjoy Unusual Service Advantages. *The Kalamazoo Gazette*,
    February 8, 1920.

Mr. Truck Buyer. *The Kalamazoo Gazette*, April 25, 1920.

Orrell Buys Harlow Garage. *The Kalamazoo Gazette*, May 28, 1920.

Three Models Comprise New Kalamazoo Line. *Automobile Trade Journal*, June 1920,
    pp. 408–10.

Auto Talk. *The Kalamazoo Gazette*, July 18, 1920.

Auto Talk. *The Kalamazoo Gazette*, August 29, 1920.

Specifications of Current Motor Truck Models. *Motor Age*, July 21, 1921, p. 45.

Sheila Buff. *Fire Engines in North America*. Secaucus, NJ: Wellfleet Press, 1991.

Hans Halberstadt. *The American Fire Engine*. Osceola, WI: Motorbooks International, 1993,
    p. 93.

Donald F. Wood and Wayne Sorensen. *Big City Fire Trucks, Volume 1, 1900-1950.*
    Iola, WI: Krause Publications, 1996.

Kalamazoo Motor Trucks: The Hand Made Truck. Company Sales Brochure, 1920.

Kalamazoo Truck Prices Down. *Motor Age*, July 28, 1921, p. 27.

Kalamazoo Lowers Prices. *Motor Age*, August 11, 1921, p. 30.

Kazoo Motors Plans for Boom. *The Kalamazoo Gazette*, December 30, 1921.

Kalamazoo Truck Increased. *Motor Age*, December 21, 1922, p. 30.

How Truck Paper Can Be Made More Attractive to Bankers. *Automotive Industries*,
    January 25, 1923, p. 171.

Kalamazoo Trucks Increase. *Motor Age*, April 5, 1923, p. 58.

American Gasoline Truck Specifications. *Automotive Industries*, February 22, 1923,
    pp. 406–407.

Receivers for Two Firms. *Motor Age*, May 17, 1923, p. 35.

Sandow Makes Purchase. *Motor Age*, April 3, 1924, p. 31.

Fig. 23-1. They came to Kalamazoo with expectations of working in the buggy factories, automobile plants, and the railway industry. This photo of the employees at the Kalamazoo Railway Supply Company, circa 1904, reveals the faces of those holding the dreams described within these pages. (DOL)

Chapter 23

Rumors, Dreams and Great Expectations

1900 – 1934

*Congratulations on your corporation just effected. Our organization and
business men would be delighted to welcome you to Kalamazoo, we know that
business conditions in our city warrant your considering us very seriously for
the permanent location of your new organization.*

—telegram to Billy Durant

As the automobile industry evolved in Kalamazoo, there were many attempts and rumors of attempts to build automobiles in the city, some by individuals and some by grand companies. Two of these concerns—Limousine Top and Reed Tractor—contributed to the local economy, while others never got beyond the dream that precipitated the rumor. These events are important, because they provide a broad background against which one might judge the struggle and the success of the major manufacturers.

THE OSWALD AUTOMOBILE: 1900

Reportedly, W. E. Oswald, a foreman at the Kalamazoo Wagon Company, built a gasoline-powered surrey in the company shop in the spring of 1900. The engine was a four-cylinder Buffalo, rated at 4½ horsepower, and the drive train was a four-wheel drive developed by Oswald. According to Kimes and Clark, the article in the April 1900 issue of *The Hub* reads, in part, as follows:

> *He believes that an automobile driven by all four wheels is better adapted to the rough roads of
> Michigan than any other.*

According to the report in *The Hub* magazine, the Oswald would have been the first gasoline-powered vehicle built in Kalamazoo. There were very few four-cylinder engines in 1900, and other sources do not verify a multi-cylinder Buffalo engine until 1908. Given the sparse amount of information on this vehicle and the lack of independent verification of the development of the car, it has not been afforded the honor of being identified as Kalamazoo's first gasoline-powered automobile.

THE BOUDEMAN-SCOTT COMPANY: 1906

The following note appeared in *Motor Age* on March 15, 1906:

> *KALAMAZOO: A new automobile company has been formed in this city to manufacture and retail automobiles. Dallas Boudeman, Jr., is president and chief stockholder in the company, while Harry Scott is secretary and treasurer. Both are young boys attending high school, but are of a mechanical turn of mind.*

Was this a hoax, a high school prank, or did the boys actually plan the construction and sale of a motorized vehicle?

At the time many blacksmiths and mechanics across the country with sufficient skill were building cars, often of crude design, to satisfy a personal interest or for a financial return. Bodies, wheels and engines were available from various manufacturers, and perhaps the boys were serious in their endeavor. Dallas was born in 1890 and was mechanically skilled, and in 1906, at the age of sixteen, he went to the Burtt Manufacturing Company and obtained the castings for the Burtt engine which he built, circa 1906. That was the same year that Dallas and Harry Scott notified the magazine that they intended to enter the automobile manufacturing business. The stationary engine that Dallas built survives, but its design is not conducive to powering an automobile and there is no evidence that an automobile was ever built. The Kalamazoo engines built by Burtt Manufacturing were guaranteed for life, and surviving members of the Boudeman family state unequivocally that they will hold to that promise.

Little is known of Dallas Boudeman, Jr.'s early career in automobile manufacturing, although he continued to show an interest in automobiles and is credited with displaying the Regal automobile at the 1910 Kalamazoo Auto Show. The Regal, built in Detroit, Michigan, from 1908 to 1918, was according to the company "the Lustiest Young Bidder on the Market." Reportedly, production was, about 3,500 cars in 1910. Dallas had his own lust for life and, on May 6, 1913, he secretly married Frieda H. Meier, a local actress. The marriage was announced on May 13, 1913. According to members of the family, she was a talented and artistic woman and was responsible for some of the advertising art work for the Kalamazoo Gasoline Engine Works that Dallas founded.

By 1915 Dallas was listed as the proprietor of the Kalamazoo Gasoline Engine Works, but was not so listed in 1914 or 1916, indicating that the company had but a one year history. That company built the Diamond gasoline pumping engine, with a two horsepower rating and a hit-and-miss governing system. The company owned by Dallas also manufactured the Diamond Marine Motor, and, according to family sources, he sold many of these engines to someone in Australia but was never paid for the merchandise, resulting in the demise of the company.

Dallas entered the service in December 1917 and served for one year with duty in England as well as Europe. He was severely injured while serving at the front when exposed to German mustard gas and returned to the States. He was discharged from the army at Camp Custer the following December and was listed simply as "an agent" following the war. His family name was associated tangentially with automobile manufacturing in Kalamazoo, and during this period he worked periodically on the Wolverine automobile with Harry Scott.

There is no evidence that Dallas continued an association with automobile manufacture in spite of his skills and his early interest in gasoline-powered vehicles. He had a reputation for mechanical ingenuity, but after the demise of the Wolverine, he apparently retired to the countryside

Fig. 23-2. The Weaver Wind Wagon was built by seventeen-year-old Clare E. Weaver and is seen here on its inaugural run in 1914. (DOL)

near Gull Lake where he busied himself with the operation of a small farm and fruit orchard.

At one time he owned a powerful Van Blerk racing boat that he called the Rainmaker. The boat was often seen on Gull Lake and he spent many enjoyable hours with Harry Parker who also had a boat at the time. His boyhood friend, Harry C. Scott, may also have been involved with boating. After their work on the Wolverine, Scott established himself as an engineer of some reputation and his story is documented within the chapter on the Wolverine.

THE SAFETY-FIRST MOTOR CAR COMPANY: 1914

The Safety-First Motor Car Company filed articles of incorporation on August 11, 1914, with a capital stock of $10,000. F. A. Young was named president, W. P. Haines, vice-president and George J. Haines, secretary-treasurer. The company planned to manufacture motorcars, and trucks based on a pattern designed by Frank Dentler of Vicksburg. The corporation had offices in room 210 of the Kalamazoo National Bank building, but also had some tie to the Reed Manufacturing Company by association with Herber Reed. George Haines, of the Kalamazoo Railway Supply Company, also had some connection to the company. News reports indicated that a prototype machine had been built, but manufacture of any substantial number of vehicles is doubted.

THE WEAVER WIND WAGON: 1914

Clare E. Weaver was a seventeen year old high school student when he designed and built a "Wind Wagon," so named because it was driven by a rear mounted airplane propeller rather than by a propeller shaft to the wheels. Clare moved to Kalamazoo from Ada, Ohio, in the spring of 1913 and lived with his parents at 275 Engleside Terrace. Apparently he had worked as a mechanic in Ada, had been given responsibility for the repair of automobiles, and had encountered and solved a number of difficult mechanical problems in that work. He arrived in Kalamazoo with strong recommendations.

Fig. 23-3. Reportedly, this photograph was taken on July 1, 1932 and the license plates are dated 1932. Employees of the Limousine Body Company, located in the old blanket factory of Michigan Buggy at 2000 Lane Blvd. are shown by their own Auburn automobiles. Limousine Body built the bodies for the Auburn seven-passenger sedan, convertible sedan, and cabriolet; and the Cord convertible sedan and cabriolet. The vehicle to the far right with the young ladies is a 1931 Auburn cabriolet from Limousine Body. (KLM)

The open car was about 12′ long and 36″ wide. It was powered by a four-horsepower motorcycle engine that drove a large propeller at about 1,000 revolutions per minute. The frame was built of wood with steel reinforcement and the vehicle was designed so that it could travel the open road in summer and then be easily adapted to winter driving on ice and snow by replacing the tires with skis. The car was first tested in February of 1914 as the temperatures hovered near the freezing point, and it reached speeds up to 37 miles an hour without difficulty.

Clare planned to enter Western Normal College (Western Michigan University) in the fall of 1914 and members of the community anticipated subsequent vehicle designs. There is no known record of other construction.

LIMOUSINE BODY: 1914–34

James D. Bobb, Jr. sold horsedrawn vehicles and was considered one of the big "cogs" in the sales machinery for Michigan Buggy Company. He was stationed for many years in Nebraska where he headed the western territory, and in 1908 he was reassigned to the sales region outside Philadelphia, Pennsylvania. When the Michigan Buggy company introduced the Michigan in 1909, Bobb's work naturally turned from buggies to cars, and in 1911 he sold four of these cars to members of the 1911 pennant-winning Philadelphia Athletics baseball team. A photograph of the baseball foursome was widely distributed and helped to increase sales of the new car. With the demise of Michigan Buggy in the summer of 1913, and the ensuing sale of the company's good will, equipment, and manufactured goods, Bobb, who had a reputation for considerable energy, turned his attention to another venture.

Charles Hays had purchased the old Michigan Buggy plant facility, and on October 3, 1914 James D. Bobb signed a lease with Hayes for use of the space that formerly served as the company's blanket mill at Lane Blvd. and Factory Street. The firm was called the Limousine Top Company and was intended to manufacture closed automobile tops that would be sold by contract to manufacturers only, as the company was not designed as a retail outlet. On April 24, 1915, articles of incorporation, with a capitalization of $25,000, were filed with the secretary of state in Michigan. James D. Bobb was named president, W. D. Milham was vice-president and L. T. Bennett was secretary-treasurer. The list of stockholders also included Frank Milham, James Dewing, and W. E. Upjohn, extending Upjohn's involvement in yet another automotive concern.

The automobile tops were designed as a demountable arrangement that could be attached to an open touring or roadster model to provide weather-tight protection in the winter months. The windows were often French crystal, giving the car an elegant appearance and in many cases creating an appearance more handsome with the top than without. The entire top was said to weigh less than 150 pounds and was easily detached, thus giving the owner an option of either an open or closed car for little more than the cost of an open car. Reportedly, the idea was so popular that many manufacturers wired in their orders when Bobb attempted to canvass them about their interest.

The company manufactured automobile tops for the local Barley Company, and the tops made by the Kalamazoo firm were a major attraction of the Roamer display at the 1917 auto shows in New York and Chicago. Similar tops also were built for Packard and Oldsmobile, and these tops can occasionally be found gracing the body of a Ford Model T or Chevrolet touring car built before 1920. In 1920, the name was changed to Limousine Body and their craftsmanship was sufficient to gain a contract to build the open car bodies for the Auburn Motor Car Company in Auburn, Indiana. Reportedly these bodies were without rattles or "canary chirps."

The success of the company attracted the attention of others, and on February 1, 1920, Charles C. Bobb, formerly associated with Michigan Buggy and not to be confused with James Bobb, announced the formation of a new Auto Top and Body company with a capital stock of $150,000. The officers of this company included Bobb as president, George Steers as vice-president, and M. R. Arnold as secretary-treasurer. The former factory of the American Carriage Company on East Willard Street was purchased and initial production was set for enclosed winter tops and the manufacture of automobile bodies.

Everett Lobban Cord was an energetic entrepreneur who revived the dying Auburn Company and in 1928 began to gather a number of companies under the newly formed Cord Corporation, including Lycoming Manufacturing Company of Williamsport, Pennsylvania; Duesenberg of Indianapolis; and Limousine Body Company of Kalamazoo. At the time, the assets of the Kalamazoo-based company were estimated at $350,000. The relationship between the two companies was cooperative, with Bobb and Bennett retaining their positions and Bobb gaining a place on the board of directors at Cord.

In July 1929, a labor dispute at Limousine Body caused a walkout. The 240 men served notice that they would return to work at the same salary scale and working agreement only if factory superintendent R. T. Nolan was dismissed. Labor grievances were exchanged with ultimatums from management, although the specific accusations against Nolan were not disclosed. Eventually Bobb capitulated and announced that in the best interests of the company, Nolan would be relieved of his duties at the plant. As promised, all 240 employees returned to work.

The "Great Crash" on Wall Street followed in the Fall and the nation's economic downturn of the early 1930s affected automobile parts suppliers as well as the manufacturers. At that time, the Cord Corporation and the Auburn Motor Car Company were chief owners of the Limousine Body making Limousine Body almost entirely dependent upon Cord and Auburn for its own success and productivity. During the first nine months of 1929, 27 percent of the Auburn cars sold were built with the cabriolet and convertible sedan bodies from Kalamazoo, but as automotive production declined at the Auburn factory, orders for Limousine Body were subsequently affected. During late 1930 and early 1931 Bobb issued a number of glowing reports about business orders. As the prices of the Auburn and Cord automobiles were reduced in an effort to stimulate sales, Bobb hinted at arrangements and contracts with other manufacturers, but layoffs in June of 1932 predicted the future. According to Henry Blommel, an E. L. Cord historian, Bobb's refusal to move the Limousine Body Company to Connersville, Indiana, at Cord's request, precipitated the company's demise. Eventually, manufacture of the Auburn open car, previously produced by Limousine Body, was moved to Central Manufacturing Company of Connersville. Central Manufacturing had been building Auburn closed bodies since 1924. Unfortunately, Limousine Body, with its dependence on the Auburn contract, suffered and the lost work could not be found elsewhere. In February 1934, the doors of the Kalamazoo plant were closed, and the company's assets were liquidated on July 27, 1935.

Undaunted, and just four days after the liquidation, the Bobb Furniture company was opened in the old Limousine Body company buildings on August 1, 1935. The new company was the first furniture manufacturer in Kalamazoo and was designed to manufacture bedroom suites for middle income buyers. The same officers, including the representatives from Cord and Auburn who held positions with the automobile supplier, assumed similar positions in the furniture company and all were said to be enthusiastic about the new venture.

TRACTION MOTOR CORPORATION: 1918

The Traction Motor Corporation filed articles of incorporation in Lansing, Michigan, in April 1918, with a capital stock of $200,000 for the purpose of building the Hans Tractor. The company was established by George I. Erwin, Edmond Hans, S. N. Biekerstaff, and C. H. Wright of Kalamazoo; and William Monroe and M. H. Pail of Muskegon. On April 17, 1918, *The Kalamazoo Gazette* reported that twenty-five machines were being built for trial in various localities around Kalamazoo. Reportedly, one of these tractors was tested in Kalamazoo and many pronounced it "one of the best tractors ever designed." The tractor was apparently well suited to heavy construction and had been used for road work in Kalamazoo county. The extent of manufacture of this tractor beyond the twenty-five machines reported in the press is unknown.

PACKARD MOTOR CAR COMPANY: 1920

Rumors of the new Packard Six created quite a stir in Kalamazoo in the winter of 1920. There was every indication that this motorcar company planned to build a new automobile series powered by a six-cylinder engine and that the car would be built in Kalamazoo. The production estimate was set at 30,000 to 50,000 units per year, and representatives from the Packard Company were looking with favor on the city as best suited for the location of a plant to manufacture their new six-cylinder cars. The company did introduce a model powered by a six-cylinder engine in

September of 1920, but the public was puzzled by its faint relationship to the traditional power and prestige of the Packard that was the basis of the company's reputation for fine motoring. Initial sales for this car lagged badly, and no new plant was destined for Kalamazoo.

DURANT MOTORS, INCORPORATED: 1921

The Durant was never manufactured in Kalamazoo, but the city was seriously considered as the site for the new company in January 1921. William Crapo Durant founded the General Motors Corporation, and it was he who designed the company structure with models that would appeal to various income levels. He lost the company not once but twice, and the second time he resigned as president following the acquisition of substantial company holdings with DuPont money. Pierre S. DuPont was subsequently elected chairman of the board.

Durant immediately sought the incorporation of his own company for the purpose of manufacturing motorcars with a market price under $1,000. That announcement was made at a meeting in New York City, while papers of incorporation with a capital stock of $5 million were filed in Albany, New York. The first announcement identified Kalamazoo as the site for a new plant, although the initial commitment was considered tentative. Competition for the company intensified during the next two days, and seven cities—including Kalamazoo—became contenders for the manufacturing plant.

The Kalamazoo Chamber of Commerce mounted an aggressive campaign to entice Durant to the city, and several prominent business leaders, some of whom apparently knew Durant personally, contacted him in New York. An invitation to visit the city was issued and representatives planned to wine and dine him while showing off the city, various plant sites, and railroad supply lines.

In addition to the private letters that were sent to Durant, the following telegram was issued by the Chamber of Commerce:

> *Kalamazoo, Jan. 15, 1921*
>
> *W.C. Durant,*
>
> *Goodrich Bldg.   New York City.*
>
> *Congratulations on your corporation just effected. Our organization and business men would be delighted to welcome you to Kalamazoo, we know that business conditions in our city warrant your considering us very seriously for the permanent location of your new organization. We would also be delighted to place the service of our Chamber of Commerce at your disposal.*
>
> *Ray C. Brundage, Secretary*

The suspense about the new plant location did not last long; apparently Durant never did visit the city. On January 18, 1921, a small article appeared on the front page of *The Kalamazoo Gazette* announcing that Durant Motors would locate in Flint, Michigan. At the same time, the company announced its intent to locate a second plant on the east coast and various trade organizations offered two hundred building sites.

The Durant corporation mimicked that of General Motors, with the Locomobile competing with Cadillac, the Flint-40 with Buick and Oldsmobile, the Durant with Pontiac, and the economical Star with Chevrolet. For a time it appeared as though Durant would work his magic once again, but the success of General Motors was not to be repeated. The Durant was the most long-lived of the lot and was produced from 1921 through 1932, but never in Kalamazoo.

Fig. 23-4. The interior of the automobile shop at Western State Normal, circa 1923. A curriculum was developed and instructors appointed to offer courses in automotive repair. The students are shown here gaining experience in repair of various automobiles. (WMU)

THE WESTERN STATE NORMAL CAR: 1923

Western State Normal School, now Western Michigan University, began to expand its manual trades program with the completion of a large modern Manual Arts Building at the base of the Oakland Hill in the fall of 1921. Courses were added in forge shop, machine shop, batteries, automobile repair, and the principles of gasoline engines. Western State Normal was a teachers college, and the intent of the curriculum was not to train mechanics, but to educate students to become teachers of automotive repair in technical programs at the high school level across the state. As the college curriculum developed, appropriately trained instructors were added to the faculty.

The program drew a large number of young men, and in the spring of 1923 a group of energetic students in that program began the construction of a race car. The engine was from a Model T Ford, modified with Dow pistons and overhead valves, and fitted with a Bosch ignition, boosting the power rating to thirty-seven horsepower. The car was mounted on wire wheels and the modified engine was capable of hurling the light racer up to speeds of eighty miles an hour. The car was painted a brilliant blue and marked with "B-4" that the college students called "mysterious yet suggestive." The meaning of the comment has been lost in translation over the years. According to

Fig. 23-5. A second view of the interior of the automotive shops at Western State Normal, circa 1923. The chassis of the Western State Normal racer is visible in the background. (WMU)

Fig. 23-6. The intrepid "water jumping" racer with the "mysterious yet suggestive B-4" on its side. (DOL)

the local press, the car was often tested on West Michigan Avenue and, because of the open exhaust, it was described as roaring like an airplane.

George Tabraham, the instructor who had been hired to guide the program, took great joy in relating the escapades with this car, particularly when he and Mack Whalen were testing it at speeds up to ninety miles an hour across the frozen surface of Gull Lake. According to George, a small crevice opened in the ice before them. Unable to brake the speeding car, they poured on the coal and hurtled the open water, although the back wheels slammed down on the edge of the ice. One wonders how the car could have become airborne, but it is a grand tale of an ingenious instructor and a crew of industrious students.

The students planned to race the car at a track in South Bend, Indiana, during the following season. The results of that venture and the eventual disposition of the car are unknown.

THE REED TRACTOR: 1917–20

The D. C. Reed and Company was founded by Dewitt Clinton Reed in 1877 for the purpose of manufacturing spring tooth harrows for agriculture. Herber C. Reed subsequently joined the firm, and within several years the name was changed to the D. C. and H. C. Reed Company. For a period of almost twenty years they manufactured harrows, rakes, and other farm implements. Clinton Reed purchased three patents for the spring harrow from David L. Garver in April of 1878, a purchase that he had to defend—which he did successfully—against legal challenges by Nehemiah Chase and Hiram Cobb in a Chicago court in December of 1888. His success in court allowed production to continue in Kalamazoo, and during the ensuing years almost every freight train that departed from the city carried spring tooth harrows bearing the Reed name of Kalamazoo for delivery throughout the agricultural world. In spite of Clinton Reed's death in 1893 and the sale of the spring harrow manufacturing business to the Standard Harrow Company of Utica, New York, in 1894, inquiries for the harrow continued to arrive at the Fulford Street foundry up until the early 1930s. The Reed Spring Tooth Harrow was a national institution before the turn of the twentieth century and its reputation continued many years thereafter.

Herber Reed resigned as president of the First National Bank in Kalamazoo in May of 1893 and succeeded Clinton Reed as president of the company after the latter's death. Herber Reed was a major figure in Kalamazoo's manufacturing community, holding the presidency of four separate companies. He purchased two-thirds of the Kalamazoo Railroad Velocipede and Car Company in January 1896, and he subsequently changed the name of the firm to the Kalamazoo Railway Supply Company on January 9, 1899. On December 13, 1900, the D. C. and H. C. Reed Company, again with Herber Reed as president, was reorganized with a capital stock of $10,000, as the Reed Manufacturing Company, for the purpose of manufacturing farm implements. On January 7, 1901, he was named director of the newly formed Superior Paper Company and then named president of the Imperial Coating Company when it was founded on February 16, 1901, with plans to build a plant west of Byrant Mill.

Herber Reed was a man of good humor as well as business accomplishment. He owned a magnificent white horse that was featured in the *Buffalo Horse Gazette* in 1903. The horse was trained to perform an array of tricks that Reed demonstrated with great enjoyment. He also loved a spirited wager, and when he lost a bet on the presidential race in 1892, he wheeled a barrel of flour

Fig. 23-7. "Power farming is the profitable way—Plowing deeper means a better seed bed and added fertility." This image of the Reed tractor showing the two-row plow is from an advertisement brochure. The difference in clarity between the image of the driver and the tractor and the noticeable line around the driver, suggests the photograph of the driver was placed on the drawing of the tractor. The same brochure included a photograph of the tractor and the driver that was much less clear. (DOL)

from the Burdick House to the Children's House in Kalamazoo. The local papers reported that he was followed by many "well wishers" in a horse-drawn hack and that his ears turned red at the halfway point on Cedar Street.

Herber Reed died on April 17, 1903, at the age of 51 in an apartment at the American House and the direction of the Reed Company was assumed by Joseph E. Brown immediately after Reed's death. The manufacture of farm implements gradually dwindled over the next several years and the name of the company, now located at 1527 Fulford Street, was changed to the Reed Foundry and Machine Company in 1910 in order to reflect the new product line of steel castings. During the next several years, improvements in equipment and technique allowed increased production of iron as well as aluminum, brass, and bronze castings.

Giant steam-powered pieces of machinery roamed the fields of America's agricultural heartland just before and after the turn of the twentieth century, both propelling themselves and moving the thresher as well as other equipment. Their purpose was to serve as mobile power sources, but it was not until late in the first decade of the century that steam power was used for plowing and other tractor work. These big, difficult machines required several men for operation, including an engineer, fireman, plow tender, water hauler, and coal hauler. Some early machines required horses to pull the front axle to the left or right to steer the tractor. Flying sparks could ignite a barn and low water levels could incite an explosion. These tractors were unparalleled for threshing, plowing straight furrows, and use with sawmills, but completely unsuited to the small "quarter section farm."

As the gasoline engine and steering mechanism were improved, the way was opened for the development of a small, versatile, yet powerful machine that was capable of traction work as well

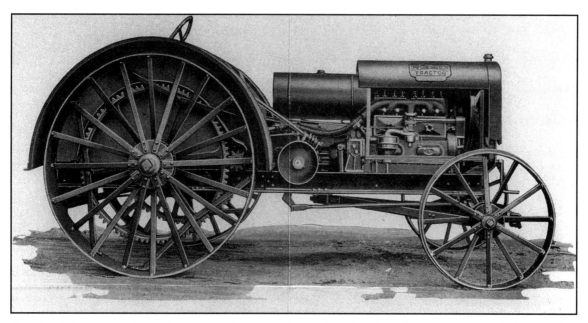

Fig. 23-8. "One man and a Reed tractor can do more work in a given time than three men and a dozen horses." This image of the Reed tractor is from an undated advertisement brochure, circa 1919. The clarity of the image suggests it was an artist drawing, rather than a photograph of the tractor. (DOL)

as belt power machine operation. The Wallis Cub, the first tractor with a unit frame, was built in 1907, Henry Ford's Fordson appeared in 1917, and John Deere's famous Waterloo Boy reached the market in 1918.

In spite of the success of the Ford Model T, Henry Ford's Fordson developed a reputation as being a bone-breaker and a killer. The hand crank would often fly back violently enough to break arms and wrists. "It kicked like a team of horses and was more stubborn than two mules," declared one farmer. Once started, the tractor had so much torque and traction that it would flip over backwards when meeting up against a rock or a resilient stump when plowing or clearing the land. A farm journal suggested that "Be Prepared to Meet Thy God" should be written in red on the side of the machine. The Fordson sold for $795, circa 1918 when Ford was granted a license by the U.S. Department of Agriculture for the manufacture of the Fordson tractor. Ford built about 38,000 of these tractors that year.

The increased availability of the tractor, the decrease in the labor force, and the increased demand for food stuffs by the government created a migration back to the farm in 1917, at least in and around the Kalamazoo area. Roy Kromdyk, owner of P. Kromdyk and Sons implement store on Portage Avenue, commented to the *Gazette* in April 1917, as follows:

> *With the back to the farm movement at its height, the farmer of earlier days [who] has been spending a few years in the city is [now] going back to the country and is taking with him some of the conveniences which he had enjoyed in the city.*

It was an auspicious hour for the development and manufacture of a farm tractor for the fertile farms raising celery, grapes, fruit, and vegetables that stretched across the Kalamazoo valley.

Sometime in late 1917 the Reed company ventured into the manufacture of farm equipment once again with the construction of a gasoline-powered tractor. The Reed tractor was available in the spring of 1918 and at least one demonstration of its prowess was held at the M. J. O'Neil farm south of Richland in March of that year. Another competition in Oshtemo with the Fordson followed in August of 1920.

There is no report on either of these competitions, but a letter from South Bend, Indiana offers some perspective on the quality of the Reed compared to other available tractors:

> *South Bend, Indiana, Sept. 26, 1919*
> *Reed Foundry & Machine Co., Kalamazoo. Mich*
> *Gentlemen:*
>
> *Today a man came into our place of business inquiring about automobiles and I might state that he was a farmer living near Mr. Rupel's farm and he was reciting to me a little instance that happened near his farm and which he was a party of. It seems that they had four tractors at this farm filling silos and before the first day's work was over, three were put out of commission.*
>
> *He went on telling me about the fourth one's performance and how it filled an 80-ton silo in a little better than four hours. After he had finished with his story I asked him what tractors were out there and I told him I was very much interested in knowing which one did all the work and went through the whole performance without trouble. He told me the name of the tractor was the REED.*
>
> *Yours very truly,*
> *SUPERIOR MOTOR SALES CO.*
> *D. A. Boswell, Mgr.*

R. C. Rupel supported Boswell's letter with one of his own that read in part as follows:

> *South Bend, Indiana*
> *Reed Foundry and Machine Co., Kalamazoo, Michigan*
> *Gentlemen;*
>
> *Some time ago I purchased one of your Reed One-Man tractors. After using the tractor on my own farm, I am very much pleased and surprised at the unusual work that it does.*
>
> *…[A]t first I ridiculed the idea of getting any kind of service out of a small machine like the Reed. Now if the Reed would only do what the Superior Motor Sales Company told me it would do, I would have been well satisfied—but the Reed positively does more than they claim for it.*
>
> *Very sincerely,*
> *R.C. RUPEL*

The tractor was equipped with high and low gears, and according to company advertisements, this arrangement allowed the operator to plow heavy ground in low gear without removing a plow, and light ground in high gear using two plows, covering the same ground as quickly as using three plows in low gear, thus saving on equipment costs, fuel, and maintenance. The automatic plow lift also allowed the operator to back into the corners of the field and thereby plow the entire field. Thus, as the company claimed, one man and a Reed tractor could do more in a given time that three men and a dozen horses.

Fig. 23-9. Advertisement brochure for the Reed "One Man" Tractor distributed by the Reed Foundry, circa 1920. (DOL)

The Reed company solved the problem of back flipping that plagued the Fordson in the following way:

> *Plows are provided with a brake-pin and automatic clutch release. When an obstruction is encountered, and the pin is broken by the impact, the motor clutch is automatically released and the tractor stops.*

After hundreds of people died or were mangled, Ford attempted to solve the same problem by making two changes. A pendulum kill switch was mounted on the magneto, stopping the engine when the front of the tractor was raised up too far. The back of the skirt on the rear fenders was also lowered so that when the front of the tractor was raised the rear fender would strike the ground and hold the tractor from flipping.

Advertisements for the Reed tractor continued at least through the spring of 1920, although little is known about the length of the production run. Published statements by the company suggest that production was limited:

> *Every Reed Tractor must be right. As a result of this policy we may not be able to supply every man who wants a REED tractor, but we will know that every REED owner has an efficient tractor, a dependable machine and a profitable investment.*

After the manufacture of the Reed tractor ceased, the Reed company continued to manufacture steel castings and by 1937 the company was producing 150 tons of such castings each month with a gross annual sales of approximately $400,000. It was a company of some standing in the community, but its flirtation with gasoline-powered tractors ended in the postwar economy. The government had ordered large numbers of tractors, particularly tracked vehicles, and with Ford producing 71,000 tractors in 1920 and 1921, the glut on the market following the end of World War I in 1919 must have been felt deeply by the Reed Company.

REFERENCES

Beverly Rae Kimes and Henry Austin Clark, Jr. *Standard Catalog of American Cars, 1805–1942* 3rd ed. Iola, WI: Krause Publications, 1996.

Ross Collier. *Ross Collier Collection*. Regional History Collections, Western Michigan University, A-1911.

Brief Business Announcements. *Motor Age*, March 15, 1906, p. 29.

R. L. Polk. *Kalamazoo Directory*, Detroit: Polk and Company, 1915.

New Truck Company Here Files Articles. *The Kalamazoo Gazette*, August 11, 1914.

Kalamazoo Boy Makes 37 Miles Per Hour. *The Kalamazoo Gazette*, February 14, 1914.

Kalamazoo Lands New Industry—To Go Into Old Blanket Factory. *The Kalamazoo Gazette*, October 3, 1914.

How a Man With Big Idea Makes Great Industry Spring Up. *Kalamazoo Telegraph-Press*, December 9, 1915.

Kalamazoo to Be Well Represented at Great National Automobile Show. *The Kalamazoo Gazette*, October 21, 1917.

Body Company One of First to Make Tops. *The Kalamazoo Gazette*, October 18, 1925.

Articles Filed by Auto Top Concern. *Kalamazoo Telegraph-Press*, April 24, 1915.

New Auto Top and Body Co. Is Organized. *The Kalamazoo Gazette*, February 1, 1920.

Tom Thinnes. "Limousine Body Company." *The Auburn-Cord-Duesenberg Experience Show Program*, Gilmore Car Museum, June 1995, pp.22–27.

Limousine Plant to Reopen Monday. *The Kalamazoo Gazette*, July 28, 1929.

240 Body Makers Return to Work. *The Kalamazoo Gazette*, August 2, 1929.

Auburn Earns $11.28 a Share in Six Months. *The Kalamazoo Gazette*, July 29, 1929.

Limousine Body's Profits Increase. *The Kalamazoo Gazette*, December 1, 1929.

Limousine Body Co. Experiencing "Production Boom." *The Accelerator*, November 1929, p. 2.

Motorcar Trade Regards 1931 as "Recovery Year." *The Kalamazoo Gazette*, December 21, 1930.

Auburn; Good News. *The Kalamazoo Gazette*, March 29, 1931.

Henry H. Blommel. *Automotive Data Collection*, Connersville, Indiana.

Furniture to Be Made Here by New Firm. *The Kalamazoo Gazette*, July 28, 1935.

First Furniture Factory Here Is Opened in 1935. *The Kalamazoo Gazette*, January 1, 1936.

$200,000 Motor Firm Organized. *The Kalamazoo Gazette*, April 17, 1918.

Packard Co. May Start Plant Here. *The Kalamazoo Gazette*, January 6, 1920.

Auto Wizard Forms $5,000,000 Concern. *The Kalamazoo Gazette*, January 14, 1921.

Eight Cities in Race for Durant Plant. *The Kalamazoo Gazette*, January 16, 1921.

Flint to Get Durant Plant. *The Kalamazoo Gazette*, June 18, 1921.

Durant Lets Contract for Motor Car Bodies. *The Kalamazoo Gazette*, August 19, 1923.

Timothy Jacobs. *A History of General Motors*, New York: Smithmark, 1992.

Brown and Gold. Yearbook of Western Michigan State Normal School, 1921.

Bulletin. Western State Normal School, 1918–21.

Bulletin. Western State Normal School, 1922–23.

Race Car Built by Students. *The Kalamazoo Gazette*, May 6, 1923.

Bulletin. Western State Normal School, 1924–26.

Bulletin. Western State Normal School, 1921–22.

Reed Company Originator of Spring Tooth Harrow. *The Kalamazoo Gazette*, January 24, 1937.

Larry Massie. Kalamazoo Helped Harness the Wind and Harrow The Earth. *Kalamazoo Gazette*, August 31, 1998.

The Harrow Cases. Opinion by Associate Justice Mathews, Circuit Court of the United States, August 14, 1885.

H. C. Reed Dead. *The Kalamazoo Gazette=News*, April 18, 1903.

Farm Tractor Now Popular. *The Kalamazoo Gazette*, April 15, 1917.

C. H. Wendel. *The Great American Farm Tractor*. Stamford, CN: Longmeadow, 1994.

Donald S. Huber and Ralph C. Hughes. *How Johnny Popper Replaced the Horse*. Moline: John Deere, 1988.

Roger Kaufman. "Breaking Ground; Henry Ford and the Fordson Tractor." *Model A News*, July-August, Vol. 46, No. 4, 1999. pp. 12-15.

Firm Here For Fifty Years Runs Foundry. *The Kalamazoo Gazette*, October 18, 1925.

Steel Castings Plant Once Makers of Farm Implements. *The Kalamazoo Gazette*, June 24, 1934.

Reed Tractor. *The Kalamazoo Gazette*, March 27, 1918.

The Reed is an Unusual Tractor. Sales Brochure, Reed Foundry and Machine Co., circa 1920.

Reed Tractors. Sales Brochure, Reed Foundry and Machine Co., circa 1919.

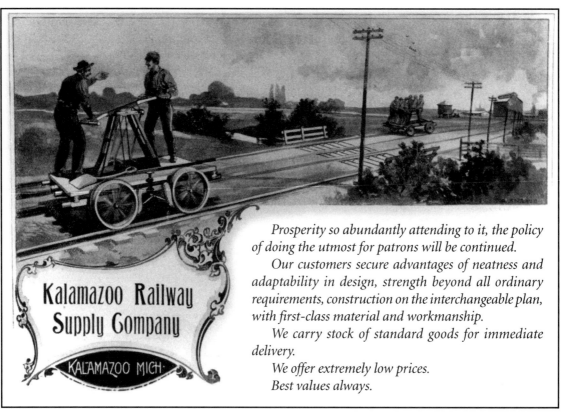

Prosperity so abundantly attending to it, the policy of doing the utmost for patrons will be continued.

Our customers secure advantages of neatness and adaptability in design, strength beyond all ordinary requirements, construction on the interchangeable plan, with first-class material and workmanship.

We carry stock of standard goods for immediate delivery.

We offer extremely low prices.

Best values always.

Fig. 24-1. When the railroads were the primary means of transportation, Kalamazoo Railway Supply was a vibrant, prosperous company. This artwork, with recreated type, from the front page of their catalog seem to reflect the strength and confidence of the company. (DOL)

Chapter 24

Kalamazoo Railway
Velocipede and Car Company

1882–1988

cable order:… steamcar, apple, banana, tomatoes
cable reply:… hyacinth, cactus, pansy
Kalamazoo means service to you.

— Cable order and reply

The Kalamazoo Railway Velocipede and Car Company was founded in 1882 by George W. Miller and Horace G. Holmes for the purpose of building the velocipede, a lightweight railway tricycle propelled by pedal power. Railroads were expanding in America; the railway supply business was very profitable; and by 1891, the company employed thirty men and enjoyed annual sales of $200,000. The product line was soon expanded to include all manner of equipment for the "maintenance-of-ways" on the railroad. Within a few years, a new plant was erected on Pitcher Street opposite the Pennsylvania Railway Station and the small factory on Kalamazoo Avenue was vacated.

George Miller sold the company in 1896 to Herber Reed, George Haines, and Elbert Ross, and in 1899, the company's name was changed to "The Kalamazoo Railway Supply Company." The company continued to grow, and in December 1902, a large parcel of land was purchased from Charles B. Hays in the South Side Land Company plat and the Pitcher Street facility was sold. The new site was just across the street from the Michigan Buggy plant, completed in October 1902, and a block east of the site that was later to become the Lane Motor Truck Company, and the Kalamazoo Motors Corporation. Frank Burtt's factory was just around the corner on Fulford Street.

Construction at the Reed Street site was begun in 1903. Unfortunately, Herber Reed died that year and failed to see the completion of the project in 1904. At the same time, the capital stock was increased to $150,000 to finance the purchase of manufacturing machinery for increased production of maintenance-of-ways equipment such as rail jacks, rail benders, rail drills, track gauges, section hand cars, conveyance vehicles, cattle guards, hand trucks, and assorted and sundry picks, shovels, and tools.

About this time D. A. Moore joined the company and brought with him a patented process for pressed steel railroad wheels. These wheels could be made with either steel or wood centers, and the patent served as the basis for much of the company's success in producing the famous velocipede, an inspection quadricycle, and utilitarian push carts that were the foundation of the business. The Kalamazoo company also produced a variety of carts and small rail cars that used these wheels and were intended to haul the material of pit mines, sugar plantations, and steel mills, as well as for transportation of work crews along the rails that were spreading like tentacles across the country just after the turn of the twentieth century.

Fig. 24-2. The Kalamazoo section hand car, built for any gauge rail, provided the early means of transportation for rail crews and inspectors across the railroads of America. The hand car was also the vehicle of choice in early film comedy taking place on the rails. (DOL)

The next major step in product development by Kalamazoo Rail was the addition of gasoline-powered rail cars. Although the exact date of the introduction of these vehicles is not known, there is some evidence that Charles B. King delivered a gasoline motor to the company in 1896.

King was the first to drive a gasoline-powered horseless carriage in the state of Michigan, an event that transpired in Detroit on the evening of March 6, 1896. The King motor was well-regarded for its simplicity and efficiency and a number of these motors were sold in west Michigan. The sales included one to Byron J. Carter of Jackson, Michigan, who built the Cartercar and another to the Kalamazoo Railway and Velocipede Company, probably making that concern the first to build a gasoline-powered railway hand car in this country.

Reportedly, King visited Kalamazoo to take part in the inaugural test run for one of Kalamazoo Rail Company's first self-powered multiple passenger rail vehicles. That test run is believed to have taken place as early as 1896. This event was marred by the explosion of the vehicle's water tank mounted below the seats which doused the occupants of the car with scalding water. There was no escape for King and his companions, since the car was perched high atop a railway trestle at the time of the accident. The explosion and the scalding water in this story make clear that the car was powered by a steam engine, rather than by the gasoline engine that King had developed and had intended on selling to the Kalamazoo Rail Company. King described this event as "an exciting

The Kalamazoo Velocipede — 1883

Fig. 24-3. The famous Kalamazoo velocipede gave rise to the company's early success and was later motorized by the Kalamazoo Rail Company as well as other companies. The Kalamazoo velocipede provided pedal-powered transportation across the rails of America for inspectors and foremen. (DOL)

Fig. 24-4. This original photograph, circa 1898, shows the Kalamazoo inspection car that is nicely trimmed for the rail inspector as well as the individual who provided the power by pumping the lever control in the middle of the car. (DOL)

Fig 24-5. This original photograph, circa 1905, is believed to capture the first gasoline-powered inspection car built by Kalamazoo Rail. Note the upholstered seating, the curtains and the decorative trim paint on the side of the vehicle. (DOL)

Fig. 24-6. This steam-powered rail vehicle built by the Kalamazoo Railway Supply Company, circa 1896, is believed to be the one that blew its tank in the King story. An artist drawing of this vehicle with the tank mounted below the seat, as was referenced in the King story, and a similar vehicle could be ordered from an early catalog. The identity of the passengers sitting so proudly in the car on rails that go nowhere is not known, but three of them are assumed to be company directors, Herber Reed, George Haines, and Elbert Ross. (DOL)

ride," and perhaps it was this "excitement" and the scalding water that convinced the Kalamazoo Rail Company to invest $400 in the gasoline-powered King motor that was used in manufacturing a small, rugged, one-man cart. Early catalogs indicate that the engine burned either gasoline or #74 stove oil, making it particularly adaptable to the use of the fuel on hand along the rails.

Many of the company's railroad products were sold through a sales catalog, but telephone service was expensive and mail delivery during the first decade of the twentieth century, particularly international orders, was slow. When possible, orders were placed by cable, and an interesting set of abbreviations was developed by the company to convey information with just a few words. The cipher code, as it was called, designated each of the company's products with a one word title and then added code for corresponding messages with vegetable and flower names. A light steam-driven rail car could be ordered by the name "steamcar," while a velocipede intended for pleasure and mail delivery was identified with the title "combination," and the basic velocipede was simply identified as "cycle." The product title followed by "apple" translated as: "Have you in stock for immediate shipment?" The word "banana" translated as: "Wire lowest price, weight and time you can ship," while "tomatoes" meant: "Our order urgent, rush shipment with least possible delay." The company might reply with "hyacinth" meaning: "We would recommend for duty stated," or "cactus" meaning: "We have in stock and can ship immediately," or finally, "pansy" meaning: "We will ship your order today and will follow with wire tracer to expedite delivery." Not all products could be ordered in this manner, of course, particularly not a railroad water tank that was offered

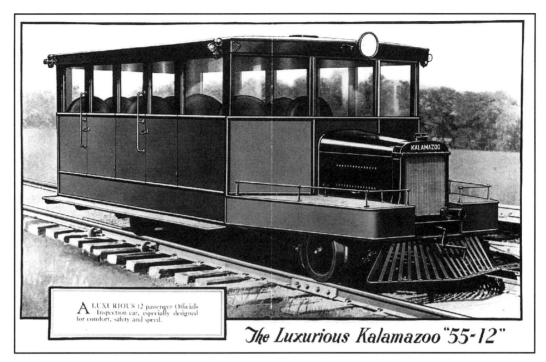

A LUXURIOUS 12 passenger Officials Inspection car, especially designed for comfort, safety and speed.

The Luxurious Kalamazoo "55-12"

Fig. 24-7. The Kalamazoo "55-12" was introduced circa 1921, and was mounted on a Kalamazoo Motors Corporation truck chassis, so that the identification across the radiator represented both company names. This car is believed to the first luxury coach of its type for which the company gained international acclaim. (DOL)

in twenty-two different sizes and three different woods. Interestingly, the cable address of "velocipede, Kalamazoo" remained in use well into the 1980s. The catalog, published circa 1910, was over one hundred pages in length with a description and picture of a separate product on each page.

The company continued to prosper in spite of the periodic changes in leadership. After Reed's death in 1904, it was headed by Frank Milham during the first decade of the century and a number of local business men served on the board of directors, including H. S. Humphrey, Frank B. Lay, Sr., Noah Bryant, and Charles B. Hayes. John McKinnon, who joined the company in 1905 as a traveling salesman, eventually rose to the presidency in 1914. He was in turn replaced by Frank E. McAllister, who was elected president of the firm in 1925. McAllister's long tenure probably strengthened the firm sufficiently to enable it to survive the 1929 Depression as well as the difficult economic times that followed during the 1930s. McAllister resigned his position in 1942, shortly after the start of World War II.

During McAllister's presidency, improvements in the gasoline engine and increased market demand for a small self-powered rail vehicle led to the construction of an enclosed gasoline-powered rail car. Production for this is believed to have started around 1921. Photographic evidence suggests that, initially, the truck chassis adapted for this use was built by the Kalamazoo Motors Corporation, located just down the street from Kalamazoo Rail. Company photographs also show that the 1928-31 Ford Model A, the 1932 Ford V-8, and the 1937 Ford V-8 truck, as well as a 1941 International truck chassis, were all used as the basis for later rail models. The interior of many of these cars was well appointed and offered either wicker chairs or wicker with a leather covering and a floor of battleship linoleum. Prices ranged from $1,100 for a six-passenger car to $6,670 for

Fig. 24-8. The company produced an array of very attractive motor rail cars. This one was built on a 1932 Ford truck chassis. (DOL)

Fig. 24-9. The sloping hood and attractive grill of the 1937 Ford truck chassis gave the Kalamazoo rail car a very distinctive and handsome appearance that year. "Kalamazoo" became a part of other languages, meaning gasoline-powered rail car, as a result of the export of this and similar rail car vehicles. (DOL)

a thirty-passenger car. It is interesting to note that the cost to railroads was about ten percent less than the cost of the same vehicle to lumber, steel, and mining companies.

The rail car was designed for supervisory personnel as well as passenger service, and about thirty percent of production was intended for export to small railroad companies. Large shipments were regularly sent to Brazil, Argentina, Peru, Cuba, India, Australia, Japan, and South Africa, and "Kalamazoo" became part of the Spanish language in Mexico to identify a motor-powered rail car. The "Kalamazoo" offered a comfortable means of rail transportation on plantations, mountain mining operations, and small railroads, as these cars were far more efficient than the large steam-driven locomotives. The initial investment was low, and they could be operated by chauffeurs rather than highly paid steam engineers. The operating cost was estimated at twenty-five cents compared to the $1 per mile for the big locomotive. In addition, the water towers, coaling stations, and roundhouse facilities required for steam locomotives were not necessary for the operation of the "Kalamazoo." Finally, these units could accelerate rapidly and could be brought to a stop from thirty-five miles an hour in two hundred feet, mak-

Fig. 24-10. The company used a 1937 Ford truck chassis to build this well finished lift truck for performing various high level work along the tracks. (DOL)

ing them suitable and economical for short-run travel.

The next development in automotive transportation for the rails was the manufacture of a rail wheel kit in 1928 that could be easily mounted on a Model A Ford so that a regular production automobile could be quickly adapted to be driven on the rails. Initially, the conversion used steel railroad wheels and the ride was naturally harsh; the next improvement came in 1933 with the use of rubber tires for rail use. Regular rubber road tires were used, with the addition of a rubberized flange attached to the rim on the inside of the wheel in order to keep the car tires on the track. The rubber-tired vehicle provided convenient transportation across the rails that was described as safe, silent, comfortable, clean, and fast. A letter dated April 13, 1933, from R. E. Keller, an engineer at

Fig. 24-11. During the 1920s and 1930s the company built both open and closed rail cars. The 65S Motor Car, with thirty-passenger capacity, had controls at each end and was powered by an 85 horsepower Ford V-8 engine. These cars were most likely used for the transport of railroad work crews. The photograph is circa 1934, the first year for the 85 horsepower Ford V-8. (DOL)

the Kalamazoo Railway Supply, to George Murray at the Grand Trunk Western in Battle Creek, Michigan, described this innovation:

> *Dear Mr. Murray,*
>
> *We have a set of Firestone Rubber Tires Wheels mounted on a Ford and are making some tests this week. Would like to have you come over to Kalamazoo on Thursday or Friday of this week to take a ride and get some first hand information on this equipment.*
>
> *The writer has had the car out today with the Rubber Tires and tests which we have made, the writer feels very enthusiastic over the Rubber Tire Equipment.*
>
> *Hoping you will be able to get over here and see this car in operation, I remain,*
>
> yours very truly,
>
> KALAMAZOO RAILWAY SUPPLY COMPANY

R. E. Keller was one of the many sales engineers who worked for the company from the late teens until well after World War II. His personal notebooks convey the image of a meticulous engineer who was knowledgeable as well as enthusiastic about his product. The letter is presented here exactly as it was written, except for the original ink pen correction in the capitalization of Ford, and it describes both the product and Keller's salesmanship. There is no evidence that he sold the product to the railroad.

After McAllister's resignation in 1942, George E. Monroe was elected president, a position he held until 1948. When World War II began, Kalamazoo Rail joined the war effort and began manu-

Fig. 24-12. Kalamazoo Rail used Ford-built chassis and engines exclusively during the 1930s, but introduced this gasoline-powered rail car on an International truck chassis in 1941. While the image is not in color, the rail car is apparently clad in a dull finish "government issue" khaki tan. This interesting photo shows that the car could be raised off the tracks with a pneumatic jack and then turned by three men to face the opposite direction on the tracks. The number of cars delivered to the Army is unknown. (DOL)

facture of passenger rail vehicles trimmed in "government issue" khaki tan that could be adapted to the various width gauge tracks throughout the world. The company also built a self-controlled gunnery target vehicle, nicknamed "Galloping Gertie," that carried a target at speed on a track that was usually laid just below the ground surface. This target was intended for ground artillery, while a second remote-controlled trackless vehicle was also built for bombing practice. Reports indicate that it was the nemesis of many a young pilot, for this trackless vehicle was never hit in target bombing. Reportedly, the army wanted to know what a direct hit would do to the target, and the elusive vehicle was stopped in the middle of a field allowing the bombardier to score a direct hit. "The bomb passed through the armor and the engine and into the ground, and that was the end of Kalamazoo's target vehicle," commented Monroe.

The company's success with these target vehicles opened new manufacturing opportunities and they entered the materials handling field in the early 1940s by producing small and versatile vehicles for unloading rail cars and for material transport inside large plants. In 1948 the change in direction was sealed with a change in the company's name to "Kalamazoo Manufacturing." Gone was any reference to the manufacture of vehicles and products for the rails.

Henry (Hank) Hawk became president in 1953 and under his direction Kalamazoo Manufacturing introduced a three-wheel gasoline-powered Speed Truck and a four-wheel Xpediter, followed by the electric runabout in 1956. In 1959, the company purchased Winkel Machine Company, founded by Herbert Winkel in Watervliet, Michigan, circa 1945. By the time of the purchase

Fig. 24-13. The Kalamazoo No. 27-42 Target Car, "Galloping Gertie," provided the perfect target for rifle, machine gun, and artillery practice during World War II. The rail car was powered by a Ford built "Jeep" four-cylinder engine. According to a company bulletin, "Cleverly devised, automatic throttle control whips up the speed or checks movement without being touched by anyone." These controls allowed for speed variation from 2 to 45 miles an hour. (DOL)

Fig. 24-14. After World War II, the company entered the materials handling field with the introduction of this small three-wheel speed truck. The company was so successful in this field that they sold the railway division in 1969 to concentrate on material handling. The Studebaker car in the background dates the photograph circa 1950. (DOL)

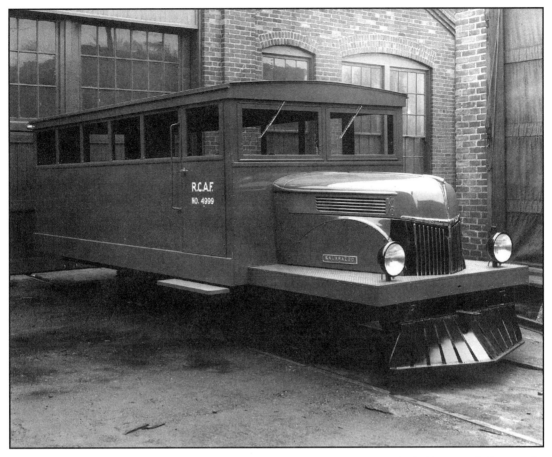

Fig. 24-15. This rail bus was built for the U. S. Army on a 1940 Ford one and a half ton truck chassis. The company continued the practice of using a truck chassis and front body work at least until 1948. After that date the rail buses used the all-steel Wayne body mounted on a Ford truck frame and powered by a Ford V-8 engine. The rough finish work on the wheelwell of the truck body suggests that the vehicle was intended for military rather than commercial use. (DOL)

Winkel had become a world leader of battery manufacturing machines. The connection between the Winkel battery equipment and the manufacturing of small electric-powered trucks was obvious and, in the early 1960s, the company again expanded its line to include a number of electric-powered vehicles. The company's postwar prosperity was based on the production of an array of three and four-wheel burden carriers in a variety of configurations, from dump carts with a sixteen-horsepower engine to a small truck powered by a four-cylinder sixty-horsepower engine. These work vehicles were well made and reliable, serving the needs of product transfer in all manner of manufacturing plants and loading docks.

In the late 1960s, commercial trucking began to dominate freight hauling, and rail transportation declined. Manufacture to support a declining industry offered little potential and the decision was made in 1969 to sell the railway division and concentrate on material handling. Competition in the material handing field, however, was severe, and as early as 1984, just six years after Blake Hawk became president and general manager, there was evidence that the company was feeling the competition. Taylor-Dunn had entered the field in 1949 and offered a wide variety of trucks for many purposes, as did Hydroelectric Lift Trucks in Ohio and Nordskog Electric Vehicles in Cali-

Fig. 24-16. The series 65 inspection car measured seventeen feet in length, with optional seating arrangements for twelve to twenty-one passengers. It was offered in October 1955, with an industrial Ford V-8 engine rated at 132 horsepower and an all-steel Wayne body. The Kalamazoo four-speed reverse-gear transmission provided equal speeds in either direction. (DOL)

fornia. The old, well-established names of E-Z-GO in Augusta, Georgia, and Cushman in Lincoln, Nebraska, also served notice of the competition. During this period, 1965 to 1979, there was great activity at the plant and a number of new developments were made in product design. Experimental vehicles built by the company included a vehicle train that might be used to escort tourists about an amusement park, a sleek passenger cart for use by the Greyhound Bus Company, and a small versatile truck. The flurry of activity and design development also makes clear that Kalamazoo Manufacturing realized that new products were needed if the firm was to survive.

After more than one hundred years, however, the company that took the name "Kalamazoo" to all parts of the world closed its doors at the Reed Street facility. Reportedly, the high maintenance and utility costs for the eighty-five year old building were excessive, but a slumping economy and the severe competition in the field may also have been the culprits. In August 1988, Kalamazoo Manufacturing was bought out by United Tractor in Chesterton, Indiana, a company that continues to offer much of the Kalamazoo product line, but without the Kalamazoo name.

Fig. 24-17. During the 1950s and 1960s Kalamazoo Manufacturing sold a number of small "in plant" fire rigs based on their speed truck chassis. This one was demonstrated May 11, 1954 and was finished by the Howe Company, a fire apparatus builder founded in 1872. The company survived until the mid 1970s using commercial trucks, such as Ford and Diamond T as a platform. This rig shows the typical fire apparatus decoration with the goldleaf trim and shaded letters on a red body. (DOL)

Fig. 24-18. (above) The company offered a complete line of small four-wheel trucks in a variety of configurations to meet the many demands in the material handling field. Many were powered by the versatile air-cooled Wisconsin engine, but the vehicle shown here was powered by a 225 cid "slant six" Chrysler engine producing 132 horsepower. (DOL)

Fig. 24-19. Kalamazoo Manufacturing also offered a very handsome "tug" that was easily adaptable to maneuver planes on the tarmac. The design, style, and purpose of the vehicle made the company's change in direction from the rails to the loading dock both clear and complete. (DOL)

Fig. 24-20. An aerial photograph of the Kalamazoo Manufacturing plant, circa 1955. The plant barely visible in the upper right was built by Michigan Buggy, later occupied by the States Motor Car Company, and then by the Barley Company that built the Roamer. The building located to the lower right, but not visible in this image, was occupied by Lane Motor Truck and then by the Kalamazoo Motors Corporation. (DOL)

Fig. 24-21. The photograph of the interior of Kalamazoo Rail is dated, March 18, 1943. This particular series of motor-driven rail cars was powered by a Buda engine and clearly identified with BUDA on the radiator. (DOL)

Fig. 24-22. In the 1970s, Kalamazoo Rail produced all manner of vehicles to remain competitive in a demanding market. This small train was intended to transport passengers through airports or amusement parks. The extent of manufacture is unknown. (DOL)

REFERENCES

Gasoline Cars for Railroads Produced Here. *The Kalamazoo Gazette*, October 18, 1924.

Ross Collier. *Ross Collier Collection*. Regional History Collections, Western Michigan University, A-1911.

Railway Supply Headed by M'Kinnon. *The Kalamazoo Gazette*, January 16, 1914.

King Motor. *The Horseless Age*, September 1896, p. 19.

King Motor, *The Horseless Age*, November 1896, p. 9.

George S. May. *A Most Unique Machine*. Grand Rapids, MI: William B. Erdmans, 1975.

Railway Inspection Car. *The Automobile*, November 5, 1904, p. 526.

Catalog No. 12. The Kalamazoo Railway Supply Company, circa 1910.

Double Railway Supply Capital. *The Kalamazoo Gazette*, November 16, 1920.

Railway Supply Firm's Equipment Spans World. *The Kalamazoo Gazette*, June 24, 1934.

Railway Supply Market Expands. *The Kalamazoo Gazette*, January 24, 1937.

The Kalamazoo. *The Kalamazoo Gazette*, October 18, 1925.

The Kalamazoo. The Kalamazoo Railway Supply Catalog, circa 1922.

Motor Trucks Taking Place of Locomotive. *The Kalamazoo Gazette*, August 19, 1923.

Firestone Pneumatic Rail Tires. Company Sales Brochure, circa 1933.

Galloping Gertie For Target Practice. Company Sales Brochure, circa 1941.

Kalamazoo Railway Motor Cars. Company Sales Brochure, circa 1946.

Kalamazoo No. 65 Inspection Car. Company Sales Brochure, circa 1946.

Kalamazoo Manufacturing Deserts Rails First Time in Long History, *The Kalamazoo Gazette*, April 18, 1948.

In Plant Fire Fighter. Company Sales Brochure, May 11, 1954.

Company Bulletins. Kalamazoo Manufacturing, circa 1955.
Company Bulletins. Kalamazoo Manufacturing, circa 1980.

Part V

WE TRY AGAIN

1915–1991

∾

Announcing the Superior States

Four cylinder type in touring car and roadster models, January 1.
Eight cylinder type in touring car and roadster models, April 1.
The car for the discriminating buyer who demands the maximum of comfort, convenience and efficiency at a moderate price.
The design and proportions are pleasing. The body is stream line; the seats deep and comfortable; wooden or wire wheels are available; the wheelbase of the "fours" will be 108 inches; of the "eights," 110 inches.
All parts are tried and true, having been subjected to the most rigid tests during the past year.
The equipment is the best. Stewart speedometer, clock, ammeter, carburetor control, ignition lock, gasoline gauge, electric lights and starter, one-man top, roll-up curtains; luxurious trimmings are listed among the many refinements and conveniences.
Interesting agency propositions are available for parties who can establish their financial and business responsibility.

STATES MOTOR CAR MFG. CO.
KALAMAZOO, MICH.

Fig. 25-1. With the decline of the light car field in 1915, the States Motor Car Company moved quickly to introduce a standard-size automobile before the close of 1915. This image of its new automobile appeared in the December 23, 1915 issue of The Automobile. (DOL)

Chapter 25

The States Motor Car

1915–1919

"Motor Car of Class, Appealing to Discriminating Buyers..."
—Company slogan

The initial development in the complex arrangements of creating the States enterprise are confusing, but at every turn William B. Smith, director of the Buckeye National Fire Insurance Company in Toledo, Ohio, was associated with the company. The initial formative step took place on July 13, 1915, when Smith purchased the Reed Street property formerly owned by the Michigan Buggy Company from Charles B. Hayes of the Kalamazoo Realty Company. The deal for the fifteen acres of land and several buildings was completed quietly by Smith and Hayes, without public announcement. On July 14, 1915, an article in *Motor World* identified the company as the States Motor Car Company, incorporated at $600,000 for the purpose of manufacturing the Greyhound light car to be sold for $600. A report in *The Automobile*, just fifteen days later on July 29, 1915, identified the company as the Crown Automobile Manufacturing Company that was incorporated for $500,000 for the purpose of building a low-priced four-cylinder car.

The Greyhound was initially introduced on November 26, 1914, in *Motor Age* as a product of the States Motor Car Company of Toledo, Ohio. The planned manufacture of these cars was set in the old Toledo tube plant. A later report indicated that a Chicago firm might produce the first lot of cars in early 1915 until the Michigan Buggy plant could be refurbished and prepared for manufacturing in the fall of 1915. The company arrived in Kalamazoo on September 30, 1915, when *The Kalamazoo Gazette* reported that the Greyhound Motor Car Company, rather than the States Motor Car Company, would soon begin manufacture of an automobile in the former Michigan Buggy plant, but little information about the car or the company was available in the local press. To add to the confusion, there was a States Cycle Car Company in Detroit, that was also building a four-cylinder States car.

The Greyhound, as its name suggests, was a small, fast vehicle of the light car design powered by a four-cylinder engine. The two engine choices—one measuring 2½" x 4" and the other 2⅞" x 4"—

Fig. 25-2. The Greyhound roadster was the first product of the States Motor Car Manufacturing Company, but was quickly dropped after the popularity of the light car waned. In the summer of 1915, the car was identified in various sources as the product of the Crown Automobile Manufacturing Company and the Greyhound Motor Car Company. Subsequently, The Greyhound was replaced by the larger and more refined States automobile. This image appeared in the November 26, 1914 issue of Motor Age. *(NAC)*

both used a two-speed gear set. The car's suspension was considered odd at the time, for the frame was only four-fifths of the length of the wheel base. Elliptical springs were cantilevered from the end of the frame at the front and the rear so that the frame was sprung between the axles instead of above them. The design was intended to lower the body, providing a comfortable ride and decreasing the amount of unsprung weight; whether these goals were met is unknown. The body was available in a tandem, side by side, coupe, or light delivery configuration, and the car's appearance was typical of the light car design: small, streamlined, and agile, with front driving lamps mounted "bug-eye" fashion above the fenders.

The Greyhound's selling price was $600 when it was introduced as the product of the Crown Manufacturing Company, July 29, 1915, although this reference is the only citation using the Crown name in association with the States Company. However, in the same publication introducing the Greyhound as a product of Kalamazoo, Henry Ford announced a $50 reduction in the price of his cars, bringing the cost of the Ford touring car down to $440 and the roadster to $390, more than $200 less than the Greyhound. Ford's price decrease was the death knell for the light car, and production of these vehicles faded quickly in 1915 as competition increased. If the States company were to survive, the board of directors needed to make changes very quickly, and sometime in the late summer of 1915, an experienced engineer was hired to design a new automobile. The new car, larger than those in the light car class, was introduced in late 1915 and early 1916. William Smith announced a new business enterprise involving two interrelated companies, one to manufacture the States and the other with exclusive rights to sell the States automobile. Smith had spent six months developing this organization and the great fanfare surrounding the introduction of the States company in Kalamazoo in the winter of 1916 provides an interesting contrast with the minimal information available in the local press concerning the Greyhound's arrival in the fall of 1915.

The States Motor Car Company was a separate entity located in Toledo, Ohio, and under Smith's supervision sold the product of The States Motor Car Manufacturing Company which manufactured all of the States pleasure cars and trucks at the former Michigan Buggy plant in Kalamazoo. The separation of the sales company from the manufacturing company was touted as the most scientific of business practices at the time; however, the idea of the connected corporation arrangement does not appear to belong to Smith, nor was the arrangement unique in the industry. The Houk Manufacturing Company and the George W. Houk Company, for example, formed a similar partnership to manufacture and sell automobile wire wheels. The two Houk concerns were incorporated in 1915; Houk wheels were respected in the industry and favored by a number of well-known automobile companies, including the States Motor Car Manufacturing Company.

The States Motor Car Manufacturing Company was organized in Kalamazoo on Thursday evening, February 10, 1916, with a capital stock of $600,000. John A. Pyl was appointed president, B. R. Barber vice-president and Samuel Hoekstra secretary-treasurer, all from Kalamazoo. James H. Johnson, president of the Johnson Pickle Company in South Haven, was appointed second vice-president. There are several references that report the company was organized much earlier in South Dakota, but that previous activity seemed to have had little impact upon the founding of the company in Kalamazoo.

The States Motor Car Company was organized in Toledo, Ohio, with capital stock of $500,000 to sell the products of the States Motor Car Manufacturing Company. The executive board was comprised of several leading capitalists, attorneys, and entrepreneurs from Michigan and Ohio, some of whom also served on the board of the States Motor Car Manufacturing Company. Members of the board were well known for their investments in real estate, fire and casualty insurance; savings and loan associations; and various manufacturing concerns, including vegetable farming, a wholesale fruit business, and a pickle cannery. None of the board members of either company had other financial interests or experience in automobile manufacturing. The description of the board gave the impression of a strong organization, but the lack of experience with automobiles was an inherent weakness of the organization's structure.

The States Motor Car Company contracted for the entire production of the States Motor Car Manufacturing Company and the former deposited $100,000 with the manufacturing company as a guarantee to fulfill the commitment with an initial delivery of five hundred cars by July 1, 1916. The lofty goals of this company were threefold: first, to divide the United States into forty selling zones with a distribution agency in each zone; second, to establish supply houses in each zone; and third, to create working capital to pay for the cars immediately on delivery. By February 11, 1916, eight of these zones had already been established in Chicago, St. Louis, and other prosperous areas of the midwest and the sales agents in these zones were stockholders and agency owners, again creating the impression of great strength in the organization.

William B. Smith was an astute businessman and a good politician. After the organization of the company in February of 1916, he immediately sought support from the Kalamazoo manufacturing community with the intent of identifying the States motorcar as "Kalamazoo's automobile" and to this end he negotiated contracts with local parts manufacturers. The universal joints were obtained from Acme Universal Joint Company, the seat springs from D'Arcy Spring Company, and the custom style tops from the Limousine Top Company. The carburetor was built by the Shakespeare Company (of fishing reel fame) and finally the axles were purchased from the Light Car Axle Company which leased 20,000 square feet of floor space in the States plant.

The Reed Avenue site provided 337,000 square feet of fire-proof construction designed for the manufacture of automobiles and was served by two railroads. The initial press release was very positive: the reports described an energetic, well-organized business enterprise. The car itself was attractive and well engineered. Plans called for the manufacture of a line of eight- and four-cylinder passenger cars with either a touring or a roadster-style body and a four-cylinder light truck with a load capacity rated at 1,000 pounds. The company expected to produce 5,000 vehicles the first year and announced a goal of 10,000 a year thereafter.

The States car was designed by Everett Cook, a graduate of the Pratt Institute of Brooklyn, New York, with fifteen years of experience at Pope-Toledo, Packard, and Warren-Detroit. He was introduced to the community in *The Kalamazoo Gazette* as a "student," presumably because of his technical and engineering education at Pratt Institute. The car that Mr. Cook designed was advertised as a "Motor Car of Class, Appealing to Discriminating Buyers," and was described as having a streamlined body, with a long tapering hood, and crown fenders. A large, slightly rounded radiator shell of heavy nickel was a dominant feature of its appearance.

The car could be fitted with either artillery style wheels or the Houk wire wheels and the tires were a 34" x 4" plain tread in front and non-skid tread in the rear. The States was finished in conventional black, with just enough gray trimming to give "snap to the color scheme." Finally, the gray trim of the body was picked up in the gray artillery style wooden wheels. The purchaser had a choice of power, either an overhead valve V-8 rated at forty-eight horsepower, or a four-cylinder engine that developed thirty horsepower. The clutch was a multiple disk and the transmission was a conventional three speed with floor-mounted control lever. The float type carburetor was guaranteed not to flood and included a primer device that sprayed fuel into the cylinder for cold starting that was controlled by a small pedal near the driver's foot. The four-cylinder powered vehicle was mounted on a 108" wheelbase and the car, powered by an eight-cylinder engine, was mounted on a 110" wheelbase. In either configuration the car weighed about 2,200 pounds. The steering wheel was mounted on the left, as was the general custom in the industry by this time. The touring model sold for $695 and the roadster for $650 with a four-cylinder engine, while the eight-cylinder car was somewhat higher.

The States car introduced at the New York show in January of 1916 had all the available amenities of the era. The steering wheel was constructed so that it would fold down out of the way for ease of entry, and it had a concealed hand warmer for winter use. The dashboard included a speedometer, clock, ammeter, oil gauge, and a dash lamp with an extension cord so it could be used as a trouble light. A tool board was hinged beneath the dash and could be opened with the release of a catch revealing a full set of tools in recessed pockets. The horn button was mounted on the door so that it could be operated by either the hand or the knee providing easy signalling and good control under demanding steering conditions. A recessed light mounted in the rear door illuminated the tonneau as well as the running board when the rear door was opened, providing a welcome entry to the car. A search light was affixed to the windshield to give additional illumination for travel on country roads.

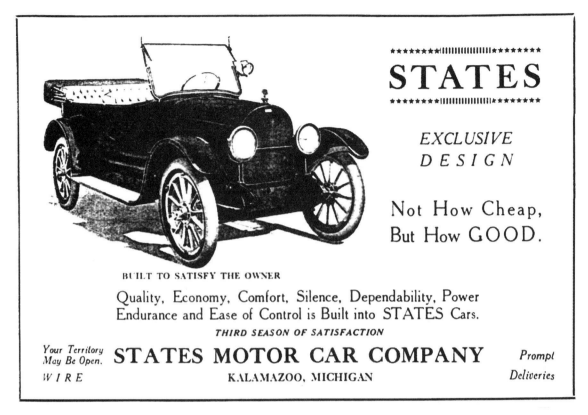

*Fig. 25-3. The armed conflict of World War I was contained in Europe, but its effect upon automobile manu-
facturing in the United States was clear in the detail of the States automobile for 1918. Most companies ceased
production during the war, suggesting that the States' production for 1918 was not substantial. Note that the
once-prominent radiator shell is painted rather than nickel plated and most of the bright work is gone. Even the
boot for the top provides only a partial cover. This image appeared in* Motor World, July 2, 1918. *(DOL)*

The display at the New York show seemed to predict great success, and on March 23, 1917, the
States Motor Car Company was refinanced in Delaware for $6 million by two New York capitalists,
Thomas B. Nevin and Son and B. F. Yoakum. Note that this sum is ten times the amount of the
original incorporation, indicating that the organization and financial stability of the company
were well regarded. The old organization of the two companies appeared to have been unwieldy,
for the new concern included both the manufacturing company and the sales company under one
title. The new company planned to manufacture a vehicle powered by a four-cylinder engine to sell
for less than $900 and another powered by a six-cylinder engine to sell for less than $1,200. The
production goal for 1917 was 6,000 vehicles. In spite of the increase in the selling price, the sales
motto of the company was changed from "The Superior States" to "Not How Cheap, But How
Good," although by 1918 the car appeared to offer less refinement than it did in 1916. The V-8
engine was no longer available; the magnificent nickel radiator had been replaced with a painted
version; the top boot did not cover the top stays; and presumably some of the other options were
dropped when the 1918 model was introduced in the fall of 1917.

An article in the January 23, 1919, issue of *Motor Age* announced that the company was "permanently out of business" and according to Kimes and Clark, President A. G. Pulfer, appointed in
1917, found another position in the city as manager of the Kalamazoo Corset Company. The sar-

casm of the remark was quite clear in its inference that the directors of the States Motor Car Manu-facturing Company were unfamiliar with the intricacies of automobile manufacturing, and found little success competing against "automobile men." An automobile was not a product in the same category as pickles, wholesale fruit, insurance, or corsets for that matter, that could be marketed in a similar manner. Those who were successful manufacturing automobiles, and many automobiles bore the name of the founder, had learned the business by developing the product themselves, building working models in a garage and testing the endurance of their labor on the track. Even many of those with considerable talent (Louis Chevrolet being a prime example) failed to main-tain a continuing position of leadership in the industry. The States company was an enterprise grown from the concepts of "economic science" and not one developed by men with grease be-neath their nails and the smell of gasoline on their clothing.

While the States company technically existed until January of 1919, the company was well on the decline when it was refinanced in March of 1917. The refinancing of the States enterprise, for an impressive $6 million, one of the highlights of the industry's year, took place almost twelve months to the day after Smith, with substantial fanfare in the press, announced the organization of the interrelated corporate enterprise. The company seemed to be posed for a major development phase, but in February of 1917, *The Kalamazoo Gazette* described competing activity in the old Michigan Buggy facility that consumed much of the space, suggesting that the concurrent manu-facture of the States motorcar in that facility in any substantial quantity was difficult. Nationally, the news was very encouraging, but locally the news from the factory was not indicative of an expanding enterprise.

On February 18, 1917, H. J. Cooper, owner of a local Dodge agency, arranged to store 1,500 Dodge cars at the States plant, a commitment that probably occupied 100,000 of the 337,000 square feet of available space. On February 24, 1917, Limousine Top leased 33,000 square feet, and on February 25, the *Gazette* announced that Barely Motor Car had a signed a contract with States Motor Car Manufacturing for 100,000 square feet of space to begin manufacture of the Roamer. The space for these three commitments, and the 20,000 square feet occupied by The Light Car Axle Company consumed over 250,000 square feet, leaving less than 100,000 square feet for manufac-turing the States, an arrangement that certainly curtailed production.

In a manner similar to the pronouncements of William B. Smith when the States Motor Car Company arrived in Kalamazoo a year before, A. C. Barley, full of optimism and energy, intro-duced the Roamer in March of 1917 and was quoted as saying, "We are going to show the people of Kalamazoo a real live going automobile concern." The former Michigan Buggy plant, touted as the most "up-to-date facility" in the area, would be active once again. The Kalamazoo Chamber of Commerce had been instrumental in enticing the Barley Company to move from Streater, Illinois, to Kalamazoo in 1917, again suggesting that the demise of the States was apparent well before the formal closure. The Commercial Club and the citizens of Kalamazoo were eagerly awaiting the availability of jobs for skilled tradesmen and the influx of salary dollars into the local economy. The demise of the States car was complete by March 1918, and local attention now turned to the Roamer, "The World's Smartest Car."

REFERENCES

States Motor Car Manufacturing Co. *Motor World*, February 23, 1916, p. 40.

New Maker for Kalamazoo. *Motor Age*, February 24, 1916, p. 12.

Crown Co. Incorporated. *The Automobile*, July 29, 1915, p. 210.

To Build Greyhound at $600. *Motor World*, July 15, 1915, p. 39.

Odd Suspension on 1915 Greyhound. *Motor Age*, November 26, 1914, p. 31.

Michigan Motor Car Plant, Now Greyhound. *Kalamazoo Telegraph-Press*,
    September 30, 1915.

States Motor Car Buys Buggy Plant. *Automobile Topics*, April 1, 1916, p. 681.

States Motor Company Soon to Appear. *Motor World*, December 16, 1914, p. 9.

Show New Trucks in Detroit, One New Passenger Car. *The Automobile*, January 21, 1915,
    p. 172.

Ford Reduces Car Prices $50. *The Automobile*, July 29, 1915, p. 210.

States Motor Car Mfg. Company is Organized. *The Kalamazoo Gazette*, February 11, 1916.

Announcing the Superior States. *The Automobile*, December 23, 1915, p. 77.

Houk Interests Merged. *Motor Age*, March 20, 1917, p. 11.

Forty Selling Agencies Handle Factory Product. *The Kalamazoo Gazette*, February 11, 1916.

States Motor Manufacturing Co. *Motor Age*, March 16, 1916, p. 47.

States Motor Car Mfg. Co. Formed—Capital $600,000. *The Automobile*, February 24, 1916,
    p. 377.

"States" Will be Motor Car of Class, Appealing to Discriminating Buyers. *The Kalamazoo
    Gazette*, February 11, 1916.

$6,000,000 Capital for States. *The Automobile*, March 22, 1917, p. 584.

Incorporates for $6,000,000. *Motor Age*, March 29, 1917, p. 11.

States Motor Co. Refinances for $6,000,000. *Motor Age*, December 27, 1917, p. 10.

States Exclusive Design. *Motor World*, July 3, 1918, p. 119.

Out of Business. *Motor Age*, January 23, 1919, p. 9.

Beverly Rae Kimes and Henry Austin Clark, Jr. *Standard Catalog of American Cars,
    1805–1942*, 3rd ed. Iola, WI: Krause Publications, 1996.

To Store 1,500 Dodge Cars Here. *The Kalamazoo Gazette*, February 18, 1917.

Limousine Top Leases 33,000 Square Feet of States Motor Car Co. *The Kalamazoo Gazette*,
    February 24, 1917.

Barley Motor Car Firm to Build Roamer Here. *The Kalamazoo Gazette*, February 25, 1917.

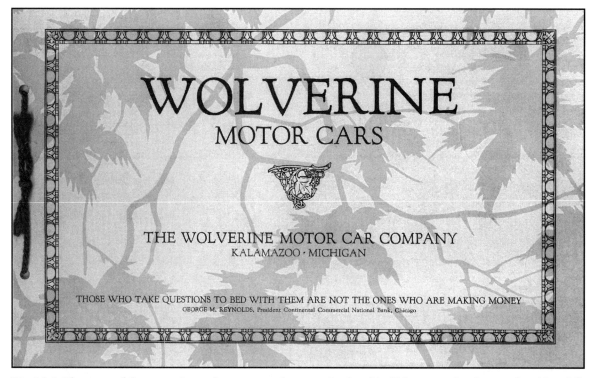

Fig. 26-1. The cover of the expensive stock prospectus that was circulated in Kalamazoo simultaneously with a full-page advertisement in The Kalamazoo Gazette *on December 2, 1917. Additional advertising followed on December 9 and 16. The prospectus contained an artist's rendition of the proposed Wolverine cars along with four letters of general financial support and several pages of text promising great profits: "There is every reason to believe that an investment in the stock of the Wolverine Motor Car Company will show an increase in value that will be most substantial."* The Kalamazoo Gazette *article reminded everyone about Billy Grove who, in 1904, invested $1,000 in the Reo Car Company and watched that investment grow to $119,050 by 1917. (DOL)*

Chapter 26

The Wolverine Motor Car Company

1917–1920

"The Car Made in Kalamazoo by Kalamazoo People"

—Company slogan

The "Wolverine" was a popular marque for motorcars manufactured in the state of Michigan during the early years of the industry, and automobiles with this title were built in Detroit (1904–1905), and in Lansing (1927–1928), as part of the Jackson product line in Jackson (1917–1918), as well as in Kalamazoo (1917–1920). The Kalamazoo-based Wolverine Motor Car Company was organized on the morning of June 29, 1917, and registry of the name "Wolverine" was established according to the legal process. Litigation against the Jackson Motor Car Company of Jackson followed, and was settled when the Jackson company published a retraction for using the Wolverine name. The notice, printed in bold, in their sales brochures read in part; "The name; 'Wolverine' applied to the Jackson car described in this catalogue is simply a model designation to distinguish this model from other Jackson eights."

The announcement of the Wolverine in the evening issue of *The Kalamazoo Gazette* in June 1917 was complete with an artist's rendering of the two-and four-seat models that constituted the dream that Albert H. Collins was selling to Kalamazoo investors. The company took as its slogan a quotation from Rudyard Kipling that appeared in their stock prospectus, revealing the eloquence and persuasive powers of Albert H. Collins:

> *They copied all they could follow,*
> *But they couldn't copy our minds,*
> *And we've left 'em waiting and toiling,*
> *A year and a half behind.*

Reportedly the Wolverine Motor Company was an outgrowth of the Wolverine-Detroit Motors Company, or at least was identified with a former employee, Albert H. Collins. He was the penultimate salesman who had been brought to the city through the efforts of several local businessmen. The award of business stipends to entice manufacturers to the city was not an uncommon

Fig. 26-2. An artist's rendition of the Wolverine "Speedway Special" as it appeared in the stock prospectus, circa October, 1917. The prospectus was not bashful in its predictions when it boasted, "Success breeds success, in which case who can doubt that the Wolverine Motor Car Company will prove to be a gigantic success and a money maker for the stock holders." (DOL)

practice at the time, although in this instance, Collins had nothing more than a set of drawings for a car and a need for investment capital.

Albert H. Collins, who was named president of the concern, was touted as having considerable experience in the industry, although his experience, with the exception of a short stint at Locomobile that survived from 1900 to 1929, was a legacy of failed enterprise. He was associated with Staver in Chicago that survived from 1907 until 1914, and he reportedly organized R. C. H. in Detroit in 1912, and was vice-president and general manager of that financially troubled firm until its demise in 1915. Collins also worked for the Wolverine-Detroit Company that produced a single cylinder express truck in 1912 and 1913. His employment with this manufacturer led the local press to cite a connection between the two companies.

Collins' prior experience was publicized locally with much fanfare in the summer of 1917 in an effort to show the heritage of the company's founder and in turn to predict the company's success, but Collins was a glib salesman and a dreamer. In 1916 he had attempted to sell his idea for an expensive speedster to investors in Indiana and then to a group of investors in Toledo, but failed on both occasions. In Kalamazoo, the legacy of the failed Michigan Buggy Company created an urgency among Kalamazoo investors to fill that void and attract automobile manufacturers. The plans and ideas expressed by Collins found a willing audience.

The company was founded with Kalamazoo capital. Harry Scott, president of the Harry A. Scott Company of Kalamazoo, was named vice-president, and Charles Bush, a director of the Home Savings Bank, was named treasurer. William H. Scott, vice-president of Western Board and Paper; Dr. J. T. Upjohn, a director of Hayes Manufacturing in Detroit; Charles Blaney, treasurer of Wheeler-Blaney Company; and James Ryder, president of the Ryder Coal Company, constituted the board of directors and provided the financial backing for the new concern. Harry C. Howard served as general counsel. The initial capitalization was reported as $125,000, and was subsequently increased to $250,000 by October of the same year.

A small, well-presented prospectus, printed on heavy paperstock decorated with maple leaf

Fig. 26-3. An artist's rendition of the "four seat touring model" as it appeared in the stock prospectus, circa October 1917. Reportedly, this car was built, although there are no known extant photographs of this model. (DOL)

outlines and tied with decorative cord, was circulated in 1917 as a part of an intense capital campaign, and coincided with full-page advertising in *The Kalamazoo Gazette*. The curious company motto—*Those who take questions to bed with them are not the ones who are making money*—was boldly printed across the cover of the prospectus. Illustrations of the Wolverine speedway special and the touring car were presented inside the prospectus that also offered the following enticement, reflecting the sales bravado of Collins:

> A full description of the car is unnecessary. It is enough to know that it is the result of years of patient and painstaking work. It is not a cheap car nor even a medium priced one; it is the 'last word' in motordom.

The Wolverine Motor Car Company was organized to manufacture two types of automobiles: a four-passenger touring model and the "Speedway Special." The latter was publicized as a "high class sport roadster," and at $3,500 it was designed to compete with hand-built automobiles in the Stutz Bearcat class. The well-known Bearcat, built in nearby Indianapolis, Indiana, could be had in 1918 for $2,550, while a Ford Model T runabout was available in classic Japanese black for only $345. Clearly, the Wolverine was expensive and was intended to appeal to a very small part of the luxury sporting car market. Production in 1918 for all models was set at six hundred vehicles, although progress toward that goal was never started, let alone realized. There was some inkling, as the United States entered World War I, that the federal government was interested in the Speedway Special for Scout Duty purposes, but those orders never materialized. The aspirations of the company were high in the fall of 1917, but demands for trucks and automotive parts and associated war material in Europe prevented the manufacture that Albert H. Collins had anticipated.

Harry Scott was the mechanical genius behind the car and the initial models of the Wolverine were to be built in his automobile garage at 432 West Main Street. Scott's interest in automobiles began early, for at the age of sixteen, he and Dallas Boudeman, a high school companion, formed a company to manufacture automobiles in Kalamazoo, although their only accomplishment in this endeavor appears to be the announcement in a national trade publication.

After high school, Harry Scott became a well known engineer and inventor in Kalamazoo, who was regarded as an authority on all types of motors, so his association with the Wolverine seemed natural to those who knew him. When the cars and drivers arrived in September 1914 for the first one hundred mile race, they met at Scott's garage and many stored their vehicles there when not at the track. When the dreams of the Wolverine finally came to an end in 1919, he continued to operate Harry S. Scott and Company on West Main Street, advertising the wonders of the Heald Cylinder grinder "to make your old car run like new again," and performing other work to maintain local vehicles when automobile parts were scarce. He built a motorized ice boat in 1924, developed a respectable reputation in dirt track racing, served as an official starter at Indianapolis, and also as a judge at many American Automobile Association events. In the latter part of the 1920s he founded the Scott Engineering Company, just off the runway at Lindbergh Field where he built the Scott airplane engine.

Harry Scott died of heart failure at the age of forty-two on September 29, 1932, in his home at 530 Horace Avenue in Kalamazoo. He had spent the previous day doing some experimental automotive work in the Edwards and Chamberlin building on East Michigan, but had returned home with complaints of an uneasiness. He was survived by his wife, Bessie; his sister, Mrs. Howard Rice; and his son, Robert W. Scott.

The 1917 year was one of great activity in Kalamazoo. During the first nine months, the States Motor Car Manufacturing Company had begun production; the Roamer was welcomed with much fanfare; and also, in June of that year, reports circulated about the birth of the Wolverine motorcar to be built in Harry Scott's garage. As late as August 6, 1917, the Wolverine Motor Car Company was still anticipating the arrival of components, but Harry Scott still managed to have a finished automobile on the road by mid-September of that year. Scott himself conducted the inaugural test run. This event was recorded by *The Kalamazoo Gazette* on Septmber 16, 1917, and provides the only evidence of the capabilities of the single model known to have been completed in Scott's garage that year. Scott's enthusiasm for the development of the car is reflected in a portion of that interview:

> *"It was some test," remarked Mr. Scott, as he paused in his work of rubbing down the car. "She ran without a hitch and rode like a Pullman. We didn't save her a bit but cut right out for the sandy, hilly roads of Barry County and did our joy riding under what would ordinarily be considered unfavorable conditions.... I might talk too much, but I will say that I am delighted with the car in every way.... The motor pulls like a truck power plant in bad places and then throttles down to the most ladylike, sweet-tempered thing on the city streets."*

Scott also reported that the car averaged twenty miles per gallon, in spite of speeds up to seventy-five miles an hour during the test. He confessed that the car was certainly capable of running faster, and many years later his son reported that the car could run up to 103 miles an hour, but speeds approaching seventy-five miles an hour were not safe on the roads in and around Kalamazoo in 1917.

The "Speedway Special" was built on a 115" wheel base and the touring model on a 125" wheel base. The car was initially fitted with a four-cylinder Wisconsin engine rated at sixty horsepower, although by 1918 this unit was replaced with one of the three Duesenberg engines delivered to Harry Scott's place of business. The 300 cid, four-cylinder Model G Duesenberg engine had a

Fig. 26-4. The distinctive lines and fender treatment are most noticeable in this three-quarter view from the rear of the car. This photograph of the Wolverine Speedway Special was used in the company's sales brochure, as well as in some of its newspaper advertising, circa 1918. (PFL)

commendable reputation in automotive racing, and most of the production for 1918 was under contract to the government. This particular engine, with a $3^{63}\!/_{64}$" bore, 6" stroke, and counterbalanced crankshaft, was rated at 80 horsepower. The Wolverine was mounted with Hartford shock absorbers with 38" springs used in front and 58" springs in the rear, supplied by Kalamazoo Spring and Axle Company. Houk wire wheels were used with 33" x 4½" racing tread Cord tires. The roadster body was fashioned from aluminum in A. L. Halperin's sheet metal shop at 215 North Rose in Kalamazoo and finished in the natural sheen of the metal. Harry's son remembers the car with black fenders and an aluminum body, but the extant photographs show the fenders in natural aluminum with only the top ridge band in black.

Standard features of the Wolverine included a thirty-gallon gas tank, a polished German silver radiator shell with motometer (to register radiator water temperatures), a 120 mph speedometer, windshield, tools, and a luggage compartment. Lights and dimming devices could be furnished if reasonable time was given, and a canopy top could also be specially ordered. Finally, the best Spanish leather seating, and the use of tungsten steel and chrome nickel steel for essential motor parts, crank shaft and bearings were specified in the company's sales brochure.

The company continued to look for production facilities in 1917 and mention was made in the press of the potential purchase of a well-known plant suitable for the production of automobiles. This was not in reference to the old Michigan Buggy plant for, as of February 25, 1917, that space served as the manufacturing site for the Roamer car. The site was not the Lull Carriage plant south of the city; this facility was subsequently sold to Dort Motor Car Company in 1920 and subsequently sold to the Checker Motors Corporation in 1923. The reference is a puzzle, but there is no evidence of a Wolverine plant outside of the Scott Company's garage.

An October 21, 1917 issue of *The Kalamazoo Gazette* reported that the Speedway Special as well as the four-passenger touring car would be on display at the national car shows during the winter

Fig. 26-5. An advertisement for the Wolverine that appeared in the February 3, 1918 issue of The Kalamazoo Gazette, *showing a photograph of the finished vehicle. (DOL)*

of 1918. Two Wolverine cars would be shown at the Astor House salon in New York, January 5–12, 1918, and at the Pompeian Room at the Congress Hotel in Chicago at the end of January. The shows were sponsored by the National Automobile Chamber of Congress, an organization of more than eighty-five member companies. Although Wolverine was not extended membership, since manufacture had not yet begun, the company was invited to display vehicles at the Importers' Show, reserved for the most exclusive models.

The New York Show issue of *Motor World* listed both two- and four-seat models for display at the Winter 1918 show, and Robert Scott confirmed that his father completed the Speedway Special, as well as a touring model and a third rolling chassis, each powered by a Duesenberg engine. The last was to have been mounted with a sedan body. Reportedly, the plant (although there was never a Wolverine plant as such) remained idle during 1918 and the firm was reported as being "out of business" in January of 1919 but then reorganized on March 24, 1919. Apparently the reorganization reported in the automotive press was a purchase by another group of investors. The investor funds came from J. W. Rider, Charles A. Blaney, and J. P. Upjohn, but legal requirements demanded that at least two of the officers from the original company must also sit on the new board. Once this legality was met, the Scott family members left the company and returned to their own concern, busying themselves with the repair and maintenance of automobiles and trucks in and around Kalamazoo.

As late as June of 1919 production news in national publications predicted the return of the sporty Wolverine, but the project was dead and the reorganized company never manufactured a single car. According to Robert Scott, President Collins absconded with company funds and made his getaway to Kentucky in the Wolverine touring car where he abandoned it. Harry Scott subsequently found the car and drove it home to Kalamazoo. When the company was reorganized, the two cars, plans, and goodwill of the company were turned over to the Upjohn group, but the rolling chassis was acquired by another party. The Duesenberg engine was gone and the chassis fitted with a Continental engine, a new radiator, and stock sedan body. Reportedly, this car was then displayed in the lobby of a local hotel as the Kalamazoo-Six Sedan for 1920. The County Sheriff arrested the two men conducting the display, charging them with "engaging in unlawful solicitation of money" and "conducting an illegal promotion," but the final destiny of the two men and the reborn Wolverine, as well as that of the original Wolverine cars, is unknown.

Meanwhile, Collins, apparently having resolved the matter of the missing Wolverine company funds, next appeared in Huntington, New York, and in 1919 persuaded William B. Brewster of the well-known New York Coach builders to join him in founding Collins Motors. The fact that Collins persuaded Brewster, who had a considerable reputation in the industry, to become a part of his enterprise is a testament to his salesmanship. Once again, Collins' intent was to build a special motorcar to compete with the finest European imports, but there is no evidence that a prototype, let alone production, was completed under this joint venture.

Undaunted, Collins moved on to Garden City, New York, with the same idea he had launched in Kalamazoo. He founded the Collinet Motor Car Company and a sporty two-seater, with a ninety-horsepower Wisconsin engine and the same high hood and open style fenders as the Wolverine, was shown at the New York Automobile Salon in November of 1920. The price tag was $5,500. This company continued until 1922, with perhaps the completion of another two prototypes, before Albert Collins disappeared from the industry.

The Wolverine was just one more failure, just one more statistic in the industry, but it was the automotive sensation of 1917 in Kalamazoo. With a racy, hand-built aluminum body, Spanish leather seating, German silver radiator, and the finest American-made Duesenberg engine, it was beautiful, fast, and agile, and even standing still "it looked like sixty miles per hour." At $3,500, it was a very expensive dream that simply could not survive the economy before and after the first global conflict. Robert Scott contends that A. C. Barley built a roadster that copied the Wolverine lines, and that may be true, but no Barley-built Roamer ever sported the distinctive ridged fenders of the Wolverine. The car's legacy remains a testament to the individual ingenuity of a Kalamazoo craftsman.

～

REFERENCES

Stock Prospectus. Wolverine Motor Cars Company, circa October 1917.

Ross Collier. *Ross Collier Collection*, Regional History Collections, Western Michigan University, A-1911.

Organize New Auto Concern. *The Kalamazoo Gazette*, June 29, 1917.

New Car Is Announced. *Motor Age*, July 1917, p. 49.

Start at Once Making New Car. *The Kalamazoo Gazette*, July 20, 1917.

Start Work on New Sport Auto. *The Kalamazoo Gazette*, August 6, 1917.

Kalamazoo's Great Money Making Opportunity. *The Kalamazoo Gazette*, December 2, 1917.

Why We Advise to Buy Wolverine Stock Now. *The Kalamazoo Gazette*, December 9, 1917.

Read These Facts About The Wolverine. *The Kalamazoo Gazette*, December 16, 1917.

Wolverine Starts Work. *The Automobile and Automotive Industries*, August 16, 1917, p. 300.

Wolverine Production Note. *Motor Age*, January 3, 1918, p. 96.

Wolverine Car Soon. *Motor Age*, August 1917.

Two Wolverine Models. *Motor Age*, August 1917, p. 43.

Harry A. Scott, Noted Motor Builder, Expires, *The Kalamazoo Gazette*, September 30, 1932.

Death Takes Heavy Toll. *The Kalamazoo Gazette*, January 2, 1933.

Wolverine Special. *Motor Age*, September 13, 1917, p. 43.

Speedway Special Is Worthy. *The Kalamazoo Gazette*, September 16, 1917.

H. Wieand Bowman and Robert J. Gottlieb. *Classic Cars and Antiques*. Los Angeles: Trend Books, 1953.

A. L. Halperin. *The Kalamazoo Gazette*, February 3, 1918.

Wolverine Custom Built Motor Cars. Company Sales brochure, February 7, 1918.

Automobile Specifications. *Automobile Trade Journal*, March 1918, p. 197.

In Their Freshman Year. *Motor*, April 1918, p. 80.

Duesenberg Stock Engine. *Automotive Industries*, December 27, 1917, pp. 1136–37.

Duesenberg 4–Cylinder engine. *Horseless Age*, February 15, 1918, p. 49.

Kalamazoo Will Be Well Represented at Great National Automobile Shows. *The Kalamazoo Gazette*, October 21, 1917.

Before The New York Show Issue. *Motor World*, December 26, 1917, pp. 24, 52.

Wolverine Cars on View. *Motor World*, October 24, 1917, p. 15.

Wolverine Now on Exhibit. *Motor Age*, October 25, 1917.

Wolverine Speedway Special on Exhibition. *Automobile*, October 25, 1917, pp. 743–44.

Recent Trade Developments. *Horseless Age*, December 1917, pp. 46–47.

Odd-Capacity Roadsters. *Automotive Industries*, January 3, 1918, p. 76.

For the Man Who Cares. *The Kalamazoo Gazette*, February 3, 1918.

Wolverine Speedster in Big Show, *The Kalamazoo Gazette*, February 3, 1918.

Heald Cylinder Grinder. *The Kalamazoo Gazette*, August 10, 1919.

Letter. Robert W. Scott to William J. Lewis. November 11, 1970.

Letters. J. W. Lewis to David Lyon. June 7, 1996 and August 10, 1996.

William J. Lewis. "The Wolverine." *Old Cars Weekly News and Market Place*, Vol. 6, #6, March 22, 1977.

Wolverine Reorganizes. *Motor Age*, March 27, 1919, p. 10.

Out of Business. *Motor Age*, January 23, 1919, p. 9.

Wolverine Reorganized, Starts Work. *Motor World*, March 26, 1919, p. 42.

Lack of Parts Slows Car Production. *Motor Age*, March 27, 1919, p. 10.

Wolverine Motor Car Company Reorganized. *Automobile Trade Journal*, May 1919, p. 180.

Revive Wolverine Car. *Motor Age*, June 19, 1919, p. 23.

Griffith Borgeson. *The Golden Age of The American Racing Car*, New York: W. W. Norton, 1966.

Beverly Rae Kimes and Henry Austin Clark, Jr. *Standard Catalog of American Cars, 1805–1942*, 3rd ed. Iola, WI: Krause Publications, 1996.

Fig. 27-1. The 1923 Dort Four Sport Touring car offered an L-head four-cylinder engine rated at 35 horsepower. Note the small lamp next to the front post, the split bumper and the disc wheels that were all characteristic of this model. Some open vehicles were built at the Dort Motor Car Company's body plant in Kalamazoo in 1920 and were similar to this model. (JCC)

Chapter 27

The Dort Motor Company Body Plant

1920–1923

"A Dort for every demand."

—Company slogan

Josiah Dallas (J. Dallas) Dort was born on February 2, 1861, in Inkster, Michigan, and was an accomplished salesman of crockery (an important item in early American households) by the age of fifteen. In partnership with William C. Durant, he purchased the Flint Road Cart Company on September 28, 1886, at the age of twenty-four following his graduation from Michigan State Normal School. They changed the name of the company to the Durant-Dort Carriage Company, and under their joint supervision it proved to be an extremely successful enterprise. The financial backing of Dort allowed Durant to purchase the Buick Motor Company in 1905 and to acquire Cadillac, Oldsmobile, and Oakland in 1910, forming the organization that eventually became the General Motors Corporation in 1917, although in the interim Durant lost control of the enterprise and spent five years retaking command of the developing corporation.

The Durant-Dort Carriage Company continued to manufacture light trucks until 1917, but in 1914, J. Dallas, then vice-president of the newly-formed Chevrolet Division, severed his relationship with Durant to build an automobile using his own surname. The first Dort was introduced at the New York Auto Show in January of 1915 and at $495, it was in direct competition with Henry Ford's Model T, which at the time commanded almost fifty percent of the market.

The Dort was initially manufactured in Flint, Michigan and by William Gray in Chatham, Ontario, Canada as Gray-Dort. The Canadian version was identical to the American model except for the name and hubcap design. The first Dort to arrive in Kalamazoo on August 10, 1915, was considered a sensation and proclaimed to be the greatest value ever offered at the price. Everyone who rode in it was quick to comment on the power and comfort of the six-cylinder sedan, and at $650, it was indeed a bargain. The car was offered by the W. O. Harlow agency, one of the first automobile agencies in the city.

Dort's reputation for quality of construction and competitive pricing continued to grow and

345

Fig. 27-2. The 1921 Dort Harvard coupe, identified by the curve at the bottom of the rear quarter window, appears in front of a government building. These closed bodies were built in Kalamazoo from 1920 to 1923, and the $1865 price for the 1921 coupe was quoted f.o.b. Kalamazoo. Note the white tires on the car, as well as the fashionable attire of the female model. (JCC)

when production peaked in 1920 with a run of 30,000 cars, Dallas Dort, anticipating continued growth, expanded the company's assembly facilities into Kalamazoo under the direction of D. M. Averill. Dort purchased the properties of the Lull Carriage Company on the corner of South Pitcher and Gibson Streets. He used one of the two brick buildings as a woodworking mill; the other was refurbished for assembling, painting, and trimming the closed bodies.

Kalamazoo was selected by Dort because of the availability of an appropriate manufacturing facility, its ability to provide a source of electricity capable of producing three hundred kilowatts of power, and its work force with a reputation for craftsmanship stemming from the production of fine horse-drawn vehicles since 1883. The Dort name was associated with the finest horse-drawn carriages, and Josiah Dallas Dort made it clear when he entered the automotive field that he would not tolerate second-class workmanship under the Dort name.

The Lull carriage facility became available on February 1, 1920, when its president, H. A. Crawford, announced his intent to move the carriage company closer to the southern market where business was flourishing. "We are too far away from our customers… and we must move further south…," he commented at the public announcement of the move. Crawford did not leave Kalamazoo for he was also president of the Kalamazoo Motors Company, founded just a year earlier.

When the Dort Motor Car Company Body Plant opened in Kalamazoo in the spring of 1920, it was a separate entity from the Dort Motor Car Company in Flint. By the fall of that year the work force of one hundred men produced twelve closed and ninety open bodies per day. By the spring of 1921, the work force grew to four hundred men and production, now limited to closed bodies, again increased substantially. The bodies were framed in wood and covered with sheet metal, a typical practice of the era,

Fig. 27-3. The second page of a two-page advertisement that appeared in the January 8, 1921 issue of the Saturday Evening Post depicts the Dort at one of the national auto shows that year. The closed bodies and some open bodies were built in Kalamazoo in 1920, but by the spring of 1921, production was limited to the closed Yale and Princeton bodies. (DOL)

and in a single day the Kalamazoo factory cut and shaped over 32,000 linear feet of lumber. Disposing of the cuttings and shavings from this operation was not a trivial problem.

There were signs that the pace at the plant was demanding, and employee performance was regulated in part by the "Non-Productive Work Ticket," a bright orange card that was given to an employee who failed to meet production goals. The card identified the employee, the department, and the account number, as well as the description of the work missed and the hours of salary to be subtracted from the individual's pay for that particular date. The card was signed by the time keeper and the foreman with approval identified as a simple "OK."

The Dort display at the 1923 Chicago Show was well received by the industry, and the "Yale" and top-of-the-line "Harvard" type closed bodies made in Kalamazoo were cited in the industry's periodicals as excellent examples of high-grade coach work. These were handsome cars offering

Fig. 27-4. An interesting advertisement from the February 13, 1920 issue of the Saturday Evening Post. The farmer chasing the turkey adds spirit and humor while the image of a family outing lends a sense of social freedom made available only by the automobile. (DOL)

such amenities as side lights, cowl ventilator, windshield visor, trunk rack, motometer, side mounted spare with cover, nickel trim, and windshield cleaner (windshield wipers). The Yale model had a rounded top, squared windows, and wood spoke wheels. The sedans offered front seating of French plaited leather and wool cloth in the rear. The Havard model had a flat roof line, with windows rounded at the bottom trailing edge and disc wheels. The interior of the Harvard model was described as "rich and tasteful," and standard amenities on this model included a dome light and heater.

Both the Yale and the Harvard offered a choice of a six-cylinder overhead valve engine rated at forty-five horsepower, on a 115" chassis, or a four-cylinder L-head engine rated at thirty-five horsepower, on a 108" chassis. The standard paint color was black, although the company also offered a "Dort Special Blue Finish."

The head of engineering at Dort was Etienne Planche, who had assisted Louis Chevrolet with the design of the first Chevrolet car. The Dort was well designed and well built. The mechanical endurance of the car, established by a touring car nicknamed "Cucumber Kate," was also well respected. "Kate" set numerous road records during a month's tour in California's summer heat, covering 4,000 miles. The Dort used a thermo-syphon cooling system that relied on the rising action of hot water rather than a mechanical pump, and "Kate" never failed on either the desert highways or the arduous mountain climbs.

On two occasions the Dort was selected to compete in the adventurous cross continent tour of Australia, carrying the Kalamazoo product around the world. This event covered 5,546 miles in sixty-seven days through desert areas, meadows of six foot high grass, flowing rivers, and incessant rain. The threat of wild animals and rumors of cannibalistic tribes in some areas of the route added both challenge to the accomplishment and color to the description of the adventure.

Fig. 27-5. The 1924 Dort Four Sport Roadster was an attractive vehicle with clean sturdy lines similar to the Kalamazoo-built body in 1920. When Dallas Dort retired from the industry in January 1925, these cars disappeared from the market place. (JCC)

In spite of the Dort's success, the Kalamazoo-based company did not last through 1923, as Dallas Dort began a progressive liquidation of the company's facilities in April of that year. In July of 1923, the company finished construction of a new $1.5 million plant in Flint, sold the old plant to the Chevrolet Division, and disposed of the Kalamazoo facility to the Checker Cab Manufacturing Company. At the same time, Checker acquired the Handley-Knight buildings.

In spite of the challenging markets and the failure of other companies, Dort was financially sound. Nevertheless, J. Dallas Dort announced his retirement in January 1925 and declared he would liquidate the entire company. He had neither sons nor trusted business partners, and some historians suggest that he simply decided that it was time to slow the pace of his life. His decision may have been too late, for he died of a massive heart attack that spring on the fairways of the Flint Country Club. More than 100,000 Dort cars had been built during the ten years of manufacture and most of the highly finished closed bodies produced during the final five years were the work of Kalamazoo craftsmen, a fact that is not well-recognized in written histories of the marque.

REFERENCES

Beverly Rae Kimes and Henry Austin Clark, Jr. *Standard Catalog of American Cars,*
  1805–1942, 3rd ed. Iola, WI: Krause Publications, 1996.

New Dort Has Reached City. *Kalamazoo Telegraph-Press,* August 10, 1915.

Beneath The Surface. Dort Company Sales Brochure, circa 1922.

Dort Doings. Dort Company Sales Brochure, 1923.

Dort Auto Co. Buys Lull Carriage Plant. *The Kalamazoo Gazette,* February 1, 1920.

Dort—Quality Goes Clear Through. Dort Company Sales Brochure, 1923.

Dort to Spend Big Sums Here. *The Kalamazoo Gazette,* February 3, 1920.

Ross Collier. *Ross Collier Collection,* Regional History Collections, Western Michigan
  University, A-1911.

City Confers With Dort Co. *The Kalamazoo Gazette,* April 11, 1920.

Dort Engineer Makes Survey. *The Kalamazoo Gazette,* April 22, 1920.

Dorts Selected as Pathmakers. *The Kalamazoo Gazette,* April 22, 1920.

Dort Plant to Be Ready Nov. 1. *The Kalamazoo Gazette,* August 1, 1920.

Connect Power to Dort Plant. *The Kalamazoo Gazette,* October 6, 1920.

Dort Plant in Kazoo Opened. *The Kalamazoo Gazette,* October 17, 1920.

Dort Plant Quadruples Labor Force. *The Kalamazoo Gazette,* April 21, 1921.

Dort Advertisement. *The Saturday Evening Post,* January 8, 1921, p. 119.

Dort Has Year of Prosperity. *The Kalamazoo Gazette,* December 10, 1922.

Local Cars in Big Display at Chicago Show. *The Kalamazoo Gazette,* February 7, 1923.

Dort Advertisement. *The Saturday Evening Post,* November 13, 1920, p. 58.

Menno Duerksen. "Dort, The Man and His Cars, Part 1." *Cars and Parts,* May 1989,
  pp. 26–30.

_____. "Dort, The Man and His Cars, Part 2." *Cars and Parts,* June, 1989, pp. 56–59.

New Dort Plant Built at Flint. *The Kalamazoo Gazette,* July 29, 1923.

A Dort for Every Demand. Company Sales Brochure, 1923.

Chapter 28

The Barley Motor Car Company

1917–1929

"Manufacturers of the Roamer, the world's smartest car...."
—Company slogan

On March 21, 1905, a patent was issued to Edwin A. Rutenber for a lightweight, high speed multi-cylinder engine, and almost immediately that patent was assigned to the Western Motor Company of Logansport, Indiana. The engines were built in both a four- and six-cylinder configuration, and the four-cylinder motor developed a reputation as the "cornerstone of the American automobile industry." Published statements claimed that many of these engines clocked more than 200,000 miles without mechanical failure, and others simply concluded that "The first mechanically good four-cylinder ever produced in this country or abroad was designed by Edwin A. Rutenber." "The Motor Makes the Car. Rutenber is the Best," read the advertisement in the March 1, 1908 issue of the *Automobile Trade Journal*.

In 1910 the Barley family obtained a financial interest in the Rutenber Motor Company, which had grown to be the largest independent manufacturer of automobile motors in the world. Alfred C. Barley was appointed secretary at a time when the company had twelve hundred employees with plants in both Marion and Logansport, Indiana. It was during this period that he began the design and development of an automobile that he would eventually manufacture. "I became familiar with the inside workings of the motor business during this period," he said, "and incidentally familiar with the automobile business."

In January of 1913 the financially troubled Streater Motor Car Company of Streater, Illinois, manufacturers of the Halladay motorcar, was sold for $56,000 to the Merchants Realization Company of Chicago. This company in turn sold the Streater Company to the Rutenber Company, placing the Halladay motorcar, powered by a Rutenber engine, under the aegis of the Barley family. The slogan for the car was a clever pun, "Everyday a Halladay," but Alfred Barley was not impressed with the automobile and commented about the Halladay enterprise that he was "amazed to find how little they understood of what the average owner really wanted and needed in his motorcar

351

Fig. 28-1. A Roamer advertisement in the December 30, 1916 issue of The Literary Digest. *The company advertisements always reflected elegance, and the use of the capital "R" at the beginning and end of Roamer was not overlooked in its similarity to the double R medallion of Rolls Royce. Note that the Barley Motor Car Company was in Streater, Illinois at the end of 1916. (DOL)*

and while I was straightening out these properties, I made use of the facilities I had in hand to build for my own use, just the kind of car I had always wanted." His own description of this period indicates that he spent time and money on all of the major aspects of the car without being hampered by "a lot of stockholders or by a bank controlled board of directors," as he later summarized the matter.

Barley was an ambitious and self-confident businessman who pursued automobile manufacturing with a vengeance. In 1914 he acquired Nyberg Automobile Works, with factories in Anderson, Indiana, and Chattanooga, Tennessee. In December of the same year, he purchased the Wahl Motor Car Company, but then sold off both Wahl and Nyberg within a year and turned his attention to the Halladay and his plans for the manufacture of a personal car that he would name the Roamer. Sometime during the same period, Barley also became vice-president of the Harwood-Barley Manufacturing Company of

Fig. 28-2. Alfred C. Barley, circa 1920, was a man of distinction who was greeted with enthusiasm when he brought the Roamer motorcar to Kalamazoo in 1917. (WMU)

Marion, Indiana, founded in 1909 by George Harwood and Charles G. Barley to manufacture the Indiana Truck. That commercial marque survived until 1939. Charles Barley later served as vice-president of the A. C. Barley Company.

Alfred C. Barley had three major complaints about the cars of that era as he began the development of a car that would appeal to his discriminating taste as well as solving the mechanical problems he found irritating. First, he complained that the frame on most cars was weak and insufficient and the resulting flexibility often resulted in squeaks, or "canary chirps," as well as rattles and loose parts. He designed a larger and more substantial frame and then tied it together with hot rivets through pre-drilled holes at all of the connecting points, a technique similar to that of the luxury hand-built Rolls Royce. Second, he claimed that the front and rear springs on most cars were usually stiff enough for a truck and gave a most uncomfortable ride. To solve this problem, he spent $100,000 and several years developing a patented double cantilever floating rear spring to provide both the comfort and the control that he sought in an automobile. Third, he charged that the bodies of most cars were neither roomy nor well appointed and certainly not comfortable. He designed the body and the interior of his car especially for his family with enough elbow space and leg room to permit driving long distances without fatigue. "The seats were fitted with the best springs, the best curled hair and the finest leather obtainable," he said, "and the car was then finished in a quiet combination of colors which expressed the family's good taste."

Soon after this personal car was finished, Cloyd Y. Kenworthy, the New York car distributor and dealer, ordered $2 million worth of these Barley-built cars. With the support of Kenworthy and Karl Martin, a coach builder in New York, the Barley Motor Car Company was founded in 1916 to produce the Roamer automobile. The name of the car was apparently suggested by Kenworthy's

Fig. 28-3. This 1916 touring car was built in Streater, Illinois, prior to A. C. Barley's move to Kalamazoo. The man at the wheel is Wilbert Robinson, manager of the Brooklyn Dodgers baseball team from 1914 to 1931 and an inductee in the Baseball Hall of Fame in 1945.(FAM)

chauffeur, who enjoyed the sporting life and was particularly found of Roamer, a famous race horse of the period. The 1916 model of the Roamer was produced in Streater, and was advertised in the October issue of *The Automobile Trade Directory* that year together with the Halladay Six. Barley built 689 Roamers and 83 Halladay automobiles in 1916. The Roamer was identified in that trade journal as "…the most beautiful light six in America," and advertised with the slogan "America's smartest car."

Kenworthy's order opened a clear avenue for success and Albert Barley quickly lost interest in the production of the Halladay, a rather undistinguished automobile that had been built in Streater, Illinois, since 1902. In 1916 he sold his interest in Halladay to a group of four investors and in so doing severed his relationship with that automobile company, then capitalized for $1 million. In March of 1917 the Halladay was moved to Mansfield, Ohio, and over the next several years, Halladay moved from one Ohio town to the another until its demise in 1922.

At the same time, in Kalamazoo, the States Motor Car Company was struggling and the Chamber of Commerce was desperately searching for another tenant to fill the Michigan Buggy plant. In early 1917 they found A. C. Barley, and with the help of a $5,000 incentive, struck a deal on February 24, 1917. The Chamber persuaded Barley to move the Roamer Company to Kalamazoo.

SETTLING IN KALAMAZOO: 1917

The city populace was ecstatic; the arrival of the A. C. Barley Company and the beautiful Roamer

Fig. 28-4. A.C. Barley began production of the Roamer in the old Michigan Buggy plant in March 1917. This photo-graph was taken circa 1920. Note the style of the roadster in the right foreground; the rumble seat opens from the flat area above the rear wheels. Note also the identification "Roamer Motor Cars" across the right front of the factory. Only the right hand portion of the original building remains today and the name has been painted over. (WMU)

in Kalamazoo in 1917 was heralded in every newspaper advertisement in the Sunday edition of *The Kalamazoo Gazette* on March 11, 1917. Each advertisement carried a picture of a Roamer with a Victoria Top, named after Queen Victoria and characterized by an open half cover over the rear seat. The message "ROAMER, WE WELCOME YOU TO KALAMAZOO," accompanied each advertisement. President Barley returned the enthusiasm with action when he fulfilled his promise. "We will show Kalamazoo a live automobile concern. We must be making cars by March 15." In fact he beat his deadline as actual manufacture had begun the week before and shipments were being readied for the end of the month. The arrival of the Roamer was applauded throughout the community and the promise and potential were summarized most succinctly by a *Gazette* writer:

> *Automobiles and prosperity go hand and hand. The wonderful progress attained in Flint, Lan-sing, Jackson, Muskegon and Pontiac was eloquent proof of that assertion. For four years Kalama-zoo has been denied those benefits. The acquisition of the Barley Motor Car Company was the last link in the golden chain of industrial awakening. The psychological effect on the community has been remarkable. Kalamazoo has talked more prosperity in the last fortnight than in the previous twelve months.*

The legacy of the Michigan Buggy failure lingered on, preying on the well-being of the commu-nity; the arrival of the Barley company was hailed as a dream that would end that nightmare. O. B. Towne, secretary of the Chamber of Commerce, pleaded for optimism among the populace. "It will mean to Kalamazoo exactly what the people of Kalamazoo want it to mean," he said. "It is a success to start with and will continue to be a success… if they will say good words about Kalama-zoo and its people, both in conversation and in correspondence and not utter or write one word which will be a discredit to the city and its future." Mayor Balch was also very enthusiastic about the Roamer's arrival. "Kalamazoo needs the Barley Motor Car Company," he said. "The concern promises to be a valuable asset for the upbuilding and the betterment of the community."

Fig. 28-5. The 1917 four-passenger touring car with the Victoria top that was featured in the advertisements and welcoming message in The Kalamazoo Gazette. *This particular image includes a "storm-top" over the driver. (FAM)*

Fuller, D'Arcy Spring and Axle, Limousine Top, Acme Universal Joint, and Lane Truck were all identified as the foundation of the community's automotive manufacturing. The list did not include the States Motor Car Manufacturing Company, although the deal for the plant was between States and the Barley Motor Car Company, and the contract called for the States company to lease 100,000 square feet of space to A. C. Barley. States was completing a well-publicized $6 million refinancing plan during the same month that the first Kalamazoo-made Roamers rolled off the line in the same plant intended for States manufacture. George B. Pulfer, chairman of the board for States, was most gracious in extending a welcome to A. C. Barley, noting that there was sufficient room in the plant for both concerns. Pulfer predicted that manufacture of the States car would begin that March, but evidence of States production was minimal at best.

A. C. Barley, other company executives, and nearly thirty employees moved with their families from Streater to Kalamazoo, and, after homes were purchased and personal lives settled, it was time to begin establishing the image of the Roamer marque within the industry.

ESTABLISHING THE MARQUE: 1917–1922

Karl Martin, coach builder from New York City and touted as a famous designer, fashioned the body style of the two models to be built in Kalamazoo during 1917. The Six-40, mounted on a 124" wheel base, was available in a touring, roadster, or closed body style and was powered by a six-cylinder Rutenber engine. The Six-90 was mounted on a 136" wheel base and was powered by a

Fig. 28-6. The 1917 formal sedan was displayed in an elegant setting at the automobile show in Chicago and drew the following comment from Motor Age: *"A new car of striking design slipped into the Chicago Show the middle of the week almost unnoticed, but due to its attractive lines, before the week was over, it was commanding large crowds and had commanded considerable comment." (FAM)*

six-cylinder Herschell-Spillman motor. This motor, built in North Tonawanda, New York, developed one hundred horsepower, and had an established reputation among airplane manufacturers. The Roamer was offered with several standard color combinations, including a medium blue body with gray upholstery or an ivory body, also with gray upholstery, but could be ordered in any combination of colors that pleased the customer. Many combinations were extravagant.

A millionaire in California ordered a bright orange exterior with white wheels and pinstripe; Dorothy Gish, film star of "Birth of a Nation," ordered a purple touring car with white leather interior, white top, and white ivory wheels. George Coates, president of a local coal company, was the first Kalamazoo resident to place an order, taking delivery of a beautiful roadster in August of 1917. Finished in bright canary yellow, trimmed in blue Spanish leather and blue wire wheels, the car was powered by a Continental engine. "Why did I buy a Roamer?" Coates commented in response to the *Gazette* reporter's inquiry. "For two reasons. First, it is a high class tailer-made *[sic]* automobile and possesses real class and distinction. Second, it is made in Kalamazoo. Every business man should buy Kalamazoo-made products whenever possible."

In the January 4, 1917, issue of *Motor Age*, a review of new models for the upcoming season claimed "the Roamer is the Halladay reincarnated." The reference to the staid Halladay could not have pleased A. C. Barley. It was an image that he sought to change immediately. The Roamer design was distinctively European, reminiscent of the Rolls Royce. Some claimed it was an un-

Fig. 28-7. The 1921 touring car is believed to be a Karl Martin design and the padded top is believed to be a product of the Limousine Top Company of Kalamazoo. Note the use of the step plates rather than a full running board. (NAM)

abashed copy of the Rolls Royce radiator, badge, hood, and styling. The similarities with the Rolls were certainly intentional, as noted in Barley's marketing strategy. He theorized that automobile sales in Europe during the disorganized postwar European economy would be slow and that directly following the conflict, European manufacturers would ship cars to the United States where they would find a ready market. That influx would in turn increase American sensitivity and appreciation of the European style. Cars that could compete with the European influx would be those with a European style, such as the Roamer, and with that reasoning, Barley anticipated good sales in the postwar market.

In spite of the scarcity of steel and automotive parts during World War I, Roamer averaged almost 1,500 cars a year from 1916 to 1922. In 1918 alone the company built 1,483 cars, including a Duesenberg-powered, seven-passenger touring car that sold for $3,250. There is no evidence of a plant shut down, or the alteration of Roamer production to meet government contracts, a circumstance that probably helped the company survive. In contrast to the Barley Company, the Interstate Motor Car Company, of Muncie, Indiana, converted its production facilities to meet government war contracts for heavy duty vehicles with Caterpillar-type treads, identified at the time as "tractors." When the war ended just six months later, however, the manufacturing facility could not be converted quickly enough for profitable production of the Interstate motorcar. After nine years of production, the Interstate name was added to the list of manufacturers that had closed and the plant was sold to the General Motors Corporation.

By 1919 the Barley company had begun to develop an international reputation for elegance of style and quality of manufacture and the Roamer had sold so well that an embargo was placed on the car by Denmark, Sweden, and Norway. In June of that year, the company's reports for the previous sixty days indicated shipments of seventy-five cars to eleven different countries including Russia, Denmark, Cuba, China, Japan, India, Brazil, and others on the European continent. Greek and Italian dealers, in particular, found that the Roamer

Fig. 28-8. (above) The cabriolet for 1919 was built at the Kalamazoo factory, while many of the other closed cars were finished by Rubay. The design is light and agile in appearance, with a European flair. Note the Rolls Royce style grill. (FAM)

was a very competitive sales option to the Rolls Royce and a large number of cars were ordered from Kalamazoo.

The company settled on two large chassis, one with a wheel base of 128" and the other 134" in length. The Rutenber and Herschell-Spillman engines were dropped at this time and customers were offered either the six-cylinder Continental Red Seal motor or the famous and more expensive Rochester-Duesenberg. The latter was available as a four-cylinder for a $1,000 premium. Duesenberg had been purchased by Rochester Manufacturing by this time, and Roamer noted rather subtly that the bore and therefore the displacement of the Rochester-Duesenberg engine had been increased to meet the size requirements of the Rochester machining tools.

A number of interesting designs were also introduced in this period, including a roadster with a unique windshield with two ovals of glass giving the impression of a large set of eyeglasses. The roadster also offered a rumble seat that was completely upholstered and had arm rests that emerged when the cover was pulled up from the rear deck. Both amenities were novel at the time. A rakish sport body was also added with cupped fenders and boat tail style that wrapped around

Fig. 28-9. (below) After he shed himself of the staid image of the Halladay motorcar, A. C. Barley sought to create a new image for the Roamer. The "eyeglasses" windshield was one of his designs, circa 1917, to gain attention for "America's Smartest Car." (NAM)

Fig. 28-10. This car was shown at the New York and Chicago shows in 1921 and has a number of interesting features. These features include an oval beveled glass rear window, strips of bright work on the body to protect the finish from abrasion by luggage mounted on the rack, and small flaps of leather on the doors to protect the bare elbows of the driver and passengers from the sting of the metal body heated by the sun. Note also the stylish side-mounted spare tire, the spot light, and the white side wall, both inside and outside, on the non-skid rear tires. (FAM)

the seats, enclosing the passengers. Between 1917 and 1922, the Roamer designs showed two distinct styles, the light open-bodied European style believed to be the work of Karl H. Martin and formal closed car designs believed to be the influence of Leon Rubay.

Reportedly, Martin had first worked in the oil fields near Lima, Ohio before moving to New York around 1918 or 1919 to design automobile coachwork for some European chassis and American manufacturers. During this period, his work included the Roamer, Kenworthy, and the Deering Magnetic before he settled in Vermont to build the Wasp from 1919 to 1924, the only car ever produced with a St. Christopher's medal built into the dash as standard equipment. All of his designs had a similar style and often attracted the monied gentry and the famous. According to legend, Douglas Fairbanks just happened to see a Wasp in the lobby of New York's Commodore Hotel and bought it on the spot as a gift for Mary Pickford. After the demise of the Wasp, Martin's career drifted into the manufacture of intricate inlaid furniture. During an interview before his death in 1954, he expressed pride in his work and his contribution to the industry. "I don't believe we really failed… we were impractical… but we did build cars and we did sell them." After Martin's departure in 1919, the Roamer roadster shed its Houk wire wheels and light body and was recast with disc wheels and heavier features, creating one of the most handsome roadsters of the period.

The Kalamazoo plant built the cabriolet and suburban bodies designed by Karl H. Martin, but the elegant closed bodies—Sedan, Limousine, Landaulet, and Town Car—were luxuriously fin-

Fig. 28-11. (top) An article in the February 1921 Roamer News *noted that the two-passenger speedster was always surrounded by admiring crowds at the New York and Chicago shows that year and described this handsome car in the following terms: "The Maroon Speedster with Duesenberg motor has steel disc wheels and is equipped for carrying three spares. Step lights, cowl lights, cowl ventilator and smooth ungrained leather upholstery in natural tan add to the distinction of this job." A special feature of the speedster was the movable rear deck that allowed the top to be completely concealed within the body retaining the trim, clean cut lines of the speedster. The design is believed to be the work of Karl K. Martin. The speedster sold for $3,985. (FAM)*

Fig. 28-12. (below) The 1921 seven-passenger sedan was a large and most impressive automobile built by the Leon Ruby company. The rear seats converted easily to a bed measuring 5'8" in length. Note the front quarter window and the wicker-style belt molding. The flip-out front glass above the windshield could be adjusted to keep rain off much of the windshield. (NAM)

Fig. 28-13. The five-passenger sport sedan was introduced in the winter of 1921 at the automobile shows in New York, Chicago and Los Angeles. The sport sedan featured entry steps and step lights, side mounted spare tires, trunk rack, luggage guards, cowl lights and cowl ventilators. This particular car was finished in Coach Painters' Green, black upper panels, white wire wheels and is painted white underneath the fenders. The interior was trimmed in Chinese gold silk tapestry. The light agile appearance is typical of the Leon Rubay design and coach work. Rubay was hospitalized for nervous exhaustion in the spring of 1923 and returned to Europe to recuperate. Only remnants of the detail that usually characterized his designs appeared on the Roamer after that time. (NAM)

ished by the Leon Rubay Company, and these cars were advertised with Rubay coachwork in the January, 1920 issue of the *Automobile Trade Journal*. Roamer advertisements always showed the graceful Roamer, often chauffeur driven, in elegant settings. "Dignified, graceful, unerringly smart, there is a fund of velvety power for every need.... Custom built to your order," read the advertising copy.

Leon Ruby emigrated to this country from France shortly after the turn of the twentieth century, and by 1908 had involved himself with several New York coach builders. In 1916 he launched his own firm, The Leon Rubay Company, and built coach bodies for some of the finest marques in the industry, including Cole, Duesenberg, Locomobile, Marmon, Pierce-Arrow, and White as well as the Roamer. The interiors were beautifully decorated with fittings of burnished nickel, lamps etched in the Adam period design, and wide cloth-covered seating complete with foot rail and arm rests. Engine make, paint color, and interior appointments were the choice of the owner, and the luxury of these automobiles found welcome buyers among the royalty in India, Japan, and other Asian countries.

The Barley company was at its pinnacle of success after World War I, building 1,630 cars in 1920; 1,310 in 1921; 1,418 in 1922; and 1,918 in 1923. Roamer was a participant of note in the New York and Chicago car shows, and published attractive color catalogs and a monthly newsletter. In 1922 the company launched an expensive advertising campaign. The packet consisted of several letters introducing the product, brochures and return postal card, costing $1.75 for each sales prospect. The campaign included two brochures, *Good Roads Included* and *The Double OK*, that described the factory, the manufacturing process and the Roamer's production standards. *The Double OK*, introduced "Lefty" to the potential customer as the company's quality engineer with the following message;

> "What I can't find in 50 miles, the owner won't find in a year."
> So says Lefty, who knows the Roamer as a surgeon knows anatomy.
> Lefty is the Roamer tester, one of the trouble shooters who spend their lives trying to hang something on the Production Department.
> No car can leave our shops until it bears their OK.

This campaign and the newsletters are indicative of a company with confidence in its image and its position in the marketplace. Indeed, the coach work was designed by two of the finest stylists of the day and the car was powered by the famous Rochester-Duesenberg engine. Roamer held the world's land speed record after 1921 and all seemed to be going well in Kalamazoo, although disaster was just around the corner.

Fig. 28-14. The 1922 sport sedan shows the distinctive characteristics of the Rubay coach work, front quarter window, front glass protector, offset belt molding and small rear quarter window with Landau accent bar. This model was introduced in the winter of 1922 and was advertised as being different from other Roamers, a car of unusual individuality with power and speed seldom found in closed cars. This model was powered by a Rochester-Duesenberg engine and equipped with a California all-weather top. The side windows were removable so the car could be used as a touring model in warm weather, a convenience that Rubay introduced on his own "Leon Rubay" car in December 1922. (NAM)

Fig. 28-15. The four-door coupe was introduced by Roamer in the winter of 1922 with the six-cylinder Continental Red Seal engine. It was four inches longer than previous coupes allowing for the four-door convenience of a sedan and the sporty appearance and agility of a coupe. This model is also believed to be a Rubay design, with front quarter window and wicker treatment on the belt molding. Note the rectangular rear quarter window with the squared off corners. (KLM)

Fig. 28-16. The 1921 Roamer standard touring at Golden Gate Park in San Francisco. The Rolls Royce radiator treatment is clearly visible in the photograph. This image was used on the cover of the September issue of the Roamer News *in 1921. (JCC)*

SPEED AND ENDURANCE: 1919–1921

After World War I ended, A. C. Barley sought to establish a reputation of speed and endurance for the Roamer, which he did primarily at the Indianapolis track, on Florida's famed Daytona Beach, and other publicized endurance runs. The Barley company sponsored a racing team in 1917 and 1918, and the Duesenberg-powered Roamer was successful, particularly after Roscoe Sarles joined the crew in 1918. Sarles led the team to victory at Ascot in 1918.

The grand brickyard at Indianapolis had been quiet during 1917 and 1918, and even the final race in 1916 was cut from five hundred to three hundred miles in length due to the impending world conflict and the escalating military action by the United States in Mexico and Panama. As World War I came to a close, many automobile manufacturers sought to establish a reputation for speed and endurance and the opening of the Indianapolis raceway in 1919 was an ideal opportunity for showcasing the Roamer, although the Roamer entries were not company sponsored. The five hundred mile race that year limited engine displacement to three hundred cubic inches, with a required minimum speed of eighty miles an hour over a one-lap time trial. The thirty-three cars with the fastest times qualified for the race.

The Duesenberg-powered Roamer speedster was very competitive and was capable of challenging the finest domestic or European built machines; two Roamers were prepared for and qualified in the 1919 Indianapolis event. The race became a friendly competition between the American

Fig. 28-17. The photograph of President Taft in the backseat of a 6-54 Sport Roamer. This photograph is believed to be one taken at the railway station in Kalamazoo, circa 1921, when Taft visited the city to talk about the League of Nations. (FAM)

and European drivers for the world's racing supremacy, many of whom had built reputations for speed and daring, flying military aircraft in the European skies. The challenge was fueled by the reporters of the day, who often compared the results of the six Indianapolis races since the inaugural 1911 event. Three races had been won by Americans and three by Europeans on the track's hallowed brick. The 1919 race was billed as the "Liberty Sweepstakes."

The most intense competition that year was between four French drivers, Louis Wagner, Rene Thomas, Albert Guyot, and Paul Bablot all driving French-built Ballot cars and all pitted against a single American folk hero, Ralph DePalma at the wheel of a big, burly Packard. His folk hero status developed in 1912 after his engine blew while leading that race. DePalma and his mechanic pushed the broken Mercedes across the finish line. He had served also in the experimental division of the United States air service during the war, and had a reputation for an "iron nerve and cool head." There was talk that the Ballot team would send one driver after another after DePalma until they tired him in the competition, but such antics could easily be deterred by the referee, Eddie Rickenbacker, another of America's war heroes. The Ballot team leader, Rene Thomas, had qualified at 104.70 miles an hour and sat on the pole at the start of the race, and it was this speed, against the wily skills of DePalma, that created much of the enthusiasm before the race. The rivalry was not settled by the race, however, for it was won by "Howdy" Wilcox, "the fearless and daring Hoosier speed demon" who averaged just over eighty-eight miles an hour to win the $20,000 prize.

The two Roamers began the event side by side in the eighth row. The first blue and gray Roamer, powered by a 299 cid Duesenberg engine, had been prepared by Roscoe Sarles, who had opted to

Fig. 28-18. Louis LeCocq sits behind the wheel and Robert Bandini occupies the "mechanician's" seat of the Duesenberg-powered Roamer. Both were cremated in a flaming roll-over accident on the twenty-fifth turn. (IMS)

drive a Barney Oldfield Special and in turn had made the Roamer available to Louis LeCocq for the race. LeCocq began his racing career on the dirt tracks of California first as a mechanic and then, in late 1917, a driver. He often finished in the money and his success was noticed by Roscoe Sarles who offered him the Roamer for the 1919 race. LeCocq's mechanic, or "mechanician" as they were called at the time, was Robert Bandini also from Los Angeles, California. Both were competing in their first, and what would prove to be their last, Indianapolis 500 race.

LeCocq qualified the car at 92.90 miles an hour, sat in twenty-fifth position at the start, and remained competitive into the ninety-sixth lap. Dramatically, the Roamer rolled over when entering the southeast turn, trapping the two men beneath it and spewing flaming gasoline on the vehicle and across the track. Newspaper reports of the tragedy were blunt when they reported that "the men burned for five minutes, before the guards and spectators extinguished the flames."

The second Roamer was also powered by the 299 cid Duesenberg engine. This car had been built for Eddie Hearne, and was purchased by C. Y. Kenworthy when Hearne had decided to drive a Durant. Kenworthy was a Roamer distributor and a vice-president of the A. C. Barley company. He had been responsible for the first large-scale purchase of the Roamer and therefore the initial success of the car in 1916. While this car was not at Indianapolis as a Roamer factory entrant, it was piloted by Kurt Hitke, a superintendent at the Roamer factory. Hitke had three years' experience as a riding mechanic but was a rookie as a driver. He qualified the second Roamer at 93.5 miles an hour to start in twenty-fourth place, but completed only fifty-six laps before a rod bearing failed and he was forced to withdraw.

Fig. 28-19. The remains of the Roamer racer, the "death carriage" for LeCocq and Bandini. Reportedly, the racer burned for five minutes before fans and guards were able to quell the flames. (IMS)

So ended the competition for Roamer at the brickyard, although Duesenberg-powered cars continued to be competitive and in 1921 the Duesenberg engine held practically all world speed records. Historians consider the 1919 race as the bloodiest in the history of Indianapolis. In addition to the tragic deaths of LeCocq and Bandini, Arthur Thurman was also killed instantly in a separate accident when his Thurman Special rolled over on the north turn of the forty-fourth lap. Nicholas Molinero, Thurman's "mechanician," suffered a skull fracture in the same accident. Elmer Shannon was also severely injured when the timing wire from Louis Chevrolet's car cut loose and flew back, slicing open his throat as he trailed Chevrolet's Frontenac racer.

The success of the Duesenberg-powered Roamer was sufficient to convince Kenworthy to embark on the manufacture of his own automobile. In November of 1919 he founded a company with a manufacturing plant in Mishawaka, Indiana, to build another Karl K. Martin-designed motorcar with the Rochester-Duesenberg engine. Advertisements introduced it as "America's Motor Car Classic" and the similarity between this car and the Roamer was unmistakable. The postwar recession was unforgiving, and after a production run of only 214 cars, Kenworthy declared bankruptcy in August of 1921.

Barley was disappointed in the showing at Indianapolis, but immediately began making plans to set the world's speed record on the sands of Daytona Beach. A letter from J. E. McQueen from Columbia, South Carolina may have precipitated the idea. In a letter dated January 19, 1921, McQueen, a Roamer distributor, reported that he had driven his Roamer to a racing event at the Columbus State Fair and had placed a sign on the back of the car proclaiming it to be the fastest car

Fig. 28-20. Kurt Hitke, a superintendent at the Roamer factory, sits at the wheel of the Duesenberg powered #12 Roamer. Hitke only finished fifty-six laps before withdrawing from the 1919 Indianapolis race due to mechanical difficulties. (IMS)

in the state. Many of the onlookers laughed at the suggestion, and to prove the doubters wrong McQueen, with permission from the promotor, drove the touring car around the mile oval track with five people aboard. He covered the mile in fifty-five seconds, one second faster than the car that subsequently won the one mile race that day.

A. C. Barley took on the racing world later that spring. A stock chassis with a special body was prepared and inspected by the American Automobile Association. A Rochester-Duesenberg engine with a 4¼" bore that the company had begun to use that January was installed in the car. Barley drafted Leland Goodspeed to drive the car. Goodspeed was then vice-president of engineering at the Barley Motor Company and had served in that capacity since the inception of the A. C. Barley company. Goodspeed was not considered a professional race driver although, with an ever-present cigar, he was as colorful as the famous Barney Oldfield. Barley was determined to show that a record could be set with a stock chassis and factory engine by a driver who was not a recognized professional. All previous record-setting events had been driven by professionals.

The event, sanctioned by the Automobile Club, took place on April 22, 1921, and Goodspeed set six speed records from one kilometer to five miles by driving 104.36 miles an hour for one mile and averaging 103.76 miles an hour over the five mile course. His speed records beat the two records set by Indianapolis driver Ralph Mulford, first driving a Hudson in 1917 and then driving a Paige in January 1921. The difference of 2.3 miles an hour between Mulford and Goodspeed's pace was a convincing victory. The Barley Company made much of the Daytona Beach records,

Fig. 28-21. The Roamer sits on the sands at Daytona Beach just before the time trial. Standing from left to right are, Alfred C. Barley, president of the company; Leland Goodspeed, driver; R. A. Leavell, official timer for the American Automobile Association; A. C. Means, secretary of the Association's contest board; and F. E. Edwards, technical inspector for the Association. Note Goodspeed's cigar and the military outfit worn by Leavell. (DOL)

including a film promotion at the Fuller Theater in Kalamazoo in conjunction with The Upjohn Motor Sales campaign, the local Roamer distributor, in June of 1921. Letters mailed over the signature of the president of the Barley Motor Car Company also proclaimed: "In exactly 2 minutes and 53.48 seconds we shattered the world's most worthwhile records, six of them—established six new speed marks for everything from the kilometer to five miles."

Following his remarkable success at Daytona Beach, Goodspeed left Kalamazoo to join the Commonwealth Motors Company in Chicago, and shortly thereafter, he had on display at the 1922 New York Automobile Show a sporty machine with a six-cylinder engine and a $5,400 price tag called the Goodspeed. Perhaps two and possibly three of these cars were built. Subsequently, the Commonwealth Company was merged with the Markin Auto Body Company to form the Checker Cab Manufacturing Company. There is reason to believe that Goodspeed found himself in Kalamazoo once again in the spring of 1923 by convincing Markin to move Checker to the city.

Leland Goodspeed was a man of reputation in Kalamazoo, and Barley was so impressed with his mechanical ability that he accused Goodspeed, rather then being born with a silver spoon in his mouth, as having been "born with a silver monkey wrench in his mouth." Goodspeed died in an automobile accident on July 14, 1925 on the country roads outside of Pittsburgh. While there is no evidence that he was racing, his history and very nature suggest that it was an accident resulting from speed rather than folly or ineptitude.

After the success at Daytona, the Roamer company built a two-passenger raceabout on a short-

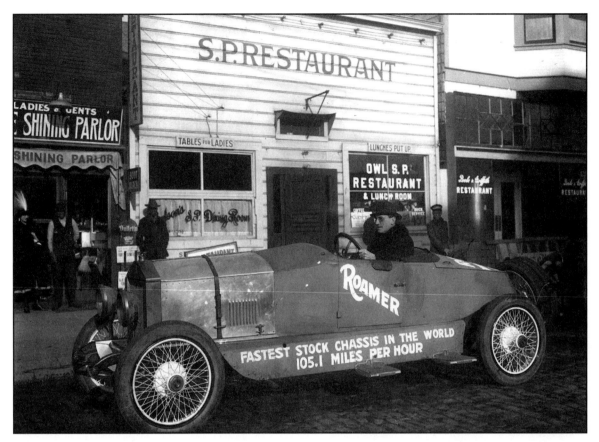

Fig. 28-22. The 1921 Roamer chassis, with Rochester-Duesenberg power, just like the one that set the world's speed records that year, sits by the curb on a street possibly in Daytona Beach or perhaps Philadelphia. This is not the race car, but one that was driven about the east coast, including a tour in Philadelphia, to advertise the victory. The driver appears to be Leland Goodspeed. Note the S. P. Restaurant in the background, a high-class place offering tables for ladies. (JCC)

ened 106" wheel base. The car was delivered without fenders and was powered by the same Rochester-Duesenberg engine that had been raced at Daytona, with the same Splitdorf magneto and dual coil ignition. It had all of the equipment required for speed, including a supply of different gear sets for various types of driving. An unusual feature of the car was that all of the floorboards and seat frames were so arranged that they could be removed in sections so as to reduce the cars weight, should the owner decide to go racing on a competitive basis. The company described the car and its place in the market in the following terms:

> [That] there is a big demand for a car of this type is shown by the number of racing type bodies that are built on mongrel chassis salvaged from standard cars whose bodies have been wrecked or worn out. Of course such equipments do not last very long because their power plant and running gear are usually worn out and unsafe for high speed at the onset.
>
> The 2-passenger Raceabout might be termed our semi-professional car, as it is not only a speedy runabout suitable for young men who want a racing type car capable of passing anything on the road, but it is also designed for competing on all kinds of speed contests, such as road races, dirt track races, hill and mountain climbing contests, etc.

This vehicle is believed to be one of the first open-wheel factory-designed and built "hotrods."

The Roamer's reputation for speed and durability was established nationally by the Daytona record. The following fall, Walter W. Rowland, automobile editor for the *Milwaukee Journal*, selected a Roamer with the same combination of engine and chassis that had set the speed records in Daytona for a tour throughout Wisconsin. The intent of the exercise was to compile a travel log to provide travel information to *Milwaukee Journal* readers. It was published under the title *The Call of the Open Road: The Adventures of "Brownie and Cuss."*

Rowland, who worked fifty-four years with the newspaper, used the pen name of "Brownie" and his traveling companion, chaperon and aide-de-camp, was dubbed "Poor Cuss." Because of its power and speed, they called the Roamer the "Greyhound." "Cuss" was responsible for resolving the mechanical difficulties on the trip, hence the moniker "Poor Cuss," and he often complained that much of his time was spent groveling under the car in the mud, changing tires on slippery soil and swinging a wicked shovel. In the early days, Brownie and Cuss carried logging chains, axes, and other such accoutrements, but by 1921 the roads had improved and their precautions had been reduced

Fig. 28-23. Leland F. Goodspeed and his ever-present cigar, circa 1921, about the time he set the record in the Rochester-Duesenberg powered Roamer. Goodspeed built a car of his own, that he called the Goodspeed, and then became involved with the Checker Cab Manufacturing Company in Kalamazoo. He died at the wheel in an automobile accident on the back roads of Pennsylvania in 1925. (DOL)

Fig. 28-24. After the success at Daytona, Roamer offered a Rochester-Duesenberg powered two-passenger roadster on a shortened, 108" chassis that was "race-ready." It is believed to be one of the first open-wheel, factory-designed and built street-legal "hotrods" offered for sale to the public in this country. (DOL)

Fig. 28-25. Brownie, the automobile editor for the Milwaukee Journal *sits at the wheel and "Poor Cuss," his traveling companion, stands with one foot on the running board. They posed for this photograph just before their departure on an 8,000 mile endurance run in a 1921 Roamer with a Rochester-Duesenberg motor. They called the car "Greyhound" because of its speed and power. (DOL)*

to a set of chains permanently affixed to the side-mounted spare tires.

Brownie, Cuss, and the Roamer covered 250 to 320 miles most days unless they encountered major difficulties—about 8,000 miles all told in twenty-eight days over Wisconsin roads that varied from concrete pavement, to sand, mud, stone, gravel, and even straw. The rain made some of the roads particularly slippery, and Cuss reported that they missed disaster several times by a "frog's hair." According to Cuss, "It is just as easy to court disaster on slippery pavements as it is showing another man's wife the lights of the city at night."

During the trip they had two mechanical problems: first, when they broke a universal joint on a culvert, and, second, when a rock sheared the cover on the crankcase. All in all, Brownie considered it his most successful trip, but he was quick to point out that Wisconsin roads were not in good shape because of all of the construction taking place at the time. He implored his readers to remember that while the detours were inconvenient and, according to Cuss, the basis for much adventure, the construction was necessary and good roads were just around the corner.

"Poor Cuss" also maintained a journal during the trip and his writings reflect both a sense of humor and a tale of adventure:

We came upon a little bridge that looked like it might hold up a mouse if he didn't drag his tail.

"Shall we?" asked Brownie, "Lead on Shylock, says I, I'm no counselor."

He led and the Greyhound bled. The bridge caved as we went over and we went down to join the Mississippi. Our rear wheels landed with such a thud against the bank that it broke our universal or something.

"We're ruined," says Brownie. "Our 8,000 mile jaunt is over for a couple of days and we won't feast on those steaks at Hotel Eau Claire this night." And he wept silently without no words.

There we was, out in the stilly night, with the rain falling loudly and a gang of jack rabbits and frogs croaking thereabouts.

The Greyhound was then rescued from the mires of highway 37 and now is on the operating table at Miller's garage, town of Alma, on the banks of the Mississippi.

It took farmer Frank McGee and six horses to bring the old boat back through the mud she had run through on her own. I wired what was wrong to the Barley Motor Co., Kalamazoo Mich., manufacturers of the Roamer and they immediately dispatched a new universal joint. In spite of the inconvenience, it gave us a good opportunity to test the Roamer service.

They were delayed for three days in Eau Claire fixing the universal joint, but Brownie was quite pleased with the Roamer and the power of the Duesenberg. "All in all," he concluded, "I characterize this, my 1921 tour, as my most successful trip."

NEW DIRECTIONS: 1923–1924

After the notoriety of the speed record in 1921 the company began a new era of development. Leon Rubay, who had been responsible for some of the earlier Roamer coach work, had moved to Cleveland to introduce a car of his own in 1923. The car was called the Leon Rubay, and it is perhaps the only car ever built with a first and last name of the manufacturer. Coincidentally with Rubay's departure, the Roamer line in 1924 began to assume a much heavier appearance, replacing the light delicate sport sedans of 1922 and 1923 with a more substantial vehicle. The distinctive front quarter window was replaced with a vertical front window pillar, and the 128" wheel base and Houk wire wheels were replaced with a 136" wheel base and massive disc wheels. Prices ranged from $2,575 up to $3,450 in 1923, as the light European cars were gradually replaced with a heavy but still a very handsome line of automobiles. Production rapidly decreased after 1924 and changes in the design culminated in the introduction of a four-door sedan powered by an eight-cylinder Lycoming engine rated at eighty-eight horsepower. Photographs of some of the sedans toward the end of this period have an almost armored car appearance to them and, while the success of this vehicle was touted in the periodicals, production plummeted after 1924.

In the fall of 1922, the company announced the manufacture of a light six, and although not disclosed immediately, the car would be named "the Barley" after the company president. This car was a good deal smaller than the Roamer, mounted on a 118" wheel base, with wood spoke wheels and powered by a fifty-horsepower six-cylinder Continental Red Seal engine. The body was made of hardwood fitted with metal panels painted in Liberty Blue, Coach Painters' Green, or Moleskin Deep, all with black fenders and matching leather seating. The line offered an innovative touring sedan with side glass windows that could be removed and stored in a handy compartment in the back of the front seat, giving an all-weather car that could be opened wide when weather permitted. A similar feature was introduced by Rubay in December 1922. The Barley was produced in

Fig. 28-26. The Barley, introduced in 1923 and continued through 1924, was marketed as a less expensive, but not cheaper, companion to the Roamer. The Barley lacked the distinctive "Rolls Royce" grill of the Roamer, but was a handsome automobile with the finest fittings and finish. The five-passenger touring shown here was termed "the most strikingly handsome car that can be maintained on a modest income." This image is from the 1923 sales brochure for the Barley. (DOL)

1923 and 1924 only.

The company also adopted the Barley chassis and running gear to a taxicab that was called the Pennant. This car was first introduced in the summer of 1923 and was displayed at the New York auto show in January of 1924 to compete with Checker, Yellow Cab, and Dodge. Apparently the introduction was so successful that an article appeared in *Motor World* the following month stating that the company had no intention of abandoning the manufacture of passenger cars which would receive as much attention as did the taxis.

REORGANIZATION AND DEMISE: 1924–1929

The introduction of new products meant the introduction of new money, and the era of the 1920s was a succession of reorganizations for the company. The first reorganization took place in 1920, when 14,000 shares of common stock with no par value were replaced with two hundred shares of common stock with a $10 par value. Each holder of the original stock would receive ten shares of the new stock. In addition, this reorganization placed the concern under the laws of Michigan succeeding the original New York corporation, and the Kalamazoo Industrial Realty Company that held the factory originally would be taken over by the Barley Motor Car Company. The States company had left the plant, and this reorganization appeared to be just a matter of tidying up the financial affairs of the company. The company had produced 1,110 cars in 1919, and was planning to manufacture 4,000 to 5,000 cars in 1920, although actual production reached only 1,630 cars that year. The payroll included about 325 employees on a regular basis and an estimated 450 employees during rush periods.

Another reorganization followed on July 5, 1923, consolidating the interests of the Barley Motor Car Company and all of the interests of the Kalamazoo Realty Company under a single entity,

Fig. 28-27. (above) The 1923 five-passenger Barley sedan was advertised as a companion to the Roamer: "It was designed by the same engineers; conceived by the same brains; is produced with the same expert skill, care and attention; is Roamer-painted and Roamer-finished." This image is from the 1923 sales brochure for the Barley. (DOL)

Fig. 28-28. (below) The Barley five-passenger sport sedan for 1923 offered "elegance without extravagance." Note the Landau bar, the padded top and oval window. The specially tailored trunk contained matching leather luggage. This image is from the 1923 sales brochure for the Barley. (DOL)

Fig. 28-29. The Barley Motor Car Company produced the Pennant cab in 1923 and 1924. The style was typical of cabs for the period and the Pennant was similar to the Yellow and Checker cabs built in the same years. This image is from a company sales brochure. (DOL)

Fig. 28-30. The company's commercial vehicle production seemed successful and the cab companies well organized. This image, from company literature, shows a line of Pennant cabs in front of a Pennant service facility in New York, circa 1923. (DOL).

Fig. 28-31. An array of 1924 Roamers, all open cars, from the Roamer Motor Car Company at 1451 Van Ness Avenue, are shown at the Chicago auto show that year. The elegant lines remain, but these are bigger and much heavier cars with larger axles and tires than the company first introduced in 1916. (JCC)

the Roamer Motor Car Company. The company was approved for 300,000 shares, with the immediate sale of 200,000 shares and a reserve of $1 million of preferred stock to be sold at a later date. The company had received an order for $19 million worth of Pennant cabs from Diamond and Murphy in New York, to be delivered over a five-year period with 1,500 cabs to be delivered during 1923. The board was a strong one and included W. S. Perkins, vice-president of Chatham and Phoenix Bank in New York; J. W. Stephenson, president of Indiana Truck in Marion, Indiana; Charles Bard, owner of a wholesale iron and steel company; and Charles Blaney of Wheeler Blaney in Kalamazoo. The financial picture appeared good, and these men were willing to subscribe $100,000 in stock to refinance the company based upon the order for the Pennant Taxi cabs and general sales of the Roamer and the Barley. The company had its best year to date in 1923 with the production of 1,918 cars.

The most productive year closed with another reorganization stemming from either undisclosed financial problems or a takeover bid by a group of local investors. In January of 1924, the board of directors returned to the table looking for another $500,000 in working capital that they claimed was to take advantage of available business. This reorganization involved a syndicate of about twenty well-known Kalamazoo investors. Charles Blaney, S. B. Monroe, Goodie Rosenbaum, William Shakespeare, and Joseph E. Brown came to the table declaring that their primary interest was the welfare of Kalamazoo. Clearly, the Roamer Motor Car Company was beginning to slip

Fig. 28-32. (above) Changes in the Roamer designs during the 1920s were substantial and are reflected in this massive car with an "armored appearance" for 1926. The style appears to be a combination of influences of Rubay and Martin, although both had left the company by this time. According to Hugo Pfau, the American consumer wanted a larger car at a competitive price and there was little interest in automobiles with a European flair. The demise of the Roamer Company was already apparent, as production fell to 137 units in 1926. (FAM)

Fig. 28-33. (below) The 1926 Eight-88 two-passenger Speedster is one of the last great cars from the Roamer line. This image was taken by the front corner of the factory in Kalamazoo and it appeared in the December 10 issue of Motor Age in 1925. Production of this model was very low, and it is doubtful that this custom-built full classic survived.

Fig. 28-34. The 1927 Eight-88 seven-passenger sedan was a massive car on a 132" wheelbase. Many Americans preferred an automobile with a large stature, and eight-cylinder engine. This one met the description of a "classic automobile." Production in 1927, however, fell to eighty-eight cars and few, if any, have survived. (FAM)

away. George C. Wigginton, of the Kalamazoo Loose Leaf Binder Company, was elected president of the Roamer Motor Car Company. A. C. Barley transferred all of his holdings to the board of directors to be used at their discretion. He was still listed as a member of the board of directors, but clearly he was no longer in control of the company he had once commanded.

The new president, with experience in making and selling looseleaf notebooks, was now in charge, and his summary of the situation was succinct: "The plant of the Roamer Motor Car Company is now down for inventory," said Wigginton. "A system will be worked out whereby the concern will be able to operate on a continuous production and on a profitable basis. There will be an entirely new organization in charge, although it is quite impossible at this time to indicate any changes that are to be made." Apparently, Wigginton was overwhelmed with the task as production fell to 723 units in 1924, the lowest since the days in Streater, Illinois.

By October of 1925, the assets of the company were owned by The Roamer Motor Car Company of Canada Limited. The Kalamazoo syndicate was gone and W. H. Parker had replaced Wigginton, who had headed the company since January 1924. Barley once again assumed an active role in the day-to-day operation of the company, moving from board member to general manager.

During 1925 and 1926, national publications introduced the new four-door Roamer, with an eight-cylinder Lycoming engine. The local press touted the car as selling well on the west coast. "With sales increasing daily since the introduction of their new straight eight models," reported the *Gazette*, "officers of the Roamer Motor Car Company of Canada are looking forward to 1926 as one of the most prosperous in the history of the company." The prosperity was a hoax. While movie stars Buster Keaton, Buck Jones, and Mary Pickford did purchase Roamers, and rumors of the construction of a west coast plant were also published, the Roamer enterprise was slowly dying.

Fig. 28-35. The 1929 Roamer seven passenger retained traces of what is believed to be details of the Rubay designs in the wire wheels and the slant of the front pillar, but this car had a far heavier appearance than the models of the early 1920s. According to the Standard Catalog of Cars, *only two cars were built in this final year of production. A similar image appeared in the New York show edition of* Motor Age, *January 1929. (FAM)*

By 1925 the Roamer Motor Car Company offered only two basic models: the Eight-88 powered by the Lycoming engine and the Six-50 with a choice of a Duesenberg or Continental engine. The car was well designed, powerful, and safe, as both series offered hydraulic brakes, but Kimes and Clark report that production fell almost by half each year for the remaining years: 212 cars in 1925, 137 cars in 1926, 88 cars in 1927, 35 cars in 1928 and then only 2 cars in 1929.

The company sought other avenues to keep the employees busy, and in the fall of 1925 advertisements included a special notice; "We specialize in overhauling, repainting and rebuilding any make of car. Phone us for prices and estimates." For almost ten years Roamer had been an international name associated with automobiles of distinction, but as the decade of the 1920s drew to a close, the grand company had turned from the manufacture of the exciting Duesenberg-powered Rubay and Martin designs to a restoration shop that built cars on the side. The onset of the Great Depression in 1929 turned the key in the lock of a door that had already closed.

REFERENCES

The Rutenber Engine. *Automobile Trade Journal*, March 1, 1908.
Advantages and Differences. Barley Motor Car Company Sales Brochure, 1921.

Fig. 28-36. Toward the end of production, the Roamer Motor Car Company built a light-duty truck. This vehicle is similar to the Pennant cab and appears to be built on the Barley chassis with the Barley radiator, setting production circa 1923–1924. MacIlvain sets the date of this truck circa 1929. Neither the production nor the mechanical specifications for these vehicles are well-documented. (WMC)

Beverly Rae Kimes and Henry Austin Clark, Jr. *Standard Catalog of American Cars, 1805–1942,* 3rd ed. Iola, WI: Krause Publications, 1996.

Auto Industry Made Its Start in 1902. *The Kalamazoo Gazette,* October 18, 1925.

Roamer—New Car of Striking Appearance. *The Automobile,* February 1916, p. 225.

Distinction Is Keynote of $1,800 Roamer. *Automobile Topics,* August 12, 1916, p. 29.

The Roamer, A New Light Six. *Horseless Age,* September 15, 1916, p. 200.

Recent Trade Developments. *Horseless Age,* November 1, 1916, p. 317.

Chicago IL—Roamer Motor Car Co. *Motor Age,* November 23, 1916, p. 55.

Roamer Price Increased. *Motor,* November, 1916, p. 98.

Before the Show Issue. *Motor World,* December 27, 1916, pp. 48, 74, 78.

The Roamer. *The Literary Digest,* December 30, 1916, p. 1743.

Barley Motor Car Firm to Build Roamer Here. *The Kalamazoo Gazette,* February 25, 1917.

Kalamazoo Extends Hand of Welcome to Roamer. *The Kalamazoo Gazette,* March 11, 1917.

Bob Lewis. "Kalamazoo Made Cars." *Kalamazoo Gazette,* October 4, 1964.

George A. Coats Buys Roamer Car. *The Kalamazoo Gazette,* August 6, 1917.

Gasoline Cars at The New York Show. *Horseless Age,* January 1, 1917, p. 27.

Over 600 Models for Prospective Motorists of 1917. *Motor Age,* January 4, 1917, p. 6.

Four Passenger Touring Cars. *Motor Age,* January 4, 1917, p. 41.

Roamer Has a Special Bracket. *Motor Age,* January 4, 1917, p. 88.

Roamer. *Motor Age,* January 4, 1917, p. 99.

Novel Runabout Body by Rubay. *Horseless Age*, January 15, 1917, p. 37.

What a Dealer Saw at The Salon. *Horseless Age*, January 15, 1917, p. 37.

For Him Who Would Have Sport Body on His Car. *Motor Age*, March 22, 1917, p. 51.

Orders Rushing Barley Company. *The Kalamazoo Gazette*, April 15, 1917.

Barley Concern Hit by Embargo. *The Kalamazoo Gazette*, May 9, 1917.

Model 38–92 Roamer Ranks with America's Highest Grade Touring Cars. *The Kalamazoo Gazette*, June 24, 1917.

Record Output At Barley Plant. *The Kalamazoo Gazette*, August 15, 1917.

Roamer. *Motor World*, December 26, 1917, p. 74.

Roamer Shown at Doubleday's. *The Kalamazoo Gazette*, February 3, 1918.

Roamer. *Motor Age*, January 23, 1919, pp. 100, 101.

Bill Truesdell. "Roamer, Flashback to an Era of Elegance." *Kalamazoo Review*, November 1976, pp. 26–28.

Roamer Competes in Foreign Field With Rolls Royce. *The Kalamazoo Gazette*, February 9, 1919.

The Chicago Show. *Automobile Trade Journal*, February 1919, pp. 145, 307.

Roamer. Barley Motor Car Co. Sales Brochure collected at the Chicago Show, Feb. 6, 1919.

Ships 75 Cars in 60 Days. *The Kalamazoo Gazette*, June 25, 1919.

The Roamer Shown at New York and Chicago. *Automobile Trade Journal*, January 1920, p. 249A.

Roamer Closed Cars. Sales Brochure, Barley Motor Car Co., 1921.

Roamer Has New Bodies at New York National Show. *Motor Age*, January 12, 1922, p. 19.

Hugo Pfau. *The Custom Body Era*. New York: Castle Books, 1970.

Two Kalamazoo-Made Cars to Be Auto Show Feature. *The Kalamazoo Gazette*, February 12, 1922.

New Roamer Light Six On Market in Thirty Days. *Motor Age*, August 31, 1922, p. 38.

Local Cars in Big Display at Chicago Show. *The Kalamazoo Gazette*, February 4, 1923.

The Double OK. Barley Motor Car Company, 1921.

Good Roads Included. Barley Motor Car Company, 1921.

Letters and Advertisements. Roamer Advertising and Selling Campaign for 1922.

Indianapolis Speedway Checkered Flag for 1919. *The Kalamazoo Gazette*, May 29, 1919.

Driver's History. Indianapolis Race Program, 1919, p. 7.

Very Fast Field for 500 Mile Race. *The Kalamazoo Gazette*, May 30, 1919.

New Record Expected on Speedway. *The Kalamazoo Gazette*, May 31, 1919.

Driver of Roamer and Mechanician Burned to Death. *The Kalamazoo Gazette*, June 1, 1919.

Griffith Borgeson. *The Golden Age of the American Racing Car*. New York: Bonanza Books, 1966

Jack C. Fox. *The Illustrated History of the Indianapolis 500*. Indianapolis: Carl Hungness, 1994.

Demonstration of Roamer Standard Touring Car Astonished Spectators at Auto Race. *The Roamer News*, March 1921, Vol. II, No. 6, p. 3.

Breaking The World's Stock Car Record. *Motor Age*, April 28, 1921, p. 23.

Roamer Establishes New World's Records. *The Roamer News*, May 1921, Vol. II, No. 7, pp. 2–7.

Record Breaking Chassis Returns to Factory. *The Roamer News*, July 1921, Vol. II, No. 8, p. 3.

Two Passenger Raceabout. *The Roamer News*, February 1922, Vol. III, No. 12, p. 6.

8,000 Miles in Twenty-Nine Days. *The Roamer News*, August, 1921, Vol. II, No. 9, pp. 2–12.

Barley Company Has New Car. *Motor Age*, August 17, 1922, p. 34.

Barley Six—Roamer Built. Company sales Brochure, Barley Motor Car Co., 1923.

We Build Them—You Sell Them. Motor World, October 4, 1922, pp. 81–82.

Barley Producing Pennant Taxicab. *Automobile Trade Journal*, June 1923, p. 88.

Dependable Performance Plus—Thousands of Miles at the Lowest Possible Cost. Sales Brochure For The Pennant Taxi, Barley Motor Car Co., 1923.

Net Profits. Sales Brochure For The Pennant Taxi, Barley Motor Car Co., 1923.

Five Good Reasons. Sales Brochure For The Pennant Taxi, Barley Motor Car Co., 1923.

Pennant Taxi. Sales Brochure For The Pennant Taxi, Barley Motor Car Co., 1923.

Roamer Not to Give Up Cars. *Motor World*, February 28, 1924, p. 39.

Barley Reports 19-Million Job For Plant Here. *The Kalamazoo Gazette*, June 24, 1923.

Reorganizing Barley Motor Co. *The Kalamazoo Gazette*, January 4, 1920.

Walter O. MacIlvain. "Roamer." *Bulb Horn*, January–February, 1978, pp. 10–15.

Roamer Motor Car Company Succeeds Barley Corp. *Motor Age*, July 5, 1923, p. 31.

Refinancing of Roamer Car Plant Begins. *The Kalamazoo Gazette*, January 4, 1924.

Wigginton to Head Roamer Car Co. *The Kalamazoo Gazette*, January 5, 1924.

Reorganization of Roamer Motor Car Co. *Motor Age*, January 10, 1924, p. 30.

Roamer Reorganization Completed. *Automobile Trade Journal*, March 1924, p. 90.

Get Canadian Charters. *Motor Age*, March 27, 1924, p. 32.

Roamer Straight Eight Is Proving a Popular Model. *The Kalamazoo Gazette*, October 18, 1925.

Roamer Automobiles. *Handbook of Automobiles*, 1925–1926, pp. 103, 318.

Roamer Eight Offered in Nine Body Styles. *Motor Age*, December 10, 1925, p. 19.

G. Marshall Naul, ed. *The Specification Book for U.S. Cars 1920–1929*. Osceola, WI: Motorbooks, 1978.

Line of 80 hp Cars Offered by Roamer. *Automobile Trade Journal*, April 1926, p. 67.

Roamer Adds New Eight Cylinder Sedan at $1,985. *Motor Age*, April 1926, p. 16.

National Show Issue. *Motor Age*, January 7, 1926, p. 29.

Larger Eight Cylinder Sedan Added by Roamer. *Automobile Trade Journal*, May 1926, p. 90.

Roamer—Total of Three Models. *Motor Age*, January 5, 1928, p. 55.

Through the Shows. *Automobile Trade Journal and Motor Age*, January 1929, p. 96.

New Roamer Plant in West. *Motor Age*, March 18, 1926, p. 35.

Screen Actor Buys Roamer. *The Kalamazoo Gazette*, September 16, 1923.

Larry Massie. "America Looked to Kalamazoo for Its Luxury Dream Car." *Kalamazoo Gazette*, November 9, 1998.

Fig. 29-1. The front elevation of the Handley-Knight deluxe seven-passenger touring car, "beautiful and distinctive from every angle" as it was described in the sales brochure dated October 13, 1921. The distinctive handles on the driving lamps are repeated on the side lights and were a topic of discussion and special mention in the reviews of the 1922 New York car show. Handles, or bails, were a popular lamp treatment on early brass cars, but only Handley continued the practice into the 1920s. (GCM)

Chapter 29

The Handley-Knight Company

1920–1923

I owned seven cars, then purchased my eighth—
the first real automobile—which is Handley-Knight.

—Dr. N. M. Schmeichel
7127 Idlewild St., Pittsburg

The Handley-Knight company was organized on December 31, 1919 and incorporated in Delaware on Tuesday, January 6, 1920, with a capital stock of $1 million, an impressive list of Kalamazoo businessmen as members of the board, and a host of company executives with experience in automobile manufacturing. The board featured W. E. Upjohn, Kalamazoo capitalist and manufacturer; C. A. Blaney, Director of the Kalamazoo City Savings Bank; and C. S. Campbell, president, and W. L. Otis, vice-president of the First National Bank of Kalamazoo. The company executives and engineers were drawn from other leading companies of the day including Cadillac, Chevrolet, Dodge, Hudson, and Willys-Overland.

James I. Handley, president of the corporation and general manager, was one of the most experienced automobile men to establish a manufacturing site in Kalamazoo. His financial past was also one of the most troubled, and his tenure as an automobile manufacturer in this city was one of the shortest. He was introduced to the Kalamazoo community on January 11, 1920 as "Big Jim," suggesting both physical size and an affable manner in addition to his long resume in the automobile industry. Handley began his career selling cars for Maxwell-Briscoe in Dallas, Texas in 1907. In 1910, he accepted a position as vice-president of the United States Motor Company of New York City, a company that Benjamin Briscoe had hoped to develop as a conglomerate that would rival General Motors. Handley remained in New York for less than a year, and in January 1911, he quietly acquired the American Motor Car Company of Indianapolis, Indiana. As the president and a major stockholder he established the American Motors Company with capitalization exceeding $1 million. V. A. Longaker, known as the "father of the underslung frame," was president of the former company and remained as general manager in the company founded by Handley that con-

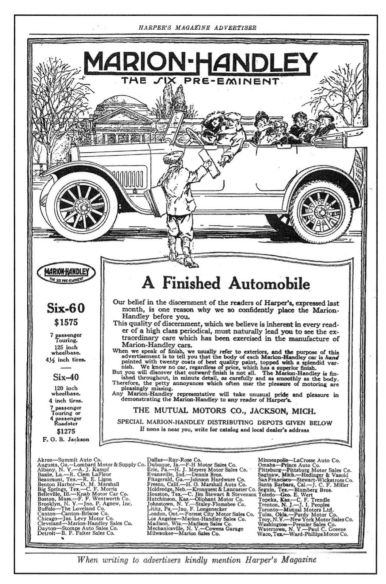

Fig. 29-2. James I. Handley purchased the factories of Imperial Motors in Jackson Michigan, and there he built the Marion-Handley from July, 1915 to December of 1917. This advertisement was intended for Harpers *Magazine, circa 1917. (DOL)*

tinued to manufacture the renowned American Underslung automobile until 1914.

In May of 1912, Handley acquired the Marion Motor Car Company from John North Willys and the acquisition was a bit of a surprise in the industry. The Marion Company built vehicles from 1904–1915 in Indianapolis, initially with air-cooled, and later with water-cooled engines. Barley kept the American and Marion companies independent of one another, and Willys continued his association with the Marion Company as an interested stock holder. Harry C. Stutz was also one of the early associates of the Marion Company, an enterprise that had not grown before 1912 because it lacked adequate working capital. When James I. Handley became president of Marion, the stock issue was increased to over $1 million and a company reorganization followed in November of 1912.

In July of 1913, all of Handley's interests were incorporated as the J. I. Handley Company and capitalized at $1.25 million. The entities in this company included the American Motors Company, the Marion Motor Car Company, American Motors Realty Company, American-Marion Sales and Service Company of Indianapolis, as well as the American-Marion Sales Company of New York and the American Motors Company of San Francisco. Announcements of a six-cylinder American Underslung and a six-cylinder Marion followed that fall, but financial difficulties continued to plague the Handley enterprise, preventing production. Subsequently, the entire conglomerate was placed in receivership.

Handley was able to pull the Marion Company from the receiver's hands in January of 1914, but was not so lucky with the American Underslung. With its low chassis designed by Longaker and rakish body designed by Fred Tone, the American Underslung was intended for the "Discriminating Few," but more than a "few" were needed to keep the company profitable. In April 1914, the American Motors Company went bankrupt. James Handley stayed in the bidding until it reached $80,000, but the final contest was between C. A. Finnegan of Buffalo, who had tried to purchase Michigan Buggy in 1913, and Samuel Winternitz, who had disposed of Michigan Buggy at auction in 1913. Winternitz triumphed once again, purchasing the American Company for $110,000. He then sold off the property, goodwill, and equipment to various Indiana companies, with a return that was sufficient to satisfy the creditors. The bankruptcy was lifted for the Marion Company, but Handley barely had time to reassess his holdings before the company was threatened again with receivership in the fall of 1914. He quickly reorganized and the Marion Company limped through production into 1915.

On July 15, 1915, Handley took over the Imperial Automobile Company of Jackson, Michigan and joined that company with the Marion Motor Company of Indianapolis to form The Mutual Motors Company of Jackson, Michigan. His intent was to manufacture both the Imperial and Marion, both selling in the $900 to $1,100 range. He purchased the facility in Jackson that had housed the Buick Motor Company before its move to Flint, and the new organization appeared to have the strength needed for survival. In a letter to prospective dealers, dated July 26, 1915, Handley expressed his intent with a quaint style: "Our energy, ambition and determination to maintain our logical place *well up in the running* stand at 'One hundred in the shade.'"

In March of 1916, John Handley introduced the Marion-Handley, a sturdy lightweight vehicle with underslung rear springs selling for $1,185. The company eventually offered two series, both powered by a six-cylinder engine. The forty-horsepower series was mounted on a 120" wheel base and sold for $1,275 and the sixty-horsepower series was mounted on a 125" wheel base and sold for $1,575. The United States had not yet entered World War I, but the war-time economy and the drain on steel and mechanical parts created difficult times for fledgling companies. The demise of Handley's Mutual Motors Company was swift. In November of 1917 the plant was shut down for inventory; on December 7, 1917, the Detroit Trust Company was named receiver; and in February of 1918, James I. Handley watched once more while his company was sold at auction. The total price was $212,000, returning about thirty cents on the dollar to the creditors. In the aftermath, he turned for help to his old friend and associate, John North Willys, and James Handley moved to Toledo with an executive position in sales at Willys-Overland. At the time Willys-Overland was building the Willys-Knight automobile powered by the sleeve-valve Knight engine.

Handley remained at Willys-Overland until 1919, but the urge to build yet another Handley car continued to gnaw at him, and he returned to Michigan to manufacture a second car that would bear his name. The story behind the choice of Kalamazoo as the city of manufacture is an interesting one, for it appeared to hinge on the work of a single man—Harry B. Parker.

Harry Parker owned a Kalamazoo automobile agency, was a legendary automobilist, and was the sales agent for the Willys-Knight automobile in the area. During one of Parker's frequent visits to the Toledo-based Willys-Knight plant in the summer of 1919, James I. Handley disclosed to Parker his ambition to build a "new Knight-powered automobile that would be unquestionably the finest in America." Handley confessed in an interview with the press, "I had my mind made up to locate in Cleveland, but this Parker boy never gave me a minute's peace and kept talking about Kalamazoo. Finally, I called his bluff, remarking, 'you have talked Kalamazoo once too often young

Fig. 29-3. The large Handley-Knight factory, measuring 80' by 800', lay north of the city running parallel to Pitcher Street, and was considered modern in design with its abundance of windows on the side walls and along the roof line. Handley-Knight was the only company attracted to Kalamazoo without the prospect of occupying an existing building. This structure was later sold to Checker Cab Manufacturing Company. (GCM)

fellow, now get busy and let me know what you can do.'" Following the challenge from Handley, Harry Parker established a committee of Kalamazoo investors to review the plans for the company and to obtain evaluations from people both in Kalamazoo and Toledo. Finally on November 26, 1919, a group of investors met and the initial stock offering was sold within twenty minutes. The next day a wire from Harry Parker arrived at Handley's office: "Everything set, come along." The Handley-Knight Company was incorporated the next month on December 31, 1919, and moved to Kalamazoo January 26, 1920.

Handley was well known in the automotive world, and as a result of his vast experience and his executive position in the sales division of Willys Overland he was able to draw investors from as far east as Wheeling, West Virginia; north to Buffalo, New York; west to Des Moines, Iowa; and south to Shreveport, Louisiana. When it came time to move to Kalamazoo, he did so with a broad financial base and men in critical positions who had a wealth of talent and experience. There was little doubt during those initial days that the new company would be successful and would become a major contributor to the city's continuing involvement in automobile manufacturing.

Progress in the development of the company was most rapid in the early part of 1920. The company of den Bleyker and Olmsted conducted an aggressive stock sale in March of 1920 selling forty-thousand of the eighty-thousand authorized shares at $32.50 each. A forty-acre site on Pitcher Street just north of the city, considered a prime location because of its proximity to the New York Central, Pennsylvania, and Grand Trunk Railroad lines, was selected for the construction of a new plant. The plant measured 80' by 800' and was designed by Mills, Rhines, Bellman and Nordhoff of Toledo, Ohio, the same firm that had planned the Willys-Knight facility. The building was a single story with row upon row of glass to guarantee sufficient natural lighting. A power station measuring 40' by 40' was built adjacent to the main plant. Groundbreaking was set for February 1, 1920 and construction work began in earnest in the latter part of March that year. The steel skeleton of

Fig. 29-4. This view of the big factory shows the 800-foot wall and the series of windows intended to provide natural light to the interior. The smaller building to the right is the power house. (JCC)

the building was raised and in place by June 20, and the entire facility was under a roof by July 15, 1920. Reportedly, an experimental model of the new Handley-Knight was completed on July 1, 1920, less than one year after Harry Parker's initial organizational meeting that brought the Handley Company to Kalamazoo.

In spite of the rapid construction and a series of quick decisions, minutes of the company meetings suggest it was a conservative organization, setting operational policy as well as financial commitments by formal vote. On September 7, 1920, for example, material inventories were set at a level sufficient to produce only one hundred cars a month although the group knew the restriction might hurt sales. At the same meeting, a purchase agreement with Willys-Overland for the Knight sleeve-valve engine was also approved and the vote of each board member recorded. The directors assumed that Willys-Knight had a capital investment of $500,000 in Handley-Knight, based upon their estimate of the cost of the necessary machinery to produce the Knight sleeve-valve engines. On this basis, they agreed to pay Willys the cost to manufacture the Knight engine, plus an additional $50. They anticipated the purchase of 10,000 engines, and with the $50 payment for each engine, the $500,000 investment would have been paid after delivery of all the engines.

On November 1, 1920 the price of the car was set at $2,985, although there was no record of manufacturing cost estimates. The selling price was set with the assumption that sales would be profitable only after production increased and the cost of parts decreased as the result of large orders.

The first Handley-Knight was finished on November 9, 1920 and was delivered immediately to I. H. Burnstine, president of the Victory Motor Sales Corporation of Chicago, Illinois. The Handley-Knight was a big handsome car, and its aluminum body, fashioned by one of America's finest coach builders was mounted on a 125" chassis. The long hood had a gentle rounded top that broke into the side panels with a distinctive line blending into the cowl. The massive fenders opened in a half circle around the wheel well and then trailed off sharply into the long running board. According to the company, the car was styled to appeal to "The fine car owner who drives from choice."

Fig. 29-5. One of the earliest Handley-Knights, clad with 32" x 4½" white sidewall tires, and sitting on a 125" wheel base; it was powered by a Knight engine, 4⅛"x 4½" rated at 48 horsepower, weighed 3200 pounds and sold for $2,985. This car has handles on the driving lamps, but not on the side lamps, the radiator is painted black rather than being nickel-plated, and there is a forward-pointing top support at the rear of the top, all characteristics of the early cars. The 1920 Ohio license plate dates the photograph and suggests that it may be one of the first cars owned by James Handley. Production in 1920 was only 115 cars. An image of the same car appeared in Motor Age, *November 18, 1920. (DOL)*

The appearance of the Handley-Knight changed little from 1920 through 1922, until the company dropped the Knight engine for 1923, returning to a series of automobiles not unlike the Marion-Handley. The 1920–1921 models are characterized by a painted radiator shell and a forward-pointing top support on the touring car. The 1922 year was regarded as sensational across the industry and Handley-Knight cars sported a wonderful nickel radiator shell and a continuance of the handles above the driving lamps. This vestige of the brass-era car also was repeated on the side lamps in 1922, a small but unique feature.

Much of the Handley-Knight advertising and sales brochures were developed under the guiding hand of D. B. Williams, who used the Knight name to make obvious reference to the traditions of medieval chivalry and the knights of the Round Table. The 1922 sales catalog, for example, described the design efforts in the following manner:

> *For the motives of our lettering, the shaping of our letters and hubcaps, the contours of our car, and the detail embodied in headlamps and side lamps, and even in terms of finish and appointments—we adhered as closely as possible to the period of the Tudors. The English royal line of this name reigned from 1485 to 1603, and it was during those six years that chivalry was at its height—champions in armor....*

Fig. 29-6. (above) The 1921 Handley-Knight was an "assembled job" on a 125" chassis with well-known components. The touring cars for 1921 are distinguished by the forward-pointing rear support for the top and the painted radiator shell, although by October 1921 the shell was nickel-plated. This image of the seven-passenger touring car appeared in Motor Age, January 27, 1921. *(DOL)*

Fig. 29-7. (below) "For a less serious enterprise than ours, it might have seemed almost amusing to an onlooker to note the models in clay and papier-mâché, and the endless drawings and sketches with which my associates and I experimented to this end." This quotation is from the 1922 company sales brochure, and refers to the development of the elegant 1922 Handley-Knight touring car with all-aluminum body and nickel trim on a 125" wheelbase. Note the handles on the driving lamps and the side lamps, the nickel-plated radiator shell and the rearward-pointing top support, distinguishing the 1922 from the 1921 models. This image first appeared in the Automobile Trade Journal, January 1922. *(GCM)*

Fig. 29-8. Powered by the famous Knight engine, the 1922 seven-passenger sedan was finished in the very distinctive Handley-Knight blue with black fenders. This car was just over 17' in length, weighed 3,800 pounds, and featured all the available accoutrements of the era. Note the rain-visor windshield extension that was used in this era when windshield wipers were not commonplace. This image appeared in Motor Age, *December 22, 1921, in an article introducing the new closed bodies of Handley-Knight; note that it does not show side lamps, although they appeared on the cars in the sales brochure, October 13, 1921.(GCM)*

Use of a single color scheme for a model year was not uncommon in the industry during this era, and the standard color was Handley-Knight blue with black top and fenders. Other colors could be ordered and the big closed sedans were featured in company advertisements with dark maroon paint. The interior was finished in hand-buffed leather for the open touring models and high-grade broadcloth for the closed sedans and coupes. The dash was polished walnut and featured a seventy-five mile an hour speedometer, an eight-day clock, ammeter, oil gauge, and dashlight with extension cord, all attractively arranged within easy view of the driver.

The seven-passenger sedan, a popular model among residents of resort towns along the Michigan lake shore, also included silken shades, satin-silver finished fixtures, toilet set and smoking outfit, ever-ready auxiliary seats, and a built-in Perfection heater for the rigors of the winter days. "The requirements of dainty raiment and of essential feminine ease were never more happily fulfilled," declared the company's advertisement copy. Command of this magnificent machine was by a massive eighteen-inch corrugated walnut steering wheel and cast aluminum spider with choke and gas levers mounted just beneath the wheel. Automobiles of this vintage and style were not inexpensive: prices ranged from $2,250 for the five-passenger touring to $3,750 for the seven-passenger sedan. In comparison, a Ford Model T touring with fewer features and accoutrements could be had for $415 in January 1922.

The cars from 1920 through 1922 were powered by the four-cylinder Knight sleeve-valve en-

Fig. 29-9. The interior of the 1922 Handley-Knight had a 75 mile an hour speedometer, ammeter, oil pressure gauge, eight-day clock, and dashlight with extension cord, all arranged by function on a polished walnut instrument panel. Note the distinctive wedge-shaped aluminum accelerator pedal and the rectangular shift lever and brake lever. This image appeared in the sales brochure, dated October 13, 1921. (GCM)

Fig. 29-10. This handsome four-passenger sedan-coupe for 1922 had a right front seat that could be tipped forward for access to the rear seat and a roomy luggage compartment easily reached from inside the car by raising the back of the rear seat. The Knight-powered car was built on a 125" wheel base and weighed 3,700 pounds. This image appeared in the company sales brochure for 1922 and also appeared in Motor Age, *December 22, 1921. (GCM)*

gine. The legacy of the Knight motored cars began in August of 1903 in a small Chicago machine shop and culminated in October 15, 1908, when Charles Yale Knight presented a paper before the Royal Automobile Club of Great Britain. That meeting of engineering experts and skeptics was later regarded as the most unique meeting in the history of that technical organization. The idea that Knight described that day was simple, ingenious, and unlike any other, although the resulting design was complex. Each cylinder was fitted with two precision-cast iron sleeves, one sliding in-

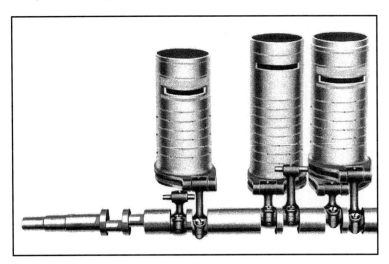

Fig. 29-11. *The Knight sleeve-valve engine is shown (from the left): with outer sleeve, inner sleeve and finally both sleeves together. The off-center, or eccentric bearings are arranged so that one sleeve is being raised as the other is being lowered. When the slots in the two sleeves coincide, an opening is created to allow either the intake of gasoline or the expulsion of exhaust gases depending upon the position in the compression cycle. (DOL)*

side the other on a film of oil. The outer sleeve moved vertically next to the wall of the engine block, and the inner sleeve moved vertically between the outer sleeve and the piston, so there were two sleeves and a piston constantly in motion inside of the cylinder. These sleeves were operated by short connecting rods working off a shaft that in turn was driven by the engine's crankshaft, and synchronized at different points in the compression cycle. The intake and exhaust valves consisted of ports or openings in the two sleeves. As the two

sleeves moved up and down, the position of these ports coincided briefly; at one point during the cycle creating an opening through which fresh gasoline could be drawn, and at another point an opening through which exhaust gases could be expelled.

The Knight engine was well received in Europe and was adopted by leaders in fine car production, including Daimler of England, Panhard-Levassor of France, Mercedes of Germany, Sigma of Switzerland, and Minerva of Belgium. The finest of Europe's royal families moved about by virtue of the silent sleeve-valve Knight engine. The Handley company made good use of this regal heritage during the advertising campaign of 1922 by publishing an historical advertising brochure entitled "Pedigreed Power." The publication cast the story of the Handley-Knight engine as a direct descendent of motors that insured comfortable and luxurious transportation for the world's aristocracy.

The engine was advertised by Knight (not known for his modesty) as "the only automobile powerplant known that improves with use." His statement was not an idle boast, however, and was backed by a 1909 engineering test by Daimler, after which the engine received the Dewar Non-stop Challenge Cup for meritorious motor performance. The Handley-Knight company was quick to note that the 1909 challenge had remain uncontested through 1921, the year of the Handley brochure. In that 1909 test, two Knight sleeve-valve engines were run at peak power on a test stand and

Fig. 29-12. "Beauty is far more than 'skin deep' in the Handley-Knight. And to insure against any possible slight annoyances from rattles, squeaks or slight adjustments every car is actually 'road tested' for a minimum of 50 miles." In the photograph, a Handley-Knight is being tested for endurance in the mud with a block of concrete over the rear wheels to insure traction. The "test track" was just outside the plant's door, at the same end of the building as the power plant. This image appeared in the Handley-Knight sales brochure, October 13, 1921.(GCM)

then at the track, totalling more than 150 hours of operation. These engines actually showed gains in horsepower as a result of the brutal treatment.

The Knight engine offered three major advantages that were first discussed in Kalamazoo on April 13, 1916, by Henry E. Hower, a member of the Society of Automotive Engineers. First, the sliding valves provided a quieter operation than the typical mechanical valve engine. (Some writers refer to poppet valves, but others define poppet valves as moving by changes in vacuum pressure and not mechanical activation.) In the mechanical design, openings in the engine block are covered by a valve, consisting of a round disk attached to a stem. That valve is held in place by a spring, and then forced off the opening by a cam attached to a shaft driven by the engine and pushing against the valve stem. The incessant opening and closing of these valves can be noisy and, when not set correctly, can create a racket. Second, the maintenance for a Knight sleeve-valve engine is less than a mechanical-valve engine. In the sleeve-valve design, there were no valve springs to break, no valve stems to warp, and no engine surfaces exposed to the pounding required to open and close the valves in a conventional engine with mechanical valves. Third, carbon deposits from burned gas built up on the bottom of the valve surface in a conventional engine, preventing complete closure and robbing power from the engine; the same deposits actually improved the seal between the sleeves in the Knight design and thus enhanced engine performance. Claims of Knight-powered automobiles reaching 300,000 miles and the remarkable trouble-free service of this motor in English and French tanks during World War I are well documented. If the engine had a fault, it was the heavy exhaust evident under power loads, and that legacy of some Knight-powered Willys cars continues.

The Knight engine was first offered in the United States in 1912 by F. B. Sterns of Cleveland, Ohio, and the Edwards-Knight Company of Long Island followed in 1912. John North Willys drove a Knight-powered car while in Ireland in 1913 and was so impressed he purchased the Edwards-Knight Motor Car Company in 1915, and under this patent license manufactured the Willys-Knight. The Willys-Knight was characteristically quiet and smooth running with impressive torque and competitive top speed, although acceleration was notably slow. According to Arch Brown, "At idle all that could be heard was the soft whistle of the carburetor, and at fifty miles an hour all that could be heard was the soft whistle of the wind." When James I. Handley, then an executive officer in sales with the Willys-Overland Company of Toledo, Ohio, decided to enter automotive manu-facturing in 1919, it is not surprising that he selected the Knight engine for his intended luxury car.

Unfortunately, the patented Knight engine was available only by license and Knight demanded a premium of $100 for each engine manufactured, almost four percent of the Handley selling price. This arrangement was not an impediment for companies that built cars for the monied gentry of Europe, but it was a considerable detriment to the promotion of sales in the United States. The engine itself was expensive to build and expensive to repair, although its durability minimized the latter cost. The engines for the Handley-Knight were built by Willys for the cost of manufacture plus $50, but the cost of manufacture is unknown. Later statements by Handley, however, suggest that the engines may have been the major portion of expensive contract commit-ments.

The year 1922 was an extraordinary one, for annual reports indicated that investment in the industry exceeded $1.4 billion and that production exceeded 2.6 million vehicles, an increase of over 60 percent compared to 1921. In spite of these very favorable conditions, signs of financial difficulty in the Handley-Knight enterprise appeared as early as March 21, 1922, less than two years after initial production. Reports in the national periodicals created a positive image, but transactions recorded in the company's record book revealed a discouraging tale. In January 1922 the board of directors attempted to raise $50,000 and had developed a plan of indebtedness that was agreeable to all of the creditors except for the Willys-Overland Company that supplied the Knight engines. The board then decided that in these circumstances they could not afford to ask the stock holders for additional cash. After some deliberation, a special stockholder meeting was called and convened in the ballroom of the New Burdick Hotel on July 27, 1922.

The major business before that body was recorded in part as follows:

> AND WHEREAS …provided a complete reorganization is effected, …for the purpose of taking over and continuing the purpose of the present company, they the said merchandize creditors will accept a compromise settlement of their claims against the present company, viz 20% of face for their present claims, payable in cash or 100% of face for present claims, payable in common shares of the proposed new company…

The vote of the stockholders was overwhelmingly in favor of the provision, thus moving toward the dissolution of the Handley-Knight company and creating the Handley Company.

The situation did not improve, and the final disposal of the company was recorded in the entries that appeared in the record book for August 31, 1922:

> WHEREAS, the Company's financial condition has been for many months, and is now such that
> it is unable to pay its indebtedness in full, or even approximately in full,
>
> AND WHEREAS, for lack of necessary capital and credit strength, the company some weeks ago
> ceased its manufacturing operations, and is now still unable to resume such operations
>
> AND WHEREAS, at said meeting, the stockholders by resolution made and adopted, authorized
> and empowered the Company's Directors to sell, transfer and set over all of the company's assets to
> a new corporation then proposed to be organized....
>
> AND WHEREAS, it is the opinion and belief of the said Directors that such transfer of the
> Company's assets to said Handley, as above described, is for the best interest of its creditors....

The secretary took the roll and all of the directors—Campbell, Otis, Upjohn, Balch, Parker, and Handley—voted yes with Woodward as the only dissenting vote.

Given the financial difficulties, it was the only option. The Handley-Knight Company, a Delaware Corporation, was liquidated, and all personal, real property, buildings, plants, machinery, bills and accounts receivable were transferred to a new company—Handley Motors—that was incorporated in Michigan. The transfer was approved on December 1, 1922 and Handley Motors Company paid all of the existing indebtedness of the Handley-Knight Company except for major creditors. In lieu of a cash payment, they were given a percentage of the 40,628 shares of no par value stock in the Handley Motors Company. The Willys-Overland Company of Toledo received 14,000 shares; Limousine Body Company of Kalamazoo received 4,952 shares; Knight American Patents Company of New York City received 3,495 shares; and so on down a list of twenty-eight major creditors. Thus the indebtedness of the old company was transferred with apparent ease to the new company, and not a hint of the internal turmoil reached the national or local press except the final resolution and transfer.

In December 1922, both the local paper and the national periodical *Motor World*, reported Handley's position as follows. "It is the opinion of Handley that the new company not being committed to any of the old high price material contracts, will be in a position to take advantage of present market levels right from the start and therefore expects to market a large car at about $1,000 less than the former price." The message was clear that the Knight engine was too expensive and once the company rid itself of that commitment, cars could be manufactured and sold at a price that was competitive in the market place.

In addition to the realignment of the stock, the company also initiated a profit-sharing plan with its dealers so dealers would share equally with the manufacturer in all profits above the manufacturer's 6 percent margin. Dealers could also implement a price reduction by agreement of 75 percent of the dealers to meet the prices of the competition. Dealers were not forced to purchase a selection of cars nor to sell both the Handley 6-40 and 6-60; instead they could concentrate on either or both of these vehicles depending on their clientele.

The new Handley company produced two cars, both powered by six-cylinder engines. The Handley 6-40 was the smaller of the two and was powered by the Falls forty-horsepower engine. It was available in touring, roadster, and closed body styles and sold in the $1,300 range. The 6-60, available as a seven-passenger sedan, seven-passenger touring, and four-passenger touring, was powered by the Midwest sixty-horsepower engine. Prices ranged from $2,150 for an open car to

Fig. 29-13. The Handley 6-60 Touring car, the larger of the two Handley offerings for 1923, sold for $2,150. The 6-60 sat on a 125" wheel base and was powered by a Midwest six-cylinder engine measuring 3⅜" x 5" and was distinguished from the smaller car by the flat radiator. This image appeared in the Automobile Trade Journal, *February 1923. (DOL)*

$2,800 for the big sedan. The larger of the two cars continued with a flat-style radiator while the Light-Six featured a European-style V-shaped radiator. The general appearance of the Handley was similar in style and presentation to the Handley-Knight. Among the most prominent features of the car were the distinctive "handles" which stood above the large round drum-style driving lamps. These handles or "bails" were reminiscent of the brass-era gas-powered lamps and the Handley company advertisement included the declaration "If it carries handles, it's a Handley."

A "Light-Six" sport, four-passenger touring, semi-custom, featured in "a snappy yellow," was very well received at the New York Auto Show on January 21, 1923. According to John Handley, hundreds of dealers inspected the car and it received more praise than any other there. The general style as well as the noiseless fabric spring shackles were two of the attributes most often mentioned. The car was shown again from January 27 through February 4, 1923 in the magnificent Coliseum at the Chicago Auto Show and again attracted considerable attention. There were no fancy advertisement brochures and the fanfare from the auto shows was short lived. In spite of the realignment and the new dealer profit sharing, the Handley Company never really got started after the loss of the Knight sleeve-valve engine and Handley was out of business by the spring of 1923.

On April 8, 1923 the Checker Cab Company purchased both the Handley plant—including the 800' x 80' manufacturing facility, the adjacent heating plant, and thirty-three acres of land—and

Fig. 29-14. The photograph of the 1923 Handley-six sedan was taken just outside of the factory presumably with four of the women from the administrative office. Note the European-style V-shaped grill, "showing its resemblance to a foreign car" that differentiated the 6-40 series Handley for 1923 from the larger 6-60 series. The handles above the driving lamps were characteristic of the Handley-Knight as well as the subsequent conventionally-powered Handley car. The Handley featured a Falls six-cylinder overhead valve engine rated at 40 horsepower and a fabric spring shackle for a quiet flexible suspension. An image similar to this one, without the young ladies, appeared in the Automobile Trade Journal, *February 1923. (DOL)*

the vacant Dort body plant. The company then moved the manufacturing plant for the Checker Cab from Joliet to Kalamazoo. Much of the impetus for Checker's relocation was due to Leland F. Goodspeed, an engineer with Checker, former employee of Barley Motor Car, and the man who set the record in the Rochester-Duesenberg-powered Roamer. Morris Markin of Checker Cab was the successful bidder for the plant in competition with Hofstetter of the Maximum Truck Company in Kansas City, Kansas, and as a result of the sale, Handley anticipated the continued manufacture of the Handley under the auspices of Checker. His statement, published in the May 2, 1923 *Motor World* read:

> *A deal is now under consideration and will probably be worked out whereby the Checker Cab Manufacturing Company will build the Handley car, of which I will direct the sales. The Handley Motors Company is now practically free from debt and has sufficient cash in the bank to operate without any extensive financing at this time.*
>
> *Had the deal to sell our plant to the Checker Cab Manufacturing failed to materialize and they had allowed their option to lapse on Friday, I would have immediately sold to another automobile concern, fully financed and ready to start immediately.*

A similar statement was made in an interview with the local press, published in the *Kalamazoo Gazette* on April 29, 1923:

I am not at liberty to tell the sales price for our property and never inquired about what was paid for the Dort plant. Suffice it to say that a deal is now under consideration… whereby the Checker Cab Manufacturing Company will in addition to their own product build the Handley car, of which I will direct the sales.

There is no evidence of manufacture of the Handley after April 1923, and the demise of the company was complete. John Handley watched his third company in nine years sold to the highest bidder. Handley left Kalamazoo and accepted a position with Simons Sales Company of Brooklyn, New York, to sell the Chrysler and Maxwell cars.

The final note about Handley is a small item appearing in *Automobile Topics*, reporting his death by suicide on a train in Texas in May of 1931. The circumstances surrounding the tragedy are unknown, but the suicide is not surprising. The market crash of 1929 devastated many. Over 28,000 banks failed in 1931 alone, and more than twelve million people were out of work. Automobile production had fallen and there were few jobs left in automobile sales. The condition of his financial affairs at the time is unknown, but if the crash had devastated his financial portfolio as it had others, Handley was not the only man at that time who solved his financial difficulties by taking his own life.

REFERENCES

Folks, Meet Jim Handley, Head of New Auto Concern. *The Kalamazoo Gazette*, January 11, 1920.

Is Director of Handley Co. *The Kalamazoo Gazette*, February 1, 1920.

Automotive Advt. Leader Director of Handley-Knight Co. in Kalamazoo. *The Kalamazoo Gazette*, February 4, 1920.

American Motors Enters Field. *The Automobile*, January 26, 1911, p. 327.

Officers of New Merger Chosen. *The Horseless Age*, February 1, 1911, p. 267.

Takes Over the American Plant. *Motor Age*, January 26, 1911, p. 80.

American Motors Succeeds American Motor Car. *Cycle and Automotive Trade Journal*, April 1911, p. 105.

American Motors Succeeds American Motor Car. *Motor*, March 1911, p. 60.

Handley in a New Deal. *Motor Age*, May 1912, p. 11.

Marion Company Reorganized. *The Horseless Age*, May 8, 1912, p. 838.

Willys-Overland Sells Marion Company. *Motor*, June, 1912, pp. 60–61.

American-Marion Sales Company Formed. -*Motor World*, August, 22, 1912, p. 8.

Reorganization of Marion Co. Completed. *Horseless Age*, September 11, 1912, p. 375.

Handley Merges Interests. *The Automobile*, July 31, 1913, p. 215.

Handley Combines Sales Companies of American and Marion Cars. *Automobile Trade Journal*, August 1913, p. 190.

Third Underslung "Six" Added to American Line. *Motor World*, September 4, 1913, p. 27.

Marion Out of Receivers' Hands. *The Automobile*, January 29, 1914, p. 337.

Mutual Plant Brings $212,000. *Motor World*, February 27, 1914, p. 52.

Chicago Man Makes Best Bid for American Motors. *Motor World*, April 2, 1914, p. 5.

A $110,000 Bid for American Motors Plant. *The Automobile*, April 2, 1914, p. 752.

Marion Motor Car Co. Threatened with Another Receivership. *The Light Car*,
    October 13, 1914, p. 9.

Marion Motor Car Co. *The Horseless Age*, November 18, 1914, p. 742.

Marion Organization Under Way. *The Horseless Age*, November 18, 1914, p. 734.

Bankruptcy Lifted From American Motors. *The Horseless Age*, December 16, 1914, p. 861.

Mutual to Market Marion and Imperial. *Horseless Age*, July 21, 1915, p. 78.

Marion-Handley Perpetuates Marion Six. *Automobile Topics*, March 18, 1916, p. 493.

Receiver for Marion-Handley. *Motor Age*, December 13, 1917, p. 15.

Letter. James I. Handley to Prospective Auto Dealers, July 26, 1915.

Deal for Handley-Knight Factory Completed. *The Kalamazoo Gazette*, January 7, 1920.

Handley-Knight Car Promised by Summer. *Motor World*, January 21, 1920, p. 44.

Handley-Knight Stockholders. *The Kalamazoo Gazette*, January 22, 1920.

Handley-Knight Builds Factory. *Motor Age*, March 11, 1920, p. 28.

Mutual Motors Moves. *The Automobile*, March 25, 1920, p. 790.

Steel Work of First Big Handley-Knight Unit Completed. *The Kalamazoo Gazette*,
    June 20, 1920.

Handley-Knight on Market in Fall. *Motor World*, June 23, 1920, p. 39.

Handley-Knight Nears Market. *Motor World*, August 18, 1920, p. 43.

New Handley-Knight Car. *Automobile Trade Journal*, August, 1920, p. 232, 234.

Handley-Knight Cars Due October 1. *Motor Age*, September 9, 1920, p. 37.

Handley-Knight on Display. *Motor World*, October 6, 1920, p. 40.

The Daddy of Them All. *The Kalamazoo Gazette*, November 9, 1920.

Handley-Knight Car Placed on Market. *The Automobile*, November 11, 1920, p. 991.

Handley-Knight Ready for Distribution. *Motor World*, November 17, 1920, p. 32.

Handley-Knight, an Assembled Job. *Motor Age*, November 18, 1920, p. 16.

Handley-Knight Features. *Motor Land*, November 1920, p. 14.

Production of Cars for 1920. *The Automobile Journal*, January 1921, p. 12.

Handley-Knight Four. *Motor*, January 1921, p. 106.

Nine of the New Ones. *Motor*, January 1921, p. 90.

Specifications. *Motor Age*, January 27, 1921, pp. 43, 82–83.

New Cars to Feature New York Show. *Automobile Trade Journal*, November 1921, p. 62.

Details of Design and Construction of Handley-Knight, Company Sales Brochure,
    circa January 1921.

Williams Joins Handley-Knight. *The Kalamazoo Gazette*, August 22, 1920.

America's Finest. Company Sales Brochure, October 13, 1921.

Handley-Knight Open cars. Advertising Brochure, circa January 1922.

The New Handley-Knight Custom-Built Enclosed Cars. Company sales brochure,
    circa January 1922.

Specifications of 1922 Passenger Cars. *Motor*, January 1922, pp. 166–67, 182–83, 192.

Handley-Knight Makes Cuts and Adds New Models. *Motor World*, January 4, 1922, p. 42.

Handley-Knight Adds Two Closed Bodies. *Motor Age*, December 22, 1921, pp. 14–15.

New Handley-Knight Gives Real Closed Car Comfort. *The Kalamazoo Gazette*,
    December 24, 1921.

Throngs See Beautiful New Handley-Knight Automobiles. *The Kalamazoo Gazette*,
    December 29, 1921.

Americas Finest Knight-Motored Car. *Automobile Trade Journal*, January 1922, p. 143.

Americas Finest Knight-Motored Car. *Automobile Topics*, March 11, 1922, p. 277.

Coupes for Fall. *Motor*, September, 1922, p. 41.

Pedigreed Power. Advertising Sales Brochure, circa January 1921.

Arch Brown. "Silent Knight." *Cars and Parts*, September 1988, pp. 37–40.

Handley-Knight Shows a Return of the Lamp Handle. *Motor*, March, 1922, p. 24.

B. M. Ikert. Some Reasons Why the 1922 Car Is the Best Ever Built. *Motor Age*,
    January 19, 1922, p. 10.

Handley Motors Company Organized to Take Over Handley-Knight Factory.
    The Kalamazoo Gazette, December 5, 1922.

Directors Record Book. The Handley-Knight Company Meetings, 1920.

Handley Reorganized Under Changed Name. *Motor World*, December 12, 1922, p. 38.

Handley Motors Inc., Takes Over Handley-Knight Business. *Motor Age*, December 14, 1922,
    p. 38.

"What New Car is That?" *Automobile Trade Journal*, January 1923, p. 155.

Handley Motors Has Profit Sharing Plan. *Automotive Industries*, January 11, 1923, p. 99.

Handley-Knight Reorganizes and Expands. *Automobile Trade Journal*, February 1923, p. 62.

New York Show. *Automotive Industries*, January 11, 1923, p. 70.

Handley Announces Two New Sixes. *Motor World*, January 17, 1923, p. 25.

Handley-Knight Develops New Light Six. *Automobile Trade Journal*, January 1923, p. 67.

Construction Details. *Motor Age*, January, 18, 1923, pp. 15–17.

Handley Auto Given Praise at New York Show. *The Kalamazoo Gazette*, January 21, 1923.

Handley Light Sixes at Show. *The Kalamazoo Gazette*, January 28, 1923.

Local Cars in Big Display at Chicago Show. *The Kalamazoo Gazette*, February 4, 1923.

Interesting Mechanical Details. *Motor World*, February 7, 1923, p. 24.

Fabric Spring Shackles on New Handley Six. *Motor*, February 1923, p. 39.

Handley Introduces Two New Sixes. *Automobile Trade Journal*, February, 1923, pp. 77–78.

Handley Mechanical Details. *Automobile Trade Journal*, February 1923, pp. 45–49.

Handley Specifications. *American Automobile Digest*, April 1923, p. 46.

Checker May Build Handley; Buys Plant. *Motor World*, May 2, 1923, p. 41.

Checker Buys Handley Plant. *Motor Age*, May 3, 1923, p. 31.

Checker Buys Kalamazoo Plants. *Automobile Topics*, May 12, 1923, p. 1228.

Handley Joins Simons in Brooklyn. *Motor World*, August 14, 1924, p. 35.
James I. Handley Obituary. *Automobile Topics*, June 6, 1931, p. 296.

Fig. 30-1. This photograph, often used to portray the early taxi, is believed to have been taken at a Hollywood studio. The vehicle shown is identified by historians as a Model D or E, circa 1923–1924, although one Checker brochure identifies it as a 1926. The car features an open driver's compartment, disk wheels, and painted drum headlights, a style that continues to appear at least through Model F. Note also the elegant coach lamps. The license plate is a 1924 California commercial issue. (NAM)

[There are a limited number of extant photographs of the early Checker cab, so histories of the company tend to use the same images, but opinions differ as to date of manufacture and model type. Five references were used to identify the Checker models. These include a brochure published by Checker Motors Corporation, Rod Walton's article in the Cars & Parts Annual, *John Heilig's history in* Automobile Quarterly, *Stanley Yost's history in* Car Classics, *and Kimes and Clark's* Standard Catalog of Cars. *Differences among these publications are noted, and dates of manufacture are cited as approximations (e.g. circa 1925–1926) to include the citations in these various references. Almost all of the disagreements among writers concern the 1920s and disappear after 1930.]*

Chapter 30

The Checker Cab

1923–1982

"Operators know it… Drivers know it…
Passengers know it… no other taxicab measures up to a CHECKER."
—Company advertisement

"Morris Markin, president of the Checker Cab Manufacturing Corporation, has enjoyed a meteoric rise, and today heads the largest factory in the United States making taxis exclusively," wrote a reporter for *The Kalamazoo Gazette* on November 23, 1930. The expression "meteoric rise," was also used by the *New York Times*, August 15, 1933, to describe the career of the flamboyant E. L. Cord, a friend and business associate of Markin, who was responsible for the rebirth of the Auburn and fashioned the legendary Cord and Duesenberg automobiles, creating one of the most powerful transportation conglomerates of the 1930s. Ultimately he purchased Checker, preventing others from wresting control of the company from Markin. Indeed, Markin's rise in the industry was "meteoric," but the road from Russia to Kalamazoo was not an easy one.

The Markin saga began in Smolensk, Russia, where, at the age of twelve, he started working in the city's largest commission house and within six years was managing the distribution of foodstuffs, produce, and dry goods. In 1912 he immigrated to the United States, landing at Ellis Island. According to his own report, he had only a $1.65 in his pocket. He persuaded a janitor at Ellis to post his $25 immigration bond, an amount that could not have been considered a casual loan at the time. His ability to obtain money from the janitor, who must have encountered scores of financially troubled immigrants, was impressive. He made his way across the country to Chicago where two uncles were living and there busied himself with odd jobs. He secured work through an advertisement in a Chicago paper that called for "an errand boy who could speak Russian and was interested in learning to be a tailor." Reportedly within a year he had earned enough to bring his parents, seven brothers, and two sisters from Russia to Chicago. In his book on E. L. Cord, Cliff Borgeson commented on Markin's secretiveness and his astounding ability to gather money in a

Fig. 30-2. Note the bullet-shaped headlights on this model with painted body and nickel trim. Walton, along with Kimes and Clark, identifies this car as a 1922 Model C, agreeing with one Checker publication, although another company brochure identifies it as a 1926 model. (NAM)

short period. In 1918, just six years after his own arrival and immediately after bringing his family to this country, Markin and a brother had sufficient capital to open their own tailor shop, a business that remained in the Markin family at least through the 1960s. He later bragged that they made the best pants in the world.

The growth of his wealth was both impressive and rapid, and in the winter of 1920, just eight years after landing at Ellis Island, he formed the Checker Taxi Cab Company of Chicago. Subsequently, he established the Markin Body Company in Chicago, Illinois, for the purpose of manufacturing the special bodies for the Checker Cabs used by his taxi company. According to his own report, he had loaned $15,000 to a business associate to build the taxi bodies, but when the business did not meet his expectations, he assumed control of the company. He contracted with the Partin-Palmer Company in Joliet, Illinois, to build the chassis and running gear and to complete the final assembly of the Checker vehicle. This company built the Partin-Palmer and then the Commonwealth automobile, and, by tracing a complex history, Stanley Yost has shown connections with the former De Schaum Motor Buggy, the Suburban Limited, and the Seven Little Buffalos automobiles. In spite of the colorful history, and the heavy-duty construction featuring a chrome-nickel alloy steel frame, five-inch channel sections, and heavily reinforced frames, the sturdy but unimaginative Commonwealth did not sell well. Because of the disappointing sales Markin assumed control of the company in October of 1921. A month later he hired Leonard Goodspeed as his vice-president of engineering. Goodspeed, former head of engineering at the Barley Company in Kalamazoo, had set the land-speed record in a Rochester-Duesenberg-powered Roamer at Daytona in 1921 and had also designed and built the Goodspeed, a beautiful car on a 124" wheelbase, trimmed in mahogany and leather, and powered by a remarkably quiet four-cylinder engine. At least four of these cars were built and shown nationally, and under Markin's direction, the Goodspeed was to be marketed by the Commonwealth Company.

Neither the sturdy Commonwealth nor the luxurious and attractive Goodspeed offered a promise of profitability, and the solid and reliable Commonwealth cab subsequently evolved into the Checker. In the spring of 1922, Markin moved quickly, asking that a receiver be appointed for the Commonwealth Company and that the Checker Cab Manufacturing Company be formed. The facilities, assets, debts, and most of the personnel from Commonwealth were assigned to the new company, and 25,000 shares of stock were offered to the public to raise operating capital. In the midst of his challenging reorganization, however, Markin was charged and then convicted of falsely listing the assets of the Checker Cab Manufacturing Company for the purpose of selling stock. He subsequently received a pardon from the courts for this charge, but the legal process had to have been a drain on his strength and his financial resources.

As 1923 opened, the story is clouded by the variety of reasons tendered for the company's move from Joliet, Illinois to Kalamazoo, Michigan, but what is known is that by July of that year Checker cabs were being manufactured at the Kalamazoo site that had previously housed the Handley-Knight Company and the Dort Body Company. Markin's own story of the move to Kalamazoo differs from other renditions, and he places the "blame" on Leland F. Goodspeed. Markin later claimed in a *Kalamazoo Gazette* interview, November 4, 1962, that he wanted Goodspeed as his chief engineer so badly that he moved the entire operation to Kalamazoo just to please him. Unfortunately Goodspeed died in 1925, two years after the move, at the wheel of a high-powered automobile on a rural Pennsylvania road just outside Pittsburgh.

The early twenties were turbulent times in Chicago, and the taxi business was highly competitive. Vicious fistfights among cabbies and violence between companies were not uncommon. The competition between the independent Checker Taxi and rival Yellow Taxi, then owned by John Hertz for whom the Hertz Rental Car Company is named, resulted in the bombing of Markin's home. Some writers claim that the intensity of this competition, with vague references to possible social persecution, was the reason for Checker's departure from Chicago. Eventually, after Hertz retired, Markin purchased Yellow Cab of Chicago and then gained control of the Parmalee Transportation Company in 1930, thus ending the competition among these giants of the streets. The Parmalee Company continued under Markin's company supervision well after World War II and was a major market for cabs of the Checker Cab Manufacturing Company. Parmalee carried passengers and baggage between railroad stations and hotels in Chicago and later to O'Hare and Midway airports. The company also operated taxi cabs in New York, Pittsburgh, and Minneapolis.

After leaving Illinois in April of 1923, the Checker Cab Manufacturing Company of Joliet completed negotiations with the Handley Motor Car Company for the purchase of the main factory (a facility measuring 800' x 80'), the adjoining power plant, and thirty-eight acres of land on North Pitcher Street. The vacant building owned by Dort, and previously owned by the Lull Carriage Company, was also purchased. The four-story Dort facility, comprising 200,000 square feet of

Fig. 30-3. A photograph of the Checker assembly line, circa 1924, showing the final match between body and chassis. Note the distinctive Checker belting, a registered trademark won in a court fight with Yellow Cab. (DOL)

space, was considered by automobile engineering experts to be one of the best arranged and equipped body plants in the industry. Local papers reported that Checker Cab Manufacturing Company had $1 million in the bank and purportedly paid $670,000 for the Dort plant, but Handley did not disclose the price paid for his plant. While he had hoped that Checker might continue to manufacture the Handley car, its production ceased after the plant was sold.

Orders for Checker cabs during that first year in Kalamazoo continued to outstrip production, and the following fall Checker took over the Scott machine shop at 432 West Main Street. Harry Scott had built the Wolverine there, and now, under his direction, the facility was reopened to produce component parts for Checker cabs on an around-the-clock schedule.

The easy transition for Morris Markin from cloth seams to metal welds is an impressive accomplishment and one not duplicated elsewhere in the industry. The automobile industry was dominated by men possessing mechanical expertise with sewing machines, bicycles, and horse-drawn vehicles. In a 1962 interview with the *Kalamazoo Gazette*, Markin admitted that he was dragged into the business to protect his investment, confessing, "I knew as much about the automobile then as I know about what's going on in heaven."

Despite Morris Markin's testimonials to his ignorance of the business, in the span of a few short years he established a taxi company, acquired an automobile body company, organized an automobile manufacturing company, purchased two factories in Kalamazoo, and then moved the entire operation from Joliet to the new site. All this activity was completed under the duress of a conviction (and subsequent pardon) for falsely listing company assets, a vicious taxi war with Hertz and Yellow Cab, and then a court fight with Yellow Cab Manufacturing to protect the checkerboard belting on Checker taxis as a trademark of the company. Few men in the industry had survived as much in such a short span of time.

Checker's success has less to do with luck than with the manufacture of a well-built product. These were difficult times when many manufacturers were closing their doors. Roamer was a prime example of the faltering industry: a company whose Pennant cab failed, in spite of enormous initial success, at the same time the Checker blossomed. Production of the Checker in Kalamazoo climbed quickly, reaching approximately one hundred cabs per month. Even in those early years when there were a number of companies building taxi cabs, Markin's vehicles earned a reputation for quality of manufacture and longevity of service, with reports of Checkers covering 140,000 miles with no signs of severe wear under the worst "stop-and-start" conditions imaginable.

Markin was tenacious in his quest for quality, and even toward the end of his career he might often be found on the Checker production line attempting to solve a problem. Various interviews reported him down on the production floor in pin stripe suit, felt hat, and work gloves pulling pieces of metal together while gesturing directions to the nearby welders. "Oh," said his son on one of these occasions, "Father is wearing his 'dammit' look," referring to his father's tendency to solve problems when they arose. He would often stop the line, idling an entire shift of workers to find the solution to a production problem or to find the bug that had crept into a new welding gun.

"We have been shut down in the past for two weeks, and we have made changes," he once commented in the 1962 *Kalamazoo Gazette* interview, "We don't know how these will work until we try them, but if they are wrong, I want them made right or I'll shut down everything until they are right.... I'm not a boss... I don't want to be. I do demand what's coming and they know it. I can't be fooled by the men on the line or by the engineers."

His rise from tailor to industrial giant was remarkable, and by 1962 Markin was president of Checker Motors Corporation, chairman of Parmalee Transportation Company, chairman of General Fire and Casualty Company, and sole owner of Checker Taxi Company of Chicago. There were 135,000 taxis on the Chicago streets in 1962, and 26 percent of them carried the Checker nameplate. Markin was also quoted in the 1962 *Gazette* interview as saying, "If I were someone else and read the story of my life, I'd say 'the s.o.b is a liar.'"

The first Kalamazoo-built Checker rolled off the line on July 15, 1923 and W. L. Kroneberger, sales manager for Checker, predicted that production between July 1923 and January 1924 would exceed $6 million. The first cab had the traditional checkered belting below the windows, the company's exclusive trademark. Its five-passenger body was built on a 117" chassis and equipped with a "Checker designed" four-cylinder Buda engine with a semi-force feed oil system. The universal joints were products of Blood Brothers Machine Company in nearby Allegan and the steering gear was from the Reed Foundry and Machine Company just south of the city. Initially the bodies were built by the Automotive Sheet Metal Company on Factory Street, until the body division for Checker could be organized. Other components were from well-known manufacturers: magnetos from Bosch, carburetors from Zenith, and a Westinghouse generator with a new type of lubricating system designed by Leonard Goodspeed. The car was mounted on 33" Budd wheels with 4.5" tires.

Fig. 30-4. While almost all historians agree that this car is a streamlined version of the Model E, this model is designated as a Model F, circa 1925–1926, except by the Standard Catalog of Cars *that lists it as an "E". The car is distinguished by an open driver's compartment, slanted windshield, triangular side window, and sloping hood. This model was powered by a four-cylinder Buda engine. (NAM)*

In 1924, for the first time ever, cab manufacturing companies were allowed to display their wares at the New York Auto Show. In the southwest corner of the Field Artillery Armory Checker Cab joined Premier, Dodge, Pennant, Rauch and Lang, Reo, Yellow and Willys-Overland to display its vehicles. A writer for *Motor Age* commented about the cabs, "There are no evidences that the four-wheel brake epidemic has obtained a foothold in this field, but there is one case of balloon tires...." At the time there was some fear that the superiority of four-wheel brakes endangered passengers, with quick stops that might throw the unwary individual against the dash resulting in injury. Four-wheel brakes were on display in 1924, and, in spite of the fear, shortly thereafter four-wheel brakes for taxis became law in New York City.

By the spring of 1924, the Checker company employed 350 to 375 people, was building one hundred cabs a week, and had introduced its product into one hundred cities across the country. A deal to supply taxis to Fuller Taxicab Company in Los Angles and a commitment by a banking group to provide $4 million for chattel mortgages on cabs—thus guaranteeing the ability of companies to purchase from Checker—placed the company in a strong position for the latter part of the decade. During this period the cab bodies were built in the old Dort plant and the final car assembly was completed in the old Handley-Knight plant. In 1930 a new facility was constructed on North Pitcher Street, adjacent to the Handley-Knight plant, and the old Dort plant was sold.

Fig. 30-5. There is general consensus among historians who use this image that it is a Model F, circa 1924–1926. Yost alone identifies this particular model as an experimental vehicle using a short wheel base and a Waukesha engine. He claims that only one was built. (NAM)

Fig. 30-6. Most historians agree that this model was introduced in 1927 and is designated as Model G-4 when built on a 117" wheel base and powered by a four-cylinder engine; when built on a 124¾" wheel base and powered by a six-cylinder engine, it is designated as a G-6, introduced that year. A company brochure sets the date for this model as 1924. This photograph must have been taken outside of the factory shortly after manufacture, as the headlamps have not yet been attached to the car. (NAM)

Fig. 30-7. This image is not a company photograph but a snapshot taken by one of the employees of the company. The cab is believed to be a G-5, the odd number designating a limousine body. One wonders about the story behind having your picture taken in a Checker cab. (KLM)

Fig. 30-8. All writers agree that this is a Model K or K-6, circa 1927, which was supplied with hydraulic four-wheel brakes. This version is completely enclosed, with a glass partition between the driver and the passenger, and is conservatively finished. Note the identification light at the top of the radiator shell, and that the front door is not a "suicide" type; it has hinges, rather than the handle, at the leading edge. The small script on the rear door reads "Quaker City Cabs," a company that was owned by the Philadelphia Rapid Transit Company. (NAM)

In 1926 the company built the first of two known open cars: a special roadster intended for advertising the official *Automobile Blue Books,* publisher of one of the primary travel directories of the period. This model was an attractive two-seat roadster built on the taxi cab chassis with the same hood and fenders as the commercial vehicle. It was probably a one-of-a-kind model built explicitly for this purpose. The second open car was built on the A2 chassis in 1950 and shown in Switzerland. Whether these two customized Checkers survive is unknown.

The Checker cabs were of a very similar design throughout the 1920s, although vehicle size gradually increased during the decade as the wheel base was stretched five inches from 117" to 122". At the end of that decade, the company was building massive cars, with vertical radiators, low windshields, and flared front fenders of "classic era" design, a style that continued into the 1940s. The handsome Model K, trimmed with optional chrome accessories or in a conservative finish, sold well enough to maintain the company's ledger on the positive side during the late 1920s. By the end of the decade, Checker had also acquired Checker Sales Corporation in New York City, and of the 21,000 cabs on the city streets, over one third wore the Checker nameplate. The company appeared to be in a strong position when the country's financial markets collapsed in October 1929, sending the nation into the Great Depression.

Fig. 30-9. In late 1929, Checker began construction of additional manufacturing facilities east of the Handley-Knight plant. The new buildings were designed by Albert Kahn and tied to the existing facilities by a bridge. Kahn was a famous industrial architect and is credited with designing 20 percent of the commercial buildings in this country, including the Packard Automobile plant; Ford Motor Company's Highland Park and River Rouge plants; the General Motors office building; and the Fisher building, often cited as Detroit's largest art object. The Detroit Free Press *and the* Kalamazoo Gazette *buildings are also Kahn's work. This photograph was taken January 21, 1930, and construction at Checker was completed in June of the same year. (GCA)*

Checker survived the initial economic crash by introducing several new vehicles that attracted the attention of cab companies in New York and Chicago and maintained sales. The Model M limousine, introduced in November of 1930, was a handsome vehicle that rivaled Packard, Cadillac, Stutz, and other cars that would later be designated classics of this era. The stylish hood tapered forward giving the appearance of speed and had a trimness of line seldom seen in commercial vehicles. The fenders were open in front, and flared back and away from the bold radiator. The polished nickel radiator harmonized with the finish on the driving lamps and matched the other hardware on the vehicle. The seating was genuine leather and the cushions were filled with down that the driver could "fluff" with a special paddle after each fare. The six-cylinder Buda engine provided ample power.

In a subsequent attempt to bolster sales the company offered a new style of convertible, perhaps the first modern station wagon, in the summer of 1931. The car resembled the typical sedan of the era with a roof line extending over the rear wheels, but it could be converted from a nine-passenger automobile to a closed sedan-delivery vehicle by folding the seat backs flat and creating ample space for freight. It was big news across the country and was advertised as a model that could be used as a delivery car during the week and a pleasure car on the weekends, or as a delivery vehicle, "where the use of an ordinary truck is objectionable." It was a utility car for "the estate," and sold for $1,795 f.o.b. Kalamazoo.

Fig. 30-10. Most historians identify this image as a Model M, and Heilig, Yost, and Checker agree that this particular vehicle was a special bullet-proof limousine ordered by Samuel Insull. According to Heilig, the steel could withstand the impact of a bullet from a 30-30 rifle and the windows were 1½" thick armored glass. The armored features added 1,500 pounds to the car. About a year after he took delivery, Insull fled to Europe to escape charges of fraud and embezzlement. Reportedly, the car disappeared. (NAM).

In 1925, Yellow Cab Manufacturing merged with General Motors Truck to form the Yellow Cab and Coach Division. Ackerson reports that when General Motors tried unsuccessfully to interest Checker in Yellow Cab in 1930, they changed the name from Yellow to General. Walton notes that Checker reported a profit in May 1931 of $665, and meager as it was, it attracted General Motors to the New York City market. The General Cab was offered to New York cabbies for a down payment of $360, but Ackerson claims that the General was poorly designed and drivers quickly returned to Checker. While General failed, Checker Cab Manufacturing received a contract to built one thousand vehicles for Chicago Yellow Cab Company for a modest profit estimated at $400,000.

Checker continued to develop new models in the early 1930s, and the popular Checker Model M was restyled and introduced as the Model T. As with its predecessor, it was very well received. In January 1933 with orders on the rise, the Checker company recalled five hundred laid-off workers, but in spite of its stylish vehicles, and acceptance by the cab companies, sales and business profits during this period began to dwindle. The Checker production line, once described as a "merry-go-round" rivaling the finest of Rube Goldberg designs, lay idle for weeks in 1932 and 1933. The company's deficit grew to $821,105, and many of the company directors blamed Markin for the company's difficulties. The economy was still depressed, profits were down, and cab fares were being cut by one quarter in New York City and other municipalities. Morris Markin was in trouble.

Markin needed to take charge of the company if he was to survive as president, and he purchased options on as much outstanding Checker stock as he could find. These options may have

Fig. 30-11. In 1931 Checker introduced the first suburban which was advertised as a vehicle that could be converted from car to light truck, "particularly when delivery in the neighborhood by truck was inappropriate." The introduction was sensational, with newspaper announcements throughout the midwest and in the east. It was a beautiful vehicle, offering style, reliability, and conversion convenience. A similar image appeared in the July 4, issue of Automobile Topics *for 1931. (DOL).*

totaled as much as 60 percent of the available stock, and most of what he purchased was stock owned by DuPont family members who had purchased a controlling interest in Checker Cab Manufacturing Company in 1930. The stock activity reverberated within the industry, and company directors soon discovered Markin's purchase and his obvious plan to gain total control of the company.

On August 4, 1933, the company's board of directors fired Markin and appointed C. A. Weymouth as president of Checker. Markin was in danger of losing his company, and the board's plan to wrest control from him might have worked if it had not been for the help of the exuberant Errett Lobban Cord. Most historians surmise that Markin did not have the funds to exercise the options on the DuPont-owned Checker stock, and without help his presidency was lost. Markin turned to E. L. Cord and was able to convince him to finance the options that Markin held and thereby purchase the controlling shares of Checker stock. The purchase was identified by *The Kalamazoo Gazette* on August 15, 1933 as an acquisition from the DuPont family and from John J. Raskob, who owned about 200,000 shares of Checker stock. The cost to Cord was never divulged, but was rumored to be less than $1 million, while Checker assets at the time were estimated at $4,546,000. For the moment, Cord was triumphant and Markin had found a safe haven.

Fig. 30-12. The Model T, a reworked Model M according to Walton, offered elegant classic lines with cutaway fenders, sporty windshield and disc wheels. This model was powered by an eight-cylinder Lycoming engine rated at ninety-eight horsepower, and was introduced in the early 1930s, although the exact date varies among historians. The open fender is believed to reflect the design influence of the engineers at the Cord company. (NAM)

The basis for the association between Markin and Cord is not obvious from historical writings. Markin began as an errand boy and Cord as a dishwasher and perhaps this small similarity in their background constituted the basis of their eventual friendship. Heilig, in his history of the Checker Company, surmises that Markin-Cord connection was tied to Markin's purchase of Cord-owned Lycoming engines that were introduced on the Model M Checker cab in 1932. Whatever the basis for the relationship, Cord's purchase of Checker was not largess but just another piece in Cord's jigsaw-puzzle transportation conglomerate. On August 3, 1933, at the age of 38, E. L. Cord was head of the Cord Corporation, and he controlled Auburn Automobile Company, Duesenberg Incorporated, Stinson Aircraft Corporation, Columbia Axle Company, Lycoming (Engine) Manufacturing Company, the Aviation Corporation, American Airways, and New York Shipbuilding, in addition to Checker. It is not surprising to find that, during this period, Lycoming engines and Columbia axles were used in Checker cabs and that American Airways flew planes built by Aviation Corporation. Cord was a very powerful influence in the transportation industry of this country, appearing on the cover of *Time* on January 18, 1932 and April 23, 1934. His association with Markin is an important piece of the history of Checker.

Within ten days after the stock purchase, Cord reinstated Markin as president of Checker Cab Manufacturing, giving Markin control of his company under Cord's oversight. Members of the

Fig. 30-13. The photograph of this 1936 Model Y was taken at the Checker factory in Kalamazoo, circa 1944. The chassis has been lengthened extending the flow of the body lines and the roof has been raised. There is a single rear-entrance door on the beautifully finished wood body. The use of the 1936 model and the Illinois license plate on the back of the car (shown in another unpublished photo) suggests that it is a concept vehicle for a postwar aerobus that an independent manufacturer had brought to the factory in hopes of selling the design. (DOL)

board for Checker included E. L. Cord, Markin, Lucius Manning of the Cord Corporation, and Ralph. E. Oakland, vice-president of Checker. With the acquisition, Cord interests then controlled three concerns in Kalamazoo: Checker Cab, the Limousine Body Company, and the air mail operators through American Airways. For the moment, Markin's presidency was secure, but Checker Cab Manufacturing Company remained in financial jeopardy for the remainder of the decade.

On May 25, 1936, Markin and Cord announced what *Time* identified as a "curious syndicate agreement," since Markin owned only 6,500 shares of the 64,000 shares of stock held by the massive Cord conglomerate. According to the two men, the agreement created a pool of stock intended as a portfolio for investing in Checker Cab, or "securities of other taxi or allied companies, including Chicago Yellow Cab and Parmalee." The Cord corporation was the source of most of the capital, but the May 1936 *Time* report inferred some uncertainty in the relationship between the two men by claiming that the agreement included "elaborate provisions to keep the two members from chiseling each other."

An investigation of the financial records of Checker as well as the other companies under the Cord umbrella by the Securities Exchange Commission followed shortly thereafter. Press reports indicate that the SEC spent a quarter of a millon dollars on the investigation and that Checker Cab was a major point of the investigation. In fact, Markin was the target of the same accusations of stock manipulation that were made against Cord in the SEC investigation.

John T. Flynn described the problem concisely in the *New Republic*, August 25, 1937:

Fig. 30-14. The series Y was introduced in 1935 and was well received by the industry. Reportedly, 980 examples were built during the first three months of production. The photograph was taken in front of the home still standing at 2003 Oakland Drive in Kalamazoo. (NAM)

> *Recently the SEC filed a complaint alleging that Cord and Mr. Morris Markin, president of the Checker Cab Manufacturing Company, were manipulating the stocks of the Checker Cab Manufacturing Company, the Parmalee Transportation Company and the New York and Chicago Yellow Cab Company....*

In brief, Cord and Markin acquired 70,000 shares of the Checker Cab—to take a single instance—at $7.00 per share. During the operation they created fictitious activity in the shares and sold 6,000 of them at $59.00 a share.

The charges claimed, according to Cliff Borgeson in his history of E. L. Cord, that "through manipulative techniques, between that date (November 7, 1935) and July 21, 1936, the defendants succeeded in provoking 59,900 shares' worth of Checker activity, and in driving the price from $7 to $69.50." Checker stock fell to $45.00 that summer and in the autumn of 1936 Markin and Cord were responsible for most of the 10,700 shares that were traded, causing a second run from $36 to $55 and then to $68 on October 22, 1936. The two men then attempted to register a two-for-one split in the stock, but the action was disapproved by the New York Stock exchange. The stock, with subsequent infrequent sales, plummeted to $14.12 on June 18, 1937. In essence, the SEC charged that "the two men had released stock on the market in a manner to effectuate an increase in price and that the two had conspired to spread rumors of a future Checker dividend."

The SEC's position was that industrial executives had no business serving as their own stock brokers, although it was a traditional practice at the time among many of the powerful manufacturing leaders in this country. Cliff Borgeson went so far as to suggest that all of the Cord managers had a small salary and earned the majority of their compensation through the manipulation and sale of stock. Since the executives—in this case Cord and Markin—had no SEC license that could be revoked, a consent decree was drawn and signed by each, in which Cord and Markin agreed to obey the law. They denied the accusations of unlawful conduct and reportedly signed the decree "to avoid long and expensive litigation that would result in irreparable damage to their business interests." In fact, the consent decree did not establish guilt, and there is no record of any suit by stockholders against either man that would have suggested guilt. There is also no evidence that their action inflicted financial loss on a third party, although as Cliff Borgeson notes, unknown claims may have been settled out of court. The decree simply set forth a document that would not allow escape from a penalty for any future violations under the guise that either Cord or Markin did not understand the law. In essence, the decree was "fair warning" of potential criminal charges in the event of any future indiscretions and attempts at manipulation in the stock market.

In August of 1937, Flynn's article in the *New Republic* offered the following social criticism about Cord, but did not directly implicate Markin. He wrote in part:

> *...people have an open admiration for fellows like the Cords. The moral values of their conduct did not interest the public. What interested the public was the enormous success in dollars and cents which attended their adventures. Cord belongs to that even larger group whose members believe that the corporations which they dominate are mere counters in the great gambling game of industry.*

Apparently it was all too much for Cord, who sold his interest in the corporation to a group of New York bankers. Some historians suggest that he "retired," but the circumstances suggest that he was forced out of a corporation that bore his name and was valued at $17 million in 1936. Lou Manning was one of the major participants in this group of bankers and was on the board of the Cord conglomerate as well as Checker Cab Manufacturing Company. He claimed responsibility for Cord's expansion into aeronautics and had little interest—some claim an actual abhorrence—for automobile manufacture. Cliff Borgeson records the following comment by Donn Hogan:

> *The first thing Lou Manning did was shut down the automotive division, because he hated the car-manufacturing business. As long as Cord was there he couldn't do it, because Cord liked cars. The thing was shut down arbitrarily by one man, because he didn't want to continue making them. It was not a case of the Depression being responsible at all.*

Perhaps Cord "retired" from the company, but the "folklore" of those last days suggests otherwise. According to Borgeson, Cord's son met his father in the parking lot of the American Airlines building in Chicago, and the son remembers the encounter as follows:

> *He told me that he had sold out, that no one knew where he was, and that he was leaving. He didn't tell me where he was going, but he said 'You'll know where to get me,' and I knew he was going to LA. I learned later that he went to Harold Ames' apartment on the North Shore. He gave Harold some cash and sent him out to buy a new Lincoln Zephyr. And he and Harold got in the car and drove to LA."*

Harold did not know it at the time, but a suitcase with $2.6 million in certified checks lay on the back seat of the Lincoln. Cord never returned to the automobile business and spent the rest of his life in Reno, Nevada. He was elected to the state senate in 1956 and died in 1974 at the age of 79.

The importance of the Cord story with its travails is its contrast to the surprisingly different outcome for Markin, whose close business association with Cord involved him and the Checker company in the disruptions within the Cord empire. In May of 1936 Cord and Markin had filed a "syndicate agreement" for the purpose of stock investment and within eighteen months, under pressure from the SEC and New York bankers, E. L. Cord, one of the most powerful men in the automobile industry, was out of the conglomerate that he had painstakingly formed. In January 18, 1932, *Time* described his presence in the following terms:

> *Not since Walter P. Chrysler strode into business for himself and built up the Chrysler Corporation to compete with General Motors all along the line, has the motor industry felt a new presence so definitely as it now feels Errett Lobban Cord's.*

The news in business periodicals of the era about Markin's fate was minimal. Somehow through all of this financial complexity, the SEC investigation, and the turmoil at the Cord Corporation, Markin miraculously survived the convoluted and bizarre circumstances and retained his presidency of Checker Cab Manufacturing Company. With E. L. Cord gone, Manning, a member of the board of directors, was in control of Checker Cab Manufacturing Company at the time of this debacle. Perhaps in the final hour Cord was able to cut a deal for Markin, or perhaps Manning wanted to rid himself of the Checker Cab Manufacturing company since it created little business opportunity beyond vehicle manufacture and taxi conveyance that Manning purportedly disdained. Cord had originally purchased the Checker stock on Markin's behalf. In the final hour, however, Markin apparently had sufficient resources, possibly money made in the market, to purchase the controlling stock of the Checker Cab Manufacturing company, or was granted a buy-out for other reasons.

The events of the mid 1930s and Markin's association with E. L. Cord, once again gave credence to Markin's wary comment in 1962, "If I was someone else and read the story of my life, I'd say 'the s.o.b is a liar.'"

Morris Markin had barely settled his life's routine after the incident with Cord and the closure of the Auburn-Cord-Duesenberg plant in Auburn, Indiana, when the bombs fell on Pearl Harbor and once again interrupted his manufacturing plans. Even before this nation entered World War II, the United States Army sought competitive bids for the manufacture of a small utility scout car. American Bantam, Willys-Overland, and Ford responded, and from this competition, with Willys as the ultimate winner, came the most famous vehicle of the war: the Army Jeep. Historians' tales of Checker's involvement in the Army's procurement of the Jeep are fraught with disagreement.

On June 19, 1940 representatives from the Army, the Cavalry, and the Office of the Quartermaster General met with engineers of the American Bantam Automobile company in Butler, Pennsylvania to discuss the applicability of the Bantam chassis for a planned quarter-ton command-reconnaissance vehicle. In the summer of 1940 Bantam's first reconnaissance vehicle was successfully tested at the Quarter Master's Holabird Depot, and in July 1940, the company was awarded a contract to built seventy vehicles, all constructed essentially by hand. In spite of Bantam's initial and successful development of the Jeep concept to meet the exacting military specifications, the ensuing government competitive bid process enticed Willys-Overland in Toledo, Ohio to enter the fray. Willys had been discussing with army officials the manufacture of military vehicles since

Fig. 30-15. The company's unique role in the production of taxicabs built specifically for commercial transport was reflected in the production of the Model A. Manufacture began in 1938 and continued until factory production was converted to support the war effort in 1942. There was nothing else like it on the city streets. The Model A featured "suicide doors," both front and rear, rakish "cutaway fenders," and a unique padded convertible canopy over the passenger seat. The Model A was powered by a six-cylinder Continental engine rated at eighty-horsepower and Yost claims that many logged over one million miles during World War II. Note the Checker design on the hubcaps. (NAM)

1938. Amid subsequent arguments about vehicle weight, cost, delivery schedules, and rights to postwar markets, the giant Ford Motor Company also entered the competition. At the direction of the quartermaster, American Bantam, Willys-Overland, and Ford each built 1,500 vehicles in the spring of 1941. After further evaluation the procurement contract for 16,000 vehicles went to the Willys-Overland that summer. Bantam, in spite of its initial development program, was not considered capable of meeting production demands because of its lack of industrial facilities and minimal financial foundation. In addition, the decision makers believed that the Bantam facilities could best be used for non-automotive production.

In the spring and summer of 1941 when the competitive process was at its height, Checker Cab also submitted a bid of $736.53 for each of 16,000 vehicles, the lowest of the four companies. According to Rifkind, however, the bid "was given scant consideration because of the excessive delivery time required—almost nine months after the date of award." That initial bid was the last of the documented involvement of Checker. Although both Ford and Bantam continued to pursue the subsequent contracts for the Jeep, only Ford was successful in gaining a contract in 1942 to manufacture a Jeep using the Willys-Overland specifications.

Checker Cab entered the picture again, apparently, in the spring of 1942. When Bantam ini-

Fig. 30-16. Checker began the cutaway styling on the front fenders in the early 1930s, when similar styling was popular on many cars from Auburn to Pierce Arrow. Checker continued this styling in its prewar Model A, long after all other major makes showed a fender treatment completely covering the front wheel. Note the placement and the art deco style of the headlight, the checker board design on the eyebrow above the lamp, the chromed flat stock used as bumper guards, and the simple wire mesh grill and hood ventilation louvers. (DOL)

tially built the first seventy Jeeps in July 1940, eight of these vehicles were equipped with four-wheel steering. Subsequent to losing the contract for the conventional front-steer Jeep to Willys-Overland, Bantam tried to interest the United States Cavalry in the four-wheel steer vehicle they initially built, and a contract for six thousand of these vehicles was written. Sometime during the period from about July 1940 to March 1942 three of these four-wheel steer vehicles were delivered to Checker Cab Manufacturing in Kalamazoo, although the source of the order for the delivery is unknown. There was considerable discussion about these vehicles between and among American Bantam, the Quarter Master Technical committee, the United States Cavalry and members of both houses of Congress. The diversion of these three vehicles to Kalamazoo and their subsequent evaluation could have benefitted the procurement interests of any one of these parties. There was much disagreement among these parties, dependent, of course, upon the degree and direction of their support for the manufacture of this vehicle. These issues included the complexity of manufacture, increased maintenance, decreased interchangeability of parts, and apparent hazards to the occupants in a vehicle with an eleven-foot turning radius. One writer described the four-wheel steer Jeep as "the closest thing on the ground to piloting an airplane."

Fig. 30-17. A single day's production of the Checker Model A, circa 1939, showing forty cars and two buses outside of the Checker plant. This model is seldom, if ever, seen in film or advertisements from the era. (DOL)

There are three major authors of Checker history written for well-known periodicals: John Heilig, writing for *Automobile Quarterly*; Rod Walton, curator at Checker, writing for *Cars and Parts;* and Stanley Yost, who spent considerable time at the plant preparing for his history that appeared in *Car Classics*. Only Yost mentions the four-wheel steer Jeep and identifies it with a photograph as an experimental product of Checker. There is a general lore in the company, although admittedly unsubstantiated by company records, that Checker built a four-wheel steer Jeep as a part of the procurement competition, fueling some uncertainty about the vehicle's heritage.

According to the descendants of Jim Stout, director of experimental vehicles at Checker during this period, the Jeeps that were delivered to Checker were tested, dismantled, parts tested again, and then reassembled in the Kalamazoo plant, creating the impression, perhaps, for all those who witnessed the reassembly that the vehicle was built by Checker. Contrary to conflicting reports the documented history of the Jeep's pedigree makes clear that Checker Cab Manufacturing never built a Jeep, but that the four-wheel steer vehicle was built by Bantam and shipped to Kalamazoo for evaluation. An example of this four-wheel steer Bantam with Checker nomenclature on the instruments survives at the Gilmore Car Museum in Hickory Corners, Michigan.

Jim Stout's daughter reports that one of these Jeeps was used around the plant for snowplowing and delivery work while another found its way to the Stout residence, where it became a central part of the "war-games" typically played by youngsters at the time. One can only imagine the expressions of surprise when bystanders saw the vehicle running cross-country on the Stout farm. The Jeep was not the only vehicle in the Stout automotive menagerie and the children were often reluctant passengers in various experimental cars that Jim drove in and around Kalamazoo. His daughter still recalls the teasing she got from her school friends about her father's novel vehicles.

Fig. 30-18. The photograph of this 1939 Model A Checker cab was taken in New York City, circa April 1948. Its ragged appearance seems to affirm Yost's estimate that many of these cabs logged over one millon miles during the period of the war economy from 1940 to 1948. (JCC)

Prior to World War II, Checker Cab Manufacturing was building truck cabs for Ford and trailers for Sears Roebuck, and the army commissioned Checker to construct a variety of self-contained trailers in both van and semi-trailer configurations. Huge tank recovery vehicles were also built at the Kalamazoo plant, and reportedly some were so large that a practical method of getting them to the front lines was never devised. The Checker name was not prominent on mechanized equipment during World War II, but the company's contribution to the war effort was substantial.

In spite of his interests in Checker, Markin lived in New York and was not a resident of Kalamazoo until after World War II, when he either purchased or built a home in the 5200 block of North Westnedge Avenue in 1947. The family "estate" was unpretentious in comparison to the living arrangements of other well-known families in the automobile industry. Perhaps it was due to his sense of "form following function," but the house on the 162-acre Markin "estate" was modest, yet comfortable. It was attractively paneled, finished with beam ceilings, and a large fireplace served as the focal point of the living room. A screened porch ran across the south side, and a two-car garage was attached to the west wall. The house, like the Checker car, was neat, functional, and nicely furnished, but without intricate showy detail. Across the street was a small cottage and an attractive wooded area where Morris Markin often entertained in the summer. Elderly neighbors still remember the strings of lights, the gaiety of the guests, and the music of those affairs. Up the hill from the house was another building—reached of course by transport in a Checker—where important visitors to the factory and family guests often stayed. It was a rural area then, a place where young David Markin could shoot blackbirds from the kitchen window without complaint and where crops were raised for commercial sale. Only the main house survives today and much of the land has been reworked. The area is owned by the city of Kalamazoo and was renamed Markin Glen Park in 1994.

Al Barberry worked at the Checker plant in those days and was a personal aid to Morris Markin, serving both as chauffeur on business trips and tractor driver on the small farm across from Markin's residence. After Al graduated from high school, he worked at an apple distribution center outside of Kalamazoo. When the season ended, the foreman, expressing an interest in what Al planned to do after the apple harvest ended, suggested that he might find work at Checker. According to Al the foreman provided a letter of introduction addressed to Vice-President Oakland at the Checker plant. When Al arrived at the company gate, there was a long line of men seeking jobs. The guard at the gate told him that Mr. Oakland was not there that day, but he would make sure that Oakland got the letter. Letters of introduction were important at the time, and the next Tuesday, Al received a call from the plant with an offer to work on the production line.

After that initial production run was over, Al was offered another job in the shipping department, and eventually worked his way up to a foreman's position as well as becoming Morris Markin's personal aide. Markin was a gentlemen farmer, and Al drew a certain amount of service tilling the fields with the tractor. He became known among some employees as "Mr. Blueberry," a name given apparently in respectful jest rather than out of spite for his favorable position with Markin.

Al served as chauffeur, and often drove Morris Markin to Elkhart, Indiana, where he caught the Twentieth Century Limited to New York. Markin owned two Cord automobiles in the late 1930s and after the war he purchased and drove Cadillacs, perhaps because his own Model A Checkers in 1939 had a distinct commercial appearance and were not well-suited for private use. Markin's choice of the Cadillac that he drove after the war may also explain the design of the postwar Checker that resembles the Cadillac of the 1940s. Markin enjoyed automobiles, and he always drove to the railway station or other destination. Al would ride along to drive the car back to Kalamazoo and then return to the railroad station for Markin on the return trip.

According to Al Barberry, Morris Markin was a good boss, an "old-fashioned" man who believed in rewards. He funded an annual trip for Al to the finest men's store in Kalamazoo and gave him his own personal car when it became available. Markin was also a fast driver; according to Al, "he loved to keep the pedal to floor, but he was not nearly as fast a driver as E. L. Cord." Al likes to reminisce about a trip to Detroit with Cord at the wheel and he admits he was scared most of the time. "I dropped him off by the river, never saw him again, and drove off about one hundred yards. I sat in the car for a long period to get my composure," he confessed. "I thought Mr. Markin was a fast driver, but Mr. Cord really liked to push it… oh!… was I scared."

Planning and design for the postwar period had continued during the war and involved two lines of experimentation: first a front-engine, front-wheel drive; and second a rear-engine, rear-wheel drive vehicle. Both Stanley Yost and Karl Ludvigsen have chronicled the development of these vehicles that Ludvigsen affectionately characterized as the "Chubby Checkers," with an obvious reference to the renowned and portly singer of the 1950s and the corresponding well-rounded lines of the two vehicles.

Fig. 30-19. The rear engine, rear drive Checker was developed under Herb Snow's supervision, but proved to be ungainly and the project was quickly dropped. (CMC)

Three well-known automobile men were associated with Checker during this period: Herb Snow, one of the few front-wheel drive experts in the United States; Jim Stout, an expert in rear-engine configurations; and Ray Dietrich, the well-known stylist. Dietrich left Chrysler in 1938 after designing the Chrysler Airstream as the replacement to the famous but unsuccessful Airflow. The collaboration of these three men led to some exciting and innovative designs at Checker for the postwar taxi, although none were realized on the production line.

Herb Snow, an acclaimed but unsung contributor to the famous Cord 810, had engineering experience at Peerless, Willys-Overland, Winton, Velie, and Auburn. When the Cord Corporation fell in 1937, he joined the Checker design group. Snow's interest in the unconventional front-wheel drive dated back to the early 1930s, and he wrote the following opinion in an unpublished position paper on alternative drives:

> *A still later variation was the automobile which featured the engine mounted in the front driving the front wheels and another which featured a rear mounted engine driving the rear wheels. These made their appearance at about the same time. While the fight for supremacy was on between the last two types mentioned, the Selden type of transmission drive was brought out and led to our present type of conventional automobile; that is, engine mounted in the front driving the rear wheels.*
>
> *For this reason the Front Engine Mounting and Drive and the Rear Engine Mounting and Drive have not received the whole-hearted support among the designers who, with few exceptions, have followed the trend of the conventional automobile. No doubt if these two types of mountings and drives were given as deep consideration, some very interesting developments would be made.*

Not surprisingly, in the late 1930's a Cord 810 appeared at the Checker plant in Kalamazoo for study and evaluation, and a series of photographs in Snow's file attest to the interest in the concept. Plans for the development of an innovative taxi vehicle, however, were interrupted by the onset of World War II.

In 1936, William Stout built the first rear-engine, rear-drive Stout-Scarab. This vehicle was completely different from anything else on the road, with the exception of Buckminster Fuller's innovative Dymaxion of 1933, and was sold by invitation to a selected list of potential customers. This sleek vehicle with rounded flowing lines was the forerunner of the modern van and, almost ten years later in Kalamazoo, Jim Stout (unrelated to William) built a vehicle with a design and configuration similar to the Scarab. The Checker was an experimental vehicle and as such, did not have the same "finished" appearance as the Scarab. This project was designated at Checker as the Model B, and reportedly two working models were built, but there is no evidence that either survives.

Snow concluded that the rear engine made handling difficult for those accustomed to the geometry of front-mounted engines driving the rear wheels of the vehicle and, according to Snow, a good weight distribution for the vehicle was impossible on the short wheel base. In addition, the vehicle included a rear-facing passenger seat that was found to be objectional by those who rode in the car at the time of the initial test.

After the experimentation with the rear-engine Model B, interest in innovation turned to the front-wheel drive configurations. Ludvigsen, in *Chubby Checkers*, reported that Snow outlined the intent of the prototype program in a memo dated May 10, 1945:

> *The primary purpose of a vehicle of this kind is to carry passengers comfortably and economically. To do this, passengers must be placed in the most advantageous seating and riding position. The vehicle must be light in weight if it is to operate economically. Keeping weight to a minimum means that the entire vehicle must be as compact as possible without any sacrifice in passenger space.*

In the summer of 1945 the design team completed a front-engine, front-wheel drive Checker, designated as the Model D. According to Ludvigsen, two designs—a five-passenger and a seven-passenger vehicle—were completed, and these fully operational prototypes were ready for road-testing in the fall of 1946. The Model D cars were well designed and provided more interior space than the 1946 Ford, although the Ford was six inches longer than the Model D. Styling was by the renowned Raymond H. Dietrich and some of the proposed designs were very sleek, featuring grill bars stretching the length of the hood and a roofline flowing down to the rear bumper. The final Checker prototypes, however, had a chubby appearance and resembled cars in the postwar Chrysler family.

According to Ludvigsen, the seven-passenger Model D design was road tested for more than 35,000 miles and the five-passenger logged more than 65,000 miles in blizzards and adverse road conditions in and around Racine, Wisconsin. Drivers were quoted as saying that the car was "easy to keep on the road, handled well in traffic and on the highway. In heavy blizzards… [i]t performed exceptionally well pulling out from curbs blocked with snow without difficulty."

The industry was stirring in the late 1950s with discussions of flat floors and front-wheel drives appearing in popular automotive periodicals. Reportedly, Ford purchased and restored a front-wheel drive Cord because of its interest in the drive train, and by 1960 *Popular Science* predicted Ford would soon market front-wheel drive cars. In July 1958, *Popular Science* quoted Peter Kyropoulos of General Motors on the subject:

> *The pros and cons of front-wheel drive, as well as the rear engine, have been discussed with more emotion than common sense. Neither arrangement poses insurmountable problems…*

Fig. 30-20. (top) Two models of the front-wheel drive Checker were built and tested under Snow's direction after World War II. The body was designed by Dietrich, who had previously worked at Chrysler. (LLL)

Fig. 30-21. (below) The Checker Cab Manufacturing plant, circa 1946. The original Handley-Knight plant is the long building on the left and is connected by a bridge to the structure designed by Albert Kahn, completed in June 1930 by Ralph Sollitt and Sons, South Bend, Indiana. (GCA)

These various public discussions and the potential application of front-wheel drive for the Checker were of major interest to Herb Snow, who kept meticulous notes about the advantages of alternative drive trains. A memo from Snow to Markin on January 17, 1961 once again stipulated the requirements for a front-wheel drive vehicle in which he noted that a short four-cylinder engine would be required and was not then available in this country. Additional notes in Snow's files after the war cited the German-made DKW as a front-wheel drive exemplar: "Jim, this is the best small car," was scrawled across the page featuring the DKW. Snow was an ardent supporter of the front-wheel drive concept, and perhaps the most knowledgeable man on the subject in the country at that time. His influence at Checker during this period was substantial, but the predicted higher cost of manufacture and maintenance, as compared to conventional taxi cabs, prevented the final development of the project and the manufacture of the front-wheel drive Checker. The postwar rear-wheel drive Checker was well received by the cab companies, and there was probably little pressure from the market place for Markin to begin consideration of a radical new drive train.

The first postwar Checker Cab was the Model A2 and A3, with the odd number designation identifying the limousine version. This car was produced until the middle 1950s and approximately six thousand units were built. The Model A4 followed, with strong beautiful lines not unlike the postwar Cadillac, Morris Markin's personal vehicle of choice. These cars were powered by a Continental engine and offered a flat floor and a turning radius that was four feet less than the competition. A minor facelift for this vehicle featuring a new horizontal grill was introduced in 1953–54 and designated as the A6.

The slab-sided Model A8 was introduced in 1956. Two hundred inches long, seventy-five inches wide and sixty-four inches tall, its 226 cid Continental engine generated eighty-nine horsepower and, given the car's curb weight of 3,720 pounds, offered a moderately slow acceleration rate from zero to fifty miles an hour in 24.2 seconds. City gas mileage was 12.5 miles per gallon and highway mileage about 16.5 miles per gallon. This model, with minor modifications in style and mechanics, defined the Checker cab until its demise some twenty-four years later. The Model A8 was well received by professional drivers, and letters from taxi companies were enthusiastic in their reply to Checker's inquiry about experience with the Model A8 cab:

…we beg to advise you that having over 80 Checkers in our fleet is testimonial to our enthusiasm for "Checkers."

—Radio Flash Cab, Chicago

We have 55 model A-8 Checkers in our operation. 35 cars have been operating for 2 years. Average mileage runs between 140–150,000 miles.

—M&S Maintenance, Brooklyn

The model A-8 Checker I bought in June 1956 is still good for another 2 years. And this after 130,000 miles—double-shifted. I've operated stock cars in the past and I've been in the red. The Checker car has really put me in the black. Checker built this car to last. That's why I don't have to plan on replacing my car for another 2 years.

—Louis Desverges, New York

Consumer Union also purchased and tested a 1958 Checker and, according to Morris Markin,

Fig. 30-22 (top). The A-2, Checker's first postwar production cab, was introduced in 1947. The signs in the "salesroom" at the Checker factory note that the overall length is only 206" and the weight is 3,795 pounds, about nine inches shorter and 700 pounds lighter than the 1946 Cadillac that this model resembles. (NAM)

Fig. 30-23 (below). The A-4 retains the same style as the postwar A series, with fender lines, high hood and massive grill similar to the Cadillac. The view of the home in the background is the south side of the Morris Markin residence on North Westnedge in Kalamazoo. (NAM)

Fig. 30-24 (top). The A-6 was the last of the "Cadillac-style" Checkers. The Cadillac was the car of choice for Morris Markin, and he often drove the same model for several years. This Cadillac-style Checker continued until the mid-1950s. Note the massive bullet-shaped bumper guards, far different from the flat guards on the prewar Model A Checker. (NAM)

Fig. 30-25 (below). The utilitarian A-8 was introduced in 1956 and this particular example shows a two-tone paint job, without the usual taxicab markings. A car very similar to this one was tested by Consumers Union and the rave reviews in Consumer Reports *convinced Morris Markin to develop a product for the consumer market. (NAM)*

Fig. 30-26. The famous Aerobus, the first postwar "stretched automobile" produced in quantity. The twelve-passenger models were popular for carrying airline passengers to and from hotels. (FAM).

as reported in the November 4, 1962 *Kalamazoo Gazette*, the very positive review appearing in *Consumer Reports* that year altered the company's marketing strategy. The report in part stated:

> *CU's reason for testing the* Checker *is a simple one—the car is full of now-vanished utilitarian virtues, like flat floors and high seats, that practical motorists cry aloud for when exposed to modern cars.*
>
> *CU feels that the auto industry, in its 1957 models, has for competitive reasons abandoned the all around type of car. Instead the industry has gone in for power and glamour… the new low cars are… hard to crawl into, hard to struggle out of, hard to house-clean, impossible to wear a hat in. Compared to most 1957 models, the Checker is a walk-in automobile. All four doors are wide, square and about 5 inches greater in height than the doors on most other cars.*
>
> *Its appearance is dignified but not dashing, its level of performance ignominious… it is designed to be economical, durable, comfortable transportation, without frivolity, without any of "geewhiz" styling that stimulates the new car sales and thereafter spends the car's life compounding repair bills.*

The exceptional *CU* review and the article's contrast between the Checker and the claimed dysfunctional glamour of the other 1957 automobiles, made clear to Markin that Checker was not exploiting the family-car market. After thirty-eight years of building automobiles exclusively for the taxi cab market, Morris Markin decided to develop a product for the consumer, and Checker entered the passenger car market in 1959. The Superba was born on June 10, 1959, although delivery was delayed by the only United Auto Workers strike in the company's history, beginning on June 12, 1959 and lasting one hundred days.

The April 1960 *Consumer Reports* again recommended the Checker as "among the most practi-

Fig. 30-27. The 1969 Marathon station wagon was advertised as a "carry-all" vehicle that could pack in a herd of sheep or provide family transportation for a weekend romp. (DOL)

cal and sensible of U.S. cars," but cautioned consumers about the lack of a dealer network. Apparently Markin read this issue also, for he turned his attention to that problem and by November 1962, the company had over two hundred active dealers. The Marathon series was added to the product line in 1961 and subsequently, the Superba nomenclature disappeared.

The Marathon series included a station wagon, a stretched aerobus in a nine- or twelve-passenger configuration, that found various uses from carrying members of the Kalamazoo College tennis team to conveying hotel guests to and from airports across the country. Checker also offered a compact limousine that had an enlarged rear-passenger area and jump seats, and with a glass partition between the chauffeur's compartment and the rear seat. The car was finished in rich gray broadcloth and passenger amenities included air conditioning, radio console, and electric sunroof. These cars were big and comfortable and very popular among the country's ambassadors. The Checker was found in London, Moscow, and thirteen other countries. Mrs. Nelson Rockefeller, and other celebrities used Checkers, as did many financiers, attorneys, and physicians. By 1962, Checker cars for the consumer market accounted for fifteen percent of Checker's production and the decade would prove to be a particularly strong one for Checker.

The advertising campaign for the consumer market was always based on quality and sensibility with never a hint of the glitz or glamour that characterized the offerings of other manufacturers. In an effort to show the load capacity—"the Checker Marathon always seems to have room for one more"—the cargo area of a Marathon station wagon was loaded with a number of full-grown sheep. David Markin had allowed the photographers to use his personal vehicle and the photographers consumed most of a three-day period attempting to coax the animals up a ramp made slippery by a protective plastic covering and into the car's cargo area. The advertising shoot was finally completed and the car returned to the Markin's garage. The plastic covering provided only partial

Fig. 30-28. Checker's advertising campaigns were always conservative, with emphasis upon the quality, driving ease, and reliability of their product. In this photograph, the female model attired in a common sundress sits in an open chassis prepared for the 1969 New York automobile show. Note the chrome valve cover, cooling fan and timing gear cover as well as full chrome hubcaps and white wall tires. This photo portrays the level of "glitz and glamour" in the company's advertising campaign. (FAM)

protection, for David's wife complained that the car recked of sheep and the unrelenting odor could not be removed regardless of the cleanser used. The vehicle was subsequently replaced with another Marathon.

Morris Markin's son David was raised in the Markin residence on north Westnedge and had always been "around the company." When his father died in 1970, David assumed control with hardly a ripple in the operation. Heilig, in his 1992 *Automobile Quarterly* history of Checker, reported that Ed Cole's wife—and Cole was president of General Motors so she had a good appreciation of the automobile industry—characterized David Markin as "tough, and determined—a hard-driving, decision making competitive fighter in the world of business." The turmoil of the 1970s needed such a leader if the company had any chance of surviving, although the overwhelming odds proved to be too much for even a "hard-driving competitor." The government regulation in 1975 led to the addition of massive aluminum bumpers on the Checker to meet the five-mile-an hour crash tests. The bumpers, together with the gas mileage requirements and the gas shortages of the same decade, made obvious the growing obsolescence of the venerable and beloved four-thousand pound Checker automobile.

A six-week long strike in 1973 did not help, and many writers point to that era as the time when

the company began to
falter. Production fell by
75 percent during the
next ten years, while the
country began searching
for answers to the "gas-
mileage" crisis. There
were national competi-
tions for fuel-efficient
cabs, and President
Jimmy Carter proposed
both a government re-
bate of $475 for buying
fuel-efficient cars and a
higher gas tax that even-
tually reached fifty cents
a gallon to penalize the
traditional American
"gas guzzler." General

Fig. 30-29. The slab-sided, practical image of the Checker is reflected here in a
1967 edition parked in front of a movie theater. (FAM)

Motors predicted that within five years, none of its cars would offer V-8 power, as government as
well as public opinion turned against vehicles with inefficient fuel ratings. In an effort to create an
economical taxi, Checker installed diesel power in some 1968 production vehicles, but finally turned
back to the front-wheel drive concepts that Carl Snow had championed just before and following
World War II.

Victor Potamkin, one of General Motors' principal stock holders, had tried on numerous occasions to gain control of Checker through stock acquisitions and had always lost to the united front
of the Markin family. In 1976, however, Potamkin and Edward Cole, former president of General
Motors, gained control of 51.4 percent of Checker stock at a cost of $6 million and planned to
develop a fuel-efficient, front-wheel drive Checker cab.

Cole joined Checker as chairman and chief executive officer with authorization to develop the
front-wheel drive concept. Cole commissioned the design and construction of a stretched version
of the Volkswagen Rabbit. Nineteen inches were added to the vehicle's length and a diesel engine
tucked under the hood. Unfortunately, Cole was killed in a crash of his small twin-engine plane in
a freshly plowed field near Mendon some eighteen miles south of Kalamazoo on May 2, 1977.
There was a heavy rainfall in the area with a three hundred foot cloud ceiling and visibility of about
one mile. Cole was on his way to an important meeting at the Checker plant that day. "We had a
busy week lined up," said Markin, "…and haven't even begun to consider what the loss of Cole will
mean in a business sense." There was no subsequent report in the press, but eventually, the
"Volkschecker" project was aborted.

In spite of the loss of Cole who was regarded as "an engineering dynamo," development of the
front-wheel drive concept continued. According to Heilig's 1992 account in *Automobile Quarterly*,
the Autodynamics Company designed a new Checker in 1980 based on the GM X-body car. Much

Fig. 30-30. The 1969 Checker Marathon: "Built to Last" and it did. The photograph was taken at the New York auto show that year. (LLL)

of the engineering, several design variations in clay models, and a seating buck were completed. Plans for construction included using a number of plastic components and reinforced injection molding panels. In retrospect these ideas do not sound impressive, but, according to Heilig, they were revolutionary concepts for the time.

David Markin and the Checker board confronted the grim reality of the industry as the 1980s began. The auto industry was in a downturn, still spinning from the government fuel economy regulations of the late 1970s, and manufacturing a new model would have meant several million dollars in development, retooling, and supplier costs. The proposed front-wheel drive cars needed new transmissions, brakes, and axles, and the investment in development costs was just too much of a gamble.

During the 1970s the Checker had used a General Motors engine, components, and platform, and when GM began to move toward a front-wheel drive geometry, Checker began to lose its ability to obtain support for the traditional rear-wheel drive vehicle. The government required extensive crash-testing, and this alone was beyond the financial resources of Checker. The company was forced to consider alternatives. A version of the front-wheel drive Chevrolet Citation, *Motor Trend's* 1980 Car of the Year, appeared tenable, as Checker could have used GM's crash data for this X-body platform. Reportedly, on occasion, during the early 1980s and usually in the late evening, stretched versions of a front-wheel drive Citation might be spotted on the streets of Kalamazoo sporting Checker nomenclature.

Changes in the industry were fast-paced however, and, the demise of the GM's X-bodied car was planned shortly after its introduction. Checker simply did not have an opportunity to develop a cab from the Citation before GM ceased production of the Citation in 1985.

In December 1980, the board of directors, including David Markin, Victor Potamkin, and Dollie Ann Cole, attempted to reorganize by

Fig. 30-31. Two Checkers at work in the big city: one a cab and the other a privately owned vehicle, circa 1964. They provide a lasting image of the grand automobile and its place in automotive history. (FAM)

purchasing all of the outstanding stock. Holders of common shares were offered $25, and preferred shareholders were offered $34.37, with an additional payment some ten years later. The following year, Checker production dipped to 2,939 units, almost a 30 percent decrease from the previous year. The company reported a loss of $448,000, although much of that was due to its taxicab operations.

On July 12, 1982, almost fifty-nine years to the day when the first Checker cab was built in Kalamazoo on July 15, 1923, the last Checker cab, with an apple green body, a rich cream top and the distinctive Checker board markings, rolled off the line. Reportedly more than 225 workers were subsequently laid off, as Checker closed its production line with plans to manufacture parts for General Motors and Chrysler. The story reported in the *Detroit Free Press* was grim:

> *"There's not much we can say from our end; it's a company decision [to halt production]," said*
> *Ken Germanson of the Allied Industrial Workers of America, which represents Checker's approxi-*
> *mate 800 workers.*
>
> *"We feel it's a sad commentary on today's times," he added.*

A letter sent the previous spring warning workers about the production halt hinted that the decision was made after the union repeatedly refused to negotiate its contract and grant concessions. Germanson rebutted the claim, noting that there were no promises or guarantees that concessions would keep the cab production going.

Although the last Checker was built in 1982, the final and most dramatic end to the manufacture of automobiles in Kalamazoo occurred some ten years later, on December 22, 1991. It was one hundred years after it all began in 1891 when Jay Rhodes drove his steam-snorting carriage across the tracks down the Rose Street.

Sunday, December 22, 1991, the *Kalamazoo Gazette* photographed a fleet of eighteen-wheel trucks leaving the Checker plant on North Pitcher Street with dies and parts for General Motors vans. Cliff McCormick, an independent trucker, told reporters that "most of the truckers involved in the transport were independents who were contacted by Steel and Machinery Transport during the past two weeks and told to be at the plant at 6:00 a.m. on Saturday." "They wanted everyone loaded and out before the union guys got there," reported Rybicki, who shared the driving with McCormick. About thirty rigs converged on the facility that day and were loaded with parts and equipment for transport to Checker's sister plant in South Charleston, West Virginia. As the *Gazette* reported:

> "This was not a proud day for Checker or Kalamazoo," said Jerry Hilton, president of the Allied Industrial Workers, Local 682, and one of the few non-management employees called to the plant that day. He predicted the loss of sixty to eighty jobs.
>
> "Merry… Christmas," he said watching a truck drive off. "They do not even have the courtesy to sit down at the table and tell us about this."

Documents filed on November 13 of that year with the SEC by International Controls, parent company of Checker, reported assets of $463 million and liabilities of $553 million. While automobile-related work continued at the plant, the removal of the manufacturing equipment on December 21, 1991 dramatically defined the end of a century of automobile experiments and manufacture in Kalamazoo, Michigan.

Activity at the plant has slowed since that fateful Sunday and weeds have punctured the test track to the north of the old plant. Steel frames lie in stacks on the blacktop, like remnants of once-proud vehicles.

Chad Elmore writing for *Old Cars*, March 18, 1999, noted that the image and the mystique of the Checker cab persists in film, including "Leaving Normal" in 1992 and "200 Cigarettes" in 1999. An advertisement for PageNet Nationwide—an enterprise wholly unrelated to automobiles and the taxicab—in the May 5, 1996 issue of *Time* shows a man with a briefcase on a busy city street, opening the door of the once-familiar, slab-sided Model A8 Checker cab. Checkers appeared in television commercials as late as June 2000.

Almost seventeen years after its demise, the Checker legacy lives on.

REFERENCES

Photographic History. Publication of the Checker Motors Corporation, circa 1975, pp. 1–6.
Checker Backs Low Fares and Long Service. *The Kalamazoo Gazette*, October 18, 1925.
Morris Markin, Ex-tailor, Heads Largest Taxi Factory in Country. *The Kalamazoo Gazette*, November 23, 1930.
Checker Cab Plant to Open Monday. *The Kalamazoo Gazette*, March 5, 1931.
Checker Cab Now Holds Parmalee's Control. *The Kalamazoo Gazette*, September 10, 1930.
Business & Finance. *Time*, January 18, 1932, pp. 39–44.

Jeff Huebner. "Kalamazoo Cab." *Michigan History*, November–December 1985, p. 45–48.

Stanley K. Yost. "Taxi! A Look at Checkers Past; Part 1." *Car Classics*, June 1974, pp. 24–26.

B. M. Ikert. Some Reasons Why the 1922 Car Is the Best Ever Built. *Motor Age*, January 19, 1922, p. 10.

Beverly Rae Kimes and Henry Austin Clark, Jr. *Standard Catalog of American Cars, 1805–1942,* 3rd ed. Iola, WI: Krause Publications, 1996.

Silver Jubilee Show Opens. *Automobile Topics*, January 3, 1923, p. 731.

Car Exhibits at Chicago Show. *Motor Age*, January 29, 1923, p. 12.

Handley-Knight and Dort Plants United. *The Kalamazoo Gazette*, April 8, 1923.

Checker Buys Handley Plant. *Motor Age*, May 3, 1923, p. 31.

Morris Markin Keeps Firm Hand in Checker Operations. *Kalamazoo Gazette*, November 4, 1962.

Checker Cab Manufacturing Company Wins Suit Against Yellow Cab Manufacturing Company. Unknown Source, circa 1923.

Stanley K. Yost. "Taxi! A Look at Checkers Past; Part 2." *Car Classics*, August 1974, pp. 18–23, 67.

Local Checker Cab Plant Now in Production. *The Kalamazoo Gazette*, July 15, 1923.

Checker Cab to Reopen Shop. *The Kalamazoo Gazette*, September 2, 1923.

New York Auto Show. *Motor Age*, January 2, 1924, p. 11.

Taxicabs. *Motor Age*, January 17, 1924, p. 21.

Checker Cab Has Two Plants. *The Kalamazoo Gazette*, October 10, 1925.

Checker Cab photograph. *Automobile Blue Book*, 1925, p. 3.

New Checker Cab Plant Ready for Rush of Business. *The Kalamazoo Gazette*, October 4, 1930.

'31 Checker Cabs in Production at Kalamazoo Plant. *The Kalamazoo Gazette*, November 16, 1930.

Convertible Taxi Has Three Set-Up Options. *St. Louis Democrat*, May 17, 1931.

Display New Car. *Toledo Ohio Times*, May 18, 1931.

Checker Offers New-Type Convertible. *Automobile Topics*, July 4, 1931, pp. 619–20.

Limousine Style Coach Used by Parmalee. *Automobile Topics*, August 1, 1931, p. 903.

Checker Utility Vehicle Is Truck or Passenger Car. *Automotive Industries*, August 8, 1931.

Rod J. Walton. "Checker! The Rolls-Royce of Taxis." *Cars and Parts Annual*, 1990, pp. 12–18.

Ackerson, Robert C. Chevy Stylelines. *Old Cars Weekly News and Market Place*, March 29, 2001, p. 33.

Taxi Fleet to Give 25% Refund on Fares, *New York Times*, August 15, 1933.

Checker Cab Works in Cord's Control. *New York Times*, August 15, 1933.

E. L. Cord and Aid Acquire Checker Cab. *The Kalamazoo Gazette*, August 15, 1933.

Aeronautics; Farley's Deal. *Time*, April 23, 1934, pp. 24–28.

John A. Heilig. "The Checkered History of the Cab From Kalamazoo." *Automobile Quarterly*, Vol. 30, No. 2, 1992, pp. 64–85.

John T. Flynn. "Other People's Money." *The New Republic*, August 25, 1937, pp. 74–75.

Borgeson, Griffith. *Errett Lobban Cord*. Princeton: Automobile Quarterly, Publications, 1989, pp. 138–39, 206, 211–16.

Filed with SEC. *Time*, May 25, 1936, p. 73.

Cord Sells Auto Holdings as SEC Files Charges. *The Kalamazoo Gazette*, August 8, 1937.

Checker Cab Co. History Filled with Twists and Turns and Taxis. *Old Cars Weekly News and Marketplace*, December 13, 1990.

Cord Out of Cord. *Time*, August 16, 1937, p. 51.

Stanley K. Yost. "Taxi! A Look at Checkers Past; Part 3." *Car Classics*, October 1974, pp. 18–24.

Herbert R. Rifkind *The Jeep—Its Procurement and Development Under the Quartermaster Corps, 1940–1942*. Washington D.C.: Historical Section, Office of the Quarter Master General, 1943. Reprinted and Titled as *Jeep Genesis*, London: ISO Publications, 1988. pp. 57, 88–92.

Autos, The Box That Tailoring Made. *Time*, August 2, 1963, p. 62.

Stanley K. Yost and Kathryn Bassett. *Taxi! A Look At Checkers Past*. Pasadena: Miscellaneous Enterprises, 1990.

Karl Ludvigsen. "Chubby Checkers, Rear Engine and FWD Prototypes." *Special Interest Autos*, August–October 1973, pp. 36–38.

Michael Lamm and Dave Holls. *A Century of Automotive Style*. Stockton, CA: Lamm-Morada Publishing Co., 1997, p. 241.

Herb C. Snow. *Rear Engine Mounting and Drive*. Unpublished position paper, circa 1930.

Michael Lamm. "The Checker King: Morris Markin and the Cabs From Kalamazoo." *Collectible Automobile*, August 1998, pp. 26–38.

Hubert Luckett. "Next Big Change in Cars: Flatter Floors." *Popular Science*, July 1958, pp. 51–55.

Joseph M. Callahan. "Interest in Front Drive Revived by U.S. Makers." *Automotive News*, January 25, 1960, pp. 20–21.

Front Wheel Drive… Is It Coming or Going? *Road and Track*, July 1956, pp. 13–15.

Will Front Wheel Drive Return To Detroit? *Mirrors of Motordom*, April 18, 1960, p. 97–98.

Michael Lamm. "1947–82 Checker: Rugged to the End." *Collectible Automobile*, June 2000, pp. 22–35.

Karl Fermoyle. "Are U.S. Front-Drive Cars Coming?" *Popular Science*, February 1960, pp. 96–100, 248.

What Owners Say About Checker Automobiles. Company Sales Brochure, circa December, 1958.

Some Special U.S. Cars. *Consumer Reports*, April 1959, p. 179.

Some Special U.S. Cars. *Consumer Reports*, April 1960, p. 188.

The Checker Cab as a Family Sedan. *Consumer Reports*, August 1957, pp. 384–87.

Checker News Release, circa 1961.

Checker News Release, circa 1965.

Special Purpose Vehicles. Promotional publication of the Checker Motors Corporation, circa 1967.

The Checker Marathon. Company Sales Brochure, August 2, 1972.

Checker Motor President Dies. *Kalamazoo Gazette*, July 8, 1970.

See and Drive America's Only Diesel Car, Checker Marathon "D". *Kalamazoo Gazette*, September 15, 1968.

End Is in Sight for V-8's. *Kalamazoo Gazette*, May 3, 1977.

AMC Opposes Rebates on Foreign Cars. *Kalamazoo Gazette*, May 6, 1977.

Higher Gas Tax Looms Over Car Buyers. *Kalamazoo Gazette*, May 8, 1977.

Robert J. Kothe "The Checker." *Chronicle*, Vol 18, No 2, 1982, pp. 26–27.

Cole Dies in Plane Crash Near Mendon. *Kalamazoo Gazette*, May 2, 1977.

Probe of Cole's Crash Continues. *Kalamazoo Gazette*, May 3, 1977.

Checker Wants to Buy Out Holders. *Automotive News*, December 1, 1980.

Chris Knape. "A Taxi That Never Was." *Kalamazoo Gazette*, June 18, 2000.

Checker Ends 60-Year History as Auto Maker. *Old Cars Weekly News and Market Place*, July 22, 1982.

Checker Ends Sixty Years of Auto Production. *Automotive News*, July 12, 1982.

Checker Plans to Continue as a Major Auto Supplier. *Automotive News*, April 19, 1982.

End Draws Near For Checker Cabs. *Detroit Free Press*, July 9, 1982.

The Last Checker. *Detroit Free Press*, July 13, 1982.

Checker Moves Production Out. *Kalamazoo Gazette*, December 22, 1991.

Checker Mum as Trucks Roll. *Kalamazoo Gazette*, December 22, 1991.

Elmore, Chad. "Where Checkers Can Still be Hailed." *Old Cars Weekly News and Market Place*, March 18, 1999, p. 17.

"Pagenet Nationwide" Advertisement. *Time*, May 5, 1996.

Fig. 31-1. The sign reads "Hale's Good Goods." The brass headlamps, right-hand steering, and open fenders date this photograph circa 1906. Apparently Mr. Hale and his son found the automobile to be a convenient conveyance for selling various items along the side of the highway in the vicinity of Kalamazoo. (WMU)

Chapter 31

Epilogue

January 1891–December 1991

*Along the way, people gawked and pointed,
squinted and saluted, did double takes, took snapshots and
lifted small children to give them a better look at what their future might be.*
—*Time*, 1990

The quotation from *Time* magazine described the occasion of the parade of solar-powered experimental vehicles built by university students across the United States and entered in a cross country race. But the passage could have as well described the occasion of Jay Rhodes' wild ride down Rose Street aboard his steam-powered carriage in 1891.

As in any other city that supported the manufacture of the gasoline motorcar, the influence of the automobile on Kalamazoo's culture was not limited to the financial success and failure of the local concerns. The automobile became an integral part of the city providing personal transportation, forming the foundation for the movement of manufactured goods, and creating work opportunities servicing the vehicles. The importance of the automobile in changing our work habits, social mores, and leisure time, is worthy of a lengthy history itself, and much has been written about it. While the treatment of these topics here is incomplete, failure to provide at least a photographic recounting of the place of the automobile in the city risks a sterile interpretation of automotive history based on factory-produced images of the motorcar. One cannot separate the manufacture of the automobile from its influence on the lives of citizens and it is here that we find a brief review of its presence on the streets of Kalamazoo.

North Rose Street was a simple dirt road in 1891 when Jay Rhodes drove his steam carriage across the tracks and the Blood brothers opened their bicycle shop at 210. A century of automobile experimentation and manufacture had begun. When the gasoline-powered horseless carriage first appeared in the spring of 1900, the motorcar primarily served the whims of the gentry and provided recreation for the monied families of Kalamazoo. These vehicles, first built by the Bloods, the Fullers, Frank Burtt, and Walter Cannon, were tall, with large wheels and engines producing

443

Fig. 31-2 (top). A group of women are found touring in and about Kalamazoo, circa 1904. Note the solid white tires, the oil side-lamps, and the bulb horn mounted on the steering wheel. The automobile is a 1904 Michigan. (DOL)

Fig. 31-3 (below). The day "Papa" brought home the family's first automobile was a time of celebration and an occasion for a family photograph. The car is a 1910 four-cylinder Reo demi-tonneau. Although the Reo was a four-passenger vehicle, the young girl has managed to squeeze in as a fifth. (WMU)

Fig. 31-4 (top). Automobiles were a favorite part of early parades in Kalamazoo. The clothing, open seating, brass features, and right-hand drive of this automobile place the photograph circa 1910. (WMU)

Fig. 31-5 (below). A group of young men display their day's catch across the top of the window of a 1910 Buick. The photograph was taken by the Clarke studio in Battle Creek and perhaps the fish are from nearby Gull Lake, an established recreational area at the time. (DOL)

ten to twenty horsepower. They were finished with the finest leather, brightly painted, and decorated with brass accouterments. The cars were started with a hand crank; illumination after dark was provided by gas and oil driving lamps, and most of the early photographs portray these grand vehicles as the center of personal leisure. Each of these companies in turn ceased automobile production, and at the heart of their demise was a lack of investment capital and established parts supply industries.

After the first decade of the twentieth century the role of the motorcar began to change. The grand automobile show and the reliability tour organized in 1910 by *The Kalamazoo Gazette* sought to establish the automobile as something more than a plaything for the rich. The delicate brass was replaced with nickel trim, and the electric self-starter and electric driving lamps began to be generally available after 1912. The Mighty Michigan, first offered in 1909, provided such electrical conveniences in 1913. The company's decision to build motorcars and its subsequent bankruptcy epitomized both the enormous changes in the industry and the incredible financial and managerial pressures that existed in such an enterprise. The brief and unsuccessful attempts in competitive racing by the Cornelian and the Roamer emphasized yet again the intensity of the competition that existed in the industry just before and after World War I.

A second major development during the teens was the arrival of the gasoline-powered vehicle intended for commercial transport. Small trucks were first introduced in this city around 1913, but it was not until after World War I that the truck became popular for purposes of cartage and in at least one unique case as a mobile store. There were three attempts to manufacture commercial vehicles in Kalamazoo between 1913 and 1925: the Kalamazoo Vehicle Company, the Lane, and the Kalamazoo truck. Each prospered for a few years, and each in turn disappeared.

The business of selling gasoline also grew exponentially between 1913 and the Great Depression of the 1930s. It was not long before one could find a gas station on almost every major corner in the city. Service station architecture varied from a simple building with pumps at the curb to intricate designs intended to attract customers in this competitive business. Standard Oil Company moved to Kalamazoo in 1887 and established a plant just south of the Lake Shore and Michigan Southern railway station. Gasoline was just a nuisance then, an explosive by-product of the cracking process necessary to produce kerosene, and it had little use until the advent of the automobile.

The first horse-drawn tank wagon appeared in 1890, and the first motorized tank truck appeared in 1914. By 1925, Standard Oil had built a large plant between the intersection of Paterson and Porter Streets and the New York Central tracks with storage facilities for 350,000 gallons of gasoline and 120,000 gallons of lubricating oils. The company owned thirteen trucks that supplied twelve Red Crown stations in Kalamazoo and another sixty privately owned dealers within a twelve mile radius of the city. Their products included Red Crown gasoline, Polarine motor oils, Perfection kerosene, and various kinds of grease.

Standard Oil finally built the first modern filling station in 1919 at the corner of Main Street and Westnedge Avenue. Three other stations followed quickly, and by 1925 their number rose to twelve, giving the company the largest dealership network in Kalamazoo, although others were soon to establish themselves. The L. V. White Company located at East Main and the railroad bridge was erected in 1923 and was considered "Kalamazoo's own."

Fig. 31-6. By 1917, automobile dealerships had grown in size and appearance, but the Stevens Buick agency still was without a show room, and cars were often displayed in front of the agency located at Edwards and South Street. (WMU)

Fig. 31-7. Four cars just outside East Hall on the campus of Western State Normal College (Western Michigan University), circa 1918. The two cars on the right are Model T Fords. By this date, almost 50 percent of the cars on the road were made by Henry Ford. (WMU)

Fig. 31-8. The Kalamazoo-built Roamer was a major part of the Kalamazoo Advertising League parade. This photograph was taken on Factory Street next to the factory, circa 1919. (KLM)

Fig. 31-9. The automobile provided an escape from urban life, but the cost and infrequent availability of lodging made overnight camps an attractive alternative for many travellers. This photograph was taken circa 1922. (WMU)

Fig. 31-10. George Reames, dressed in tie and vest, drove this "Store at Your Door" grocery-on-wheels for the Art Trathan grocery store located in the 300 block of South Burdick Street. The truck is easily identified as a Kalamazoo, since the name appears clearly on the radiator. Equipped with hard rubber tires, neither the steering nor the ride could have been easy, although flat tires were never a problem. The photograph is circa 1921. (RRC)

Fig. 31-11. The Kalamazoo Savings Bank, located on West Main Street at the Portage Street intersection, paid three percent interest on savings, circa 1925, when this photograph was taken. The distinctive shape of the coupe in the foreground identifies it as Model T Ford. (DOL)

The decade of the 1920s seemed to predict great successes for Kalamazoo. Checker Cab Manufacturing, Kalamazoo Railway Supply, A. C. Barley, and Handley-Knight Motor Car built gasoline-powered vehicles during this period. Some of the most stunning and renowned automobiles in America's history were built during the financial struggles of the Great Depression, including flashy Auburn open cars at Limousine Body Company. Only Checker Cab Manufacturing and Kalamazoo Railway Supply,whose products were essentially commercial vehicles, survived the financial troubles of the 1930s, the former with the support of E. L. Cord and the latter by the financial inventiveness of the named receiver after declared bankruptcy. Both later obtained defense contracts that brought them through World War II.

After World War II, the automobile took on a new look with the extravagant use of chrome trim and a variety of designs and styles that might appeal to a financially secure consumer. Many purchased a new automobile every two years. Street scenes during the 1960s seem to sparkle with new cars, tri-color paint, and opulent chrome. Automobiles grew more reliable between 1950 and 1970, and many small gas stations and other roadside services were no longer in demand. The gas shortages of the 1970s caused many of the remaining independent owners to close their doors and most of these buildings were converted into small convenience stores. Automobile safety and the gasoline shortages convinced the United States Congress to become involved in the regulation of the automobile industry and by the early 1980s Checker Motors, unable to meet the gasoline mileage and crash-test requirements, ceased automobile manufacturing. Much of the major stamping equipment was moved from the Checker plant and rumblings of the closure of the General Motors stamping plant followed. The "dramatic closure" of the era of automobile manufacture in Kalamazoo was recorded on December 22, 1991.

One might ask if the story of automobile manufacture in Kalamazoo is simply a tale of failure, for the account seems to document the demise of one company after another. Certainly there were failures, and the demise of Michigan Buggy was a very regrettable time in the history of the city. But Kalamazoo was not alone in its record of automobile manufacturing bankruptcies; in fact the city did better than most in this highly competitive industry. Indianapolis, Cleveland, Chicago, and New York, all far larger than Kalamazoo, also tried to support automobile manufacturers and each in turn failed.

Automobiles are no longer exclusively manufactured in certain cities, or countries for that matter, as companies spread their manufacturing facilities and draw their component parts from around the world. The companies that survive are large conglomerates with international subsidiaries and manufacturing interests around the globe. The origin of manufacture for some cars is best estimated by the percentage of parts made in a particular country. As of 2002, General Motors, Ford Motor Company, and Chrysler Corporation are the only three that remain in the United States, and Daimler-Chrysler is actually a German-owned, rather than an American-owned, enterprise. Ford Motor Company, once confined to building cars in Detroit, now consists of a family of fine cars including Aston Martin (Great Britain), Ford (USA), Jaguar (Great Britain), Lincoln (USA), Mercury (USA), Mazda (Japan) and Volvo (Sweden).

There are no surviving independent manufacturers in this country and, in addition to Checker in Kalamazoo, Michigan (1923–82), there are only five independent companies with any considerable history: Studebaker in South Bend, Indiana (1902–64); Nash in Kenosha, Wisconsin (1902–

Fig. 31-12 (top). Inman's gas station and refreshment stand was located in Galesburg, Michigan just to the east of Kalamazoo. The owners provided travelers with cold Cokes and Orange Crush and dispensed Sinclair gasoline for their cars. The Kalamazoo River is in the background of this photograph, circa 1930. (RRC)

Fig. 31-13 (below). The Goodrich Silvertown tire store and gas station stood at 136 South Westnedge Avenue. This photograph is believed to be on the occasion of the opening of the store in the spring of 1931. The trees appear to be covered with buds and there is just the remnant of snow near the sidewalk. The three cars at the pumps are 1931 Auburn cars from the nearby dealership owned by Harry Parker. The car in the service bay is a 1931 Model A Ford. Texaco gas was dispensed from the Gilbert and Baker meter-style pumps. (DOL)

Fig. 31-14 (top). Gerlines' extravagant windmill service station was located at 924 East Michigan Avenue. Owned by Robert and Edward Fleckenstein, they dispensed Sunoco gasoline from the Tokheim Volunteer Model 950 clock-face pumps. Complete lubrication using Franklin and Pennzoil motor oils was provided in a separate structure. The photograph is circa 1935. (DOL)

Fig. 31-15 (below). The Seydel Brothers' station, circa 1940, was located on West Main Street. They dispensed D-X gasoline from Wayne pumps for thirteen cents a gallon, sold Goodyear tires, and provided mechanical repairs. (DOL)

54); Hudson in Detroit (1909–53); Packard in Detroit (1903–54); and Willys-Overland in Toledo, Ohio (1914–55). Willys Jeeps still survive, but the company lost its independent standing in 1954 when it was purchased by Kaiser. Packard moved from Warren, Ohio, in 1899 and survived in Detroit from1903 until 1954 when it was joined with Studebaker. Rambler built cars in Kenosha from 1902–13 and was transformed into the Jeffery (1914) and then Nash (1917), finally dissolving into American Motors in 1954. Hudson began manufacture in Detroit in the summer of 1909 and survived until 1954 when it, too, lost its identity as an independent by becoming part of Nash in 1953, and then American Motors in 1954. Only Checker remained independent through the difficult economic times of the '50s and '60s when other marques attempted to survive by joining forces.

Considering the worldwide competition, the financial pitfalls, the host of government regulations, and consumers' fickleness, the record for Kalamazoo is not one of failure but one of commendable success. No other independent manufacturer carries a legacy as successful as that of the Checker. Willys continues to be associated with the four-wheel drive Jeep, the Packard name is synonymous with opulence, and Studebaker stirs visions of radical styling. But Checker and only Checker survives in advertisement and film as the epitome of a taxi cab more than seventeen years after its demise. How long this image and reputation continue will be interesting to observe.

What does the future hold for Kalamazoo? At Western Michigan University, groups of faculty and students experiment with automobiles powered by the sun's rays. Perhaps one day the fruits of these endeavors will prove vital to manufacturing the next evolution of the personal means of transportation we now call the automobile.

REFERENCES

Racing Along on Sunshine. *Time*, July 23, 1990, p. 67.

Ross Collier. *Ross Collier Collection*, Regional History Collections, Western Michigan University, A-1911.

Beverly Rae Kimes and Henry Austin Clark, Jr. *Standard Catalog of American Cars, 1805–1942*, 3rd ed. Iola, WI: Krause Publications, 1996.

Seven Firms Distribute Oil. *The Kalamazoo Gazette*, October 18, 1925.

Tad Burness. *American Truck and Bus Spotters Guide, 1920–1985*. Osceola, WI: Motorbooks International, 1985.

John A. Gunnell, ed. *Standard Catalog of Light Duty Trucks*. Iola, WI: Krause Publications, 1987.

Oil Firm Is Conducted by Local Men. *The Kalamazoo Gazette*, October 18, 1925.

Standard Oil in Kalamazoo Since 1887. *The Kalamazoo Gazette*, October 18, 1925.

Eight Handle Motor Trucks Here. *The Kalamazoo Gazette*, October 18, 1925.

Gas Shortage? Not Then. *The Kalamazoo Gazette*, April 7, 1974.

Scott Anderson. *Check the Oil*, Lombard, IL: Wallace-Homestead, 1986.

Fig. 31-16. The 5:00 p.m. rush hour traffic heads south into Kalamazoo on Burdick Street, as the camera looks north. The bullet nose Ford in the middle of the picture and the Kaiser just before the intersection set this photograph circa 1949-50. Note the Doubleday building on the right and the street lamps which are tall overhead rather than the older style short column globe light. (WMU)

Fig. 31-17. The view is at Main Street and Burdick, looking east toward Portage Street. The 1960–61 Corvair is in the middle of the picture facing west. The other vehicles—a 1961–62 Imperial, a 1962 Oldsmobile, and a 1962 Chevrolet—set the date of the photograph circa 1962. (WMU)

Fig. 31-18. The inside of the Orrin B. Hays automobile agency, circa 1953, when new automobiles were introduced with great fanfare. (DOL)

First Garage Started Here Twenty Years Ago. *The Kalamazoo Gazette*, October 18, 1925.

Michael K. Witzel. *The American Gas Station*, Osceola, WI: Motorbooks International, 1992.

John A. Gunnell, ed. *Standard Catalog of American Cars, 1946–1975*, 2nd ed. Iola, WI: Krause Publications, 1982.

General Motors to Build Here. *Kalamazoo Gazette*, March 18, 1964.

Tom Bell and P. J. Storm-Artis. *Thirty Years of Kalamazoo: From Fisher Body to Metal Fabrication Division*, Kalamazoo, MI: Amerikal, circa 1994.

Sunseeker Gears Up for Big Race Finish. *Kalamazoo Gazette*, July 19, 1990.

Fig. 31-19. Western Michigan University's Sunseeker competed in the national race for solar-powered cars, once again giving Kalamazoo a chance to contribute to the automobile industry. (WMU)

Appendix A

DEFINITION of TERMS

The following terms were used with reasonable consistency in the automobile industry prior to World War II and are based upon the definitions approved by the Society of Automotive Engineers (S.A.E.) as published in 1941 or taken from era automotive trade journals. Various manufacturers used some license in their nomenclature, and the unbridled use of terms has grown since publication of these S.A.E. definitions. Fortunately, most of the vehicles described in this book were built before 1941. Terms in italics have their own definitions in the listing.

Aerobus—an eight to twelve passenger closed *sedan* with six to eight doors. The chassis was built longer than standard to accommodate the additional body length and seating.

Brougham—a *limousine* with no roof over the chauffeur's compartment; the windshield offered the only permanent protection, and a waterproof covering and side curtains were provided as an option for the driver's protection in inclement weather. The term was used by some manufacturers rather than *town car* to suggest a certain elegance of finish, or to identify *sedans* that had special trim and/or amenities but which were not necessarily intended to be chauffeur driven.

Buggy—an early open car with four tall hard rubber wheels (thirty-six to forty-two inches in diameter), and front and rear seating, usually with entry doors on the rear *tonneau* only. When there were no doors on either the front or the rear compartment, the style was called a *surrey,* although the tall hard rubber wheels were the predominant characteristic of the buggy.

Burden carrier—a four-wheel vehicle designed to carry small loads inside factory buildings or on the loading dock.

Cabriolet—a closed body with two entry doors, seating for two, a folding top and retractable roll-down glass windows in the doors, *i.e.,* a true convertible. An open *rumble seat* was typical, differentiating the cabriolet from *convertible coupe.*

Carry-cycle—an early open vehicle with three wheels; the driver's position was over a single rear-drive wheel behind the passengers. Steering was controlled by bicycle handlebars and the passenger seat turned as the vehicle turned.

Coach—a popular term in the 1920s and 1930s for a two-door closed vehicle with retractable roll-down glass windows, (*i.e.,* a two-door sedan).

Commercial car—a large car, usually built on a truck chassis with multiple seating, that functioned as a small bus.

Convertible coupe—a closed body with two entry doors, seating for four, and a folding top with retractable roll-down glass windows in the doors.

Convertible sedan—a closed body with four entry doors, seating for five, and a folding top with retractable roll-down glass windows in the doors.

Coupe—a closed body with two entry doors, retractable roll-down glass windows in the doors, seating for two to three, and an optional rumble seat.

Cowl—the top part of the automobile body, forward of the front doors, below the windshield and above the instrument panel or dashboard.

Custom—a general term for vehicles with special trim components or other amenities that varied among manufacturers.

Cyclecar—a vehicle with four wheels, an engine displacement less than seventy-one cubic inches, and design characteristics more similar to a motorcycle than to an automobile, (*e.g.,* tandem seating, air-cooled engine, no fenders (or motorcycle fenders) and an exterior belt or chain drive).

Flyer—a general term used by various manufacturers to identify an open sporting car, usually without a top, and having seating for two.

King of Belgium—an early open car in which the body structure for the rear seating area, or *tonneau,* extended or bulged outward over the rear fenders to provide a large seating area. Reportedly, it was named after the King of Belgium whose physical stature required a larger seating area than normal.

Landau—a four-door sedan with a convertible rear quarter; *i.e.,* the roof area behind the rear seat could be folded down. Some automobiles are fitted with Landau bars (decorative hinged bars on the rear quarter) that are non-functional.

Landaulet—a closed car with a folding top, seating for three or more passengers in the back seat, and a glass separation between the chauffeur and passenger compartments. Usually, only the roof over the rear compartment folded down.

Light car—a vehicle with four wheels, an engine displacement of less than 100 cubic inches and weighing less one thousand pounds, but which had characteristics similar to a full-size car—*e.g.,* automobile body with doors, full fenders, full running boards, and side-by-side seating.

Limousine—a closed car seating three to five in the rear compartment, usually with *jump seats* and a separate covered chauffeur's compartment. A glass partition separated the rear compartment and the chauffeur's compartment.

Phaeton—a term preferred in the 1920s and 1930s for identifying the card known as *touring* prior to World War I.

Platform truck—a small open truck with four wheels and a flat loading deck intended to carry loads inside a factory or on the loading dock.

Quadricycle—an early type of four-wheel vehicle that combined two bicycle-type frames mounted side by side with horizontal and diagonal stiffening members. Steering was most often controlled by a tiller.

Race car—a car intended for racing that eliminated non-essential features, (e.g., fenders, headlamps, upholstery and extra seating), that would add unnecessary weight to the car. It usually had space for only a single occupant.

Roadster—an open car with two entry doors, seating for two, folding top and no retractable roll-down glass side windows. A *rumble seat* was optional. The roadster, lacking glass windows, offered minimal protection from wind and rain. Consumers turned to the convertible, and the roadster disappeared by 1938.

Rumble seat—a seat attached to the trunk lid, hinged at the bottom rather than the top of the lid, that created an open seating space for two when opened from the top. Rumble seats, offering no protection from wind or rain, disappeared by 1939.

Runabout—an early car having seating for two, no doors, and typically offered without a top or windshield. When tops were added, the optional windshield might be made of plastic-like material.

Sedan—a closed car with permanent top, retractable roll-down glass windows, and seating for four or five, all in the same compartment. Sedans had either two or four entry doors; in the former variation it was identified as a Tudor sedan, coach, or coupe sedan.

Speedster—an open race car with the addition of fenders, lights and other accoutrements enabling it to be legally driven on the street.

Sport touring—a *touring* car with special amenities depending on manufacturer, *e.g.,* folding tan top, wire wheels, two rear-mounted spare tires, side-mounted spare tires, chromium-plated trim, folding rear windshield, and/or choice of paint color.

Special—a general term for vehicles with special trim components or other amenities that varied among models and manufacturers.

Speed truck—a small three-wheel vehicle with bicycle handlebar steering, designed to move small loads inside a warehouse or on a loading dock.

Station wagon—a closed vehicle with retractable roll-down glass windows and a flat top extending from the top of the windshield to the rear of the vehicle. The rear compartment was accessed through either the rear window or tailgate.

Standard sedan—a vehicle meeting the definition of a sedan but without special amenities or decorative detail (as compared to models designated as "special" or "custom").

Stretched—a standard-size vehicle with extra seating capacity added by cutting the chassis and body behind the driver's compartment and inserting additional frame members and passenger body components.

Suburban—a closed *sedan* with retractable roll-down glass windows and rear seating designed to convert for specific purposes. In the Roamer, the rear seat converted to a bed; in the Checker, the rear seat converted to a flat surface for cargo.

Surrey—an early open *touring* car having no doors on either the front or rear passenger compartments, with or without tall hard rubber wheels.

Taxi—a body style designed for carrying passengers on a commercial basis, characterized by distinctive paint schemes and special identification lamps. A "mileage/price" meter to record the cost of the trip was mounted in the front compartment, and most often there was a glass partition between the driver and the passenger compartments.

Tonneau—an early term referring to the rear seating compartment of an automobile body. Some early cars had a single entrance door at the rear of the compartment ("rear entrance tonneau"). As car bodies grew larger, doors were placed on the side ("side entrance tonneau").

Torpedo touring—a touring body with four entry doors, folding top, and no retractable roll-down glass windows. It was designed as a single compartment to create a straight visual line from the top of the cowl to the end of the rear tonneau; see also "toy tonneau."

Touring—an open car, with folding top, four entry doors, with no retractable roll-down glass windows, and seating designed for four or more. Depending upon the trim and amenities, the touring might be designated as standard, deluxe or sport.

Touring sedan—a vehicle that met the definition of a *sedan,* but having additional passenger amenities, *e.g.,* liquor cabinet, smoking accessories or a lady's cosmetics bar in the rear compartment.

Town sedan (or Town)—a typical closed four-door sedan with a glass separation between the chauffeur and the rear compartment. The area above the chauffeur was open, but could be covered with a folding top. The town car resembled the *landaulet,* but without the folding top over the rear compartment; it also resembled the *limousine,* but did not have jump seats in the rear compartment. Some manufacturers preferred the term *brougham* for this car.

Toy tonneau—an open touring car having four doors, no retractable roll-down glass windows, and a rear *tonneau* added to the front compartment, rather than the car being built as a single unit. This arrangement created a tonneau that was smaller than the touring car.

Tudor sedan—a closed *sedan* with permanent top, retractable roll-down glass windows, and two doors. Typically, entrance was through the passenger side, and the front seat tipped forward to allow easy access to the rear compartment.

Victoria touring—an open *touring* car with four doors and without retractable roll-down glass windows; a Victoria top formed a half shell that covered only the rear seat of the otherwise open car. A separate folding windshield was usually mounted in front of the rear passenger compartment.

Appendix B

SUMMARY of
AUTOMOBILE PRODUCTION
in KALAMAZOO

≈

The new cars for each year were traditionally introduced at the grand car shows in New York and Chicago during the month of January, and the specifications of new releases appeared shortly thereafter in national publications. Announcements of pending developments and specifications for the following year often appeared in periodicals in late fall, October through December, when the first models were shipped to the agencies and made available to the public. Contrary to current practice there was no typical model year and many manufacturers introduced new models throughout the year. The Michigan Automobile Company Ltd., for example, sold a small runabout in January 1904, introduced a new model D in June of that year, which was then followed by a modification to that vehicle without a change in model designation. They then introduced a completely new car in January of 1905. The succession of these modifications makes year designation difficult. For some early vehicles, the specifications in the following summary are made according to the year and the month of the reference source to make clear the period during which the vehicles were built. The information is limited at best. Some of the detail is the compilation of tidbits of information published during the period. Some specifications are difficult to trace because of periodic changes that were neither annual model changes nor well documented in the press and annual publications of vehicle specification. Finally, the vehicle prices also varied. In one example, the Barley Company changed the prices of the Roamer several times in the early 1920s with the complaint that government requirements made it impossible to maintain a permanent price schedule for any length of time.

MAKE & MANUF.		APPEARANCE			MECHANICAL 1		
Year	Model	Body Type and # Passengers	Steering	Engine Manufacturer	Cooling #Cyl & Conf.	Fuel	Bore & Stroke

Barley — *Barley Motor Car Company (Roamer), 200 Reed Ave. (s.e. corner of Reed and Factory St. in old Michigan Buggy plant)*

1923

	6-50	Touring–5p	Lh-w	Continental	lqd 6-L	gas	3 1/8 x 4 1/4
		Sedan–5p	Lh-w	Continental	lqd 6-L	gas	3 1/8 x 4 1/4
		Sport Sedan–5p	Lh-w	Continental	lqd 6-L	gas	3 1/8 x 4 1/4
		Tour Sedan–5p	Lh-w	Continental	lqd 6-L	gas	3 1/8 x 4 1/4

1924

	6-50	Phaeton–5p	Lh-w	Continental	lqd 6-L	gas	3 1/8 x 4 1/4
		Sport Sedan–5p	Lh-w	Continental	lqd 6-L	gas	3 1/8 x 4 1/4
		Special Sport–5p	Lh-w	Continental	lqd 6-L	gas	3 1/8 x 4 1/4
		Touring Sedan–5p	Lh-w	Continental	lqd 6-L	gas	3 1/8 x 4 1/4
		Sedan–5p	Lh-w	Continental	lqd 6-L	gas	3 1/8 x 4 1/4

Production totals for the Barley are unknown, and are included in the production figures for the Roamer. Total production of the Barley is estimated at 600 cars.

Blood — *Kalamazoo Cycle Company, 208–210 N. Rose Street*

1902

June	na	Quadricycle–1p	Tiller	de Dion Boutan	air 1	gas	3 x 3 1/4
Sept	na	Carry-cycle–3p	Tiller	Blood	air 1	gas	na

1903

Jan	na	Runabout–2p	Tiller	Blood	air 1	gas	na

The 1903 Blood runabout became, with some refinements, the Michigan produced by Michigan Automobile Company Ltd., owned by the Fullers and the Bloods and founded in December 1902.

Blood — *Blood Brothers Automobile and Machine Company, 114 N. Edwards Street*

1904

June	na	Buggy Side Entr–6p	Rh-w	Blood	lqd 2	gas	5 x 5

1905

Jan	na	Buggy Side Entr–6p	Rh-w	Blood	lqd 2	gas	5 x 5

The Blood brothers appear to have built a single model automobile in 1904, 1905 and 1906. Confusion persists between the Blood vehicle and the numerous Michigan vehicles built by the Fullers in the same period.

Blood — *Blood Brothers Machine Company, 623 W. Ransom Street.*

1913

Aug	na	Cyclecar tandem–2p	Lh-w	Blood	na	gas	na

Reports indicate that this was an experimental vehicle designed and built by Maurice Blood, Howard Blood's father.

Boudeman — *450 W. Main St.*

Dallas Boudeman founded an automobile company in 1906 at the age of 16. There is no evidence of manufacture beyond a single Kalamazoo engine from the Burtt Company that he built at that time.

Burtt — *Burtt Manufacturing, southeast corner of Clinton and Fulford Streets*

1909

Dec	na	1/2 ton truck	na	Burtt	air 4	gas	na

MECHANICAL 2				CHASSIS			PRODUCTION	
CID	Hp	Transmission & Gearing		Wheelbase & gauge (in.)	Tire Size	Weight	Production	Cost
196	50b	sld-gear	3f-r	118	32x4	na	na	$1,395
196	50b	sld-gear	3f-r	118	32x4	na	na	$1,850
196	50b	sld-gear	3f-r	118	32x4	na	na	$1,495
196	50b	sld-gear	3f-r	118	32x4	na	na	$1,225
196	50b	sld-gear	3f-r	118	32x4	na	na	$1,395
196	50b	sld-gear	3f-r	118	32x4	na	na	$1,495
196	50b	sld-gear	3f-r	118	32x4	na	na	$1,685
196	50b	sld-gear	3f-r	118	32x4	na	na	$1,695
196	50b	sld-gear	3f-r	118	32x4	na	na	$1,850
23	3.3	plant-ch	na	48x30	28x1.75	360	1	$ na
na	3.5	plant-ch	2f	45	28x1.75	300	100	$ 400
na	3.5	plant-ch	2f-r	na	28x2	400	25	$ 450
205	20	sld-gear	4f-r	90x54.5	30x3.5	1700	na	$1,500
205	20	sld-gear	4f-r	90x54.5	30x3.5	1700	na	$na
na	na	friction	na	narrow	na	na	1-2	$na
na	40	na	na	na	na	na	1-3	$na

MAKE & MANUF.		APPEARANCE			MECHANICAL 1		
Year	Model	Body Type and # Passengers	Steering	Engine Manufacturer	Cooling #Cyl & Conf.	Fuel	Bore & Stroke

Cannon —*Burtt Manufacturing, 1214 North Edwards Street*

1903

Sept	Flyer	Runabout–2p	Tiller	Cannon	lqd 1	gas	5 x 5

1904

Sept	#3	Side-Tonneau–5p	Rh-w	Cannon	lqd 2	gas	5 x 5

1905

Feb	#3	Side-Tonneau–5p	Rh-w	Cannon	lqd 2	gas	na
	Custom	Side-Tonneau–5p	Rh-w	Cannon	lqd 4	gas	5 x 4

Checker — *Checker Cab Manufacturing Company, 1850 North Pitcher (at the city limits)*

1920

	C	Taxi–5p	Lh-w	Lycoming	lqd 4	gas	na

1921

	C	Taxi–5p	Lh-w	Herschell-Spillman	lqd 4	gas	na

1922

	C-44	Limo Taxi–5p	Lh-w	na	lqd 4	gas	na
	C-44	Lan Taxi–5/7p	Lh-w	na	lqd 4	gas	na

1923

	H	Lan Taxi 4 dr.–5p	Lh-w	Buda	lqd 4	gas	na
	H	Limo Taxi 4 dr.–5p	Lh-w	Buda	lqd 4	gas	na

The factory in Kalamazoo began production in July 1923, and total production for the year is estimated at 450 vehicles. Other publications claim production of 4, 500 vehicles, an impressive total in a six-month period for a new factory.

1924

	E	Lan Taxi 4 dr. 5p	Lh w	Buda	lqd 4	gas	na
	E	Limo Taxi 4 dr.–5p	Lh-w	Buda	lqd 4	gas	na

1925

	E	Taxi 4 dr.–5p	Lh-w	Buda	lqd 4	gas	na

A righthand-drive taxi was also built in 1925 for export to England. Checker Cab built a roadster in 1925 as the Official Car of the Automobile Blue Books, *a popular touring guide of the era.*

1926

	E	Taxi 4 dr.–5p	Lh-w	Buda	lqd 4	gas	na
	F	Taxi 4 dr.–5p	Lh-w	Buda	lqd 4	gas	na

1927

	F	Taxi 4 dr.–5p	Lh-w	Buda	lqd 4	gas	na
	G-4	Lan Taxi 4 dr.–5p	Lh-w	Buda	lqd 4	gas	na
	G-4	Limo Taxi 4 dr.–5p	Lh-w	Buda	lqd 4	gas	na
	G-6	Lan Taxi 4 dr.–5p	Lh-w	Buda	lqd 6	gas	na
	G-6	Limo Taxi 4 dr.–5p	Lh-w	Buda	lqd 6	gas	na

MECHANICAL 2			CHASSIS			PRODUCTION	
CID	Hp	Transmission & Gearing	Wheelbase & gauge (in.)	Tire Size	Weight	Production	Cost
98	7	comb-ch	2f-r	72x54	28x2.5	na	50	$ 650
196	15	comb-ch	4f-r	84.5x54	30x3	1500	250	$1,350
na	24	comb-ch	na	104x54	na	na	na	$1,650
314	40	comb-ch	4f-r	120x54	na	na	2	$3,500
na	na	sld-gear	3f-r	na	na	na	100	$1,595
na	na	sld-gear	3f-r	na	na	na	100	$1,595
na	40	sld-gear	3f-r	na	na	na	na	$2,680
na	40	sld-gear	3f-r	na	na	na	na	$2,785
na	na	sld-gear	3f-r	na	na	na	4500	$2,340
na	na	sld-gear	3f-r	na	na	na	4500	$2,440
na	22.5	sld-gear	3f-r	127	na	na	600	$2,440
na	22.5	sld-gear	3f-r	127	na	na	600	$2,340
na	22.5	sld-gear	3f-r	na	na	na	930	$2,690
na	22.5	sld-gear	3f-r	117	na	na	na	$2,500
na	22.5	sld-gear	3f-r	117	na	na	na	$2,500
na	22.5	sld-gear	3f-r	117	na	na	na	$2,500
na	22.5	sld-gear	3f-r	117	na	na	na	$2,592
na	22.5	sld-gear	3f-r	117	na	na	na	$2,600
na	27.3	sld-gear	3f-r	124 3/4	na	na	na	$2,692
na	27.3	sld-gear	3f-r	124 3/4	na	na	na	$2,700

MAKE & MANUF.		APPEARANCE			MECHANICAL 1		
Year	Model	Body Type and # Passengers	Steering	Engine Manufacturer	Cooling #Cyl & Conf.	Fuel	Bore & Stroke

Checker — *continued*

1928

	G-4	Lan Taxi 4 dr.–5p	Lh-w	Buda	lqd 4	gas	na
	G-4	Limo Taxi 4 dr.–5p	Lh-w	Buda	lqd 4	gas	na
	G-6	Lan Taxi 4 dr.–5p	Lh-w	Buda	lqd 6	gas	na
	G-6	Limo Taxi 4 dr.–5p	Lh-w	Buda	lqd 6	gas	na

1929

	K-6	Town Car 4 dr.–6p	Lh-w	Buda	lqd 6	gas	na

1930

	K-6	Town Car 4 dr.–6p	Lh-w	Buda	lqd 6	gas	na

1931

	K-6	Town Car 4 dr.–6p	Lh-w	Buda	lqd 6	gas	na
	M	Town Car 4 dr.–6p	Lh-w	Buda	lqd 6	gas	na
	MU6	Suburban 4 dr.–6p	Lh-w	Buda	lqd 6	gas	na

1932

	K-6	Town Car 4 dr.–6p	Lh-w	Buda	lqd 6	gas	na
	M	Town Car 4 dr.–6p	Lh-w	Buda	lqd 6	gas	na
	MU6	Suburban 4 dr.–6p	Lh-w	Buda	lqd 6	gas	na

Approximately 1,000 Suburban Utility cars were built in 1931–32.

1933

	T	Taxi–6p	Lh-w	Lycoming	lqd 6	gas	na
	T	Suburban 4 dr.–6p	Lh-w	Lycoming	lqd 6	gas	na

Approximately 500 Model T trucks were produced during the year. Total production is unknown.

Reportedly, E. L. Cord, who was in control of Checker, produced the Saf-T-cabs for the Auburn Motor Company.

1934

	T	Taxi 4 dr.–6p	Lh-w	Lycoming	lqd 6	gas	na
	T	Suburban 4 dr.–8p	Lh-w	Lycoming	lqd 6	gas	na

Approximately 1,000 models were manufactured in 1934.

1935

	Y-6	Taxi 4 dr.–5p	Lh-w	Continental	lqd 6	gas	na
	Y-6	Taxi 4 dr.–9p	Lh-w	Continental	lqd 6	gas	na
	Y-6	Taxi 4 dr.–5p	Lh-w	Lycoming	lqd 8	gas	3.06 x 4.75
	Y-6	Taxi 4 dr.–9p	Lh-w	Lycoming	lqd 8	gas	3.06 x 4.75

Checker was under E. L. Cord's control, and the Lycoming is the same engine used in the Auburn 850.

1936

	Y-6	Taxi 4 dr.–5p	Lh-w	Continental	lqd 6	gas	na
	Y-6	Taxi 4 dr.–9p	Lh-w	Continental	lqd 6	gas	na
	Y-6	Taxi 4 dr.–5p	Lh-w	Lycoming	lqd 8	gas	3.06 x 4.75
	Y-6	Taxi 4 dr.–9p	Lh-w	Lycoming	lqd 8	gas	3.06 x 4.75

MECHANICAL 2			CHASSIS			PRODUCTION	
CID	Hp	Transmission & Gearing	Wheelbase & gauge (in.)	Tire Size	Weight	Production	Cost
na	22.5	sld-gear 3f-r	117	na	na	na	$2,592
na	22.5	sld-gear 3f-r	117	na	na	na	$2,600
na	27.3	sld-gear 3f-r	124 3/4	na	na	na	$2,692
na	27.3	sld-gear 3f-r	124 3/4	na	na	na	$2,700
na	27.3	sld-gear 3f-r	127	na	na	na	$2,500
na	27.3	sld-gear 3f-r	127	na	na	na	$2,500
na	27.3	sld-gear 3f-r	127	na	na	na	$2,500
na	61.5	sld-gear 3f-r	122	na	na	na	$na
na	61.5	sld-gear 3f-r	122	na	na	na	$1,800
na	27.3	sld-gear 3f-r	127	na	na	na	$2,500
na	61.5	sld-gear 3f-r	122	na	na	na	$na
na	61.5	sld-gear 3f-r	122	na	na	na	$1,800
na	98b	sld-gear 3f-r	122	na	na	na	$na
na	98b	sld-gear 3f-r	na	na	na	na	$1,800
na	98b	sld-gear 3f-r	na	na	na	na	$na
na	98b	sld-gear 3f-r	na	na	na	na	$na
na	80b	sld-gear 3f-r	na	na	na	na	$na
na	80b	sld-gear 3f-r	Lwb	na	na	na	$na
279	148b	sld-gear 3f-r	na	na	na	na	$na
279	148b	sld-gear 3f-r	Lwb	na	na	na	$na
na	80b	sld-gear 3f-r	na	na	na	na	$na
na	80b	sld-gear 3f-r	Lwb	na	na	na	$na
279	148b	sld-gear 3f-r	na	na	na	na	$na
279	148b	sld-gear 3f-r	Lwb	na	na	na	$na

MAKE & MANUF.		APPEARANCE			MECHANICAL 1		
Year	Model	Body Type and # Passengers	Steering	Engine Manufacturer	Cooling #Cyl & Conf.	Fuel	Bore & Stroke
Checker — *continued*							
1937							
	Y-6	Taxi 4 dr.–5p	Lh-w	Lycoming	lqd 8	gas	3.06 x 4.75
1938							
	Y-6	Taxi 4 dr.–5p	Lh-w	Lycoming	lqd 8	gas	3.06 x 4.75
1939							
	Y-6	Taxi 4 dr.–5p	Lh-w	Lycoming	lqd 8	gas	3.06 x 4.75
1940							
	A	Taxi 4 dr.–5p	Lh-w	Continental	lqd 6-L	gas	na
1941							
	A	Taxi 4 dr.–5p	Lh-w	Continental	lqd 6-L	gas	na
1942–44							
		In the production hiatus for automobiles during World War II, Checker tested a four-wheel drive, four-wheel steer Jeep built by American Bantam. Checker submitted a bid to the U.S. Army Quartermaster to build a Jeep, but never built a Jeep-type vehicle.					
1945							
	B	Taxi–5p	Lh-w	Continental	lqd 6-L	gas	na
1946							
	D-ftwd	Taxi–5p	Lh-w	Buda	lqd 4	gas	na
	D-ftwd	Sedan–7p	Lh-w	Continental	lqd 6-L	gas	na
		The rear engine Model B and the front-wheel drive Model D were experimental models. Reportedly, a Model C was developed, but it was short-lived and there is scant information available.					
1947		**The A-2 series was the first of the "Cadillac-style" Checkers designed by Dietrich and built on a 124" chassis.**					
	A-2	Taxi 4 dr.–7p	Lh-w	Continental	lqd 6-L	gas	na
	E	Transit bus; 42–44p	About 1,000 of these were built between 1947 and 1951				
1948							
	A-2	Taxi 4 dr.–7p	Lh-w	Continental	lqd 6-L	gas	na
	A-3	Limo 4 dr.–8p	Lh-w	Continental	lqd 6-L	gas	na
1949							
	A-2	Taxi 4 dr.–7p	Lh-w	Continental	lqd 6-L	gas	na
	A-3	Limo 4 dr.–8p	Lh-w	Continental	lqd 6-L	gas	na
		Approximately 6,000 A-2, & A-3 vehicles had been built when production ceased in June 1950.				.	
1950		**Production of the A-4 and A-5 began in June 1950.**					
	A-4	Taxi 4 dr.–7p	Lh-w	Continental	lqd 6-L	gas	na
	A-5	Limo 4 dr.–8p	Lh-w	Continental	lqd 6-L	gas	na
1951							
	A-4	Taxi 4 dr.–7p	Lh-w	Continental	lqd 6-L	gas	na
	A-5	Limo 4 dr.–8p	Lh-w	Continental	lqd 6-L	gas	na

MECHANICAL 2			CHASSIS			PRODUCTION	
CID	Hp	Transmission & Gearing	Wheelbase & gauge (in.)	Tire Size	Weight	Production	Cost
279	148b	sld-gear 3f-r	na	na	na	na	$na
279	148b	sld-gear 3f-r	na	na	na	na	$na
279	148b	sld-gear 3f-r	na	na	na	na	$na
na	80b	sld-gear 3f-r	124	na	na	na	$na
na	80b	sld-gear 3f-r	124	na	na	na	$na
na	na	sld-gear 3f-r	100	na	na	2	$na
na	60b	sld-gear 3f-r	112	na	na	1	$na
na	60b	sld-gear 3f-r	112	na	na	1	$na
na	80b	sld-gear 3f-r	124	na	na	na	$2,370
na	80b	sld-gear 3f-r	124	na	na	na	$na
na	80b	sld-gear 3f-r	124	na	na	na	$na
na	80b	sld-gear 3f-r	124	na	na	na	$na
na	80b	sld-gear 3f-r	124	na	na	na	$na
na	80b	sld-gear 3f-r	124	na	na	na	$na
na	80b	sld-gear 3f-r	124	na	na	na	$na
na	80b	sld-gear 3f-r	124	na	na	na	$na
na	80b	sld-gear 3f-r	124	na	na	na	$na

MAKE & MANUF.		APPEARANCE			MECHANICAL 1		
Year	Model	Body Type and # Passengers	Steering	Engine Manufacturer	Cooling #Cyl & Conf.	Fuel	Bore & Stroke
Checker — *continued*							
1952							
	A-4	Taxi 4 dr. –7p	Lh-w	Continental	lqd 6-L	gas	na
	A-5	Limo 4 dr.–8p	Lh-w	Continental	lqd 6-L	gas	na
1953							
	A-6	Taxi 4 dr.–7p	Lh-w	Continental	lqd 6-L	gas	na
	A-7	Limo 4 dr.–8p	Lh-w	Continental	lqd 6-L	gas	na
1954							
	A-6	Taxi 4 dr.–7p	Lh-w	Continental	lqd 6-L	gas	na
	A-7	Limo 4 dr.–8p	Lh-w	Continental	lqd 6-L	gas	na
1955	**The 1955 model was the last of the "Cadillac-style" Checkers on a 124" wheelbase.**						
	A-6	Taxi 4 dr.–7p	Lh-w	Continental	lqd 6-L	gas	na
	A-7	Limo 4 dr.–8p	Lh-w	Continental	lqd 6-L	gas	na
1956	**The 1956 model was the first year of the "slab-sided" Checker on a 120" wheelbase.**						
	A-8	Taxi 4 dr.–6p	Lh-w	Continental	lqd 6-L	gas	3 5/16 x 4 3/8
	No single individual has been credited with the A-8 design.						
1957							
	A-8	Taxi	Lh-w	Continental	lqd 6-L	gas	3 5/16 x 4 3/8
	A-8	Taxi	Lh-w	Continental	lqd 6-ov	gas	3 5/16 x 4 3/8
	Reportedly, an American Motors over-head valve six, with a reputation for low gas consumption at idle, was installed in twenty-five vehicles apparently as a trial run.						
1958	**The company name was changed to Checker Motors Corporation in 1958.**						
	A-8	Taxi	Lh-w	Continental	lqd 6-L	gas	3 5/16 x 4 3/8
	A-8	Taxi	Lh-w	Continental	lqd 6-ov	gas	3 5/16 x 4 3/8
1959							
	A-9	Taxi	Lh-w	Continental	lqd 6-L	gas	3 5/16 x 4 3/8
	A-9	Taxi	Lh-w	Continental	lqd 6-ov	gas	3 5/16 x 4 3/8
	A-9	Aerobus 6 dr.–9p	Lh-w	Continental	lqd 6-ov	gas	3 5/16 x 4 3/8
	A-9	Aerobus 8 dr.–12p	Lh-w	Continental	lqd 6-ov	gas	3 5/16 x 4 3/8
	Reportedly, from 1959 through 1961 the Aerobus was a stretched version of the Checker built by Armbruster-Stageway in Ft. Smith, Arkansas.						
1960	**Checkers were available to private citizens, but the first Checker designed for the consumer market appeared in late 1959 and is considered a 1960 model year vehicle.**						
	A-10	Superba Sedan–8p	Lh-w	Continental	lqd 6-L	gas	3 5/16 x 4 3/8
	A-10	Superba Sta. Wagon	Lh-w	Continental	lqd 6-ov	gas	3 5/16 x 4 3/8
	A-10	Superba Sp. Sed–8p	Lh-w	Continental	lqd 6-L	gas	3 5/16 x 4 3/8
	A-10	Superba Sp. Sta. Wagon	Lh-w	Continental	lqd 6-ov	gas	3 5/16 x 4 3/8
	A-10	Aerobus 6 dr.–9p	Lh-w	Continental	lqd 6-ov	gas	3 5/16 x 4 3/8
	A-10	Aerobus 8 dr.–12p	Lh-w	Continental	lqd 6-ov	gas	3 5/16 x 4 3/8
	A-10	Taxi	Lh-w	Continental	lqd 6-L	gas	3 5/16 x 4 3/8
	A-10	Taxi	Lh-w	Continental	lqd 6-ov	gas	3 5/16 x 4 3/8

Total production for all models is estimated at 6,980, including 1,050 for the consumer market.

MECHANICAL 2			CHASSIS			PRODUCTION	
CID	Hp	Transmission & Gearing	Wheelbase & gauge (in.)	Tire Size	Weight	Production	Cost
na	80b	sld-gear 3f-r	124	na	na	na	$na
na	80b	sld-gear 3f-r	124	na	na	na	$na
na	80b	sld-gear 3f-r	124	na	na	na	$na
na	80b	sld-gear 3f-r	124	na	na	na	$na
na	80b	sld-gear 3f-r	124	na	na	na	$na
na	80b	sld-gear 3f-r	124	na	na	na	$na
na	80b	sld-gear 3f-r	124	na	na	na	$na
na	80b	sld-gear 3f-r	124	na	na	na	$na
226	95b	sld-gear 3f-r	120	6.70x15	3410	na	$1,805
226	95b	sld-gear 3f-r	120	6.70x15	3410	na	$na
226	95b	sld-gear 3f-r	120	6.70x15	3410	na	$na
226	95b	sld-gear 3f-r	120	6.70x15	3410	na	$na
226	125b	sld-gear 3f-r	120	6.70x15	3410	na	$na
226	95b	sld-gear 3f-r	120	6.70x15	3410	na	$na
226	125b	sld-gear 3f-r	120	6.70x15	3410	na	$na
226	125b	sld-gear 3f-r	152.5	na	5000	na	$na
226	125b	sld-gear 3f-r	189	na	5000	na	$na
226	80b	sld-gear 3f-r	120	6.70x15	3410	na	$2,542
226	122b	sld-gear 3f-r	120	6.70x15	3780	na	$2,896
226	80b	sld-gear 3f-r	120	6.70x15	3410	na	$2,650
226	122b	sld-gear 3f-r	120	6.70x15	3780	na	$3,004
226	122b	sld-gear 3f-r	152.5	na	5000	na	$na
226	122b	sld-gear 3f-r	189	na	5000	na	$na
226	80b	sld-gear 3f-r	120	6.70x15	3410	na	$na
226	122b	sld-gear 3f-r	120	6.70x15	3780	na	$na

MAKE & MANUF.		APPEARANCE			MECHANICAL 1		
Year	Model	Body Type and # Passengers	Steering	Engine Manufacturer	Cooling #Cyl & Conf.	Fuel	Bore & Stroke

Checker — *continued*

1961   The Marathon line was announced in the fall of 1960 for the 1961 model year.

	A-10	Superba Sedan–8p	Lh-w	Continental	lqd 6-L	gas	3 5/16 x 4 3/8
	A-10	Superba Sta. Wagon	Lh-w	Continental	lqd 6-ov	gas	3 5/16 x 4 3/8
	A-10	Marathon Sedan–8p	Lh-w	Continental	lqd 6-L	gas	3 5/16 x 4 3/8
	A-10	Marathon Sta. Wagon	Lh-w	Continental	lqd 6-ov	gas	3 5/16 x 4 3/8
	A-10E	Aerobus 6 dr.–9p	Lh-w	Continental	lqd 6-L	gas	3 5/16 x 4 3/8
	A-10E	Aerobus 8 dr.-12p	Lh-w	Continental	lqd 6-L	gas	3 5/16 x 4 3/8
	A-10	Taxi	Lh-w	Continental	lqd 6-L	gas	3 5/16 x 4 3/8
	A-10	Taxi	Lh-w	Continental	lqd 6-ov	gas	3 5/16 x 4 3/8

Total production for all models is estimated at 5,683, including 860 for the consumer market.

1962   Checker added the Town custom limousine to its offerings, then withdrew the model for 1967–68. It returned in 1969.

	A-10	Superba Sedan–8p	Lh-w	Continental	lqd 6-L	gas	3 5/16 x 4 3/8
	A-10	Superba Sta. Wagon–8p	Lh-w	Continental	lqd 6-ov	gas	3 5/16 x 4 3/8
	A-10	Marathon Sedan–8p	Lh-w	Continental	lqd 6-L	gas	3 5/16 x 4 3/8
	A-10	Marathon Sta. Wagon–8p	Lh-w	Continental	lqd 6-ov	gas	3 5/16 x 4 3/8
	A-10E	Town Custom Limo	Lh-w	Continental	lqd 6-L	gas	3 5/16 x 4 3/8
	A-10E	Aerobus 6 dr.–9p	Lh-w	Continental	lqd 6-ov	gas	3 5/16 x 4 3/8
	A-10E	Aerobus 8 dr.-12p	Lh-w	Continental	lqd 6-ov	gas	3 5/16 x 4 3/8
	A-10	Taxi	Lh-w	Continental	lqd 6-L	gas	3 5/16 x 4 3/8
	A-10	Taxi	Lh-w	Continental	lqd 6-ov	gas	3 5/16 x 4 3/8

Total production for all models is estimated at 8,173, including 1,230 for the consumer market

1963   The Continental overhead valve six-cylinder engine was now rated at 141 hp—last model year in the post-war period with no eight-cylinder engine option.

	A-12	Superba Sedan–8p	Lh-w	Continental	lqd 6-L	gas	3 5/16 x 4 3/8
	A-12	Superba Sta. Wagon–8p	Lh-w	Continental	lqd 6-ov	gas	3 5/16 x 4 3/8
	A-12	Marathon Sedan–8p	Lh-w	Continental	lqd 6-L	gas	3 5/16 x 4 3/8
	A-12	Marathon Sta. Wagon–8p	Lh-w	Continental	lqd 6-ov	gas	3 5/16 x 4 3/8
	A-12E	Town Custom–9p	Lh-w	Continental	lqd 6-ov	gas	3 5/16 x 4 3/8
	A-12E	Aerobus 6 dr.–9p	Lh-w	Continental	lqd 6-ov	gas	3 5/16 x 4 3/8
	A-12E	Aerobus 8 dr.–12p	Lh-W	Continental	lqd 6-ov	gas	3 5/16 x 4 3/8
	A-11	Taxi	Lh-w	Continental	lqd 6-L	gas	3 5/16 x 4 3/8
	A-11	Taxi	Lh-w	Continental	lqd 6-ov	gas	3 5/16 x 4 3/8

Total production for all models is estimated at 7,050, including 1,080 for the consumer market.
During 1963–64, Chrysler 326 cid V-8 engines were mounted in some Checkers; estimate of 100 vehicles.

1964   The first year with an eight-cylinder engine option since the 1930s, using the Chrysler V-8 engine. The Superba line was dropped.

	A-12	Marathon Sedan–8p	Lh-w	Continental	lqd 6-L	gas	3.31 x 4.38
	A-12	Marathon Sta. Wagon–8p	Lh-w	Continental	lqd 6-L	gas	3.31 x 4.38
	A-12E	Town Custom–9p	Lh-w	Continental	lqd 6-L	gas	3.31 x 4.38
	A-12E	Aerobus 6 dr.–9p	Lh-w	Chrysler	lqd V8	gas	na

MECHANICAL 2			CHASSIS			PRODUCTION	
CID	Hp	Transmission & Gearing	Wheelbase & gauge (in.)	Tire Size	Weight	Production	Cost
226	80b	sld-gear 3f-r	120a	6.70x14	3410	na	$2,542
226	122b	sld-gear 3f-r	120	7.10x15	3670	na	$2,896
226	80b	sld-gear 3f-r	120	6.70x14	3410	na	$2,650
226	122b	sld-gear 3f-r	120	7.10x15	3720	na	$3,004
226	122b	sld-gear 3f-r	152.5	na	5000	na	$na
226	122	sld-gear 3f-r	189	na	5000	na	$na
226	80b	sld-gear 3f-r	120	6.70 x 15	3410	na	$na
226	122b	sld-gear 3f-r	120	na	3410	na	$na
226	80b	sld-gear 3f-r	120	6.70x15	3410	na	$2,542
226	122b	sld-gear 3f-r	120	7.10x15	3670	na	$2,896
226	80b	sld-gear 3f-r	120	6.70x15	3485	na	$2,650
226	122b	sld-gear 3f-r	120	7.10x15	3720	na	$3,004
226	80b	sld-gear 3f-r	129	na	5000	na	$na
226	122b	sld-gear 3f-r	154.5	na	5000	na	$na
226	122b	sld-gear 3f-r	189	na	5000	na	$na
226	80b	sld-gear 3f-r	120	6.70 x 15	3410	na	$na
226	122b	sld-gear 3f-r	120	na	3410	na	$na
226	80b	sld-gear 3f-r	120	6.70 x15	3485	na	$2,642
226	141b	sld-gear 3f-r	120	7.10 x15	3625	na	$2,991
226	80b	sld-gear 3f-r	120	6.70x15	3485	na	$2,793
226	141b	sld-gear 3f-r	120	7.10x15	3625	na	$3,140
226	141b	sld-gear 3f-r	129	na	3625	na	$4,638
226	141b	sld-gear 3f-r	154.5	na	na	na	$na
226	141b	sld-gear 3f-r	189	na	na	na	$na
226	122b	sld-gear 3f-r	120	na	3485	na	$na
226	141b	sld-gear 3f-r	120	na	3410	na	$na
226	80b	sld-gear 3f-r	120	6.70x15	3485	na	$2,793
226	80b	sld-gear 3f-r	120	7.10x15	3625	na	$3,140
226	80b	sld-gear 3f-r	129	na	3625	na	$4,638
326	na	sld-gear 3f-r	154.5	na	na	na	$na

MAKE & MANUF.		APPEARANCE			MECHANICAL 1		
Year	Model	Body Type and # Passengers	Steering	Engine Manufacturer	Cooling #Cyl & Conf.	Fuel	Bore & Stroke

Checker 1964— *continued*

	A-12E	Aerobus 8 dr. –12p	Lh-w	Chrysler	lqd V8	gas	na
	A-11	Taxi	Lh-w	Continental	lqd 6-L	gas	3.31 X 4.38
	A-11	Taxi	Lh-w	Continental	lqd 6-ov	gas	3.31 X 4.38

Total production for all models is estimated at 6,310, including 960 for the consumer market.

The 266 cid, overhead valve engine, measuring 3 5/16 x 4 3/8, and rated at 141 brake hp was an option for all series.

1965   **Checker Motors Corporation turned to the Chevrolet Division of General Motors for its engines. These engines, all with overhead valves, became the standard offering through 1982.**

	A-12	Marathon Sedan–6p	Lh-w	Chevrolet	lqd 6-ov	gas	3.88 x 3.25
	A-12	Marathon Sedan–8p	Lh-w	Chevrolet	lqd 6-ov	gas	3.88 x 3.25
	A-12	Marathon Sta. Wagon–6p	Lh-w	Chevrolet	lqd 6-ov	gas	3.88 x 3.25
	A-12E	Town Cust Limo–6p	Lh-w	Chevrolet	lqd 6-ov	gas	3.88 x 3.25
	A-12E	Aerobus 6 dr.–9p	Lh-w	Chevrolet	lqd V8-ov	gas	3.88 x 3
	A-12E	Aerobus 8 dr. –12p	Lh-w	Chevrolet	lqd V8-ov	gas	3.88 x 3
	A-11	Taxi Sedan–6p	Lh-w	Chevrolet	lqd 6-ov	gas	3.88 x 3.25

The V-8 engine was an available option for all models and is shown here with the larger and heavier Aerobus models.

Total production for all models is estimated at 6,136, including 930 for the consumer market.

1966

	A-12	Marathon Sedan–6p	Lh-w	Chevrolet	lqd 6-ov	gas	3.88 x 3.25
	A-12	Marathon Sedan–8p	Lh-w	Chevrolet	lqd 6-ov	gas	3.88 x 3.25
	A-12	Marathon Sta. Wagon–6p	Lh-w	Chevrolet	lqd 6-ov	gas	3.88 x 3.25
	A-12E	Town Custom Sedan–8p	Lh-w	Chevrolet	lqd 6-ov	gas	3.88 x 3.25
	A-12E	Aerobus 6 dr.–9p	Lh-w	Chevrolet	lqd V8-ov	gas	3.88 x 3
	A-12E	Aerobus 8 dr. –12p	Lh-w	Chevrolet	lqd V8-ov	gas	4 x 3.25
	A-11	Taxi Sedan 6p	Lh w	Chevrolet	lqd 6 ov	gas	3.88 x 3.25

The V-8 engines were an available option for all models and are shown here with the larger and heavier Aerobus models.

Total production for all models is estimated at 5,761 including 1,056 for the consumer market.

1967   **The limousine was replaced with a deluxe sedan without a window separating the front and rear seats.**

	A-12	Marathon Sedan–6p	Lh-w	Chevrolet	lqd 6-ov	gas	3.88 x 3.25
	A-12	Marathon Sta. Wagon–6p	Lh-w	Chevrolet	lqd 6-ov	gas	3.88 x 3.25
	A-12E	Marathon Del. Sedan–8p	Lh-w	Chevrolet	lqd 6-ov	gas	3.88 x 3.25
	A-12	Marathon Aerobus–9p	Lh-w	Chevrolet	lqd V8-ov	gas	4 x 3.25
	A-12	Marathon Aerobus–12p	Lh-w	Chevrolet	lqd V8-ov	gas	4 x 3.25
	A-11	Taxi Sedan–6p	Lh-w	Chevrolet	lqd 6-ov	gas	3.88 x 3.25

Total production for all models is estimated at 5,822 including 950 for the consumer market.

1968   **The new emission controls were fitted to all Checker gasoline engines and the company introduced the first diesel power option.**

	A-12	Marathon Sedan–6p	Lh-w	Chevrolet	lqd 6-ov	gas	3.88 x 3.25
	A-12	Marathon Sta. Wagon–6p	Lh-w	Chevrolet	lqd 6-ov	gas	3.88 x 3.25
	A-12	Marathon Del. Sedan–9p	Lh-w	Perkins	lqd 4	diesel	3.875 x 5.0
	A-12	Aerobus–9p	Lh-w	Chevrolet	lqd V8-ov	gas	na

MECHANICAL 2			CHASSIS			PRODUCTION	
CID	Hp	Transmission & Gearing	Wheelbase & gauge (in.)	Tire Size	Weight	Production	Cost
326	na	sld-gear 3f-r	189	na	na	na	$na
226	80b	sld-gear 3f-r	120	na	3485	na	$na
226	141b	sld-gear 3f-r	120	na	3485	na	$na
230	140b	sld-gear 3f-r	120	8:25 x 15	3360	na	$2,874
230	140b	sld-gear 3f-r	120	8:25 x 15	3406	na	$3,567
230	140b	sld-gear 3f-r	120	8:25 x 15	3400	na	$3,075
226	155b	sld-gear 3f-r	129	8:25 x 15	3578	na	$na
283	195b	sld-gear 3f-r	154.5	8:25 x 15	3578	na	$na
283	195b	sld-gear 3f-r	189	8:25 x 15	3578	na	$na
230	155b	sld-gear 3f-r	120	8:25 x 15	3268	na	$na
230	155b	sld-gear 3f-r	120	8.15 x 15	3390	na	$2,874
230	155b	sld-gear 3f-r	120	8:15 x 15	3390	na	$3,567
230	155b	sld-gear 3f-r	120	8:15 x 15	3480	na	$3,075
226	155b	sld-gear 3f-r	129	na	3800	na	$4,541
283	195b	sld-gear 3f-r	154.5	na	na	na	$na
327	250b	sld-gear 3f-r	189	na	na	na	$na
230	155b	sld-gear 3f-r	120	8:25 x 15	3268	na	$na
230	155b	sld-gear 3f-r	120	8:25 x 15	3400	na	$2,874
230	155b	sld-gear 3f-r	120	8:25 x 15	3500	na	$3,075
230	155b	sld-gear 3f-r	129	8:25 x 15	na	na	$na
283	195b	sld-gear 3f-r	154.5	8:20 x 15	na	na	$na
327	275b	sld-gear 3f-r	189	8:20 x 15	na	na	$na
230	155b	sld-gear 3f-r	120	8:25 x 15	3400	na	$na
230	155b	sld-gear 3f-r	120	8:25 x 15	3390	na	$3,221
230	155b	sld-gear 3f-r	120	8:25 x 15	3480	na	$3,491
236	88b	sld-gear 3f-r	129	na	3700	na	$3,915
307	na	sld-gear 3f-r	154.5	na	na	na	$na

MAKE & MANUF.		APPEARANCE			MECHANICAL 1		
Year	Model	Body Type and # Passengers	Steering	Engine Manufacturer	Cooling #Cyl & Conf.	Fuel	Bore & Stroke

Checker — *continued*

	A-12	Aerobus—12p	Lh-w	Chevrolet	lqd V8-ov	gas	4 x 3.25
	A-11	Taxi Sedan–8p	Lh-w	Perkins	lqd 4	diesel	3.875 x 5.0
	A-11	Taxi Sedan–6p	Lh-w	Chevrolet	lqd 6-ov	gas	3.88 x 3.25

Total production for all models is estimated at 5,477 including 992 for the consumer market.

A Ghia-designed Checker was shown at the 1968 automobile show in Paris.

1969   Checker offered the Medicar in 1969–70, with high roof profile convenient for transporting medical equipment and the wheelchair-bound passenger.

	A-12	Marathon Sedan–6p	Lh-w	Chevrolet	lqd 6-ov	gas	3 7/8 x 3 17/32
	A-12	Marathon Sta. Wagon–6p	Lh-w	Chevrolet	lqd 6-ov	gas	3 7/8 x 3 17/32
	A-12	Marathon Sedan–8p	Lh-w	Chevrolet	lqd 6-ov	gas	3 7/8 x 3 17/32
	A-12	Marathon Limo–8p	Lh-w	Chevrolet	lqd V8-ov	gas	3 7/8 x 3 17/32
	A-12	Aerobus 6 dr.–9p	Lh-w	Chevrolet	lqd V8-ov	gas	4 x 3 1/4
	A-12	Aerobus 8 dr.–12p	Lh-w	Chevrolet	lqd V8-ov	gas	4 x 3 15/16
	A-11	Taxi Sedan–6p	Lh-w	Chevrolet	lqd 6-ov	gas	3 7/8 x 3 17/32

Checker offered two optional V-8 engines; one at 300 bhp was the highest hp rating in the history of the company. These engines are listed for the larger, heavier Aerobus.

Total production for all models is estimated at 5,417 including 760 for the consumer market.

1970   Disc brakes were offered as an option.

	A-12	Marathon Sedan–6p	Lh-w	Chevrolet	lqd 6-ov	gas	3 7/8 x 3 17/32
	A-12	Marathon Sta. Wagon–6p	Lh-w	Chevrolet	lqd 6-ov	gas	3 7/8 x 3 17/32
	A-12	Marathon Sedan–8p	Lh-w	Chevrolet	lqd 6-ov	gas	3 7/8 x 3 17/32
	A-12	Marathon Limo–8p	Lh-w	Chevrolet	lqd 6-ov	gas	3 7/8 x 3 17/32
	A-12	Aerobus 8 dr.–15p	Lh-w	Chevrolet	lqd V8-ov	gas	4 x 3 15/16
	A-11	Taxi Sedan–6p	Lh-w	Chevrolet	lqd 6-ov	gas	3 7/8 x 3 17/32

Checker offered only one 350 cid V-8 engine option which was now rated at 250 hp.

Total production for all models is estimated at 4,000 of which 397 were for the consumer market.

1971   The six- and eight-cylinder models were each marketed as a separate series.

	A-12	Marathon Sedan–6p	Lh-w	Chevrolet	lqd 6-ov	gas	3.88 x 3.53
	A-12	Marathon Sta. Wagon–6p	Lh-w	Chevrolet	lqd 6-ov	gas	3.88 x 3.53
	A-12	Marathon Sedan–6p	Lh-w	Chevrolet	lqd V8-ov	gas	4 x 3 15/32
	A-12	Marathon Sta. Wagon–6p	Lh-w	Chevrolet	lqd V8-ov	gas	4 x 3 15/32
	A-12	Marathon Sedan–8p	Lh-w	Chevrolet	lqd 6-ov	gas	3.88 x 3.53
	A-12	Marathon Limo–8p	Lh-w	Chevrolet	lqd 6-ov	gas	3.88 x 3.53
	A-12	Marathon Sedan–8p	Lh-w	Chevrolet	lqd V8-ov	gas	4 x 3 15/32
	A-12	Marathon Limo–8p	Lh-w	Chevrolet	lqd V8-ov	gas	4 x 3 15/32
	A-12	Aerobus 8 dr.–15p	Lh-w	Chevrolet	lqd 6-ov	gas	4 x 3 15/32
	A-11	Taxi Sedan–6p	Lh-w	Chevrolet	lqd 6-ov	gas	3.88 x 3.53

Total production unknown, but estimated at 4,500 for all models.

MECHANICAL 2			CHASSIS			PRODUCTION	
CID	Hp	Transmission & Gearing	Wheelbase & gauge (in.)	Tire Size	Weight	Production	Cost
327	275	sld-gear 3f-r	189	na	na	na	$na
236	88b	sld-gear 3f-r	120	na	na	na	$na
230	155b	sld-gear 3f-r	120	8:25 x 15	3390	na	$na
250	155b	sld-gear 3f-r	120	8.25 x 15	3390	na	$3,290
250	155b	sld-gear 3f-r	120	8:25 x 15	3480	na	$3,560
226	155b	sld-gear 3f-r	129	8:25 x 15	3590	na	$3,984
226	155b	sld-gear 3f-r	129	8:25 x 15	3802	na	$4,969
327	235b	sld-gear 3f-r	154.5	8:20 x 15	na	na	$na
350	300b	sld-gear 3f-r	189	8:20 x 15	na	na	$na
250	155b	sld-gear 3f-r	120	8:25 x 15	3268	na	$na
250	155b	sld-gear 3f-r	120	8:25 x 15	3268	na	$3,671
250	155b	sld-gear 3f-r	120	8:25 x 15	3470	na	$3,941
250	155b	sld-gear 3f-r	129	8:25 x 15	3378	na	$4,364
250	155b	sld-gear 3f-r	129	8:25 x 15	3578	na	$5,338
350	250b	sld-gear 3f-r	189	na	na	na	$na
250	155b	sld-gear 3f-r	120	8:25 x 15	3268	na	$na
250	145b	sld-gear 3f-r	120	G-78 x 15	3400	na	$3,843
250	145b	sld-gear 3f-r	120	G-78 x 15	3600	na	$4,113
350	245b	sld-gear 3f-r	120	G-78 x 15	3500	na	$3,958
350	245b	sld-gear 3f-r	120	G-78 x 15	3700	na	$4,228
250	125b	sld-gear 3f-r	129	G-78 x 15	3700	na	$4,536
250	145b	sld-gear 3f-r	129	G-78 x 15	3700	na	$5,510
350	245b	sld-gear 3f-r	129	G-78 x 15	3800	na	$4,651
350	245b	sld-gear 3f-r	129	G-78 x 15	3800	na	$5,626
350	245b	sld-gear 3f-r	189	G-78 x 15	5300	na	$na
250	145b	sld-gear 3f-r	120	G-78 x 15	na	na	$na

MAKE & MANUF.		APPEARANCE			MECHANICAL 1		
Year	Model	Body Type and # Passengers	Steering	Engine Manufacturer	Cooling #Cyl & Conf.	Fuel	Bore & Stroke
Checker — *continued*							
1972	**Automatic transmission and power disc brakes become standard for all models.**						
	A-12	Marathon Sedan–6p	Lh-w	Chevrolet	lqd 6-ov	gas	3.88 x 3.53
	A-12	Marathon Sta. Wagon–6p	Lh-w	Chevrolet	lqd 6-ov	gas	3.88 x 3.53
	A-12	Marathon Sedan–6p	Lh-w	Chevrolet	lqd V8-ov	gas	4 x 3 15/32
	A-12	Marathon Sta. Wagon–6p	Lh-w	Chevrolet	lqd V8-ov	gas	4 x 3 15/32
	A-12	Marathon Sedan–8p	Lh-w	Chevrolet	lqd 6-ov	gas	3.88 x 3.53
	A-12	Marathon Sedan–8p	Lh-w	Chevrolet	lqd V8-ov	gas	4 x 3 15/32
	A-12	Aerobus 8 dr.–15p	Lh-w	Chevrolet	lqd V8-ov	gas	4 x 3 15/32
	A-11	Taxi Sedan–6p	Lh-w	Chevrolet	lqd 6-ov	gas	3.88 X 3.53

Total production unknown, but estimated at 4,500, including 850 vehicles for the consumer market.
The six cylinder engine was rated at 110 S.A.E. Net horsepower, and the eight cylinder was rated at 165 S.A.E Net.

1973	**Beginning in 1973, horsepower is reported as S.A.E Net rather than braking horsepower. The S.A.E. figures are lower than the braking horsepower.**						
	A-12	Marathon Sedan–6p	Lh-w	Chevrolet	lqd 6-ov	gas	3.88 x 3.53
	A-12	Marathon Sta. Wagon–6p	Lh-w	Chevrolet	lqd 6-ov	gas	3.88 x 3.53
	A-12	Marathon Sedan–6p	Lh-w	Chevrolet	lqd V8-ov	gas	4 x 3 15/32
	A-12	Marathon Sta. Wagon–6p	Lh-w	Chevrolet	lqd V8-ov	gas	4 x 3 15/32
	A-12	Marathon Sedan–8p	Lh-w	Chevrolet	lqd 6-ov	gas	3.88 x 3.53
	A-12	Marathon Sedan–8p	Lh-w	Chevrolet	lqd V8-ov	gas	4 x 3 15/32
	A-12	Aerobus 8 dr.–15p	Lh-w	Chevrolet	lqd V8-ov	gas	4 x 3 15/32
	A-11	Taxi Sedan–6p	Lh-w	Chevrolet	lqd 6-ov	gas	3.88 x 3.53

Total production of all models is estimated at 5,900.

1974	**The massive bumpers required by Federal regulations appear on all Checkers.**						
	A-12	Marathon Sedan–6p	Lh-w	Chevrolet	lqd 6-ov	gas	3.88 x 3.53
	A-12	Marathon Sta. Wagon–6p	Lh-w	Chevrolet	lqd 6-ov	gas	3.88 x 3.53
	A-12	Marathon Sedan–6p	Lh-w	Chevrolet	lqd V8-ov	gas	4 x 3 15/32
	A-12	Marathon Sta. Wagon–6p	Lh-w	Chevrolet	lqd V8-ov	gas	4 x 3 15/32
	A-12E	Marathon Sedan–8p	Lh-w	Chevrolet	lqd 6-ov	gas	3.88 x 3.53
	A-12E	Marathon Sedan–8p	Lh-w	Chevrolet	lqd V8-ov	gas	4 x 3 15/32
	A-12E	Aerobus 8 dr.–15p	Lh-w	Chevrolet	lqd V8-ov	gas	4 x 3 15/32
	A-11	Taxi Sedan–6p	Lh-w	Chevrolet	lqd 6-ov	gas	3.88 x 3.53

Total production of all models is estimated at 5,880.

1975	**Checker dropped the station wagon and the 129" long wheel base models, but retained the Aerobus with its 189" wheel base.**						
	A-12	Marathon Sedan–6p	Lh-w	Chevrolet	lqd 6-ov	gas	3.88 x 3.53
	A-12	Marathon Sedan–6p	Lh-w	Chevrolet	lqd V8-ov	gas	4 x 3 15/32
	A-12	Marathon Deluxe–6p	Lh-w	Chevrolet	lqd V8-ov	gas	4 x 3 15/32
	A-12E	Aerobus 8 dr.–15p	Lh-w	Chevrolet	lqd V8-ov	gas	4 x 3 15/32
	A-11	Taxi Sedan–6p	Lh-w	Chevrolet	lqd 6-ov	gas	3.88 x 3.53

Total production for all models is estimated at 3,005, including 450 for the consumer market.

MECHANICAL 2			CHASSIS			PRODUCTION	
CID	Hp	Transmission & Gearing	Wheelbase & gauge (in.)	Tire Size	Weight	Production	Cost
250	145b	automatic 3f-r	120	G-78 x 15	3522	na	$3,654
250	145b	automatic 3f-r	120	G-78 x 15	3725	na	$3,910
350	245b	automatic 3f-r	120	G-78 x 15	3623	na	$3,769
350	245b	automatic 3f-r	120	G-78 x 15	3816	na	$4,025
250	145b	automatic 3f-r	129	G-78 x 15	3722	na	$4,312
350	245b	automatic 3f-r	129	G-78 x 15	3823	na	$4,427
350	245b	automatic 3f-r	189	G-78 x 15	5300	na	$na
250	145b	automatic 3f-r	120	G-78 X 15	na	na	$na
250	100sae	automatic 3f-r	120	G-78 x 15	3622	na	$3,955
250	145sae	automatic 3f-r	120	G-78 x 15	3825	na	$4,211
350	145sae	automatic 3f-r	120	G-78 x 15	3723	na	$4,070
350	145sae	automatic 3f-r	120	G-78 x 15	3916	na	$4,326
250	100sae	automatic 3f-r	129	G-78 x 15	3822	na	$4,612
350	145sae	automatic 3f-r	129	G-78 x 15	3923	na	$4,727
350	145sae	automatic 3f-r	189	G-78 x 15	na	na	$na
250	100sae	automatic 3f-r	120	G-78 x 15	na	na	$na
250	100sae	automatic 3f-r	120	G-78 x 15	3720	na	$4,716
250	100sae	automatic 3f-r	120	G-78 x 15	3925	na	$4,966
350	145sae	automatic 3f-r	120	G-78 x 15	3723	na	$4,825
350	145sae	automatic 3f-r	120	G-78 x 15	3916	na	$5,074
250	100sae	automatic 3f-r	129	G-78 x 15	3920	na	$5,394
350	145sae	automatic 3f-r	129	G-78 x 15	3923	na	$5,503
350	145sae	automatic 3f-r	189	G-78 x 15	na	na	$na
250	100sae	automatic 3f-r	120	G-78 x 15	na	na	$na
250	100sae	automatic 3f-r	120	G-78 x 15	3774	na	$5,394
350	145sae	automatic 3f-r	120	G-78 x 15	3839	na	$5,539
350	145sae	automatic 3f-r	120	G-78 x 15	4137	na	$6,216
350	145sae	automatic 3f-r	189	G-78 x 15	na	na	$na
250	100sae	automatic 3f-r	120	G-78 x 15	na	na	$na

MAKE & MANUF.		APPEARANCE			MECHANICAL 1		
Year	Model	Body Type and # Passengers	Steering	Engine Manufacturer	Cooling #Cyl & Conf.	Fuel	Bore & Stroke

Checker — *continued*

1976 Horsepower ratings are now indicated as braking instead of S.A.E Net, but the ratings show minimal or no change.

	A-12	Marathon Sedan–6p	Lh-w	Chevrolet	lqd 6-ov	gas	3.88 x 3.53
	A-12	Marathon Sedan–6p	Lh-w	Chevrolet	lqd V8-ov	gas	4 x 3.48
	A-12E	Marathon Deluxe–6p	Lh-w	Chevrolet	lqd V8-ov	gas	4 x 3.48
	A-12E	Aerobus 8-dr.–15p	Lh-w	Chevrolet	lqd V8-ov	gas	4 x 3.48
	A-11	Taxi Sedan–6p	Lh-w	Chevrolet	lqd 6-ov	gas	3.88 x 3.53
	A-11E	Taxi Sedan	Lh-w	Chevrolet	lqd V8-ov	gas	4 x 3.48

Total production is estimated at 4,790, including an estimated 400 for the consumer market.

1977

	A-12	Marathon Sedan–6p	Lh-w	Chevrolet	lqd 6-ov	gas	3.88 x 3.53
	A-12	Marathon Sedan–6p	Lh-w	Chevrolet	lqd V8-ov	gas	3.74 x 3.48
	A-12	Marathon Deluxe–6p	Lh-w	Chevrolet	lqd V8-ov	gas	3.74 x 3.48
	A-12E	Aerobus 8-dr.–15p	Lh-w	Chevrolet	lqd V8-ov	gas	4 x 3.48
	A-11	Taxi Sedan–6p	Lh-w	Chevrolet	lqd 6-ov	gas	3.88 x 3.53

Total production is estimated at 4,568, including 450 for the consumer market.

The 350 cid V-8 was an option and is shown here in the Aerobus.

1978

	A-12	Marathon Sedan–6p	Lh-w	Chevrolet	lqd 6-ov	gas	3.88 x 3.53
	A-12	Marathon Deluxe–6p	Lh-w	Chevrolet	lqd V8-ov	gas	3.74 x 3.48
	A-12E	Marathon Deluxe–6p	Lh-w	Chevrolet	lqd V8-ov	gas	3.74 x 3.48
	A-12E	Aerobus 8-dr.–15p	Lh-w	Chevrolet	lqd V8-ov	gas	4 x 3.48
	A-11	Taxi Sedan–6p	Lh-w	Chevrolet	lqd 6-ov	gas	3.88 x 3.53

Total production is estimated at 5,503, including 307 for the consumer market.

The 350 cid V-8 was an option and is shown here in the Aerobus.

1979

	A-12	Marathon Sedan–6p	Lh-w	Chevrolet	lqd 6-ov	gas	3.88 x 3.53
	A-12	Marathon Deluxe–6p	Lh-w	Chevrolet	lqd V8-ov	gas	3.74 x 3.48
	A-12E	Marathon Deluxe–6p	Lh-w	Chevrolet	lqd V8-ov	gas	3.74 x 3.48
	A-12E	Aerobus 8-dr.–15p	Lh-w	Chevrolet	lqd V8-ov	gas	4 x 3.48
	A-11	Taxi Sedan–6p	Lh-w	Chevrolet	lqd 6-ov	gas	3.88 x 3.53
	A-11E	Taxi Deluxe–6p	Lh-w	Chevrolet	lqd V8-ov	gas	3.5 x 3.48

Total production is estimated at 5,231 including 270 for the consumer market.

1980 The Checker line featured new engines, and the return of the diesel engine option.

	A-12	Marathon Sedan–6p	Lh-w	Chevrolet	lqd V6-ov	gas	3.74 x 3.48
	A-12	Marathon Deluxe–6p	Lh-w	Chevrolet	lqd V8-ov	gas	3.5 x 3.48
	A-12E	Marathon Deluxe–6p	Lh-w	Chevrolet	lqd V8-ov	gas	3.5 x 3.48
	A-12E	Aerobus 8-dr.–15p	Lh-w	Chevrolet	lqd V8-ov	gas	3.74 3.48
	A-11	Taxi Sedan–6p	Lh-w	Chevrolet	lqd V6-ov	gas	3.74 x 3.48
	A-11E	Taxi Deluxe–6p	Lh-w	Chevrolet	lqd V8-ov	gas	3.5 x 3.48

Total production is estimated at 2,574 for all models.

A V-8 Diesel engine, 4.06 x 3.39, rated at 125 bhp was also available this year.
  These models were priced at $10,473 and $11,310.

MECHANICAL 2			CHASSIS			PRODUCTION	
CID	Hp	Transmission & Gearing	Wheelbase & gauge (in.)	Tire Size	Weight	Production	Cost
250	105b	automatic 3f-r	120	G-78 x 15	3775	na	$5,749
350	145b	automatic 3f-r	120	G-78 x 15	3839	na	$na
350	145b	automatic 3f-r	120	G-78 x 15	4137	na	$6,736
350	145b	automatic 3f-r	189	G-78 x 15	na	na	$na
250	105b	automatic 3f-r	120	G-78 x 15	na	na	$na
350	145b	automatic 3f-r	120	G-78 x 15	4137	na	$na
250	110b	automatic 3f-r	120	G-78 x 15	3775	na	$na
305	145b	automatic 3f-r	120	G-78 x 15	na	na	$na
305	145b	automatic 3f-r	129	G-78 x 15	4137	na	$an
350	170b	automatic 3f-r	189	G-78 x 15	na	na	$na
250	110b	automatic 3f-r	120	G-78 x 15	na	na	$na
250	110b	automatic 3f-r	120	G-78 x 15	3740	na	$6,419
305	145b	automatic 3f-r	120	G-78 x 15	3862	na	$na
305	145b	automatic 3f-r	129	G-78 x 15	3999	na	$7,472
350	160	automatic 3f-r	189	G-78 x 15	na	na	$na
250	115b	automatic 3f-r	120	G-78 x 15	na	na	$na
250	110b	automatic 3f-r	120	P215/75R	3740	na	$7,314
305	145b	automatic 3f-r	120	P215/75R	3862	na	$7,515
305	145b	automatic 3f-r	129	P215/75R	3999	na	$8,389
350	160b	automatic 3f-r	189	P215/75R	na	na	$na
250	115b	automatic 3f-r	120	P215/75R	na	na	$na
267	120b	automatic 3f-r	129	P225/75R	na	na	$na
229	115b	automatic 3f-r	120	P215/75R	3680	na	$8,118
267	120b	automatic 3f-r	120	P215/75R	na	na	$na
267	120b	automatic 3f-r	129	P225/75R	3999	na	$9,192
305	155b	automatic 3f-r	189	P225/75R	na	na	$na
229	115b	automatic 3f-r	120	P215/75R	na	na	$na
267	120b	automatic 3f-r	129	P225/75R	na	na	$na

MAKE & MANUF.		APPEARANCE			MECHANICAL 1		
Year	Model	Body Type and # Passengers	Steering	Engine Manufacturer	Cooling #Cyl & Conf.	Fuel	Bore & Stroke

Checker — *continued*

1981

	A-12	Marathon Sedan–6p	Lh-w	Chevrolet	lqd V6-ov	gas	3.73 x 3.48
	A-12	Marathon Deluxe–6p	Lh-w	Chevrolet	lqd V8-ov	gas	4 x 3 15/32
	A-12E	Marathon Deluxe–6p	Lh-w	Chevrolet	lqd V8-ov	gas	4 x 3 15/32
	A-12E	Aerobus 8-dr.–15p	Lh-w	Chevrolet	lqd V8-ov	gas	4 x 3 15/32
	A-11	Taxi Sedan–6p	Lh-w	Chevrolet	lqd V6-ov	gas	3.73 x 3.48
	A-11E	Taxi Deluxe–6p	Lh-w	Chevrolet	lqd V8-ov	gas	4 x 3 15/32

Total production for the year is estimated at 2,950.
The V-8 Diesel engine was also available in 1981.

1982   The last Checker was built July 12, 1982.

	A-12	Marathon Sedan–6p	Lh-w	Chevrolet	lqd V6-ov	gas	3.73 x 3.48
	A-12	Marathon Deluxe–6p	Lh-w	Chevrolet	lqd V8-ov	gas	4 x 3 15/32
	A-12E	Marathon Deluxe–6p	Lh-w	Chevrolet	lqd V8-ov	gas	4 x 3 15/32
	A-12E	Aerobus 8-dr.–15p	Lh-w	Chevrolet	lqd V8-ov	gas	4 x 3 15/32
	A-11	Taxi Sedan–6p	Lh-w	Chevrolet	lqd V6-ov	gas	3.73 x 3.48
	A-11E	Taxi Deluxe–6p	Lh-w	Chevrolet	lqd V8-ov	gas	4 x 3 15/32

Total production for the year is estimated at 2,000.
The V-8 Diesel engine was also available in 1982.

Clark — *Clark brothers, Vicksburg, Michigan*

1901

June		Runabout–2p	na	Clark	lqd 1	stm	na

Cornelian — *Cornelian Department, Blood Brothers Machine Company, 623 W. Ransom Street*

1913

Aug		Cyclecar side/side–2p	Lh-w	Mack	air 2	gas	3 3/8x3 29/32

1914

Jan		Cyclecar side/side–2p	Lh-w	Spacke	air 2	gas	na

1914

Feb		Cyclecar side/side–2p	Lh-w	Sterling	lqd 2	gas	2 3/4x4

In February 1914, Howard Blood replaced the 2-cylinder Spacke air-cooled engine with a 95 cid Sterling 4-cylinder water-cooled engine.

1914

Apr		Lightcar side/side–2p	Lh-w	Sterling	lqd 4	gas	2 7/8x4

In April 1914, the Cornelian was reconfigured to meet the "light-car" definition.

1914

Sept		Race car–2p	Lh-w	Sterling	lqd 4	gas	2 7/8x4

In September 1914, Howard Blood entered a stock Cornelian in the Kalamazoo race; descriptions of the mechanics of this car vary slightly depending on publication.

MECHANICAL 2			CHASSIS			PRODUCTION	
CID	Hp	Transmission & Gearing	Wheelbase & gauge (in.)	Tire Size	Weight	Production	Cost
229	110b	automatic 3f-r	120	P215/75R	3680	na	$9,632
267	115b	automatic 3f-r	120	P215/75R	na	na	$9,869
267	115b	automatic 3f-r	120	P215/75R	3999	na	$10,706
267	115b	automatic 3f-r	189	P225/75R	na	na	$na
229	110b	automatic 3f-r	120	P215/75R	na	na	$na
267	115b	automatic 3f-r	129	P215/75R	na	na	$na
229	110b	automatic 3f-r	120	P215/75R	3839	na	$10,950
267	115b	automatic 3f-r	120	P215/75R	4137	na	$11,187
267	115b	automatic 3f-r	120	P215/75R	4137	na	$12,025
267	115b	automatic 3f-r	189	P225/75R	na	na	$na
229	145b	automatic 3f-r	120	P215/75R	na	na	$na
267	115b	automatic 3f-r	129	P215/75R	na	na	$na
na	na	na continuous	na	na	na	2	$750
69.9	9	sld-gear 2f-r	100x56	28x3	600	4	$400
70	9	sld-gear 2f-r	96x55	28x2.5	1000	10	$425
95	12.1	sld-gear 2f-r	96x55	28x3	1000	25	$425
103	13.2	sld-gear 2f-r	96x55	28x3	1000	100	$425
103	13.2	sld-gear 2f-r	96x55	28x3	1000	1	$na

MAKE & MANUF.		APPEARANCE			MECHANICAL 1		
Year	Model	Body Type and # Passengers	Steering	Engine Manufacturer	Cooling #Cyl & Conf.	Fuel	Bore & Stroke

Cornelian—*Blood Brothers Machine Company, Allegan, Michigan*

1915   The Blood Brothers Company moved to Allegan in December 1914.
Howard Blood's Cornelian Department remained as a separate entity in the company.

Mar		Light car side/side–2p	Lh-w	Sterling	lqd 4	gas	2 7/8 x 4

By 1915 the Cornelian had a roadster style body with full running boards.

1915

Apr		Indy-500 race car–2p	Lh-w	Sterling	lqd 4	gas	3.04x4 est.

Production of the Cornelian ceased in September 1915.

Crown

Early reports in the local paper identified the Greyhound as being built by the Crown Automobile Manufacturing Company. The source for this reference is unknown; please refer to Greyhound.

Dort — *Dort Body Company, northeast corner of S. Pitcher and Gibson Streets*

1921

		14-C Coupe 2p	Lh-w	Lycoming	thm 4-L	gas	3 1/2 x 5
		19-S Sedan 5p	Lh-w	Lycoming	thm 4-L	gas	3 1/2 x 5

The Dort Body Company was established in Kalamazoo in late 1920 and began production of closed bodies in the old Lull Carriage plant for the 1921 model year. The Dort company manufactured cars in Flint from 1915–24, but advertisements identified the "Finer Dort Models" as being built in Kalamazoo, and prices for these two models were given as F.O.B. Kalamazoo.

Total production in 1921 was 17,438; the number of closed bodies built in Kalamazoo is unknown, but estimated at 3,000.

1922

		14-C Coupe 2p	Lh-w	Lycoming	thm 4-L	gas	3 1/2 x 5
		19-S Sedan 5p	Lh-w	Lycoming	thm 4-L	gas	3 1/2 x 5

Dort advertisements imply that the 1921 series of cars was continued through 1922 with little or no change.

Total production for Dort in 1922 was only 6,582 vehicles, one fifth of the production in 1920. The number of closed cars built in Kalamazoo is unknown, but is estimated at 600.

1923

		Yale Coupe 2p	Lh-w	Lycoming	thm 4-L	gas	3 1/2 x 5
		Yale Sedan 5p	Lh-w	Lycoming	thm 4-L	gas	3 1/2 x 5
		Harvard Coupe 3p	Lh-w	Lycoming	thm 4-L	gas	3 1/2 x 5
		Harvard Sedan 5p	Lh-w	Lycoming	thm 4-L	gas	3 1/2 x 5
		Yale Coupe 2p	Lh-w	Falls	thm 6-ov	gas	3 1/2 x 4 1/4
		Yale Sedan 5p	Lh-w	Falls	thm 6-ov	gas	3 1/2 x 4 1/4
		Harvard Coupe 3p	Lh-w	Falls	thm 6-ov	gas	3 1/2 x 4 1/4
		Harvard Sedan 5p	Lh-w	Falls	thm 6-ov	gas	3 1/2 x 4 1/4

In 1923 Dort offered two series identified as the Yale and the Harvard, and two engine options were offered for both. Advertising material for that year does not clarify the origin of the two series, but closed bodies were still being built in Kalamazoo until the plant was sold to Checker Cab Manufacturing Company in the spring of that year. Both the Yale and the Harvard series are listed here.

Total production for Dort in 1923 was 5,592. The number of closed cars built in Kalamazoo is unknown, but is estimated at 200.

MECHANICAL 2				CHASSIS			PRODUCTION	
CID	Hp	Transmission & Gearing		Wheelbase & gauge (in.)	Tire Size	Weight	Production	Cost
103	13.4	sld-gear	2f-r	96x55	28X3	1000	100	$410
116	30 est.	sld-gear	2f-r	96x55	30x3 1/2	980	1	$na
192	30b	sld-gear	3f-r	108	31x4	na	na	$1865
192	30b	sld-gear	3f-r	108	31x4	na	na	$1995
192	30b	sld-gear	3f-r	108	31x4	na	na	$1,865
192	30b	sld-gear	3f-r	108	31x4	na	na	$1,995
192	35b	sld-gear	3f-r	108	31x4	na	na	$1,020
192	35b	sld-gear	3f-r	108	31x4	na	na	$1,070
192	35b	sld-gear	3f-r	108	31x4	na	na	$1,240
192	35b	sld-gear	3f-r	108	31x4	na	na	$1,370
145	45b	sld-gear	3f-r	115	31x4	na	na	$1,145
145	45b	sld-gear	3f-r	115	31x4	na	na	$1,195
145	45b	sld-gear	3f-r	115	31x4	na	na	$1,365
145	45b	sld-gear	3f-r	115	31x4	na	na	$1,495

Year	Model	Body Type and # Passengers	Steering	Engine Manufacturer	Cooling #Cyl & Conf.	Fuel	Bore & Stroke
MAKE & MANUF.		**APPEARANCE**			**MECHANICAL 1**		

Durkee — *Durkee Hotel, Vicksburg, Michigan*
1903

| Summer | | Runabout–2p | Rh-w | na | air / na | gas | na |

Ells — *Ells Confectionery Store, Vicksburg, Michigan*
1902

| Aug | | Runabout–2p | na | na | na / na | na | na |

Greyhound — *States Motor Car Company, 2000 Reed Ave.*

The Greyhound was built but the States Motor Co. refer to States.

Handley-Knight — *Handley-Knight Company, 1850 N. Pitcher Street*
1920

| Nov | | Touring–7p | Rh-w | Knight | ths 4-sl | gas | 4 1/8 x 4 1/2 |

The first Handley-Knight touring was completed in the fall of 1920 and was followed by a sedan model in 1921.

1921

| Jan | B | Touring–7p | Rh-w | Knight | ths 4-sl | gas | 4 1/8x4 1/2 |
| | | Sedan–7p | Rh-w | Knight | ths 4-sl | gas | 4 1/8x4 1/2 |

1922

Jan		Touring–5p	Rh-w	Knight	ths 4-sl	gas	4 1/8x4 1/2
		Standard Touring–7p	Rh-w	Knight	ths 4-sl	gas	4 1/8x4 1/2
		Deluxe Touring–7p	Rh-w	Knight	ths 4-sl	gas	4 1/8x4 1/2
		Sedan Coupe–5p	Rh-w	Knight	ths 4-sl	gas	4 1/8x4 1/2
		Custom Sedan–7p	Rh-w	Knight	ths 4-sl	gas	4 1/8x4 1/2

In December 1922, the Handley-Knight company was reorganized, the Knight engine dropped and the company name changed to Handley Motors Inc.

Handley— *Handley Motors, Inc., 1850 N. Pitcher Street*
1923

Feb	6-40	Runabout–2p	Rh-w	na	ths 6-vh	gas	3 1/8x4 1/4
	6-40	Touring–4p	Rh-w	na	ths 6-vh	gas	3 1/8x4 1/4
	6-40	Coupe	Rh-w	na	ths 6-vh	gas	3 1/8x4 1/4
	6-40	Sedan	Rh-w	na	ths 6-vh	gas	3 1/8x4 1/4
	6-60	Touring	Rh-w	na	ths 6-vh	gas	3 3/8 x 5
	6-60	Sedan	Rh-w	na	ths 6-vh	gas	3 3/8 x 5

In May 1923, the Handley plant was sold to the Checker Cab Manufacturing Company.

Hans Tractor—*Traction Motor Corporation, 210 Kalamazoo National Bank Building*

This firm was incorporated in April 1918 to build tractors; apparently some models were built and tested, but serious manufacture is doubted.

Kalamazoo—*Michigan Buggy Company, 2000 Reed Ave. (southeast corner of Reed and Factory Street)*
1903

| July | | Runabout–2p | na | na | lqd 1 | gas | na |
| | | Runabout–2p | na | na | lqd 1 | gas | na |

There is no evidence of a Kalamazoo automobile being manufactured beyond these few reported examples.

MECHANICAL 2				CHASSIS			PRODUCTION	
CID	Hp	Transmission & Gearing		Wheelbase & gauge (in.)	Tire Size	Weight	Production	Cost
na	na	planetary	na	na	na	1500	1	$na
na	na	na	na	na	na	na	1	$na
240	48b	na	na	125	na	na	115	$2,850
240	48b	na	na	na	32x4 1/2	3200	na	$2,985
240	48b	na	na	na	32x4 1/2	3200	na	$2,985
240	48b	sld-gear	3f-r	125	32x4 1/2	na	na	$2,250
240	48b	sld-gear	3f-r	125	32x4 1/2	na	na	$2,450
240	48b	sld-gear	3f-r	125	32x4 1/2	na	na	$2,650
240	48b	sld-gear	3f-r	125	32x4 1/2	na	na	$3,750
240	48b	sld-gear	3f-r	125	32x4 1/2	na	na	$3,730
240	48b	sld-gear	3f-r	115	34x4 1/2	na	na	$1,350
240	48b	sld-gear	3f-r	115	34x4 1/2	na	na	$1,350
240	48b	sld-gear	3f-r	115	34x4 1/2	na	na	$1,750
240	48b	sld-gear	3f-r	115	34x4 1/2	na	na	$1,750
268	na	sld-gear	3f-r	125	34x4 1/2	na	na	$2,150
268	na	sld-gear	3f-r	125	34x4 1/2	na	na	$2,850
na	5	plant	2f	72-54	na	600	1–3	$na
na	7	plant	2f	72-54	na	600	1–3	$na

MAKE & MANUF.		APPEARANCE			MECHANICAL 1		
Year	Model	Body Type and # Passengers	Steering	Engine Manufacturer	Cooling #Cyl & Conf.	Fuel	Bore & Stroke

Kalamazoo — *Kalamazoo Railway Supply Co., 1827 Reed Street*
1922–29

	55-12	Inspection car–12p	na	Kalamazoo	lqd 6	gas	3 3/4 x 4 1/2

The Kalamazoo reverse transmission allowed the rail car to be driven in either direction as "forward."

Kalamazoo — *Kalamazoo Manufacturing, 1827 Reed Street, the name was changed in 1946.*
1972

	K-45A	Platform truck-1p	Mid-w	Continental	lqd 4	gas	na
	K-45B	Platform Truck-1p	Mid-w	Chrysler	lqd 6slnt	gas	na
	2500	Burden Carrier-1p	Mid-w	Wisconsin	lqd 4-ov	gas	na
	2XRG-20	Speed Truck–2p	Lh-w	Wisconsin	air 2	gas	na

Kalamazoo Manufacturing produced all manner of small platform trucks, burden carriers and speed trucks from 1946 to 1988. The four listed models are intended to show the range of vehicles. Kalamazoo Manufacturing was purchased by United Tractor of Chesterton, Indiana in 1988.

Kalamazoo Truck — *Kalamazoo Motor Vehicle Company, 416–430 North Church Street*

1913

Sept	B	1 1/2 ton truck chassis	Rh-w	Rutenber	lqd 4	gas	3 3/4 x 5 1/4
Dec	B	1 1/2 ton truck chassis	Rh-w	Rutenber	lqd 4	gas	3 3/4 x 5 1/4

1914

Dec	B	1 1/2 ton chassis	Rh-w	Buda	lqd 4	gas	3 3/4 x 5 1/2

1915

Sept		1 1/2 ton chassis	Rh-w	Buda	lqd 4	gas	3 3/4 x 5 1/2

In July, 1915 the company's name was changed to Columbia Motor Truck & Trailer Company and the company moved to Flint at the end of the year. It was not the predecessor to the Kalamazoo Motors Corporation.

Kalamazoo Truck — *Kalamazoo Motors Corporation, southeast corner Reed Ave. and Fulford Street*

1919 (est.)

	F	1 1/2 ton chassis	Lh-w	Continental	lqd 4	gas	3 1/2 x 5
	B	2 1/2 ton chassis	Lh-w	Continental	lqd 6-L	gas	3 1/2 x 5 1/4
	C	3 1/2 ton chassis	Lh-w	Continental	lqd 6-L	gas	3 3/4 x 5 1/4

The 1919 models of the Kalamazoo truck are believed to be a continuation of the Lane. In 1920 Kalamazoo dropped the six-cylinder engine in favor of the four-cylinder.

Total production estimated at 240 trucks.

1920

Aug	G	1 1/2 ton chassis	Lh-w	Continental	lqd 4	gas	3 3/4 x 5
Aug	H	2 1/2 ton chassis	Lh-w	Wisconsin	lqd 4	gas	4 x 6
June	K	3 1/2 ton chassis	Lh-w	Wisconsin	lqd 4	gas	4 1/4 x 6

1921

July	G-1	1 1/2 ton chassis	Lh-w	na	lqd 4	gas	3 3/4 x 5
	G-2	2 ton chassis	Lh-w	na	lqd 4	gas	3 3/4 x 5
	H	2 1/2 ton chassis	Lh-w	na	lqd 4	gas	4 x 6
	K	3 1/2 ton chassis	Lh-w	na	lqd 4	gas	4 1/4 x 6

MECHANICAL 2				CHASSIS			PRODUCTION	
CID	Hp	Transmission & Gearing		Wheelbase & gauge (in.)	Tire Size	Weight	Production	Cost
298	65b	sld-gear	3f-r	na	24" steel	na	na	$na
162	60b	sld-gear	3f-r	96	6.50 x 10	2650	na	$na
225	132b	sld-gear	3f-r	95	6.50 x 10	3200	na	$na
na	45b	automatic	3f-r	82 1/4	4.80 x 8	1700	na	$na
na	16b	sld-gear	3f-r	61	4.80 x 8	1450	na	$na
232	23	sld-gear	na	110-56	36x4	2500	6	$1,690
232	23	sld-gear	na	110-56	36x4	2500	25	$1,690
232	23	sld-gear	3f-r	126-56	37x4	3000	100	$1,590
232	23	sld-gear	na	119-59	37x4	3200	200	$1,650
192	19.6	na	na	144	34x4	3940	na	$2,250
303	33.5	sld-gear	na	150	na	na	na	$na
303	33.5	sld-gear	na	160	36x5	5870	na	$3,700
221	22.5	sld-gear	4f-r	144-58	36-4	5080	na	$na
302	25.6	sld-gear	4f-r	160-58	36-4	6200	na	$na
340	28.9	sld-gear	4f-r	160-62	36-5	7300	na	$na
221	22.5	na	na	na	34-4	na	na	$2,495
221	22.5	na	na	na	36-4	na	na	$3,100
302	25.6	na	na	na	36-4	na	na	$3,700
340	28.9	na	na	na	36-5	na	na	$4,300

MAKE & MANUF.		**APPEARANCE**			**MECHANICAL 1**		
Year	Model	Body Type and # Passengers	Steering	Engine Manufacturer	Cooling #Cyl & Conf.	Fuel	Bore & Stroke

Kalamazoo Truck — *continued*
1922–23

	T	1 ton chassis	Lh-w	Hercules	lqd 4-L	gas	4 x 5
	G1	1 1/2 ton chassis	Lh-w	Continental	lqd 4-L	gas	3 3/4 x 5
	LC	2 ton chassis	Lh-w	Hercules	lqd 4	gas	4 x 5
	DH	3 ton chassis	Lh-w	Wisconsin	lqd 4	gas	4 x 6
	HD	3 ton chassis	Lh-w	Wisconsin	lqd 4	gas	4 1/4 x 6
	Sk	4 ton chassis	Lh-w	Wisconsin	lqd 4	gas	4 1/4 x 6
	CK	5 ton chassis	Lh-w	Wisconsin	lqd 4	gas	4 1/2 x 6

Kalamazoo Motors Corporation was sold to Sandow Motor Truck Co. of Chicago, Illinois in April, 1924.

Lane Truck — *Lane Motor Truck Company, southeast corner of Lay and Fulford Streets*
1916

March		3/4 ton chassis	na	Wisconsin	lqd 4	gas	3 1/4 x 5

1917

April		commercial car–12p	Lh-w	Wisconsin	lqd 4	gas	na

1917

Nov		1 1/2 ton chassis	Lh-w	Continental	lqd na	gas	na
		2 1/2 ton chassis	Lh-w	Continental	lqd na	gas	na
		3 1/2 ton chassis	Lh-w	Continental	lqd 6-L	gas	3 3/4x 5 1/4

Total production is estimated at 800 trucks.
1918

July	F	1 1/2 ton chassis	Lh-w	Continental	lqd 4	gas	3 1/2 x 5
	B	2 1/2 ton chassis	Lh-w	Continental	lqd 6-L	gas	3 1/2 x 5 1/4
	C	3 1/2 ton chassis	Lh-w	Continental	lqd 6-L	gas	3 3/4 x 5 1/4

The Lane Motor Truck company was purchased by the Kalamazoo Motors Corporation in March, 1919.
Total production is estimated at 240 trucks.

Michigan — *Michigan Automobile Company Ltd, corner Prouty and North Pitcher Streets (old Montgomery Ward wagon plant)*
1903

May		Runabout-2p	Tiller	Blood	air 1	gas	3 1/4 x 3 1/2

1904

May		Runabout-2p	Tiller	Blood	air 1	gas	3 1/4 x 3 1/2

The 1903–04 Michigan was a refinement of the Blood runabout built in early 1903. While the Michigan was built by the Fullers, it has a Blood brothers heritage. The Bloods left the company in Spring 1904.

June	D-	Buggy Rear-Tonneau 5p	Rh-w	Fuller	liq 2	gas	4 1/2 x 5
	D-	Buggy Rear-Tonneau 5p	Rh-w	Fuller	liq 2	gas	4 5/8 x 5
	D-	Runabout-2p	Rh-w	Fuller	liq 2	gas	4 5/8 x 5

1905   **In May, 1905, and with much fanfare, the company introduced a Model D doctor's coupe selling for $1,000.**

Jan	E	Buggy Side-Tonneau 5p	Rh-w	Fuller	liq 2	gas	4 5/8 x 5

1906–07

Jan	E	Buggy Side-Tonneau 5p	Rh-w	Fuller	liq 2	gas	4 5/8 x 5

Advertisements indicate the continuation of the Model E with little change.

MECHANICAL 2				CHASSIS			PRODUCTION	
CID	Hp	Transmission & Gearing		Wheelbase & gauge (in.)	Tire Size	Weight	Production	Cost
251	25.6	na	na	134	34-5	3600	na	$1,685
221	22.5	na	na	144	34-5	4400	na	$2,100
251	25.6	na	na	144	36-4	5000	na	$2,775
302	25.6	na	na	160	36-4	6200	na	$3,350
340	32.4	na	na	160	36-4	6400	na	$3,500
340	32.4	na	na	160	36-4	7800	na	$4,000
382	32.4	na	na	160	36-6	8700	na	$4,550
166	16.9	na	na	120	34x4	na	na	$na
na	25	na	na	120-56	na	na	12	$na
na	na	na	na	na	na	na	na	$na
na	na	na	na	na	na	na	na	$na
232	33.8	na	na	160	36x5	na	800	$3,250
192	19.6	na		144	34x4	3940	na	$2,250
303	29.4	sld-gear	na	150	na	na	na	$na
303	33.8	sld-gear	na	160	36x5	5870	240	$3,700
29	3.5	plant-c	2f	54x55	28x2	570	100	$450
29	3.5	plant-c	2f	54x55	28x2	575	50	$475
159	12	plant-c	2f-r	78-55	28x3	1400	30	$1,000
168	14	plant-c	2f-r	80x55	30x3.5	1675	125	$1,100
168	14	plant-c	2f-r	80x55	30x3	na	na	$ 950
168	14	plant-c	2f-r	86x55	30x3.5	1700	125	$1,250
168	14	plant-c	2f-r	86x55	30x3.5	1700	na	$na

MAKE & MANUF.		APPEARANCE			MECHANICAL 1		
Year	Model	Body Type and # Passengers	Steering	Engine Manufacturer	Cooling #Cyl & Conf.	Fuel	Bore & Stroke

Michigan — *Michigan Buggy Company, 2000 Reed Ave., southeast corner of Reed and Factory Street*

1909

Nov	B	Buggy Touring–5p	Rh-w	Hazard	liq 4	gas	4 x 4 1/2

1910

	B	Buggy Touring–5p	Rh-w	Hazard	liq 4	gas	4 x 4 1/2

1911

	B	Buggy Touring–5p	Rh-w	Hazard	liq 4	gas	4 x 4 1/2
	D	Buggy Roadster–2p	Rh-w	Falls	liq 4-L	gas	4 x 4 1/2
	E	Buggy Touring–5p	Rh-w	Falls	liq 4-L	gas	4 x 4 1/2
	H	Touring 4 dr.–5p	Rh-w	Falls	liq 4-L	gas	4 x 4 1/2

Total production for the model year was 1,000.

Michigan — *Michigan Motor Car Company, founded in 1912, was owned by the Michigan Buggy Company. Address varies from 1909 to 1913. Factory was at the southeast corner of Reed and Factory Street, but in various advertisements is listed as 116; 121; 135; 138; 169; 172; 206; 211; or 214 Lay Street, or as 232 Lay Boulevard.*

1912

	G	Roadster–2p	Rh-w	Sandusky	liq 4	gas	4 1/16 x 4 1/2
	H	Torpedo-tour–5p	Rh-w	Sandusky	liq 4	gas	4 1/16 x 4 1/2
	K	Touring–5p	Rh-w	Buda	liq 4	gas	4 1/4 x 5 1/4
	M	Flyer–2p	Rh-w	Buda	liq 4	gas	4 1/4 x 5 1/4

The 1912 model offered an optional 60 gauge (wheel base width) for the "southern trade." Reportedly, many southern states adopted a wider gauge so the wheel ruts would hinder the advance of invading armies. Total production for the model year was 1700.

1913

	L	Touring–5p	Lh-w	Sandusky	liq 4-L	gas	4 1/16 x4 1/2
	O	Roadster–2p	Lh-w	Sandusky	liq 4-L	gas	4 1/16 x4 1/2
	R	Touring–5p	Lh-w	Buda	liq 4 L	gas	4 1/4 x 5 1/4
	S	Roadster–2p	Lh-w	Buda	liq 4	gas	4 1/4 x 5 1/4

Total production during the model year was 4000; production of the Michigan ceased in August, 1913.

Oswald

1900

	na	Canopy-top Surrey	na	Buffalo	na 4	gas	na

Reportedly an article from the elusive periodical The Hub *stated that a four-wheel drive automobile was built by W. E. Oswald.*

Pennant — *Barley Motor Car Company (Roamer) south east corner of Read and Factory Streets (old Michigan Buggy plant)*

1923

Jan	6-50	Taxi–5p	Lh-w	Buda	liq 4	gas	3 3/4 x 5 1/8

1924

Jan	6-50	Taxi–5p	Lh-w	Buda	liq 4	gas	3 3/4 x 5 1/8

1925

Jan	6-50	Taxi–5p	Lh-w	Buda	liq 4	gas	3 3/4 x 5 1/8

MECHANICAL 2			CHASSIS			PRODUCTION	
CID	Hp	Transmission & Gearing	Wheelbase & gauge (in.)	Tire Size	Weight	Production	Cost
226	36	sld-gear 3f-r	112x56	34x3.5	2300	100	$1,750
226	36	sld-gear 3f-r	112x56	34x3.5	2300	500	$1,750
226	25.6	sld-gear 3f-r	112x56	34.3.5	2300	na	$na
226	33	sld-gear 3f-r	112x56	34x3.5	na	na	$1,350
226	33	sld-gear 3f-r	112x56	34x3.5	na	na	$1,500
226	33	sld-gear 3f-r	112x56	34x3.5	na	na	$1,600
233	33	sld-gear 3f-r	114x56	34x3.5	2300	na	$1,400
233	33	sld-gear 3f-r	114x56	34x3.5	2300	na	$1,400
299	40	sld-gear 3f-r	116x56 (60)	34x4	na	na	$1,500
299	40	sld-gear 3f-r	116x56 (60)	34x4	na	na	$1,500
233	33	sld-gear 3f-r	114x56	34x4	2850	na	$1,400
233	33	sld-gear 3f-r	114x56	34x4	2850	na	$1,400
297	40	sld-gear 4f-r	118x56 (60)	34x4.5	3100	na	$1,585
297	40	sld-gear 4f-r	118x56 (60)	34x4.5	3100	na	$1,585
na	4.5	4-whldrve na	na	na	na	1	na
196	50	sld-gear 3f-r	115	33x4.5	na	na	$na
196	50	sld-gear 3f-r	115	33x4.5	na	na	$na
195	50	sld-gear 3f-r	115	33x4.5	na	na	$na

MAKE & MANUF.		APPEARANCE			MECHANICAL 1		
Year	Model	Body Type and # Passengers	Steering	Engine Manufacturer	Cooling #Cyl & Conf.	Fuel	Bore & Stroke

Reed Tractor — *Reed Foundry, 1527 Fulford Street*
1918–20

		Tractor	w	Waukesha	liq 4	gas	4 1/2 x 5 3/4

Roamer — *Barley Motor Car Company, 2000 Reed Ave., southeast corner of Reed and Factory St. (old Michigan Buggy plant)*
1916

	Six	Light-six-Touring 4p	Lh-w	Rutenber	liq 6-L	gas	3 1/8 x 5

Reportedly, total production of all models for 1916 was 689.

1917

	6-40	Touring–4p	Lh-w	Rutenber	liq 6-L	gas	3 1/8 x 5
	6-40	Roadster–2/4p	Lh-w	Rutenber	liq 6-L	gas	3 1/8 x 5
	6-40	Sport–2p	Lh-w	Rutenber	liq 6-L	gas	3 1/8 x 5
	6-40	Tudor Sedan	Lh-w	Rutenber	liq 6-L	gas	3 1/8 x 5
	6-40	Sedan	Lh-w	Rutenber	liq 6-L	gas	3 1/8 x 5
	6-40	Limousine	Lh-w	Rutenber	liq 6-L	gas	3 1/8 x 5
	6-40	Landaulet	Lh-w	Rutenber	liq 6-L	gas	3 1/8 x 5
	38-92	Touring–6	Lh-w	Hershal-Spillman	liq 6-T	gas	4 x 5 1/2

A six-cylinder Continental engine was available for an additional $150 on the model 6–40.
Some roadsters were equipped with the special "eyeglass" windshield. The Sport body had rakish fenders, and a boat-tail body. Reportedly, total production of all models for 1917 was 898.

1918

	6-54	Touring–7p	Lh-w	Continental	liq 6-L	gas	3 1/2 x 5 1/4
	6-54	Touring–4p	Lh-w	Continental	liq 6-L	gas	3 1/2 x 5 1/4
	6-54	Sport–4p	Lh-w	Continental	liq 6-L	gas	3 1/2 x 5 1/4
	6-54	Roadster–2/4p	Lh-w	Continental	liq 6-L	gas	3 1/2 x 5 1/4
	6-54	Cabriolet–3p	Lh-w	Continental	liq 6-L	gas	3 1/2 x 5 1/4
	6-54	Touring Sedan	Lh-w	Continental	liq 6-L	gas	3 1/2 x 5 1/4
	6-54	Standard Sedan	Lh-w	Continental	liq 6-L	gas	3 1/2 x 5 1/4
	4-75	Touring–6p	Lh-w	Duesenberg	liq 4	gas	4 x 6
	4-75	Touring–7p	Lh-w	Duesenberg	liq 4	gas	4 x 6
	6-90	Touring–6p	Lh-w	Duesenberg	liq 6	gas	3 3/4 x 5 3/4

The company announced that only a few orders would be accepted due to the material restraints created by the war in Europe. Reportedly, total production of all models in 1918 was 1,483.

1919

	6-54	Touring–4p	Lh-w	Continental	liq 6-L	gas	3 1/2 x 5 1/4
	6-54	Roadster–2/4p	Lh-w	Continental	liq 6-L	gas	3 1/2 x 5 1/4
	6-54	Touring–7p	Lh-w	Continental	liq 6-L	gas	3 1/2 x 5 1/4
	6-54	Vic Touring–4p	Lh-w	Continental	liq 6-L	gas	3 1/2 x 5 1/4
	6-54	Sport Touring–4p	Lh-w	Continental	liq 6-L	gas	3 1/2 x 5 1/4
	D-4-75	Touring–4p	Lh-w	R-Duesenberg	liq 4-ov	gas	4 1/4 x 6
	D-4-75	Touring–7p	Lh-w	R-Duesenberg	liq 4-ov	gas	4 1/4 x 6

The Duesenberg engine became the property of John North Willys' Rochester Motors Corporation in late 1919.
The company adopted the overhead valve configuration for the engine at about the same time.
Total production of all models in 1919 was 1,110.

MECHANICAL 2				CHASSIS			PRODUCTION	
CID	Hp	Transmission & Gearing		Wheelbase & gauge (in.)	Tire Size	Weight	Production	Cost
466	32	sld-gear		96	60 x 12	5000	na	$na
231	23	sld-gear	3f-r	124	34 x 4	na	na	$1800
231	23	sld-gear	3f-r	124	34 x 4	na	na	$1850
231	23	sld-gear	3f-r	124	34 x 4	na	na	$2150
231	23	sld-gear	3f-r	124	34 x 4	na	na	$na
231	23	sld-gear	3f-r	124	34 x 4	na	na	$2350
231	23	sld-gear	3f-r	124	34 x 4	na	na	$2550
231	23	sld-gear	3f-r	124	34 x 4	na	na	$na
231	23	sld-gear	3f-r	124	34 x 4	na	na	$2850
553	100b	sld-gear	3f-r	135	34 x 4	na	na	$2950
303	29.4	sld-gear	3f-r	128	32x4	na	na	$2475
303	29.4	sld-gear	3f-r	128	32x4	na	na	$na
303	29.4	sld-gear	3f-r	128	32x4	na	na	$na
303	29.4	sld-gear	3f-r	128	32x4	na	na	$na
303	29.4	sld-gear	3f-r	128	32x4	na	na	$na
303	29.4	sld-gear	3f-r	128	32x4	na	na	$na
303	29.4	sld-gear	3f-r	128	32x4	na	na	$na
302	25.6	sld-gear	3f-r	128	32x4 1/2	na	na	$3250
302	25.6	sld-gear	3f-r	128	32x4 1/2	na	na	$3250
381	43.4	sld-gear	3f-r	138	32x4 1/2	na	na	$3650
303	29.4	sld-gear	3f-r	128	32x4	na	na	$2750
303	29.4	sld-gear	3f-r	128	32x4	na	na	$na
303	29.4	sld-gear	3f-r	128	32x4	na	na	$na
303	29.4	sld-gear	3f-r	128	32x4	na	na	$na
303	29.4	sld-gear	3f-r	128	32x4	na	na	$na
340	28.9	sld-gear	4f-r	128	32x4 1/2	na	na	$na
340	28.9	sld-gear	4f-r	128	32x4 1/2	na	na	$na

MAKE & MANUF.		APPEARANCE			MECHANICAL 1		
Year	Model	Body Type and # Passengers	Steering	Engine Manufacturer	Cooling #Cyl & Conf.	Fuel	Bore & Stroke

Roamer — Barley Motor Car Company, *continued*

1920

	C-6-54	Touring–4p	Lh-w	Continental	liq 6-L	gas	3 1/2 x 5 1/4
	C-6-54	Sport touring–4p	Lh-w	Continental	liq 6-L	gas	3 1/2 x 5 1/4
	C-6-54	Roadster–2/4p	Lh-w	Continental	liq 6-L	gas	3 1/2 x 5 1/4
	C-6-54	Roadster–2p	Lh-w	Continental	liq 6-L	gas	3 1/2 x 5 1/4
	C-6-54	Touring–7p	Lh-w	Continental	liq 6-L	gas	3 1/2 x 5 1/4
	C-6-54	Cabriolet–3p	Lh-w	Continental	liq 6-L	gas	3 1/2 x 5 1/4
	C-6-54	Coupe–4p	Lh-w	Continental	liq 6-L	gas	3 1/2 x 5 1/4
	C-6-54	Sedan–5p*	Lh-w	Continental	liq 6-L	gas	3 1/2 x 5 1/4
	C-6-54	Limousine–7p*	Lh-w	Continental	liq 6-L	gas	3 1/2 x 5 1/4
	C-6-54	Landaulet–7p*	Lh-w	Continental	liq 6-L	gas	3 1/2 x 5 1/4
	D-4-75	Touring–4p	Lh-w	R-Duesenberg	liq 4-ov	gas	4 1/4 x 6
	D-4-75	Touring–7p	Lh-w	R-Duesenberg	liq 4-ov	gas	4 1/4 x 6

* These bodies were built by Leon Rubay.

Reportedly, total production for all models in 1920 was 1,630.

1921

	C-6-54	Touring–4p	Lh-w	Continental	liq 6-L	gas	3 1/2 x 5 1/4
	C-6-54	Roadster–4p	Lh-w	Continental	liq 6-L	gas	3 1/2 x 5 1/4
	C-6-54	Sport–4p	Lh-w	Continental	liq 6-L	gas	3 1/2 x 5 1/4
	C-6-54	Cabriolet	Lh-w	Continental	liq 6-L	gas	3 1/2 x 5 1/4
	C-6-54	Touring–7p	Lh-w	Continental	liq 6-L	gas	3 1/2 x 5 1/4
	C-6-54	Speedster–2p	Lh-w	Continental	liq 6-L	gas	3 1/2 x 5 1/4
	C-6-54	Coupe–5p	Lh-w	Continental	liq 6-L	gas	3 1/2 x 5 1/4
	C-6-54	Sedan–5p	Lh-w	Continental	liq 6-L	gas	3 1/2 x 5 1/4
	C-6-54	Town Car–5p	Lh-w	Continental	liq 6-L	gas	3 1/2 x 5 1/4
	C-6-54	Landaulet	Lh-w	Continental	liq 6-L	gas	3 1/2 x 5 1/4
	C-6-54	Suburban Sedan–7p	Lh-w	Continental	liq 6-L	gas	3 1/2 x 5 1/4
	D-4-75	Roadster–4p	Lh-w	R-Duesenberg	liq 4-ov	gas	4 1/4 x 6
	D-4-75	Sport–4p	Lh-w	R-Duesenberg	liq 4-ov	gas	4 1/4 x 6
	D-4-75	Touring–7p	Lh-w	R-Duesenberg	liq 4-ov	gas	4 1/4 x 6
	D-4-75	Speedster–2p	Lh-w	R-Duesenberg	liq 4-ov	gas	4 1/4 x 6

Reportedly, total production of all models in 1921 was 1,310.

The Sport model was a touring body with a second windshield to protect rear seat passengers.

The Rochester-Duesenberg engine was used in the Roamer chassis that set the world speed record (105 mph) at Daytona in April, 1921.

Photos in an advertising brochure for 1921 show the town car with right-hand drive.

MECHANICAL 2				CHASSIS			PRODUCTION	
CID	Hp	Transmission & Gearing		Wheelbase & gauge (in.)	Tire Size	Weight	Production	Cost
303	54b	sld-gear	3f-r	128 1/4	32 x 4	na	na	$2750
303	54b	sld-gear	3f-r	128 1/4	32 x 4	na	na	$2875
303	54b	sld-gear	3f-r	128 1/4	32 x 4	na	na	$2875
303	54b	sld-gear	3f-r	128 1/4	32 x 4	na	na	$2850
303	54b	sld-gear	3f-r	128 1/4	32 x 4	na	na	$2950
303	54b	sld-gear	3f-r	128 1/4	32 x 4	na	na	$3550
303	54b	sld-gear	3f-r	128 1/4	32 x 4	na	na	$3750
303	54b	sld-gear	3f-r	128 1/4	32 x 4	na	na	$3950
303	54b	sld-gear	3f-r	128 1/4	32 x 4	na	na	$3950
303	54b	sld-gear	3f-r	128 1/4	32 x 4	na	na	$3950
340	28.9	sld-gear	4f-r	128 1/4	32x4 1/2	na	na	$na
340	28.9	sld-gear	4f-r	128 1/4	32x4 1/2	na	na	$na
303	54b	sld-gear	3f-r	130	32 x 4 1/2	na	na	$3250
303	54b	sld-gear	3f-r	130	32 x 4 1/2	na	na	$3375
303	54b	sld-gear	3f-r	130	32 x 4 1/2	na	na	$3375
303	54b	sld-gear	3f-r	130	32 x 4 1/2	na	na	$na
303	54b	sld-gear	3f-r	130	32 x 4 1/2	na	na	$3450
303	54b	sld-gear	3f-r	130	32 x 4 1/2	na	na	$3450
303	54b	sld-gear	3f-r	130	32 x 4 1/2	na	na	$425
303	54b	sld-gear	3f-r	130	32 x 4 1/2	na	na	$4400
303	54b	sld-gear	3f-r	130	32 x 4 1/2	na	na	$4500
303	54b	sld-gear	3f-r	130	32 x 4 1/2	na	na	$na
303	54b	sld-gear	3f-r	130	32 x 4 1/2	na	na	$4500
340	75b	sld-gear	4f-r	130	32 x 4 1/2	na	na	$4375
340	75b	sld-gear	4f-r	130	32 x 4 1/2	na	na	$4375
340	75b	sld-gear	4f-r	130	32 x 4 1/2	na	na	$4475
340	75b	sld-gear	4f-r	130	32 x 4 1/2	na	na	$4475

MAKE & MANUF.		APPEARANCE			MECHANICAL 1		
Year	Model	Body Type and # Passengers	Steering	Engine Manufacturer	Cooling #Cyl & Conf.	Fuel	Bore & Stroke

Roamer — Barley Motor Car Company, *continued*

1922

	6-54	Touring–4p	Lh-w	Continental	liq 6-L	gas	3 1/2 x 5 1/4
	6-54	Touring–7p	Lh-w	Continental	liq 6-L	gas	3 1/2 x 5 1/4
	6-54	Cabriolet–3p	Lh-w	Continental	liq 6-L	gas	3 1/2 x 5 1/4
	6-54	Coupe 4 dr. –5p	Lh-w	Continental	liq 6-L	gas	3 1/2 x 5 1/4
	6-54	Sport–4p	Lh-w	Continental	liq 6-L	gas	3 1/2 x 5 1/4
	6-54	Sedan–5p	Lh-w	Continental	liq 6-L	gas	3 1/2 x 5 1/4
	6-54	Sedan–7p	Lh-w	Continental	liq 6-L	gas	3 1/2 x 5 1/4
	4-75	Roadster–4p	Lh-w	R-Duesenberg	liq 4-ov	gas	4 1/4 x 6
	4-75	Sport–4p	Lh-w	R-Duesenberg	liq 4-ov	gas	4 1/4 x 6
	4-75	Touring–4p	Lh-w	R-Duesenberg	liq 4-ov	gas	4 1/4 x 6
	4-75	Speedster–2p	Lh-w	R-Duesenberg	liq 4-ov	gas	4 1/4 x 6

Reportedly, total production of all models in 1922 was 1,418.

Roamer — *Roamer Motor Car Company (reorganization) 2000 Reed Ave., southeast corner of Reed and Factory St. (old Michigan Buggy plant)*

1923

	6-54	Touring–4p	Lh-w	Continental	liq 6	gas	3 1/2 x 5 1/4
	6-54	Roadster-4/2p	Lh-w	Continental	liq 6	gas	3 1/2 x 5 1/4
	6-54	Touring–7p	Lh-w	Continental	liq 6	gas	3 1/2 x 5 1/4
	6-54	Town Sedan–5p	Rh-w	Continental	liq 6	gas	3 1/2 x 5 1/4
	6-54	Touring Sedan–5p	Lh-w	Continental	liq 6	gas	3 1/2 x 5 1/4
	6-54	Std. Sedan–5p	Lh-w	Continental	liq 6	gas	3 1/2 x 5 1/4
	6-54	Coupe–5p	Lh-w	Continental	liq 6	gas	3 1/2 x 5 1/4
	6-54	Cabriolet–3p	Lh-w	Continental	liq 6	gas	3 1/2 x 5 1/4
	6-54	Limousine	Lh-w	Continental	liq 6	gas	3 1/2 x 5 1/4
	4-75	Roadster–4p	Lh-w	R-Duesenberg	liq 4-ov	gas	4 1/4 x 6
	4-75	Sport–4p	Lh-w	R-Duesenberg	liq 4-ov	gas	4 1/4 x 6
	4-75	Touring–4p	Lh-w	R-Duesenberg	liq 4-ov	gas	4 1/4 x 6
	4-75	Speedster–2p	Lh-w	R-Duesenberg	liq 4-ov	gas	4 x 6
	6-90	Touring–6p	Lh-w	R-Duesenberg	liq 6	gas	4 1/4 x 6
	6-90	Touring–7p	Lh-w	R-Duesenberg	liq 6	gas	4 1/4 x 6

Reportedly, total production of all models, including Barley, in 1923 was 1,918.

Roamer — *Roamer Motor Car Company of Canada (reorganization) 2000 Reed Ave., southeast corner of Reed and Factory St. (old Michigan Buggy plant)*

1924

	6-54	Touring–4p	Lh-w	Continental	liq 6	gas	3 1/2 x 5 1/4
	6-54	Roadster–2/4p	Lh-w	Continental	liq 6	gas	3 1/2 x 5 1/4
	6-54	Touring–7p	Lh-w	Continental	liq 6	gas	3 1/2 x 5 1/4
	6-54	Town Sedan–5p	Rh-w	Continental	liq 6	gas	3 1/2 x 5 1/4
	6-54	Tour Sedan–5p	Lh-w	Continental	liq 6	gas	3 1/2 x 5 1/4
	6-54	Std. Sedan–5p	Lh-w	Continental	liq 6	gas	3 1/2 x 5 1/4

MECHANICAL 2			CHASSIS			PRODUCTION	
CID	Hp	Transmission & Gearing	Wheelbase & gauge (in.)	Tire Size	Weight	Production	Cost
303	54b	sld-gear	3f-r	130	32 x 4 1/2	na	na	$2485
303	54b	sld-gear	3f-r	130	32 x 4 1/2	na	na	$2750
303	54b	sld-gear	3f-r	130	32 x 4 1/2	na	na	$3650
303	54b	sld-gear	3f-r	130	32 x 4 1/2	na	na	$3850
303	54b	sld-gear	3f-r	130	32 x 4 1/2	na	na	$2650
303	54b	sld-gear	3f-r	130	32 x 4 1/2	na	na	$3950
303	54b	sld-gear	3f-r	130	32 x 4 1/2	na	na	$3420
340	75b	sld-gear	4f-r	130	32 x 4 1/2	na	na	$4375
340	75b	sld-gear	4f-r	130	32 x 4 1/2	na	na	$4375
340	75b	sld-gear	4f-r	130	32 x 4 1/2	na	na	$4375
340	75b	sld-gear	4f-r	130	32 x 4 1/2	na	na	$3650
303	54b	sld-gear	3f-r	128	32 x 4	na	na	$2575
303	54b	sld-gear	3f-r	128	32 x 4	na	na	$2650
303	54b	sld-gear	3f-r	128	32 x 4	na	na	$2750
303	54b	sld-gear	3f-r	128	32 x 4	na	na	$3350
303	54b	sld-gear	3f-r	128	32 x 4	na	na	$3450
303	54b	sld-gear	3f-r	128	32 x 4	na	na	$3350
303	54b	sld-gear	3f-r	128	32 x 4	na	na	$3450
303	54b	sld-gear	3f-r	128	32 x 4	na	na	$3250
303	54b	sld-gear	3f-r	128	32 x 4	na	na	$3450
340	75b	sld-gear	4f-r	130	32 x 4 1/2	na	na	$4375
340	75b	sld-gear	4f-r	130	32 x 4 1/2	na	na	$4375
340	75b	sld-gear	4f-r	130	32 x 4 1/2	na	na	$4375
302	80b	sld-gear	4f-r	130	32 x 4 1/2	na	na	$3650
510	43b	sld-gear	4f-r	na	na	na	na	$3450
510	43b	sld-gear	4f-r	na	na	na	na	$3450
303	54b	sld-gear	3f-r	128	32 x 4	na	na	$2575
303	54b	sld-gear	3f-r	128	32 x 4	na	na	$2650
303	54b	sld-gear	3f-r	128	32 x 4	na	na	$2750
303	54b	sld-gear	3f-r	128	32 x 4	na	na	$3350
303	54b	sld-gear	3f-r	128	32 x 4	na	na	$3450
303	54b	sld-gear	3f-r	128	32 x 4	na	na	$3350

MAKE & MANUF.		APPEARANCE			MECHANICAL 1		
Year	Model	Body Type and # Passengers	Steering	Engine Manufacturer	Cooling #Cyl & Conf.	Fuel	Bore & Stroke

Roamer — Roamer Motor Car Company of Canada (reorganization), 1924 *continued*

	6-54	Coupe–2/4p	Lh-w	Continental	liq 6	gas	3 1/2 x 5 1/4
	6-54	Cabriolet–3p	Lh-w	Continental	liq 6	gas	3 1/2 x 5 1/4
	6-54	Limousine–7p	Lh-w	Continental	liq 6	gas	3 1/2 x 5 1/4
	4-75	Roadster–4p	Lh-w	R-Duesenberg	liq 4-ov	gas	4 1/4 x 6
	4-75	Sport–4p	Lh-w	R-Duesenberg	liq 4-ov	gas	4 1/4 x 6
	4-75	Touring–4p	Lh-w	R-Duesenberg	liq 4-ov	gas	4 1/4 x 6

Reportedly total production of all models, including Barley in 1924 was 723.

1925

	6-54	Touring–4p	Lh-w	Continental	liq 6	gas	3 1/2 x 5 1/4
	6-54	Roadster–2/4p	Lh-w	Continental	liq 6	gas	3 1/2 x 5 1/4
	6-54	Touring–7p	Lh-w	Continental	liq 6	gas	3 1/2 x 5 1/4
	6-54	Town Sedan–5p	Rh-w	Continental	liq 6	gas	3 1/2 x 5 1/4
	6-54	Tour Sedan–5p	Lh-w	Continental	liq 6	gas	3 1/2 x 5 1/4
	6-54	Std. Sedan–5p	Lh-w	Continental	liq 6	gas	3 1/2 x 5 1/4
	6-54	Coupe–2p	Lh-w	Continental	liq 6	gas	3 1/2 x 5 1/4
	6-54	Cabriolet–2/4p	Lh-w	Continental	liq 6	gas	3 1/2 x 5 1/4
	6-54	Limousine–7p	Lh-w	Continental	liq 6	gas	3 1/2 x 5 1/4
	8-80	Coupe–2p	Lh-w	Lycoming	liq 8-L	gas	3 1/2 x 5 1/4
	8-80	Roadster–2p	Lh-w	Lycoming	liq 8-L	gas	3 1/2 x 5 1/4
	8-80	Tudor Sedan–5p	Lh-w	Lycoming	liq 8-L	gas	3 1/2 x 5 1/4
	8-80	St Sedan 5p	Lh-w	Lycoming	liq 8-L	gas	3 1/2 x 5 1/4
	4-75	built to order	Lh-w	R-Duesenberg	liq 4-ov	gas	4 1/4 x 6

The 1925 year was one of change, as local reports cite the introduction of the straight eight 8-80 series in 1925 with the continuation of the six-cylinder Continental powered cars. The 4-75 series Duesenberg-powered cars were apparently built by special order only.

Reportedly total production of all models in 1925 was 212.

1926

	8-80	Coupe–2p	Lh-w	Lycoming	liq 8-L	gas	3 1/2 x na
	8-80	Roadster–2p	Lh-w	Lycoming	liq 8-L	gas	3 1/2 x na
	8-80	Tudor Sedan–5p	Lh-w	Lycoming	liq 8-L	gas	3 1/2 x na
	8-80	Std. Sedan–5p	Lh-w	Lycoming	liq 8-L	gas	3 1/2 x na
	8-88	Touring–5p	Lh-w	Lycoming	liq 8-L	gas	3 3/16 x 4 1/4
	8-88	Roadster–2/4p	Lh-w	Lycoming	liq 8-L	gas	3 3/16 x 4 1/4
	8-88	Sedan–5p	Lh-w	Lycoming	liq 8-L	gas	3 3/16 x 4 1/4
	8-88	Coach–5p	Lh-w	Lycoming	liq 8-L	gas	3 3/16 x 4 1/4
	4-75	built to order	Lh-w	R-Duesenberg	liq 4-ov	gas	4 1/4 x 6

The 8-88 series was announced in Kalamazoo in October 1925 as a new series for 1926 and the 6-54 series appears to have been dropped at this time.

Reportedly the total production of all models in 1926 was 137.

MECHANICAL 2				CHASSIS			PRODUCTION	
CID	Hp	Transmission & Gearing		Wheelbase & gauge (in.)	Tire Size	Weight	Production	Cost
303	54b	sld-gear	3f-r	128	32 x 4	na	na	$3450
303	54b	sld-gear	3f-r	128	32 x 4	na	na	$3250
303	54b	sld-gear	3f-r	128	32 x 4	na	na	$3450
340	75b	sld-gear	4f-r	130	32 x 4 1/2	na	na	$4375
340	75b	sld-gear	4f-r	130	32 x 4 1/2	na	na	$4375
340	75b	sld-gear	4f-r	130	32 x 4 1/2	na	na	$4375
303	54b	sld-gear	3f-r	128	32 x 4	na	na	$2575
303	54b	sld-gear	3f-r	128	32 x 4	na	na	$2650
303	54b	sld-gear	3f-r	128	32 x 4	na	na	$2750
303	54b	sld-gear	3f-r	128	32 x 4	na	na	$3350
303	54b	sld-gear	3f-r	128	32 x 4	na	na	$3450
303	54b	sld-gear	3f-r	128	32 x 4	na	na	$3350
303	54b	sld-gear	3f-r	128	32 x 4	na	na	$3450
303	54b	sld-gear	3f-r	128	32 x 4	na	na	$3250
303	54b	sld-gear	3f-r	128	32 x 4	na	na	$3,450
303	54b	sld-gear	3f-r	128	32 x 6.00	na	na	$1,985
303	54b	sld-gear	3f-r	128	32 x 6.00	na	na	$1,895
303	54b	sld-gear	3f-r	128	32 x 6.00	na	na	$1,985
303	54b	sld-gear	3f-r	128	32 x 6.00	na	na	$1,985
340	75b	sld-gear	4f-r	na	na	na	na	$na
na	80b	sld-gear	3f-r	128	32 x 6.00	na	na	$1,985
na	80b	sld-gear	3f-r	128	32 x 6.00	na	na	$1,895
na	80b	sld-gear	3f-r	128	32 x 6.00	na	na	$1,985
na	80b	sld-gear	3f-r	128	32 x 6.00	na	na	$1,985
287	88b	sld-gear	3f-r	128	32 x 6.00	na	na	$na
287	88b	sld-gear	3f-r	128	32 x 6.00	na	na	$na
287	88b	sld-gear	3f-r	126	32 x 6.00	3580	na	$an
287	88b	sld-gear	3f-r	126	32 x 6.00	3580	na	$na
340	75b	sld-gear	4f-r	na	na	na	na	$na

MAKE & MANUF.		APPEARANCE			MECHANICAL 1		
Year	Model	Body Type and # Passengers	Steering	Engine Manufacturer	Cooling #Cyl & Conf.	Fuel	Bore & Stroke

Roamer — Roamer Motor Car Company of Canada (reorganization), *continued*
1927

	8-80	Coupe–2p	Lh-w	Lycoming	liq 8-L	gas	3 1/2 x na
	8-80	Roadster–2p	Lh-w	Lycoming	liq 8-L	gas	3 1/2 x na
	8-80	Tudor Sedan–5p	Lh-w	Lycoming	liq 8-L	gas	3 1/2 x na
	8-80	Std. Sedan–5p	Lh-w	Lycoming	liq 8-L	gas	3 1/2 x na
	8-88	Sedan–5p	Lh-w	Lycoming	liq 8-L	gas	3 1/4 x 4 1/2
	8-88	Speedster–2p	Lh-w	Lycoming	liq 8-L	gas	3 1/4 x 4 1/2
	8-88	Touring–5p	Lh-w	Lycoming	liq 8-L	gas	3 1/4 x 4 1/2

Reportedly total production for all models in 1927 was 88.

Roamer — Roamer Consolidated Corporation (reorganization), 2000 Reed Ave., southeast corner of Reed and Factory St. (old Michigan Buggy plant)
1928

	8-88	Sedan–5p	Lh-w	Lycoming	liq 8-L	gas	3 1/4 x 4 1/2
	8-88	Speedster–2p	Lh-w	Lycoming	liq 8-L	gas	3 1/4 x 4 1/2
	8-88	Touring–5p	Lh-w	Lycoming	liq 8-L	gas	3 1/4 x 4 1/2
	8-88	Touring–5p	Lh-w	Lycoming	liq 8-L	gas	3 1/4 x 4 1/2
	8-88	Sport Touring–5p	Lh-w	Lycoming	liq 8-L	gas	3 1/4 x 4 1/2
	8-88	Roadster–2/4p	Lh-w	Lycoming	liq 8-L	gas	3 1/4 x 4 1/2

Although historical sources differ in citation of the year of change, the 8-80 series was apparently dropped circa 1928, coinciding with another company reorganization.

Reportedly, total production of all models in 1928 was 35.

1929

	8-88	Sedan–5p	Lh-w	Lycoming	liq 8-L	gas	3 1/4 x 4 1/2
	8-88	Sedan–7p	Lh-w	Lycoming	liq 8-L	gas	3 1/4 x 4 1/2
	8-88	Speedster–2p	Lh-w	Lycoming	liq 8-L	gas	3 1/4 x 4 1/2
	8-88	Touring–5p	Lh-w	Lycoming	liq 8-L	gas	3 1/4 x 4 1/2
	8-88	Sport Touring–5p	Lh-w	Lycoming	liq 8-L	gas	3 1/4 x 4 1/2
	8-88	Roadster–2/4p	Lh-w	Lycoming	liq 8-L	gas	3 1/4 x 4 1/2

Reportedly, total production for all models in 1929 was 2.

1930

	8-88	Sedan–5p	Lh-w	Lycoming	liq 8-L	gas	3 1/4 x 4 1/2
	8-88	Speedster–2p	Lh-w	Lycoming	liq 8-L	gas	3 1/4 x 4 1/2
	8-88	Touring–5p	Lh-w	Lycoming	liq 8-L	gas	3 1/4 x 4 1/2

The 8-88 models were listed in trade magazines, but production is doubtful.

Rhodes — *Rhodes residence, 612 Douglas Avenue*
1891

Mar		Wagon	na	Rhodes	water 1	steam	na

Rhodes reports that one example was built and that a subsequent illness prevented him from developing the vehicle further.

MECHANICAL 2			CHASSIS			PRODUCTION	
CID	Hp	Transmission & Gearing	Wheelbase & gauge (in.)	Tire Size	Weight	Production	Cost
na	80b	sld-gear 3f-r	128	32 x 6.00	na	na	$1,985
na	80b	sld-gear 3f-r	128	32 x 6.00	na	na	$1,895
na	80b	sld-gear 3f-r	128	32 x 6.00	na	na	$1,985
na	80b	sld-gear 3f-r	128	32 x 6.00	na	na	$1,985
299	88b	sld-gear 3f-r	136	32 x 6.20	na	na	$2,985
299	88b	sld-gear 3f-r	136	32 x 6.20	na	na	$2,985
299	88b	sld-gear 3f-r	136	32 x 6.20	na	na	$2,485
299	88b	sld-gear 3f-r	136	32 x 6.20	na	na	$2,985
299	88b	sld-gear 3f-r	136	32 x 6.20	na	na	$2,985
299	88b	sld-gear 3f-r	136	32 x 6.20	na	na	$2,485
299	88b	sld-gear 3f-r	136	32 x 6.20	na	na	$2,485
299	88b	sld-gear 3f-r	136	32 x 6.20	na	na	$2,750
299	88b	sld-gear 3f-r	136	32 x 6.20	na	na	$2,985
299	88b	sld-gear 3f-r	136	32 x 6.20	na	na	$2,985
299	88b	sld-gear 3f-r	136	32 x 6.20	na	na	$3,285
299	88b	sld-gear 3f-r	136	32 x 6.20	na	na	$2,985
299	88b	sld-gear 3f-r	136	32 x 6.20	na	na	$2,485
299	88b	sld-gear 3f-r	136	32 x 6.20	na	na	$2,750
299	88b	sld-gear 3f-r	136	32 x 6.20	na	na	$2,985
299	88b	sld-gear 3f-r	136	32 x 6.20	na	na	$2,985
299	88b	sld-gear 3f-r	136	32 x 6.20	na	na	$2,985
299	88b	sld-gear 3f-r	136	32 x 6.20	na	na	$2,485
na	na	continuous na	na	na	na	1	$ 150

Year	Model	Body Type and # Passengers	Steering	Engine Manufacturer	Cooling #Cyl & Conf.	Fuel	Bore & Stroke
		MAKE & MANUF.		APPEARANCE		MECHANICAL 1	

Safety First — *210 Kalamazoo National Bank Building*
1914

The firm was incorporated in 1914 to manufacture a gasoline-powered vehicle, but there is no evidence of any manufacture.

Sunseeker — *Western Michigan University, 1903 West Michigan Avenue, Kalamazoo Michigan*
1991

		Race car–1	w	QMC	na	electric	na

This single-passenger vehicle was driven by electric motors, one at each rear wheel, and powered by solar-energy cells mounted on top of the vehicle. Several cars were built; specifications are listed for the #77 car, built in 1990.

States Motor Car Company — *2000 Reed Ave., southeast corner of Reed and Factory St. (old Michigan Buggy plant)*
1915

| | H | Greyhound Cycle car | Lh-w | na | lqd 4-L | gas | 2 1/2 x 4 |
| | I | Greyhound Cycle car | Lh-w | na | lqd 4-L | gas | 2 7/8 x 4 |

The Greyhound was available in tandem, side-by-side, coupe or delivery bodies. The "Greyhound Motor Car Company" (actually, the States Motor Car Co., Toledo, Ohio) was welcomed to Kalamazoo in September, 1915. The announcement of the 1916 States automobile with either V-8 or 4 cylinder power appeared in The Automobile *on December 23, 1915.*

1916

		Touring	Lh-w	na	lqd 8ov	gas	3 x 3 1/2
		Roadster	Lh-w	na	lqd 8ov	gas	3 x 3 1/2
		Touring	Lh-w	na	lqd 4	gas	3 x 3 1/2
		Roadster	Lh-w	na	lqd 4	gas	3 x 3 1/2
		1/2 ton – chassis	Lh-w	na	lqd 4	gas	3 x 3 1/2

1917

		Touring	Lh-w	na	lqd 6	gas	na
		Roadster	Lh-w	na	lqd 6	gas	na
		Touring	Lh-w	na	lqd 4	gas	na
		Roadster	Lh-w	na	lqd 4	gas	na

1918

| Feb. | B | Touring | Lh-w | GB&S | thm 4-L | gas | 3 3/4 x 4 1/4 |

1918

| Mar. | 6-37 | Roadster | Lh-w | na | lqd 6 | gas | na |
| | 6-37 | Touring | Lh-w | States | thm 6-L | gas | 3 x 4 1/2 |

Specifications for 1916 may reflect "planned autos," for in spite of the variety of models and anticipated manufacture of 6,000 vehicles, production was never extensive. The company was out of business by January 1919.

Windwagon — *275 Engleside Terrace, Kalamazoo, Michigan*
1914

| | | Windwagon–1p | na | motorcycle | air na | gas | na |

The Weaver Windwagon was built by Clare Weaver in 1914. Details of construction, other than power by a motorcycle engine-driven propeller, are unknown.

MECHANICAL 2				CHASSIS			PRODUCTION	
CID	Hp	Transmission & Gearing		Wheelbase & gauge (in.)	Tire Size	Weight	Production	Cost
na	16	continuous		na	1/75 x 20	578	1	$400,000
78.5	10	na	na	104x44	28 x 3	na	na	$600
97.5	13	na	na	106x56	28 x 3	na	na	$600
198	48b	sld-gear	3f-r	110	34 x 4	2200	na	na
198	48b	sld-gear	3f-r	110	34 x 4	2200	na	na
99	14.4	sld-gear	3f-r	108	33x3 1/2	2200	na	na
99	14.4	sld-gear	3f-r	108	33x3 1/2	2200	na	na
99	14.4	sld-gear	3f-r	108	na	na	na	na
na	na	sld-gear	3f-r	112	na	na	na	na
na	na	sld-gear	3f-r	112	na	na	na	na
na	na	sld-gear	3f-r	112	na	na	na	na
na	na	sld-gear	3f-r	112	na	na	na	na
188	22.5	sld-gear	3f-r	112	32x3 1/2	na	na	$ 895
na	na	sld-gear	3f-r	112	na	na	na	$ 995
191	21.6	sld-gear	3f-r	110	31x4	na	na	$1,195
na	na	na	na	144	na	na	2	$na

MAKE & MANUF.		APPEARANCE			MECHANICAL 1		
Year	Model	Body Type and # Passengers	Steering	Engine Manufacturer	Cooling #Cyl & Conf.	Fuel	Bore & Stroke

Western Race car — Department of Manual Arts, Western State Normal School, Kalamazoo, Michigan

1922

	B-4	Race car–1p	W	Ford	thm 4-ov	gas	3 3/4 x 4

The students in the automotive class built a small racer powered by a modified Ford Model T engine. Evidence suggests only one was built.

Wolverine — Wolverine Motors Inc., 434–440 West Main Street

1917

Dec		Speedway Special–2p	Lh-w	Duesenberg	lqd 4-ov	gas	3 63/64 x 6
		Touring–4p	Lh-w	Duesenberg	lqd 4-ov	gas	4 3/8
		Chassis Touring–6p	Lh-w	Duesenberg	lqd 4-ov	gas	3 63/64 x 6

In December, 1917, the company claimed that material was on hand to build 600 cars and that 454 models had been sold. Three Duesenberg engines were delivered to Wolverine, but there is no evidence that more than one Speedway, one touring car, and one chassis were ever built. Reports in May 1919 claim the completion of a roadster and a four-passenger model. The only extant photographs are of the Speedway Special roadster.

CATEGORY ABBREVIATIONS

Body type	*see definitions*
# of passengers	refers to the number that can ride in the vehicle including the driver. Exception is Taxi which refers to paying passengers.
Steering	type of steering, either Tiller (tiller) or steering wheel (W) and location of mechanisms on either right (R) or left (L) side of the vehicle.
Engine manufacturer	name of company manufacturing engine. No abbreviations are used.
Cooling	type of engine cooling used; air (air), or liquid (lqd). The liquid cooling system is either by thermosyphon (thm) or by a mechanical pump, which is indicated by (lqd). The thermosyphon system depends on the upward movement of heated water to circulate the coolant through the radiator and engine.
# Cyl	number of cylinders. This number is followed by the type of valve arrangement used for the engine.
Conf	configuration arrangement of the intake and exhaust valves relative to the top of the cylinder.
L	L-head, a flat head engine with intake and exhaust on the same side of the cylinder.
T	T-head, a flat head engine with intake and exhaust valves on the opposite sides of the cylinder.
F	F-head, an engine with one overhead valve and one side-mounted valve.
ov	overhead valves. An engine with both intake and exhaust mounted above the cylinder.
slv	sleeve valves. Openings in the side of two cylinders that move outside of the piston's cylinder creating openings for exhaust and intake when the openings in these two cylinders coincide.
fuel	power source for the engine: gas, diesel, electric or steam. Terms are not abbreviated.
Bore & stroke	bore and stroke of the engine expressed in inches (e.g., 4" x 5").
CID	cubic inch displacement of the engine. When not provided, CID was calculated using the formula: *bore squared x .7854 x stroke x the number of cylinders.*
HP	horsepower. Engine horsepower was initially calculated by the S.A.E. formula: *the bore squared x number of cylinders and dividing that product by 2.5.* This calculation is referred to the S.A.E. horsepower (Society of Automotive Engineers). In the late teens, engineers began measuring horsepower under actual test conditions using a dynometer, and this hp rating, called *braking horsepower,* is almost always greater than the S.A.E hp. Braking horsepower is indicated by a "b" following the rating. No initial indicates S.A.E. hp.
Transmission	There are four types of transmissions: 1) planatary (plant), in which bands are tightened by a foot pedal or lever around a turning hub holding the orbiting gear, like a planet circulating the earth, and transferring power from the middle gear to the drive shaft; 2) friction, a type of transmission in which two wheels are placed at 90° angles to one another, with the drive gear pressed against the face of the other gear. As the

MECHANICAL 2			CHASSIS			PRODUCTION	
CID	Hp	Transmission & Gearing	Wheelbase & gauge (in.)	Tire Size	Weight	Production	Cost
177	37	planetary na	na	na	na	1	$na
298	25.3	sld-gear na	115	32 x 4 1/2	2340	1	$3,500
361	30.6	sld-gear na	125	32 x 4 1/2	na	1	$3,700
298	25.3	sld-gear na	127	na	na	1	$na

drive gear speeds up, it moves to the outside of the gear face and changes the ratio of the gearing from low, a small gear driving a large gear, to high, a large gear driving a small gear; 3) the sliding gear (sld-gear), later called a standard transmission, in which gears are selected by moving a lever, either floor-mounted or column-mounted, according to a pattern to select the appropriate gear ratio for the power/speed desired; 4) automatic, in which gears are changed according to the speed of the vehicle, but only Checker was built late enough to offer this option; 5) continuous: steam and electric-powered vehicles do not require transmissions used to select gear ratios. Power to the drive wheels is continuous and determined by engine speed. Almost all transmissions provide power to the drive wheels by a rotating shaft. Those that use a chain are identified with the abbreviation "ch". Comb. refers to a combination of plant and sld-gear.

Gearing — indicates the number of forward gears (3f) and, if applicable, the presence of a reverse gear (r).

Wheelbase — the distance from the centerpoint of the front axle to the centerpoint of the rear axle. The second number given for some of the vehicles is the width of the tread—the distance between the center points on the front wheels. Some measurements are unknown, but have a long wheelbase (Lwb).

Tire Size — diameter and width of tires.

Weight — vehicle weight in pounds.

Production — number of vehicles built; most of these figures are estimates.

Cost — reported selling price or advertised price.

REFERENCES

References for the Automobile Technical Specifications were taken from period publications and original advertising literature and sales brochures as listed in the chapters. The *Standard Catalog of Cars, Volumes 1, 2, & 3* were used as verification in many cases, and in the case of the Roamer and the Checker, the catalog was relied upon heavily. In some of the early cars, particularly the Blood cars, the Kalamazoo-named vehicles and the Michigan cars, there is a difference between the information in this text and in the *Standard Catalog*. The listed specifications for these vehicles were compiled from extant sales brochures and articles from the local papers. This information is well documented and believed to be correct.

Index

In parentheses following the index heading for Kalamazoo entries are manufacturing company location and residence addresses that correspond quite closely to the era of the cited references. Addresses for people employed in Kalamazoo, for whom there is no record in local directories, are noted as; "no rec." Addresses outside of Kalamazoo are noted by city or country when known, and left blank when unknown. The years of vehicle production for Kalamazoo-built vehicles are also noted in parentheses following the entry. The page numbers for entries citing photographs are in bold and those entries for color photographs are preceded by the letter "C".

abbreviations: a.k.a., *also known as*; Ave., *Avenue*; bds., *beds*; Blvd., *Boulevard*; Co., *Company*; cor., *corner*; e., *east*; Ltd., *Limited*; f.o.b., *freight-on-board from point of origin*; no rec., *no record*; n., *north*; rms, *rooms*; St., *Street*; s., *south*; vs, *versus*; w. *west*;

Abbott Detroit Motor Car Co.: (Detroit, MI, 1906-16); Gerber purchases, 255-56

advertisements: Auto Show, 1910, **89**; Auto Show, 1914, **76**; Brush, **90**; Burtt Manufacturing, **34**; Cornelian cyclecar, **110**; Crown bicycle, **22**; Dort automobile, **347, 348**; Lane truck, **271, 272, 274**; Kalamazoo Manufacturing, **321**; Marion-Handley automobile, **386**; Michigan Model A, **48**; Michigan Model B, **57**; Michigan Model D, **56**; Michigan Model R, **169**; Mighty Michigan "33", **166**; Michigan with electric lights, **239**; Orient Buckboard, **13**; Reed tractor, **304**; Roamer automobile, **352**; States automobile, **326, 331**; Wolverine automobile, **340**

Advocate, Kalamazoo Daily, (230 N. Burdick St.): Harlan Babcock editor, **223**; Henry Lane and, 258

American Motors Co., (Indianapolis, IN): James Handley and, 385-87

American-American (Underslung) automobile, (Indianapolis IN, 1906-14): V. A. Longaker and, 385, 386; Fred Tone and, 386

Auburn automobile, (Auburn, IN, 1900-36): convertible sedan, **C-17**; *see also* Limousine Body Co.

automobile: Auburn, **C-17**; Cadillac, **C-7**; Clarkmobile, 265-66; Cord, **C-17**; Ford cyclecar, 104-105; Delage, **C-9**; earliest in Kalamazoo, 3-4; Ford Model T, **C-8**; Locomobile, 10-11, **11**, 15, **C-3**; Mercury cyclecar, **98**; Mobile steam powered, 11-12, **12**; Murray, 12-13, **11**; no longer a luxury, 91; Oldsmobile 13-14, **14**; Orient Buckboard, **13**, **C-4**; Peugeot, **C-10**; Sun, 258; White steam powered, **15**; *see also* automobiles built in Kalamazoo area; buses built in Kalamazoo area; tractors built in Kalamazoo area; trucks built in Kalamazoo area; race cars; race cars built in Kalamazoo area

automobiles built in Kalamazoo area: *see* Auburn; Barley; Blood; Boudeman-Scott; Burtt; Cannon;

507

try, 443, 446; *see also* automobile firsts in Kalamazoo; service stations

Bablot, Paul: drives French-built Bablot racer, 365

Babcock, Harlan, (721 Academy St.): editor of Advocate, **223**; editor of the Kalamazoo Telegraph-Press, xii

Bandini, Robert: Roamer mechanician, 366-67, **366**

Banyon, W. John: bankruptcy referee, 183; quiets the atmosphere in court, 196

Barberry, Al: Markin's chauffeur, 425; trip with E. L. Cord described, 425

Bardeen, George, (Otsego, MI): bondsman for M. H. Lane, 225

Barley, Albert. C., (208 Stuart Ave.): appearance 1920, **353**; complaints about cars, 353; Daytona at, **369**; Kenworthy and, 353-54; incentive to move to Kalamazoo, 354-55; Indiana Truck Co. and, 353, 377; Rutenber engine and, 351; *see also* Barley automobile; Barley Motor Car Co.; Roamer automobile; Pennant cab

Barley automobile, (Kalamazoo, 1923-24): closed cars, **385**; description of, 373-74; Pennant cab and, 374, 376; touring model, **374, C-23**; *see also* Barley, Albert C.; Barley Motor Car Co.; Roamer automobile

Barley Motor Car Co., (2000 Reed Ave., s.e. cor. Reed Ave. & Factory St.): advertisement for, **352**; international reputation, 358-59; Kalamazoo welcome, 354-55; Michigan Buggy legacy and, 355-56; move from Streater IL, 354-56; production, 358, 362, 377, 380; States and, 356; *see also* Barley automobile; Barley, Albert. C.; Kenworthy, Cloyd Y.; Martin, Karl; Pennant cab; Roamer automobile; Roamer racing; Rowland, Walter; Rubay, Leon

Bennett, Milo, (120 East Walnut St.): brought libel suit, 256; complains to county board, 224-25; criticism of conduct, 228-29, **229**; replaced, 223

Bergdoll, Grover: at Kalamazoo, 120-21; failed to qualify at Indianapolis 500, 130

bicycle: Blood Brothers' business, 20-22; Frank Burtt and, **32**; Burtt's eastern trip, 34; carry cycle, 24; history of, 21-22; Kalamazoo club, 33-

34; Kalamazoo Cycle Co., 19; lithograph of, **22**; Dr. Rush McNair's adventures with, 21; ordinary style, 21, **32**; technology and automobile, 23-24

Bird, Miss, (no rec.): employed by Detroit Trust, 248; Michigan Buggy Beauties and, **205**; Michigan Buggy secretary, 212

blacksmith: shop in Kalamazoo circa 1891, **18**

Blood automobiles, (Kalamazoo, 1902-03, 1904-06, 1913): carry cycle is second auto, 24-25, **24**; cyclecar built in 1913, 97-98; de Dion Boutan and, 23-24; driving the 1905 model, 28-29, **28**; Michigan Model A, 26-27, **25**, **26**, **48**, **50**; sold 100 before Henry Ford, 25; horseless carriage is third auto, 25-26, **25**; quadricycle is first auto, 23-24; *see also* Cornelian automobile

Blood Brothers: credited with many firsts, 22-23; Fuller family and, 20, 25-28; Michigan Automobile Co. and, 25; *see also* Blood automobiles; Kalamazoo Cycle

Blood Brothers Automobile Co., (114 N. Edwards St.): name change, 29; separation from Fullers, 27-28, 51-52; *see also* Blood automobiles; Kalamazoo cycle

Blood Brothers Machine, (633 West Ransom St.): incorporated, 29; merge with Cornelian Co., 101; move to Allegan, 109; *see also* Blood Brothers Machine Co., Cornelian; Kalamazoo Cycle Co.

Blood Brothers Machine Co., (Allegan, MI): advertisement, **110**; Clarence Blood severs relationship with, 111; move to Allegan, 109; Rockwell International and, 111; *see also* Blood Brothers Automobile Co.; Blood Brothers Machine; Cornelian; Kalamazoo Cycle Co.

Blood, Clarence, (132 Catherine St.): death, 20; dredging machine, 96; early life, 19-20; severs relationship with company, 111; *see also* Blood Brothers Machine Co.

Blood, Howard, (724 W. Kalamazoo Ave.): celebration with Rickenbacker, **140**; Louis Chevrolet and, 129, **128, 134**; college graduate, 102, **103**; commander at McCook Field, 111, 141; Cornelian cyclecar and, **104**; defines cyclecar, 100-101; demise of cyclecar movement and, 104-

Cannon, Walter, (429 Park Place & Vicksburg, MI): builds Cannon car, 35; joins Burtt Manufacturing, 34-35; *see also* Burtt Manufacturing; Burtt Manufacturing Co.

Carlson, "Coal Oil" Billy or Willie: Maxwell and, **125**; Indianapolis 500, 136; races in Kalamazoo, 120, 124

Carney, Claude, (218 W. Walnut St.): attorney, 180, 186, **196**; bankruptcy hearing, 183-84; defends Palmer, 239, 242-43

Checker automobile & cab, (Kalamazoo, 1923-82): Aerobus, 432, **C-30**; Art Deco cabs, **416**, **417**, **418**, **421**, **422**, **C-28**, **C-29**; Blue Book model, 412; Buda engine, 268, 409, 413; "Built to last", **436**; catalog cover, **C-29**; Consumers Union review, 432-33; diesel power, 437; Ray Dietrich stylist, 426; extant photographs explained, 404; first cab built in Kalamazoo, 409, **C-27**, **C-28**; four-wheel brake epidemic, 410; GM X-body Citation, 436-37; Hollywood and, 438, 452, **404**; in the city, **437**; last Checker, 437, **C-31**; legacy, 438, 452; Marathon series, 433-34; Model A, **421**, **422**, **423**, **424**; Model A2 to A6, 429, **430**, **431**; Model A8, 429, **431**, **C-30**; Model B rear-engine, **426**; Model C, **406**; Model D front-wheel drive, 427, 429, **428**; Model E, **406**, **411**; Model F, **410**, **411**; Model G, **411**; Model K, 412, **412**; Model M, **414**; Model T, 414, **416**, **C-29**; Model Y, **417**, **418**, **C-28**; model for 1967, **435**; model for 1969, **436**; open cars, 412; production, 409, 410, 437, **423**; suburban model, 413, **415**; testimonials, 429, 432; *see also* Checker Cab Manufacturing; Checker Motors Corp.

Checker bus, (Kalamazoo, circa 1939-58): part of day's production, **423**

Checker Cab Manufacturing, (2016 N. Pitcher St.): E. L. Cord controls, 416-17; deficit, 414; did not build Jeep, 420-23; Dort plant purchased by, 349, 399-400, 407, 410; Fuller taxi deal, 410; Leland Goodspeed and, 407; Handley plant purchased by, 349, 398-99; Kahn designed plant, 410, **413**, **428**; Partin-Palmer and, 406; plant interior, **408**; production, 409, **423**; production during World War II, 424; Reed Foundry and, 409; Harry Scott's machine shop and, 408; survives initial economic crash, 413; Yellow Taxi and, 407, 409, 410; *see also* Checker Motors Corp.; Checker automobile & cab; Markin, Morris

Checker Motors Corp., (2016 N. Pitcher St.): advertising campaign, 433-34, **434**; annual report cover, **C-31**; dramatic end of manufacture, 437-38; last automobile, 437, **C-31**; semi-trucks roll with dies and parts, 438; stock certificate, **C-31**; strike by UAW, 432; Volkschecker aborted, 435; *see also* Checker Cab Manufacturing; Checker automobile & cab

Chevrolet, Gaston: Cornelian and, 132-33, **134**; death, 141

Chevrolet, Louis: beat up Albert Champion, 132; Cornelian and, 138, **128**, **134**, **133**; death, 141; 138; early life, 130-32; holding Sterling engine, **136**; later life, 141, 332; prepares Cornelian for Indianapolis 500, 132-34

Clark automobile, (Vicksburg, MI, 1901): driven to Ohio, 43-44

Clark, Omer, (RFD 6, Vicksburg, MI): designed and built two cars, 43-44

Cole, Edward: death, 435; front-wheel drive Checker and, 435-36; wife's comments about David Markin, 434

Collins, Albert H., (Park-American Hotel): absconded with funds, 341; penultimate salesman, 335-37; president of Wolverine Motor Car Co., 336

Continental -Red Seal- engine, (Continental Motors Corp., Muskegon, MI): Barley and, 373; Roamer and, 357, 359, 373, 380

Cooper, Joe: Indianapolis 500 and, 136

Cord automobile, (Auburn, IN, 1929-32, 1936-37): convertible sedan, **C-17**; Limousine Body and, 295, 296

Cord, Errett Lobban: conglomerate, 416; death, 420; Limousine Body and, 294, 295; Lucius Manning and, 417, 419, 429; Morris Markin and, 405, 415-19, 420; out of Cord Co., 419-20; people's admiration for, 419; *see also* Auburn automobile; Cord automobile; Markin-Cord

Cornelian automobile, (Kalamazoo, MI, 1913-15, Allegan MI, 1915): Bushong Hill and, 109; cyclecar, 103-105, **99**, **102**, **104**, **105**; cyclecar to light car, 100; demise of, 110-111; cyclecar

511

described, **103, 105, 106**; drive train, 103, **99, 137**; impressed Henry Ford, 104-105; light car described 107-108, **107, 108**, 110; little gem, 102-103; Mack engine and, 103; "Made in Kalamazoo" tour, 108-109; Model T Ford and, 105; named after, 102-103; patent drawings of, **106**; production of, 107, 110; Sterling engine and, 106, 107; Spacke engine and, 103; trip to Detroit in, 104-105; whimsy, 100-101; *see also* Blood, Howard; Cornelian Co; Cornelian race car

Cornelian race car: characteristics of, 138-39; Howard Blood and, **128, 134**; Louis Chevrolet and, 129-30, **128, 134, 135**; Indianapolis 500 race and, 136, 138, **135**; sold to Roscoe Dunning, 139-40; *see also* Blood, Howard; Chevrolet, Louis

Cornelian Co., (635 West Ransom St.): merges with Blood Brothers Machine, 101; moves to Allegan, 109-110

Crawford, H. A., (Park-American Hotel): buys Lane Motor Truck, 275-76; business forecasts by, 287-88; closes Lull Carriage, 275; Dort and, 346; moves carriage business, 346-47; named president of Kalamazoo Motors Corp, 280; *see also* Kalamazoo Motors Corp.

Crown automobile, (1915): confusion with Greyhound automobile, 327; *see also* Greyhound automobile; States automobile

cyclecar: concept and history, 98-101, 104-105, **98, 99**; Cornelian as, **99, 102, 104, 105, 106**; Mercury, **98**; whimsical names for, 100; *see also* Cornelian automobile

Dawson, Joe: races at Indianapolis, 137

De Alene, Wilbur: races at Kalamazoo, 121

de Dion Boutan, Count Albert, (France): Kalamazoo and, 23

de Dion Boutan engine and drive train, (de Dion Boutan Co., France): Blood and, 23-24; Cornelian race car and, 117-18, 133; drive train, 23, 133, **137**; Ferrari and, 23, 118

DePalma, Ralph: career, 124; folk hero, 120, 137, 365; Indianapolis race and, 136-37, **126, 139**; Kalamazoo race and, 117, 120, 121, 124

Depression, Great: Checker Cab and, 413-15; Fuller Co. and, 56-58; Kalamazoo Railway Supply and, 313; Sandow Truck Co. and, 288; Roamer production and, 380

Dietrich, Ray: Checker stylist, 426

Dingley, Edward N., (S. West St. Heights): arrives in Kalamazoo, xii; buggy trial sordid affair 179-80; charged with contempt, 220; death, 256; sentenced by Judge Stewart, 229-30, 256, **230**; What's the matter with Kalamazoo, 258

Dort automobile, (Kalamazoo, 1920-23, Flint, MI, 1915-24): advertisement, **347, 348**; "Cucumber Kate," 348; f.o.b. Kalamazoo, 346; Gray Dort, 345; Harvard body, 347-48, **346**; Kalamazoo and, 347, 275; Etienne Planche and, 348; sport roadster, **349**; touring model, **345**; Yale body, 348-49

Dort, Dallas J., (Flint, MI): death, 349; Kalamazoo and, 275, 346, 347

Dort Motor Car Company Body Plant, (n.e. cor. S. Pitcher St. & Gibson St.): sale to Checker Cab, 339, 349

Dunning, Roscoe: Cornelian and, 139-40

Durant, William Crapo: Chevrolet Motor Car Co. and, 131-32; Dort and, 345; Kalamazoo and, 297

Durkee automobile, (Vicksburg, MI, 1903): description, 45-46, **45**

Durkee, Carson, (Vicksburg, MI): Bloods and, 46; builds automobile, 43-46; Michigan Buggy and, 46; Durkee House and, 44-45

Duesenberg engine, (Duesenberg Motors, Inc., Elizabeth, NJ): Wolverine and, 338, 338-39, 340; *see also* Rochester-Duesenberg engine

Eldred, Fred C., (rms 435 W. South St.): indicted 227-28; indictment thrown out, 255

Ells automobile, (Vicksburg, MI, 1902): Brecht auto body and, **44**; *see also* Ells, Theodore, A.

Ells, Theodore A., (Vicksburg, MI): appearance, **43**; builds automobile, 41-43

endurance run, (Kalamazoo to South Haven, 1910): automobiles represented, 149; James S. Gilmore drives in, 151; Michigan auto and, 150-51; purpose and rules of, 149-50; George J. Sharker dies in, 150

Greyhound automobile, (Kalamazoo & Toledo, OH, 1914-15): arrives in Kalamazoo, 327; confusion with Crown, 327; light car, 327-29, **328**

Griswold, Florence M., (rms 627 S. Rose St.): Harem house and, 204-205; Michigan Buggy Beauties and, **205**

Gull Lake: Allendale Hotel, **C-8**

Gumbinsky, Nathan, (bds 214 Portage St.): Fred Eldred and, 227-28; purchases good will of Michigan Buggy, 217

Guyot, Albert: drives French-built Bablot racer, 365

Halladay automobile, (Streator, IL & other cities, 1905-22): Barley and, 351, 353; sale of, 354

Halperin, A. L.: Wolverine sheet metal, 339

Hamilton, Burritt, (Battle Creek, MI): attorney for Palmer, 180, 183, 242

Handley automobile, (Kalamazoo, 1923): fabric spring shackles, 398; Falls engine, 397; "if it carries handles it's a Handley," 398; Midwest engine, 397; not built by Checker, 399-400; sedan, 397-98, **397**; touring model, 397-98, **398**; *see also* Handley, James I.; Handley Company; Handley-Knight automobile; Handley-Knight Co.

Handley Co., (1850 N. Pitcher St.): factory purchased by Checker Cab, 399-400; incorporated, 396-97; profit sharing and, 397; *see also* Handley automobile; Handley-Knight automobile; Handley-Knight Co.

Handley, James I., (617 South St.): bankrupt, 387; "Big Jim" introduced to Kalamazoo, 385; death of, 400; Marion-Handley auto and, 386-87, **386**; Willys-Knight and, 387-88; *see also* Handley automobile; Handley Co.; Handley-Knight automobile; Handley-Knight Co.

Handley-Knight automobile, (Kalamazoo, 1920-22): advertising for, 390, 394-95, **C-24, C-25**; color, 492; design of, 390-92; first delivery, 389, **390**; front view, **384**; interior, 392, **393**; Knight sleeve-valve engine, 392, 394-96, **394**; medieval chivalry and, 390; road testing of, **395**; sedan, **392, 393**, C-25; touring model, **C-24, C-26**; touring models compared, 391; *see also* Handley automobile; Handley Co.; Handley, James I.; Handley-Knight Co.

Handley-Knight Co., (1850 N. Pitcher St.): board of directors, 385; board minutes of, 496-97; catalog for, **C-26**; liquidation of, 397; reorganization of, 396-97; incorporated, 385; plant construction in Kalamazoo, 388-389, **388, 389**; stock sale, 388; stock certificate, **C-26**; "test track," **395**; *see also* Handley automobile; Handley Co.; Handley-Knight automobile; Handley, James I.

Hans tractor, (Kalamazoo, 1918): builds 25 machines, 296

harem house, (1216 S. West St.): Lay Jr. testifies about, 206-207; Miss Griswold and, 204-205; Palmer testifies about, 204-205, **207**; some Michigan Buggy beauties and, **205**

Harlow, William, (822 Egleston Ave.): Kalamazoo's first automobile dealer, 85-87, **86**; bicycle racer, 85; sold Cadillacs, 86, **C-7**

Hatfield, James C., (417 W. Main St.): buys Cannon auto, 337-38; slow race and, 83

Haupt, Willie: Indianapolis 500 and, 136

Havers Motor Car Co., (Port Huron, MI, 1911-14): possible tenant in Michigan Buggy plant, 257

Hays, Charles B., (427 Stuart Ave.): buys Cannon autos, 37; buys Michigan Buggy plant, 257; honored, 254-55, **254**; indicted, 227, 250, **250**; indictment set aside, 253-54; organizes Kalamazoo Land Co., 255; sells factory to States Motor Car Co., 257-58

Hazard engine, (Rochester, NY): Michigan and, 148, 161; out of business, 151-52

Herschell-Spillman engine, (North Tonawanda, NY): Roamer and, 356-57

Hill, George: qualifies Bugatti, 136

Hitke, Kurt: Roamer race car and, **366, 368**

homes: Frank Burtt, 39; harem house, **207**; M. Henry Lane, 66, **C-15**; Frank B. Lay, Sr., 65, **C-13**; George T. Lay, Sr., 64; Victor L. Palmer, 67

horse-drawn vehicles: in Kalamazoo, 63; *see also* Michigan Buggy after 1902 fire; Michigan Buggy before 1902 fire

horse racing: auto race and, 116; National Park and, 66; Recreation Park and, **114, C-11**

Imperial Automobile Co., (Jackson, MI, 1908-16): James Handley and, 387

Indianapolis 500 race: Ralph DePalma and Mercedes in 1913, **126**; Ralph DePalma folk hero, 120, 137, 365; start in 1913, **C-11**; track, **C-10**; World War I and, 364-65; *see also* Indianapolis 500 race in 1915; Indianapolis 500 race in 1919

Indianapolis 500 race in 1915: cars that failed to qualify, 129-30; Cornelian and, 129, 136, 138, **134, 135, 137**; ole maw superstition, 134-35; program, **C-10**; start, **138**; *see also* Cornelian race car

Indianapolis 500 race in 1919: Kurt Hitke and, **368**; LeCocq & Bandini death at, **366, 367**; Roamer at, 365-67; *see also* Roamer racing

Jacobus, Everett E., (1231 Clinton Ave.): testifies, 199, 241

Jeep engine, (Ford Motor Co., Detroit, MI): Kalamazoo rail and, 318

Jeep vehicle, (1940-42): Army procurement process for, 420-23, 433; Checker's bid, 421; Checker did not build, 423-24; four-wheel steer and, 422-23;

Kahn, Albert: architect for Checker Cab Manufacturing plant, 413, 428; architect for Kalamazoo Gazette Building, xi, 413

Kalamazoo: automobile, 34, 36, 72, 145; Burdick Hotel, **C-14**; Burdick St., **C-7, C-15**; failure of Michigan Buggy and, 224, 231; Hotel Rickman, **C-12**; Main Street, **182, C-2, C-15**; means gasoline-powered rail car, 315; name soiled with gossip and scandal, 258; oil dispensing bottle, 6; rail car, **311, 312, 313, 314, 315, 316, 317, 319**; river, **C-1**; rush hour, **453**; roads, **C-3, C-6**; Savings Bank, **448**; street cars, **C-2**; street scenes, **174, 182, 453, C-2, C-4, C-5**; unemployment in 1914, 233; what's the matter with, 258

Kalamazoo area vehicles: *see* automobiles built in Kalamazoo area; buses built in Kalamazoo area; race cars built in Kalamazoo area; tractors built in Kalamazoo area; trucks built in Kalamazoo area

Kalamazoo automobile, (Kalamazoo, 1903): announcement of, 34, 36, 72; Michigan Buggy and, 145-46

Kalamazoo County Fairgrounds, (2900 Lake St.): Grand Circuit horse racing and, 114, **C-9**; *see also* Recreation Park

Kalamazoo Cycle Co., (210 N. Rose St.): automobile dealership, 22; automobile manufacturing, 23-29; bicycle shop, 20-22; carry cycle is second auto, 24-25, **24**; de Dion Boutan and, 23; Fortune, Crown & Waverley bicycles, 20, **22**; horseless carriage is third auto, **25**; quadricycle is first auto, 23-24; *see also* Blood automobiles; Blood brothers

Kalamazoo Evening Press, (114-18 South St.): combined with *Kalamazoo Telegraph*, xii; Edward Dingley Editor, xi-xii

Kalamazoo Gasoline Engine Works, (116 N. West St.): Dallas Boudeman proprietor, 292

Kalamazoo Gazette (The), (401 S. Burdick St.): charges against *Kalamazoo Telegraph-Press*, 250; first newspaper, xi; building designed by Albert Kahn, 425; *Michigan Statesman*, xi; purchases *Kalamazoo Telegraph-Press*, 250; sponsors auto show; 87; sponsors endurance race, 149-51; style of reporting, 249-50; "The" in title, xi

Kalamazoo Manufacturing, (1907 Reed Ave.): factory, **322**; factory interior, **322**; fire rig, **321**; "Galloping Gertie," 317, **318**; Greyhound Escorter, 320, **C-19**; platform truck, **327, C-19**; President Blake Hawk, 319-20; President Hank Hawk, 317, 319; sold to United Tractor, 320; speed truck, **318**; tug, **321**; vehicle train, 320, **323**; Winkle Machine, 317, 319; *see also* Kalamazoo Railway Supply Co.; Kalamazoo Railway Velocipede and Car Co.

Kalamazoo Motors Corporation, (1800 Reed Ave., s.e. cor. Reed Ave. & Fulford St.): business forecast for, 287-88; dealership in Baltimore, 281; factory, **280**; production of, 280-81; sold to Sandow Motor Truck Co., 288; *see also* Kalamazoo truck

Kalamazoo Motor Vehicle Co., (416-430 N. Church St.): founded, 266; name changed to Columbia Truck & Trailer, 268-69; removed to Pontiac, 266, 268-69; *see also* Kalamazoo vehicle

Kalamazoo platform truck, (Kalamazoo, circa 1975): built by Kalamazoo Manufacturing, 321, **C-19**

Kalamazoo race 1914, (Recreation Park, 2900 Lake St.): Howard Blood and, 122-24; Bob Burman and, 115-16, 119, **116**; Willie Carlson and Maxwell, 124, **125**; cars and drivers in, 115-16, 121; Cornelian at, 117-19, 120, 122-24, **120**; Delage at, **118**, **C-9**; Ralph DePalma at, 120, 123, 124, **126**; Duesenberg and Eddie O'Donnell, **117**; Lawrence Blood at, 117, 123-24, **120**; Peugeot and Bob Burman, 124, **116**, **C-10**; race card, 121; reputation of drivers, 115-16, 120-21; Harry Scott as host, 118-19; Vern Shobe of Zenith and, 117; success and future of, 124-25; Teddy Tetzloff at, 116, 118-19, **122**; winners, 124; *see also* Cornelian race car

Kalamazoo rail car: built by Kalamazoo Railway Supply, 311, 312, 313, 314, 315, 316, 317, 319, **C-18**; Firestone tires on rail car, 315-16; first gasoline-powered inspection car, **311**; Ford Model A and, 313, 315; Ford-powered rail car, **316**; Ford truck chassis, 313, **314**, **315**; inspection car, **311**, **312**, **316**, **320**; International truck chassis and, 313, **317**; *see also* Kalamazoo Railway Supply Co.

Kalamazoo Railway Supply Co., (1907 Reed Ave.): catalog cover, **308**; change in name and focus, 317-20; construction on Reed Ave., 309; employees, **390**; Galloping Gertie, 317, **318**; Great Depression and, 313; Kalamazoo Motors and, 313, **313**, **C-18**; orders placed by cable, 312-13; plant interior, **322**; Presidents, 313, 316; salesman R. E. Keller, 315; section-hand car, **311**; steel railroad wheel patent, 310; World War II production and, 313, 316-17, **318**; *see also* Kalamazoo Manufacturing; Kalamazoo rail car; Kalamazoo Railway Velocipede and Car Co.

Kalamazoo Railway Velocipede and Car Co., (122 S. Pitcher St.): founded, 309; hand car, **310**; Charles King and, 310-12; change name & factory, 309; steam-powered rail car, **312**; velocipede, **311**; *see also*, Kalamazoo Railway Supply Co.; Kalamazoo Manufacturing

Kalamazoo River: boating party on, **C-1**; Kalamazoo and, xix; train bridge and, **C-1**

Kalamazoo Six sedan, (Kalamazoo, 1920): displayed, 341; *see also* Wolverine automobile; Wolverine Motor Car Co.

Kalamazoo Telegraph, (116-18 South St.): combined with *Evening Press*, xii; Edward Dingley editor, xi; purchased by Henry Lane and Victor Palmer, xi-xii

Kalamazoo Telegraph-Press, (114-18 South St.): Lane president, 73; October 1913 issue, **194**; publishes fiction, 250; "sensational and reckless afternoon daily," 258; style of reporting, 249-50

Kalamazoo truck, (1919-24): drive to Baltimore by Major Evans, 284-87, **285**, **287**; Kalamazoo fire truck, **282**; testimonials to, 281; truck owned by Celery City Moving, **288**; truck owned by Shawnee Milling, **281**; truck owned by Upjohn Co., **278**; trucks sold locally by Thomas Orrell, 281; trucks sold to various local firms, **283**; *see also* Kalamazoo Motors Corp.

Kalamazoo vehicle, (1913-15): at loading dock, **267**; Buda engine and, 268; description of, 267-68; name changed from Superior to Kalamazoo, 267; Model B, **266**; not predecessor to Kalamazoo Motor Truck Co., 269; trailer, **269**; truck & trailer combination, **268**; *see also* Kalamazoo Motor Vehicle Co.

Kennedy, Cap: Cornelian and, 119, 123, 124

Kenworthy automobile, (Mishawaka, IN): "America's Motor Car Classic," 367

Kenworthy, Cloyd Y.: bankruptcy, 367; Barley-built cars and, 353-54; Duesenberg engines and, 357, 367; Indianapolis 500, 366; Karl Martin and, 367

King, Charles: drives first car in Michigan, 310; Kalamazoo test run, 310-11

Kline, Dutch: Cornelian riding mechanic, 119, 124, 129, **133**, **134**, **135**

Knight engine: Dewar trophy, 394-95; first discussed in Kalamazoo, 395; first offered in U.S., 396; Indianapolis 500 and, 130; major advantages of, 395-96; sleeve-valve design explained, 394-96, **394**

Ladd, Sanford, (Detroit, MI): attorney for receiver, 180, 183; questions Gerber, 186-88, 199-202; questions about harem, 204-207; questions Lay

Jr., 196, 199-202, 204, 207-209; questions Palmer, 196, 201, 204-206; speaks against Gerber, 212; "peevish puppy," 196; "shyster lawyer," 183; velvet payroll and, 202-204;

Lane automobile, (Kalamazoo, 1917): twelve-passenger commercial car, 273

Lane, M. Henry, (507 W. Main St.): death, 251; deposed as president, 251; early life, 63-64; founding of Michigan Buggy, 64; incorporates Lane Motor Truck Co., 271; indicted, 225; Lane Castle, 203, **66, C-15**; marries Ida Lay, 64; relationship with Lay family, 73, 251; retires, 275; *see also* Lane Motor Truck Co.; Michigan Buggy after 1902 fire; Michigan Buggy before 1902 fire; Michigan Buggy bankruptcy

Lane Motor Truck Co., (1800 Reed Ave., s.e. cor Reed Ave. & Fulford St.): "Ask The Man Who Owns One," 274; incorporated, 271; production, 275; sold to Crawford, 275-76; World War I and, 275; *see also* Lane truck

Lane truck, (Kalamazoo, 1916-18): advertisement for, **272, 274**; production of, 275; "These Trucks put Ginger in Your Business," **271**; truck series, 273-74, 276; twelve-passenger car, 273; *see also* Lane automobile; Lane Motor Truck Co.

Lay Sr., Frank Barber, (523 W. South St.): at local hotel, **248**; death, 252; early life, 65; emerged from bankruptcy trial, 251-52; founding of Michigan Buggy, 64; indicted, 225-26, **226**; mood at son's trial, 252; residence, **65, C-13**; relationship with Lane, 73, 251; *see also* Michigan Buggy after 1902 fire; Michigan Buggy before 1902 fire; Michigan Buggy bankruptcy

Lay Jr., Frank B., (611 W. Lovell St.): guilty, 252-53; harem and, 206-207; indicted 226; sale of cars, 199-200; velvet payroll, 202-203; *see also* Michigan Buggy bankruptcy

Lay Jr., George T., (738 W. South St.): indicted, 226; missing, 194, 195; guilty, 252-53; velvet payroll and, 202-203; *see also* Michigan Buggy bankruptcy

Lay, Sr., George T., (Allegan, MI): Allegan farm, **64**; death 65; early life, 64-66

LeCocq, Louis: Roamer and, 365-66, **366, 367**

Leon Rubay automobile, (Cleveland, OH, 1923): introduced, 373

Lewis, D. D., (122 W. South St.): patent for oil dispensing bottle, 6

light car: Cornelian as, 105, 106, 107-108, **107, 110**; decline of, 104-105, 110, 341; defined, 100; Greyhound as, 339-40; States and, 338

Limousine Body Co., (2000 Lane Blvd., s.e. cor. Lane Blvd. & Fulford St.): Auburn and Cord bodies, 296; automobile tops, 295; E. L. Cord and, 295; factory, **294**; Great Depression and, 295-96

Limousine Top Co., (2000 Lane Blvd., s.e. cor. Lane Blvd. & Fulford St.): founded, 294-95; name changed to Limousine Body in 1920, 295; Roamer and, 358; *see* Limousine Body, Co.

Little Motor Car Co., (Flint, MI): built Little auto, 131; *see also* Little, William

Little, William: Buick and, 135; Durant and, 131; Howard Blood and, 132; Little auto, 135; Louis Chevrolet and, 131-32

Lull Carriage Co., (n.e. cor. S. Pitcher St. & Gibson St.): Checker purchases, 399-400, 407; Crawford president of, 280, 346-47; Dort purchases, 346-47

Lycoming engine, (Lycoming Manufacturing Co., Williamsport, PA): Checker and, 416; Roamer and, 379, 380

Mack engine, (manufacturing site unknown): Cornelian and, 102-103

Marion-Handley automobile, (Jackson, MI, 1916-18): advertisement, **386**; James Handley and, 386-87

Marion Motor Car Co., (Indianapolis, IN): James Handley and, 386-87

Majestic Theater (118 East South St.): New Year's eve of 1913 and, **232**

Manning, Lucius: Checker director, 417; demise of Cord automobile and, 419; Morris Markin and, 420

Markin-Cord: John Flynn comments on, 418-19; friendship between, 405, 416; Markin survives, 420; SEC investigation of, 417-18; stock

518

manufacturing plants, **68, 69**; "rule of the rails", 68; Portland Cutter, **C-5**; value 65-66; *see also* Michigan Buggy Bankruptcy

Michigan Buggy sold, (2000 Reed Ave., s.e. cor. Reed Ave. & Factory St.): auction, 216-17; Commercial Club and, 213-14, 216; Finnegan bids, 216, 219; gloom of collapse, 211; real estate of, 216, 217-18; three groups sought purchase of, 212, 213; Winternitz purchase of, 214-15

Michigan Central Railroad Station, (459 N. Burdick St.): circa 1914, **C-16**

Michigan Motor Car Company, (2000 Reed s.e. cor. Reed Ave. & Factory St.): expand manufacturing plant, 158; factory goes to Barley Co., 354-55; factory sold to States Motor Car Co., 257-58; in advertisements, **144**; of California, 158; *see also* Michigan Buggy after 1902 fire

Midwest engine, (Midwest Engine Co., Indianapolis IN): Handley auto and, 398

Molinero, Nicholas: at Indianapolis, 367

Monroe, Stephen B., (445 Academy St.): indicted, 228; resigns presidency of Kalamazoo Savings Bank, 255

Mulford, Ralph: races at Indianapolis 500, 136

Mutual Motors Co., (Jackson, MI): James Handley and, 387

Newhouse, Claude, or Charles, "Jack": places third in Kalamazoo race, 121, 124, **C-9**

Newspapers: compared, 249-50; *see also* Advocate; *Kalamazoo Evening Press*; *Kalamazoo Gazette, (The)*; *Kalamazoo Telegraph*; *Kalamazoo Telegraph-Press*; *Progressive Herald*

Nichols, Charles: replaces Milo Bennett, 223; no authority charge, 231

O'Donnell, Eddie: death, 124; drives Duesenberg at Kalamazoo, 116, 124, **117**; replaced Rickenbacker, 117, 121

Oldfield, Barney: failed to qualify at Indianapolis in 1915, 130

Orrell, Thomas M., (725 Elm St.): sells Kalamazoo truck, 281; sells Brush, K-R-I-T, Mitchell, Oldsmobile and & Detroit Electric, 88; sells Lane truck, **274**

Oswald automobile, (Kalamazoo, 1900): described, 291

Oswald, William C., (833 W. Main St.): builds automobile, 291

Packard Motor Car Company, (Warren, OH, & Detroit, MI): de Palma races Packard, 365; Lane uses same advertisement, 274; rumors of building in Kalamazoo, 296-97

Palmer Criminal trial: chronology of, 244; prosecutions's case, 239-41; Palmer's defense, 241-42; scheme to defraud, 243; verdict read, 242

Palmer, Victor, L., (320 S. West St.): annual report of company, 196-97; attempt to leave city, 197; death, 251; declares bankruptcy, 197; discrepant reports, 196-207; early life, 66-67; felt brunt of bankruptcy, 250-51; harem and, 204-206; indicted, 226-27; "I will not be goat any longer," 193; Levenworth and, 243-45, 250; testifies about financial condition, 189-90; photograph of, **248, 239**; residence, **67**; retains best lawyers, 223; testify against Frank Lay Jr. and George Lay, 244-45; velvet payroll and, 195, 202-204; *see also* Palmer criminal trial

Park-American Hotel, (313-325 E. Main St.): banquet in honor of Charles Hays, 254-55

Parker, Harry, (1546 Spruce Dr.): accident, 89-91; automobile dealer, 89; death, 91; father's fatal accident, 83; tales of the Stanley, 89-90

Pennant Cab, (Kalamazoo, 1923-25): compare to Checker, 409, **C-27**; introduced, 374; order for $3 million of, 377; typical style, **376**

people, photographs of: Harlan Babcock, **223**; Alfred C. Barley, **353**; Prosecutor Milo Bennett, **229**; Clarence Blood, **25, 97**; Edward Blood, **97**; employees of Kalamazoo Railway Supply, **290**; Howard Blood, **103, 104, 128, 134, 140**; Lawrence Blood, **104, 120, 134**; Maurice Blood, **25, 104**; Wallace Blood, **134**; Bob Burman, **116**; Willie Carlson, **125**; Frank Burtt, **32, 34**; W. H. Cameron, **164**; Claude Carney, **196**; Arthur Chevrolet, **134**; Gaston Chevrolet, **134**; Louis Chevrolet, **128, 134, 135, 136**; Ralph DePalma, **126, 139**; Edward N. Dingley, **230**; Theodore A. Ells, **43**; Charles B. Hays, **227, 254**; Dutch Kline, **133, 134, 135**; Frank Lay, Sr., **226, 248**; Michigan Buggy Beauties, **205**; Eddie O'Donnell, **117**; Victor Palmer, **190**, **240**, **245**; Ray Perrigo, **133**; Jay B. Rhodes, **4**; Eddie Rickenbacker, **140**; Judge Nathaniel H. Stewart, **230**; Teddy Tetzloff, **122**; Rene Thomas, **118**; Roscoe Turner, **140**; W. E. Upjohn, **15**; W. H. Upjohn, **16**

Perrigo, Ray, (Allegan, MI): Cornelian and, **133**; Cornelian moves to Allegan, **109**

Planche, Etienne: Chevrolet and, **131-32**; Dort and, **132**, **348**

Potamkin, Victor: Checker and, **435**

Progressive Herald, (211 Peck Bldg.): bizarre ending of Grand Jury, **230**; bankruptcy a sordid affair, **179-80**; editor in contempt of court, **229**; Editor Edward Dingley, **238**; founded, **xii**; Michigan Buggy sale and, **211**, **216**; "What's the matter with Kalamazoo?" editorial, **258**; *see also* Dingley, Edward

race card: Kalamazoo race in 1914, **121**

race cars: Blitzen Benz, **120**; Bugatti, **136**; Cornelian, **120**, **133**, **134**, **135**, **C-11**; Delage, **120**, **123**, **124**, **118**, **C-9**; Duesenberg, **124**, **141**, **120**; Erwin, **121**; Frontenac, **141**; Keeton, **119**, **117**, **123**; Marmon, **123**; Maxwell, **121**, **123**, **124**, **130**, **122**, **125**; Mercedes, **117**, **121**, **125**, **123**, **133**, **136**, **135**, **126**, **138**, **139**; National, **137**; Peugeot, **120**, **121**, **123**, **124**, **133-34**, **137**; **116**, **138**, **C-10**; Roamer, **365-67**; **368-70**; **366**, **367**, **368**, **369**, **370**, **371**; Sebring, **136**; Stutz, **138**; *see also* Cornelian race car; race card; race car drivers; SunSeeker

race car drivers: *see* Paul Bablot; Grover Bergdoll; Lawrence Blood; Joe Boyer; Bob Burman; Jack Callahan; Billy "Coal Oil" Carlson; Gaston Chevrolet; Louis Chevrolet; Joe Cooper; Joe Dawson; Wilbur De Alene; Ralph DePalma; Roscoe Dunning; Albert Guyot; Leland Goodspeed; George Hill; Kurt Hitke; Cap Kennedy; Louis LeCocq; Ralph Mulford; Claude "Jack" Newhouse; Eddie O'Donnell; Barney Oldfield; Dario Resta; Eddie Rickenbacker; Roscoe Sarles; Teddy Tetzloff; Rene Thomas; Arthur Thurman; Roscoe Turner; Howdy Wilcox; *see also* race card; race car mechanicians

race car mechanicians: *see* Robert Bandini; Louis Fountaine; Dutch Kline; Nicholas Molinero; Vern Shobe

race cars built in Kalamazoo area: *see* Cornelian race car; Roamer racing; SunSeeker

Ready, Willard, (Niles, MI): thinks he buys Michigan Buggy plant, **256-57**

Recreation Park, (County Fairgrounds, 2900 Lake St.): Blitzen Benz at, **120**; campaign for new track, **125**; careful preparation of, **117**; horse racing at, **116**, **C-9**; inaugural 100-mile automobile race at, **115-16**; Lane & Lay interests in, **66**; third place auto race trophy from 1915, **C-9**; *see also*

Kalamazoo Race, 1914

Reed Foundry and Machine Co., (1527 Fulford St.): founded, **301**; *see also* Reed tractor

Reed, Herber, (423 E. Main St.): death, **300**, **301**, **309**, **313**; buys Kalamazoo Railway Supply, **300**, **309**; man of good humor, **300-301**; spring tooth harrows, **300**

Reed tractor, (Kalamazoo, 1917-20): compare to Fordson, **302**; compare to steam machines, **301-302**; one man tractor, **301**, **302**, **304**; production run, **305**; testimonials for, **303**; *see also* Reed, Herber

Resta, Dario: at Indianapolis 500 in 1915, **136-37**

Reynolds, George J., (Pittsburgh, PA): Gerber's attorney, **180**, **184**; Commercial Club and, **190-91**, **213**

Rhodes, Bert. O., (1407 Egleston Ave.): oil dispensing bottle, **6**

Rhodes Co., (145 E. Kalamazoo Ave.): manufactured thousands of bottles, **6**

Rhodes, Jay B., (612 Douglas Ave.): appearance, **4**; compressed-air dumping car and Panama Canal, **4**; death, **7**; oil dispensing bottle, **5-6**, **5**; road guide, **5**; drives steam carriage on Rose St., **3-4**; steam snorting carriage, **437**, **443**

Rhodes steam carriage, (Kalamazoo, 1891): drives down Rose Street, **3-4**, **437**, **443**

Rickenbacker, Eddie: Borg-Warner Trophy and, **140**; Indianapolis 500 and, **136**, **140**; Kalamazoo race and, **117**, **121**; race referee, **365**

Rickman Hotel, (345 N. Burdick St.): departure point for Michigan auto endurance run, **149**, **C-12**